IET SECURITY SERIES 10

# Nature-Inspired Cyber Security and Resiliency

**Other volumes in this series:**

# Nature-Inspired Cyber Security and Resiliency

## Fundamentals, techniques and applications

Edited by
El-Sayed M. El-Alfy, Mohamed Eltoweissy,
Errin W. Fulp, and Wojciech Mazurczyk

The Institution of Engineering and Technology

Published by The Institution of Engineering and Technology, London, United Kingdom

The Institution of Engineering and Technology is registered as a Charity in England & Wales (no. 211014) and Scotland (no. SC038698).

The Institution of Engineering and Technology
Michael Faraday House
Six Hills Way, Stevenage
Herts, SG1 2AY, United Kingdom

www.theiet.org

**British Library Cataloguing in Publication Data**
A catalogue record for this product is available from the British Library

**ISBN 978-1-78561-638-9 (hardback)**
**ISBN 978-1-78561-639-6 (PDF)**

Typeset in India by MPS Limited
Printed in the UK by CPI Group (UK) Ltd, Croydon

# Contents

**11 Nature-inspired approaches for social network security**    **277**
*Indu Valsaladevi and Sabu M. Thampi*

# Preface

The rapid evolution of cyberspace, computing, and communications has given rise to numerous new applications, services, and business opportunities. Over the past decade, several advancements of potentially significant benefits have emerged, such as fog and cloud computing, smart infrastructure systems and environments, Internet of Things (IoT), collaborative computing, virtual and mixed reality environments, etc. These systems are often characterized as complex, highly dynamic, and distributed. As a result, they require efficient, robust, distributed, and cooperative monitoring, measurement, control, and management for communication and data processing. As organizations and individuals rely more on these systems, it has become substantially crucial to maintain their security, trustworthiness, and resilience to attacks. These issues raise new design and operational challenges that require innovative and creative sustainable solutions for cyber security and resilience.

For many years, nature has been a magnificent source of inspiration for solving complex problems. Many computing models and algorithms have been developed to mimic the operation of natural processes, phenomena, and organisms. Examples include artificial neural networks, artificial immune systems (AISs), swarm intelligence, evolutionary computation, deep learning systems, DNA and molecular computing, quantum computing, amorphous computing, cellular automation, membrane computing, simulated annealing, biomimicry, etc. The characteristics of these systems offer a plethora of novel methodologies to cope with the emerging cyber challenges. Several problems have been addressed using these algorithms including, but not limited to, intrusion and malware detection, intelligent threat detection and traffic analysis, evolutionary and self-healing security systems, nature-inspired confidential data protection, cooperative and self-configurable cyber defenses, adaptive resilient and evolvable security platforms, moving-target defense mechanisms, biomimetics and digital ants, immunity-based defense systems, deception, and optimization.

The aim of this book is to provide a timely review of the essential fundamentals, latest developments, and diverse applications of nature-inspired algorithms in cyber security and resilience. The book targets IT professionals, engineers, software developers and academic educators, graduate students and postdocs in the field of computing and cyber security. It also targets scientists, engineers, and professionals in other related disciplines who are interested in exploring nature-inspired applications in cyber security.

Calls for book chapters have been distributed to selected researchers and educators based on their contributions to the field. After a thorough peer review of each

xvi   *Nature-inspired cyber security and resiliency*

chapter by experts in the field, 16 chapters have been selected. A summary of each chapter is provided below.

Chapter 1 concentrates on investigating the most notable nature-inspired analogies and metaphors for cyber security. Particularly the authors draw the analogies between current offensive/defensive techniques in cyber security and nature. Other less obvious metaphors like nature-based interactions are also analyzed. For example, the malware-host scenario found in computer science is shown to have many resemblances to the parasite-host scenario found in nature.

Chapter 2 reviews the basics of evolutionary theory that shapes the algorithms formed in nature. Then, it discusses how these types of emergent designs can provide insight into human-designed systems. The authors considered a handful of real-world cases in cyber security in which nature-inspired algorithms have been employed with success and look for underlying commonality in the challenges addressed. Most critically, they explained the properties of systems that suggest a nature-inspired algorithm might be appropriate and contrasted them with systems in which nature is unlikely to have produced an algorithm that could compete with a human-designed solution.

Chapter 3 reviews existing work on different levels of collaboration schemes that are inspired by nature and examines mutual influences between bioinspired collaboration and cyber security. For successful collaboration, it is critical to have proper mechanisms to search the most eligible and available objects, organize groups with communication channels between members, and coordinate their collaboration in order to achieve a common goal. The authors described various impacts of bioinspired schemes on cyber security and cyber security technologies used to protect bioinspired collaboration systems. Then, they discussed research challenges on both sides.

Chapter 4 first introduces the main mechanisms of natural immunity: innate vs. acquired immunity, the discussed concept of self and nonself, as well as the three-signal model. These mechanisms highlight how a fully decentralized system can protect an organism against unknown actors, taking the actual damage they generate into account and memorizing previous aggressions for quicker response. A key insight into the analysis of the natural immune systems is the idiotypic network model, which shows how its multi-scale organization ensures the resilience of the immune system: lymphocytes react together to build a reactive network that is constantly regenerated, thus maintaining the immune reaction and memory although individual cells live and die. Understanding the immune properties of natural organisms is the key to leverage them in artificial systems. The application of these rich principles for building defensive and resilient systems is known as immunoengineering. The main product of this approach is the AIS and its application to intrusion detection. The first generation of AIS provides suitable event perceptors for classification of aggressions. The second generation introduces the concept of danger perception in artificial environments. An architecture common to most AIS distinguishes between the local layer, at the environment endpoints, for detection and reaction, a monitoring layer, in gateways or user machines, for vaccination and user interface, and a control layer, that collects status, generates metrics, and shares information at a central appliance. In this chapter, the authors summarized the immune properties of artificial organisms and how they relate to natural ones. They also presented and discussed the current limitations of AISs.

Chapter 5 explores four biologically inspired dimensions of network traffic analysis: (1) macroscale trends across networks, (2) microscale features of endpoints expressed through their network traffic, (3) mesoscale coordination and organization that occurs through networks, and (4) natural language constructs that embody key features across scales. Specifically, this discussion includes recent advances along each of these areas including algorithms focusing on, for example, biosequence alignment, biosequence complexity, genetic algorithms, neural nets and computational learning, social insect coordination and control, network organization and structure, natural language constructs, processing, recognition, and cognition. Specific applications in research and case studies for the above topics are presented and their applicability to network traffic is illustrated. This chapter also includes a discussion on limitations of these methods as applied to network traffic and a discussion about possible future work in this area.

Chapter 6 illustrates the critical role of nature as a source of inspiration to many successful security and resilience techniques. It starts by a discussion for the moving-target defense (MtD) as the fundamental concept for diversity, which is the pillar supporting MtD concept. The authors then discussed different technologies presented to enable diversity applications across some layers in the OSI (Open Systems Interconnection) layer in a top-down approach. They discussed about the driver by listing the various MtD applications exploiting such technologies to induce diversity for defense. Then, we discussed various nature-inspired heuristics and artificial intelligence techniques presented across the literature. As a demonstrative example, this chapter focused on swarm intelligence, genetic algorithms, neural networks, and some of the other popular techniques. Such techniques are the base driver that controls most of the smart systems solutions being deployed nowadays.

Chapter 7 provides an insight into bioinspired techniques applying machine learning and feature extraction in the area of cyber security. The focus is on the fundamental aspects of the intelligent systems, namely, how relevant information can be extracted in order to build the knowledge and how then knowledge could be maintained and represented to solve various cyber security problems. Moreover, this chapter provides some practical examples and quantitative results to reveal the usefulness of the presented algorithms to the reader.

Chapter 8 studies and analyzes multilayer-encryption anonymity networks. Multilayer-encryption anonymity networks aim to enable users to access the Internet without being tracked or traced. To achieve this, the authors use technologies to resist traffic analysis and network surveillance—or at least making it more difficult. However, for various reasons—from network operations to security—network packet and flow analysis have been employed to identify multilayer-encryption anonymity networks. It also includes a discussion of the usage of traditional and nature-inspired artificial intelligence and data analytics techniques to classify encrypted anonymity network traffic.

Chapter 9 explores how nature/bioinspired algorithms are applied in intrusion detection against different threats and attacks for various networks. First, it gives an introduction and in-depth explanation of how the most popular nature/bioinspired algorithms operate. Both the theoretical and practical concepts are explained and how these algorithms operate to detect malicious behavior in the context of cyber security. Then, it includes a selection of the most notable and complete studies of anomaly detection using nature/bioinspired algorithms in networks and in low-resources systems such as cyber-physical systems and IoT. The techniques used and the results produced are discussed next. Finally, future directions on how nature-inspired algorithms could be applied in detecting anomalies in such systems is presented.

Chapter 10 reviews the evolutionary characteristics found in a new type of social spambots. The spambot behavior mimics several human-like characteristics and as a result is able to escape detection counter-measures put in place by social network providers, users, and state-of-the-art detection algorithms. To cope with this new threat, recent scientific literature has highlighted the dawning of an emerging and promising trend of research devoted to perform malicious accounts detection via global or collective analyses. Inspired by this new research trend, the authors described a novel, nature-inspired, behavioral modeling technique. Such technique exploits historic behavioral data of an account, in order to produce a compact and efficient behavioral representation for such an account. The obtained behavioral representation is particularly suitable to be compared against other ones, thus supporting efficient group analyses. An extensive experimental campaign on Twitter supports our proposal, showing its effectiveness, efficiency, and viability.

Chapter 11 aims to uncover some of the nature-inspired approaches that find application in social network security. It gives an overview of the different categories of bioinspired algorithms that can be used for social network analysis such as information diffusion, community detection, link prediction, influence maximization, and rumor detection and also for trust management and enhance the security of these networks. This chapter also outlines the state-of-the-art nature-inspired techniques prevailing in social network security, their open challenges and future research directions in this area. It also aims to explore the scope of novel bioinspired algorithms for deciphering issues concerned with social network security that are not addressed by the existing techniques. Since cyberattacks and cyber terrorism are increasing at an alarming rate, the need for developing algorithms that enhance the secure use of these networks is of great significance.

Chapter 12 is inspired by the close relationship between diversity of species and resilience of ecosystems and its application to software diversity security. Due to the dominant trend of the monoculture software deployment, attackers have taken high advantages of their existing intelligence using a single attack to more efficiently compromise other homogeneous system components, such as operating systems, software packages, and/or hardware packages. In this chapter, the authors developed a software diversity metric that measures the node's software diversity based on its neighbors' software diversity as well as its own software diversity. In addition, they used the node's software diversity to develop percolation-based adaptation strategies which can increase adaptability of a network under highly hostile, dynamic, and large-scale network environments. By using the proposed adaptation strategies, they aimed to achieve the following: (1) maximizing the software diversity of a given network based on the developed software diversity metric; (2) maximizing the size of the giant component, which has been used as a metric to represent the degree of network resilience (i.e., higher connectivity with more nodes leads to attaining better resource/service availability); and (3) minimizing adaptation cost caused by removing or adding edges from an original network to the network that has adapted by the proposed adaptation strategies (i.e., removing or adding edges) and an intrusion detection mechanism (i.e., removing all edges of a detected attacker).

Chapter 13 is motivated by the urgent need for secure software to construct new testing methods inspired by biology to improve current development lifecycles. The authors connect probability theory with current testing technologies by formulating feedback-driven fuzzing in the language of stochastic processes. This mathematical model allows translating deep results from probability theory into algorithms for software testing. Exploring the full capabilities of the presented model has led to the application of reinforcement learning methods, which turns out to be a fruitful new direction in software testing.

Chapter 14 provides an overview of how nature-based solutions can be used to safeguard critical infrastructures. These infrastructures, such as the smart grid, are increasingly difficult to manage and secure due to their large scale, distributed nature, and heterogeneous composition. However, given that problems with similar characteristics can be found in nature, several nature-inspired solutions have been developed and, some cases, successfully used as management approaches and cyber defenses. These include solutions based on the immune system and ant swarms. This chapter also includes a discussion of future challenges.

Chapter 15 is structured into four parts. After the brief introduction into the importance of nature-inspired cryptology given above, some background and preliminary information is presented. The central parts cover general ideas (including classical approaches) and recent developments in nature-inspired cryptography and cryptanalysis, respectively.

Chapter 16 addresses another problem in cyber security where nature-inspired methods are widely used to solve complex problems when classical mathematical ones fail. This problem concentrated on the optimization of access-control schemes in computer networks. A common example of such problem is the generation of access-control schemes in databases which use role-based access control (RBAC) models. This problem was singled out in a separate direction and received the name "role mining problem." The problem is NP-complete, and a set of different methods is offered to solve it. However, none of them can be considered as universal. At the same time, genetic algorithms, which are one of the most characteristic representatives of nature-inspired methods can be the basis for such universal solutions. The chapter shows that the generation of access control schemes in computer networks is a difficult optimization problem which belongs to the class of Boolean matrix factorization problems. It also suggests using genetic algorithms and offers some enhancements to significantly increase the speed of the algorithm and accuracy of decisions. The attained results are generalized in the conclusion, the possible fields of their application are defined, and the directions of further research are defined.

To wrap-up, nature is replete with astonishing concepts and methodologies providing us with frameworks, metaphors, and systems to model and design solutions for several complex problems in cyber security and resiliency. The field is steadily growing. Though we attempted to address some important issues and selected topics in this book, several interesting challenges remain. For instance, how to effectively and seamlessly integrate and evaluate the nature-inspired computing paradigm within traditional software engineering methodologies and processes? How to affect generational learning across bioinspired platforms? How to manage heterogeneity and handle constraints at large-scale in computing systems? How to design systems to permanently reverse the asymmetry between cyberattackers and defenders? How to formulate the theory and essence of the underlying principles and mechanisms at broader perspectives? How to optimally infuse nature into cyber and vice versa in a secure and resilient manner?

*The Editors,*
*El-Sayed M. El-Alfy*
*Mohamed Eltoweissy*
*Errin W. Fulp*
*Wojciech Mazurczyk*

# About the editors

**El-Sayed M. El-Alfy** is a Professor at College of Computer Sciences and Engineering, King Fahd University of Petroleum and Minerals (KFUPM), Saudi Arabia. He has accumulated over 25 years of academic and industrial experience. He has been actively involved in research, development, teaching, and assessment of areas related to intelligent systems and computational intelligence, pattern recognition and biometrics, data mining and security analytics, networking and information security. He has participated in several funded research projects and published numerously, with 170+ refereed journal and conference papers, patents, book chapters, and technical reports on various research topics in his field. El-Alfy has founded and coordinated the Intelligent Systems Research Group (ISRG) at KFUPM. He has co-translated four textbooks and coedited ten book volumes and six journal special issues. He contributed in the organization of many world-class international conferences and workshops. He is a senior member of IEEE; an ex-member of ACM, IEEE CS, IEEE SMC; and a member of IEEE CIS, ACS, Egyptian Syndicate of Engineers. He has served on the editorial boards of a number of international journals including *IEEE/CAA Journal of Automatica Sinica*, *IEEE Transactions on Neural Networks and Learning Systems*, *International Journal on Trust Management in Computing and Communications*, *Journal of Emerging Technologies in Web Intelligence*. He has also participated in various academic committees and chaired the ABET/CAC Accreditation Committee in the Computer Science Department (KFUPM) in 2010. He received several awards and recognitions including Outstanding Undergraduate Student (1986–91); listed in Marquis Who's Who in the World (2009); listed in Marquis Who's Who in Science and Engineering (2011–12); received Distinction Award for Excellence in Teaching from KFUPM (2011); won The Custodian of the Two Holy Mosques King Abdullah bin Abdulaziz International Award for Translation (2012).

**Mohamed Eltoweissy** is Department Head and Professor of Computer and Information Sciences at The Virginia Military Institute, USA. He is also an affiliated Professor with The Bradley Department of Electrical and Computer Engineering at Virginia Tech. Prior to joining VMI, Eltoweissy served as Chief Scientist for Secure Cyber Systems at Pacific Northwest National Laboratory. Additionally, he founded and directed cyber security research centers and cofounded several start-up companies throughout his career. His current interests crosscut the areas of network security and resilience, cooperative autonomic systems, and networking architecture and protocols. He has over 175 publications in archival journals, books, and conference proceedings. He has an extensive funding record and has also served on the editorial board of IEEE Transactions on Computers (the flagship and oldest Transactions of the IEEE Computer Society) as well as other reputable journals. In addition, he is active as an invited speaker at both the national and international levels. He has organized and cochaired many national and international conferences and workshops. Eltoweissy received several awards and recognition for research, education, service, and entrepreneurship, including best paper awards, top placements at Cyber Security competitions, and nomination for the Virginia SCHEV Outstanding Faculty Awards, the highest honor for faculty in Virginia. He is a senior member of IEEE and ACM.

**Errin W. Fulp** is a Professor of Computer Science at Wake Forest University, USA. His research interests include computer security with emphasis bioinspired solutions. This work has by funded by various agencies including US Pacific Northwest National Laboratory (PNNL), Department of Energy (DOE), and National Science Foundation (NFS). This has resulted in multiple patents as well as several workshop, conference, and journal publications. Errin Fulp is also the cofounder of Great Wall Systems, a network security start-up in Winston-Salem, NC, and the head of the Network Security Group at Wake Forest University. While at Wake Forest University he has received several awards and recognition for his research and teaching, including best paper, faculty fellowships, and early career research awards. He is an associate editor for the *Telecommunications* journal, and also a reviewer for several ACM/IEEE journals, conferences, and workshops. He is a member of ACM and a senior member of IEEE.

**Wojciech Mazurczyk** is an Associate Professor at the Cybersecurity Division, Institute of Telecommunications (IT), Faculty of Electronics and Information Technology, Warsaw University of Technology (WUT), Poland. He is also the cofounder of the Cybersecurity Division and Head of the Bioinspired Security Research Group (BSRG). He holds a B.Sc. (2003), an M.Sc. (2004), a Ph.D. (2009, with honors), and a D.Sc. (habilitation, 2014) all in Telecommunications from WUT. He works also as a Researcher at the Parallelism and VLSI Group at Faculty of Mathematics and Computer Science at FernUniversitaet, Germany. He is the author or coauthor of 2 books, over 130 papers, 2 patent applications, and over 35 invited talks. He has been involved in many international and domestic research projects as a principal investigator or as a senior researcher. He is also a guest editor of many special issues devoted to network security (among others: IEEE TDSC, IEEE S&P, IEEE Commag). He has served as a Technical Program Committee Member of (among others): IEEE INFOCOM, IEEE GLOBECOM, IEEE ICC, IEEE LCN, IEEE CNS, IEEE WIFS, and ACM IH&MMSec. Since 2016 he has been Editor-in-Chief of an open-access *Journal of Cyber Security and Mobility*. From 2018, Associate Editor of the *IEEE Transactions on Information Forensics* and Security and Mobile Communications and Networks Series Editor for *IEEE Communications* magazine. He is an accredited cybercrime expert and trainer for Europol EC3 (European Cybercrime Center). A founder and a coordinator of the Criminal Use of Information Hiding (CUIng) Initiative launched in cooperation with Europol EC3. He is also a founding member of EURASIP "Biometrics, Data Forensics and Security" (B.For.Sec) Special Area Team, an IEEE Senior Member (2013–), and EURASIP member (2015–). For over 10 years, he has been serving as an independent consultant in the fields of network security and telecommunications. Between 2003 and 2007, he was also a deployment specialist for the telecom company Suntech. His research was covered by worldwide media numerous times including in "IEEE Spectrum," "New Scientist," "MIT Technology Review," "The Economist," "Der Spiegel," etc.

## Chapter 1
# Nature-inspired analogies and metaphors for cyber security

*Elżbieta Rzeszutko[1] and Wojciech Mazurczyk[1]*

The soaring number, growing complexity and the diversity of network attacks is overwhelming. The big picture is further affected by the increasing sophistication of modern malicious software. The observed state of matters call for action. The security community is urged to seek for other, promising directions which cyber security research and development should follow. We are currently in a state where current countermeasures are progressively showing their limitations and are unable to withstand new waves of threats – consider, for example, the recent plague of ransomware. It is now time for security professionals and researchers to turn to nature in the search for inspirations for the next-generation defence systems.

Humankind has an extensive history of benefiting from nature-based inspirations. Many everyday inventions that are today mundane are the result of biomimicry. Consider, for example, the Velcro which is a fabric hook-and-loop fastener that was invented by closely inspecting burdock burrs. Success of this and the multitude of other bio-inspired inventions is not surprising since nature has over three billion years of experience in the evolution of various types of organisms and adapting them to the diverse environmental conditions.

In the Internet, it has been already discovered that many current offensive and defensive solutions (unconsciously) mimic the ongoing arms' race between various species in nature. Moreover, many of the virtual world's current network attack schemes have been, in fact, long known. Worms, spam campaigns, botnets, and others, along with defensive techniques such as firewalls and intrusion detection/prevention systems (ID/PSs), have been found to have counterparts in nature [1].

Additionally, it must be noted that we had already been on the right path once: the first generation of cyber security solutions was, in fact, nature-inspired. For example, the human immune system inspired threat detection based on signature analysis. However, since then the threats have evolved significantly to make these first-generation defences obsolete. What is worse, we ceased to follow the biomimicry path – the countermeasures did not evolve effectively and fast enough. Therefore, in order to 'survive', cyber security defences must be adapted, with the aid of nature-based inspiration, to be able to efficiently counter the new threats. Fortunately, the next generation

[1]Cybersecurity Division, Institute of Telecommunications, Warsaw University of Technology, Poland

of nature-inspired cyber security research is now emerging (see, e.g. the recent detection systems taking inspiration from ants' [2] or bees' behaviour [3]). However, we also find that the newly achieved developments and knowledge are scattered because the field lacks a more general framework and a general overview.

Obviously, the mappings from nature to the cyber world will not be faithful copies as exact mappings are not realistic in practice. Some of the reasons why exact mappings are not always possible include:

- Many mechanisms and relationships in nature are very complex and not yet sufficiently understood to correctly map them to the virtual world.
- In nature, individual organisms within a species are replaceable, and death is a critical driver of evolutionary adaptation, but for many security-critical systems (e.g. military, utilities and other critical infrastructure), any loss, compromise or corruption is unacceptable. Honeynets/honeypots may seemingly escape this rule as they are employed to 'impersonate' a real host/network and their compromise is permissible – for the sake of obtaining knowledge regarding the enemy, but they are not a target *per se*. Breach of their security does not result in the loss of sensitive data.
- The main aim of each organism is to reproduce and survive, whereas computers/networks have many different goals (specific tasks and functions).

Despite these imperfect mappings, we strongly believe that there are still many important lessons from nature that can benefit and improve cyber security. Moreover, if we follow a Sapir–Whorf hypothesis [4], which states that the language has a direct impact on thoughts, then finding analogies between cyber security and nature with its accompanying terminology, concepts and solutions can have a tremendous impact on the way we think about solving cyber security problems.

Nevertheless, drawing inspirations from the organisms' characteristic features or defence mechanisms is a must. Considering the pace at which new threats are evolving it is an even more urging necessity than before.

This chapter will be focused on investigating the most notable nature-inspired analogies and metaphors for cyber security. Particularly, we first show how inspirations from nature had influenced the history of inventions and then we point out nature-based systems' features that are extremely important from the cyber security perspective. On this ground, we describe *cyber security ecology* (CSE) in order to understand better the main actors and their interactions. Next, we review some of the recent and interesting nature-inspired analogies and metaphors for cyber security and provide an example of the generalised attack scenario. Finally, the last subsection concludes this chapter.

## 1.1  Historical examples of the nature-inspired inventions

Nature and technology are intertwined, sometimes inseparably. Through deliberate actions or through mere accident, nature's ways are reflected in the everyday life of any human. People have sought inspiration in nature for as long as historical accounts date back.

A brief glimpse into ancient history gives us the feeling how it must have been to observe the environment and replicate its mechanisms to solve real-life problems. Ancient Romans have noticed that trees use resin to seal their wounds and cut off entrance pathways for pathogens. Resin also prevents decay and reduces the amount of water stored in the tissues. Not surprisingly, the Romans have put this knowledge to use. Burial sites in Great Britain reveal that bodies were preserved with resin, and it was used in ancient medicine as an antiseptic.

Moving even further back in time, to ancient Greece, we can name one other invention that strikes much resemblance living organisms. It is highly likely that the antique Archimedes screw pump was inspired by the helical shape of mollusc's shells.

Sometimes the design process was carried out with the ultimate goal of replicating nature's formula for solving a particular problem. This was the case with flying, which long, fascinated people. Many have attempted to replicate how birds fly, among them the notable Leonardo da Vinci, but the ones to succeed were the Wright brothers, who learned the aerodynamics of the wing. In other cases, it was a mere accident that showed how a phenomenon occurring in nature can be put to use in a completely new situation. One notable example is how a Japanese engineer, Nakatsu, had tackled the problem of abrupt pressure changes that the Shinkansen bullet train was undergoing. He transferred his knowledge of birds and adapted the train engine shape to reflect that of a kingfisher. Currently, scientists and designers from different fields look into the ingenuity of nature to find solutions for their challenges. The influence can be seen from architecture, through product design, medicine, up to more surprising areas, such as space technology.

The motivation is sometimes for aesthetic reasons, sometimes it is mere pragmatism that drives the creative process. British architect Laurie Chetwood built his house to mimic the life cycle of a butterfly [5]. The structure reflects the stages of development from an egg, through caterpillar, chrysalis, to an adult. It is partly a work of art, partly a fully functional home. At the other side of the spectrum, there is the coral reef–inspired housing put forward by Vincent Callebaut in 2011 [6], after the Haiti earthquake. The modular housing would be self-sustainable and serve as a replacement for the homes devastated by the 2010 catastrophe. The French architect mimicked the structure of the coral reef to ensure good ventilation, exposure to sunlight and ensure low-cost construction. The modules for the building are prefabricated and joined together to form a coral-like mesh.

Biomimicry is also visible in product design. The most notable example is the Velcro. George de Mestral replicated in 1941 the burdock burr to create a strong and easy to use fastener. A more recent example would be the work of Jean-Marie Massaud who is an unprecedented advocate of organic design. Among his work is a volcano-shaped sports stadium or a faucet imitating a waterfall. Massaud noticed that using a water mixer with a wide, waterfall-like stream will decrease the amount of wasted water.

Yet another field reaching for inspiration to nature is robotics. It is probably hard to find a discipline more oriented towards mimicking nature. Not only do walking robots reflect the structure of their model organisms, but they also mimic their gait. In some cases, even a central pattern generator (CPG) is used to provide a rhythmic walking pattern. The CPG is made to replicate a biological neural network. In other cases, whole groups of robots are made to behave like groups of real animals. Reynolds, in 1987 [7], modelled the flocking behaviour of birds, thus establishing a whole new concept in robotics – the swarm robotics. The application of swarm intelligence algorithms enables the robots to collectively achieve a predefined goal through series of interactions between each other and the environment.

Looking further, into material science, biomimicry has spurred the development of multiple new materials. The honeycomb structure is exemplary of how versatile can the applications of one biological structure be [8]. Due to its durability, the honeycomb is used as a rigid mesh-type filler for furniture, heat insulation brick structure pattern and as a replacement for tubes in airless car tyres. Such tyres are resistant to punctures and, at the same time, retain the flexibility characteristics of an ordinary pressurised tyre. At the same time, the same honeycomb is used in micro-scale and nano-scale for a multitude of other applications. Biomedicine, photonics and electronics are just a few of the other fields, where this structure is exploited.

Nature-inspired materials are not only used in engineering but also find application in medicine. Jeffrey Karp is at the forefront of bioengineering solutions for surgical procedures. He investigated the exceptional adhesiveness of gecko feet and developed special tape, consisting of glue-covered pillars [9]. His tape could bind soft tissues without damaging them, facilitating faster recovery from complex surgeries. Other Karp's projects involve porcupine quill-inspired staples that create smaller punctures in the skin and provide a better barrier for bacteria entering the wound, and marine-worm-inspired glue, that is capable of binding tissue in moving organs, such as the heart.

It would be extremely hard to name one field that would not be influenced by the intricate inventions of nature. Even very theoretical fields, such as maths, delve into the intricate fractal structures that can be seen in nature. Another discipline that might seem a surprising location to spot bio-inspiration is space technology. Recently, a group of Hong Kong scientists led by Dr Jing Xing-jian have devised a vibration damping system that mimics the limb structure of birds and insects. Their active vibration system, which counters the vibration forces with equal opposing force, can be used in spacecraft and satellites [10].

## 1.2   Classification of the nature-inspired inventions

The number of emerging biomimetic inventions is soaring in the recent years. Surveying the areas where bio-inspiration is present, it is possible to discern three groups of purposes driving the replication of nature's creations.

The first area of research is geared towards the *recreation of natural materials' physical characteristics*. The ultimate goal is to enhance such properties as adhesiveness, heat conductivity, heat insulation, durability, low friction or others. One of such solutions is the aforementioned Velcro or fabric functioning like Morpho butterflies' wings, which contain no pigment but still appear vividly coloured. These butterflies owe their so-called structural colour to optical interference. The Morphotex textile fibre is a commercialised product that employs the same mechanism. The lack of dying in the manufacturing process makes the fabric an eco-friendly alternative to conventional products [11].

The second area of research is aimed at *modelling the physical interactions between different organisms or between organisms and their environment*. This may involve the replication of techniques that the species employ to function in their environment. One such example would be the structure of animal skeletons and joints, which is recreated in robots, to help them tackle obstacles the same way as animals do.

The third area where science *takes inspiration from algorithms and models of interactions*. Nature-inspired computing is a broad term that encompasses a whole range of algorithms that recreate the phenomena of the living world. AIS, neural networks, genetic algorithms and artificial life are some of the examples of nature-inspired computing methods.

When it comes to computer sciences, most of the nature-inspired solutions fall into the third category. Cyber security follows this pattern. New models and algorithms for cyber security have emerged giving birth to the so-called nature-inspired cyber security. Recently, a shift in the terminology used to describe the attacker-victim relationships can be observed. The employed models are currently geared towards employing biological nomenclature, rather than using military metaphors. The barricade-from-outside-threats mindset is gradually replaced by an approach of sensing the aggressor from within. This is achieved with the aid of artificial intelligence and immune systems, among others.

## 1.3 Nature-inspired analogies and metaphors for cyber security: needed or not?

The alarming rise in the quantity of network attacks in the last few years poses a serious challenge to the security community. Though, it must be noted that nowadays defensive systems are no longer as effective as prior. It is estimated that current commercial anti-virus solutions are able to detect only 45% of the new malware samples that Internet users are exposed to each day [12]. It should also be noted that, according to Verizon's '2017 Data Breach Investigations Report', the time between the initial infection within a network and its discovery is continuously growing and is now measured in months, and, in the case of more complex attacks, even years. This situation is caused by largely static and not sufficiently adaptable defence systems in use today which are unable to cope with the ever evolving attackers' tactics and tools. As a result, there is an enormous asymmetry between the attackers' and the defenders' costs and efforts. Today it is more than obvious that defenders are at a loss in this adversarial game.

The growing complexity, diversity and proliferation of malicious software and network attacks make it imperative to find a new direction for cyber security research and development to follow. This challenge needs to be addressed urgently. It is high time for researchers and security experts to turn (again) to nature in the search for novel inspirations for defence systems.

As mentioned in the previous subsection, people have long sought inspiration in nature. It is probably the most amazing and recognised invention machine on Earth with about three billion years of experience in evolution by natural selection, genetic drift and mutations. Biomimicry has been the propelling power of human invention and in science many biologically inspired techniques have proven useful, e.g. genetic algorithms, neural and sensor networks, etc.

In [1], it was shown that many astounding analogies between nature and cyber security exist. The main concepts of multiple network security threats have their counterparts in the actions of real predators. It was also pointed out that the ongoing evolution of offensive and defensive techniques seen in nature finds an analogy in network attacks and their countermeasures (an 'arms race'). The evolution is also visible in the process of current malware formation. Symantec in its latest Internet Security Threat Report (April 2017) informs about 400 million unique malware samples discovered in 2016 of which nearly 90% are modified variants of previously known malicious code. Note that this fact had been used by a start-up company CyActive (later acquired by PayPal) to distinguish 'malware DNA' with the aid of bio-inspired algorithms. Their program was capable of predicting how future threats can evolve and use this knowledge to improve malware detectors to proactively anticipate and prevent attacks on network and endpoint devices.[1]

Obviously, from the cyber security perspective, bio-inspiration is not a completely novel idea. It must be noted that the first generation of cyber security systems was mostly inspired by nature. For example, the immune system metaphor inspired creation of detection systems based on signature analysis, as well as solutions to counter polymorphic threats. However, since then, these first-generation defences' performance has deteriorated due to the continuous evolution of the Internet threats. In order to improve, cyber security should adapt and evolve to counter the new threats and to form the next generation of nature-inspired cyber security solutions.

As seen above, there are various aspects in nature that can serve as inspiration for cyber security purposes. Unfortunately, these inspirations are heavily underestimated and security community does not make enough efforts to benefit from them, especially considering the increasing ineffectiveness of current defence systems. It seems like we are 'stuck' somewhere in the middle – the knowledge of nature mechanisms is continuously increasing, but we ceased to adapt current cyber security measures or to seek for completely novel approaches. It must be emphasised that in other computer science subfields, nature-inspired algorithms have emerged as novel and innovative ways to conveniently address existing challenges, and new solutions are continuously derived from machine learning, optimisation or data mining – take for instance firefly, bat or flower pollination algorithms [13].

Clearly, nature serves only as a source of inspiration as mappings from nature to the cyber world are not always perfect. Nevertheless, the nature-based approach allows

---

[1] https://www.daniweb.com/digital-media/digital-marketing/news/493293/paypal-buys-into-bio-inspired-security-with-cyactive.

taking a look at cyber security from a different perspective, which can potentially result in new discoveries and conclusions. What we think that cyber security is lacking right now, among others, is a generalised review of how different solutions can be utilised together to form an efficient layered approach.

That is why in the remaining of this section, we will inspect what main features known from nature can be "reused" to the benefit of cyber security.

## 1.3.1   Adaptability as a key factor in nature

In [14], a nature-inspired framework called PROTECTION (see Figure 1.1) had been introduced. The purpose of PROTECTION is to show the direction which the evolution of existing security solutions and the design of future ones should pursue. Close inspection of rules and techniques present in living organisms' interactions permitted to identify five vital features that cyber security solutions should employ in order to attain higher effectiveness. What is more, after an analysis of the evolving communication networks and security measures, which responded to various historical challenges and threats, it is notable that their improvements (mostly unconsciously) fulfilled the framework's features.

In nature, the answer to the ever-changing conditions is an organism's ability to adapt, i.e. adjust its structure, behaviour and/or interactions, triggered in response to challenges or threats potentially endangering its survival. Adaptability facilitates proper reaction to challenges and threats as they arise in a particular organism's environment. In order to be efficient, the reaction must be adequate and timely. An organism's evolution is the result of its adaptation to the changing environment. Evolution, in turn, is responsible for ensuring that the organism's offspring is prepared for the threats encountered by its predecessors. Sagarin *et al.* [15,16] identified three crucial characteristics that have allowed organisms to survive and adapt throughout billions of years – namely decentralisation, redundancy and cooperation – and showed how they generally relate to public security and the information and communication technology (ICT) world. However, the big picture of adaptability was missing some other relevant factors. It should be noted that Sagarin *et al.* sketched up some general considerations on how organisms' functioning had been improving over time and how it related to societal and homeland security [15,16]. Additionally, Sagarin *et al.* pointed three main features necessary for adaptability to be put to life and they project onto the general success of a security solution.

However, it must be pointed out that, apart from the mentioned components, two more features are vital for adaptability: responsiveness and heterogeneity. Hence,

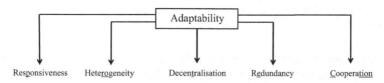

*Figure 1.1   PROTECTION framework for ensuring adaptability*

instead of three, there are five capabilities that comprise an effective defence mechanism. All five factors collectively form the PROTECTION framework (Figure 1.1). Using the PROTECTION framework, we gain a broad outlook as to how knowledge about nature can be practically projected onto cyber security. The more components a given solution covers, the more adaptable and, in turn, effective it becomes.

The building blocks of the PROTECTION framework are as follows. Each feature is illustrated with a concrete example from nature:

- *Responsiveness* – The ability to act upon an arising alarming condition, the response to a sensed danger is accurate and reactive, not proactive. Prognosing challenges are seen as too costly, inaccurate and inefficient. Human body is a marvellous example of responsiveness put to action. Biology has equipped us with means to escape danger without overanalysing it. Although we heavily rely on our brain to govern our well-being, we are at the same time equipped with special neural pathways, or reflex arcs. Reflex arcs can be compared to an emergency shortcut, which permits us to react instantaneously when danger arises. The electric impulses from a trigger point do not take the longer route from the sensor via the brain to the effector. Instead they only reach the spinal cord, where appropriate reaction is automatically triggered. Thus, the reaction time is as short as possible.
- *Heterogeneity* – The genotypic diversity of a species is its safety net. The number of genotypic variations in a given species corresponds to the higher cumulative chances of survival. Differentiation and specialisation of roles is of significance as well. Heterogeneity enables evasion of the attacker's interest – the greater the diversity, the higher is the ratio between the effort required to breach safety measures and the potential benefit of targeting a rare entity of an organism or a computer system. Certain species of moths have benefited from their natural diversification of phenotypes, or the set of observable characteristics. Peppered moths have developed a speckled camouflage that came in many hues as an antipredatory measure for bird attacks. Industrial Revolution altered their habitat – trees became sooted and devoid of any lichens. The species as a whole survived because natural selection favoured the darker shaded variant of the peppered moth, which reproduced freely to rebuild and sustain the population.
- *Decentralisation* – It comes in many forms, among others, diversified localisations (habitats) or distributed control (increased autonomy). Decentralisation allows for prompt response to an emerging peril. Its benefits are particularly visible in non-solitary species. Most notably, ants and bees, which form social relationships, have developed complex means of communicating information provided by other members of the community to the collective benefit of all.
- *Redundancy* – Nature sometimes seems to employ suboptimal solutions, but in fact it complies to the rules of game theory. Following the Minimax decision rule, organisms minimise their losses in a worst case scenario. That might result in a more 'costly design' of an organism but such behaviour increases the chance of success (survival and reproduction). Redundancy is seen as the source of resilience: surplus resources allocated to a task prove essential when critical

events occur. There are varied approaches to redundancy in nature, consider these two examples – some lizards perform tail autotomy to evade capture, the lost limb is not vital for survival and can be regrown over time; animals living in communities duplicate certain roles; thus, the loss of a single individual is not significant from the group perspective.

* *Cooperation* – It is seen as means to push the limits of adaptability. Species forming symbiotic relationships with others can jointly overcome problems, which they could not tackle on their own. Take ants as an example. These insects protect vulnerable aphids from predators in exchange for nutritious honeydew produced by the latter. The benefits of this relationship are mutual.

Noting the parallelism between relationships and challenges present in nature and in the virtual world [1], the proposed PROTECTION framework can be conveniently projected to illustrate historical challenges, as well as current trends and developments, in communication networking and cyber security. Ideally, a proposed security solution should display as many characteristics of the PROTECTION framework as possible. The larger the subset of possessed features, the more robust the system, which in turn decreases the risk of data leakage.

When looking into the development of communication networks one can observe that they consecutively introduce features from the PROTECTION framework to improve their overall effectiveness. An overview of the communication networks' evolution in this context is necessary. The bird's eye view of network development is the 'canvas', or a virtual environment, for the threats. Thus, it shall have significant influence on the cyber security measures.

### 1.3.1.1 Communication networks and adaptability

The evolution of communication networks follows a steady transition from centralised and homogenous systems towards a dispersed architecture. Prominent examples are the P2P (peer-to-peer) networks. P2P network design was the response to the single point of failure weakness of centralised networking and the client–server limitations. The decentralisation was achieved by distributing control and transport functions between the peers. At the same time, responsiveness was ensured by remediating the previous design's vulnerabilities, i.e. resiliency increased as the network became capable of undisrupted operation even if its fragment was malfunctioning.

Decentralisation was also crucial for the development of a particular service – let us consider IP telephony. Classical, centralised VoIP (voice over IP) solutions have been suffering issues stemming from the complexity of NAT (network address translation) and firewall traversal. On the contrary, Skype, due to its P2P design, experiences no such problems. These pitfalls were resolved with the aid of decentralisation and heterogeneity. Each Skype node can be assigned either a super node (SN) or an ordinary node (ON) role. These functions are differentiated depending on the node's network capabilities. Typically, SNs cooperate while determining user's location in a Skype network. Moreover, they participate during the signalling phase of any call, and they help ONs establish and relay a call if they are behind a NAT.

Meanwhile, another P2P service – the BitTorrent has employed the redundancy feature to its benefit. This resulted in a significantly improved transmissions' effectiveness compared with previous P2P file-sharing systems. From the network perspective, every BitTorrent resource is partitioned into many duplicate fragments. The data is made available at multiple sources (the so-called seeds and leechers). The more copies of the original resource present in the network, the better. Thanks to that different fragments of the same item can be downloaded simultaneously.

### 1.3.1.2   Cyber security and adaptability

As written previously, PROTECTION framework comes in handy when describing the evolution of cyber security – both the threats and the countermeasures, as well as the aspect influencing the design of new security mechanisms. It must be noted that according to this concept, the more features of this framework are going to be incorporated into a security solution, the more adaptable, effective and, as a result, the more secure it will become.

Looking into current CSE, or the threats and modern countermeasures, it becomes visible that parts of the PROTECTION framework are already put to use. In some cases, even a few of the framework's building blocks can be already found. In many cases, these parallelisms have emerged spontaneously in the process of evolution. In the rest of this section, we provide examples from cyber security (both offensive and defensive techniques) which refer to the five previously introduced features of the PROTECTION framework.

Let us look into botnets in search of the use of the decentralisation feature. Primarily, botnets relied on a centralised architecture. However, it was quickly proved that, this way, they were easy to defeat. This, in turn, prompted a shift towards the P2P design. Botnets became difficult to detect and eliminate. At the same time, from the security solutions' standpoint, the appearance of ID systems (IDSs) confirmed that decentralisation is a good approach. Employing multiple 'probes', or IDS sensors, increased the chances of successful threat detection.

Similarly, both offensive and defensive techniques in cyber security make use of responsiveness. However, many security measures are designed to forecast future threats rather than to effectively react to the existing ones as they arise. SPIT (spam over Internet telephony) can serve as illustration to this phenomenon. Few years back, SPIT was envisioned to pose a serious threat to future IP telephony systems, and some efforts have even been made to counter it before its appearance [17]. All in all, it turned out that the scale of the problem was incomparably smaller than the spam issue, and currently not many countermeasures are utilised in practice. When it comes to offensive techniques, responsiveness is somewhat more natural. From the attacker's perspective, the main challenge is to find a vulnerability, preferably a zero-day, which always involves reacting and accommodating to the current security measures. Attack scenario is adapted to match the conditions – an attacker must find a single vulnerability or a limited number of them in order to breach a network. The defender faces a much more challenging task. He is forced to coordinate the whole, often complex and heterogenic security system with an unknown number of security gaps. On the defence side of the cyber security battle, reactive behaviour is present in the intrusion prevention system (IPS) part of IDS/IPS system. Until recently, the typical response to a new threat was to create a new malware signature, which enabled future detection and prevention (similarly to the way, an immune system behaves). However, with the inundation of new malware samples, each with a different signature, this approach for combating malware is no longer effective. Things are made worse by the emergence of polymorphic and metamorphic malware, which never bears the same signature more than once.

In general, cooperation between cybercriminals, especially until a few years ago, has been more notable and more effective than among cyber security experts (luckily the situation finally starts to change). The Black Hat community has shown more interest in sharing knowledge, experience and malware tools than the White Hat community. An example of an attack that strongly depends on cooperation is the notorious black hole attack on MANETs' (mobile ad-hoc networks) popular routing algorithms. It relies on a rogue node deliberately injecting bogus routing information into the network to redirect the legitimate traffic to a non-existent node. The negative impact is reinforced when multiple malicious nodes cooperate with each other while generating falsified routing information. On the opposing side, from the security solutions' perspective, SocialScan [18] is a recently proposed security solution that benefits from cooperation. SocialScan enables distributed, friend-to-friend suspicious object scanning service with priorities governed by levels of social altruism.

Heterogeneity on the cyber security side is the result of increasing diversity of devices, systems and services in communication networks. Typically, a combination of various security solutions is employed to defend a network. At the same time, heterogeneity is used to the benefit of cybercriminals who have a whole range of malware tools in their portfolio. There is a plethora of malware variants that continuously evolve to exploit new security vulnerabilities. Most frequently, the Black Hats exploit heterogeneity to conceal the true nature of their malware – polymorphism, variable "decoy" parts of source code or instruction substitution are meant to obfuscate the true purpose of the program, evade detection, and stall the reverse-engineering process.

In the ICT world, redundancy is considered as profoundly related to resilience, rather than security. Applied to the latter case, it is viewed as an additional, dispensable cost. Employing numerous auxiliary security systems at the same location frequently results in ambiguous behaviour (e.g. multiple firewalls on the same device). The honeypot is an example of a cyber security solution employing redundancy. It is basically a clone of some existing system but established and tuned with the aim of learning the behaviour and/or the tools of cybercriminals. The recent trend in malware evolution implies that redundancy is a valued trait. Previously, worms typically exploited a single zero-day vulnerability, but more recent malware, like the infamous Stuxnet, attacked Windows systems using four unprecedented zero-day vulnerabilities. Likewise, it has been observed that certain attacks are conducted through double injection of the same malicious code by means of two different exploits – just to ensure that the infection takes hold.

## 1.4    Cyber security ecology

### 1.4.1    Cyber ecosystem

From the biology standpoint, the term 'ecology' is defined as the field of life sciences analysing interactions among organisms and/or between the organisms and their environment. This signifies that ecology deals with the structure and the functioning of ecosystems. An ecosystem is basically a community of living organisms (biotic components) together with the nonliving (abiotic) components of their environment, which interact as a system. Besides the biotic and abiotic components, linked by various interactions, the ecosystem is fuelled by energy in the form of electromagnetic radiation (if production in an ecosystem is sun-driven, i.e. accomplished by green plants) or chemical energy (if an ecosystem relies on chemosynthetic bacteria). Both the biotic and abiotic factors have influence on an organism. For example, abnormally low temperatures, a drought or an exceptionally large number of predators will negatively impact some species [19].

The energy flow is crucial to understanding an ecosystem. Every ecosystem is energy based and performs its transformation, accumulation and circulation. In nature, the flow of energy is represented as a food chain, and the concept of trophic levels is utilised to illustrate the position that an organism occupies in a food chain. Depending on how energy is obtained, two groups of organisms can be distinguished: producers (who are able to manufacture their own food using inorganic components and chemical or radiation energy) and consumers (who feed on producers and/or other consumers) [20].

Ecology can be viewed as a good starting point to study complex and evolving systems. Understanding how ecosystems and the related concepts map onto the cyber security field, we can evaluate the usefulness of various ecological methodologies. If such mappings are accurate, the application of mathematical models of ecologic systems for cyber systems can be investigated.

Stemming from the above ecology terms and definitions, we want to systematically create an analogous taxonomy for the cyber world.

Let us define the cyber ecosystem [21] as a community of cyber organisms, i.e. non-human actors. This includes applications, processes, programs, defensive and offensive tools (analogues to the biotic components) that interact between each other and the environment (abiotic components). Let us also assume that the biotic components' environment is a communication network, e.g. the Internet, and it constitutes a nonliving (abiotic) component with its hardware, links and interconnections.

In the cyber ecosystem, just like in its natural counterpart, both biotic and abiotic factors impact a cyber organism. For instance, malicious software can be utilised to breach a user's device defences and to obtain his/her confidential data. On the other hand, a link failure, network device breakdown or network congestion influence a cyber organism by limiting its ability to communicate and exchange information.

Considering a cyber ecosystem defined in this manner, we are particularly interested in the network of interactions among cyber organisms, and between cyber organisms and their environment.

As mentioned above, the crucial resource in nature is energy. The corresponding key resources in communication networks are the different kinds of information, including personal user- or user-generated data, as well as information regarding his/her behaviour. In a cyber ecosystem defined as above, information is transformed, accumulated and/or circulated similarly to energy circulation in real-life ecosystems.

To have a clear overview of the analogies between ecosystems and cyber ecosystems, the role of humans in the present context is constrained to the following:

- Producers who possess and generate information that forms the target resource for the consumers (e.g. the tools that attackers or digital marketing companies use to obtain the sought-after information).
- Components of the offensive/defensive solutions. For instance, a bot herder typically issues commands for a bot that he controls. Thus, he is inevitably a 'par' of the botnet. At the other extreme is an ID/PS which is configured and monitored by a security specialist.
- The invisible hand of the 'evolutionary force'. Humans influence cyber organisms by changing their code, functionalities and applications, thus carrying out the evolution process. At the other extreme, attackers try to outwit defenders by developing malicious software that would circumvent existing defence mechanisms/systems. Conversely, defenders develop their defences to be 'immune' to existing threats. This way, both sides are taking turns in a cyber 'arms race'.

## 1.4.2  Cyber-ecology and its subtypes

With the aid of this simple analogy, we can define the following terms that precisely outline the toolbox of the CSE:

- Cyber ecology (CE) is a field that analyses and studies the interactions between cyber organisms and/or their environment.
- CSE analyses and studies interactions between cyber organisms and among cyber organisms and their environment that influence their security. CSE is a subfield of CE.
- Attacker–defender ecology (ADE) describes interactions between cyber organisms taking the attacker and defender roles in a specific cyber ecosystem (e.g. on the Internet). This type of relationship can be regarded not only as predation but also as parasitism. It is worth noting that such interactions are linked to different stages in the cyber food chain and depend on the trophic level. ADE is a part of CSE.
- Attackers' ecology (AE) illustrates interactions among attackers (cyber organisms) in a given cyber ecosystem. The possible interactions encompass both antagonistic and non-antagonistic behaviours, depending on the context. Attackers can predate or parasite on each other, but the relationship can be of symbiotic or cooperative nature. AE is a part of CSE.
- Defenders' ecology (DE) provides insights into possible interactions among the defenders (cyber organisms). It mostly incorporates non-antagonistic ties. It

encompasses both: the external defence mechanisms (interactions between malware and the defence systems resulting in defence) and the internal properties (analogous to animal immune systems). DE is a part of CSE.

## 1.4.3   Cyber ecosystem interactions

In nature, the structure and stability of an ecosystem are determined by the set of interactions that link different entities. We can roughly group interactions as antagonistic interactions (between species; mainly predation and parasitism), non-antagonistic interactions (between and within species; cooperation, symbiosis) and sexual selection–driven interactions (within species). In all of the three classes, interacting entities co-evolve as they respond reciprocally to their current states in a positive/negative feedback loop mechanism (also known as the arms-race dynamics for antagonistic interactions) [19]. The interactions can be defined as follows:

- *Predation*: A way of obtaining resources by killing/eating other organisms; results in the death of the prey; predation involves complex cycles of prey and predator abundance and scarceness modelled in mathematics by such equation systems as the Lotka–Volterra equations' system [19,22]. The Lotka–Volterra model can be utilised to design optimal strategies of defence or offense, depending where in the predator–prey system the cyber organism of interest lies. In communication networks, ransomware may be considered a predator, since it 'kills' the victim device by encrypting vital information that it stores and, unless a ransom is paid, the resource is 'destroyed/lost', i.e. user's data cannot be retrieved.
- *Parasitism*: Interaction involving acquiring resources through eating other entities without killing them [19,22]; it gave rise to a fruitful field of epidemiological parasitology, with mathematical models and defence systems that could be directly transferred onto the context of cyber epidemics. As noted before, the current trend, especially considering sophisticated malware such as the advanced persistent threats (APTs), bears more resemblance to a parasite-host scenario than a predation–prey one. This means that there is a high probability that malicious software will reside on an infected host for a long time and will keep obtaining its resources in a transparent manner.
- *Symbiosis*: Positive impact relationship, involving obligatory interaction of two or more entities, crucial for the survival of all parties and their successful propagation. In cyber security symbiosis is present on both attackers' and defenders' sides. For example, a common malware infection scenario is as follows. The first infection is initially performed by exploiting a vulnerability on the host machine, which subsequently allows for the download and execution of the second part of malware in order to perform malicious actions on behalf of the cybercriminal. On the defender's side, the integration of intrusion defence systems (IDS) and firewalls is an example of symbiosis. IDS finds suspect packets and informs the firewall to block traffic from that source. In turn, the IDS sees less traffic.
- *Cooperation*: Facultative interaction of an individual within one species or members of different species, increasing the fitness and survival of other individuals (the acceptors of cooperation) often at the cost of the focal individual (the giver

of cooperative behaviour) [19,23,24]. In communication networks, cooperation should be perceived not only as means of reinforcing defence mechanisms but also as a possible threat (deceiver malware might exploit system's willingness to cooperate, wreaking havoc in its structures). A recent real-world example is the sharing of cyber threat indicators as prescribed in the US Cybersecurity Information Sharing Act of 2015.

- *Sexual interactions*: It occur exclusively within species and are channelled towards combining, in the most desired and effective way, the genes of opposite sexes to maximise the fitness of the offspring [25]; from the point of view of cyber ecosystems, the models of sexual selection based on compatible genes [26] are particularly interesting, since they may serve as mechanisms for producing dynamic sets of optimal combinations of entities and their mutations. Such hybrids should provide maximum protection against evolving malware. What is more, the knowledge of the mechanisms of sexual selection can spur an interesting study how to become the most 'unappealing' victim to the potential attacker.

- *Competition*: This relationship is symmetric and involves multiple organisms competing for the same pool of resources. Inherently, the relationship between the entities can be broken off without any harm to any of the sides. Since the effect on both organisms is negative, the cessation of the link benefits both competitors. In communication network environment, this interaction can occur e.g. between two types of malware trying to simultaneously infect a single host, when one of them succeeds, it tries to 'secure' the host by patching the exploit used by the other type of malicious software. Competition can be also spotted among defenders, when a few similar defence systems (e.g. antivirus software) are run in parallel and they negatively impact each other.

A CE-based point of view may be to treat these interactions as purely mechanistic descriptions of cyber systems – without delving into the consequences of interactions themselves and into the dynamics they describe. However, growing evidence suggests that the interactions not only influence the fitness and performance of entities but also significantly modify their physiology/performance in the interaction, altering the final outcome of competition/synergy [21]. Such elastic responses of the interacting entities to the interaction itself may have a significant role in cyber ecosystems, as they may aid the design of more efficient ways of controlling cyber ecosystems and reacting to the unknown, emerging threats.

## 1.5 Early nature-inspired terminology in cyber security

During the long period of time before computers became common, the terminology around them varied. The birth of computing is strongly linked to the mathematical field; thus, it is no surprise that the earliest programmable devices designed by Charles Babbage were christened with the names: Difference Engine and Analytical Engine. When the World Wars gave a sudden boost to the development of computing, first analogue and electromechanical, and later digital, computers were mostly considered counting machines. Their primary role was to calculate ballistic trajectories (ENIAC) or to break cyphers (Colossus).

The mid-1960s brought about a shift in the perception of computers. Multiple working groups had been concentrating their efforts on connecting devices to each other, in order to exchange information, for the past 15 years. The most notable computer network is the ARPANET, which became the tipping point in the development of wide area networks.

The first noted use of the term network understood as a concept where social interactions would be possible by means of computers, was in a series of memos by J.C.R Licklider of MIT, referring to his 'Intergalactic Computer Network' idea. The thought that entities should communicate and exchange information is strongly biologically linked. With the emergence of first computer malware, it became visible that we are speaking of something intricate and bearing a strong resemblance to the world of living things.

When John von Neumann was writing in the 1940s about self-replicating machines, he had no idea that this will become the foundation stone for the rise of computer viruses. Later, in the 1960s, self-replicating programmes were referred to as 'organisms'. It was 1983 when Frederic Cohen and Len Adleman, have coined the term 'computer virus' for their self-replicating software, thus acknowledging its similarity in behaviour to a biological virus.

Computer worms, just like viruses, mimic their biological namesakes. The worm is understood here as a parasite exploiting a chain of various organisms to reach its final host. The electronic counterpart behaves in a similar manner, undertaking its journey through a network of connected devices (typically, the Internet) to reach its victim. In both cases, we utilise the same term to describe the resulting outcome – an infection.

Not surprisingly, the biologically linked malware had triggered the creation of defences stemming from the observation of the living immune systems. This approach enables an automatic reaction to an emerging threat, as opposed to the tedious browsing through a signature database. Modern ID/PSs employ artificial intelligence algorithms to build cyber immunity.

## 1.6   Recent nature-inspired analogies and metaphors for cyber security

Currently, in the literature there have been many proposals to map concepts known from nature onto cyber security. It must be noted that many of such attempts have been successfully transformed into efficient and effective security technologies, and systems that are in use nowadays, including ID/prevention, antivirus software, threat behaviour analysis, honeypots, counterattack, etc. [1]. However, it must be emphasised that the current nature-inspired cyber security research is mostly fragmented and lacks a systematic approach. This is due to the fact that a lot of various aspects from nature can become inspiration for cyber security solutions.

Therefore, current efforts on nature-inspired cyber security can be broadly divided into two groups, depending on how an inspiration is drawn:

- An inspiration is drawn from an *organism's characteristic feature/defence mechanism internal or external* – Internal mechanisms include, e.g., an immune system, while an example of external feature can be represented by various camouflage and mimicry techniques.
- An inspiration is drawn from *various inter-organism interactions* – which includes, for example, predator–prey associations.

In the next two subsections, we will provide more details on the existing literature for both these groups of nature-inspired classification.

## 1.6.1  Nature-inspired cyber security inspired by an organism's characteristic feature/defence mechanism

In nature when an organism wants to hide or conceal its presence in order to effectively avoid detection/observation, it uses camouflage or mimicry techniques that modify the organism's external appearance [27].

Camouflage embraces all solutions that utilise individual's physical shape, texture, colouration, illumination, etc. to make animals difficult to spot by the predator. This makes the information about their exact location to remain ambiguous. Exemplary organisms which are able to easily blend into the background include the *chameleon* (family Chamaeleonidae) that is able to shift its skin colour to make it similar to ambient lighting and background colouration; *stick and leaf insects* (order *Phasmatodea*) that take the physical form of a wooden stick or a leaf or *orchid mantis* (*Hymenopus coronatus*) that resembles a tropical orchid that, although under normal conditions should be quite noticeable, is challenging to spot against a background of developed flowers. Camouflage often occurs on levels other than visual recognition, for example many viruses code pathways and molecular signalling systems that mimic host cell transduction mechanisms in order to easily invade the cell and in result take control of the metabolism and immunological system of an individual [28].

It must be also noted that another flavour of such techniques is represented by various information hiding techniques, e.g. steganography, that can be utilised to provide means to hide the location of confidential data within the innocent-looking carriers or to otherwise enable covert communication across communication networks [29].

Colourations and/or patterns can be also used to confuse the potential predator, i.e., to make information about the prey hard to interpret. Such techniques are commonly named as "disruptive" camouflage, and they can be seen in, for example, zebras (*Equus quagga*) where it is difficult for an attacking predator, e.g. a lion to identify a single animal in a herd when they flee in panic. Patterns of contrasting stripes purportedly degrade an observer's ability to judge the speed and direction of the moving prey. Such an effect is possible by exploiting specific mechanisms associated with the way brain processes visual information on movement [30]. A similar solution is used by many moving target techniques/defence in cyber space, which focus on distributing the uncertainty between the attacker and the defender in a more fair manner. It must be noted that, e.g., some first-generation solutions made periodic changes in a host's appearance from the network perspective, in order to mitigate the effectiveness of target reconnaissance [31]. Then the second-generation solutions include, e.g., an ant-based cyber defence which is a mobile resilient security system that removes attackers' ability to rely on prior experience, without requiring motion in the protected infrastructure [2].

Mimicry incorporates techniques which allow an organism's characteristic features to be obfuscated by adopting the attributes of another living organism. In particular, this means that the prey is able to evade attack by making the predator believe it is something else, e.g. a harmless species can mimic a dangerous one. The prey conceals information about its own identity by impersonating something that it is not. For example, harmless milk snakes (*Lampropeltis* sp.) mimic venomous coral snakes (*Micrurus* sp.) in order to confuse predators. In result, their attack is less probable as they fear potential venomous harmful bite. Cyber security solutions that utilise the same idea include various traffic type obfuscation techniques, for example traffic morphing [32].

Organisms' internal systems can also serve as an inspiration for the new cyber security solutions. There are many recent studies attempting to map features and functions of the human immune system to the defensive cyber security system ([33–36]). Immune systems utilise a variety of receptors to spot external antigens (alien proteins). These variations are not inherited but instead are generated via recombination in the process of V(D)J (somatic) recombination. It generates repertoires of receptors undergoing clonal selection and reinforcement – preparing them for effective action against antigens, with the lowest possible level of autoagression (e.g. reaction against an organism's own proteins) [37]. The resultant artificial immune systems (AIS) are designed to mimic certain properties of the natural immune system. In communication networks, their main application is detection of misbehaviour and anomalies. AIS typically rely on one of four major paradigms: (i) negative selection algorithm [33]; (ii) clonal selection algorithm [34]; (iii) dendritic cell algorithm [35]; or (iv) idiotypic networks models algorithms [36]. The first-generation AIS (i and ii) used only simple models of human immune systems, so the resulting performance was not comparable with its human counterpart. More recent AIS (iii and iv) are even more rigorous and better correspond to natural immune systems.

## 1.6.2   *Nature-inspired cyber security inspired by organisms' interactions*

It must be noted that in nature, there are many inter-organism interactions that can potentially serve as inspirations to reinforce cyber security.

In the literature, there have been several studies focused on various aspects of predator–prey associations. In [38], the authors make the predator–prey analogy for the Internet and investigate how different levels of species diversification can serve as a defensive measure. They consider each type of a vulnerable device as a heterogeneous species and investigated what level of species diversification is necessary to prevent a malicious attack from causing a failure to the entire network. Next, in [39], it was discovered that the cost to the predator in seeking its prey drastically impacts the predation process. In particular, it has been observed that even fairly simple strategies for raising the cost of predation can result in significant reduction in outbreak size. Other studies utilise biological models of epidemic spreading (a special case of antagonistic interaction between the pathogen and the victim) to predict or analyse malicious software outbreaks [40,41].

Finally, the relationships and interactions between existing malware (so-called malware ecology) have been investigated in [42]. Numbers of interactions, both accidental and intentional, between different types of malicious software were analysed, and the main conclusion was to seek ecologically inspired defence techniques, because many ideas from ecology can be directly applied to all aspects of malware defence.

From the related work presented above, it may be concluded that nature-inspired cyber security is an emerging, wide, evolving and diverse research area. However, it must be also pointed out that from the research perspective, a lot of loose ends are present that should be tied using a more systematic approach. In the next subsection, we review a generalised attack scenario for nature and for cyber world and then we make an analogy between three lines of defence present in nature and then we make an effort to map it for cyber security purposes.

## 1.6.3   Generalised attack scenario analogy

Currently, in ecology, the term 'natural enemy ecology' has been coined [43] to encompass all interactions involving detrimental effects of one organism (aggressor) on another (victim), be it a direct or indirect (e.g. via shared resources) effect. It incorporates predator–prey interactions which by analogy can be referred to a typical network attack and parasite–host interactions which pertain to an APT attack (it is more likely that the attacker will be active on an infected host for a long time and obtaining its resources in a transparent manner).

In nature and more specifically in the aggressor–victim scenario, the attacker must undertake several steps in order to succeed (Figure 1.2). First of all, it must

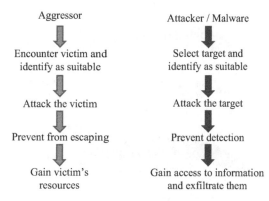

*Figure 1.2   Generalised attack scenario in nature (left) and in the cyber world (right)*

encounter a suitable victim which means that considering its offensive techniques, resources and determination, the successful attack is probable. This can be achieved by means of e.g. luring the victim or relocating the attacker to try to spot it. If a suitable target is identified then the aggressor launches an attack to prevent its escape. Finally when it succeeds, the attacker will acquire resources necessary for survival. It must be noted that in this scenario, at any of above-mentioned steps, the victim can utilise defence measures to obstruct the attack.

The analogous scenario can be derived for the attacker/malware – host scenario where each step is similar to the aggressor–victim case. First of all, an attacker must select a suitable target, i.e. he is convinced that he will be able to overcome its defence systems. This can be achieved by means of luring the victim (e.g. via phishing or social engineering) or by actively/passively searching for it (e.g. via network scanning or traffic inspection). If a suitable target is identified, the attack will be performed to prevent too early detection (here also many offensive techniques can be used to cloak the presence of infections, e.g. obfuscation or information hiding techniques). In result of successful attack, an access to the infected host resources, e.g. the information stored there is gained and exfiltration, is possible.

### 1.6.3.1    Three lines of defence in nature

From the victim's perspective, in nature, typically three lines of defence are utilised in reaction to the potential aggressor attack (Figure 1.3). Note that with each line, the victim's cost for utilisation of the particular technique increases; thus, with the rising risk of attack, the victim activates more complex and energy-consuming responses.

The aim of the first line of defence is to avoid being detected or spotted by the aggressor, i.e. to reduce the probability of encounter. The common techniques for this case include camouflage, mimicry or aposematism. Camouflage embraces all solutions that utilise physical shape, texture, colouration, illumination, etc. in making animals hard to spot. This causes the information about their exact location to remain

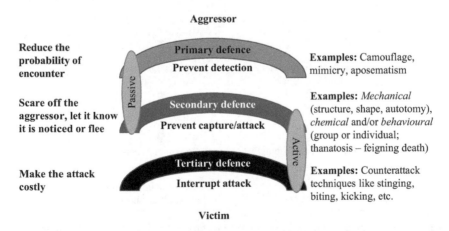

*Figure 1.3    Three lines of defence in nature*

ambiguous (examples include a chameleon which can make itself look similar to a leaf or a jellyfish that is almost transparent to hide in water). Mimicry obfuscates organism's attributes by adopting the characteristics of another living organism. In result, the victim can avoid an attack by making the attacker believe it is something else. For example, harmless milk snakes bear significant resemblance to venomous coral snakes which is their protective measure because the predators are less likely to attack if they can be harmed. Finally, aposematism describes techniques in which a warning signal (e.g. a warning colouration, sound or smell) is associated with the unprofitability of a victim to the potential aggressor. It involves advertising signals that the victim has defences such as being unpalatable or poisonous which may be enough to prevent an attack.

The aim of the second line of defence is to prevent the capture/attack. It is achieved by trying to scare off or distract the aggressor to be able to flee or to let it know it is noticed. Defensive techniques often utilised at this point can be grouped into mechanical, chemical or behavioural. Mechanical solutions include predatory structures, spines and hairs or a body shape that could resemble something dangerous for the attacker. A particular type of this defensive technique is autotomy where an animal sheds or discards one or more of its own body parts to elude or distract the attacker. Chemical techniques include noxious substances because they irritate, hurt, poison or drug the aggressor. Finally, behavioural actions include techniques like e.g. fleeing or changing flight patterns but also less obvious like feigning death (thanatosis) or making a startle display. The latter is executed by a victim upon discovery and involves exposure of a startling colour pattern or display, such as eyespots. Behavioural defences can be also executed collectively in groups. For example, chemically defended, aposematic insects tend to cluster rather than spread out in the environment to maximise appearance and position themselves to optimally disseminate noxious chemicals. They can also form aggregations in defensive circles (cycloalexy).

When two previous lines of defence fail, then the ultimate solution is to interrupt the attack by making it costly to the aggressor. This incorporates techniques to counterattack like stinging, biting or kicking, etc. It must be noted that typically the defensive techniques used as tertiary defence bear the highest energetic costs for the victim.

### 1.6.3.2 Mapping nature lines of defence to cyber security – main findings

First, it must be emphasised that the majority of currently widely deployed security solutions seen in both hosts and communication networks (i.e. firewalls, ID/PS or antivirus systems) that rely on the long-established reactive paradigm cannot be treated as direct analogies for the victim lines of defence characterised above. Moreover, it should be noted that in nature, every member of a species has practically the same set of defensive measures. Note, however, that on the Internet, the level of security of hosts and networks is often budget dependent. Despite this, small businesses and individual users are no less prone to cyber attacks than enterprises. These obvious gaps force to rethink our current reactions to potential cyber attacks.

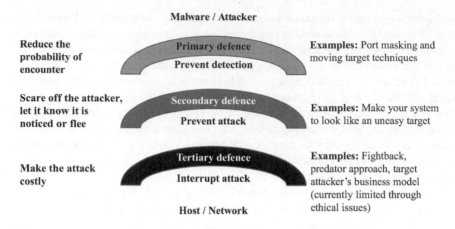

Figure 1.4   Three lines of defence in cyber world

One possible solution is to reorganise the responses to cyber threats, using a mix of existing as well as some of the next-generation, nature-inspired solutions. We review below some of these security measures and point to new directions, which novel techniques should pursue.

If we apply the same analogy of three lines of defence to the cyber world, then (Figure 1.4) the primary defence should be focused on preventing the attacker from easily identifying/learning the details of host/network architecture/setup. This, in turn, would lower the probability of launching a successful attack. The main aim here is to make the reconnaissance phase of the attack harder. Equivalents of nature's camouflage and mimicry techniques could be a solution. Introducing camouflage could mean, for example, that the network hosts are not easily identified by services like Shodan or Censys, which make attacker's work significantly easier. This can be achieved by deceptively responding to any suspicious network/host scans or to advertise a host/network as an uninteresting target. An alternative approach and a ready-to-be-deployed nature-inspired technique could base on cyber aposematism combined with mimicry, i.e. to use deception and decoys on the potential aggressor by intentionally manifesting the presence of the advanced security systems and tools (even if this is not true) or mimicking responses from heavily guarded systems, or the ones that the attacker would like to evade (e.g. a sandbox). It turns out that in some real-life malware cases, e.g. in Andromeda or Simda families, such behaviour could lead to continuous blockage or limitation of malicious activities on the infected host to avoid being spotted [44].

When considering existing techniques that can be deployed in this vein, one should look at e.g. port masking or a recently more and more popular moving target defence methods which can be utilised at network, host and/or application levels and are aimed to create uncertainty on the attacker's side, by constantly shifting the attack surface [31].

The secondary defence should focus on trying to scare off the attacker by making the defended host/network to look like an uneasy target or to let the attacker know that his actions/presence is noted.

Obviously, the solution combining aposematism and mimicry proposed for the primary defence is also valid here. Even if it does not withhold the aggressor from attacking in the first place, then it can be used to stop or limit the damage. However, other techniques can be devised as well. Making an analogy to nature, a cyber autotomy can be considered. This means, we intentionally prepare decoys for the network attacker that will look like easier targets by comparison to other devices. When malicious activity is spotted (here well-known IDS systems or similar techniques can be utilised), the decoys are shut down or disconnected from the network ('detachable network parts'). Alternatively, some kind of scareware can be utilised on the attacker to let him know he has been discovered (this also resembles startle display mechanical defence) or the machine can appear as already infected with other types of malware (analogy to thanatosis), then it is less rewarding for some aggressors to conquer it. The decoy can be organised basing on honeypots/honeynets or it can be a real physical machine. It can also be a network location that appears to be attractive for the aggressor because of its (fake) structure and information presented that is luring attacker's attention and focusing much of his efforts.

Other existing nature-inspired security mechanisms for the secondary defence include recently proposed detection systems based on inspirations from ants' [2] or bees' [3] behaviour. What is more, even if the aggressor has not resigned from launching an attack, the moving target defence techniques mentioned earlier can be used to confuse him or disrupt his actions by making it difficult for the attacker to predict victim's next move – in this sense, such techniques can be treated as an analogy to fleeing.

The tertiary defence involves counterattack techniques, i.e. proactive offensive measures. Such approaches should be treated as an ultimate solution, and they involve among others predator approach [45] (i.e. using benevolent, self-propagating programs which have the ability to clean up systems infected by malware), disturbing attacker's business model (e.g. by intentionally feeding attacker with fake data [46]) or performing network attacks on his infrastructure (e.g. index poisoning or Sybil attacks on a botnet [47]). It must be noted that such actions are currently treated as ethically questionable as attackers tend to utilise third-party machines as relays to perform their malicious activities. Thus, fighting back means compromising or disturbing machines of innocent users. However, an example of Google's reaction to Aurora operation (multiple security breaches in US institutions and companies) proves that such solutions are utilised [48]. In cooperation with the NSA (National Security Agency) Google developed a sophisticated tool – Turbine – for attack detection and response. It was intended to suppress the flow of unwanted traffic or, more proactively, to launch a counterattack if necessary [48].

## 1.7 Conclusion and outlook

Since nature has a profound experience in developing solutions to the challenges that organisms face living in extremely diverse conditions, the next-generation cyber security should seek inspiration there. Obviously, the mappings from nature to the cyber world will be not faithful copies as exact mappings typically prove unrealistic in practice. Nevertheless, drawing inspirations from the organisms' characteristic features or defence mechanisms is necessary. Moreover, careful observation of nature can help us rethink current cyber security paradigms and interplays between various security mechanisms. This, considering the number of incidents and threats that the Internet users face today, is inevitable.

# References

[1]   Mazurczyk W, Rzeszutko E, Security – a perpetual war: lessons from nature. IEEE IT Professional, 17(1): 16–22, 2015.

[2]   Fink GA, Haack JN, McKinnon AD, Fulp EW. Defense on the move: ant-based cyber defense. IEEE Security & Privacy, 12(2): 36–43, 2014.

[3]   Korczynski M, Hamieh A, Huhx JH, Holmy H, Rajagopalanx SR, Fefferman NH. Hive oversight for network intrusion early-warning using DIAMoND (HONIED): a bee-inspired method for fully distributed cyber defense. IEEE Communications, 54(6): 60–67, 2016.

[4]   Whorf BL. Language, thought, and reality: selected writings of Benjamin Lee Whorf. In: Carroll JB, editor. Cambridge, MA: MIT Press, 1956.

[5]   Bradbury D. New Country House. London: Laurence King Publishing Ltd., pp. 198–201, 2005.

[6]   Callebaut V. Coral Reef – Matrix and Plug-In for the Construction of 1000 Passive Houses. Port-au-Prince, Haiti, 2011. http://vincent.callebaut.org/object/110211_coral/coral/projects/user.

[7]   Reynolds CW. Flocks, herds, and schools: a distributed behavioral model, In Proceedings of Computer Graphics 21(4) (SIGGRAPH '87), pp. 25–34, 1987.

[8]   Zhang Q, Yang X, Li P, *et al.* Bioinspired engineering of honeycomb structure – Using nature to inspire human innovation. Progress in Materials Science, 74: 332–400, 2015.

[9]   Parker L. Inspired by nature: the thrilling new science that could transform medicine. The Guardian, October 2016, https://www.theguardian.com/science/2016/oct/25/bioinspiration-thrilling-new-science-could-transform-medicine.

[10]  Pan H, Jing XJ, Sun W, Li Z. Analysis and design of a bio-inspired vibration sensor system in noisy environment. IEEE/ASME Transactions on Mechatronics, 23(2): 845–855, 2018. 10.1109/TMECH.2018.2803284.

[11]  Eadie L, Ghosh TK. Biomimicry in textiles: past, present and potential. An overview. Journal of the Royal Society Interface, 8: 761–775, 2011. rsif20100487.

[12]  Yardon D, Symantec develops new attack on cyberhacking. Wall Street Journal, May 2014, URL: http://www.wsj.com/articles/SB1000142 4052702303417104579542140235850578

[13]  Yang XS, Cui Z, Xiao R, Gandomi AH, Karamanoglu M. Swarm Intelligence and Bio-Inspired Computation: Theory and Applications. Amsterdam: Elsevier Science Publishers, 2013.

[14]    Rzeszutko E, Mazurczyk W. Insights from nature for cybersecurity. Biosecurity and Bioterrorism: Biodefense Strategy, Practice, and Science, 13(2): 82–87, 2015.

[15]    Sagarin R, Taylor T. Natural security: how biological systems use information to adapt in an unpredictable world. Security Informatics, 1: 1–14, 2012.

[16]    Sagarin R. Bio-hacking: tapping life's code to deal with unpredictable risk. IEEE Security & Privacy, 11(4): 93–95, 2013.

[17]    Dantu R, Kolan P. Detecting SPAM in VoIP networks, In Proc. of USENIX, SRUTI Workshop, pp. 31–38, July 2005.

[18]    Probst M, Park JC, Kasera SK. Exploiting altruism in social networks for friend-to-friend malware detection, In 2nd IEEE Conference on Communications and Network Security (CNS), October 2014.

[19]    Krebs CJ. Ecology: The Experimental Analysis of Distribution and Abundance. Bejamin Cummings, San Francisco, CA, USA, 2009.

[20]    Rooney N, McCann KS. Integrating food web diversity, structure and stability. Trends in Ecology and Evolution, 27(10): 40–46, 2012.

[21]    Mazurczyk W, Drobniak S, Moore S. Towards a systematic view on cyber-security ecology, combatting cybercrime and cyberterrorism. Challenges, Trends and Priorities, Akhgar Babak, Brewster Ben (Eds.), Advanced Sciences and Technologies for Security Applications. Cham: Springer International Publishing, pp. 17–37, 2016.

[22]    Ings TC, Montoya JM, Bascompte J, Blüthgen N, Brown L, Dormann CF, Review: ecological networks – beyond food webs. Journal of Animal Ecology, 78(1): 253–269, 2009.

[23]    Axelrod R, Hamilton WD. The evolution of cooperation. Science, 211(4489): 1390–1396, 1981.

[24]    Riolo RL, Cohen MD, Axelrod R. Evolution of cooperation without reciprocity. Nature, 414: 441–443, 2001.

[25]    Andersson M. Sexual Selection. Princeton, NJ: Princeton University Press, 1995.

[26]    Neff BD, Pitcher TE. Genetic quality and sexual selection: an integrated framework for good genes and compatible genes. Molecular Ecology, 14(1): 19–38, 2005.

[27]    Ruxton GD, Sherratt TN, Speed MP. Avoiding Attack: The Evolutionary Ecology of Crypsis, Warning Signals and Mimicry. Oxford: Oxford University Press, 2004.

[28]    Moore PS, Boschoff C, Weiss RA, Chang Y. Molecular mimicry of human cytokine and cytokine response pathway genes by KSHV. Science, 274(5293): 1739–1744, 1996.

[29]    Zielinska E, Mazurczyk W, Szczypiorski K. Trends in Steganography. Communications of the ACM, 57(2): 86–95, 2014.

[30]    How MJ, Zanker JM. Motion camouflage induced by zebra stripes. Zoology, 117(3): 163–170, 2014.

[31]    Okhravi H, Hobson T, Bigelow D, Streilein W, Finding focus in the blur of moving-target techniques. IEEE Security & Privacy, 12(2): 16–26, 2014.

[32]    Moghaddam HM, Li B, Derakhshani M, Goldberg I. SkypeMorph: protocol obfuscation for Tor bridges, In Proceedings of the 2012 ACM Conference on Computer and Communications Security (CCS '12). ACM, New York, NY, USA, pp. 97–108, 2012.

[33]    Hofmeyr SA. An Immunological Model of Distributed Detection and Its Application to Computer Security, Ph.D. Thesis, University of New Mexico, 1999.

[34]    de Castro LN, Von Zuben FJ. The clonal selection algorithm with engineering applications, In Genetic and Evolutionary Computation Conference (GECCO), pp. 36–37, Las Vegas, USA, 2000.

[35]    Greensmith J. The Dendritic Cell Algorithm, PhD Thesis, University of Nottingham, UK, 2007.

[36]    Hart E, Timmis J. Application areas of AIS: the past, the present and the future. Applied Soft Computing, 8: 191–201, 2008.

[37]    Delves PJ, Martin SJ, Burton DR, Roitt IM. Essential Immunology. Hoboken, NJ: Wiley-Blackwell, 2011.

[38]    Gorman SP, Kulkarni RG, Schintler LA, Stough RR. A predator prey approach to the network structure of cyberspace, In Proceedings of the Winter International Symposium on Information and Communication Technologies (WISICT '04), Trinity College Dublin, 1–6, 2004.

[39]    Ford R, Bush M, Bulatov A. Predation and the cost of replication: new approaches to malware prevention? Computers & Security, 25(4): 257–264, 2006.

[40]    Kephart J, White S. Measuring and modeling computer virus prevalence, In Proceedings of the 1993 IEEE Computer Society Symposium on Research in Security and Privacy, Oakland, California, pp. 2–14, May 24–25, 1993.

[41]    Pastor-Satorras R, Vespignani A. Epidemic spreading in scale-free networks. Physical Review Letters, 86: 3200, 2001.

[42]    Crandall JR, Ladau J, Ensafi R, Shebaro B, Forrest S. The ecology of malware, In Proceedings of the New Security Paradigms Workshop (NSPW '08), pp. 99–106, Lake Tahoe, CA, USA.

[43]    Raffel R, Martin LB, Rohr JR. Parasites as predators: unifying natural enemy ecology. Trends in Ecology and Evolution, 23(11): 610–618, 2008.

[44]    Lindorfer M, Kolbitsch C, Comparetti PM. Detecting environment-sensitive malware, In Proc. of the 14th International Symposium on Recent Advances in Intrusion Detection (RAID), 2011.

[45]    Gupta A, DuVarney DC. Using predators to combat worms and viruses: a simulation-based study, In 20th Annual Computer Security Applications Conference, pp. 116–125, 2004.

[46]   Leder F, Werner T, Martini P. Proactive botnet countermeasures – an offensive approach, In Proc. of 1st CCDCEO Conference on Cyber Warfare, Tallinn, Estonia, 17–19 June 2009.

[47]   Davis CR, Fernandez JM, Neville S, McHugh J. Sybil attacks as a mitigation strategy against the Storm botnet, In 3rd International Conference on Malicious and Unwanted Software, pp. 32–40, 2008.

[48]   Harris S. @War: The Rise of the Military-Internet Complex. New York: Eamon Dolan, 2014.

## Chapter 2

# When to turn to nature-inspired solutions for cyber systems

### *Nina H. Fefferman[1]*

Nature-inspired algorithms have given us elegant solutions across a broad spectrum of design challenges [1]. Efforts within cyber systems are equally replete with cases in which algorithms either adapted from, or at least inspired by, observations of natural biological systems, ranging from efficient packet routing [2], to anomaly detection [3], and beyond [4]. It is tempting to turn to nature for many reasons, both esthetic and practical. At the most basic of practical reasons, these algorithms are already proven techniques, avoiding the potential for catastrophic failure (so long as the application is sufficiently similar to the natural setting). Of course, simple assurance of sufficient function is very different from assurance of locally maximized, or globally optimal performance, and (as we will discuss in detail below) it is rare for a natural system to truly optimize algorithms in ways that allow for straightforward adaptation outside their native environment. Natural systems can also function as "black boxes" where design effort can be bypassed by demonstrable success. Of course, black box solutions are not without their own requisite investment of effort. To be assured that algorithms from natural settings function adequately in human-designed settings, the analogy between the settings must be sufficiently robust, including likely bounds on constraints in both the behaviors of the system's components and system-wide acceptable outcomes. Constructing these analogies is often itself time-consuming, and it may be impossible to understand (at least initially) how any departure from natural algorithms may affect performance outcomes. Ideally, exploitation of systems that are initially treated as black box solutions can lead to discovery via fruitful interrogation into why a seemingly unlikely solution actually works, then allowing purposeful design that leverages that insight.

In this chapter, we will discuss how natural systems achieve robust and efficient solutions and the implications this ontology has for helping inform how and when it may be most fruitful to exploit them, and when instead we should probably forgo analogy and instead build tailored tools from scratch. Further, we will consider how it might be possible to move beyond this case-by-case analogy paradigm to exploit

[1]Departments of Math & Ecology and Evolutionary Biology, University of Tennessee, Knoxville, USA

the deeper design elements that make natural systems successful at converging on sufficient solutions and then employ these more fundamental tools in purposeful design.

## 2.1  Why natural systems are tempting

To begin to determine which types of challenges may be served well by turning to natural systems for the best source of inspiration, we first need to consider explicitly the features that make them attractive potential solutions.

### Promising characteristics of natural systems

*Many interdependent components*
Many natural systems involve the collective function of many interdependent pieces [5,6]. The immediate logical implication is that, if a solution truly requires a large set of component contributors, any algorithm or design that results in their all working seamlessly in concordance represents a solution to a potentially combinatorially expansive problem. Rather than exhaustively searching among freely varying, independent parameters or functions, inspiration drawn from such systems can reliably fall within the coordinated degrees of freedom that still permit the entire system to function.

*Extrinsic physical rules and constraints*
While there may be combinatorial complexity in the interactions among chemical or biological components of natural systems, they are all constrained by universal physical laws. This extrinsic control ensures global constraint on the bounds of outcome of the system. While this can potentially be manipulated in the designed analogous problem, it also allows for clear limitations on design specifications for use. For example, thermal limits and oxygen exchange may be critical in determining the possible range of animal body sizes [7]. A designed system that relied on gas exchange in animal bodies for insight can therefore be assured of the same bounds in tolerance due to the same physical laws, even if the analogy fails to assure similar performance of the design in other ways.

*Intrinsic behavioral rules and constraints*
Within natural systems, in addition to extrinsic laws of physics, there can also be easily identifiable physiological and/or behavioral rules that are intrinsic to the system that may also provide useful constraints on potential outcomes. For example, density dependence-driven criteria for acceptable nest site selection in birds assure sufficient average expected available resources without requiring direct assessment of environmental resource availability [8]. These types of intrinsic rules allow for internal control of outcome tolerance in a way that can complement the physical, extrinsic bounds.

*Emergent behaviors*

Building on the existence of both extrinsic and intrinsic rules, natural systems frequently exhibit efficient emergent global behaviors; systems in which the outcome is the logical necessity of the set of (potentially independent) rules that apply to each of the components, but the outcome itself requires the interaction enacted by each of those components, according to those rules. In other words, there are many natural systems in which the full range of system behaviors could not be achieved without the complete diversity of components (and their associated rules). For example, ecosystems fail at nutrient cycling without a sufficiency of species able to exploit "earlier" species waste products and produce their own exploitable waste for the "next" species [9]. The stability of the ecosystem emerges from the interaction of the individual rules for exploitation and production of waste for each species. Critically, these emergent system behaviors can be unpredictable based on simply knowing the starting conditions and individual rules (i.e., "complex systems," in the formal sense [10].)

*Stochastic perturbations in environment and input*

Many natural systems routinely experience different types of stochastic perturbation and continue to function potentially even returning to their initial condition. This ability to be challenged at irregular intervals and to inconsistent extents without system collapse is frequently highly desirable in human-designed systems in which there is incomplete control of system input or environment.

*Dynamic environments and constraints*

In addition to stochastic perturbation, the baseline nature of the environment in which the system functions, or the constraints under which it acts, can be deterministically dynamic. For example, energetic resource availability to animals in temperate climates varies predictably with season. These fluctuations are not perturbations from a normal condition, but they can nonetheless drastically affect the ongoing processes and outcomes.

## 2.1.1 Analogous qualities in engineered cyber systems

It may be only natural to feel drawn toward these natural systems for inspiration when faced with the challenges of cyber security and resilience. Cyber systems themselves have emerged from the distributed efforts of the past 50 years of technological research and ingenuity, independently and iteratively developing new hardware and new protocols that exploit that each other in ways the initial designers never anticipated. There are similar extrinsic physical rules that govern the hardware and/or networking infrastructure just as there are intrinsic behavioral rules that arise from common standards of practice, social norms in engineering practice, communally derived functional goals, and regulatory systems (e.g., the National Institute of Standards and Technology). Perhaps most importantly, the threats to cyber systems are themselves continuously evolving. Whether the result of innovation in purposeful attacks or novel inadvertent anomalies introduced by reliance on new technologies or shifting technological environments, the very definition of what it means to be a secure and resilient system shifts. These dynamic constraints mirror our understanding of the evolution of natural systems. Faster rabbits can only be caught by faster foxes, who in turn then fail to catch only the very fastest of the "already faster" rabbits. The arms race among emergent, dynamic, and interdependent systems begs for the parallel in description. It is only natural to try and leverage these analogies to supply algorithmic solutions.

## 2.2 How biological systems develop solutions

To explore how natural systems arrive at solutions to problems, we will focus on the traits of living things simply for clarity of language; however, it is worth noting that these same basic concepts apply to physical/chemical systems.

### 2.2.1 Darwinian evolution

#### 2.2.1.1 Fitness

"Evolutionary fitness" is the term employed in the language of biology to attempt to characterize the ability of a biological unit (e.g., gene, individual, population, species, etc.) to persist over time. The concept of fitness boils down to only two critical, interdependent accomplishments: survival and reproduction. For a population/species to persist over time, individuals in that population must survive at least long enough to replace themselves, and their children must similarly minimally replace themselves, and so on. Additional longevity is "useful" if it allows an increase in expected cumulative reproductive success. Using this metric of success, we can then consider the relative fitness of two individuals, two populations, two species, etc., incorporating variation between them in their ability to survive and reproduce. A population that achieves an expected 1.3 offspring per individual is relatively more fit than a population that achieves only an expected 1.1 offspring per individual given the same environment and resources. Both of these populations would be considered sufficiently fit to persist, but fitness metrics such as this allow us to see that sufficient success at persistence that does not indicate a maximally efficient solution has been attained. In fact, any fitness that allowed for at least replacement value of each parental generation into the next would be sufficient for persistence.

#### 2.2.1.2 Competition

Of course, in the scenarios mentioned immediately above, the populations being compared were considered in the context of equivalent hypothetical environments. In real natural settings, relative fitness is considered between competitors within the same environment. In this way, relative success at garnering and exploiting environmental resources contribute to the expected realized fitness of each individual/population. Perhaps two individuals of the same population would be able to achieve the same number of offspring if only they both had the same access to nutritional resources, but one of them is better at locating food than the other and therefore is functionally able to secure the resources needed to have four offspring, whereas the other is left unable to find enough food and starves, dying before reproducing at all. While there were sufficient available resources in the environment for each of the individual to have had two offspring, only one of them had a competitive advantage, allowing them to monopolize the resources.

In fact, we can relax the severity of this example and allow the better searcher to have three children while the worse searcher can still have one. If we assume that food search algorithms are inherited genetically or else learned directly from one's parent, then this inequality is expected to persist in subsequent generations. Although in real settings species must satisfy many different sufficiency criteria and are always in competition with others for access to finite resources, we nonetheless expect that more successful algorithms will increase in representation with each next generation and less successful algorithms will decrease, eventually disappearing altogether. The evolutionary term for this is "selection," and the "selective pressure" of competition for food resources is said to result in the "adaptation" of the population to increase their ability to succeed in finding food over generations.

While vastly oversimplified to focus on an environment in which the only relevant competition boils down to food search algorithms, this situation illustrates how a better algorithm can persist in nature, while an algorithm that is sufficiently worse will fail to persist. This phenomena is encapsulated in the phrase "survival of the fittest."

**Important note**

The phrase "survival of the fittest" is actually somewhat misleading since, in a world with sufficiently rich resources, there would be very little selective pressure. In this case, a diversity of resource gathering algorithms could persist for a long, long time, so long as they were each independently sufficiently fit to allow for expected replacement value in each generation, even if they were all relatively less fit than one, existing, very efficient solution. Although they would decrease as a percentage of the total set of behaviors, they would continue. Of course, as the number of generations increases, in any finite universe, there will be successive loss of the relatively least fit algorithms as the absolute number of individuals increases, increasing the anticipated severity of competition, and therefore the strength of selection. This is referred to as the "principle of competitive exclusion" [11].

## 2.2.2  Avoiding a common trap: best may not be good

There is a common logical fallacy into which the language of evolutionary biology lures many unsuspecting thinkers: that the gradual elimination of all but the least fit algorithms in natural systems leaves only algorithms that must themselves be highly effective and/or efficient. This is untrue for a number of reasons that are stated below:

- There may be insufficient constraint to have imposed a strong enough selective pressure for a sufficiency of generations to eliminate even quite poorly performing algorithms. In a world of functionally infinite resources, being a terrible competitor barely matters in any finite amount of time.

- Competition exists among variants. If no genetic or heritably learned variation exists, then there is no more fit competitor to gradually displace a poorly performing algorithm.
- There may be multiple constraints that are satisfied by being efficient or effective in different ways. Therefore, traits that perform poorly under one metric may be the best option under another metric. If the stronger constraint operates on the metric under which the trait performs well, we would expect the gradual dominance of that trait, even though it is a poor competitor under the other constraint. An unsuspecting designer may not be able to envision all the selective pressures in nature acting on that trait and falsely assume that it is a good solution to the type of problem for which the trait actually performs quite poorly.
- Even if we can assume a single constraint acting on a trait/algorithm/solution, natural systems are almost never in a long-term stable state. As a result, the intensity and direction of that selective pressure can be expected to fluctuate over time. This inconsistency means that the duration/efficiency of gradual competitive exclusion may be drastically extended and/or compromised. Further, relaxing that assumption of the single pressure, as each of the more realistic multitude of selective pressures acting on a system vary, which solutions are "best" or "most fit" may fluctuate (even oscillating back and forth), depending on timing and environmental context.
- Perhaps most importantly, the gradual increased representation of the "best" competitor is still limited by the available variants. So long as the "best" is still sufficiently fit as to maintain itself, it can actually be a very poor performer in absolute terms. In the evolution of biological systems, nature does not purposefully seek out better and better options, and new variants (arriving by emigration, mutation, or recombination [12]) are rare (even though they may have a relative probabilistic advantage for increasing their representation in a population over generations [13]). The result is that a ubiquitous terrible-but-just-good-enough solution is difficult to displace, even in the unlikely event that a better solution is discovered by chance.

Rather than optimizing, or even maximizing the performance of an evolved solution, evolutionary dynamics instead usually "satisfice" [14]. It is critical to remember this when turning to nature for inspiration in designing human systems. While sometimes satisficing algorithms will meet our needs, many times we are more interested in trying to optimize some aspects of performance. This is especially true in cyber systems facing threats to security and resilience, in which we are battling not only the current threats but the next generation of threats/attacks to come.

This is not to suggest that no work has been done to develop evolutionary theory in ways that relax these assumptions, as very elegant work has explored precisely these themes (e.g., [15]). These assumptions are nonetheless widely undertaken, and more importantly, implicit and unconsidered in many of the cases in which engineering has

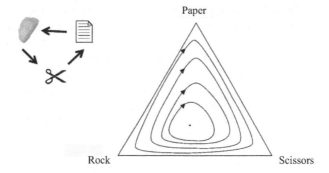

*Figure 2.1    In an evolutionary game of rock, paper, scissors the success of any one
strategy depends on the density of players using the other strategies.
There is clearly no long-term stable, best strategy that wins against the
others, as evidenced by the shown cyclic orbits of the system. For
complete mathematical analysis of this evolutionary game, see [16]*

turned to natural systems, expecting that evolutionary processes will have acted as a
functional search to discover effective or efficient processes.

### 2.2.2.1    An illustrative example of evolution failing to converge
on a single "best" solution

Consider an evolutionary system in which three morphs play against each other
according to the rules of the game "Rock, Paper, Scissors" [16]. In this game, each
player ties when playing against another player of his own morph, loses against one
of the other two morphs, and wins against the third. In this context, the determination
of the fitness of each morph is the relative density of the morph against which it wins.
This creates an ever-shifting evolutionary environment in which constant selective
pressures on a static set of rules yield stable oscillations among the three morphs
(see Figure 2.1). There is no best or worst, but the relative success of each strategy
fluctuates predictably.

Again, this is a clear situation in which looking to a scenario such as this from the
natural world for inspiration may lead to very misleading conclusions unless the full
dynamics are understood and are themselves analogous to the desired human system.

## 2.2.3    Does this make natural systems poor sources of inspiration?

It would be easy to be slightly disheartened at this point, but I do not at all mean
to suggest that nature-inspired design is a poor plan. While we have now discussed
many of the reasons why nature itself may not have produced optimally efficient or
effective solutions to complex problems, this in no way restricts natural solutions
from inspiring us to design optimally efficient or effective solutions in ways that
we might otherwise have not considered. Importantly, however, this analysis does
suggest that rather than always being a net time- or energy-saving endeavor, drawing
inspiration from nature requires a great deal of work and care to ensure that all

will function as desired: ensuring that the scope/dimensions of the systems are in agreement, ensuring that the ranges of environments/parameter spaces in which the solutions are proposed to function are sufficiently similar, and still potentially tailoring the function of the design/algorithm/solution itself to more specifically address the dynamics of human system of concern. While these are all challenging, this last is potentially also promising. It suggests that there might be productive ways in which we might structure our thoughts about how to adapt natural solutions that leverage the process of evolving itself the driving force in having honed the observed method to help exploit their strengths and avoid their weaknesses.

**Important note**

Taking a slightly different perspective on how nature-inspired design might lull us into a false sense of security, it is worth remembering that very few systems in nature are without constantly evolving direct and indirect challenges to their success. Unfortunately, while designers are used to testing whether a proposed solution behaves in ways they desired and anticipated, it is much harder to envision how seemingly unrelated behaviors or challenges can affect system function. In essence, nature "red-teams" [17] its solutions, and it is probably a wise course of action to mimic that effort at creative destruction in a purposeful way before truly having faith in any cyber security or resilience inspired by natural solutions.

## 2.3   Evidence of success from nature-inspired efforts

For all of the reasons discussed above, many designers have already turned to natural systems for inspiration when facing challenging problems and have some truly beautiful and amazing results to show for their efforts. Borrowing insights from head, wing, and feather shape of diving and hunting birds to increase aerodynamic efficiency allowed the designers of Japan's second-generation high speed train to improve energy efficiency and meet urban design noise requirements [18]. Engineers wondering how to design germ-resistant surfaces in hospitals turned to the skin of sharks and were able to build self-cleaning materials [19]. Researchers working to increase robustness in routing protocols for mobile ad hoc networks turned to attractor selection in gene expression [20].

### 2.3.1   A standard pattern in nature-inspired design research

The multitude of problems with demonstrably successful solutions due to turning to natural systems is truly astonishing. However, while both the challenges and solutions are as diverse as the natural world itself, there is a fairly uniform pattern in the progression of the research that leads to the development of the solution.

1. **Identify an open, challenging design problem**
   There is frequently no requirement for, or inclusion of, any discussion about why the particular design challenge might best be addressed by turning to nature for

inspiration. The tautological truth that "all good solutions are good" frequently obviates the need for justification, relying instead on the idea that if a good design results, why not use any of the methods available to produced it. This is clearly valid, but it also does nothing to help advance understanding of best practices that might be of use in developing a more general methodology for nature-inspired design.

2.  **Identify an analogous problem from the natural world**

    Again, most frequently, the discovery/construction of these analogies are the result of accidental overlap in knowledge, rather than being able to establish particular underlying criteria that would enable a thorough classification or search among natural systems. No method of common description or abstraction currently exists that would allow designers to know where to begin a search. Further, most frequently (and for perfectly understandable reasons), the analogies sought are in the nature of the problem, rather than the type of solution required to try and address it. While similar problems are most likely to benefit from similar solutions, it may instead be the case that seemingly dissimilar problems share common underpinnings that allow them to be susceptible to common solutions, despite seeming to share little in the description of the problems themselves. Characterizing these types of cases remains almost entirely undiscussed, even though we have existing successful cases in which a nature-inspired algorithm is now broadly employed to great success way beyond the scope of the initial analogy (e.g., genetic algorithms began in direct analogy for general optimization and have now been employed very successfully across a giant array of problems; [21–23]).

3.  **Carefully characterize the algorithm/design observed to be the solution in the analogous natural system**

    While again equally valid and effective in the context of discovering particular solutions to isolated problems, this step focuses on making rigorous the steps or calculations needed to blindly reproduce the observed natural solution.

4.  **Assume the solution observed in nature is efficient and/or effective within its own context**

    Perhaps this step is a bit overstated as, slightly later in the progression, testing will show whether or not the natural algorithm is at least somewhat successful in achieving its goal. However, it is nonetheless true that by focusing on the particular solution in nature, we (myself included) generally bypass asking questions about what makes the solution appropriate to the problem, instead relying on the continued existence in nature to at least provide evidence of success within the natural constraints on the system.

5.  **Tailor the natural solution to fit the design problem**

    In this step, the characterized solution from nature is tailored or adjusted to accommodate the constraints/parameters (whether broader or narrower) of the human system. These adjustments can cause cascading problems in the success of the algorithms (i.e., "fixing" one limited function accidentally compromises the function either locally elsewhere, or else fundamentally globally). This can lead to a series of minor adjustments that keep the same basic logic of a system but may compromise the principles that led the system to emerge within nature in the first place. While such compromise may not become problematic, again, the focus is phenomenological. We reject systems that cannot be appropriately tailored as "failed candidates for inspiring solutions from nature" and move on to other candidates or give up entirely on natural systems as inspiration.

As we will discuss in detail below, there might be a valuable alternative: identifying which features enabled the solution to perform sufficiently within the constraints of the original problem and then adapting those, rather than attempting to replicate the entire solution/algorithm itself.

6.  **Test the solution in the human-designed context**
    This is usually a fairly straightforward, if potentially time-consuming, step.

7.  **Iterate refinement of tailoring step based on testing**
    This iteration helps ensure that having brought the solution "out of its native environment" has not compromised its utility. As mentioned above, it is crucial in these iterations to ensure that patching identified gaps does not accidentally introduce other failures in function elsewhere. This can be both tricky and time-consuming.

    It is worth noting that this iteration can be both about ensuring non-native function but also about improving effectiveness and efficiency in performance. Again, this is usually done by considering small "tweaks" rather than fundamentally reanalyzing the appropriateness of the design unless something goes terribly wrong.

8.  **Declare victory and publish/deploy**
    This step, by design, focuses on the successes rather than the promising starts that seem to be the perfect analogies between natural and human systems but ultimately fail to provide a functional solution to the human problem at hand. As with all science, this bias against negative publication is entirely natural but severely hampers our communal ability to improve methodological best practices.

This entire protocol should seem very familiar to anyone familiar with nature-inspired research. To be completely clear, I absolutely do not mean to suggest that anything is wrong with this protocol. (I myself have been and remain an enthusiastic practitioner of this method.) However, it is not without room for improvement. This protocol is entirely *ad hoc*. It is my hope that by pointing out some of the common ways in which we have all been exploring from scratch, we might together discover some better practices to enable us to use the collective experience we have now achieved in the consideration of natural systems to streamline the process of inspiration and discovery.

Despite the discussion above, exploring why natural solutions need not be either efficient or effective, many solutions are, in fact, highly effective in a surprising number of contexts and over a tantalizing breadth of parameter space. Again mirroring discussion above, natural algorithms may not always maximize their efficiency in a particular axis of a solution space but are routinely amazing at achieving sufficiency in multi-objective criteria under multiple rigid constraints and are frequently robust to sudden, larger perturbations [24].

I argue that, for all of these reasons, it is time to switch the main focus of research into nature-inspired algorithms away from individual analogy developed on an *ad hoc* basis, and instead to explore whether or not we can discover the abstract and universal rules that might function as the building blocks of natural solutions. **In doing so, perhaps we can move beyond analogy to purposeful design using nature-inspired tools, rather than nature-inspired solutions.**

## 2.4 A few of nature's tools

Clearly, building a full understanding of nature's toolkit is an ambitious, long-term endeavor. That said, there are already some glaring commonalities among some of the best studied and most successful sources of inspiration. I propose three features that appear over and over again in nature and have been critical to the success of human designs that have borrowed from natural systems:

- **Proximate cues**
- **Distributed decisions**
- **Error convergence**

(Note that I do not mean to suggest that these are the only, or even the most important features of effective or efficient natural algorithms, they were simply the ones that most obviously suggested themselves to me as I considered the problem. It is my hope that future perspectives will increase this list and therefore enlarge our toolkit until we have the ability to build a well-tailored solution, from an appropriate set of components, for any problem that arises.)

Here, I will explore each of these three and consider why it might be so broadly included in natural solutions across systems and types of particular challenges. The goal is to understand not only why these are useful features in the natural settings in which they occur but to then be able to envision how these same tools might be employed to tackle problems in scenarios even where analogue cases in nature do not actually employ the techniques themselves. *In this way, we may be able to move beyond the happy accidents of evolved solutions.*

### 2.4.1 Proximate cues

Exactly as it sounds, the definition of a proximate cue is a signal that reflects information about system, but it is not a direct manifestation of the actual desired information: a proxy signal. To be useful, these are frequently easier to observe or measure directly than would be direct information about the focal system or process. (For example, fever patterns can be good proximate cues for identifying specific medical problems in humans; [25].)

Many natural systems make extensive use of proximate cues. Identifying which features may act as efficient proximate signals is already itself a useful endeavor.

- To rigorously characterize what information or feature of the system you actually need to understand is already a meaningful research endeavor.

While this sounds trite, narrowing the information set desired to precisely and only that which is required can help to focus identification of whether or not the desired understanding or outcomes can actually be achieved from that information set in the first place (e.g., is the system itself too noisy or inconstant for even direct observation to inform action).

- Is a potential proximate cue an actual reflection of the information you really want from the system?

  How reliable is the cue? Is the cue always correlated with the desired information? If so, how strong is that correlation? If not, are there specific, identifiable contexts in which the cue fails to accurately represent the information in ways that might be isolated and excluded? Perhaps there is no single effective cue, but a suite of cues, used in combination or each according to relevant context could provide the desired information.

- How easily or efficiently can the proximate cue itself be observed, measured, or analyzed?

  Of course, this is only effective and efficient if the proximate cue is itself readily accessible to observation and analysis.

By appropriately leveraging clever proximate cues, many natural systems demonstrate the ability to evaluate and respond to some mind-bogglingly complex scenarios easily and efficiently.

As one example, mosquitoes (a short-lived species with relatively little direct observational capacity about seasonal weather patterns) must be able to determine whether to lay eggs that will hatch quickly or else diapause (a mosquito's version of winter hibernation). If asked to design a system that restricted itself to the types of information accessible to, and processable by, a mosquito that could indicate whether or not winter is coming (thereby compromising the potential survival and success of eggs that will hatch in a few weeks due to colder temperatures and decreased food sources), the directly salient information might be completely unattainable. The ability to predict the temperature weeks into the future, or anticipate the availability of nectar produced by different flowers as the season changes require the ability to forecast and extrapolate beyond the life experience of an individual mosquito. Instead, mosquitoes rely on well-informed proximate cues of day length and current temperature to decide whether or not they should prepare for winter and change their egg-laying strategy [26]. These features are directly observable by the mosquito in real time and, over the course of the mosquitoes evolutionary life history, have served as relatively accurate and reliable signals of coming winter. (It is fascinating to note that global climate change has been decreasing the accuracy of day length signals as indicators of forthcoming temperature drops, thereby potentially compromising the utility of this signal in some species of mosquito; [27].)

## 2.4.2 Distributed decisions

Again, distributed decisions are exactly what they sound like. Rather than relying on a single, centralized decision-maker to whom all relevant information must be funneled and who then must be able to analyze and interpret that information, distributed decision systems use the contributions of local analysis of subsamples of the complete set of relevant information to lead to a decision. This process can feel like scientific magic. For example, birds flying together in a flock are making distributed decisions about where to fly, even if no one bird or set of birds is "in charge" of direction or speed, and yet flocks can be highly cohesive and zoom around the sky together in truly beautiful patterns [28,29].

As with proximate cues, exploring the ways in which distributed decision systems work might allow us to abstract and generalize this tool for use in human systems:

- Which individuals or units require what information and when?

     By their very nature, in distributed decision systems, most collaborating decision-makers are unlikely to have access to the same set of information as anyone else. Such systems work by leveraging the complementary sets of information to inform local decisions that function together, without the need for hierarchical control, to lead to successful emergent global outcomes [30]. This naturally leads to the need to consider who requires what subset of information and at what times, to enable the emergence of an effective and efficient global outcome. (Note that there are some distributed decision systems in which failure of sufficient information or coordination in timing prevents the system from converging to a common solution at all, whereas in others, the system instead converges to a poor solution. It may also be important to characterize which of these types of system is being analyzed if lack of convergence constitutes critical failure, or if an inability to differentiate a good solution from a poor solution until the actual results from the decision are known would be catastrophic.)
- What, if anything, do individuals/units need to share with each other to enact the distributed decision-making?

     In some cases, they may share independent decisions about local information. In others, they may have to take actions based on their independent decisions that cause changes in the system (these changes may then alter the information that others use to make their own local decisions). In still other cases, perhaps there is neither a decision nor an action affecting the system that needs to be made/taken, but instead the critical role for an individual/unit is to propagate a signal or generate a proximate cue for use in the local decision-making of others.

     Distributed decision systems have a number of fascinating properties. They eliminate the need for accurate and rapid collection of (potentially giant amounts of) relevant data, enabling faster, more flexible updates in information assimilation and decision-making. They relieve the need for the cognitive or computational capacity to store (e.g., remember) and analyze collected data. They help avoid single points of failure (although, of course, they increase the capacity for coordination failures). (In fact, a large part of the field of complex systems focuses research explicitly on the form and function of distributed decision-making, including those systems seen in nature [31,32].)

     Honey bee foraging is an excellent example of surprising capability in a natural system enabled by distributed decision-making [33,34]. In nature, honey bee colonies rely on designated foragers to gather resources from outside of the hive. Some of these foragers are tasked with discovering new resource sites, but all are then responsible for transporting those discovered resources to the colony. This would be an incredibly challenging task for individual bees. Success involves repeated searches of the landscape over time (since different flowers bloom and fade at different times, etc.), the ability to detect resources, to identify and then be able to accurately communicate their position to others (since single bees making lone trips cannot carry very much), and also to incorporate some mechanism for abandoning a site when the resource has been sufficiently exploited to deplete the site. If bees were to operate in parallel isolation, most of each bee's time would be spent in searching for a new resource site. Instead, honey bees employ a distributed decision process in which the bees who search for new sites ("scout" bees) return to the colony and communicate the existence of a resource site to other foragers by means of an elaborate dance that encodes both the level of enthusiasm for the resource abundance at the site and the location of the site. Foragers can observe the dances of multiple scouts and are more likely to follow the directions of more enthusiastic scouts. Once they return from a trip to a site, a forager can dance along with the scout, reinforcing the signal, continue to make trips without reinforcing the dance, or actively interrupt the dance (thereby signaling that the site may no longer be as resource rich as the dance seemed to indicate [35]), before making another independent choice about which directions to follow on their next trip from the hive [34]. This ongoing resource gathering system leverages time-saving parallel search by a few with the independent evaluation of those who act on the communicated information. These evaluations then act to enhance or degrade the signal indicating the location of resources and allows the foragers to deploy themselves with seamless efficiency to exploit the best of the already discovered sites while gradually shifting to the next best site as they exploit and deplete the resources they have found. This distributed decision-making process is so successful that it can support an order of magnitude more bees than the number that act as foragers, even in relatively resource poor seasons/environments.

### 2.4.3    Error convergence

While slightly less straightforward than either proximate cues or distributed decisions, an equally common and critical tool found in natural systems is the feature of error convergence: when any errors made in information analysis, communication, or action work synergistically with other errors/features of the system to maintain (or even enhance) overall function. Mirroring the above example in foraging honey bees, we consider a frequently ignored concept: what happens when foragers get lost? Analysis of foraging behaviors in ant colonies has shown that, under the right circumstances of colony size and need, ants getting lost can add critical efficiency to the discovery of new resource sites [36].

What are the mechanisms nature has evolved to exploit error to benefit the system? Are these also methods we can understand and exploit? The common aspects needed to appropriately leverage error convergence include

- How (in)accurate is the information analysis, communication, and or action likely to be?

Although I am arguing that errors can be useful, it is likely that they are only useful in particular ways, and under particular assumptions. For example, in many natural systems, expected inaccuracy tends to be bounded within a small range around the truth (e.g., systems that consider speed versus accuracy trade-offs in decision-making; [37,38]). Decisions or actions taken in response to information that is completely independent of reality are unlikely to be exploitable errors; however, small errors that enable the equivalent of local search around a current output as an iterative search toward an objective can increase the probability of efficient convergence to a local maximum [23].

• Do errors compound or self-correct?

In some systems (e.g., sensitivity to allergens [39]), single errors are more likely to trigger additional errors, whereas in other cases (e.g., attenuation of stress responses due to exposure therapy [40]), each additional error decreases the likelihood of perpetrating the same error again. This question essentially becomes one of identifying whether systems rely predominantly on feedback or feedforward protocols. Both can be useful, but it is important to identify which type of mechanism for error handling is in use.

• How many measurements/decisions are needed for convergence?

Almost by definition, single errors are not helpful. The ability to leverage the expected outcome from errors requires some useful probabilistic estimate to result from multiple or iterated errors (i.e., biased noise). Some systems, (e.g., dynamical resonance [41]) can achieve surprising outcomes from small amounts of noise, whereas others (e.g., emergence of multidrug antibiotic resistance among pathogens [42]) may need huge numbers of parallel trials and errors that must work synergistically to yield a benefit.

Of course, ideally, tailored error convergence could exploit both feedforward and feedback mechanisms to ensure outcomes within desired bounds. While ambitious, this is not without natural precedent. In a well-functioning synaptic system, neurons maintain stable patterns in activity. Neuron firing patterns are themselves determined by type and number of membrane-bound ion channels. Amazingly, these channels are actively created when firing activity is insufficient to maintain stability and are similarly actively degraded when activity is too high [43]. (In biology, these systems are frequently referred to as homeostatic due to their ability to return to function after deviation in either direction [24].)

## 2.5 Synergy among nature's tools

Each of these tools is clearly already of great potential use as isolated and independent features of any system. However, their most lucrative potential may come to fruition by leveraging synergies between/among them. Even focusing only on these three example features, there are compelling natural systems that leverage these synergies.

In the honey bee example mentioned above as a clear case of distributed decision-making, those distributed decisions are based on communicated information that bees make using proximate cues to estimate distance of the site from the hive (changes in angles of shadows [44]) and to communicate information about site quality (relative vigor of "waggling" during a dance [33]). Similarly, the errors made by ant foragers getting lost in our example above for error convergence [36] would also be "wasted" were there is not a system of distributed decision-making ready to act on newly discovered sites. Even the fundamental stochasticity of phenotypic expression of individual genes due to cumulative life history experience (including both epigenetic modifications [45] and individual experiences [46]) can be considered as the combined impact of proximate cues and error convergence together producing greater possible variation and thereby increasing expected sufficient fitness for the individual carrying those genes across a broader range of environments.

When all three of even just these few factors are present in a system, the outcomes are generally more robust to critical failures (i.e., they are able to persist in some form), more resilient to perturbations (i.e., they can return to their initial state), and they maintain efficiency across a diversity of contexts.

## 2.6    Potential pitfalls in nature-inspired algorithms specific to cyber security and resilience

Thus far, we have discussed evolutionary principles that shape natural systems and general algorithmic design that can borrow from those systems. Now let us consider more specifically the design challenges faced when trying to borrow from nature to inform the areas of cyber security and resilience.

### 2.6.1    Coevolutionary arms races

The construction of cyber security systems are, by nature, adversarial (whether concerned with active or passive attacks), and it is tempting to look toward adversarial systems in nature for inspiration. In nature, however, adversarial systems frequently result in coevolutionary arms races (e.g., the "Red Queen hypothesis" [47]) in which each mutation/escalation on one side provides the increased selective pressure that selects for a more extreme mutation/adaptation on the other side. These dynamics easily result in some extreme systems that are excellent at precise defense against the escalating mechanism of attack (e.g., bats and moths have highly coevolved sonic traits [48], but moths are light colored and would likely be highly susceptible to a visual night-hunter). Turning naively to these systems leaves us open to the possibility of building an impregnable fortress but forgetting to close the gate as it may be tempting to focus on creating designed analogies for these extreme defenses without realizing that those are the ontogenic response of generations of a specific direction of escalation, but not the only possible direction in which an attack could have happened.

**Recommendation:** It may be a wise and useful step when borrowing from any evolved adversarial system to consider vulnerability to challenges that remain unexploited by the natural adversary before these become apparent in testing after all the hard work of designing the inspired system has already been completed.

## 2.6.2 Designed threats versus evolved threats

Along similar lines as above, evolution works predominantly by exploring small variations around an already functional set of traits. Of course, mutations or recombinations can result in large leaps in form and/or function, but they are rare, and the most frequent outcome is inviability of the organism. As a result, truly uniform exploration of the space of parameters governing the behavior of an evolved trait is biologically rare. (It should be noted that it is more common in physical systems with phase transitions/bifurcations.) As a result, systems that have evolved to be secure or robust to adversarial threats need only (on expectation) be secure and robust to those adversarial threats already seen, or those very similar to the ones already in existence. In other words, there is frequently no evolved mechanism to defend against zero-day attacks. These constraints on the nature of attack are utterly untrue in human-designed systems.

**Recommendation:** Systems in nature that have evolved under threat from a greater diversity of extant adversaries or have survived novel challenges (e.g., from previously unfamiliar invasive species) may provide a better source for inspiration. It may be most profitable to see if we can isolate common tools in algorithms from systems that have been able to meet these broader challenges rather than focusing on systems that seem truly analogous to any one specific threat model.

## 2.6.3 Trade-offs between security and privacy may be different for each design component

### 2.6.3.1 Proximate cues must be relatively "leak-proof"

Cyber security design is used to the challenges faced in allowing only authorized agents to have access to private or sensitive information, but the challenges expand rapidly when we first need to understand the full array of information being encoded in proximate cues. Are there additional, accurate correlations encoded in the proximate cue beyond the feature we intend to capture and exploit? The same proximate cue an animal might use to indicate a food source can be exploited by a predator as a cue that the prey animal is likely to be near.

**Recommendation:** Carefully consider why likely proximate cues are useful, and if there are other signals, they might also capture/reveal.

### 2.6.3.2 Distributed decision-making

These systems are naturally susceptible to bad actors (either legitimate participants acting in bad faith or else infiltration by illegitimate participants). Luckily, these are common challenges considered within cyber systems. Less frequently considered, but of equal or potentially greater concern, is the ability to purposefully exceed the natural parameter space (e.g., range of environments or cues) in which the system functions and thereby cause critical failure by self-destruction. One famous example of a human-designed critical failure for a natural system is the "death spiral" (also called a "circular mill") in army ants [49]. In this case, the algorithm ants use to coordinate movement in a swarm can be tricked by purposefully manipulating the proximate cue they use to detect where others have been before and then also recommend going. By connecting the pheromone trail back onto itself, these ants can be tricked into literally running to death in a circle they themselves reinforce as they run.

**Recommendation 1:** Purposefully consider the impact of bad actors internal to the distributed decision-making process.

**Recommendation 2:** Anticipate the impact on the algorithm of exceeding design specifications (especially if those parameters are also drawn direction from the natural system).

### 2.6.3.3    Error convergence

Cascading amplification of errors is often fatal. Feedforward systems without compensatory feedback safety protocols are responsible for such critical failures as thyroid storm (in which endocrinological malfunction causes a series of increasingly life-threatening failures in the human body [50]).

**Recommendation:** While it is not likely to be practical to incorporate compensatory feedback mechanisms every time there is the potential for error, it is always critical to consider how amplification or resonance in seemingly minor individual errors can act together to compromise an entire system.

## 2.7    When NOT to use nature-inspired algorithms

We have now discussed why nature-inspired algorithms might be tempting, how their ontology makes them both well suited and also potentially challenging for adaptation to suit the needs of human-designed challenges, what common design components might be responsible for their strengths, and what types of weaknesses might be especially important to consider in the context of cyber security and resilience. In each of these considerations, we have focused on picking apart the nuances of how to exploit strengths while avoiding failure and suggested how to maximize the likelihood of success. But are there any cases in which we can definitely save ourselves the trouble of these careful analyzes and reject the possibilities of nature-inspired design on its face?

While unlikely to occur with any frequency, it is true that there are a few cases we can probably eliminate fairly rapidly from consideration for nature-inspired solutions. For example, it is likely we can eliminate any case in which the set of design components that could be used in tackling the problem each have inherent, exploitable susceptibilities to designed attack. This would leave us with the only recourse toward security to be in keeping secret the inspirational designs themselves. This type of "security by obscurity" is obviously flawed as any attacker who can figure out the design can then instantly understand how to overcome any secure features [51]. Similarly, when the system we are trying to secure or make resilient has constant, narrow constraints on the diversity of its function it is unlikely that we should turn to nature-inspired solutions. In this case, it is not that nature-inspired solutions cannot work well, it is rather that the types of solutions that are most likely to emerge in nature have themselves been constrained to deal with a minimally sufficient breadth in system behavior that they are optimized for flexibility and are therefore likely to be inefficient for application to narrowly defined cases. Of course, even these examples do not provide any truly rapid or guaranteed-sufficient criteria for rejection.

## 2.8 Conclusions

Nature-inspired algorithms are truly beautiful, elegant, impressive, and they have in the past provided the spark of creativity that allowed researchers to solve previously intractable problems with startling efficiency. However, now that we have seen that wheel can be invented in this way, it is time for us to step back from the processes by which we have fumbled about in the early stages of discovery and provide nature-inspired algorithmic design with a rigorous, scientific methodology of its own. We should analyze effective and efficient natural systems to discover fundamental functional components. We should not hope to find analogies for human-design challenges that accidentally leverage these components, either independently or synergistically. We should learn when nature-inspired design may be helpful and when instead the tools and techniques shaped in nature may not yield the best solutions. It is time to use the functional components of nature's designs, learning by example, but growing beyond mimicry to true inspiration. Thus far, we have followed or adapted nature's blue prints, it is time instead for us to master the principles of design that nature can teach us and begin to draft our own plans.

## Acknowledgments

The author is grateful for support for this work from the NSF: Grant CNS-1646890.

## References

[1]   Vierra S. Biomimicry: designing to model nature. Whole Building Design Guide; 2011. http://www.wbdg.org/resources/biomimicry-designing-model-nature

[2]   Mahadevan V, Chiang F. iACO: a bio-inspired power efficient routing scheme for sensor networks. International Journal of Computer Theory and Engineering. 2010;2(6):972.

[3]   Korczynski M, Hamieh A, Huh JH, *et al.* Hive oversight for network intrusion early warning using DIAMoND: a bee-inspired method for fully distributed cyber defense. IEEE Communications Magazine. 2016;54(6):60–67.

[4]   Mazurczyk W, Moore S, Fulp EW, *et al.* Bio-inspired cyber security for communications and networking. IEEE Communications Magazine. 2016;54(6): 58–59.

[5]   Kaneko K. Life: an introduction to complex systems biology. Berlin: Springer; 2006.

[6]    Ma'ayan A. Complex systems biology. Journal of The Royal Society Interface. 2017;14(134):20170391.

[7]    Verberk WC, Bilton DT. Can oxygen set thermal limits in an insect and drive gigantism? PLoS One. 2011;6(7):e22610.

[8]    Doligez B, Cadet C, Danchin E, *et al.* When to use public information for breeding habitat selection? The role of environmental predictability and density dependence. Animal Behaviour. 2003;66(5):973–988.

[9]    DeAngelis D. Energy flow, nutrient cycling, and ecosystem resilience. Ecology. 1980;61(4):764–771.

[10]   Nicolis G, Nicolis C. Foundations of complex systems: emergence, information and predicition. Singapore: World Scientific; 2012.

[11]   Hardin G. The competitive exclusion principle. Science. 1960;131(3409): 1292–1297.

[12]   Dlugosch K, Parker I. Founding events in species invasions: genetic variation, adaptive evolution, and the role of multiple introductions. Molecular Ecology. 2008;17(1):431–449.

[13]   Frank SA, Slatkin M. Evolution in a variable environment. The American Naturalist. 1990;136(2):244–260.

[14]   Wierzbicki AP. A mathematical basis for satisficing decision making. Mathematical Modelling. 1982;3(5):391–405.

[15]   Noor E, Milo R. Efficiency in evolutionary trade-offs. Science. 2012; 336(6085):1114–1115.

[16]   Hofbauer J, Sigmund K. Evolutionary game dynamics. Bulletin of the American Mathematical Society. 2003;40(4):479–519.

[17]   Wood BJ, Duggan RA. Red teaming of advanced information assurance concepts. In: DARPA Information Survivability Conference and Exposition, 2000. DISCEX'00. Proceedings. vol. 2. IEEE; 2000. pp. 112–118.

[18]   Primlani RV. Biomimicry: on the frontiers of design. Vilakshan: The XIMB Journal of Management. 2013;10(2):139–148.

[19]   Liu K, Jiang L. Bio-inspired self-cleaning surfaces. Annual Review of Materials Research. 2012;42:231–263.

[20]   Leibnitz K, Wakamiya N, Murata M. A bio-inspired robust routing protocol for mobile ad hoc networks. In: Computer Communications and Networks, 2007. ICCCN 2007. Proceedings of 16th International Conference on. IEEE; 2007. pp. 321–326.

[21]   Houck CR, Joines J, Kay MG. A genetic algorithm for function optimization: a MATLAB implementation. Ncsu-ie tr. 1995;95(09):1–10.

[22]   Davis L. Handbook of genetic algorithms. New York: Van Nostrand Reinhold; 1991.

[23]   Mitchell M. An introduction to genetic algorithms. Cambridge, MA: MIT Press; 1998.

[24]   Tregonning K, Roberts A. Complex systems which evolve towards homeostasis. Nature. 1979;281(5732):563.

[25]   Cunha BA. The clinical significance of fever patterns. Infectious Disease Clinics. 1996;10(1):33–44.

[26] Bradshaw WE. Geography of photoperiodic response in diapausing mosquito. Nature. 1976;262(5567):384.

[27] Bradshaw WE, Holzapfel CM. Genetic shift in photoperiodic response correlated with global warming. Proceedings of the National Academy of Sciences. 2001;98(25):14509–14511.

[28] Genone J, Van Buskirk I. 8 Complex Systems and Effective Interaction. Building the Intentional University: Minerva and the Future of Higher Education. 2017; p. 109.

[29] Hildenbrandt H, Carere C, Hemelrijk CK. Self-organized aerial displays of thousands of starlings: a model. Behavioral Ecology. 2010;21(6): 1349–1359.

[30] Jensen HJ. Self-organized criticality: emergent complex behavior in physical and biological systems. vol. 10. New York: Cambridge University Press; 1998.

[31] Deneubourg JL, Goss S. Collective patterns and decision-making. Ethology Ecology & Evolution. 1989;1(4):295–311.

[32] Couzin ID. Collective cognition in animal groups. Trends in Cognitive Sciences. 2009;13(1):36–43.

[33] Winston ML. The biology of the honey bee. Boston, MA: Harvard University Press; 1991.

[34] Seeley TD. The wisdom of the hive: the social physiology of honey bee colonies. Boston, MA: Harvard University Press; 2009.

[35] Pastor KA, Seeley TD. The brief piping signal of the honey bee: begging call or stop signal? Ethology. 2005;111(8):775–784.

[36] Deneubourg JL, Aron S, Goss S, *et al.* Error, communication and learning in ant societies. European Journal of Operational Research. 1987;30(2):168–172.

[37] Passino KM, Seeley TD. Modeling and analysis of nest-site selection by honeybee swarms: the speed and accuracy trade-off. Behavioral Ecology and Sociobiology. 2006;59(3):427–442.

[38] Chittka L, Skorupski P, Raine NE. Speed–accuracy tradeoffs in animal decision making. Trends in Ecology & Evolution. 2009;24(7):400–407.

[39] Rivas MN, Burton OT, Wise P, *et al.* A microbiota signature associated with experimental food allergy promotes allergic sensitization and anaphylaxis. Journal of Allergy and Clinical Immunology. 2013;131(1):201–212.

[40] Watson J, Gaind R, Marks I. Physiological habituation to continuous phobic stimulation. Behaviour Research and Therapy. 1972;10(3):269–278.

[41] Beck F, Blasius B, Lüttage U, *et al.* Stochastic noise interferes coherently with a model biological clock and produces specific dynamic behaviour. Proceedings of the Royal Society of London B: Biological Sciences. 2001;268(1473): 1307–1313.

[42] Martinez J, Baquero F. Mutation frequencies and antibiotic resistance. Antimicrobial Agents and Chemotherapy. 2000;44(7):1771–1777.

[43] Marder E, Prinz AA. Modeling stability in neuron and network function: the role of activity in homeostasis. Bioessays. 2002;24(12):1145–1154.

[44] Srinivasan MV, Zhang S, Altwein M, *et al.* Honeybee navigation: nature and calibration of the "Odometer". Science. 2000;287(5454):851–853.

[45]   Zhang YY, Fischer M, Colot V, *et al.* Epigenetic variation creates potential for evolution of plant phenotypic plasticity. New Phytologist. 2013;197(1): 314–322.
[46]   Biro PA, Stamps JA. Are animal personality traits linked to life-history productivity? Trends in Ecology & Evolution. 2008;23(7):361–368.
[47]   Van Valen L. The red queen. The American Naturalist. 1977;111(980): 809–810.
[48]   Fullard JH. The sensory coevolution of moths and bats. In: Comparative hearing: insects. New York: Springer; 1998. pp. 279–326.
[49]   Schneirla TC. A unique case of circular milling in ants, considered in relation to trail following and the general problem of orientation. New York: American Museum of Natural History; 1944.
[50]   Chiha M, Samarasinghe S, Kabaker AS. Thyroid storm: an updated review. Journal of Intensive Care Medicine. 2015;30(3):131–140.
[51]   Mercuri RT, Neumann PG. Security by obscurity. Communications of the ACM. 2003;46(11):160.

*Chapter 3*

# Bioinspired collaboration and cyber security

*Youna Jung[1]*

Throughout history, collaborative approaches have been regarded as one of the most efficient solutions to complex and large-scale problems. Collaboration enables distributed and heterogeneous things to achieve a complicated goal through rich interactions. That is why many emerging technologies, such as multi-agent systems, cloud computing, crowdsourcing, and collective intelligence, are leveraging collaboration to address complicated problems at different levels. For successful collaboration, it is critical to have proper mechanisms to search the most eligible and available members, organize a group with communication channels between members, and control their collaboration. However, current solutions to distributed computing do not deeply concern about collaboration. To support collaboration between distributed smart things, many researchers have studied the organization and collaboration strategies. The bioinspired collaboration that we will explore in this chapter is one of the target research areas. Indeed, we can easily find actual examples of effective and well-organized collaboration in nature. To get ideas, many researchers have studied patterns of collaborative behaviors of insects and birds and applied their models to computer systems.

In this chapter, we focus on collaboration schemes inspired by nature and examine cyber security technologies used to protect bioinspired collaboration systems and discuss research challenges and future research directions.

## 3.1 Collaboration

Many group-based approaches have been proposed in the literature to address the large-scale and complex problems. In fact, the group-based problem-solving approach has been a good way to solve a problem requiring diverse resource and capabilities and perform a highly resource-consuming and time-consuming task [1].

Before we introduce existing work on group-based solutions, let us first clarify the difference between relevant terminologies, such as *coordination*, *cooperation*, and *collaboration*. Blank *et al.* [2] defined three terminologies as follows. By adopting

[1]Department of Computer and Information Sciences, Virginia Military Institute, USA

their work, we define three strategies as shown below to distinguish the different type of group efforts throughout this chapter.

- *Coordination*—It models the simplest group efforts. The goals of coordination must be compatible with the goals of organizations that each member belongs. In general, interaction between members lasts for only limited-time for a specific project or task. All communication and resources of each member are controlled by a member's organizations.
- *Cooperation*—A group can be organized to address a new mission or goal. Normally, cooperation addresses a longer term effort than coordination and has a centralized authority dealing with negotiation between organizations. Members' resources are maintained by individual organization but can be shared as needed.
- *Collaboration*—It models the most comprehensive and dedicated group efforts. Similar to cooperation, a group is organized to achieve one or more mission(s) newly created. However, unlike cooperation, it assumes a strong commitment between organizations to share resources and supports joint-planning and joint-evaluation. In many cases, dedicated communication channels are established for collaboration.

Among three strategies, in this chapter, we focus on cooperation and collaboration only. As mentioned above, the group-based strategies have been applied to emerging areas, such as the computer-supported cooperative work (CSCW), the service-oriented architecture (SOA), online social networks (OSNs), and multi-agent systems.

## 3.1.1   Computer-supported cooperative work

CSCW is a methodology for small or medium size teamwork and its computer support. In [3], Wilson *et al.* defined CSCW as stated below:

*CSCW is a generic term that combines the understanding of the way people work in groups with the enabling technologies of computer networking, and associated hardware, software, services and techniques.*

The objective of CSCW is to develop a groupware allowing individual users to perform a common task through information sharing. At this time, groupware is a software system consisting of software, hardware, and services. It supports teamwork by coordinating necessary resources and tasks. The popular groupware in CSCW are the video-conferencing systems and the multiauthor editing systems.

Typically, groups are small-size project-oriented teams. Members in a team share the same task environment and interact with other members to perform a common task [4,5]. Typically, cooperation in CSCW is designed as ad hoc group processes. A group process specifies necessary information, activities, and communication between members. A group process usually consists of a static part and a dynamic part. A static part identifies a group's goal, organization, communication protocol, and environment. At this time, group organization is defined with team members and their roles. Group protocol specifies a way to communicate between members, and group environment describes necessary hardware and software systems.

A dynamic part contains frequently changing components like current state and group activities. All possible activities and dependencies between activities are defined in the group activities component, and the current state changes according to the execution of group activities. Note that members' activities are tightly coupled in CSCW. Therefore, it is critical to define activity dependencies to manage cooperation in groupware.

## 3.1.2 Service-oriented architecture

SOA is introduced by Gartner Groups in 1996 as an evolutionary approach of the distributed component architecture. There are many definitions of SOA, but in this chapter, we use the following definition proposed by Erl [6]:

> ***Service-oriented Architecture (SOA)*** is a form of technology architecture that adheres to the principles of service-orientation. When realized through the Web services technology platform, SOA establishes the potential to support and promote these principles throughout the business process and automation domains of an enterprise.

Because of its great reusability of components on a same system, the distributed component approach had been spotlighted. However, its strong dependency with specific platform and language caused serious problems. To remedy the problem, SOA published standardized interfaces. By using XML-based messaging protocol, SOA then supports loosely coupled connections between services using [6–9]. Now, we can use SOA to integrate and reuse services across heterogeneous systems. Note that, the granularity of services in SOA is relatively bigger than the granularity of components in traditional distributed component architecture.

Typically, SOA applications can be characterized as follows: (1) standardized service infrastructures and services, (2) loosely coupled service connection, and (3) service reusability. First, SOA provides standard service infrastructures including Web Service Definition Language for service interface, Simple Object Access Protocol for messaging format, Universal Description Discovery and Integration or US-Discovery for Service Discovery, as well as standardized services for messaging, transaction, security, and diverse business executions. In addition, SOA separates service interfaces from service implementation in order to reduce dependency between services and environments. Finally, in SOA, applications can dynamically discover and composite necessary services at runtime.

## 3.1.3 Online social networks

The rapid growth in mobile and networking technologies has significantly improved the level of connectivity and interactions among people around the world, and it has resulted in the explosive growth of OSNs such as Facebook and Twitter. The objective of OSNs is to enable social users to share information and resources with their friends and make new friends. OSNs have influenced in the patterns of communication and cooperation with rich communication methods (e.g., wall posting, photo sharing, messaging, and tagging).

Recently, OSNs are used as a basis for immediate and effective cooperation among people because of their huge pool of users and support for rapid dissemination of information. In fact, we can easily find real-world examples cooperation through OSNs. When Hurricane Irene occurred and tsunami hit Japan, people in the distressed areas actively shared critical information about Irene's path and evacuation plans and warned residents about possible damages through Facebook and Twitter. The aid organizations such as the Red Cross also rushed to use OSNs in order to help the victims and recruit volunteers. In addition, people have been using OSNs to find their lost pets by sharing information. Through the *Lost Dog Found* and the *Fidofinder* in Twitter, users distribute information about lost pets to their followers and try to find lost pets together. In the healthcare domain, an immediate cooperation between medical team and a patient's family through OSNs saved a patients' life. As we can see in actual examples above, OSNs have provided an innovative way to organize people and promote immediate cooperation.

### 3.1.4   Multi-agent systems

Multi-agent systems are frequently developed to provide services requiring complex interactions because of agents' features such as flexible and autonomous problem solving behavior and the richness of interactions [1]. Toward this, many researchers have conducted research on goal-oriented group organization and collaboration between intelligent agents. A group's collaboration procedure is predefined or dynamically determined using members' intelligence at runtime.

The objective of multi-agent approaches is to design and implement necessary agents to satisfy a given requirements. It is different from an approach that intends to offer services using collaboration among existing agents. At this time, the later approach assumes that participating agents are predefined. It might be a reason that most of multi-agent approaches do not concentrated on cooperation. For the better understanding of collaboration in multi-agent systems, we introduce some notable existing work below.

- *Community in PICO*—The pervasive information community organization (PICO) is a middleware framework [10,11]. It creates a goal-oriented community using existing objects at request time. In the PICO, hardware devices are clearly distinguished from software agents. The hardware devices are represented as *camileuns* while agents are represented as *delegents*. The PICO focuses on how to meet the requirement for proactive collaborations using agent communities but it does not provide specific organization and cooperation models for multi-agent systems.
- *Groups in active space*—The active space [12] introduced Gaia, a distributed middleware infrastructure that coordinates software agents and heterogeneous networked devices. Using the Gaia middleware, we can represent a cyberspace as a programmable environment rather than a collection of individual and disconnected heterogeneous devices. Four years later, the same research team proposed an improved middleware, called super space [13]. Super space focuses on how to manage and orchestrate groups in heterogeneous active spaces created by different Gaia middleware.

- *Groups in AALADIN*—AALADIN is an organization model for multi-agent systems [14]. It allows us to specify the role-based groups and interactions in a group. In this model, each agent takes a role, which is an abstract of an agent's function and service, in a group. AALADIN was evolved to the AGR model (Agent/Group/Role model) that considers a dynamic aspect of an organization [15]. Using the AGR model, we can describe a group creation process, a membership mechanism of agents within a group, and a role acquisition mechanism additionally.
- *Community in community computing* [16]—Community computing is a multi-agent based framework to develop a cooperative ubiquitous system that offers dynamic services through collaboration between existing agents. This framework proposed a conceptual model to abstract agents' communities and role-based situation-aware collaborations in a community and a development process based on the model-driven architecture from the most high-level abstraction model to source code. For the practical use of the framework, the project team provides a development toolkit, called CDTK, for developers' convenience.

## 3.2 Bioinspired cooperation

As the level of intelligence and autonomy of computing elements has been increased and the connections between elements are highly distributed, researchers have studied the coordination and cooperation schemes of living things (e.g., animals, insects, and cells) to understand underlying principles of their interaction and cooperation. In fact, cooperation between software agents or networking nodes in computer sciences shares many similarities with coordination/cooperation in ant colonies, bird flocking, fish schooling, bacterial growth, and chemical reaction.

Before proceed further, let me first define the eight characteristics of cooperative living things in nature as follows: (1) *Perception/Awareness*—A living thing is aware of environment changes, (2) *Intelligence*—A living thing has own knowledge and use it to solve a problem or achieve a goal, (3) *Autonomy*—A living thing has complete control over its own actions and internal states, hence it is able to act without direct intervention from other organisms, (4) *Reactiveness*—A living thing is capable of reacting appropriately to events or information from its environment or other living things, (5) *Adaptivity*—A living thing is capable of changing its own behavior flexibly based on environment changes and/or previous experiences, (6) *Interoperability/Sociability*—A living thing is capable of interacting with others in a peer-to-peer manner, (7) *Goal-oriented*—A living thing continuously tries to achieve its own goals or a common goal of a group, and (8) *Partially/fully decentralized control*—A living thing is capable of achieving a common goal without centralized control.

Because of the characteristics of organisms, most bioinspired systems involve interactions and cooperation. By analyzing complexity of cooperation in biological systems, Mano *et al.* [17] has defined four cooperative mechanisms as follows.

- *Parallelism*—Parallelism is the basic level of cooperation. All elements in a system share a common goal but each element performs independent activity based on its role. Therefore, elements carry out different activities in parallel, without frequent communication between different role groups. The most well-known example of parallelism is shown in Polistes Wasps' nest construction [18]. Wasp workers share a same goal, building the nests, and the performance of their activities depends on the number of elements in the worker group.

- *Coordination*—Unlike parallelism, coordination requires administrative activities to observe and adjust cooperative activities among two or more elements. To achieve a common goal, each element interacts with others and sometimes adjust its activity depending on others' activities. We can find a good example in ant colonies. When a group of ants tries to take a branch off an entrance of their nest, ants perform coordinated activities. For example, the first ant lifts up the branch while other ants catch the branch lower and then lift it up on their turn.

- *Specialization*—Specialization is a cooperative mechanism that assign a particular task to some groups of elements to achieve a common goal. An administrative mechanism is required to decide specialized tasks and a group of elements that perform the tasks. The bust example of the specialization is the specialization of cells in cellular streams [19]. To produce more metabolites for other cells and the whole organisms, some cells can modify their structure and/or develop particular abilities (e.g., gas transportation in blood read corpuscles, production of antibodies in immunity cells, production and propagation of spikes in neurons, or chemical energy storage in lever cells).

- *Recruitment*—Recruitment represents collective behaviors to achieve a common goal. Note that, in this mechanism, single element's goal matches a goal of group cooperation. In general, each element performs the same task in order to produce mass effect. There exist many examples in nature like fish schooling to protect themselves from predators, temperature regulation in penguin colonies, or predator detection in sheep flock.

As mentioned above, many researchers have applied the cooperative mechanisms of biology systems to solve problems in computer sciences because of the similarities between biology systems and computer systems. In this chapter, we introduce two popular research areas in bioinspired collaboration, swarm intelligence (SI) and chemical reaction.

## 3.2.1 Cooperation in swarm intelligence

SI refers to a problem-solving scheme using decentralized and collective behavior [20]. Note that, in SI, we assume that each element in a swarm is capable of processing simple information and adapting its activities to achieve a goal. The type of elements can vary (e.g., insects, birds, robots, networking nodes, or standalone workstations), but regardless of their types, elements interact and cooperate with each other to solve a common problem. So far, many cooperation schemes in SI have been used in computer science areas, for example, clustering, multi-agent systems, robotics, and networks, but in this section, we focus on two of the most popular research areas, self-organized network (SON) and robotics.

- *SI in SON*—Self-organization is one of well-known features in artificial communication systems, especially in wireless ad hoc and wireless sensor networks [21]. The main objectives of the SON systems are to achieve better scalability, availability, and reliability [22–24]. To meet these requirements, many cooperative algorithms in SI have been used, for example, the pulse-coupled oscillators and the ant colony optimization. The bioinspired cooperative algorithms have produced good performance on different networking problems, such as load balancing (e.g. *BeeHive* routing algorithm [25,26]), adaptive routing, cooperative transmission [27,28], distributed synchronization, cooperative beam-forming [29], network coding [30], cognitive spectrum sensing [31], and coordinated multipoint transmission/reception (CoMP) [32].

- *SI in robotics*—Many researchers in robotics have been inspired by cooperation in nature. The characteristics of cooperative living things defined above perfectly fit in the robot systems. Similar to biological systems, the robots' perception of their environment directly affects their action. Each robot can obtain local information, but the overall behavior of a robot system is decided by coordinating local information from each robot [33]. Based on the similarity between cooperation in nature and robot systems, researchers have applied several SI algorithms to robot-based exploration [34], robot swarms [35,36], and decentralized robots for cooperative transport [37].

## 3.2.2 Coordination in chemistry

Chemistry has been another source of inspiration. Researchers have identified the coordination rules from chemical reactions in biological organisms and meteorological systems.

Two remarkable works on this area are the *GAMMA* model and the *chemical abstract machine (CHAM)* model. The *GAMMA* model governs coordination using chemical-like rules defined in a space [38]. The *CHAM* model supports coordination between floating molecules according to reaction rules [39]. Besides the two models introduced above, most models use the chemical reaction metaphor that represent a system's state as a fluid in which reactants are coordinated with others based on predefined reaction rules. Currently, several coordination models are used in computer science areas. The *Fraglets* model uses chemistry-based coordination models to data distribution and aggregation [40]. In addition, some service composition approaches in SOA are using chemical models [41]. Recently, a chemistry-inspired coordination approach has been proposed for pervasive systems that can support multi-missioned coordination by utilizing the concept of *chemical affinity* between networked objects [42].

## 3.3 Access control for bioinspired cooperation

As seen in the previous section, the bioinspired coordination/cooperation mechanisms have significantly influenced emerging technologies by supporting advance features such as self-organization and decentralized control. To realize its full potential, however, security must be guaranteed in the bioinspired cooperative systems. Without proper security solutions, their vulnerability to security threats may become a barrier to further progress. Security encompasses several aspects and topics, but in this chapter, we focus on access control only.

### 3.3.1   Traditional access control models

Before interaction and cooperation become the norm, access control models focused on users' identities [e.g., the discretionary access control (DAC) and the mandatory access control (MAC)], roles [e.g., the role-based access control (RBAC)], or attributes [e.g., the attribute-based access control (ABAC)]. The details about each model are below:

- *DAC*—DAC is an identity-based access control model, controls access to an object based on an owner's permissions. It allows individual users to grant or revoke access to any of the objects under their control [43]. DAC has been used in many systems and networks. For an instance, the Windows operating system is using DAC to enable the owners of a file or directory to grant or deny access to other users.
- *MAC*—MAC is based the Bell–LaPadula model. In this model, permissions are associated with security labels attached to users and objects. A user can access objects in the security label assigned to the user and lower levels. A system enforces all the control and users are not able to modify their access rights [44]. MAC is frequently used in government and defense information systems in which the resource owner must not make authorization decisions on their resources.
- *RBAC*—RBAC controls accesses based on users' roles rather than identifications or security labels. A user can have permissions by having appropriate roles. In RBAC model, system administrators can create roles, grant permissions to the roles, and then assign users to one or more roles based on job responsibility and organization policy. By employing the concept of role, RBAC dramatically reduces the complexity of system maintenance and security enforcement. In fact, the role-based approach is more realistic than user-based approach since the structure of access right is mainly depending on roles in most organizations. Due to such advantages, RBAC became popular in most large-scale and complex systems. RBAC model has evolved from $RBAC_0$ to $RBAC_3$ $RBAC_0$ identifies the minimal requirements of RBAC systems. $RBAC_1$ added role hierarchies into $RBAC_0$, while $RBAC_2$ added constraints to $RBAC_0$. $RBAC_3$ combined $RBAC_1$ and $RBAC_2$ [45].
- *ABAC*—ABAC control accesses according to attribute-based policies. The policies can be specified with a variety of attributes, such as user attributes, resource attributes, object attributes, and environment attributes. Unlike the RBAC model, ABAC can evaluate not only subjects' roles but also many different attributes [46]. Because of its dynamic and context-aware control, ABAC is currently used in many web and cloud applications.

## 3.3.2   Access control models for bioinspired collaboration

### 3.3.2.1   Existing access control models for cooperation

As we can see, traditional access control models focus on individual users (subjects) and do not consider interaction or cooperation between users. As the level of connectivity has been increased, researchers have been interested in access controls for interactive and cooperative systems. Let me introduce some recent access control models considering cooperation.

- *Task-based Access Control (TBAC)*—TBAC controls accesses from a task-oriented (TO) perspective rather than the traditional subject-object perspective. Using TBAC, we can control authorizations at various points during tasks [47]. Because of its TO view, TBAC is used in some distributed computing systems and workflow management systems. However, as pointed out in [48], TBAC is not suitable for cooperative systems due to the difficulty in dividing cooperation into separate tasks with usage counts. Moreover, TBAC allows specifying restricted context information related to tasks, activities, or workflows but not cooperation-related contexts.
- *Team-based access control (TMAC)*—TMAC [49] and context-based TMAC [50] provide access control schemes for a group/team of users taking different roles in a team. However, they do not have a flexible access control and administration models for dynamic cooperation. In addition, they capture only limited context information about teams.
- *Group-based RBAC (GB-RBAC)*—GB-RBAC has been proposed to support access control for intergroup collaboration. It assumes that many groups, called *virtual groups* (*VG*), already exist in a system. A VG is created dynamically by gathering roles and permissions required for the VG and terminated as soon as it accomplishes its goal. Each VG has one or more administrators governing accesses in the VG [51]. However, GB-RBAC does not consider an organization mechanism for VGs and context-aware cooperation. Moreover, there is no clear mechanism to resolve conflicts between administrators in a VG. The most critical problem is that all members in a VG have all permissions assigned to the VG. However, it could cause a serious security threat.

As you can see above, understanding of context/situation-aware cooperation is required for dynamic and effective control in cooperative systems. To the best of our knowledge, only few models support context-aware dynamic interaction and cooperation: the role-interactionbased access control (RiBAC), the community-centric RiBAC (CRiBAC), and the community-centric property-based access control (CPBAC).

### 3.3.2.2   Role-interaction-based access control

RiBAC mainly focuses on accesses during interaction between subjects (e.g., human users, software agents, etc.). It controls access to users' tasks as well as traditional resource objects. Note that, RiBAC defines an interaction as access to a partner's task or to the partner itself and propose the interaction permissions in addition to the traditional definitions of permission in RBAC [52].

## Interaction permissions

RiBAC defines two types of role interactions, the *role-oriented (RO)* interaction and the *task-oriented (TO)* interaction. An *ro* interaction indicates that a subject role ($R_s$) initiating an interaction performs its operation on a targeted object role ($R_o$), while the TO interaction means that $R_s$ commands its $R_o$ to perform $R_o$'s tasks [52]. To perform a task on a user or ask a user to perform his/her tasks, a subject user must have a corresponding interaction permission, either a *task-oriented permission (tprms)* or a *role-oriented permission (rprms)*. To support traditional permission associated to object resources, RiBAC has the *Object-oriented permission (oprms)* also. A valid pair of an object and an operation on that object forms an oprms. A valid pair of an operation of a subject role and its target role forms an rprms. A tprms is represented as a pair of a role and its task that can be invoked by others. Since RiBAC is a variation of RBAC, users must be assigned to a particular role to interact with others through *user assignment* and the *permission assignment (PA)*.

## RiBAC family

RiBAC has four variations: *basic RiBAC (RiBAC-B)*, *hierarchical RiBAC (RiBAC-H)*, *constrained RiBAC (RiBAC-C)*, and *constrained hierarchical RiBAC (RiBAC-CH)*. The formal definitions for each RiBAC models are shown in [53].

- *RiBAC-B*: This basic model deals with interactions between users with two types of interaction permissions.
- *RiBAC-H*: RiBAC-H allows that permissions can be inherited through a role hierarchy (RH) for better permission management and inheritance. In the definition of RiBAC-H, there is a small change in the role definition.
- *RiBAC-C*: RiBAC-C adds the *separation of duty (SoD)* and the *cardinality* constraints to RiBAC-B. SoD is a mechanism to prevent fraud and errors that could be caused by simultaneous accesses. In RiBAC-C provides the static and dynamic SoD (DSoD) constraint. The *static SoD (SSoD)* constraints specify that no agent can be assigned to more than a specific number of roles in a role set and typically, they are enforced in the *agent-role assignment (AA)*. The *DSoD* constraints affect role activation and make sure that an agent cannot activate certain roles together in one session. In addition, RiBAC-C supports cardinality constraints that limit the number of users that may be assigned to a role. The cardinality constraints can be static or dynamic. Similar to the SoD constraints, the *static cardinality* constraints are applicable to AA, while the *dynamic cardinality* constraints limit the total numbers of active roles across sessions of a user. For each type of SoD constraints, RiBAC-C defines the minimum and the maximum constraints as well.
- *RiBAC-CH*: RiBAC-CH is a combination of RiBAC-H and RiBAC-C. RiBAC-CH adopt the concept of *hybrid hierarchy (HH)* [54] that differentiates permission usage from role activation in a hierarchy by defining three types of relationships: *permission inheritance*, *activation*, and *inheritance-activation*. By leveraging the *activation* and *permission inheritance* of HH relationships, RiBAC-CH provides more flexible policy specification.

### 3.3.2.3   Dynamic role-interaction based access control

DRiBAC is an improved version of RiBAC, which captures dynamic aspects of inter-actions [55]. A key limitation of RiBAC is that there is no way to distinguish each user assigned to the same interaction role. It brings a serious problem that a user has permissions for all the users assigned to its partner role. To avoid such oversharing and guarantee the principle of the least privilege, in RiBAC, we must create a new role for each interacting user but it is unrealistic solutions

DRiBAC enables us to capture actual interactions between users and supports exclusive accesses for their actual partners only based on context. Toward this, DRiBAC defines four types of context-based constraints: the assignment constraint, the activation constraint, the cardinality constraint, and the SoD constraint. DRiBAC uses ontologies to describe its model including policies (*DRiBAC ontology*) and a variety of context (*DRiBAC context ontology*) [56]. Those ontologies are written in OWL1.0 and provides means for well-formed, reusable knowledge sharing among users and systems.

*Context-aware dynamic constraints*

DRiBAC assigns roles, permissions, and role interactions to users based on context, not only environment context such as time and location but also user-specific and object-specific context. By doing so, only qualified users can be assigned to a role and get permissions. If a user is disqualified by changes in his/her context, the user's roles, permissions, and interaction relationships are deactivated to prevent potential errors. Toward this, DRiBAC defines four context-aware constraints as follows [55].

*   *Assignment constraints*—An assignment constraint represents a context-based condition for role/permission/interaction assignment. It specifies a minimum qualification of a user to be assigned. If an assignment condition is associated with user context, a system can recommend some candidates for the assignment automatically. If there are two or more users who satisfy a corresponding condition, an administrator selects the most suitable one. For an interaction assignment, we need to perform agent-role assignments (AA) twice for two interacting roles, $ri.r_i$ and $ri.r_j$, in a role interaction. If the user is disqualified due to the change of its context later, the assigned role, permission, and interaction are automatically de-assigned for security.
*   *Activation constraints*—An activation constraint describes a condition to activate the assignment relations. If the condition is not satisfied, the assignment cannot be activated. Even if an assignment is activated, it is automatically deactivated. If a user assigned to one of interaction roles in an *ri* is deactivated, then the interaction is temporarily deactivated until all the participating users are activated again. Note that some assignment may not have activation constraints. In this case, an assignment is immediately activated right after assignment.
*   *Cardinality constraints*—This constraint limits the maximum number of users, role interactions, or interacting users assigned to a particular interaction role in a system. The cardinality constraints have two types: *static cardinality con-straint* and *dynamic cardinality constraint*. The static constraints are applied to

the interaction assignment to users, while the dynamic constraints are used on the interaction activation.

- *SoD constraints*—DRiBAC supports both the *SSoD* and the *DSoD* constraints. Using the SoD constraints, we can prevent problems that might occur by *mutually exclusive roles* and *exclusive role interactions*. DRiBAC uses the SSoD constraints to prevent users from assigning to *exclusive role interactions* at the same time. To prevent simultaneous activations of *exclusive role interactions*, DRiBAC uses the DSoD constraints ($ri_i.IA_a^{active} \leftrightarrow ri_j.IA_a^{active}$). The *mutually exclusive roles* are represented as follows: $r_i \leftrightarrow r_j$. DRiBAC help us avoid simultaneous assignment and activation of *mutually exclusive roles* by using SSoD and DSoD constraints.

### 3.3.2.4 Community-centric role-interaction-based access control

Unlike RiBAC and DRiBAC that focus on interaction only, CRiBAC support not only interaction within a system but also cooperation among users within a community. CRiBAC assumes that a community is created upon a user's request, and members actively cooperate with each other to achieve a common goal. In CRiBAC, cooperation is defined as a set of interactions among members who are taking particular roles in a community. CRiBAC extends the idea of RiBAC to support secure cooperation among users using diverse context information and goal-oriented communities. To conceptualize the communities and their cooperation, CRiBAC employs the organization model and the cooperation model of *community computing* [16].

By adopting the community computing model, CRiBAC represents a cooperative system as a *society* that consists of communities and users. Every user and community that belongs in a society must register with a society in advance. When registering in a society, each user is assigned to one or more *society roles (SRs)* depending on the agents' contexts and capabilities. All social roles must be predefined at the time that a society is established. A society has *society objects (OBJ_s)*, similar to objects in traditional RiBAC, and *society contexts (CONT_s)* that represent context information relate to a society. A user needs to register with a society to gain access to the society's context and objects, or interact with other users in the society. An SR will be revoked, when an agent leaves the society.

A user can participate in one or more communities by taking *community role (CR)*. A *community (c)* consists of a set of CRs *($CR_c$)*, a set of participating user taking one or more CRs *($A_c$)*, and the *community context (CONT_c)*. At this time, $CONT_c$ includes information related to a community *c*, such as community type, the creation time, and the number of members. A community type is defined with community goal, necessary roles *(cr)*, and constraints on corresponding CR assignments *(CRAs)*. According to the CRAs, a community instance selects and invites suitable users for each *cr*. After receiving an invitation from a community, every user must decide whether or not participate in the community. This decision will be made based on a user's availability and preference. After gathering enough number of users, a community needs to select the most appropriate agents based on users' contexts and capabilities. The CRs are revoked from members when the community is terminated or a user leaves the community or society.

When an administrator assigns roles to users, he/she should consider the relationships between the users' tasks and permissions and must assign the *least privileges*. Note that CRiBAC does not allow changes in the CRA after cooperation has been initiated. It allows early leave only. A user has its own *resources*, *context*, and *tasks* that it can perform. A user's resources are a set of objects that belong to the user and fully controlled by the user. The user context captures user-specific information, such as status and identification. A user's tasks represent the capability of a user. As we mentioned above, a user can play both SRs and CRs at the same time. When a role, whether *cr* or *sr*, is assigned to a user, the user have all the permissions that are assigned to the role.

### Interaction permissions in CRiBAC
In the previous section, we learned about the interaction permissions of RiBAC. CRiBAC has similar interaction permissions, but there is a slight difference. CRiBAC defines two types of interaction permissions, the traditional *OPRMS* and the *interaction permissions*. The *interaction permissions* include the *resource-oriented permission (SPRMS), RPRMS*, and *TPRMS*. The RPRMS and TPRMS are the same as those in RiBAC, but CRiBAC adds SPRMS to the interaction permissions of RiBAC. A *sprms* is a permission that allows access to a user's resources. To interact with others, users must have interaction permissions. Note that, in CRiBAC, some permissions are parameterized based on roles. In such a case, the parameterized permissions must be interpreted with users who are actually assigned to the role, after the role assignment. Additionally, CRiBAC assume that members of a community are able to share information about their tasks, contexts, and permissions, during cooperation. Similar to RiBAC family, CRiBAC has four variations: CRiBAC-B, CRiBAC-H, CRiBAC-C, and CRiBAC-CH. If you want to know the details about each model, please refer to the original paper [53].

### Analysis on interaction permissions
For a decade, potential problems related to permissions in access control models have been studied. For the traditional OPRMS, we may be able to use existing solutions but the interaction permissions that CRiBAC proposed additionally have not been analyzed yet. Constrained CRiBAC supports the SoD constraints including SSoD and DSoD. The SoD constraints are the same as those in RiBAC-C. To limit the number of users (represented as agents in the model) that can be assigned to a certain role, CRiBAC refine the cardinality constraints of RiBAC-C into the *agent cardinality (AC)*. An *ac* constraint is applied to the agent-role assignments (*AA*). Besides cardinality problems, several potential problems may result from the interaction permissions. CRiBAC defines four problems: the *self-referencing interaction (SRI)*, the *single-role and single-agent interaction (SRSA)*, the *single-role and multi-agent interaction (SRMA)*, and the *implicit TPRMS* problems. The definitions of each problem and corresponding solutions are below.

**Definition 3.1.** *SRI problem is that a tprms recursively invokes itself. The formal definition is as follows:*

*If tprm = (ops, obj-prms) ∈ TPRMS & obj-prms ≡ tprm where obj-prms ∈ TPRMS*

The SRI problem happens when a tprms and its object permission (*obj-prms*) are actually the same. If the obj-prms of a tprms invokes to another tprm, a referencing chain is formed. If the end of the chained referencing refers to its beginning, the original tprms is a chained *sri*. If a user agent has an interaction permission experiencing the SRI problem, it recursively carries out referencing. If an *sri* problem is discovered, then the corresponding PA relationship(s) has to be modified.

**Definition 3.2.** *SRSA problem is that only one user agent is assigned to both a subject role and an object role. The formal definition is as follows:*

1.  *In the case of RPRMS, If (sub-role, rprms)* $\in$ *PA & sub-role* $\equiv$ *obj-role & agt_card(sub-role) = 1, where sub-role, obj-role* $\in$ *R & agt_card(sub_role)* $\in$ *AC.*
2.  *In the case of TPRMS, If (sub-role, tprms)* $\in$ *PA & (sub-role, tprms.final-obj-prms)* $\in$ *PA & sub-role* $\equiv$ *final-obj-role & agt_card(sub-role) = 1, where sub-role, obj-role* $\in$ *R & final-obj-prms* $\in$ *P & agt_card(sub_role)* $\in$ *AC.*

The SRSA problem occurs when a user is assigned to a subject role. If the subject role refers to itself as its object role or its tprms eventually invokes itself as its object permission, then the SRSA problem occurs. The SRSA problem leads to the abnormal situation where a user agent interacts with itself; in truth, this is not an interaction. This situation is not different from that of a user who plays a subject role in executing its own tasks. This problem might not directly relate to serious security fraud or system error, but it is logically incorrect. To resolve it, an administrator should check the role-PAs and AC constraints. If an *srsa* is found, the administrator should modify the corresponding policies.

**Definition 3.3.** *SRMA problem is similar to SRSA, but in this problem, two or more user agents are assigned to a subject role and an object role, simultaneously. The formal definition is as follows:*

1.  *In the case of RPRMS, if (sub-role, rprms)* $\in$ *PA & sub-role* $\equiv$ *obj-role &* $2 \leq agt\_card(sub-role)$ *& {(a$_i$, sub-role)|$1 \leq i \leq n$, $n \geq 2$}* $\in$ *ARA, where sub-role, obj-role* $\in$ *R & agt_card (sub-role)* $\in$ *AC*
2.  *In the case of TPRMS, if sub-role* $\equiv$ *final-obj-role & (sub-role, tprms)* $\in$ *PA & (sub-role, tprms.final-obj-prms)* $\in$ *PA & $2 \leq agt\_card(sub-role)$ & {(a$_i$, sub-role)|$1 \leq i \leq n$, $n \geq 2$}* $\in$ *ARA, where sub-role, obj-role* $\in$ *R & agt_card(sub-role)* $\in$ *AC*

CRiBAC interprets the SPMA problem as a situation where all the users who are assigned to a subject role have a corresponding interaction permission to interact with each other. In order to solve this problem, CRiBAC distributes an interaction permission having an *srma* problem to all the users who are assigned to the subject role of the interaction permission. We define this process as the permission distribution.

**Definition 3.4.** *Implicit TPRMS problem means that we can determine a new tprms, if a tprms invokes other roles' tasks in a sequence. The formal definition is as follows:*

*If {(r$_i$,p$_j$)|$1 \leq i \leq n$, $1 \leq j \leq m$, $3 \leq n$}* $\in$ *PA & {p$_j$ |$1 \leq j \leq nm$, $3 \leq n$}* $\in$ *TPRMS & {(p$_j$.obj-prms)|$1 \leq j \leq nm-2$, $3 \leq n$}* $\in$ *TPRMS & !(p$_j$.final-obj-prms* $\in$ *TPRMS)'.*

We refer to such a tprms obtained from a chain of tprmss as implicit tprms. If an implicit tprms is found, then it should be replaced with an existing tprms. We define the process as the TPRMS replacement. To guarantee the security of a system, an administrator should extract all implicit tprmss. If a user agent participates in multiple communities, a chain of tprmss might be spread over several communities. In this case, an administrator should check all the implicit tprmss across communities. Note that a tprms chain can be formed although tprmss are assigned to different roles that are involved in different communities. To solve the Implicit TPRMS problem, we should extract all implicit tprmss across the communities and then replace existing tprmss with implicit tprmss.

*Administration of CRiBAC*

For practical use of CRiBAC, an administration model is necessary. Existing administration models for RBAC are well-defined, but they are not able to manage the interaction permission and cooperation of CRiBAC, because RBAC does not deal with them. To meet the requirement, the same team that proposed CRiBAC developed an administration model for CRiBAC, called ACRiBAC.

ACRiBAC employs the concept of *society manager (SM)* and *community manager (CM)*. An *SM* takes responsibility for controlling nine different tasks including *agent registration in a society (ARG)*, *community registration in a society (CRG)*, *society role-to-society assignment/revocation (RSA)*, *agent-to-society role assignment and revocation (SRA)*, *community role to community assignment and revocation (RCA)*, *agent to community role selection (CRS)*, *role to permission assignment (PA)*, *CM creation and deletion*, and *RH maintenance*. On the other hand, a *CM* has responsibility for community-specific tasks including *the creation and termination of a community*, *agent to community role assignment (CRA)*, and *permission realization (PR)*. The definitions of each administrative tasks are described in [53].

### 3.3.2.5  CPBAC

CRiBAC has a definite advantage of ensuring secure interaction and cooperation on role-based cooperative systems. To support secure collaboration on emerging systems, such as cloud computing systems and OSN systems, an access control model must consider a variety of aspects of subjects, objects, and actions as well as subjects' roles. To address the requirements, the community-centric property-based access control model (CPBAC) has been proposed [57]. CPBAC defines four types of user (subject) properties as follows.

- *User contexts (u.CNT)*—A user context represents a user $u$'s status such as age, gender, job, reputation, and social relationships.
- *User task (u.TSK)*—A user task that $u$ can carry out in a system (e.g., in an OSN, data uploading and message posting).
- *User resource (u.RSC)*—A user resource that $u$ creates and owns in a user's private space (e.g., in an OSN, users' photos and postings).
- *User policies (u.POL)*—A user policy that $u$ specifies to control accesses to own *context*, *tasks*, *resources*, and *policies*. The user policies are of two types, the *access control policy (u.AC)* and the *filtering policy (u.FP)*. The access control

policies specify the conditions of subjects to be authorized to access to a user's own properties, while the filtering policies define the rules to filter unwanted contents out using a user's preferences. An access control policy is represented as a combination of an eligibility rule that is represented by *status predicate* functions defined below and permissions to be assigned. If a subject is eligible, in other words, the corresponding predicate functions return "*True*," then the permission is assigned to the subject. A filtering policy is specified as a combination of a filtering condition and resources and a filtering function (*hide* (*x.prop*)). At this time, a filtering condition is specified by status predicate functions, especially, intended for subjects' contexts, tasks, and resources. If the filtering condition is satisfied, a system filters out the specified properties from the subject's space.

Similar to CRiBAC, CPBAC defines a community as a mission-oriented cooperative group of users who are eligible and willing to cooperate with other members. As an occasion demands, a community is created dynamically and terminated when its goal is achieved. A community has five properties: (1) *community contexts (c.CNT)* such as community goal and CRs, (2) *community tasks (c.TSK)* such as community creation and termination, (3) *community resources (c.RSC)* shared with members, (4) a *cooperation process (c.COP)* which describes the cooperation between community members, (5) *community policies (c.POL)*, and (6) *user to community role assignments (c.CRA)*.

CPBAC leverages the situation-based cooperation model [58] to specify a community's cooperation. This model defines a cooperative process as a fine-state machine in which each state represents a situation of a community. For each community situation, different task sets are assigned to members. Since the situation-based cooperation model is a role-based cooperation model, the members' tasks are defined, based on their CRs. If a different cooperation model that is not based on roles is utilized in a system, then CPBAC does not specify CRs in *c.CNT*.

A community can have three types of policies: (1) the *access control policy (c.AP)*, (2) the *recruiting policy (c.RCP)*, and (3) the *SoD policy (c.SoD)*. The access control policy specifies authorize accesses to a community's properties, and the recruiting policy defines the eligibility rules for CRs. If a user is eligible for a CR, then a system is able to assign the role to the user. Once a user takes a role in a community, the assignment relationship is specified in *c.CRA* and then the user can have the permissions necessary to cooperate with others. If necessary, a community can have its own SoD policies (*c.SoD*) to prevent assigning conflicting CRs (e.g., the *patient* role and the *helper* role in an emergency community) to the same member. A system must check the *SoD* policies when assigning CRs. A system is represented as a society *s* having four properties shown below:

- *Society contexts (s.CNT)*—A society has environment context and society-specific information such as the registered users and their social roles.
- *Society tasks (s.TSK)*—The society tasks represents services provided by a system to promote social activities (e.g., in OSNs, displaying of friends who are online, recommending potential friends, and notifying friends' updates).
- *Society resources (s.RSC)*—The society has its own resources that users can use based on their social roles.

- *Society policies (s.POL)*—A system can enforce a set of policies on its social users (e.g., in an OSN, users who are under age are prohibited to access the contents tagged "*adult only*").

In CPBAC, a permission consists of an operation and one or more object properties. The target objects could be varied. According to the types of the object properties, the permissions are categorized into five types: (1) the *context-oriented permission (CP)*, (2) the *tasks-oriented permission (TP)*, (3) the *resources-oriented permission (RP)*, (4) the *policies-oriented permission (PP)*, and (5) the *users-oriented permission (UP)*. An entity including society, community, and user can have permissions through the *PA*. If it is necessary to grant permissions for every object properties that belong to a particular type or subtype, CPBAC allows us to specify a PA based on the type of object properties (e.g., *CNT, TSK, RSC*, or *POL*) or subtype (using a prefix "*subtype*"). If a subject has a *type-based permission*, it has all the permissions that belong to that type. The type-based permission increases the efficiency of policy specification and enforcement in CPBAC.

*Status predicate*

The *status predicate* functions represent the status of a subject's property. In general, those functions are used to examine if a subject has a particular property at execution time. CPBAC defines four status predicate functions: (1) *hascnt (subject, condition of the subject's context)*, (2) *hastsk (subject, condition of the subject's task)*, (3) *hasrsc (subject, condition of the subject's resource)*, and (4) *haspol (subject, condition of the subject's policy)*. If a subject has a property satisfying a condition, then the corresponding predicate function returns "*True*," otherwise, it returns "*False*." The status predicate functions are categorized into two groups, *the property-based predicate* and *the attribute-based predicate*. The definitions for each type of predicate are as follows.

**Definition 3.5.** *A property-based predicate examines if a property has a particular value. Its formal definition is stated below:*

> *predicate_function (subject, (subtype_name | property_name), property_value), where subject = (society | community | user) and property_value = (enumeration | range | set).*

It consists of a subject, a subject's property, and a property's value. To inspect all the properties that belong to a subtype, a subtype of properties should be specified instead of the property. For example, *hascnt (u, Gps.location, "Times Square"), hascnt (u, Cooperation.communityrole, "Helper"), hascnt (u, Friends), hascnt (c, Cooperation.situation, "Initiation"), hastsk (u, Regulartsk.takePicture), hastsk (u, Admintsk), hasrsc (u, Photos.profilephoto), haspol (u, Filtering policies)*.

**Definition 3.6.** *An attribute-based predicate checks if a property has a particular attribute value. Its formal definition is below:*

> *predicate_function (subject, property_name.attribute_name, (property_value.) attribute_value) or predicate_name (subject, (subtype_name.attribute_name, attribute_value)), where subject = (society| community|user) and attribute_value = (enumeration | range | set).*

It consists of a subject, an attribute name that is associated with a subject's property, and an attribute value. A subtype should be specified to examine attributes of all the properties that belong to the subtype. By using the subtype-based description, we can specify a predicate at an abstract level and examine all the properties of a particular subtype at once. For example, *hascnt (u, Gps.location, "Times Square"), hascnt (u, Cooperation.communityrole, "Helper"), hascnt (u, Friends), hascnt (c, Cooperation.situation, "Initiation"), hastsk (u, Regulartsk.takePicture), hastsk (u, Admintsk), hasrsc (u, Photos.profilephoto), haspol (u, Filtering policies).*

### Administration model of CPBAC

To administrate a system effectively, ACPBAC has been proposed [57]. ACPBAC is a decentralized model that manages a cooperative system using three types of administrators: *society manager (SM), community manager (CM)*, and *User*. An *SM* manages *CRS* and $PA_s$, while a *CM* deals with *CRG*, *CRA*, and $PA_c$ for the associated community. Each user handles *URG* and $PA_u$.

First, a user registers in a system (*URG*) and takes the responsibility of controlling accesses to his own properties ($PA_u$). A CM creates and deletes a community by handling the assignment of users to CRs (*CRA*). A CM also registers a community that it created in a system (*CRG*) and controls accesses to the community's properties during cooperation ($PA_c$). Once an SM receives a registration or withdrawal request from a user or CM, it creates or deletes a virtual space for a requester, respectively. At the same time, the SM must manage accesses to the society's properties ($PA_s$). If a CM asks an SM to recommend candidates for members, an SM examines the registered users and sends recommendation to the CM (*CRS*). The detailed explanation of each administrative task in ACPBAC is as follows.

- *URG (user to society registration)*—A user who wants to join in a society must register the information about user properties (e.g., a user's contexts, tasks, resources, and policies) with a society. All the user property information are saved in the *user definitions* of CPBAC description. If an SM receives a *registration* request from a user, it creates a virtual space and stores the requester's properties in the created space (*SM.createUser*()). Once a user joins a society, the user can access a society's properties by having permissions on society properties ($PA_s$). If an SM receives a *withdrawal* request from a user, it removes all properties that are associated with the user and removes the requester's space (*SM.deleteUser*()).
- *CRG (community to society registration)*—All communities existing in a society must register the information about community properties including community contexts (*c.CNT*), the user to CR assignment relationships (*c.CRA*), community tasks (*c.TSK*), sharable community resources (*c.RSC*), cooperation processes (*c.COP*), and policies (*c.POL*) with a society at the onset. If a user requires to create a community, then an *SM* performs *createComm*() that creates a virtual space for a community, stores the community's properties, and recruits a CM for the community. When a community goal is accomplished, the SM deletes the community at a request from the corresponding *CM*.

*Table 3.1   Analysis on existing access control models for cooperative systems to check their applicability for bioinspired systems*

|  | TBAC | TMAC | Context TMAC | GB-RBAC | RiBAC DRiBAC | CRiBAC | CPBAC |
|---|---|---|---|---|---|---|---|
| Perception | X | X | √ | X | X | √ | √ |
| Intelligence | X | X | X | X | √ | √ | √ |
| Autonomy | X | X | X | X | √ | √ | √ |
| Reactiveness | √ | √ | √ | √ | √ | √ | √ |
| Adaptivity | X | X | X | X | X | Δ[a] | Δ[a] |
| Sociability | √ | √ | √ | √ | √ | √ | √ |
| Goal oriented | X | X | X | √ | X | √ | √ |
| Decentralized control | X | X | X | X | X | √ | √ |

[a]In CRiBAC and CPBAC, communities are capable of changing their own behavior flexibly based on changes in community situations, but a society's adaptivity has not considered yet.

- *CRS (user to CR selection)*—An SM can recommend candidates who are suitable for a CR by examining the user properties at execution time (SM.*recommendMember*()). *CRS* must be preceded before the user to *CRA*. Due to the privacy issue, only the *SM* can inspect the user-property information.
- *CRA (user to CR assignment)*—A *CM* can assign/deassign the most suitable user(s) among candidates selected by *SM* to a *CR* (CM.assignCR()/deassignCR()). Each CRA relationship is specified in the *CR_Assignment* of a community description.
- *PA (user to PA)*—The PAs are divided into three types based on target objects: (1) the *PA on the society properties (PA$_s$)*, (2) the *PA on the community properties (PA$_C$)*, and (3) the *PA on the user properties (PA$_U$)*. Each PA is administrated by an owner of an object property by using two administrative functions, *assignP()* and *deassignP()*. It means that an *SM* manages *PA$_s$*, a *CM* manages the PA on a community $c$, $PA_c \in PA_C$, and a user manages the PA on itself, $PA_u \in PA_U$. All PAs are specified in the *Permission_Assignments*.

In this section, we introduced several access control models for cooperative systems. To select the most suitable access control model, we first need to define a cooperative system's features. The eight characteristics of cooperative living things introduced in Section 3.2 could be reasonable criteria. The analyzed result using the eight characteristics of cooperative living things is shown in Table 3.1. According to a cooperative system's features, you can select a right access control model.

## 3.4   Conclusions and future work

In this chapter, we learned the characteristics of bioinspired cooperative living things and research trend in the cooperative bioinspired systems domain. In addition, we introduced traditional and innovative access control schemes that have been proposed for cooperative systems and analyzed them based on the characteristics of cooperative bioinspired systems.

Note that, in this chapter, we focused on cooperation and collaboration. However, coordination might be required depending on the characteristics of application domains. To address this issue, we need to research the coordination strategies for emerging technologies in future. In addition, we discussed one of security aspects only, access control. To complete a comprehensive analysis on security mechanisms for collaboration, we need to examine other aspects including confidentiality, availability, and integrity, in near future.

# References

[1]    Wooldridge M., Nicholas R. J. 'The Gaia methodology for agent-oriented analysis and design'. *Autonomous Agents and Multi-Agent Systems*. 2000;3: 285–312.

[2]    Blank M., Kagan S., Melaville A., Ray K. *Collaboration: What Makes It Work. A Review of Research Literature on Factors Influencing Successful Collaboration*. St. Paul, MN, Amherst H. Wilder Foundation, 1992, pp. 59–61.

[3]    Wilson P. *Computer Supported Cooperative Work: An Introduction*. Oxford, UK: Intellect Books; 1991.

[4]    Johansen R. *Groupware: Computer Support for Business Teams*. New York: Free Press; 1988.

[5]    Borghoff U. M., Schlichter J. H. *Computer-Supported Cooperative Work: Introduction to Distributed Applications* Berlin: Springer-Verlag; 2000.

[6]    Erl T. *Service-Oriented Architecture: Concepts, Technology, and Design*. Upper Saddle River, NJ, Prentice Hall PTR; 2005.

[7]    Krafzig D., Banke K., Slama D. *Enterprise SOA: Service-Oriented Architecture Best Practices*. Upper Saddle River, NJ, Prentice Hall PTR; 2005.

[8]    Erl T. *Service-Oriented Architecture: A field Guide to Integrating XML and Web Services*. Upper Saddle River, NJ, Prentice Hall PTR; 2004.

[9]    Reitman L., Ward J., Wilber J. *Service Oriented Architecture (SOA) and Specialized Messaging Patterns*. Technical White Paper published by Adobe Corporation USA, 2007.

[10]   Kumar M., Shirazi B., Das S. K., Singhal M., Sung B., Levine D. 'Pervasive Information Communities Organization PICO: A Middleware Framework for Pervasive Computing'. *IEEE Pervasive Computing*. 2003, July–September, pp. 72–79.

[11]   Sung B., Shirazi B., Kumar M. *Pervasive Community Organization*. Tehran: Eurasia; 2002.

[12]   Román M., Campbell R. H. 'GAIA: Enabling Active Spaces'. *Proceedings of the 9th ACM SIGOPS European Workshop*, Kolding, Denmark: ACM; 2000. pp. 229–234.

[13] Al-Muhtadi J., Chetan S., Ranganathan A., Campbell R. 'Super Spaces: A Middleware for Large-Scale Pervasive Computing Environments'. *Proceedings of the IEEE International Workshop on Pervasive Computing and Communications*; Orlando, FL, March. IEEE; 2004.

[14] Ferber J., Gutknecht O. 'A Meta-Model for the Analysis and Design of Organization in Multi-Agent Systems'. *Proceedings of the 3rd International Conference on Multi-agent Systems (ICMAS'98)*; 1998.

[15] Ferber J., Gutknecht O., Michel F. *From Agents to Organizations: An Organizational View of Multi-agent Systems*. Berlin Heidelberg: Springer-Verlag LNCS 2935; 2003. pp. 214–230.

[16] Jung Y., Kim M. 'Situation-aware community computing model for developing dynamic ubiquitous computing systems'. *Journal of Universal Computer Science*. 2010;16(15):2139–2174.

[17] Mano J., Bourjot C., Lopardo G., Glize P. 'Bio-inspired mechanisms for artificial self-organised systems'. *Informatica*. 2006;30(1):55–62.

[18] Theraulaz G., Bonabeau E., Deneubourg J. L. *The mechanisms and rules of coordinated building in social insects*. Birkhäuser, Basel: Springer; 1999. pp. 309–330.

[19] Detrain C., Deneubourg J. L., Pasteels J. M. *Information Processing in Social Insects*. Birkhauser: Verlag; 1999. pp. 309–330.

[20] Bonabeau E., Dorigo M., Theraulaz G. *Swarm Intelligence: From Natural to Artificial Systems*. New York: Oxford University Press; 1999.

[21] Kennedy J. *Swarm Intelligence. Handbook of Nature-Inspired and Innovative Computing: Integrating Classical Models with Emerging Technologies*. Boston, MA: Springer US; 2006. pp. 187–219.

[22] Caro G. D., Dorigo M. 'AntNet: distributed stigmergetic control for communications networks'. *Journal of Artificial Intelligence Research*. 1998;9: 317–365.

[23] Dressler F. *Self-organization in Sensor and Actor Networks*. Hoboken, NJ, Wiley; 2007.

[24] Dorigo M., Birattari M., Stutzle T. 'Ant colony optimization- artificial ants as a computational intelligence technique'. *IEEE Computational Intelligence Magazine*. 2006;1:28–39.

[25] Goyal M., Xie W., Hosseini H., Bashir Y. 'AntSens: An Ant Routing Protocol for Large Scale Wireless Sensor Networks'. *Proceedings of the International Conference on Broadband, Wireless Computing, Communication and Applications*; 2010. pp. 41–48.

[26] Seeley T. D., Towne W. F. 'Tactics of dance choice in honey bees: do foragers compare dances?'. *Behavioral Ecology and Sociobiology*. 1992;30: 59–69.

[27] Farooq M. *From the wisdom of the hive to intelligent routing in telecommunication networks: a step towards intelligent network management through natural engineering*. Ph.D. Dissertation. University of Dortmund, 2006.

[28] Zhang Z., Tellambura C., Schober R. 'Improved OFDMA uplink transmission via cooperative relaying in the presence of frequency offsets part I: ergodic

information rate analysis'. *European Transactions on Telecommunications*. 2010;21:224–240.

[29]  Ahmed M., Vorobyov S. 'Collaborative beamforming for wireless sensor networks with Gaussian distributed sensor nodes'. *IEEE Transactions on Wireless Communications*. 2009;8:638–643.

[30]  Du J., Xiao M., Skoglund M. 'Cooperative network coding strategies for wireless relay networks with backhaul'. *IEEE Transactions on Communications*. 2011;59:2502–2514.

[31]  Jovicic A., Viswanath P. 'Cognitive radio: an information-theoretic perspective'. *IEEE Transactions on Information Theory*. 2009;55:3945–3958.

[32]  Sawahashi M., Kishiyama Y., Morimoto A., Nishikawa D., Tanno M. 'Coordinated multipoint transmission/reception techniques for LTE advanced'. *IEEE Wireless Communications*. 2010;17:26–34.

[33]  Cheng G., Zelinsky A. 'Real-time visual behaviours for navigating a mobile robot'. *Proceedings of the IEEE/RSJ International Conference on Intelligent Robots and Systems*; Osaka, Japan; IEEE; 1996. pp. 973–980.

[34]  Thakoor S., Morookian J. M., Chahl, J., Hine, B., Zornetzer, S. 'Bees: exploring mars with bioinspired technologies'. *Computer*. 2004;37(9):36–47.

[35]  Levi P., Kernbach S. *Symbiotic Multi-Robot Organisms*. Cognitive Systems Monographs. vol. 7. Springer, Berlin, 2010.

[36]  Dorigo M. *et al.* 'Swarmanoid: a novel concept for the study of heterogeneous robotic swarms'. *IEEE Robotics & Automation Magazine*. 2013;20(4):60–71.

[37]  Ronald K. C. *Collective robotics: from local perception to global action*. Dissertation for the Doctoral Degree, University of Alberta; 1998.

[38]  Banˆatre J., Le M'etayer D. 'The GAMMA model and its discipline of programming'. *Science of Computer Programming*. 1990;15(1):55–77.

[39]  Berry G. 'The chemical abstract machine'. *Theoretical Computer Science*. 1992;1:217–248.

[40]  Monti M., Meyer T., Tschudin C. F., Luise M. 'Stability and sensitivity analysis of traffic-shaping algorithms inspired by chemical engineering'. *IEEE Journal on Selected Areas in Communications*. 2013;31(6):1105–1114.

[41]  Banˆatre J., Priol T. 'Chemical programming of future service oriented architectures'. *JSW*. 2009;4(7):738–746.

[42]  ElGammal M., Eltoweissy M., 'A novel chemistry-inspired approach to efficient coordination of multi-mission networked objects'. *International Journal on Advances in Intelligent Systems*, IARIA, 2015;8(3&4):385–397.

[43]  United States Department of Defense, *Trusted Computer System Evaluation Criteria*. DoD Standard 5200.28-STD, December 1985.

[44]  Bell D. E., LaPadula L. J. *Secure computer system: unified exposition and MULTICS*. Technical Report ESD-TR-75-306. The MITRE Corporation, 1976.

[45]  Sandhu R. S. 'Role-based access control'. *IEEE Computer*. 1996;29(2):38–47.

[46]  Hu V. C., Kuhn D. R., Ferraiolo D. F. 'Attribute-based access control'. *IEEE Computer*. 2015;48(2):85–88.

[47]   Thomas R. K., Sandhu R. S. 'Task-Based Authorization Controls (TBAC): A Family of Models for Active and Enterprise-Oriented Authorization Management'. *Proceedings of the IFIP TC11 WG11.3 11th International Conference on Database Security XI: Status and Prospects*; London, UK; 1997. pp. 166–181.

[48]   Tolone W., Ahn G., Pai T., Hong S. 'Access control in collaborative systems'. *ACM Computing Surveys*. 2005;37(1):29–41.

[49]   Thomas R. K. 'Team-Based Access Control (TMAC): A Primitive for Applying Role-Based Access Controls in Collaborative Environments'. *Proceedings of the 2nd ACM workshop on Role-based access control (RBAC '97)*; 1997. pp. 13–19.

[50]   Georgiadis C. K., Mavridis I., Pangalos G., Thomas R. K. 'Flexible Team-Based Access Control Using Contexts'. *Proceedings of the 6th ACM Symposium on Access Control Models and Technologies (SACMAT '01)*; 2001. pp. 21–27.

[51]   Li Q., Zhang X., Xu M., Wu J. 'Towards secure dynamic collaborations with group-based RBAC model'. *Computers & Security*. 2009;28(5):260–275.

[52]   Jung Y., Masoumzadeh A., Joshi J. B. D., Kim M. 'RiBAC: Role Interaction Based Access Control Model for Community Computing'. *Lecture Notes of the Institute for Computer Sciences, Social Informatics and Telecommunications Engineering*. Berlin Heidelberg: Springer; 2009, Vol. 10, pp. 304–321.

[53]   Jung Y., Joshi J. B. D. 'CRiBAC: community-centric role interaction access control model'. *Computers & Security*. 2012;31(4):497–523.

[54]   Joshi J. B. D., Bertino E., Latif U., Ghafoor A. 'A generalized temporal role-based access control model'. *IEEE Transactions on Knowledge and Data Engineering*. 2005;17(1):4–23.

[55]   Jung Y., Kim M., Joshi J. B. D. 'DRiBAC: Context-Aware Dynamic Role Interaction Access Control'. *Proceedings of the 12th IEEE International Conference of Information Reuse and Integration (IRI)*, 2011. pp. 88–93.

[56]   Jung Y., Kim M. 'Ontology based dynamic role interaction access control'. *Journal of Research and Practice in Information Technology*. 2011;43(3): 209–225.

[57]   Jung Y., Joshi J. B. D. 'CPBAC: property-based access control model for secure cooperation in online social networks'. *Computers & Security*. 2014;41:19–39.

[58]   Jung Y., Lee J., Kim M. 'Community situation based strict cooperation model for cooperative ubiquitous systems'. *Journal of Convergence Information Technology*. 2007;2(1):93–97.

## Chapter 4
# Immune-based defence and resiliency

*Pierre Parrend[1,2,3]*

The natural immune system is a prototypical example of a natural system that supports defence and resilience. It is thus a powerful metaphor for building artificial systems that exhibit such properties. In this chapter, we first introduce the main mechanisms of natural immunity: innate vs. acquired immunity, the (discussed) concept of self and non-self as well as the three-signal model. These mechanisms highlight how a fully decentralized system can protect an organism against unknown actors, taking the actual damage they generate into account and memorizing previous aggressions for a quicker response. A key insight into the analysis of the natural immune systems is the idiotypic network model, which shows how its multi-scale organization ensures the resilience of the immune system: lymphocytes interact together to build a reactive network that is constantly regenerated, thus maintaining the immune reaction and memory, although individual cells live and die. Understanding the immune properties of natural organisms is the key to leverage them in artificial systems.

The application of these rich principles for building defensive and resilient systems is known as immuno-engineering. The main product of this approach is the artificial immune system (AIS) and its application to intrusion detection. The first generation of AIS provides suitable event perceptors for classification of aggressions. The second generation introduces the concept of danger perception in artificial environments. An architecture common to most AIS distinguishes between the local layer for detection and reaction, at the environment endpoints, a monitoring layer for vaccination and user interface, in gateways or user machines and a control layer, that collects status, generates metrics and shares information at a central appliance. We summarize the immune properties of artificial organisms and how they relate to natural ones. To conclude this chapter, we present and discuss the current limitations of AISs.

## 4.1  Introduction

Immune systems are capable of 'sensing' very scarce modifications of their environments, detecting new bacteria or other antigens previously unknown, memorizing

[1]ECAM Strasbourg-Europe, France
[2]ICube Laboratory, University of Strasbourg, CNRS, France
[3]Complex System Digital Campus UNESCO Unitwin, France

these encounters and even reacting to round them off. Moreover, they do so not only locally but also at large scale throughout the organism. All these features would be very desirable for monitoring and protecting *IT ecosystems*, especially *multi-scale* ones, if one could enforce immune properties in artificial environments. Indeed, the properties of *natural multi-scale ecosystems* are intuitively highly relevant for monitoring and protecting *artificial multi-scale ecosystems*.

The field of immunity modelling was pioneered in the mid-1970s by the work of Jerne [1] and made popular by Varela *et al.* [2]. Among the fields bound with the simulation of life [3], it is probably one the most worked on, but also one where more questions remain than answers have been provided. The perspective of replicating the capability of detecting ill behaviours and being able to react to them has fascinated the research community. However, though radical breakthroughs have been done for understanding and modelling immunity and rich applications have been proposed, creating artificial systems capable of an efficient immune response in production-scale systems is still an open challenge.

One of the core challenges in modelling natural immune systems or producing their artificial counterpart is the significant size of the natural immune system[1] [4]. Reproducing its features requires that it can be emulated, although at a significantly smaller scale, as some figures on human immunity highlight:

- $10^{15}$ different types of lymphocytes may be produced, based on the genetic heritage which is at play,
- $10^{12}$ lymphocytes are available at any moment, per batches of 2,000 clones,
- each of them is able to recognize $10^5$ antigens and
- a repertoire of $10^7$–$5.10^8$ different types of lymphocytes is active at any moment.

A suitable abstraction level is therefore required to enforce immune properties in artificial systems without the need for data modelling and analysis at such a scale. The efforts for identifying this suitable abstraction level is the subject of this chapter, which discusses principles, models and implementations of natural immune systems and of their artificial counterparts. The chapter is organized as follows. Section 4.2 provides the definition of terms from the immunity vocabulary used in this chapter. Section 4.3 presents the core scientific contributions in the domain of immunity and immune system modelling. Section 4.4 gives an overview of the most representative applications of immunity in artificial systems and discusses their current limitations.

## 4.2   Definitions

Common definitions related to immunity and useful for understanding the current chapter are recalled here.

---

[1]Personal discussions with Véronique Thomas-Vaslin, CNRS, Paris, France

**Antibody:** An immunoglobulin, a specialized immune protein, produced because of the introduction of an antigen into the body and which possesses the remarkable ability to combine with the very antigen that triggered its production.[2]

**Antigen:** A substance that the immune system perceives as being foreign or dangerous. The body combats an antigen with the production of an antibody.[3]

**B lymphocytes:** A type of white blood cells at the core of adaptive immunity. Most B lymphocytes mature into what are called plasma cells that produce antibodies (proteins) necessary to fight off infections, while other B lymphocytes mature into memory B lymphocytes. B lymphocytes mature in the bone marrow.[4]

**Dendritic cells:** A special type of cells that is a key regulator of the immune system, acting as an antigen-presenting cell capable of activating naïve T cells and stimulating the growth and differentiation of B cells.[5]

**Pathogen:** An agent of disease. For example, *Bacillus anthracis* is the pathogen that causes anthrax.[6]

**T lymphocytes:** A type of white blood cells at the core of adaptive immunity. T lymphocytes can produce substances called cytokines which further stimulate the immune response. T lymphocytes mature in the thymus.[7]

## 4.3 Core contributions

This section introduces the main concepts which are useful for understanding the complex mechanics of the immune system. First, the basic principles are introduced, both for setting the historical context of research efforts on immunity and to build the link between approximate but broadly known concepts such as the 'self' and more accurate models of the immune systems. Second, the complexity aspects of the immune systems are presented and discussed. Please note that this section does not intend to provide a systematic view on immunity research. A comprehensive history of the models of the natural immune system can be found in [5]. A summary of the mechanisms of immunity is provided by Vaz and Varela in [2]. An introductory presentation of the main mechanisms is given in [6], and a more formal comprehensive introduction for non-biologists is provided by Perelson [7]. Only issues relevant for understanding defence and resiliency mechanisms are presented here; the interested reader is invited to consult these external sources to broaden his/her understanding of the mechanisms of immunity.

### 4.3.1 Immunity basics

The immunity models which can be considered to be part of a 'classical' approach base on the immunity mechanisms found in vertebrate organisms, *acquired* or *adaptive*

---

[2]http://www.medicinenet.com/script/main/art.asp?articlekey=19101
[3]http://www.medicinenet.com/script/main/art.asp?articlekey=2282
[4]http://www.medicinenet.com/script/main/art.asp?articlekey=2413
[5]http://www.medicinenet.com/script/main/art.asp?articlekey=19035
[6]http://www.medicinenet.com/script/main/art.asp?articlekey=6383
[7]http://www.medicinenet.com/script/main/art.asp?articlekey=11300

*immunity*, rather than on *innate immunity* already present in invertebrate organisms, since the former supports specific response to pathogens rather than the generic, non-specific and slower response of the latter. These immunity models have been developed in three major phases. First, the very existence of an immune system and the principle of a distinction between a 'self' and a 'non-self' are stated and investigated by Ehrlich at the end of the nineteenth century [8,9]. Next, the impact of genetics is discovered and leads to the breakthrough by Burnet who describes the process for the generation of antibodies, in particular through clonal selection [10]. Lastly, the impact of tissue decay, which greatly increases the intensity of the immune reaction, is discovered by Matzinger [11].

### 4.3.1.1   Innate and acquired immunity

Immunity is built by two complementary mechanisms: *innate immunity*, which is already present in plants, fungi and insects, and *acquired immunity*, which appeared in the first vertebrates [12]. In vertebrates, both coexist to provide a suitable immune response. Figure 4.1 shows the steps involved in fighting pathogens: protection by anatomical barriers like the skin, the gastrointestinal tract or the eyes, physiological conditions like pH or temperature which provide inappropriate living conditions for foreign organisms, the innate immune system and the acquired immune system [6].

*Innate immunity* is the most primitive type of immunity [6]. It focuses on non-specific immune perception and response, i.e. the handling of unknown pathogens, and typically occurs on a local scale. Its mechanism can be simplified as built of four main steps:

- First, the *complement system* binds to certain pathogens like specific bacteria and triggers either lysis or opsonization processes. Lysis is the rupture of the cell membrane, which results in the rapid destruction of the bacteria. Opsonization is a specific binding between the complement and the bacteria which eases the activation of macrophages.

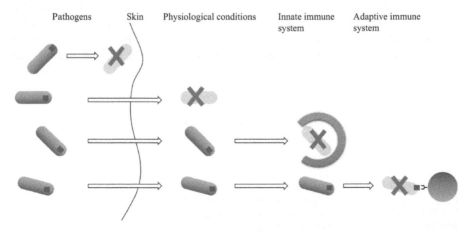

*Figure 4.1   Immune steps involved in fighting pathogens in vertebrates [6]*

- Second, *macrophages* 'detect' and engulf bacteria: they are considered as 'scavenger' cells which have receptors for certain kinds of bacteria or can be activated by opsonization in the case of bacteria bound with the *complement system*. They then secrete a molecule called *cytokine*.
- Third, *cytokine* is responsible for facilitating the immune response through inflammation of the tissues which consists in increased blood flow and temperature. Increased blood flow eases the arrival of immune cells in the tissue, and increased temperature both reduces the activity of the pathogen and increases the intensity of the immune response.
- Lastly, *natural killer cells* are another key component in the innate immune response. They bind with a large spectrum of cells but are inhibited by healthy cells of the organism. In the absence of inhibitors such as in virus-infected cells, they activate the cells they bind with. This triggers *apoptosis*, i.e. programmed death cell, in these cells.

*Acquired immunity* [6] learns to 'recognize' certain kinds of pathogens through a memory mechanism. It is also known as *adaptive immunity*. The first encounter with a pathogen is known as the *primary response*. Subsequent encounters are known as *secondary response* and are typically much quicker and more intense. In a *primary response*, several days are required before the response becomes visible, and up to three weeks are necessary to clear an infection. A *secondary response* is often rapid and efficient enough so that no clinical sign of infections can be perceived. *Lymphocytes* are primary actors of the *acquired immunity* mechanism. They circulate *via* the blood and the lymph system, which enables organism-wide detection of pathogens. *Acquired immunity* builds the focus of immune models dealing with specific immune perception and response mechanisms, i.e. the handling of known pathogens, which are mainly encountered through infection or vaccination.

### 4.3.1.2   Self and non-self

In the early days of immunology, Ehrlich postulated that the body is able to distinguish between self-components and non-self components [8,9], i.e. between the organism and alien substances. This distinction should explain the reactivity between the antigens, i.e. the substances which trigger an immune reaction, and the antibodies, i.e. the molecules that play an active role in this immune reaction. However, he already identified the challenges that pose to his theory the fact that not all cells trigger an immune response, in particular that an organism is indifferent to its own substance.

Ehrlich model poses two issues: (1) how to actually detect the presence of an antigen? and (2) how to support evolution? Issue 1 is highlighted by the fact that vaccines made out of weakened antigens do not operate by themselves but require adjuvant as calcium phosphate or aluminium – at the time of Ehrlich's publication, Pasteur is vaccinating sheep against anthrax for 10 years. Issue 2 is blatant in the pregnancy process, where the foetus has a different genotype from his mother but does not trigger an immune response. Recent research underlines the fact that microchimerism, where mother cells survive in the child body and child cells survive in the mother's body, goes on well after birth or miscarriage [13].

### 4.3.1.3    Selection, cloning and deletion

The discovery of the structure of the DNA in 1953 [14] and of related messenger-RNA-based protein generation by Watson and Crick introduces new insights to the creation of antibodies, which is explored by Burnet [10]. Antibodies can only be created based on the m-RNA pattern, and not based on antigen patterns, this is called the 'selective aspect' of antibody synthesis. Moreover, a mechanism is required to let antigen molecules 'elect' the cells which happen to fit with them so as to ensure a suitable intensity of the immune reaction, which Burnet postulates appear through cloning of the antibodies reactive to available antigens. This is the 'clonal aspect' of antibody synthesis. This model of immunity is in particular successful in explaining autoimmune diseases. However, it needs to be complemented to explain the variety of antibodies in organisms, and thus the variety of antigens that can trigger an immune reaction, whereas very few trigger autoimmune reactions. This requires that a mechanism for massive destruction of self-reactive clones is available: this is 'clonal deletion'. Indeed, it is considered that more than 95% of generated antibodies are destroyed in the thymus before they are released in the organism.

However, Burnet model does not explain how the gut flora lives in harmony with its host: it is considered that half of the cells in a human body, accounting for 10% of its weight, are non-human living entities, some simply harmless and some necessary for the equilibrium of the organism.

### 4.3.1.4    Danger

The first radical challenge on the modelling of the immune system as a system focusing on the distinction of self and non-self comes from the danger theory. In the danger context, it is not the antigen that builds the key trigger for the immune response but the presence of actual harm to the body [11,15]. However, the conservation of a strong dichotomy between safe and non-safe state, even though finer than the self/non-self distinction, still fails to account for the auto-reactivity of cells between them, and to explain the distinction between antibodies and antigens during the immune reaction.

### 4.3.1.5    The three-signal model

This framework is summarized as the three-signal model by [16]:

- The one-signal model, as shown in Figure 4.2, depicts immunity as the (simplified) process of T cells carrying antibodies that match antigens [10], as in Burnet model of acquired immunity.
- The two-signal model, as shown in Figure 4.3, introduces the fact that the antigens are actually presented to T cells by dendritic cells, which moreover require pathogen associated molecular patterns (PAMPs) for their activation [17]. This mechanism is typical of innate immunity. This activation provokes the emission of co-stimulatory molecules. This mechanism is known as co-stimulation [18,19].
- The three-signal model, as shown in Figure 4.4, considers that the concept of danger, i.e. of actual degradation of tissues, that manifests itself through apoptosis and necrosis, is central to the activation of the dendritic cells [11].

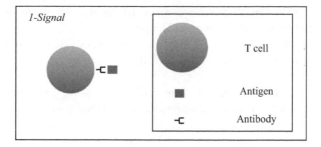

*Figure 4.2   The one-signal model [11]*

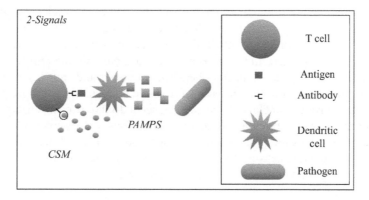

*Figure 4.3   The two-signal model [11]*

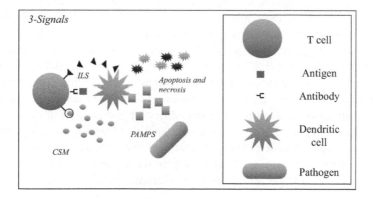

*Figure 4.4   The three-signal model [11]*

However, these models fail to explain several important developments in immunology:

- the genetic control of immune events, i.e. the fact that the immune responsiveness is depending on so-called Ir-genes (immune response genes) which control the elicitation of very specific immune responses;

- the importance of interactions between cells for the regulation of quality and magnitude of these immune events [2]; and
- the fact that some autoimmune diseases are bound not with an excess of immune activity, but with immunodeficiencies [20].

An alternative analysis path is here required to solve these challenges: the science of complexity provides new significant insights, as well as radically new models.

## 4.3.2   Complexity aspects of the immune system

The inability of classical immunity models to solve key puzzles related to immune reactions necessitates to radically switch the hypothesis underlying immune system models. Major investigations highlight the importance of the meshes emerging out of the point-to-point interactions between the entities building the immune system. A first mesh is built by the interactions between antibodies and antigens: N different antibodies are activated in the presence of a single antigen; similarly, M different antigens can activate a single antibody sort. A second kind of mesh emerges: antibody molecules, which contain several variable regions, are reactive to regions of other antibodies. This mesh of inter-reacting antibodies is called the idiotypic network [1]. The idiotypic network arouses a very strong interest in efforts to solve the inconsistencies of previous models of the immune system.

### 4.3.2.1   The idiotypic network

In his model of the immune system as an idiotypic network, Jerne postulates that the immune detectors, the antibodies (more precisely the immunoglobulin), are not by default reacting outwards to non-self objects, but rather reacting inwards to known immunoglobulins only [1]. The intensity of the reaction between two immunoglobulins is function of the *affinity* between these immunoglobulins. The type and magnitude of reaction then depend of the strength of the perturbation induced by the *affinity* of antibodies with antigens encountered in the organism. Consequently, in the Jernian network, 'foreign' is described as a perturbation of the system above a certain threshold [21]. A model for the construction of such a network is proposed by [22]. The theory of idiotypic networks induces new explanations for tolerance as well as for immune affinities, which are a prerequisite to the immune response. It also provides a new insight w.r.t. multi-scale mechanisms of the immune system.

### 4.3.2.2   Modelling self-assertion and immune tolerance

The shift from classical models of immunity to the idiotypic framework is in particular symbolized by the distinction between *self-recognition*, where a 'self' would be distinguished from a 'non-self', and *self-assertion*, where asymmetric autoreactive mechanisms build tolerant and reactive zones which can model the dynamic of immune cell populations in a satisfactory way [23]. The self-assertion model underlines the importance of inter-cell interactions for the regulation of immune events.

The author proposes a compact theoretical model to evaluate the relevance of the self-assertion model for modelling the populations of immune cells.

$$if \ (low < Aff_j < high) \ then$$

$$C_{cell}(t+1) = C_{cell}(t) + 1$$

$$else$$

$$C_{cell}(t+1) = C_{cell}(t) - 1$$

(4.1)

$$if \ (low < Aff_j) \ then$$

$$C_{antigen}(t+1) = C_{antigen}(t) - k \times (Aff_j/low)$$

(4.2)

$$Aff_j = \alpha \sum_i affinityOfCell_i + \beta \sum_i affinityOfAntigen_i$$

(4.3)

The network is characterized by the level of *affinity* $Aff_j$ for any given cell, the population of immune cells $C_{cell}(t)$ at a time $t$, the population of antigens $C_{antigen}(t)$ at a time $t$, *low* and *high* minimum and maximum bounds of *affinity* for the reactive zone. When the value of *affinity* $Aff_j$ lies between these *low* and *high* values, the immune cell population increases incrementally as defined in (4.1). When it lies outside these boundaries, it decreases at the same pace. In the reactive domain, the population of antigens decreases faster when the *affinity* $Aff_j$ is big with regard to the *low* boundary, and slower when it nears this threshold, as given by (4.2). The overall *affinity* value depends on both the *affinity* of individual immune cells as well as the *affinity* of antigens as given in (4.3).

If $C_{cell}(t) = 0$, the cell disappears from the system.

If $C_{antigen}(t) = 0$, the antigen disappears from the system.

If $\alpha = 0$, the model amounts to *self-recognition*, and immune cells react to antigens only.

The simulation of this model enables to visualize the immune properties which are put in the foreground in the idiotypic framework. Figure 4.5 shows a visualization of tolerant and reactive zones in a case of *self-assertion*: from a random population, a clear delimitation appears between a tolerant zone characterized by a high density of receptors (on the bottom left), and a reactive zone on the upper right which is symmetric to the former [23]. This delimitation is built by self-sustained cells. Other cells mutually simulate themselves. For this simulation, Figure 4.6 shows the evolution of the number of cells according to time. The population of reactive cells first increases dramatically then slightly decreases before it stabilizes [23]. The consistency of these results with experimental observations underscores the theoretical relevance of the idiotypic framework to depict the evolution of populations of immune cells.

### 4.3.2.3  Empirical validation of immune affinities

The role of *affinity*, i.e. the reactivity level when the organism faces antigens, explains why some autoimmune diseases are bound with immunodeficiencies rather than with

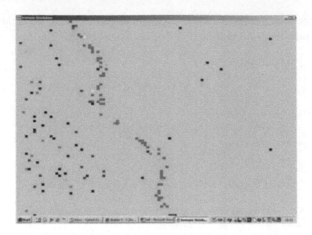

*Figure 4.5   Visualization of tolerant and reactive zones in a case of self-assertion [23]*

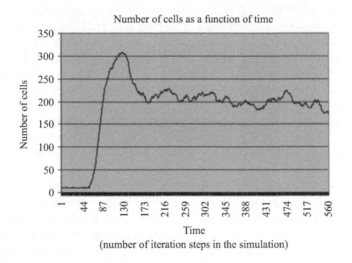

*Figure 4.6   Evolution of the number of cells during the time in a case of self-assertion [23]*

an excess of immune activity: insufficient inter-cell reactivity induces a loss of equilibrium in the immune system. The reactivity level is depicted by matrices of affinities. Using pre-existing experiments on B-lymphocytes by Kearney *et al.* [24], Stewart *et al.* compare *in vivo* affinities of observed cells with a simulated model [20,25]. They first highlight the fact that observed affinities between immunoglobulin M (IgM) antibodies and affinities simulated according to an ideal idiotypic network

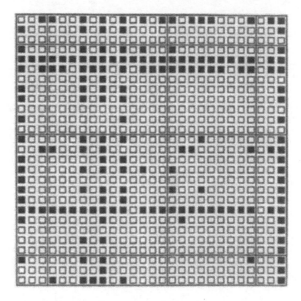

*Figure 4.7   The matrix of empirical affinities between all pairs of 27 foetal and neonatal IgM antibodies [25]*

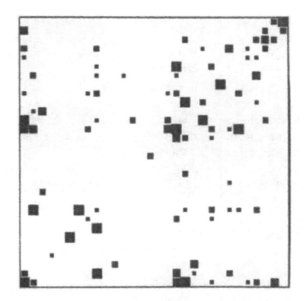

*Figure 4.8   The matrix of simulated affinities [25]*

show a similar overall structure: Figure 4.7 shows the matrix of affinities between all pairs of 27 foetal and neonatal IgM antibodies in the Kearney experiment; Figure 4.8 shows the matrix of simulated affinities. The size of each square is proportional to the *affinity* above a threshold of 11%.

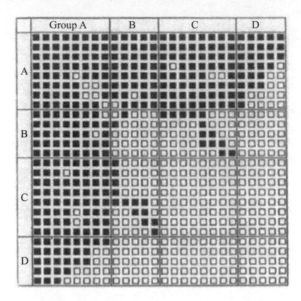

*Figure 4.9   The restructured matrix of empirical affinities [25]*

Stewart next highlights that the matrices from both observed and simulated data can be restructured to extract four groups of lymphocytes: a multi-affinity group A, two mirrors groups B and C with low within-group *affinity*, but where single clones of B have a related clone in C to which they are reactive, and a group D with low *affinity*. The A-group builds the core of the tolerant immune system. Groups B and C are reactive to specific immunoglobulins. Lymphocytes from the D-group are not connected to the idiotypic network and have very limited reactivity. Figure 4.9 shows the restructured matrix of affinities in empirical data. Figure 4.10 shows the restructured matrix of affinities in simulated data.

The comparison between simulated and empirical data enables to validate the theoretical assumptions of idiotypic networks while highlighting the mechanisms at play.

### 4.3.2.4   Multi-scale mechanisms

The idiotypic model continues to be refined and consolidated using recent experimental results. In particular, the hierarchy of lymphocyte groups is refined to four groups, instead of three in Stewart's model. The *core* of the idiotypic network is built by strong idiotype/anti-idiotype interactions that are rare events. This is the A-group of Stewart's model. The *periphery* of the network is built by interactions with one idiotype only, or 'self' antigens. This is the case for the C-group and D-group of Stewart's model. On the outer bound of the network, *singletons* survive in absence of connection to the central network. Such events have a high frequency and characterize 'non-self' reactivity . This is Stewart's D-group. Lastly, *holes* are lymphocyte clones which have to low or too much affinity and thus die. Figure 4.11 shows the structure

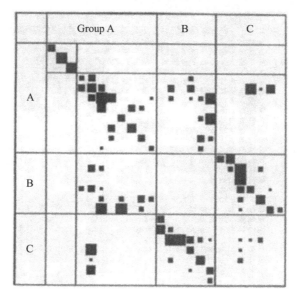

*Figure 4.10   The restructured matrix of simulated affinities [25]*

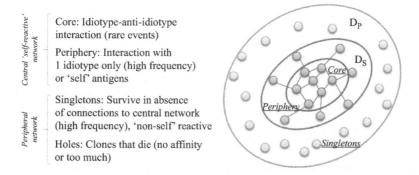

*Figure 4.11   The structure of the idiotypic network [26]*

of the idiotypic network [26], using the four categories of B-lymphocytes defined in [25].

This model enables a refined understanding of the complexity aspects of the immune system as shown in Figure 4.12 [27]. A first factor of heterogencity of lymphocytes is the diversity and selection of the cells. The high number of cell deaths during the inception of a new repertoire enables the generation of a population with a very high variability. When considering the T-cell population, the multiplicity lies in their various functions such as naïve-state cells, memory cells, regulation cells as well as in the numerous perturbations, they are exposed to ageing, diseases, treatments or immunosuppression.

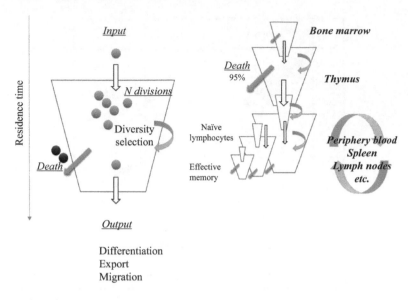

*Figure 4.12    The complexity aspects of the immune system [27]*

### 4.3.2.5  The contributions of idiotypic networks

Two major aspects of the immune response become blatant in the idiotypic model [2]:

- The individual clones of cells which are stimulated by the antigens, the B cells, are not primarily designed to react with them, which is the role of killer-T cells or macrophages. Rather, these stimulated cells reacts with internal components of the network, which Jerne denominate the 'internal image' of the antigen.
- A primary disturbance causes perturbation not only at a local scale but on different magnitudes and at different scales of the network.

The operations of perception of and reaction to antigens are thus supported not by individual cells but by the whole network which exhibits both local and multi-scale interactions.

Idiotypic networks have experienced a regain of interest both for clinical applications [28] and in the domain of theoretical immunity [26]. Some autoimmune diseases can be healed by restoring a dense network, through the injection of numerous antibodies [28]. Moreover, new network types are considered: after successful models based on B-lymphocytes, networks of T-lymphocytes also appear to be highly sensitive to cell-to-cell interactions. This approach opens promising perspectives to better understand not only immune reactions but also their regulation mechanisms.

### 4.3.3  Immune properties of natural organisms

The objective of our work on the mechanisms of immunity is to identify the core properties of immunity, to characterize them and to identify the ones which are susceptible

*Table 4.1   Immune properties of natural organisms*

| Immune property | Main-involved cells/organisms part | Classical model | Idiotypic model | Three-signal model |
|---|---|---|---|---|
| Anatomical barriers (skin; gastrointestinal tract; eyes) | Sweat; gastric acid, gut flora; tears | – | – | – |
| Perception | Immunoglobulin (antibodies), T-killer cells | Ehrlich self/ non-self distinction [8] | Antibody–antigen interference if reactive antibodies are present or T-killer-cell action for low-affinity D-Group [25] | One-signal |
| Reaction | Phagocytes | – | – | – |
| Memory | B cells, T cells | Burnett selection/ deletion [10] | – | – |
| Perceptor generation | B cells: bone marrow T cells: thymus B-cell cloning: lymph nodes | Burnett selection/deletion [10] Lafferty–Cunningham costimulation [18,19] | See classical model | Two-signals |
| Perceptor regulation | T cells | Burnett selection/ deletion [10] | Affinity with the network [25], density of the idiotypic network [28] | – |
| Reaction regulation | T cells | Matzinger's Danger [15] | – | Three-signals |

of providing useful analogies for building artificial systems capable of exhibiting similar properties. We therefore summarize the immune properties of natural organisms in Table 4.1.

The first protection in the immune process is built by the anatomical barrier. Its role is not addressed in the classical or idiotypic models of the natural immune system. The second aspect corresponds to immune perception, reaction and memory. The third aspect deals with regulation issues, i.e. the generation and regulation of the population of perceptors, as well as the regulation of the immune reaction.

In the model, detectors in immune systems are called perceptors. This word is chosen instead of 'detector' which is often used in the immunity community but has a very specific meaning (runtime analysis) in the domain of intrusion detection which we intend to be compliant with for applications. The term 'sensor' is also not suitable since perceptors do more than just sensing information and transferring them. They play a precise role in the recognition of pathogens. Please also note that no characterization of the distinction between perception and reaction is formalized in the natural immune system.

A mapping between immune properties and the three-signal model is also proposed. The one-signal model can be mapped to a simple perception mechanism. The two-signal model is related to the issue of perceptor generation, since the modelling of PAMPs strongly depends on the type of perceptors considered. The three-signal model is considered to be related to the issue of reaction regulation, since safe signals play an inhibitor role in the model which is a core feature of regulation, and danger signals play a stimulator role.

## 4.4  Applications

Natural immunity is a complex field which defines a highly consistent set of perception, reaction, memory and regulation mechanisms. It therefore induces a very high interest beyond the immunity community and especially in computer science. As in the case of other nature-inspired algorithms like genetic algorithms for optimization or neural networks for pattern recognition [29], the community is attracted to exploit the analogy with natural processes to propose innovative and powerful mechanisms for identifying outliers or to fight aggressions by malicious actors. However, contrary to mentioned examples and despite qualitatively and quantitatively highly significant contributions [30], a simple expression of an algorithm for artificial immunity as well as a flagship application is still missing [23]. The situation has not radically evolved since this statement made at the beginning of the 2000s.

The application of principles taken from natural immunity to artificial systems builds the field of immuno-engineering. It produced several models of AISs as a clustering, classification and anomaly-detection approach. These models have been in particular, but not exclusively, applied to intrusion detection. An overview of the immune properties as applied to artificial systems as well as a summary of the current limitations of proposed AIS conclude this chapter.

### 4.4.1  Immuno-engineering

Numerous principles can be identified and reused from immunity and immune systems [31] such as mechanisms for modelling the immune network, its memory properties or its adaptability. Reaction and tolerance are considered to emerge and to reinforce themselves from the interactions with the environment – this is *self-assertion* – rather than being the result of *a priori* dichotomy between self and non-self – the *self-recognition* [22]. This original approach lays the foundation for a conceptual framework for bio-inspired computational research [32] as shown in Figure 4.13.

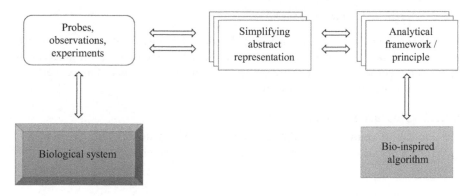

*Figure 4.13 Conceptual framework for bio-inspired computational research [32]*

The objective is to draw analogies between immune properties and artificial systems so as to devise algorithms which would provide efficient bio-inspired algorithms suitable for artificial ecosystems. The analogies should first lay on models of the natural immune system which is to be simplified through an abstract representation. An analytical framework for enforcing the principles of interest can then be defined. Three complementary approaches are defined: immuno-ecology, immunoinformatics and immuno-engineering.

**Immuno-ecology** is 'the study of immunological principles that permit effective immunological function within the context of the immensely complex immunological network … the principles serve mainly to provide an infrastructure for the immune system' [33].

**Immunoinformatics** is 'the study of the immune system as a cognitive, decision-making device … addresses mechanisms by which the immune system converts stimuli into information, how it processes and communicates that information, and how the information is used to promote an effective immuno-ecology … how the immune system generates, posts, processes, and stores information about itself and its environment' [33].

**Immuno-engineering** is 'the abstraction of immuno-ecological and immunoinformatics principles, and their adaptation and application to engineered artefacts (comprising hardware and software), so as to provide these artefacts with properties analogous to those provided to organisms by their natural immune systems' [34].

To express it in the context of this framework, the careful conclusion of authors w.r.t. the field of AISs [23] leads us to consider that the community has spent too much effort on building algorithms derived from natural immune behaviour at the level of immuno-engineering without having given enough attention at the principles underlying these algorithms, i.e. to immuno-ecology. A likely reason is the complexity of the mechanisms at play, which led the community to build artificial immune solutions almost synchronously with models of natural immunity.

## 4.4.2 Artificial immune systems

AISs are versatile algorithms which are capable of performing various operations such as clustering, classification or anomaly detection. Their principles are introduced, and an overview of the research activity in the AIS domain is provided. First-generation and second-generation systems are presented.

### 4.4.2.1 Research efforts on AIS

The application domains of AISs are quite vast, which underlines the adaptability of the algorithmic solutions based on the immunity analogy proposed by the community [35]:

- clustering and classification,
- anomaly detection,
- computer security,
- numeric function optimization,
- combinatoric optimization,
- learning and
- minor application domains: bio-informatics, image processing, control, robotics, virus detection, web mining or novelty detection in time series [36].

The research domain of AISs is a domain which has been very active since the mid-1990s and continues to be the focus of major research events, even though the rhythm of conferences dedicated to the subject has slightly slowed down in recent years. Figure 4.14 shows the number of scientific publications per year (1) according to a reference AIS bibliography [blue] [37], (2) according to Google Scholar results for 'AISs' [green] and (3) for all indexed PubMed articles [red] per year. The results show a relative growth in the domain based on both AIS bibliography and Google Scholar results until 2008, when the survey (which has been published in 2013) stops. The exponential fits are validated using the $R^2$ coefficient [30]. Figure 4.15

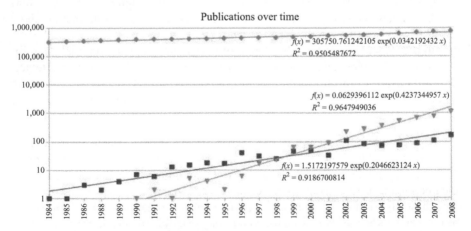

*Figure 4.14   Number of publications per year in the AIS domain [30]*

| Rank | Author | Publications | Author | Degree | Author | Betweenness | Author | Closeness |
|---|---|---|---|---|---|---|---|---|
| 1 | Timmis | 83 | Timmis | 50 | Timmis | 86260 | Timmis | 0.22405 |
| 2 | Dasgupta | 71 | Forrest | 35 | Dasgupta | 35531 | R-Smith | 0.22391 |
| 3 | Forrest | 68 | Castro | 29 | Forrest | 20535 | Bentley | 0.22390 |
| 4 | Castro | 58 | Dasgupta | 28 | Castro | 18859 | Nicosia | 0.22389 |
| 5 | Zuben | 42 | Perelson | 28 | X-Wang | 17737 | Tyrrell | 0.22389 |
| 6 | Aickelin | 38 | X-Wang | 24 | A-Freitas | 17628 | Chow | 0.22386 |
| 7 | Perelson | 35 | D-Lee | 22 | Chow | 16984 | Y-Liu | 0.22386 |
| 8 | Hart | 20 | Zuben | 20 | Hart | 16183 | Clark | 0.22385 |
| 9 | Gonzalez | 19 | J-Kim | 18 | R-Smith | 15714 | Neal | 0.22385 |
| 10 | Stibor | 18 | Lamont | 18 | Tyrrell | 15451 | Lau | 0.22384 |
| 11 | Neal | 17 | Aickelin | 17 | Y-Liu | 14936 | Forrest | 0.22384 |
| 12 | Hunt | 17 | Tarakanov | 16 | Bentley | 14827 | Cutello | 0.22384 |
| 13 | Bersini | 17 | A-Freitas | 15 | Perelson | 13960 | Pavone | 0.22384 |
| 14 | Lamont | 16 | Nicosia | 15 | Stewart | 13312 | Goncharova | 0.22384 |
| 15 | Lau | 16 | Faro | 15 | Aickelin | 12671 | Knight | 0.22384 |
| 16 | Esponda | 15 | Bentley | 13 | Gao | 12462 | Stepney | 0.22384 |
| 17 | J-Kim | 15 | Oliveira | 13 | Carvalho | 11618 | Dasgupta | 0.22383 |
| 18 | Bentley | 15 | Hart | 13 | Jackson | 11594 | Castro | 0.22383 |
| 19 | Greensmith | 15 | Clark | 12 | Huang | 11481 | Hart | 0.22383 |
| 20 | Tarakanov | 15 | Gonzalez | 12 | Bersini | 11119 | A-Freitas | 0.22382 |

*Figure 4.15   AIS authors [30]*

shows an overview of most prolific AIS authors ranked according to their number of publications, degree (or number of unique collaborators), betweenness and closeness. Timmis, Dasgupta, Forrest, Castro, Zuben, Aickelin, Perelson and Hart are the most prolific authors, and often qualitatively the ones who have brought much insight to the community.

A further survey on AIS would bring little new information here, we will therefore not attempt to provide yet another extensive survey on AIS research. The reader is invited to refer to [38–40] for reference works.

### 4.4.2.2   First-generation artificial immune systems

First-generation AISs address the challenge of providing suitable perceptors for supporting classification issues and of regulating their population. Figure 4.16 shows the process for a string-matching detector in early AISs [41]. Candidate perceptors are first generated as random bit strings. They are then matched against 'self strings' representing specific behaviours of the systems as ranges of source or target machines, network packet parameters or system commands. Of course, it is necessary that they can be represented as a bit string and that a meaningful matching metric such as a distance can be computed between the candidate perceptor and the 'self string'. As in the deletion process of natural immunity, self-matching strings are discarded and strings with few affinity with the 'self strings' are added to the detector set. The detectors then undergo a maturation life cycle as shown in Figure 4.17 [42]. The selected detectors are first in an immature state, where they are waiting to be activated through an encounter with a corresponding antigen. Should this encounter not occur at all or not occur enough during a given timespan, the detector is discarded and dies. Should this encounter occur frequently enough to exceed a given count threshold, the

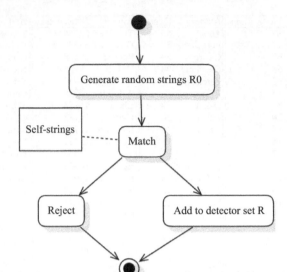

*Figure 4.16 Process for a string-matching detector in early artificial immune systems [41]*

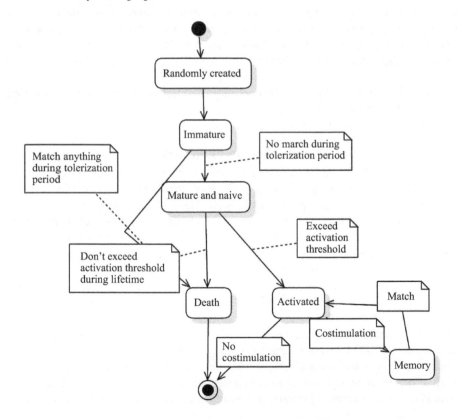

*Figure 4.17 Detector life cycle in a computer immune system [42]*

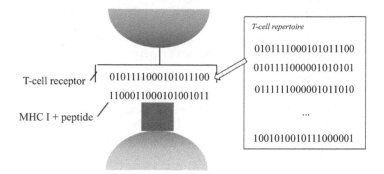

*Figure 4.18   The string-matching process used for emulating antibody–antigen affinity [44]*

detector becomes activated. It then becomes reactive to costimulation signals such as known anomalies. Should this costimulation not occur, the detector is finally discarded. Should this costimulation occur, the detector is labelled as a detector of an actual system issue and included in the AIS memory. This process is also known as clonal selection, for which De Castro proposed the CLONALG algorithm [43] as a refinement of this model.

Figure 4.18 shows the string-matching process used for evaluating antibody-antigen affinity [44]. The T-cell receptor, i.e. the detector, is represented as a string where individual characters are taken from the binary set {0,1}. The antigen consists in the MHC (major histocompatibility complex) and a peptide. It is compared to all available T-cell receptors: all antigens which binary distance with one antibody of the repertoire being below a given threshold are considered as a match.

A similar approach is proposed by Dasgupta to leverage the complementarity of the positive characterization for identifying 'self' behaviour and negative characterization for abnormal behaviours [45], using genetic algorithms for the generation of detection rules. Both models suffer from the limitations of these first-generation algorithms: new behaviours can appear throughout the system life-cycle, making the generation of the 'self' data a never-ending task. Moreover, even if one assumes that the current 'self' state is satisfactory, basing the identification of anomalies on a string distance between binary 'antibodies' and system traces imply that this distance is significative of the level of threat posed by identified abnormal traces. This assumption is far from obvious, and not evaluated by the authors.

### 4.4.2.3   Second-generation artificial immune systems

Following the reference work that builds the first generation of AIS, the mechanics of the natural immune system were explored with a still greater precision to refine the model. One major refinement is the integration of the concept of danger, which has been defined in the immunology community concurrently to the inception of first AIS. Danger means that the actual impact of an aggression is considered for evaluating the

*Table 4.2   Biological signals and their artificial counterparts [48]*

| Signal | Biological property | Abstract property | Computational example |
|---|---|---|---|
| PAMP | Indicator of microbial presence | Signature of likely anomaly | Error message per second |
| Danger signal | Indicator of tissue damage | High levels indicate *potential* anomaly | Network packets per second |
| Safe signal | Indicator of healthy tissue | High levels indicate normally functioning system | Size of network packets |
| Inflammation | Indicator of general tissue distress | Multiplies all other input signals | User physically absent |

threat, rather than just a distance to non-self antibodies. This shift enables to consider the system to be protected by the AISs in a more systematic manner. It also implies that a concept of danger can be defined, thereby invalidating applications such as classification to favour the detection of system anomalies or of malicious attacks. The application of danger to artificial immunity is proposed by the dendritic cell algorithm (DCA), where dendritic cells are responsible for presenting antibodies to B or T lymphocytes so as to influence their behaviour [46,47]. DCA leverages the three-signal model of natural immunity: Table 4.2 summarizes biological signals and their artificial counterparts involved in DCA [48].

Beside the antigen themselves, the PAMPs, provide known signatures of probable anomalies. Danger signals indicate the presence of a damage to the tissue. Safe signals are an indicator of healthy tissues. Inflammation indicates a general tissue distress and amplifies the immune reaction. To accurately simulate an immune reaction, all these information should be considered. Figure 4.19 shows a state chart for the natural immune system showing the possible states and transitions between the immature, semi-mature and mature states of a dendritic cell [48].

The DCA itself only considers antigens under the form of process IDs and a signal matrix entailing both safe and danger signals. Figure 4.20 shows the DCA process [48]. When antigens match significant danger signals, a dedicated immature dendritic cell is generated. In the presence of safe signals, it becomes a semi-mature cell. In the presence of danger signals, it becomes activated and triggers suitable reaction. The DCA algorithm has been validated experimentally by its authors for distributed denial of service [48], NMAP port scanning [47] as well as for misbehaviours in sensor networks [49]. Its main advantages are low CPU requirements as well as a reduced training period [46].

The main limitation of DCA lies in its highly stochastic character: the algorithm is hard to analyse and its behaviour is hard to predict, both with regard to performance as well as to detection ability. These issues lead to the development of a deterministic version of the DCA [50]. The deterministic approach provides results which are more

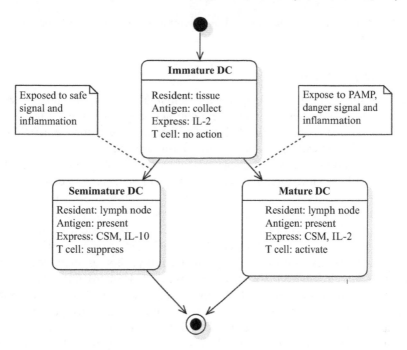

Figure 4.19  *State chart showing the possible states and transitions between these states for a dendritic cell [48]*

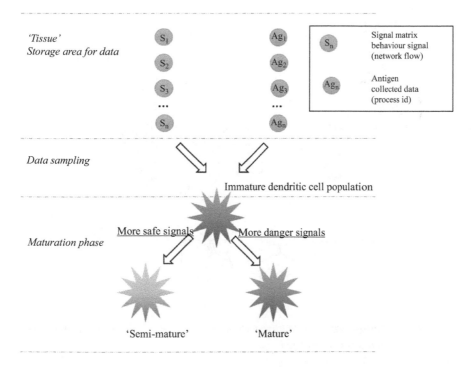

Figure 4.20  *The dendritic cell algorithm process [48]*

consistent from a run to another, and less dependent on the underlying stochastic process.

### 4.4.3  AIS for intrusion detection

Since the analogy with the natural immune system intuitively implies some protection against aggressive entities, AIS were naturally and very early applied to intrusion detection in computer networks. Both first-generation and second-generation AIS have been evaluated with satisfactory results in this context.

The main additional contributions in the context of IT security applications are the particular architectural solutions which are implemented to deploy the AIS. The algorithm themselves are used with no major adaptations. Several authors have proposed architectures for applying the AIS approach to the detection of computer intrusions [42,51,52]. Figure 4.21 shows a three-level architecture with differentiated actions at local, network and system level [51]. The local level is responsible for virus detection, system response and system memory. It transfers resource requests, user interactions and virus alerts to the upper layer of the architecture. It receives resource allocation as well as virus alerts from the upper layer. The network level controls local activities, collects local status, dispenses vaccination against viruses and provides a user interface for monitoring. It transmits information regarding user interactions and virus alerts towards other network-level nodes. The system level supports status

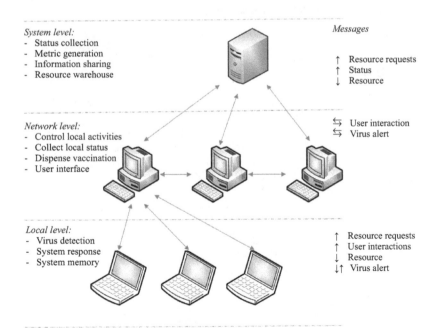

*Figure 4.21   Three-level architecture with differentiated actions at local, network and system level [51]*

collection, metric generation and information sharing. It manages the resource ware-house. Figure 4.22 shows the various sessions used for managing the interactions between these levels [51]. The local sessions entail detectors, killers, classifiers and helpers. The network session supports monitoring and binds local and system levels. The system session performs the controller role.

The proposed three-level model is pervasive throughout the literature, well accepted and validated through various implementations. However, we consider that the terminology used does reflect neither the functional objectives nor the reality of AIS implementations – and still less in the case of recent architectures like the one of Internet of Things infrastructures. For instance, the concept of 'network level' proposed by [51] is not compliant with user-interaction features, and the concept of 'system' can apply at the same time to embedded local systems, network devices and central control appliances. We therefore propose to categorize the layers of AISs as the following:

**The local layer,** typically located in the endpoint nodes. It is responsible for detection, memory and response.

**The monitoring layer,** typically located in gateways or in user machines. It is in charge of controlling local activities, dispensing vaccinations and providing a first-level interface with the user.

**The control layer,** typically a central appliance. It collects status, generates metrics, shares information and store resources.

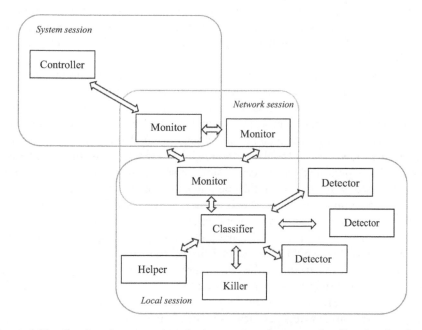

*Figure 4.22   Session for managing the interactions between the three levels of an AIS [51]*

In the AIS literature, the term 'architecture' is also used to denote the protection process made of the subsequent steps: anatomical barriers, physiological conditions, innate immunity and acquired immunity [6]. However, in computing science terms, we consider this as a process, i.e. a succession of consecutive steps, rather than an architecture, i.e. a static structure supporting the system's features.

One can note that on the contrary to natural immune systems which are highly non-hierarchical in nature [6], artificial ones require a well-defined hierarchy to map the actual architecture of the system to be protected. This non-hierarchical structure ensures a very high resilience level to the natural immune system. Artificial counterparts exhibit a weakness here which needs to be addressed.

### 4.4.4    *Immune properties of artificial systems*

AISs exhibit properties similar to natural ones, especially because the underlying mechanisms are very directly inspired from natural cell-level mechanisms. In particular, an adaptation of the three-signal model for AISs is proposed by [16]

- the one-signal model is characterized by negative and clonal selection [41,43],
- the two-signal model introduces costimulation [42] and
- the three-signal model introduces the concept of danger by considering safe and non-safe behaviours of networks and systems [47].

Research efforts on AIS tend to map quite tightly the underlying molecular mechanisms of immunity. However, no explicit framework focusing on immune properties rather than on immune mechanisms is used in the literature to compare and classify contributions. In Table 4.3, we therefore propose to summarize the immune properties of artificial systems.

As expected, perception and memory are well addressed both at the operational as well as at the regulation level. The basic perception mechanisms match the one-signal model, whereas regulation addresses two-signal and three-signal models according to the comprehensiveness of information which is taken into account during the maturation process. In any case, maturation is a feature entailed in most AIS models of the literature. However, the framework highlights interesting facts. First, the issue of reaction, that is presented as self-explanatory in several reference works, is almost never addressed explicitly. Given the operational difficulties to automate a security response in a computer network, this is actually hardly surprising but underlines a significant discrepancy between the promises and the actual scope of proposals. Second, anatomical barriers, that build a first protection against aggressions, are almost never addressed. One could consider that the central firewall of any organization plays this role, but this would neglect the complexity of the natural anatomical barriers analogy – and the actual openness of real IT ecosystems. Lastly, the role of an AIS controller is defined, but its features such as status collection and information sharing are far from drawing a consensus in the community.

*Table 4.3   Immune properties of artificial systems*

| Immune property | Three-signal model | AIS model | AIS layer |
|---|---|---|---|
| Anatomical barriers | – | – | – |
| Perception | One-signal | Bitwise distance [41] Signatures of processes and protocols [47] | Local |
| Reaction | – | Mentioned, but no solution specified | Monitoring |
| Memory | – | Conservation of perceptors | Monitoring |
| Perceptor generation | Two-signals | Selection-deletion [41], Clonal selection [53], Knowledge-based [47] | Monitoring |
| Perceptor regulation | Two-signals<br><br>Three signals | Maturation process, vaccination [41,47], Costimulation [42], Danger in dendritic cell algorithm (DCA) [47] | Monitoring |
| Reaction regulation | – | – | – |
| Status collection, information sharing | – | Mentioned, but no solution specified | Control |

## 4.4.5   Limitations and perspectives of AIS applications

The natural immune system provides a rich analogy for building high-tuned bio-inspired algorithms: the research community actually provided an extensive effort in this domain since the mid-1990s. However, fewer focus on the issues of artificial immunity exists in the last couple of years. This is underlined by the fact that several properties of the immune system appear to be of interest but actually bring little insight for building operational systems, at least ones which introduce radical improvements in field solutions [23]. Examples of such systems are

- two classes classification and pattern recognition systems, as would in older models of the immune system be the distinction between 'self' and 'non-self';
- Clustering and self-organizing systems, as would the immune system create markers of 'self'; and
- Protective system, as would the immune system protect the body from external damages.

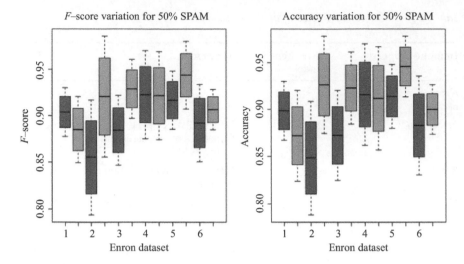

*Figure 4.23    Comparison between the Agent-Based Cross-Regulation Model [54]
(dark grey) and Naïve Bayesian classifier (light grey) for detecting
intrusion detection*

Based on their earlier models such as the immune recruitment mechanism,
Bersini *et al.* consider that such models, aiming at reproducing search and memory
features of the natural immune system, actually build a variant of hill-climbing
meta-heuristics [31].

Some authors went further by acknowledging the limitation of their own implementations to highlight the limit they see in the immune approach. Figure 4.23 shows
the relative performance of the immune-based Agent-Based Cross-Regulation Model
(ABCRM) and a Naïve Bayesian network [54]. It is worth noting that the ABCRM
model provides slightly better results than the Naïve Bayesian network for some
specific problems using suitable parameters, but that the solution does not bring a
spectacular improvement which would warrant non-specialists to learn such a method.
The great scientific honesty of the authors must be acknowledged for the insight
they bring.

Based on these discussions as well as on the classification of immune properties
in natural and artificial systems in Tables 4.1 and 4.3, we summarize the challenges
of existing solutions in AISs as follows:

- AIS algorithms are actually designed for perceptions at a single place, i.e. the
  proposed solution are intrinsically centralized rather that distributed, even though
  the models claim to address this issue. Moreover, the suitable validity domains
  for the proposed algorithms are not specified.
- Distribution issues are considered to be addressed by the model, whereas the
  control layer, in charge of information sharing, is only scarcely specified.

- The variety of inputs is not addressed in the AIS models. Each model addresses a specific representation of the system behaviour, often for online detection, by considering system states and network packets. However, the application domains are not discussed, and the interconnection with existing IT infrastructures (system logs) and security solutions (SIEMs) is not considered.
- Reaction is mentioned, but to the best of our knowledge never specified – and it is not a trivial task.
- The role of the interaction with the user (Reporting? Integration of expert knowledge? Analysis of complex events? Manual reaction?) is mentioned but not specified.
- Although natural immune systems enforce a very high resilience level through a totally non-hierarchical structure, artificial ones typically enforce a simpler, pyramid-like architecture. Resilience is therefore not embedded in AIS, on the contrary to natural-immunity processes.

The analogy between a natural approach to protection, i.e. immunity, and the protection of artificial ecosystems makes the exploration of the capabilities of the former to solve issues posed by the latter an appealing domain, which is far from being covered. However, identified challenges highlight the difficulties that research effort have met so far, such as the high cost of development with regard to the efficiency of proposed algorithms for concrete problems. Actually, the fundamental differences in scale, number of considered entities or cost for generating a single perceptor between the natural and the artificial worlds need to be better characterized. Moreover, reproducing a fully emergent natural process to solve very targeted and technology-specific goals like performing classification or protecting IT systems from viruses may not be as easy as AIS pioneers have thought.

## 4.5   Conclusions and perspectives

The immune system provides a promising framework for modelling an approach that, far beyond the mapping of specific mechanisms such as immunoglobulin affinities or dendritic cells maturation processes which provide revolutionary insights but failed to find a path towards broad acceptation so far, would ensure that immune properties are supported as a mean of protecting the overall stability of IT ecosystems on the long-term. A path for further investigation on these immune properties would be to address not the properties of the immune system themselves, but the cognitive mechanisms at play, which have long attracted significant interest from the community [55,56]. Varela proposes to consider the immune system as a prototypical example of advanced cognition, which would go beyond cybernetics, symbolism and even emergence to focus to the actual impact of the cognition process and to the interactions between the individual and the environment: the enactment process [57]. This framework has been defined through the 4E properties [58–61] of cognitive systems: embodied, embedded, enacted and extended. In a 4E cognitive AIS, these 4E properties should be supported, and the cognition mechanisms should be

**embodied,** since the analysis capability of a system cannot be parted from its capability to sense its environment, and its reaction capacity is strongly conditioned by built-in features;
**embedded,** since the analysis capability of a system is tightly bound with its ability to work in symbiosis with the intelligence transmitted from its environment, which should support efficient processing;
**enacted,** as the capability of the system to handle the messages from its environment and to react to them is the key to its survival in hostile environments; and
**extended,** as the analysis and reaction capability of a system is highly dependent on its capacity to leverage intelligence from peer systems or from external actors such as human IT administrators.

The enaction concept marks a major shift in scientific method: based on the relative failure of models striving for comprehensive understanding of the world under study, which become ever more complex and experience increasing difficulties to percolate outside the scientific community, researchers focus more and more on the identification of critical interactions susceptible to break the resilience of systems [62], so as to understand how to make them secure and resilient.

# References

[1]  Jerne NK. Towards a network theory of the immune system. Annales d'immunologie. 1974;125:373–389.
[2]  Vaz NM, Varela FJ. Self and non-sense: an organism-centered approach to immunology. Medical Hypotheses. 1978;4(3):263–267.
[3]  Barricelli NA. Esempi numerici di processi di evoluzione. Methodos. 1954;6(21–22):45–68.
[4]  Perelson AS, Oster GF. Theoretical studies of clonal selection: minimal antibody repertoire size and reliability of self-non-self discrimination. Journal of Theoretical Biology. 1979;81(4):645–670.
[5]  Carneiro J. Towards a comprehensive view of the immune system. PhD thesis, University of Porto; 1997.
[6]  Hofmeyr SA. An interpretative introduction to the immune system. In: Design Principles for the Immune System and Other Distributed Autonomous Systems. Oxford University Press, vol. 3; 2001. p. 28–36.
[7]  Perelson AS, Weisbuch G. Immunology for physicists. Reviews of Modern Physics. 1997;69(4):1219.
[8]  Ehrlich P. Experimentelle untersuchungen über immunität. I. Ueber ricin. DMW – Deutsche Medizinische Wochenschrift. 1891;17(32):976–979.
[9]  Ehrlich P. Experimentelle untersuchungen über immunität. II. Ueber abrin. DMW – Deutsche Medizinische Wochenschrift. 1891;17(44):1218–1219.

[10] Burnet SFM. The clonal selection theory of acquired immunity. Vanderbilt University Press, Nashville; 1959.

[11] Matzinger P. Tolerance, danger, and the extended family. Annual Review of Immunology. 1994;12(1):991–1045.

[12] Buchmann K. Evolution of innate immunity: clues from invertebrates via fish to mammals. Frontiers in Immunology. 2014;5:459–466.

[13] Gammill HS, Stephenson MD, Aydelotte TM, *et al.* Microchimerism in women with recurrent miscarriage. Chimerism. 2014;5(3–4):103–105.

[14] Watson JD, Crick FH. Molecular structure of nucleic acids. Nature. 1953;171(4356):737–738.

[15] Matzinger P. The danger model: a renewed sense of self. Science. 2002; 296(5566):301–305.

[16] Greensmith J, Aickelin U. Artificial dendritic cells: multi-faceted perspectives. In: Human-Centric Information Processing Through Granular Modelling. Berlin, Heidelberg: Springer; 2009. p. 375–395.

[17] Lederberg J. Genes and antibodies. Do antigens bear instructions for antibody specificity or do they select cell lines that arise by mutation? Science (Washington). 1959;129:1649–1653.

[18] Lafferty KJ, Cunningham A. A new analysis of allogeneic interactions. Australian Journal of Experimental Biology & Medical Science. 1975; 53(1):27–42.

[19] Gill RG, Coulombe M, Lafferty KJ. Pancreatic islet allograft immunity and tolerance: the two-signal hypothesis revisited. Immunological Reviews. 1996;149(1):75–96.

[20] Stewart J, Varela FJ, Coutinho A. The relationship between connectivity and tolerance as revealed by computer simulation of the immune network: some lessons for an understanding of autoimmunity. Journal of Autoimmunity. 1989;2:15–23.

[21] Tauber A. The biological notion of self and non-self. In: Zalta EN, editor. The Stanford Encyclopedia of Philosophy. Winter 2016 ed. Metaphysics Research Lab, Stanford University, Standford, CA, USA; 2016.

[22] Detours V, Bersini H, Stewart J, *et al.* Development of an idiotypic network in shape space. Journal of Theoretical Biology. 1994;170(4):401–414.

[23] Bersini H. Self-assertion versus self-recognition: A tribute to Francisco Varela. In: Published in the Proceedings of 1st International Conference on Artificial Immune Systems (ICARIS), University of Kent at Canterbury, UK; 2002.

[24] Kearney J, Vakil M, Nicholson N. Non-random VH gene expression and idiotype anti-idiotype expression in early B cells. In: Evolution and Vertebrate Immunity: The Antigen Receptor and MHC Gene Families. University of Texas, vol. 1; 1987. p. 175–190.

[25] Stewart J, Varela FJ. Exploring the meaning of connectivity in the immune network. Immunological Reviews. 1989;110(1):37–61.

[26] Thomas-Vaslin V. A complex immunological idiotypic network for maintenance of tolerance. Frontiers in Immunology. 2014;5:369–371.

[27]    Thomas-Vaslin V, Six A, Pham HP, *et al.* Immunodepression and immunosup-
        pression during aging. In: Immunosuppression-Role in Health and Diseases.
        InTech; 2012.
[28]    Behn U. Idiotypic networks: toward a renaissance? Immunological Reviews.
        2007;216(1):142–152.
[29]    Bersini H. The endogenous double plasticity of the immune network and the
        inspiration to be drawn for engineering artifacts. In: Artificial Immune Systems
        and Their Applications. Berlin, Heidelberg: Springer; 1993. p. 22–44.
[30]    Haidar AA, Ganascia JG, Six A, *et al.* The artificial immune systems domain
        identifying progress and main contributors using publication and co-authorship
        analyses. In: ECAL. vol. 12; 2013.
[31]    Bersini H, Varela FJ. Hints for adaptive problem solving gleaned from immune
        networks. In: International Conference on Parallel Problem Solving from
        Nature. Springer; 1990. p. 343–354.
[32]    Stepney S, Smith RE, Timmis J, *et al.* Conceptual frameworks for artifi-
        cial immune systems. International Journal of Unconventional Computing.
        2005;1(3):315–338.
[33]    Orosz CG. (2001, June). An introduction to immuno-ecology and immuno-
        informatics. In Santa Fe Institute Studies in the Sciences of Complexity.
        Reading, Mass.; Addison-Wesley; 1998. p. 125–150.
[34]    Timmis J, Hart E, Hone A, *et al.* Immuno-engineering. In: Biologically-
        Inspired Collaborative Computing. Boston, MA: Springer; 2008. p. 3–17.
[35]    Hart E, Timmis J. Application areas of AIS: The past, the present and the future.
        Applied Soft Computing. 2008;8(1):191–201.
[36]    Dasgupta D, Forrest S. Novelty detection in time series data using ideas from
        immunology. In: Proceedings of the International Conference on Intelligent
        Systems; 1996. p. 82–87.
[37]    Dasgupta D. Artificial immune systems: a bibliography. In: Technical report.
        University of Memphis, Memphis, USA; 2007. CS-07-004.
[38]    Dasgupta D, Attoh-Okine N. Immunity-based systems: a survey. In: Systems,
        Man, and Cybernetics, 1997. Computational Cybernetics and Simulation.
        1997 IEEE International Conference on. vol. 1. IEEE; 1997. p. 369–374.
[39]    Dasgupta D. Advances in artificial immune systems. IEEE Computational
        Intelligence Magazine. 2006;1(4):40–49.
[40]    Sotiropoulos DN, Tsihrintzis GA. Artificial immune systems. In: Machine
        Learning Paradigms. Paris: Springer; 2017. p. 159–235.
[41]    Forrest S, Perelson AS, Allen L, *et al.* Self-nonself discrimination in a computer.
        In: Research in Security and Privacy, 1994. Proceedings. 1994 IEEE Computer
        Society Symposium on. IEEE; 1994. p. 202–212.
[42]    Hofmeyr SA, Forrest S. Architecture for an artificial immune system.
        Evolutionary Computation. 2000;8(4):443–473.
[43]    De Castro LN, Von Zuben FJ. Learning and optimization using the
        clonal selection principle. IEEE Transactions on Evolutionary Computation.
        2002;6(3):239–251.
[44]    Forrest S, Beauchemin C. Computer immunology. Immunological Reviews.
        2007;216(1):176–197.

[45] Dasgupta D, González F. An immunity-based technique to characterize intrusions in computer networks. IEEE Transactions on Evolutionary Computation. 2002;6(3):281–291.

[46] Greensmith J. The dendritic cell algorithm. University of Nottingham, Nottingham, UK; 2007.

[47] Greensmith J, Aickelin U, Twycross J. Articulation and clarification of the dendritic cell algorithm. In International Conference on Artificial Immune Systems. Springer, Berlin, Heidelberg; (2006, September). p. 404–417.

[48] Greensmith J, Aickelin U, Cayzer S. Detecting danger: the dendritic cell algorithm. In: Robust Intelligent Systems. London: Springer; 2008. p. 89–112.

[49] Kim J, Bentley P, Wallenta C, *et al.* Danger is ubiquitous: detecting malicious activities in sensor networks using the dendritic cell algorithm. Artificial Immune Systems. 2006:390–403.

[50] Greensmith J, Aickelin U. The deterministic dendritic cell algorithm. In International Conference on Artificial Immune Systems. Springer, Berlin, Heidelberg; (2008, August). p. 291–302.

[51] Harmer PK, Williams PD, Gunsch GH, *et al.* An artificial immune system architecture for computer security applications. IEEE Transactions on Evolutionary Computation. 2002;6(3):252–280.

[52] Kim J, Bentley PJ. Towards an artificial immune system for network intrusion detection: an investigation of clonal selection with a negative selection operator. In: Evolutionary Computation, 2001. Proceedings of the 2001 Congress on. vol. 2. IEEE; 2001. p. 1244–1252.

[53] de Castro LN, Timmis J. Artificial immune systems: a novel paradigm to pattern recognition. Artificial Neural Networks in Pattern Recognition. 2002;1:67–84.

[54] Haidar AA. An adaptive document classifier inspired by T-cell cross-regulation in the immune system. (Doctoral dissertation, Indiana University), Citeseer; 2011.

[55] Maturana HR, Varela FJ. Autopoiesis and cognition: the realization of the living. vol. 42. Dordrecht, Holland, Springer Science & Business Media; 1991.

[56] Bourgine P, Stewart J. Autopoiesis and cognition. Artificial Life. 2004;10(3):327–345.

[57] Francisco V. Invitation aux sciences cognitives. Seuil; 1988.

[58] Menary R. Introduction to the special issue on 4E cognition. Phenomenology and the Cognitive Sciences. 2010;9(4):459–463.

[59] Rowlands M. The new science of the mind: from extended mind to embodied phenomenology. Cambridge, MA: MIT Press; 2010.

[60] Froese T, Di Paolo EA. The enactive approach: theoretical sketches from cell to society. Pragmatics & Cognition. 2011;19(1):1–36.

[61] Harvey MI, Gahrn-Andersen R, Steffensen SV. Interactivity and enaction in human cognition. Constructivist Foundations. 2016;11(2):602–613.

[62] Jacquemart F, Thomas-Vaslin V. L'évaluation globale des technologies. Villeneuve-d'Ascq: Presses Universitaires du Septentrion; 2016.

*Chapter 5*

# Bio-inspired approaches for security and resiliency of network traffic

*Christopher S. Oehmen[1] and Elena S. Peterson[1]*

## 5.1 Introduction

Computational networks are proliferating at an ever-increasing rate to provide functionality for critical aspects of modern life. Interactions among data, sensors, computing and humans through communication networks have made it possible to control, analyse and optimize many activities that until now have been impossible or labour-intensive. Traditional information technology (IT) networks make it possible for people to access data and services worldwide almost instantaneously. Operational technology (OT) networks make it possible to sense and control very complex systems such as the power grid and smart buildings and cities. As more and more devices such as smartphones, mobile sensors and even appliances (e.g. the Internet of Things or IoT) connect to these networks, a highly complex and organic macrocosm of digital entities is emerging. Networks can serve as a communication fabric that is the connective tissue among all of these bits of functionality, and so it is natural to study networks from the standpoint of biological systems.

This book chapter is organized into two main sections. The first describes several biological approaches that have led to applications in computational and computer science for computer networks, with particular emphasis on the aspects of those biological approaches that are essential for capturing the method's benefit. This section also includes discussions on how or under what conditions biological methods do not apply to computer networks. The second section describes recent work done in applying biological methods at several levels of network operations. Several examples of historical and recent research are given in these sections to illustrate the ways in which biology has been used to inspire novel applications for computer networks. These two main sections are introduced briefly below.

### 5.1.1 Biological approaches

Several different aspects of biological systems have been brought to bear on various aspects of network traffic. Specifically, because network traffic is constantly reacting

[1]Computing and Analytics Division, Pacific Northwest National Laboratory, USA

to changes in availability of resources and other environmental demands (like bandwidth traffic jams), one useful category of biological strategies heavily leveraged in computer networks focuses on control and coordination. Examples of such methods include swarm intelligence, flock dynamics and social insect coordination models employed by ants or bees, for instance. Such models make it possible for large numbers of dynamic entities to coordinate and seek optimal solutions across complex, changing terrains while minimizing the need for information transfer, preserving precious bandwidth. A second class of useful biological strategies for improving networks focuses on computational learning from complex network data. This class includes neural nets, machine learning, artificial intelligence, deep learning and other forms of learning. These algorithms have arisen from various biological strategies for discovering complex patterns in data, largely derived from neural architectures, and have resulted in numerous methods for designing, operating and analysing network traffic. A third category of biological approaches that has wide applicability in computer networks focuses on automaticity, self-healing and autonomic aspects of complex biological systems. Such methods enable subsystems to work independently of central control, automatically detect and mitigate incorrect functionality and faults and otherwise locally react to changing conditions. There are many other biological approaches that have made meaningful contributions to the regimes described in this chapter and for which more focused applications have been developed. Examples of these include information flow, multi-organism coordination, collective decision-making, autonomy and autonomous control, redundancy, diversity, programmed cell death and learning/cognition. Each of these will be discussed in more detail in Section 5.2.

## 5.1.2    Network regimes

Traffic between computer IT systems or OT control systems exhibits both macroscopic and microscopic behaviours that operate under principles analogous to those that govern biological systems. At the micro scale, network traffic is a collection of data bits that are sent between systems and interpreted by the receiving application for some predetermined purpose. This flow of information is a complex interplay between traffic that is highly dynamic and reactive to a changing network terrain and simple, repeatable, predictable information that flows through a terrain that is static or very slowly changing. This combination is in many ways reminiscent of how information flows through biological systems to give information about the state of the system or to help communities solve hard problems like finding food. At the macro level, planning and managing networks looks very analogous to biological processes for control, in part because of the need for hierarchical control of constantly evolving systems. This can happen in either an ad hoc fashion, such as for mobile wireless sensors, or in a more static fashion, such as how neural systems behave. Also at the macro scale, the real-time dynamic properties of how traffic is routed through networks can be thought of from the standpoint of several different biological approaches to optimization and organization. Finally, neural networks that make it possible for organisms to learn, reason and draw associations between elements in the dynamic natural world can also be used to help networks learn optimal strategies and find anomalies.

In the network traffic analysis section, biological approaches are explored for suitability in three different regimes:

- Micro-scale features of endpoints expressed through their network traffic.
- Planning and management of networks.
- Routing traffic through networks.

The applicability of biological approaches is discussed in more detail for each of these regimes in Section 5.3, with example historical and current research that illustrates the many ways that biological methods have been used to inspire various features of computer networks.

## 5.2   Biological methods as models for network traffic analysis

Many features of biological systems can serve as models for aspects of cyber security, in particular how to control, regulate and protect network traffic. These can be taken from molecular and cellular levels or from higher organisms and collections of organisms and from organs themselves like the vertebrate brain. These biological models can be used to solve a variety of challenges in the cyber world, but they must be understood well before they can be used effectively. In some cases, it is important to capture all of the biological features to get the benefit from such an approach. In other cases, the biological metaphors break down, and it is important to understand when to treat the cyber world differently. The following sections contain more detailed descriptions of several biological approaches, including some key features that are essential to capture with fidelity in computational cyber security. In addition, some aspects that do not apply are also discussed.

### 5.2.1   Information flow

At the molecular level, biological organisms expend great effort to manage and propagate data or information. Long strands of deoxyribonucleic acid (DNA) contain repeating subunits of four constituent types, each having molecular properties that drive production of molecular machinery, and by extension, cellular behaviour. This molecular data that resides in every living cell, along with many contextual inputs, enables and also sets boundaries for all possible behaviours of each cell. For this reason, it is essential that organisms perform two information-related tasks with great fidelity: (1) protect the integrity of the DNA sequence during the lifetime of an organism and (2) pass this information on to future generations of organisms while providing flexibility for new functionality in these future generations [1].

There is a direct linkage between the molecular sequence of a DNA strand and the chemistry that cellular machinery can engage in using those DNA 'instructions'. More specifically, DNA is transcribed and translated into worker molecules known as proteins, which also have a primary structure that is best described as long chains of repeating units of 20 constituent types. The sequence of DNA subunits that comprise a section of DNA is directly related to the sequence of protein subunits that section of DNA encodes for. These proteins are often further modified by their chemical environment and folded into higher order structures that perform most of the work needed in cells. For example, proteins serve as the cellular skeleton, transport specific chemicals and even are used to build part of the apparatus that 'reads' the DNA itself. During a cell's lifetime, DNA is protected and auto-repaired by a collection of complex molecular processes (executed by proteins), and when it is time to pass this information on, the information is partitioned and packaged appropriately by the cell. This flow of information from DNA to protein to cell function is illustrated in Figure 5.1.

Because of their simple linear primary structures, DNA and proteins can be represented as sequences of text, where each character of text corresponds to a molecular subunit. Standard DNA sequences typically have an alphabet of four characters, while standard protein sequences are described using an alphabet of 20 characters. As a result, there is a very strong relationship between computational methods for matching text strings and detecting similarity in biological molecules. This opens the door to use strings of text to describe sequences of network activities and then apply biological models for quantifying inheritance similarity and even build family trees of related events.

Edit distance and more flexible measures of string similarity including dynamic programming have been used for decades to detect similarity in gene or protein sequences across organisms [2,3]. When applying this technique to cyber security, it is essential that the events being captured by the method (for instance, network traffic packets) can be roughly categorized into a small number of types (either 4 types or 20 types would be simplest for adapting DNA or protein sequence analysis, respectively). It is also essential that the sequences that are associated with entities being studied are at least tens of characters long. Finally, it is important that the sequences have complexity, meaning that nearly all of the characters of the alphabet will be found in any string, although potentially in different relative amounts. In this approach, sequences that have a high degree of similarity can be associated into 'families' or collections of sequences that refer to behaviours that are similar. Long

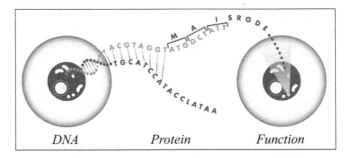

*Figure 5.1    Information flows from DNA to proteins and ultimately results in cellular function*

sequences that do not use the whole alphabet fall into a category of 'low complexity' and are actually often ignored by biosequence methods that rely on text similarity. However, the complexity filters themselves can be used as an alternative model for cyber events that lack the complexity required for full-blown biosequence analysis. Short-length or low-complexity sequences may be very important for biological systems, but because these do not adhere to the mathematical models used in string similarity methods, they must be handled by alternative algorithms. All of these methods are relevant for cyber security because they can be used to characterize sequences of behaviour or events in a format that can be easily searched for similarity.

### 5.2.2 Multi-organism coordination: flocking, swarming and social insects

Above the cellular level, many biosystems need to behave as a collective. This need can be an essential survival feature for solving ill-posed optimization problems such as finding dynamic food supplies in a changing terrain or swimming or flying in a large group to evade predators. In all cases, the concept of having a single leader would force a centralized communication and decision-making strategy that would be a single point of failure, and it would not scale well. Nature has devised several alternatives to centralized control that are remarkably efficient. These alternatives include concepts such as flocking, swarming, and other models that social insects follow [4] and are illustrated in Figure 5.2.

Flocking and swarming are very interesting approaches for coordinated control because they allow for a collective to follow a general trajectory, where at any moment one may identify a single leader organism. But at each turn, because of the three-dimensionality of the flock, the leading organism may change. This behaviour allows

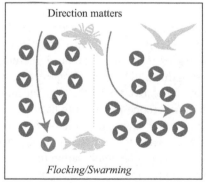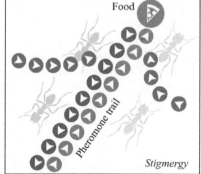

*Figure 5.2    Biosystems that operate collectively without centralized control: the leader of flocks and swarms changes as the collective direction changes. Stigmergic communication between ants biases their motion towards desired targets*

the flock or swarm to constantly survey its surroundings using different functions (i.e. different animals have different biases and perspectives), while not getting stuck in any local minima for long. This approach is a good model for searching a complex parameter space for a global good solution (not necessarily the 'best solution') where it is important to avoid local maxima. The physical extent of flocks and swarms when manifested in a computational search domain acts as a fuzzer to force a sampling over some dimensions. It is this sampling that, in conjunction with changing the leader organism, allows efficient searching for a global good solution. Note that swarming is NOT a good strategy for finding a pernicious (i.e. narrow in parameter space or fragile in biological parlance) global optimal solution. Such solutions rarely exist for biological systems; therefore, biological strategies are not well suited for finding such solutions. This is true because biological systems must react to constantly changing environments. If they settle in deep but narrow optimal solutions, slight changes in the parameter space have very large implications for survival. Fortunately, when applied to network traffic, this biological approach for finding good solutions that are not fragile is often desired.

Some social insects also exhibit additional behaviours that are related to flocking and swarming but have implications in terms of communications overhead. Ant systems also have leaderless control, where ants are semi-autonomous units traversing a complex terrain. However, in some cases, they do not coordinate using physical proximity (or flocking) but instead need to search a wide space. In this case, they must communicate, but the overhead and latency of this communication must be negligible because overhead of communication is related to energy consumption, and latency of communication lengthens the time it takes to survey the terrain (i.e. find food). This is not unlike the requirements imposed on operating a distributed communications network, or coordinating across geographically dispersed devices.

Stigmergy is the model employed by ants to achieve these goals. In stigmergic communication, each ant is tasked with finding something such as a food supply. While traversing the terrain, ants will walk in a staggered random walk. This walk is not a pure random walk because the shape of their bodies forces them to bias the walk in the direction they are already going while sampling from right- or left-leaning changes. When an ant finds what it is looking for, it begins releasing a chemical pheromone trail as it returns to the nest. Other ants crossing this trail begin biasing their right- or left-sampling to line up with the trail, creating a positive feedback that concentrates other ants at the same location. Because the pheromone has a finite half-life, once the food supply is exhausted and ants are no longer laying down new pheromone, it will dissipate and the colony will naturally disperse to continue foraging. All of this happens without the need for centralized control. The combination of staggered random walk, dynamic pheromone and directional bias results in a highly effective sampling of the whole terrain and simultaneous ability to concentrate activity on locations of interest (while those locations remain interesting). When applying this technique to computational systems, a 'terrain' must be defined to support all of the directionality that is required for stigmergic communication to result in the desired emergent colony behaviour. It is important to maintain fidelity with respect to many of the details about population interactions, such as how long ants looking for a certain feature will survive when they have not found the feature, the randomness with which new ants are generated and physical details about ant movement, because implementation details in any one of these features have dramatic impact on the effectiveness of the algorithm.

### 5.2.3   Collective decision-making: thresholds, consensus and feedback

The previous section described low-level interactions among organisms that were mainly focused on optimizing collective survivability. Several other mechanisms for collective decision-making are employed by cells and communities primarily to change the state of individuals in those communities (and as a result, frequently the collective as well). Although many systems in the natural world behave as a continuum (e.g., the force between two electrical charges varies smoothly as the distance between them changes), many biological systems employ thresholding as an alternative method for sudden state changes. Figure 5.3 illustrates the difference between continuous and threshold responses. Thresholding occurs when inputs to an element do not cause any change in state. But these sub-threshold changes accumulate until a critical criteria has been reached, at which point a Boolean change in state occurs.

As an example, a neuron may receive input from several adjacent cells, but it will not pass input along until a threshold of excitation is crossed, which may happen when input from two adjacent cells occurs simultaneously. At this point, the neuron dramatically changes its state, passing along the state change very rapidly as input to the next cell. Thresholds allow for systems to adopt a small number of states that can have very different properties. This thresholding accentuates the differences between geographically close cells for important higher level effects such as localizing the source of a distant sound. Thresholding using nearly identical chemical mechanisms, albeit connected in very different distributions, also results in contraction in skeletal

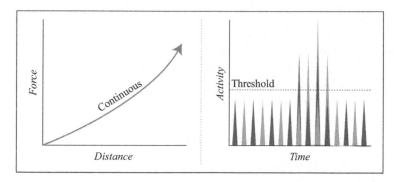

*Figure 5.3*   *Continuous processes vs. threshold processes: continuous processes such as force and distance have a smooth relationship between variables. Threshold processes are harder to predict but can drive optimized nonlinear responses*

muscle cells (a rapid state change triggered by neural input resulting in physical locomotion); autonomous pacing and contraction of heart cells; and coordinated peristalsis or wave-like contractions that push nutrients along the digestive tract. These are all examples of how cells work together using threshold responses to enact rapid and extreme state changes under certain conditions. Single cells can also use thresholding with respect to changes in their environment to dramatically change their internal molecular composition, resulting in extreme changes in behaviour, like changing from an active cell to a protected but relatively inert spore [5].

Thresholding also is a key prerequisite for some coordinated responses when such drastic state changes are required at a macro level. In this case, consensus-based approaches can ingest multiple complex forms of input across a population, and when key conditions arise, the whole population can be incited to share a response based on consensus. Consensus occurs when a group of organisms or cells all synchronize a state change based on some collectively experienced input. For survival reasons, it may be ideal to ensure that a whole population achieves consensus in near lockstep because outliers are often vulnerable in biological systems. Consensus can also concentrate the energy that can be collectively applied to achieving a particular survival strategy.

The final component of coordinating control in complex cooperative systems is feedback. In many cases, it is important for large state changes to be accompanied by some process that resets or reverses the large state change (i.e., a bistable oscillator) once it has been achieved. Additionally, it may be important to prevent the same state change from happening for a certain time (i.e. a refractory period), while the cell recovers from the state change. This delay may include time needed to rebalance materials or rebuild energy supplies needed for the next state change. Feedback can happen at any of the several levels, including changing gene expression or protein translation (which occurs over a slower time scale) or molecular signals that change the operation of a protein for a time (which can unfold over much more rapid time scales) [6].

With respect to computational environments, threshold and consensus responses are not often employed because they do not typically follow simple continuous equations, which are much simpler to express and calculate. As a consequence, they can be harder to predict, coordinate and control. However, for instances when large state changes are desired as a result of multiple complex inputs, thresholding could be a useful approach. As examples, thresholding and consensus could be used to balance network traffic away from areas of congestion, while feedback could ensure that threshold events do not happen in succession to the detriment of the system.

## 5.2.4  Autonomy and autonomic control

Long-term coordination between distal elements of an organism or across communities requires the ability to flexibly manage that coordination because strategies and solutions that work in one environment may not work at all in another. For example, some mammals shiver when they are cold to generate additional heat. The same response in hot weather would raise body temperature to a dangerous level. The same cells and organs that under one condition have a certain behaviour may have to change their behaviour greatly under another condition. Thus, organisms and populations are left with a challenging problem of autonomy – how to control disparate components when not all of them have direct access to environmental context.

Again staying as far as possible away from strategies of central control, many instances of autonomy exist in biological systems. Autonomy allows subsystems to operate under generally reasonable assumptions of environment, while key inputs from environment changes trigger deviations on this baseline behaviour. For instance, mammalian hearts contain an endogenously pacing tissue group known as the sino-atrial node. If this tissue is physically removed from the rest of the heart and maintained in an environment having the same chemistry as its native environment, then the tissue will continue to rhythmically pace, even in the complete absence of inputs from the nervous system. In the functional heart system, brain impulses can slow down or speed up the heart to respond to external stimuli via neural input, but the baseline behaviour of pacing is dependent only on local chemistry of the sinoatrial node (including gene expression, protein abundance and ion concentrations inside and outside the cell). In other words, the sinoatrial node serves as a simplistic, local sub-brain that is subject to governance from the higher authority of the nervous system only as a modification on its local activity. It is essentially a 'good enough' solution for most cases, freeing the brain for higher cognitive functions and using a minimum of energy and communication bandwidth for control [7]. This model plays out in other centres of the body such as the gut, where a similar endogenously pacing cell group creates a baseline of coordinated muscular contraction, or peristalsis, to push nutrients through intestines, and which is subject to speed up or slow down from neural input [7]. This is a remarkably efficient decentralized control system that works well when a 'normal' or 'resting' state can be defined, and only deviations from that state require input from a central authority.

A second low-level layer of control drives the delocalized autonomous control layer. This second layer achieves autonomic control. While it is possible to consciously control breathing and heart rate (to some extent), many other functions in the body are much more difficult or impossible to control via conscious means. This autonomic functionality in mammals is achieved through a similar strategy of autonomous control, but in this case, the functions respond to input that arrives through systemic molecular messages such as hormones and neurotransmitters. By defining a subsystem that is essentially closed to conscious control (at least at a small time scale), mammalian systems effectively partition themselves into functions that are allowed to be controlled without conscious input and functions that are subject (or entirely reliant) on conscious input.

Autonomy and autonomic control may apply to computer networks when key functionality can be defined that can be performed without active control. This control must be flexible enough to respond to a variety of environments and communicate the desired response to environmental changes to constituent components. In this model, activities that can be automated should be automated, and only control signals for deviations from that baseline behaviour should be allowed. This may require a great degree of planning to understand how to construct such a system to have desired behaviour under potentially unknowable environments. One key challenge in adapting these methods for use in computational networks is that it can be hard to determine which functions could and should be automated and how autonomous control should be exerted over them.

## 5.2.5   Redundancy, diversity and programmed death

Many strategies are employed by biological systems that are anything but straight-forward measures of efficiency but do impart essential resilience into the system and therefore are reasonable models to pattern cyber systems on. Redundancy, diversity and programmed death including apoptosis are examples. Programmed death is often exhibited by cells in particularly hostile environments such as the highly acidic lining of the mammalian intestine or in the topmost layers of skin [6,7]. When cells must die in this way, mechanisms of apoptosis ensure that their death does not cause unintended side effects for neighbouring cells. (A dead cell can be toxic to neighbours if its internal contents are not packaged properly.) When occurring through apoptosis, high cell turnover rate is actually a good feature, making it possible to ward off breaches through containment and isolation. If a foreign object becomes stuck in the topmost layers of skin, it is only a matter of time before it is carried away from the body by skin cells that die and are pushed away by newly generated layers of cells below. Similarly, the intestine's high degree of deliberate turnover in the interior-facing cells prevents damage from the acidic environment from reaching the body cavity. In both cases, the expectation for cells to die off is built in and consumes resources deliberately to achieve the higher mission of system integrity.

The mammalian brain has many examples of redundancy to preserve function. For instance, many cognitive functions map to multiple areas of the brain. Sometimes this is because the cognitive function requires multiple sub-functions that are all localized to different areas. But this redundancy also provides a survival function because in certain kinds of brain damage, functionality that was lost can actually be accentuated by the remaining areas to help compensate (sometimes completely).

Diversity, while also expensive in terms of resources, can also be employed to support higher level objectives of biological systems. A simple example is the additional degrees of freedom that are imparted by skeletal motion. A person can drink from a cup of coffee from multiple trajectories and with either hand. This makes it possible to still have some range of motion when a particular region of the range of motion is limited. For instance, when sitting on an airplane, one may have to hold the elbow very close, limiting motion to only forearm and wrist. But when there is more space to move, the wrist may not be used at all for tipping, and nearly all locomotion may come from the shoulder. This is not perfectly efficient because there are different muscle and bone groups that can be used to achieve the same end, but the diversity makes it possible to cope with many changes in environment including some loss of locomotion. Another example of diversity is population diversity. A tragic example of this is the Irish potato famine, which occurred in the mid-nineteenth century. As a result of a single species of potato becoming a widespread primary staple, the whole population of potato was susceptible to blight that wiped out Ireland's food supply causing widespread starvation.

Interestingly, both redundancy and diversity often exist together in biological systems. In the skeletal motion example above, redundancy is present (left and right arms that are highly similar) and so is diversity (overlapping degrees of freedom in each arm). Redundancy and diversity can be a very synergistic pair of strategies to help biological systems cope with hostile and dynamic environments. However, these features (as well as programmed death) come at the expense of some efficiency, as it takes resources to build, maintain and operate these overlapping resources, and the chance for injury or compromise is also larger because of the larger, more complex attack surface. Translating this to computer networks, there is a trade-off space between redundancy (such as failover systems), diversity (such as similar functionality being provided on different operating systems), turnover (including deliberately switching between redundant and/or diverse systems) and security/functional efficiency and the lifespan of attacks that make it past outer defences. If achieving the overall mission of the system is paramount and one can sacrifice efficiency, then these biological strategies may be ideal. However, if efficiency or minimizing exposure (attack surface) is the driving requirement, then they may not be good strategies. It is worth noting (and discussed in other sections of this book chapter) that highly efficient strategies also impart fragility on systems, so it is worth a detailed analysis of the trade-off between the efficiencies gained and the overall robustness of the resulting cyber system.

## 5.2.6 Learning and cognition

At the topmost level of sophistication, one can adapt how biological systems learn and think to apply in computer networks. Cognition and learning are very complex processes, requiring high-level organization, control, information handling and compute capacity. The mammalian brain is an enormously dense tissue full of interconnected neurons that feed back into one another to produce an astounding array of emergent behaviours. For instance, mammals perform streaming visual processing in real time, combined with image categorization, facial recognition (including information content of mood and emotion embedded in those faces), consequence prediction and a host of coordinated activities to integrate visual input with memory, motor activities, problem-solving, emotion processing and other critical functions. Mammals concurrently perform streaming audio processing (also in real time and integrated in many cases with visual processing) that can locate the source of a sound in a 3D environment, understand language (including intent, mood, emotion, truthfulness and sophisticated nuances such as sarcasm on top of raw information extraction), tie that sound to memories and perform other tasks it might be very difficult to train computers to do. These two examples highlight the ability of cognitive processing to handle sensory input. Cognitive processes also allow for complex and abstract problem-solving, imagination, long and short-term memory and drawing associations between highly diverse inputs [7].

While input processing aspects of mammalian cognitive systems are quite impressive, it is the abstraction and associative aspects that inspire most computer network applications. For decades, machine learning and its derivative fields have striven to capture the essential features of learning and cognition to develop algorithms for training and classification of complex features from diverse datasets. A wealth of public information about machine-learning applications exists, so the comments here are restricted to key insights with impact to computer-network applications.

Although many of the implementation details vary widely, the domain of computational learning is driven by the key aspects of biological systems that make it possible to infer 'connections' between events or measurements and very high-level system state. For example, in baseball or cricket, a ball is thrown at high speed towards a person attempting to hit it with a bat. The thrower wants to trick the hitter into swinging in the wrong place to miss the ball. A hitter must engage in processing visual and other input, followed by decision-making (swing high vs. low; swing early vs. late) and actual muscle movement – each of which takes time for the brain to process and execute. So when a ball is thrown at very high speed, the person batting has to make a guess as to where the ball will be at a certain time because waiting for all that processing to occur would delay the decision to swing until the ball was already beyond the hitter. As a result, the batter swings based on a complicated collection of state information that includes any clues from the rotation of the ball, the trajectory of the thrower's arm before releasing the ball and many others. The result of these measurements is tied directly to a response that is highly tuned based on prior experience.

Capitalizing on the model of mammalian learning typically requires capturing this essential ability to tie diverse inputs to an output, which could be a direct response such as in the ball-hitting analogy, or it could be simply to alert humans under certain conditions such as a dangerous event happening in one's environment. In general, making this conceptual leap to capture the essence of mammalian learning involves a large amount of training observations and some knowledge of the desired outputs. The more one can cover the space of possible inputs using training, the more likely the trained system is to behave as desired when deployed.

One key difference between the physical world and the computer network world is that in the physical world, biosystems enjoy the benefit of largely continuous physical laws, whereas in the network world, many events happen in discrete state changes. This is important because continuity allows one to say something definitive about the coverage of an input space achieved by a sampling strategy in a physical case. However, it may be difficult or impossible to say with any certainty how broadly and at what level of granularity a cyber space is sampled when applying cognitive approaches.

### 5.2.7    A few notes of caution when applying biological concepts to computer networks

Many computer applications have been derived from biological systems. These cover a wide range of utility; this chapter emphasizes computer network applications. Although there are many opportunities to apply the benefits gained from biological approaches to computer network applications, there are many pitfalls to avoid. In some cases, biological principles are applied in name only, and the underlying algorithms do not actually contain the key ingredients inspired from biology. In some cases, biological principles are used but in applications where they do not make sense. Further, sometimes biological concepts are not understood well and the resulting implementations may either miss the benefit of biological inspiration, or in the worst case, they may fail altogether. In the spirit of educating readers to correctly determine if biological algorithms are right for their application, the following discussions highlight some key areas of common misconception and misinterpretation that can easily be avoided. There are many other opportunities for such confusion, so it is always advantageous to engage biological scientists knowledgeable in the field to truly understand an underlying process before jumping to computer science applications.

### 5.2.7.1 Equilibrium vs. homeostasis

Many physical systems tend to minimize certain kinds of energy. For example, a ball rolling down a hill will settle at a low point. Having reached this point, one can perturb it from this location, but once such a small disturbance is removed, the ball will naturally tend back towards the same point of equilibrium. At this point, no energy is required to keep the ball in its location, and essentially the energy state of the system does not change unless external factors intervene, as illustrated in Figure 5.4.

Biological systems take this one step further with the concept of homeostasis. In homeostasis, a biosystem seeks to achieve a certain state that is conducive to survival. Homeostasis is importantly different than equilibrium because (1) it is context-dependent and (2) it typically requires continued energy input to maintain. One example of homeostasis in mammals is regulation of an internal set temperature. Many of the core functions in mammalian systems require a certain temperature range to operate correctly [7]. Systemic processes are in place to maintain this internal temperature, but the particular processes used at any given time depend on the external temperature and other factors. When it is hot outside, mammals typically use evaporative cooling via sweating in humans, or panting in dogs, to reduce internal temperature. This cooling requires energy and expends water (another precious resource), but it can help prevent overheating. In cold weather, by contrast, blood

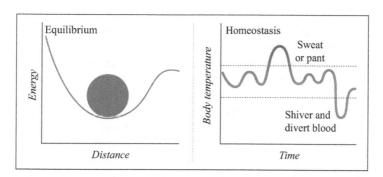

*Figure 5.4 Equilibrium vs. homeostasis: equilibrium results in a neutral energy state, whereas homeostasis requires continued energy input to maintain an operating state*

circulation patterns change to conserve heat in the core, and shivering can occur, which raises temperature. Shivering requires energy to sustain, and diverting blood moves heat away from extremities but preserves internal temperature. In both hot and cold cases, there is no low-energy state for achieving homeostasis as there is in equilibrium; rather, an organism expends resources to ensure a meta-state that is conducive to survival.

Always keep in mind that biological systems exist in hostile, dynamic environments from their inception and that it is very hard to change their 'programming' (or primary DNA sequence) in response to environmental input. To be clear, the regions of the DNA that are expressed can be highly dynamic with respect to environmental conditions, but adding new functionality that is not present anywhere in a DNA sequence is very hard if not impossible after inception. Consequently, all molecular strategies for coping must be present at the beginning of life, even if the organism may later be exposed to something it was not explicitly 'programmed' to respond to. Homeostasis is a layer of abstraction for organisms to seek general states that are conducive to survival as opposed to developing specific strategies to deal with every possible environmental factor separately.

Homeostasis is an interesting metaphor for computer networks because several of the prerequisite features apply for both biosystems and computer networks: (1) there is an overall desire for global 'health' of the system that can generally be defined in terms of its ability to achieve its mission goals, but environmental factors can dramatically change the means by which these systems would achieve those goals; (2) decisions made to achieve goals frequently involve complex trade-offs between resources, and in some cases, local sacrifices must be made to support overall system health; (3) flexibility to make these trade-offs must be included in the system at inception as it is frequently difficult or impractical to make on-the-fly changes in response to a particular environmental factor; and (4) due to the dynamic demand that drives network traffic, there may be no equilibrium state even though there may be a point of homeostasis that the overall system drives towards.

### 5.2.7.2    Trade-off between optimality and robustness

In computer science, often the goal is to devise a new algorithm to achieve a stated objective. Typically, an algorithm's quality and effectiveness is measured by the computational complexity (memory and arithmetic required as a function of problem size), time to solution as a function of input size or other algorithmic parameters and for algorithms designed to find a solution in a complex space, the optimality of solution or solutions found. The first two criteria (computational and time performance) are analogous in biological systems to the physical resources required and the time required to perform a function, respectively. However, the criteria of optimality do not translate directly from biological approaches. For a general computational algorithm, one can dream up very complex and indeed pathological inputs that have very specific global optima (i.e., a best overall solution that is much better than other good solutions but is very hard to 'find'). In many of these cases, smaller 'local optima' appear to be better solutions than others in their vicinity in parameter space, but the extremely narrow and pronounced global correct solution may be much 'better'. Computational

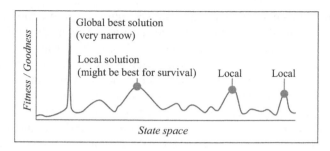

*Figure 5.5*   *The global solution (tallest peak) is often fragile (narrow), whereas other less optimal solutions (lower peaks) may be more stable (broad) over a range of environmental inputs*

algorithms that fail to find such global solutions are penalized, being judged as incapable of breaking free from the local good solutions to find that one hidden global optimum. Figure 5.5 illustrates examples of narrow global optimal solutions and more robust, local solutions.

While this approach is reasonable for the theoretical world of computer science, it is very much at odds with how the biological world operates, and this dichotomy can lead highly versed computer and computational scientists to dismiss biological solutions that may actually be ideal. The reason for this dichotomy is that biological systems must adapt dynamically to a constantly changing environment. The notion of global, narrow optimal solutions also would impart fragility on a biological system that seeks that solution. For instance, if a particular chemical reaction essential for life were 10× more efficient at a temperature of exactly 36 °C but fell to only 0.1× efficiency more than 0.1 °C away from 36 (i.e. a narrow but very good optimum), then any organism that had adapted its internal machinery to rely on this 10× efficiency would fail during even daily fluctuations of temperature. Certainly, biological systems could sometimes take advantage of having such a global optimum, but if they rely on it, then they become fragile. As a result, biological systems often gravitate towards 'good solutions' that are also characterized by minor changes in performance under wide perturbations from the solution. In the example above, if similar molecular machinery for the same essential process were only 2× efficient at 30 °C (a lower quality solution) but never dropped below 1× efficiency for a range of ±20 °C (and is therefore a local optimum that is more robust to changes), then the organism's likelihood of being able to maintain homeostasis would be much better under the second solution. This second solution is not the global optimum, but it is a 'good solution' and for survival reasons under changing environments, this may actually be the solution that is sought. This second solution has a significantly higher robustness, because it can withstand orders of magnitude and larger changes in environment without such a significant loss of functionality.

Translating this concept to computer networks, there may be perfectly useful algorithms that fail to find, for example, a particularly efficient method of routing network traffic to its destination under certain conditions. These algorithms may yet be more useful than other algorithms that do succeed in finding that global solution for routers if their performance is more robust with respect to changes in the network environment. The key is to understand the trade-off between optimality and robustness for a given algorithm so that a good solution can be found even though it may not operate at the highest efficiency. For the reasons described here, one may even assert that the desire to operate at 100% efficiency often drives systems towards fragility, so networks should have built-in allowances for unused efficiency to gain the advantage of robustness. The point is to take care when applying biologically inspired algorithms for use in computer network applications. When narrow but pronounced efficiencies are sought, biology is not a good model for optimization. However, if broad but robust solutions are desired that can continue core functionality in the presence of a wide array of environmental factors, then biological optimization may be very useful indeed.

### 5.2.7.3 Latent vs. expressed properties

DNA, as discussed in Section 5.2.1, contains instructions for building functional proteins in a living cell, providing the cell with properties needed to survive depending on the current environment. However, at any point in time, only a small fraction of the possible functionality may actually be built. To put it another way, functionality may refer to a possible, or latent, state; or it may refer to a currently observed, or expressed, state. Measures of latent state provide information about what a biological system might do, but it may be extremely difficult to reliably link external environmental conditions to the corresponding latent state that would become functional. Conversely, expressed state measures give information about what is happening now in a cell but do not describe what might happen if conditions were to change. As an example, consider a microbe that has the capacity to exist in an active (normal) state or to become a spore (hibernate) by encapsulating itself in a protective outer layer with minimal other functionality. In such a case, the protein coating required to protect the organism in the spore state, and the molecular machinery needed to synthesize this coating, may not be present in the active state. When the organism senses environmental changes that cause it to switch to a spore state, most of the normal molecular processes would 'turn off', and new machinery would be made that makes and transports protective coating to the cell's outer layer. The DNA, which contains all of the cell's latent state information (i.e. the possible behaviours the cell can engage in), did not change, but the expressed state (i.e. whether the cell had machinery to support active life vs. becoming a spore) is very different.

This concept bears directly on measures of computer networks drawn from biological sciences and from other domains, in fact. For example, one could construct a graph of traffic traversing a networked system where nodes are devices such as computers, phones, routers, control systems; and edges indicate that a pair of systems is exchanging data during a specified time interval. Graph theoretical measures applied to such a structure could be used as metrics for the system. One might be interested in how many graphical shortest paths between any pairs of nodes traverses a single node (i.e. a measure of graph centrality). This is a common calculation to extract from such graphs and might lead one to assert that a node of high centrality is also a critical node because if it fails, a large number of shortest paths are severed. This might lead a cyber defender or network architect to take specific steps to harden or provide redundant capabilities around the critical node. However, criticality is a latent property and so would not be evident from a graph constructed from expressed behaviours. In this case, the expressed traffic graph fails to capture the already redundant nature of the physically connected system. A node in an expressed traffic graph may be very busy, but losing the node does not imply that other communications would be disrupted because there may be other fibre links or connection paths that are simply not being used at the moment. These edges would be entirely absent from an expressed traffic graph, yet their presence as possible data paths means that the system has the latent property of robustness with respect to failure in the critical node. Very similar to the difficulties in interpreting biological results when working with systems that have both expressed and latent properties, this example illustrates the care that must be taken when interpreting measures and model results for computer networks because they also have expressed and latent properties.

## 5.3 Applying biological methods to network traffic

### 5.3.1 Identifying normal and anomalous network traffic

Traditional enterprise networks include wired and wireless components and are configured or maintained from a central location. Other types of networks that are also very widespread include IoT and wireless sensor networks (WSNs), which comprise a large number of small, low-cost, independent, intelligent sensors that can sense and communicate with each other. These sensor nodes have limited memory, computational capacity and power to support processing. Because all of these network types can connect high-value assets and are designed to facilitate access (sometimes globally), they are also vulnerable to numerous attacks [8]. As a result, biological approaches have been used to analyse the data traversing traditional and wireless networks to look for anomalous activity.

At the most basic level, one can begin to extract meaning from the bits and bytes traversing networked systems. In doing so, it becomes important to understand 'normal' traffic so that abnormal traffic or anomalies can be found. Though anomalies are often benign, they can sometimes indicate an attack and even the nature of the attack. There are a variety of ways to model traffic using biological methods to improve security of a network.

#### 5.3.1.1 Machine learning

As noted above, there is a class of learning techniques roughly modelled on human cognition. In this section, these methods are generally referred to as 'machine learning', although these techniques also include deep learning, neural networks and recent innovations in artificial intelligence. General machine-learning techniques have been applied to anomaly detection in both wired and wireless networks with limited success.

Historically, several machine-learning techniques have been applied to the problem of finding anomalies in network traffic, including reinforcement learning, neural networks, support vector machines and decision trees. These are often used for some sort of intrusion detection, event detection and query processing [9]. They are also often used for traffic classification, flow prediction and routing management.

There are several barriers to developing machine-learning enabled approaches for anomaly detection on networks [10]. First, attack-free data is hard to find. Obtaining enough 'normal' data to train on means either generating representative data sets that are often not accurate enough or training on live data and hoping there are not events in them. Even with that problem solved, the issue of defining normal data in a system that is naturally variable makes it hard to find a stable sense of 'normal' and often returns a very high false positive rate. Finally, there is the notion that with continuous training, the learning system can be fooled into accepting abnormalities as normal. These issues tend to make real-world analysts not trust these kinds of systems.

However, some real applications of machine learning on networks exist for cyber security. They tend to focus on very specific attacks, such as a selective forwarding attack as described in [11]. Advancements in deep learning show much more promise in becoming truly applicable [9]. There is evidence that deep learning techniques can help mitigate some of the constraints that come with general machine learning such as the need for labelled data and accurate classifiers [12]. Some other impacts of deep learning approaches are that they can support transfer learning, which can increase performance and scale [9].

### 5.3.1.2   Swarm intelligence

Swarm intelligence (e.g. ant colony optimization and flocking) is particularly adaptable to WSN because of the need for coordinated control, and because the sensors are small, have limited power and are not connected to a central command and control [13,14]. Swarm intelligence can be used to help organize a network and perform efficient routing, but it is very well suited to detect certain kinds of intrusions. This section discusses the applicability of swarm intelligence to distributed denial of service (DDoS) or jamming attacks, secure beaconing/location and sinkhole attacks.

Generally, swarm intelligence can be used to help defend against DDoS and related attacks by presenting a constantly shifting routing infrastructure that is dynamically reorganized over time. This makes it possible to route traffic around infected nodes or potentially infected nodes while constantly keeping the potential DDoS target in motion. This provides a resilient approach to defence in allowing for continued response even though some parts of the network are dead or dying.

Non-biological mechanisms for mitigating infected nodes are many and include malicious traffic detection, overlay networks and indirection infrastructures, and modelling of legitimate user behaviour, among others. Swarm intelligence-based approaches have been shown to have limited successes. One example creates a nonstationary transport network using the intelligent water-drop methodology to determine the fastest and most efficient route to relay messages between nodes using speed and latency of the nodes as features [15].

Another example which is an application of ant colony optimization is used in detecting sinkhole attacks in WSNs that are vulnerable because of their communication patterns. In WSNs, sensor nodes send packets to a base station, and sinkhole attacks prevent this base station from obtaining complete and correct sensing data, which could become a threat to higher layer applications. Sinkhole attacks are difficult to detect because compromised nodes can send the wrong information in validly signed routing packets.

To combat sinkhole attacks, an ant-colony inspired method was developed which shares data across many elements in the network to locate compromised elements and raise alerts. By spreading quality information across the system, an adversary must compromise many nodes to avoid detection. An algorithm was developed to generate alerts by the sensor nodes of the WSNs based on the node IDs and the link quality defined in the ruleset. A voting analysis method also was used to identify the intruder. Neighbouring nodes share a list of suspect nodes that is signed using a key. An ant colony optimization approach is used to generate the minimum number of keys for signing the suspect list, and another ant-based algorithm distributes the keys to the alerted nodes to sign the suspect list. Each node that receives the list counts the occurrences in the list, and the node ID with the highest count is identified as the intruder. In this way, problems at a single location can be identified by the distributed, vote-based calculation that is much harder to corrupt. Some advantages to this approach are that false positive hits based on node IDs are eliminated and the storage requirements in each alerted sensor node are minimized [14].

### 5.3.1.3 Sequence analysis and other methods

The concept of sequence-based alignments such as DNA and/or protein sequences has been used to detect anomalies in network traffic. Some methods need to be 'trained' in some way with known 'normal' behaviour but others have had success without *a priori* knowledge. They are able to model normal traffic and quickly identify potential anomalies using these bio-based approaches. In one approach, network traffic was represented as protein strings on which analysis was performed to detect anomalies resulting in an operational tool [16,17]. This approach only uses the metadata of netflow and not full packet inspection to perform in a realistic timeframe and not be overwhelmed with the volume of data that full packet capture would present. The results show that using the concepts of protein similarity and building families of similar proteins allowed the authors to recognize behaviours, both human and automated, and types of payload on an operational network.

Fuzzy logic is often used to lower false positive rates of anomaly detection with some success. Research has been conducted using chromosome representations and genetic operations to both speed up the process of applying fuzzy rules and make the rules easier to interpret [18].

Tools for network traffic analysis can give results that have very different interpretations depending on where in the network they are being applied. Bringing context from multiple layers can be a particularly potent combination. For example, in one application, a genetic algorithm was applied at the physical layer to obtain the optimal schedule of transmission codes without the restriction of a cost function, and anti-phase synchronization (observed from the calling behaviour of Japanese tree frogs) at the media access control layer, and then uses an ant colony optimization at the network layer to establish intrusion-resistant routing. The final step puts these algorithms together in two phases using cross-layer neural networks for intrusion detection and machine learning for identifying attack types [19,20].

## 5.3.2   Network design and management

Managing computer networks involves designing network elements to have the properties desired for a system to achieve a specified goal and effectively monitoring and enabling resources to respond to dynamic demand within a specified performance tolerance. This approach includes devising and enacting policies to govern utilization of network resources. Resources managed include the services provided by endpoint systems, the applications on host systems that interact with these services and the physical connections between systems that enable up to a certain amount of traffic per unit time (bandwidth), provided with a certain delay or latency. There are many best practices for designing a computer network to achieve desired functionality for a given use.

Several biological principles have been applied to designing and managing networks, which can vary between ad hoc WSNs and more rigid networks such as traditional IT networks.

### 5.3.2.1   Automaticity and autonomic control

Imparting automaticity and autonomic control on computer networks often starts with an understanding of the purpose of the network [21–23]; however, in some cases, the survival of the network itself is used as the fitness criterion [24]. In either case, the overall goal of the autonomic control apparatus drives an active loop (or loops) that senses state of the system, prioritizes options subject to policy constraints and takes actions.

In some cases, the biological inspiration for autonomic control exists only at the level of designing autonomic control loops that sense and control resources across a variety of vendors [23]. But in some cases, autonomic control draws inspiration from the biological world more tangibly. In [22], a virtual chemical gradient is created that carries information about resource utilization by location. In this model, differing chemical amounts in different 'locations' drives a bio-inspired chemotaxis response, which is an automatic tendency to move away from areas of high chemical concentration. Although tracking an overall chemical gradient requires global information, the decision to migrate resources away from a location based on this gradient can be made using only local and near-neighbour information. This approach also achieves network homeostasis by using a virtual chemical signal to change the balance between positive and negative feedback loops regulating the behaviour of devices. The result is that changing the bias on these loops can change the emergent behaviour based on a simple signal (digital chemical level), which is the means of transmitting changes in the environment to the autonomic controller. Bias through virtual chemical signals has been effective for medium-term resource allocation via simplistic predictions of use based on historical data in short-term situations where extreme demands are placed on scarce resources [25], which can be thought of as a surge-mode that can only be sustained for a short time but that allows systems to withstand temporary resource exhaustion dynamically.

In [26], a similar strategy is demonstrated whereby concentration of virtual chemical helps packets 'decide', via chemotaxis, what route to take through a potentially congested environment. A secondary bio-inspired method of quorum sensing is also used to help packets choose a new route when nodes fail. This method uses localized consensus calculations to provide coarse context for the packets.

Another aspect of autonomic control in biosystems that is used by these approaches is that of hierarchical control, such as in [21]. At the lowest layer, local control is exerted over small domains using local information only. But many autonomous domains can be connected in a global system that has a management layer that oversees activities in each domain. The key here is ensuring proper behaviour inside each autonomous domain without having too much control exerted by the central authority.

One key challenge for widespread adoption of autonomous network control strategies is how to control the emergent properties of the system. Dressler describes this as a balance between determinism that arises from centralized strategies and scalability that is possible through self-organization [27]. It may be that for known input ranges, the behaviour and dynamics of the system can be asserted. But autonomic systems will continue to make decisions when inputs are outside these planned ranges, and complex feedback loops can interact producing widely varying behaviours. So when employing these methods, care must be taken to truly understand the range of behaviours the system can adopt.

### 5.3.2.2   Information exchange

One very interesting method for self-organizing was proposed in [28], which outlines a method for using information exchange inspired by cell-to-cell communication. In this model, a cell's internal state (which on a network could be characterized by any of a number of state measures, intrusion alerts, etc.) can trigger DNA to be transcribed and then translated into proteins that are released into the environment. This higher level data unit can only be received by other cells (i.e. devices or services) that have an appropriate receptor for the protein. In this way, routers, devices, services and other components could share information about their internal state, potentially leading to emergent responses, without having to explicitly communicate point-to-point. Additionally, the abstraction of using the DNA/protein representation allows for very flexible sensing and communication using a concise language.

### 5.3.2.3   Other methods

In [29], the authors demonstrate a method using genetic algorithms and the cellular life cycle to optimize collective interconnected services in an on-demand environment. In this approach, real-time demands for services on a network are used as state information to drive population dynamics (service replication or termination), and multiple performance measures determine the fitness of the parameters that drive service agents' behaviours (i.e. how they replicate or terminate). Genetic algorithms are applied to populations of agents to result in varying agent behaviour to enable different strategies to accommodate dynamic environmental conditions. One advantage of genetic algorithms is that if they are properly incentivized, they may find optimal strategies without repeated input from operators or subject matter experts.

## 5.3.3   Routing

One key functionality provided by computer networks that makes them useful and robust to dynamic environments is routing. This is the process whereby information destined for a certain system is delivered to the correct system through a network (or networks) via potentially numerous possible physical paths. Many computer applications and processes rely on external routing fabric to ensure that data arrives at the intended destination. For instance, when accessing a web page on a distant server, a host's web browser is a local application that issues a request to retrieve the data from the remote system. Both the request and the returned data require routing fabric that exists outside the browser for the data to be correctly exchanged. Each link, or physical connection between systems, is connected through systems that are usually routers, which are computers dedicated to handling and sending data nearer to a destination machine. Each link that must be traversed in an overall route between two systems imposes its own physical limitations, including bandwidth (how much data can traverse a link in a given time period), latency (how much time delay is associated with data entering and leaving the link) and accuracy (the likelihood that data going into the link leaves without modifications or omissions).

Firewalls and other control points in the network can act as filters or provide other enrichment or protection to network data. Such systems are often configured with rules of what sort of traffic and behaviours to allow or prohibit and can have a large impact on the ability of traffic to reach its destination.

Although routing is often seen as one aspect of network management, discussed in the previous section, it has a substantial body of algorithm and applied research, relying on many different biologically inspired strategies for a wide range of applications [30–34], so it receives a deeper treatment here.

### 5.3.3.1   Autonomic control

One strategy for achieving a higher collective function in a complex routing and firewall environment is to employ chemical-signalling strategies similar to hormone and cell-to-cell communications used by biosystems to regulate collective autonomic behaviours [35]. This allows firewalls and routers with their own local rulesets to function with a predefined behaviour. But coordinating between them without extensive communication or central control can be achieved by translating network events and state into a cell communication model, which provides higher level abstractions to be shared and acted upon by components in the system.

Though autonomic strategies can be powerful means to achieve localized but controllable routing, these strategies run the risk of producing unpredictable emergent responses in some cases. These emergent behaviours correctly follow the system's rules given system history and the current environment but are not the ones intended by system architects. One solution to controlling the emergence problem is to apply a policy layer on top of the autonomic routing fabric, as outlined in [36]. In this approach, autonomic routing results from a combination of bio-inspired elements that automatically send traffic around problem areas or respond to congestion without intervention from a centralized authority. A policy layer serves as the interface between human users and administrators (who only have to author high-level policy boundaries for expected behaviour) and the underlying system, for which those authored policies are converted into constraints used by the subsystems to limit emergent behaviours to only desired system behaviours.

### 5.3.3.2   Machine learning

Routing algorithms have historically focused on continuously updating information about the current performance of different links and routers in a network to effectively send traffic through a highly performing pathway. Learning approaches have been demonstrated to significantly enhance selection of good routes over random searches of the routing fabric [37]. As learning techniques advance, the sophistication of strategies for route selection do as well. In [38], the authors propose a deep learning technique and apply it to the challenge of route selection. They demonstrate that learning routes based on states observed from edge routers can significantly improve overall route selection.

With increased sophistication in learning algorithms, challenges in applying these methods to routing in particular is also increasing. First, they tend to presume that a 'normal' state exists and that it can be quantified using some state measures. One could define normal as 'all traffic having acceptable latencies, delivered with a high enough reliability, and balanced across links with respect to their available bandwidth', but this definition is so abstract that the state space that satisfies it may be too large to sample exhaustively. However, knowledge of the state space is required for machine-learning applications to yield usable information because if they are exposed to states far from their training data, their reliability tends to drop.

### 5.3.3.3   Coordination without centralized control: swarms and social insects

Perhaps the most compelling biological strategy that applies to routing comes from how swarms, social insects and other communities coordinate without a centralized leader [39,40]. Just as cells, insects or animals working together must coordinate collective decision-making based on local sensing, so too must data bundles travers-ing complex computer networks 'make decisions' that serve their own goals while simultaneously using precious shared resources wisely.

Swarm intelligence has been applied to routing strategies in ad hoc networks [41–44], including WSNs [19,45,46], vehicular networks [47] and cognitive radio sensor networks [48], paving the way for a variety of uses in smart devices, and even the IoT.

Exploring one specific example, mobile ad hoc networks are collections of delib-erately mobile and transient devices that can serve as a routing fabric between each other and additional endpoints. This is a less constrained version of conventional computer networks because elements can physically move, and they are more likely to be connected and disconnected from the network than physically static routing networks. As a consequence, they represent a 'worst case scenario' for the complexity of routing traffic through them and stand to gain the most by efficient biologically inspired control models. Social insect colonies like ants and termites have similar characteristics and thus have been used as inspiration for routing in ad hoc networks [43,49]. Ant-inspired strategies can reduce communication overhead for sensing and coordination and, for larger systems, reduce the control overhead required to maintain the network and correctly route traffic. Stigmergy enables improved performance by providing a model for passive communication that transiently biases traffic away from areas of congestion and towards areas having capacity to handle more traffic. This eliminates the need for more heavy-handed monitoring of the health of various paths and the communication that would be required to support it.

Multiple aspects of bee behaviour including genetic selection of highly fit parameters [48] and leader-free communication using scouts [47] have been applied to routing in smart grid and vehicle networks, respectively.

As with autonomic control, social insects and swarms in the real world are both informed and constrained by the physical world they are embedded in. The digital world does not have all of the same constraints, so care must be taken to control for potentially unwanted emergent behaviour when using these methods to develop routing applications. Although much of the benefit of using stigmergy is the lack of an overall leading agent, there is some value in implementing a hierarchical scheme in which low-level decisions are made that may result in large-scale emergent behaviours, but a higher level of control is exerted at this macro-scale. In this way, policies about the overall behaviour of the system might be developed and enforced to control for emergence, making the applications more likely to be provable and therefore adopted in real scenarios.

## 5.4 Conclusions and future directions

Similar to the biological world, all computer systems are 'born' into a hostile, resource-constrained environment. Coordinating in such an environment for a specific goal or mission outcome requires flexible strategies that can be encoded simply to account for a wide range of environmental states including hardware and software errors and malicious use. In addition, the low-level details of quantum state are akin to the bits and bytes exchanged over computer networks in which they are essential for understanding some low-level behaviours, and by extension through many layers of aggregation, the high-level intent of users and systems. As a result, without some layers of abstraction, it is very difficult to peer into network traffic or systems at the bit level to make good decisions. Biology provides a robust toolkit of strategies and associated abstractions that have been explored for decades to enhance and optimize the functionality of computer networks. Biology has therefore been a source of inspiration for many applications in cyber security in general and specifically for ensuring that essential features of computer networks are preserved under a multitude of environmental conditions. In many cases, biological metaphors translate directly to the computer world, but in some cases very important differences between the two worlds (such as the lack of an underlying spatial organization in cyber systems) compel researchers to cautiously apply biological principles. These differences can also lead to unwanted behaviours, particularly through emergence, whereby biological systems can use physical constraints to control for unwanted behaviour. Where no such constraints exist for computer networks, alternative solutions for imposing limits on the organic models are needed.

Biological inspiration has been discussed in this chapter at a range of levels: from the molecular level where information content drives decision-making and detection to the system level where cognition and high-level functionality can be applied to decision-making and pattern matching. Two key changes in the networking world are driving the future of how biological strategies apply: (1) rapid penetration of technology further and further away from traditional IT networks, such as IoT, internet of nano-things, smart buildings and cities, and vehicle networks and (2) the constant exponential increase in bandwidth, computing and data (roughly following Moore's Law) that makes new methods possible when historically data has not been available but that simultaneously drives the need for greater scaling and efficiency of the methods being used. The push to more heterogeneous and distant devices will drive solutions towards hierarchical and autonomous control. The increasing availability of compute cycles, bandwidth and data may enable new machine-learning and data-analysis approaches to provide new abstractions for planning and managing networks. These trends likely will continue to push biological strategies to the forefront because they come from systems that have been trained for very long times to result in good enough solutions to very complex and dynamic problems like foraging for food in a changing environment, and they must operate at tissue and community scales efficiently. As more people look to biology as a source for inspiration, a community of increasingly bio- and cyber-savvy researchers will emerge with a common language and toolkit to develop novel and highly impactful solutions.

# References

[1]  Voet D, Voet JG, Pratt CW. Fundamentals of biochemistry. New York, NY: Wiley; 1999.

[2]  Altschul SF, Gish W, Miller W, Myers EW, Lipman DJ. Basic local alignment search tool. Journal of Molecular Biology. 1990;215(3):403–410. Available from: https://doi.org/10.1016/S0022-2836(05)80360-2.

[3]  Needleman SB, Wunsch CD. A general method applicable to the search for similarities in the amino acid sequence of two proteins. Journal of Molecular Biology. 1970;48(3):443–453.

[4]  Liu Y, Passino KM. Swarm intelligence: Literature overview. Columbus, OH: Department of Electrical Engineering, The Ohio State University; 2000. Available from: http://www2.ece.ohio-state.edu/~passino/swarms.pdf.

[5]    Setlow P. Spore germination. Current Opinion in Microbiology. 2003;6(6):550–556.

[6]    Lodish H, Berk A, Zipursky SL, Matsudaira P, Baltimore D, Darnell J. Molecular cell biology. 4th ed. Bethesda, MD: National Center for Biotechnology Information Bookshelf; 2000. Available from: https://www.ncbi. nlm.nih.gov/books/NBK21475/.

[7]    Tortora GJ, Grabowski SR. Principles of anatomy and physiology. 9th ed. Hoboken, NJ: John Wiley and Sons Google Scholar; 2011.

[8]    Qureshi S, Asar A, Rehman A, Baseer A. Swarm intelligence based detection of malicious beacon node for secure localization in wireless sensor networks. Journal of Emerging Trends in Engineering and Applied Sciences. 2011;2(4):664–672.

[9]    Fadlullah Z, Tang F, Mao B, *et al.* State-of-the-art deep learning: Evolving machine intelligence toward tomorrow's intelligent network traffic control systems. IEEE Communications Surveys and Tutorials. 2017;19(4): 2432–2455.

[10]   Sommer R, Paxson V. Outside the closed world: On using machine learning for network intrusion detection. In: 2010 IEEE Symposium on Security and Privacy (SP2010). 2010:305–316.

[11]   Kaplantzis S, Shilton A, Mani N, Sekercioglu YA. Detecting selective forwarding attacks in wireless sensor networks using support vector machines. In: 2007 International Conference on Intelligent Sensors, Sensor Networks and Information (ISSNIP 2007). 2007:335–340.

[12]   Javaid A, Niyaz Q, Sun W, Alam M. A deep learning approach for network intrusion detection system. In: 9th EAI International Conference on Bio-inspired Information and Communications Technologies (formerly BIONETICS). 2016:21–26. Available from: https://dl.acm.org/citation.cfm?id=2954780.

[13]   Muraleedharan R, Osadciw LA. Jamming attack detection and countermeasures in wireless sensor network using ant system. In: SPIE Wireless Sensing and Processing. vol. 6248. 2006:62480G.

[14]   Sreelaja N, Pai GV. Swarm intelligence based approach for sinkhole attack detection in wireless sensor networks. Applied Soft Computing. 2014; 19:68–79.

[15]   Lua R, Yow KC. Mitigating DDoS attacks with transparent and intelligent fast-flux swarm network. IEEE Network. 2011;25(4):28–33.

[16]   Peterson E, Curtis D, Phillips A, Teuton J, Oehmen C. A generalized bio-inspired method for discovering sequence-based signatures. In: IEEE International Conference on Intelligence and Security Informatics. 2013:330–332.

[17]   Teuton J, Peterson E, Nordwall D, Akyol B, Oehmen C. LINEBACkER: Bio-inspired data reduction toward real time network traffic analysis. In: 6th International Symposium on Resilient Control Systems (ISRCS). 2013: 170–174.

[18]   Gomez J, Dasgupta D, Nasraoui O, Gonzalez F. Complete expression trees for evolving fuzzy classifier systems with genetic algorithms and application to network intrusion detection. In: Keller J, editor. Annual Meeting of the North

American Fuzzy Information Processing Society (NAFIPS). 2002:469–474. Available from: http://ieeexplore.ieee.org/document/1018019/.

[19] Saleem K, Fisal N, Baharudin MA, Ahmed AA, Hafizah S, Kamilah S. Ant colony inspired self-optimized routing protocol based on cross layer architecture for wireless sensor networks. WSEAS Transactions on Communications. 2010;9(10):669–678.

[20] Hortos WS. Bio-inspired, cross-layer protocol design for intrusion detection and identification in wireless sensor networks. In: 37th Conference on Local Computer Networks Workshops (LCN Workshops). 2012:1030–1037.

[21] Agoulmine N, Balasubramaniam S, Botvich D, Strassner J, Lehtihet E, Donnelly W. Challenges for autonomic network management. In: 1st IEEE International Workshop on Modelling Autonomic Communications Environments (MACE). 2006.

[22] Balasubramaniam S, Botvich D, Donnelly W, Foghlu M, Strassner J. Biologically inspired self-governance and self-organisation for autonomic networks. In: 1st Bio-Inspired Models of Network, Information and Computing Systems. 2006:1–7.

[23] Jennings B, Van Der Meer S, Balasubramaniam S, *et al.* Towards autonomic management of communications networks. IEEE Communications Magazine. 2007;45(10):112–121.

[24] Tizghadam A, Leon-Garcia A. Autonomic traffic engineering for network robustness. IEEE Journal on Selected Areas in Communications. 2010;28(1):39–50.

[25] Balasubramaniam S, Botvich D, Mineraud J, Donnelly W, Agoulmine N. BiRSM: Bio-inspired resource self-management for all IP-networks. IEEE Network. 2010;24(3):20–25.

[26] Foley C, Balasubramaniam S, Power E, *et al.* A framework for in-network management in heterogeneous future communication networks. In: Van Der Meer S, Denazis S, Burgess M, editors. 3rd IEEE International Workshop on Modelling Autonomic Communications Environments (MACE). 2008:14–25.

[27] Dressler F. Benefits of bio-inspired technologies for networked embedded systems: An overview. In: Dagstuhl Seminar. Wadern, Germany: Schloss Dagstuhl-Leibniz-Zentrum für Informatik. 2006.

[28] Dressler F. Bio-inspired mechanisms for efficient and adaptive network security mechanisms. In: Dagstuhl Seminar Proceedings. Schloss Dagstuhl-Leibniz-Zentrum für Informatik. 2005.

[29] Nakano T, Suda T. Self-organizing network services with evolutionary adaptation. IEEE Transactions on Neural Networks. 2005;16(5):1269–1278.

[30] Dressler F, Akan OB. A survey on bio-inspired networking. Computer Networks. 2010;54(6):881–900.

[31] Dressler F, Akan OB. Bio-inspired networking: From theory to practice. IEEE Communications Magazine. 2010;48(11):176–183.

[32] Leibnitz K, Wakamiya N, Murata M. Biologically inspired networking. In: Cognitive Networks: Towards Self-Aware Networks. John Wiley & Sons, 2007:1–21.

[33]   Pavai K, Sivagami A, Sridharan D. Study of routing protocols in wireless sensor networks. In: International Conference on Advances in Computing, Control, and Telecommunication Technologies (ACT'09). 2009:522–525.

[34]   Dressler F. Efficient and scalable communication in autonomous networking using bio-inspired mechanisms-an overview. Informatica. 2005;29(2): 183–188.

[35]   Kruger B, Dressler F. Molecular processes as a basis for autonomous networking. IPSI Transactions on Advances Research: Issues in Computer Science and Engineering. 2005;1(1):43–50.

[36]   Balasubramaniam S, Botvich D, Jennings B, Davy S, Donnelly W, Strassner J. Policy-constrained bio-inspired processes for autonomic route management. Computer Networks. 2009;53(10):1666–1682.

[37]   Choi SP, Yeung DY. Predictive Q-routing: A memory-based reinforcement learning approach to adaptive traffic control. In: Mozer MC, Jordan MI, Petsche T, editors. Advances in Neural Information Processing Systems (NIPS 1996). 1996:945–951.

[38]   Kato N, Fadlullah ZM, Mao B, *et al.* The deep learning vision for heterogeneous network traffic control: proposal, challenges, and future perspective. IEEE Wireless Communications. 2017;24(3):146–153.

[39]   Zhang Z, Long K, Wang J, Dressler F. On swarm intelligence inspired self-organized networking: Its bionic mechanisms, designing principles and optimization approaches. IEEE Communications Surveys and Tutorials. 2014;16(1):513–537.

[40]   Zungeru AM, Ang LM, Seng KP. Classical and swarm intelligence based routing protocols for wireless sensor networks: A survey and comparison. Journal of Network and Computer Applications. 2012;35(5):1508–1536.

[41]   Roth M, Wicker S. Termite: Ad-hoc networking with stigmergy. In: 2003 Global Telecommunications Conference (GLOBECOM'03). vol. 5. 2003:2937–2941. Available from: http://ieeexplore.ieee.org/document/1258772/.

[42]   Arabshahi P, Gray A, Kassabalidis I, *et al.* Adaptive routing in wireless communication networks using swarm intelligence. In: AIAA 19th Annual Satellite Communications System Conference. Reston, VA: The American Institute of Aeronautics and Astronautics. 2001. Available from: http://hdl.handle.net/2014/12434.

[43]   Zhang M, Yang M, Wu Q, Zheng R, Zhu J. Smart perception and autonomic optimization: A novel bio-inspired hybrid routing protocol for MANETs. Future Generation Computer Systems. 2018;81:505–513.

[44]   Villalba LG, Cañas DR, Orozco ALS. Bio-inspired routing protocol for mobile ad hoc networks. IET Communications. 2010;4(18):2187–2195.

[45]   Saleem M, Di Caro GA, Farooq M. Swarm intelligence based routing protocol for wireless sensor networks: Survey and future directions. Information Sciences. 2011;181(20):4597–4624.

[46] Saleh AMS. Bio-inspired technique: An adaptive routing for reliability and energy efficiency method in wireless sensor networks. International Journal of Communication Networks and Information Security. 2017;9(2):247.

[47] Bitam S, Mellouk A, Zeadally S. HyBR: A hybrid bio-inspired bee swarm routing protocol for safety applications in vehicular ad hoc networks (VANETs). Journal of Systems Architecture. 2013;59(10):953–967.

[48] Fadel E, Faheem M, Gungor VC, *et al.* Spectrum-aware bio-inspired routing in cognitive radio sensor networks for smart grid applications. Computer Communications. 2017;101:106–120.

[49] Rieck K, Laskov P. Language models for detection of unknown attacks in network traffic. Journal in Computer Virology. 2007;2(4):243–256.

*Chapter 6*

# Security and resilience for network traffic through nature-inspired approaches

*Mohamed Azab[1,2], Effat Samir[3], Esraa M. Ghourab[3], Mohamed El-Towessiy[1], Marwan Nabil[4], Ahmed Mansour[3], Ahmed Hamdy[4], and Ayah Yasser[4]*

## 6.1  Introduction

There is no doubt that cyber systems and optimization mechanisms are everywhere, from engineering design to networking, to healthcare, Internet services, and gaming. Nature has always been the primary source of inspiration toward many of the greatest advances that we rely on in our daily life. Most of the information technology (IT) research is somehow inspired by living beings and natural processes. Artificial intelligence (AI), machine learning (ML), computer networks, and cyber security are perfect examples.

As creatures of nature, it makes sense that the largest fraction of our nature-inspired algorithms, for good or bad purposes, is based on some successful characteristics of some biological system. It is worth noting that nature inspiration in computer security and resilience dates, at least, to the definition of the term "computer virus" in the early 1980s [1].

Replication has emerged as an example for biologically inspired computing and communication mechanisms. For instance, viruses and cells use replication and mutation to withstand changes around them. Typically, a virus life cycle relies on spreading via continuous replication of their genetic material, and DNA/RNA to be well hosted inside the cells. Once a virus is inside the body, it searches for a host cell and then gets attached to its surface. After that, the virus takes control over the cell by installing its RNA to drive the cell and deviate its behavior from the normal form. After taking control over the cell, it starts producing copies of the virus until the cell bursts and dies from the huge amount of copies staying inside it and releasing those copies to neighboring cells. Every virus that enters a cell repeats this process, yielding millions

[1]Computer and Information Sciences Department, Virginia Military Institute, Lexington, USA
[2]The City of Scientific Research and Technological Applications, IRI, Computer and Information Science Department, Alexandria, Egypt
[3]Electrical Engineering Department, Alexandria University, Egypt
[4]Computer and Communication SSP Department, Alexandria University, Egypt

of replicas for each infected body. Projecting this process to the cyber security space, we can see the stages of virus attacks: reconnaissance, initial compromise, command and control, and, finally, corruption and lateral movements.

Resilience is another example. Resilience can be defined as the ability of a system to absorb external stresses within an acceptable degradation threshold [2]. Cyber resilience has been inspired by nature. Individuals die, species disappear and get extinct, those species that are highly resilient are the ones who can stay alive during the ongoing process of natural selection. Highly resilient species can withstand changes caused by humans, natural disasters, and attacks. Living species strive to keep their kind from extinction. Reproduction and replication are the main methodologies employed by living species to keep their kind. As an application, in today's world of 99.999% uptime, resilience in systems has become a very demanding requirement. System and security engineers have made a huge amount of effort to keep the systems up and running under those highly demanding uptime rates. Replication is a key methodology in order to achieve this uptime of cyber systems [3]. Many of us nowadays use cloud to keep their data and are sure that it will always be available and will never get lost. In the cloud, data is stored and replicated across many hard drives to insure the maximum amount of availability and fault tolerance.

Diversity is another natural characteristic with huge impact on the cyber world. Computer viruses and worms achieve their goals once executed. Then they can do a lot of damage from deleting files, to DOS attacks. Viruses and worms are programed to do particular functions, so the more diverse the security mechanisms of a system, the stronger the system will be and the harder it will be for a virus to take it down. Surely, dealing with a computer virus is easier than a biological virus, since it needs to be told exactly what to do, but the biological virus depends on chances and random replication.

In this chapter, we will illustrate the critical role of nature as a source of inspiration to many successful security and resilience techniques. Our context is providing security and resilience as a service. We model the service delivery process to encompass two main players; service delivery vehicle and a driver. We use moving-target defense (MtD) as a service delivery vehicle, while the various AI and ML algorithms construct the driver driving such vehicle.

MtD is a relatively recent concept presented as a transformative solution to the several limitations of our conventional defense techniques. This chapter starts by a discussion for the MtD as the fundamental concept for diversity, which is the pillar supporting MtD concept. We will discuss different technologies presented to enable diversity applications across some layers in the OSI layer in a top-down approach. We will conclude this section talking about the driver by listing the various MtD applications presented exploiting such technologies to induce diversity for defense. Moving to the driver, in this section, we will discuss various nature-inspired heuristics and AI techniques presented across the literature. As a demonstrative example, we will focus on swarm intelligence (SI), genetic algorithms (GAs), neural networks, and some of the other popular techniques. Such techniques are the base driver that controls most of the smart systems solutions being deployed nowadays.

## 6.2 Service delivery vehicle—Moving-target Defense (MtD) technique

Current network security systems are progressively showing their limitations. One credible estimate suggests that only about 45% of the new threats are detected. Additionally, current defense systems are largely static and not sufficiently adaptable to cope with the attackers' changing tools and tactics. Therefore, it is vital to find a new direction that cyber security development should follow. We argue that the next generation of cyber security systems should seek inspiration in nature. This approach has been used before in the first generation of cyber security systems; however, since then, cyber threats and environment have evolved significantly, and accordingly the first-generation systems have lost their effectiveness. A next generation of bioinspired cyber security research is emerging, but the progress is hindered by the lack of a framework for mapping biological security systems to their cyber analogies.

Indeed, the network security community should look into nature for new approaches to cyber security, both offensive and defensive. Current and future cyber security solutions should be designed, developed, and deployed in a way that will fully leverage the experience, learning, and knowledge from ongoing biological evolution. Conversely, the community should also look to nature to anticipate how the threat may evolve and respond accordingly.

### 6.2.1 Diversity concept

Everything in nature points to diversity as an effective self-defense mechanism. Since humans get their inspiration from how the world works, this seems to be applicable to technology as well. The tiniest concepts which lead to the evolution of technology are inspired from the rules of the universe and from nature. Therefore, diversity is the root fundamental concept of MtD in most of the recent cyber security systems. Diversity could be applied starting from the stand-alone software to network system. For example, dynamically changing the software or system configuration to add uncertainty, unpredictability, and diversity causes the system's attack surface to change continuously leading to an increase in the attackers cost. As a result, the system is unpredictable to attackers, hard to be exploited, and is more resilient to attacks [4].

Diversity using confusion (camouflage) and replication as well as running was studied several years ago. In [5,6], deception/camouflage categories were identified as distasteful tools that are rarely used to achieve national interests, unless in relation to the deployment of military force.

From the literature, we can notice two main techniques inspired from Mother Nature trying to implement the concept of diversity for security, which are **Confusion and Replication**. Confusion is a simple self-defense mechanism, which relies on just staying there and confusing the attacker, rather than fighting back. When it comes to "confusion," one of the most popular examples from nature is chameleon. This creature camouflages itself by taking on various colors similar to the environment, in order to blend into its surroundings and hide in plain sight from its predator.

In order to effectively avoid detection/observation, an organism can hide or conceal its presence by using camouflage or mimicry techniques that modify the organism's external appearance [7]. Camouflage embraces all solutions that utilize individual's physical shape, texture, coloration, illumination, etc. to make animals difficult to spot. This causes the information about their exact location to remain ambiguous. Examples of animals that can easily blend into the background include the chameleon (family Chamaeleonidae) which can shift its skin color to make it similar to ambient lighting and background coloration; stick and leaf insects that take the physical form of a wooden stick or a leaf; orchid mantis that resembles a tropical orchid which, although quite conspicuous, is difficult to detect against a background of developed flowers.

Another example from nature is Cephalopods, which incorporate octopuses, squid, and cuttlefish. Cephalopods are capable to change both the shading and surface of their skin within seconds to mix into their surroundings, which keeps them from being attacked. Therefore, cephalopods change their appearance fundamentally for disguise (Camouflage). Therefore, camouflage in cephalopods can be utilized both for predator shirking and to help with chasing prey. Foundation likeness, tricky similarity, countershading, and troublesome designing are for the most part techniques utilized for cover. When this fails and the cephalopod is still threatened, it applies other strategies like stun to give itself imperative seconds to get away. Moreover, it was found that changing their appearance also could be their way of communication to each other. Cephalopods have numerous utilizations for shading change, for example, in courtship, acts of aggression, and cautioning different individuals from a social gathering of risk.

Camouflage often occurs on levels other than visual recognition: e.g., many viruses code pathways and molecular signaling systems that mimic host cell transduction mechanisms—by doing so the virus can easily invade the cell and take control of the metabolism and immunological system of an individual. In cyberspace, various information hiding techniques, e.g., steganography, can be utilized to provide means to hide the location of confidential data within an innocent looking carrier or to otherwise enable covert communication across communication networks [8].

Another nature-inspired defense mechanism is to simply RUN. Any creature at the bottom of the food chain has to deal with predators. While cephalopods hide and viruses replicate, most creatures can do neither and just have to run. This predator–prey model has been used in security for a while now, and a lot of work has been done on it. It relies on hiding from an attacker and hoping that the attacker does not catch up. In fact, self-propagating malware and computer worms have clear life-like properties [9]. In nature, diversity provides a defense against such self-propagating threats by maximizing the probability that some individuals will survive and replenish the population with a defense against that particular threat. It has been noted that much of the vulnerability of our networked computing systems can be attributed to the monoculture or lack of diversity in our software systems [10]. It is practically inevitable that a software will contain flaws. The software monoculture makes it easier for attacks to spread, thus exposing the systems to large-scale attacks by well-informed attackers.

Finally, the relationships and interactions between existing malware (so-called malware ecology) have been investigated in [11]. Numbers of interactions, both accidental and intentional, between different types of malware were analyzed, and the main conclusion was to seek ecologically inspired defense techniques because many ideas from ecology can be directly applied to all aspects of malware defense.

From the studies presented above, we can conclude that bioinspired cyber security is a wide, diverse, emerging, and evolving research field. However, from the research perspective, we see many "loose ends" that need to be tied by using a more systematic approach, which we next propose.

## 6.2.2   Diversity as a fundamental concept for moving-target defense (MtD)

In fact, there is no standard definition of what an MtD is, what is meant by attack surface or metrics to define the effectiveness of such systems. MtD aims at creating asymmetric uncertainty on the attacker's side, by changing the attack surface. In other words, MtD is the concept of controlling change across multiple system dimensions in order to increase uncertainty and apparent complexity for attackers, reducing their window of opportunity and increasing the costs of their probing and attack efforts. Specifically, MtD assumes that impeccable security is unattainable. Given the beginning point and the hypothesis that all systems are compromised, research in MtD concentrates on authorized the continued integrity of operation in a compromised environment and to have systems that are defensible rather than perfectly/completely secure.

In order to address the security challenges in any system, a theoretical framework for MtD must be characterized. This framework is supposed to analyze simple points like a description of what MtD does and its characteristic features, like its adaptation, diversification, and randomization. It is expected to illustrate how knowledge is acquired and lost, and show the contrasting classes of attacks. The way the attacker interacts with the MtD system must be moderated by the suggested framework. This is done by defining key concepts like the attacker, adaptation, and engagement surfaces. On this basis, MtD system designers have to be permitted by the framework to make their decisions regarding using already existing configuration as well as diversification in functionality in order to improve security. The framework must give them the ability to evaluate how effective it is to adapt different aspects regarding configuration, to stop various attack classes. Therefore, a proper defense strategy was needed, like MtD. That is the role of the driver mentioned in Section 6.3.

## 6.2.3   MtD techniques and applications in the OSI layer

MtD describes how an adaptive environment can be used to prevent or delay an attack on a system that would otherwise be easier to compromise or attack. Researchers applied MtD techniques across multiple layers to maintain the overall system security, starting with the advantages of using MtD in some essential wireless systems, such as the cooperative Vehicle Cloud Communication wireless network and the network-based Internet of Things (IoT). Besides, MtD, as a concept, has historically been used in warfare along with various wireless communication systems to avoid signal jamming attacks. As an example, authors in [12] describe basic research problems and how MtD can be deployed using asymmetric cost techniques that are advantageous for the defenders and disadvantageous for the attackers. The techniques include virtualization, workload migration, network redundancy and instruction set, and address space randomization. As a result, MtD has gained significant traction within the IT security community.

### 6.2.3.1    MtD in the cloud layer

Cloud computing is the main pillar supporting most of the applications that we rely on daily. The innovation is resource virtualization technologies revolutionized how computing resource are exploited by users. **Resource virtualization** facilitated decoupling the tightly coupled link between logical software and the underlying hardware enabling real-time elastic response. The availability and ease of re-configurability for such elastic virtual environment enabled security researchers to present multiple **applications** for MtD through runtime diversification of such resources. However, increasing the number of users and the software-based programmability opened the door for new attacks and threats.

There is a desperate need to use MtD approach in the higher layer of OSI layer and study the effect of exploiting it in cloud computing techniques, in both containers and virtual machines (VMs). Virtualization is the creation of substitutes for real resources that have the same functions and external interfaces as their counterparts, but that differ in attributes, such as size, performance, and cost [13]. Virtualization and resource sharing are commonly applied to physical hardware resources by combining multiple physical resources into shared pools from which users receive virtual resources. Computing clouds provides convenient, on-demand network access to a large pool of shared configurable computing resources through various complicated, service-provider-managed virtualization tools. Services are provided to the cloud users through virtualization capsules based on the type of service needed. These capsules used to be a full-fledged VMs with its own operating system operating on the cloud shared hardware resources. Therefore, virtualization achieved running multiple machines on a single hardware, where the real hardware is invisible to OS, which sees an abstracted out picture. Only VM monitor talks to hardware.

Resource sharing in cloud computing has a lot of pros, but its cons are mostly security related. The reason is that we have multiple users on the same machine, so if one of them is malicious, it is quite possible for them to manage and obtain private information about other users. This kind of attacks is called co-residency attack. Most of the addressed solutions toward such attacks present customized solutions that often required significant modifications to the hardware, client VMs, or hypervisors. Such solutions are not generic and will not succeed with mutating versions of these attacks.

MtD applications were presented repeatedly in the literature to secure cloud-based applications. In a very simple way, many MtD applications assume that if a user on a certain machine is being/is suspected to be under attack, that machine is supposed to be "moved" or "migrated" to another safer one. The main challenge in this case is the downtime involved in this process [14]. OSDF was presented as an

MtD application on OpenStack clouds to secure mission critical applications [15]. OSDF frequently migrates running machines between various hosts to complicate the target traceability. Further, OSDF, guided by a smart IDS, moves suspicious machines to isolated quarantine zone. The main issue with OSDF was the extensive cost of migration and application downtime.

To address such problem, MIGRATE was proposed in [14]. MIGRATE was inspired from the camouflaging process of the sea chameleons to evade predators. MIGRATE exploited a lightweight virtualization technology, Linux containers, to introduce a more efficient MtD application. In this work, authors presented MIGRATE as a container-management framework that employs resource efficient, scalable, real-time MtD to obfuscate the container execution behavior complicating the attacker's task to locate their targets. This technique offers generic defense against side-channel attacks and employs efficient real-time probabilistic random migrations of cloud tenants' applications to minimize the probability of attacker–victim co-residency on the same host. Eliminating the stable co-residency issue eliminates most of the side-channel attacks that face such a platform. Figure 6.1 shows MIGRATE-enabled system architecture.

MIGRATE lacked the awareness and guidance of an informed driver. It simply moves in a random fashion to minimize attack surface. In a game like fashion, another informed MtD mechanism for cloud containers called ESCAPE was presented in [16] to address this issue. ESCAPE models the interaction between attackers and their target containers as a "predator searching for a prey" search game. Live migration of Linux containers (prey) is used to avoid attacks (predator) and failures. The entire process is guided by a novel host-based behavior-monitoring system that seamlessly monitors containers for indications of intrusions and attacks. The model showed results indicating a high container survival probability with minimal added overhead. The main concept of ESCAPE relied on three main modules, which are the behavior monitoring module, the checkpoint/restore module, and the live migration module.

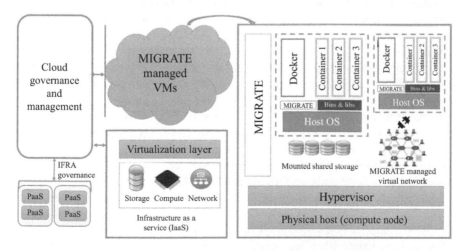

*Figure 6.1    MIGRATE technique architecture [14]*

The behavior monitoring module was adopted by the same authors in [17] and is used for monitoring the operating containers from the suspicious intrusion. The system depended on the fact that Linux containers communicates with the host kernel and the outer world by using system calls issued to the host kernel. The second module which is called checkpoint and restore was adopted to avoid any container customization, by leveraging the encapsulated state of the application; finally, the live migration module. The containers migration process starts by check pointing the container, killing the process on the original host, change the MAC/IP assignment of the old server network interface to match the new one while mainlining the IP value, and restore the container and all enclosed applications on the destination server. The entire process occurs in matter of milliseconds. Following the aforementioned processes guarantees almost zero downtime unless the source host fails completely during the process.

### 6.2.3.2    MtD in the network layer

State, enterprise, and service provider organizations have focused attention on how computer networks and systems can use MtD in order to provide more secure services. As an example, some researchers such as in [18] introduce Moving Target IPv6 Defense (MT6D) that hides and rotates IPv6 assignments by implementing MT6D tunneled packets. To form the tunnels, MT6D requires the endpoint interface identifier, a secret key and a nonce which makes them difficult to deploy in existing networks.

The main challenge faced researchers trying to deploy MtD as a service within computer networks was always the tight coupling between network configuration and control plan and the data plan presented as hardware and connections.

Further, MtD mechanisms usually depend on central control and monitoring units. For example, address randomization or network tunnel creation requires a central entity that controls them. Other MtD schemes need a central station to be able to evaluate and optimize the network routes shape. Apparently, these MtD mechanisms call for new network paradigm to enable more flexibility and to deliver highly customizable services. The exciting traditional network infrastructures cannot be a suitable choice.

The introduction of software-defined networking (SDN) was a game changer. SDN is a flexible architecture, based on open standards, that separates the network control plane and data plane entities [12]. SDN adopts the concept of programmable networks by using a logically centralized management, which represents a simplified solution for complex tasks such as traffic engineering, network optimization, and orchestration [19]. This enables the network control to become flexible and abstract the infrastructure for applications and network services. Therefore, SDN could be a successful technology enabling MtD applications [12].

Despite the great advantages of the SDN paradigm, it came with new set of attacks and threats that were never considered before in conventional networks. The SDN controller is a single point of failure and a target for attackers. The situation is even worse when we consider the tight coupling and lack of isolation between the controller as a software component and the underlying hosting hardware.

Such lack of isolation limits the controller resilience against host-based attacks and failures.

MtD was presented as an application and a solution to secure SDN controllers, and to resolve such challenge [14,20]. As mentioned before, Linux containers is a successful thin virtualization technique that enables encapsulated, host-isolated execution environments for running applications. In [20], a successful technique called proactive attack-and-failure resilience (PAFR) technique was presented as a controller sandboxing mechanism based on Linux containers.

PAFR enables controller/host isolation, plug-and-play operation, failure- and attack-resilient execution, and fast recovery. The objective of PAFR technique is to loosen the coupling between SDN controllers and their hosting servers by employing a lightweight virtualization technology, Linux containers. It employs and manages live remote check-pointing and migration between different hosts to evade failures and attacks. This could be achieved by accessing the shared storage only at container load-time, either as a fresh start or after a check-pointed restore. Once the container is instantiated, all system operations occur in the host memory. The only files that have to be synchronized between the source and destination servers are the memory dump files. These are tiny files that require extremely small amount of time to be sent to the destination server. The entire process is summarized in Figure 6.2. The frequent employment of PAFR's live-migration showed great results in minimizing the chance of successful attack/failure with limited to no impact on network performance.

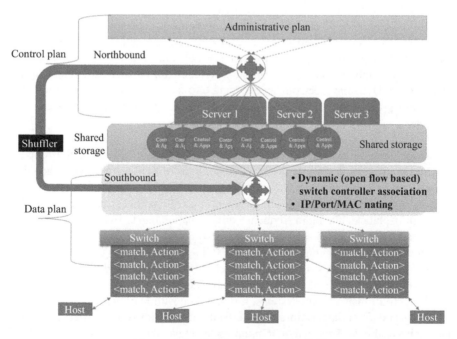

*Figure 6.2   PAFR architecture [20]*

### 6.2.3.3    MtD in the signals and communication layers

Last decades witnessed increasing demand for devices/services that can provide high data rates over different wireless communication bands. Therefore, wireless communication technology struggles to cope with such increasing demands to facilitate and secure resource sharing during the transmission process in wireless systems. Several concepts are applied to optimize resource utilization and provide optimal performance for different wireless systems [21,22].

Today, wireless communication deals with two main problems: spectrum scarcity and deployment delays. These problems are caused by the centralized manner and static in nature of frequency assignment. This scheme cannot adapt to the changing needs of spectrum by users from the military, governmental, and commercial purposes.

Spectrum is no longer sufficiently available because it has been assigned to primary users that own the privileges to their assigned spectrum. However, it is not used efficiently most of the time. In order to use the spectrum in an opportunistic manner and increase the spectrum availability, the unlicensed users can be allowed to utilize licensed bands of licensed users, without causing any interference with the assigned service. The licensed bands of primary users are allocated to the unlicensed users only under the protocol of no interference with the assigned services. As per spectrum has limited frequencies, so we cannot increase spectrum frequencies, but we try to improve spectrum efficiency by the help of different technologies and methodologies. Cognitive radio (CR) and software-defined radio (SDR) play an important role to improve spectrum efficiency, but interference, false alarm, and low detection is a problem that can reduce by diversity technologies.

This paradigm for wireless communication is known as an opportunistic spectrum access and this is considered to be a feature of CR. CR is an emerging wireless communication paradigm in which either the network or the wireless node itself intelligently adapts particular transmission or reception parameters by sensing the environment. Dynamic spectrum access using CR is an emerging research topic. CR techniques provide the capability to use or share the spectrum in an opportunistic manner.

The concept behind SDR is that the radio can be fully configurable by software. A software uses to modify or change the configuration of radios for the function required at given time. One of the main advantages of SDR is to provide reconfigurable it and another is waveform portability and benefits of waveform portability are cost saving, interoperability, and obsolescence mitigation. It contains a number of functional blocks like radio frequency amplification block, frequency conversion block, and digital conversion baseband processor.

One of the most common topics of CR is spectrum management. Spectrum management is the process of regulating spectrum usage among different users over time, within receivers, and can use spectrum more efficiently than under conventional spectrum-management systems. It is attached with SDR, where the radio's key operating is defined largely in software. SDR along with software-defined antennas is the enablers of the CR. CR requires an expandable radio device and SDR provides platform for CR. CR is comprised of a control layer on "top" of an agile

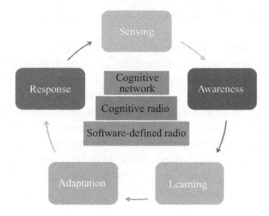

*Figure 6.3    Cognitive cycle with SDR*

SDR. Combination of a cognitive "engine" and the SDR together comprise a "CR." Cognitive cycle contains five phases, i.e., sensing, awareness, learning, adaptation, and response that are shown in Figure 6.3.

As abovementioned, CR technology emerged as one of the most promising and efficient solution to expand the channel spectrum utilization. CR is a subset of wireless communication networks, which are vulnerable to attacks, and eavesdropping, as there are no static end-to-end paths. Therefore, these networks desperately need to consider security mechanisms to defend and mitigate such kind of attacks. In some CR cases, eavesdroppers can be hidden within the network as a user (PU or SU).

From this context, due to the broadcast nature of the wireless communication systems, legal user's data can be easily overheard, altered, or blocked by malicious parties (eavesdropping attacks). Therefore, current wireless protocols have addressed the privacy issues but have failed to provide effective solutions against cyberattacks; such as denial-of-service attacks, session hijacking, and the jamming attacks. Additionally, researchers proved that even with computationally expensive resources, eavesdropper can still decrypt heavily encrypted data. Therefore, researchers addressed several approaches to enable secure data transfer within wireless communication networks. They present a resilient wireless communication approach to achieve highly dependable and resilient wireless networks and services based on MtD.

As mentioned before [13–17], MtD is based on the concept of manipulating system characteristics across multiple system dimensions in order to increase uncertainty and apparent complexity for attackers. Moreover, the impact of MtD is the reduction of the attacker's window of opportunity and the increase in the costs of probing and attacks. MtD creates asymmetric uncertainty for the attacker. MtD aims to alter the way the system is configured in order to make the attacker's information invalid, forcing the attacker to put extra time and effort to locate ways to exploit system vulnerabilities. Although this seems to be reassuring, this technique is innovative, and consequently, there is no standardized description of what MtD, diversification, and randomization are, and which metrics can help evaluating the performance of such systems [23].

Runtime diversification mechanism as an MtD approach is one of the new and appropriate mechanisms used to increase the level of diversification in the wireless networks. This approach efficiently ensures legitimate security by dynamically changing the runtime behavior of the system, spectrum, and the transmitted data. The main disadvantage of this approach is based on the need for high synchronization between source and destination nodes. Therefore, SDR Technology was presented as a paradigm solution to efficiently reprogram/reconfigure the attached communication equipment. SDR allows different radio-communication protocols and signal-processing mechanisms to be implemented in software rather than being dependent on hardware implementation. Therefore, CR is used to enable more spectrum availability.

Despite that SDR has the power to improve the wireless network security. When the communication link properties do not change as it is normally the case, the attacker will have enough time to probe the communication channel, identify its vulnerability and then launch an attack as shown in the successful attack scenario. Therefore, to insure wireless communications resiliency, SDR functions are used to change the properties of the communication links between two nodes at random. The easy reprogrammability enabled by SDR technology to support dynamic real-time change needed by MtD applications to randomly change the communication link properties to hide the transmitted data from attacker reach.

The role of SDR and CR appears in many important and various MtD applications presented by the literature.

The first application [24] relies on a benign employment of false-data injection to confuse the attacker. Such technique disorients attackers from compromising user's information, as the attacker will not be able to discriminate between real and fake data, due to the randomization and dynamic data transmission patterns.

To further complicate signal traceability, this mechanism senses the whole band spectrum and applies a dynamic frequency hopping between the available operating bands according to the running channel characteristics. The main disadvantage of the presented approach is the need for multiple antennas to enable frequency bands manipulation.

Authors [24] introduced a more complicated mechanism to enhance the system security using a real-time multiband diversification hopping. This technique works by dividing the transmitted message across the list of dedicated transmission frequency bands. A legal user receives the data fragment using a multiband frequency circuit and then recombines such data to reconstruct the message. This additional diversification dimension increases the confusion efficiency and ensures the secrecy of the system.

Authors [25] introduced an additional diversification layer by further changing the transmission characteristics. In this work, they introduced real-time signal modulation change. Their future work included a plan to merge such dimension into one dynamic system. This type of confusion is quite hard to be detected or attacked. It employs fast SDR reconfigurability offering a wide CR spectrum. Furthermore, the transmitted data is diffused in a wide space that is contentiously changing, making it almost impossible to be attacked.

## 6.3 The driver—artificial intelligence (AI) fundamentals

AI is a rapidly growing field that includes a wide range of subfields, including knowledge representation, reasoning, planning, decision-making, optimization, ML, and metaheuristic algorithms. Thereof, it can be considered as the core of most of engineering problems. For example, security and privacy problems are major issues for cyber systems due to the lack of resilience and risk of misuse of private data. High levels of security for Internet communications usually require analysis of users' data by accredited individuals or organizations. Paradoxically, these security measures themselves invade personal privacy and organizational needs for confidentiality. That is why the adequate balance between security and privacy is the central issue for institutional design of the modern information society. Building a machine-learning algorithm like in [26] could facilitate a suitable modeling for optimizing such problem.

In MtD, coevolution is a powerful heuristic approach. It can be employed to evolve adaptive strategies for the defender and all adversaries, leveraging the analytical insight from simpler models to provide initial strategy seeding [27]. For instance, in [28], authors used GA to guide MtD in allocating temporally and spatially diverse solutions. They used GA to select a set of diverse computer configurations to induce MtD. Such configurations were modeled as chromosomes, where individual configuration settings were traits. The general concept was that good chromosomes are used to generate better chromosomes using a series of selection, crossover, and mutation processes. These processes also incorporate randomness that also can provide diversity. The generated configuration was initially tested for feasibility, which determines if the configuration provides the desired functionality.

Originally, most of the developed heuristic techniques are inspired from the Mother Nature. Some algorithms were developed by mimicking a certain physical or chemical behavior. However, the largest fraction of nature-inspired heuristic algorithms is based on some successful characteristics of biological system "bioinspired algorithms." In fact, biologically inspired algorithms form the majority of all nature-inspired algorithms that have been considerably studied in the past decades. As indicated by [29], bioinspired solutions to the problems related to computing and communications fields can be classified into three application domains which are bioinspired computing, bioinspired systems, and bioinspired networking. Bioinspired computing, which represents a class of algorithms focusing on efficient computing, can be effectively used for a great number of problem spaces, such as optimization problems, exploration and mapping, pattern recognition, etc. Most of the biologically inspired systems relies on massively distributed, and collaborative systems to enable functionalities like distributed sensing, and exploration.

Algorithms based on SI are among the most popular biologically inspired systems. SI algorithm was first introduced in 1989 and inspired from the behavior of a

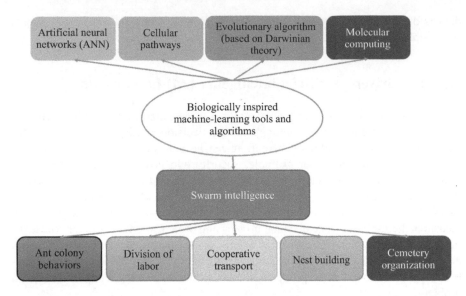

*Figure 6.4    Some examples for Nature-Inspired algorithms and their classifications [33]*

collective emerging of agents that follow some simple rules. Despite each agent may not show any sort of intelligence, the whole group can have a certain organizational strategy. Therefore, any SI-based algorithm uses multiple agents for self-organization, coevolution, and learning to provide an efficient optimum solution [30]. Some of the SI algorithms were inspired from the behavior of insects, such as ants, bees, and wasps, while other SI algorithms were inspired from the behavior of some animals such as flocks of birds or fish. Fish and birds swarming behavior was the inspirational spies for the classical particle swarm optimization algorithms. Another algorithm like firefly algorithm was inspired from the fireflies swarming behavior. Cuckoo search and bat algorithm were inspired from the brooding parasitism of some cuckoo species and the echolocation of foraging bats respectively. One of the most famous optimization techniques is the ant colony algorithm which was inspired from the social interaction of ants [31]. In fact, not all of the bioinspired algorithms are inspired from the swarming behavior, for instance, GAs are biologically inspired from the human genetic science, but it is not SI based. Another example is an algorithm developed in [32] and was inspired from the flower pollination. This algorithm is biologically inspired and cannot be considered as a SI algorithm. Figure 6.4 shows a simple classification of various nature-inspired applications [33].

## 6.3.1    Natural-inspired AI fundamentals and techniques

Bioinspired systems and optimization algorithms are the main pillars supporting quick, accurate, and efficient solutions to many problems that were impossible to be solved using the traditional techniques. Such techniques are widely utilized in many applications in the computing and communication fields. There is no doubt that the main reason for achieving most of the aforementioned diversification techniques to enhance the system security and reliability are credited to such biologically inspired optimization and AI techniques. That is why we mentioned the AI techniques as the driver for our hypothetical vehicle which is MtD through diversity to enhance system's resilience and security. As an example, resources allocation in the clouds must be determined accurately to avoid resource contention, scarcity of resources, resource fragmentation, and over-provisioning [34]. Therefore, a well-defined algorithm for resources allocation verifying the system's constraints decreases the probability of the systems failure. In addition, in order to avoid most of the cloud security issues that virtualization and migration mechanisms are attempting to solve, a well-defined optimization algorithm and machine-learning techniques are needed to guide this process. The following section sheds the light on the fundamental and techniques of some of the most popular biologically inspired AI systems.

### 6.3.1.1 Ant colony algorithms

For thousands of years, insects utilize their dense population as a central strategy for survival. One of the most well-known examples for cooperation and applying a well-defined strategy is ants. Ant colony optimization (ACO) algorithm is one of the popular heuristic approaches that were inspired from the behavior of some ant species in finding the shortest paths. As defined in [35], "ACO algorithm depends on a number of artificial ants build solutions to an optimization problem and exchange information on their quality via a communication scheme that is reminiscent of the one adopted by real ants." Therefore, the fundamental source beyond this definition returns back to the ants' strategy in finding food. Ants initially search for the source of food randomly, while depositing a substance called pheromone to remark the paths they passed by [36]. In order to get more food, other ants follow the suggested path by perceiving the presence of the highest pheromone concentration, while depositing more pheromone to reinforce the path for other ants. Based on this strategy, ants can transport food to their nest in a remarkably effective way. From this context, ACO approach was inspired and developed to solve some of the heuristic problems.

General ACO algorithm for solving optimization problems can be summarized in three main stages by which the system continues to iterate over, until finding the optimum solution. In the first stage, a number of solutions are constructed by some of the assumed artificial ants. These solutions can be improved through a stage called local search stage, which can be used as an optional stage. These assumed ants generate pheromone that is used for remarking the fittest solution. These processes continue to update the generated pheromone until obtaining the optimal solution [35].

### 6.3.1.2 Genetic algorithms

Most of the bioinspired optimization techniques exploit ideas of biological evolution, such as reproduction, mutation, and recombination, for searching the solution of an optimization problem. They apply the principle of survival on a set of potential solutions to reach the optimum solution quickly. Evolutionary algorithms fundamentally rooted on the Darwinian theory of evolution. They can be categorized into many classes including, GAs, evolution strategies, evolutionary programming, generic programming, and classifier systems [37]. Evolutionary algorithms represent a set of search techniques used to find an optimal or approximate solution to optimization problems.

GA as an example is considered as a very popular stochastic global search method used for solving optimization and machine-learning problems. GA is a bioinspired algorithm that is inspired of the metaphor of natural biological evolution and genetic science [38]. It follows the principles of Charles Darwin theory that illustrates the concept of survival of the fittest [39]. Despite the efficient and great performance shown in solving the optimization problems, GA are objective-function-based algorithm. It relies on a population of individuals, where the fitted individual ensures the maximum fitness and minimizes the cost of the objective function. Selection, crossover, and mutation are the essence processes that GA relies on. Selection process means selecting the fittest individuals in the current population to form a stronger generation of the population. Crossover depends on exchanging a portion of the structure of two individuals to produce a new individual that might replace the weaker individuals in the next population. Mutation is a local operator used to alter the value of a random position in the generated individual and is applied with a very low probability of occurrence [40]. This process leads to the evolution of populations of individuals that are better suited to their environment than their ancestors. The main loop of GAs includes the following steps:

1. Evaluate the initial population.
2. Perform competitive selection from the objective function.
3. Apply genetic operators (crossover and mutation) to generate new solutions.
4. Obtain the fitness solutions in the population.
5. Start again from point 2 and repeat until some convergence criteria is satisfied.

### 6.3.1.3   Artificial neural network

A neural network traditionally refers to a network of biological neurons, and the term is now used to refer to an artificial neural network (ANN). ANN primary objective is to acquire knowledge from the environment (i.e., a process of self-learning is performed). In most cases, an ANN is an adaptive system that is capable of changing its structure based on external or internal information that flows through the network, where the complex relationships between inputs and outputs can be modeled [33]. The spectrum of application domains for the ANNs is wide and includes, among others, applications in industry and business, data mining, civil engineering, and fire safety. In the field of ML, the ANNs are used in classification and regression tasks [30].

The first mathematical model of neurons was devised by McCulloch and Pitts. ANN algorithm simulates the electrochemical signals in the brain by which these signals are amplified and propagated along neuronal chains, whereby each neuron receives a number of input signals through ramified sensors (dendrites) and forward an output signal through its single extension (axon) [41,42]. According to this nature model, a neuron "fires," when a linear combination of weighted inputs exceeds some threshold. In the most widely used type of ANNs, the neurons are organized in layers. The outputs of one layer become the weighted inputs to the next layer, with no interconnections of neurons within the layer. Network training is executed in a supervised fashion by introducing the inputs to the network, observing the output error with respect to the target values, and adjusting the connection weights to improve the performance in the next round.

### 6.3.1.4   Others

There are many other biological swarm indigence techniques that are recently used in many of the optimization and machine-learning problems. Fireflies algorithm, for example, is one of the recent algorithms that is used in many of the networking and communication applications. The source of inspiration beyond this algorithm returns to the rhythmic illuminance of fireflies, which is an amazing demonstration of this kind of communication [43]. The fireflies illuminate using the process of biolumi-nescence, in which oxygen, calcium, and adenosine triphosphate and the chemical luciferin are combined with, bioluminescent enzyme, luciferase to efficiently pro-duce light without loss of any heat energy. Fireflies appear to produce light for a wide range of reasons; a warning sign against potential predators, to uniquely identify their members and communicate with potential mates in mating seasons. Self-organized behavior presents itself in some tropic where fireflies flashing patterns are synchro-nized [44]. The FA runs in a framework of three idealized rules stated in Xin-She's original paper:

* Each firefly can produce light and attract less bright one.
* Attractiveness is directly proportional to the brightness of a firefly. And they are both inversely proportional to distance.
* The brightest firefly moves randomly.
* The brightness is directly proportional to the fitness function.

Initially, the fireflies are assigned random location, where each location represent a solution. The fitness of each is represented by their brightness, updating their brightness to correlate with the quality of their solution. Communicating the solution is achieved using light as a medium. However, what makes the FA different from other swarm-based algorithm is the variable importance of a solution against the distance. Inspired by nature, Yang decided to model the physics of lights, mainly the inverse square law. This law shows the importance of reaching the optimal solutions by using the nearest fireflies while enabling repeated enhancements to prevent a single solution to influence other candidate solutions. such prevention gives the swarm the ability to create sub-swarms and exploit multiple good solutions in the neighboring space. Thus, if we have enough number of fireflies we can find in all local and global optima [45].

Another technique is inspired from the bats communicating behavior, that is why this algorithm is called bat algorithm. Bats utilize echolocation to avoid obstacles, search for food, and navigate to their roosts [46]. Echolocation is the active use of sound that enables bats to "see" their environment. In the case of microbats, they calculate time delay from emission to detection of the echo, the temporal distance between their ear, and the amplitude variations to construct three-dimensional model of their surrounding thus achieving "vision." When searching for a prey, bats vary the rate of bursts and loudness depending on the target's proximity. Reaching the target, the bat decreases the echolocation loudness while increasing the burst's rate reaching about 200 pulses per second [47]. As a swarm-based metaheuristic technique, the bat algorithm consists of two steps, which are exploration and exploitation. The exploration step is realized using loudness, frequency, and rate of pulse in each iteration. Frequency defines the interest in exploitation of best solution. Loudness defines the interest of the current local solution on next iteration solution. The rate of pulses defines the probability of accepting a candidate solution as the best solution. As iterations elapse interest in exploration dissipates by increasing the rate of pulses and while the interest in exploitation accumulates as the frequency increases. Moreover, increasing the exploitation and decreasing the exploration could influence the user-defined linear variables [48].

## 6.3.2    *Artificial intelligence applications across some OSI layers*

AI showed great advances in various fields especially in computing and communication fields. For instance, demanding a good switching strategy, to achieve the concept of MtD when switching between multiple configurations for the web application stack. Evolutionary algorithms can be utilized in wireless networks by solving problems of the location management and channel-assignment procedure [49]. In this section, we will show how AI and SI techniques proved to be good drivers in achieving better performance and efficiency across the OSI layers. AI and ML approaches have been widely used for solving various problems such as routing, traffic classification, flow clustering, intrusion detection, load balancing, fault detection, quality of service (QoS) and quality of experience optimization, admission control, and resource allocation [19].

As mentioned before, SDN architecture, a central management of the forwarding elements (i.e., switches and routers) is accomplished by a central unit, which can be programmed directly to perform fundamental networking tasks or implementing any other additional services. Combining both central management and network programmability opens the door to employ more advanced techniques such as AI in order to deal with high-demand and rapidly changing networks [19,50]. Therefore, AI reveals a huge potential in SDN innovation. A large variety of metaheuristic algorithms were widely adopted in SDN. ACO, for example, is used for solving various networking problems such as routing [51,52], load balancing [51,53], video surveillance [54], network security [55], and maximizing network utilization [56]. GAs are used for networking routing, virtual network planning, optimizing the cost of deploying deep packet inspection functions in SDN, load balancing, and designing optimal observation matrices. Simulated annealing and artificial bee colony (ABC) are used for solving controller placement problem [20] and dynamic controller provisioning, besides solving traffic engineering for SDN-based video surveillance systems issues.

Another popular application utilizes AI and SI techniques, what is called self-organizing systems. Artificial self-organized networking (SON) systems are expected to exhibit some intelligent features for the network such as flexibility, robustness, decentralized control, and self-evolution. In [33], authors served the utilization of SI techniques like ACO, fireflies optimization, ABC technique, and others in designing such SON systems. They showed the application of such biologically inspired techniques in designing the SON across the IOS layers including the physical, MAC, and networking layers. Compared to the conventional SON techniques, bioinspired SON algorithms may lead to a more effective system in terms of networking, maintenance, control, and optimization. Besides, the capability of adapting to environmental changes in bioinspired SON systems comes from the inheritance of biological species, and this capability is much higher than the conventional solutions. Among the studied SI techniques, ACO showed emphasis scalability and better performance metrics for the network routing protocols for SON systems such as wireless sensor networks and delay tolerant networks. Different from it, another bioinspired algorithm like the firefly inspired algorithm, may obtain a cost-effective physical-layer synchronization by simply depending on the local pulse interactions among individuals based on the pulse-coupled oscillators [33].

Furthermore, AI and SI play a very important role for cloud and networks managing resources and allocations. Managing resource, by applying approaches to load balance the utilization of hosts (servers) and of network resources, can greatly improve the system performance. Traditional load balance methods are usually inefficient and inflexible since there are no effective ways to obtain network statistics from each network device. Authors in [57] adopted SDN approach as a technique to overcome these issues and increase the system's QoS. They proposed a comprehensive dynamic load balance module for SDN, which aims to load balancing both the servers and the paths leading to such servers. They implemented ant colony system to select the best routing path in order to reach the chosen server, in addition to a dynamic server load balance algorithm to choose the best server. This presented module showed exceptional system performance while achieving both higher network throughput and lower delay.

Moving to the concept of applying MtD in cloud computing. Migration process as we discussed before is a very successful technique to achieve high security and resilience for users in public cloud hosts. This technique relies on changing the position of the users host to avoid co-residency attack. However, it is not a simple process; there are many dimensions to it and it depends on an IoT. Decisions have to be made to decide where to place that machine, based on the security of the new location. These decisions require applying a sophisticated AI algorithm that decides where will be the new hosted machine. This algorithm plays the role of confusing the attacker in order to reduce the probability of having a shared machine hosting both the user's and the attacker's VMs.

In the communication level, MtD as mentioned before could be applied through the suggested multiband diversification technique in communication and signals level to avoid eavesdropping and signals jamming. The mentioned techniques required selecting different relays to manipulate the communication signals through it. Nevertheless, there is a tradeoff between the system reliability and the required security enhancement [25], as the wrong selection of such relays might cause a huge system failure. Therefore, an intelligent paradigm must be applied to verify the concept of

MtD with reducing the possibilities for the system failure. Such paradigm definitely relies on AI technique, ML, and optimization techniques such as GA to introduce such smartness and reduce chance of failure.

# References

[1]   Spafford, Eugene H. "Computer viruses as artificial life." Artificial Life 1, no. 3 (1994): 249–265.

[2]   Haimes, Yacov Y., Barry M. Horowitz, James H. Lambert, Joost R. Santos, and Kenneth G. Crowther. "Harmonizing and uniting the key technical disciplines for risk management of cyber security." New Hampshire: Institute for Information Infrastructure Protection, Dartmouth College, 2008.

[3]   Colombo, Armando W., Thomas Bangemann, Statmatis Karnouskos, *et al.* "Industrial cloud-based cyber-physical systems." The IMC-AESOP Approach, Springer, 2014.

[4]   Azab, Mohamed Mahmoud Mahmoud. "Cooperative autonomous resilient defense platform for cyber-physical systems." PhD diss., Virginia Polytechnic Institute and State University, 2013.

[5]   Bell, J. Bowyer. "Cheating and deception". New York: Routledge, 2017. https://www.taylorfrancis.com/books/9781315081496

[6]   Whaley, Barton. "Toward a general theory of deception." The Journal of Strategic Studies 5, no. 1 (1982): 178–192.

[7]   Mazurczyk, Wojciech, Szymon Drobniak, and Sean Moore. "Towards a systematic view on cybersecurity ecology." In Combatting Cybercrime and Cyberterrorism, pp. 17–37. Springer, Cham, 2016.

[8]   Rabah, Kefa. "Steganography-the art of hiding data." Information Technology Journal 3, no. 3 (2004): 245–269.

[9]   Azab, Mohamed, Riham Hassan, and Mohamed Eltoweissy. "ChameleonSoft: a moving target defense system." In Collaborative Computing: Networking, Applications and Worksharing (CollaborateCom), 2011 7th International Conference on, pp. 241–250. IEEE, 2011.

[10]  Williams, Daniel, Wei Hu, Jack W. Davidson, Jason D. Hiser, John C. Knight, and Anh Nguyen-Tuong. "Security through diversity: leveraging virtual machine technology." IEEE Security & Privacy 7, no. 1 (2009).

[11]  Smith, Reginald D. "Malware "Ecology" Viewed as Ecological Succession: Historical Trends and Future Prospects." arXiv preprint arXiv:1410.8082 (2014).

[12]  Kampanakis, Panos, Harry Perros, and Tsegereda Beyene. "SDN-based solutions for moving target defense network protection." In World of Wireless, Mobile and Multimedia Networks (WoWMoM), 2014 IEEE 15th International Symposium on a IEEE, pp. 1–6. 2014, June.

[13]  Lombardi, Flavio, and Roberto Di Pietro. "Secure virtualization for cloud computing." Journal of Network and Computer Applications 34, no. 4 (2011): 1113–1122.

[14] Azab, Mohamed, and Mohamed Eltoweissy. "Migrate: towards a lightweight moving-target defense against cloud side-channels." In Security and Privacy Workshops (SPW), 2016 IEEE, pp. 96–103. IEEE, 2016.

[15] Kashkoush, Mona, Azab, Mohamed, Mohamed Eltoweissy, and Gamal Attiya. "Towards online smart disguise: real-time diversification evading co-residency based cloud attacks." In Collaboration and Internet Computing (CIC), 2017 IEEE 3rd International Conference on, pp. 235–242. IEEE, 2017.

[16] Azab, Mohamed, Bassem Mokhtar, Amr S. Abed, and Mohamed Eltoweissy. "Toward smart moving target defense for Linux container resiliency." In Local Computer Networks (LCN), 2016 IEEE 41st Conference on, pp. 619–622. IEEE, 2016.

[17] Abed, Amr S., Charles Clancy, and David S. Levy. "Intrusion detection system for applications using Linux containers." In International Workshop on Security and Trust Management, pp. 123–135. Springer, Cham, 2015.

[18] Dunlop, Matthew, Stephen Groat, William Urbanski, Randy Marchany, and Joseph Tront. "Mt6d: a moving target ipv6 defense." In Military Communications Conference, 2011-Milcom 2011, pp. 1321–1326. IEEE, 2011.

[19] Latah, Majd, and Levent Toker. "Artificial Intelligence Enabled Software Defined Networking: A Comprehensive Overview." arXiv preprint arXiv:1803.06818 (2018).

[20] Azab, Mohamed, and José A.B. Fortes. "Towards proactive SDN-controller attack and failure resilience." In Computing, Networking and Communications (ICNC), 2017 International Conference on, pp. 442–448. IEEE, 2017.

[21] Zou, Yulong, Jia Zhu, Liuqing Yang, Ying-Chang Liang, and Yu-Dong Yao. "Securing physical-layer communications for cognitive radio networks." IEEE Communications Magazine 53, no. 9 (2015): 48–54.

[22] Shu, Zhihui, Yi Qian, and Song Ci. "On physical layer security for cognitive radio networks." IEEE Network 27, no. 3 (2013): 28–33.

[23] DeLoach, Scott A., Xinming Ou, Rui Zhuang, and Su Zhang. "Model-driven, moving-target defense for enterprise network security." In Models@ run. time, pp. 137–161. Springer, Cham, 2014.

[24] Ghourab, Esraa M., Ahmed Mansour, Mohamed Azab, Mohamed Rizk, and Amr Mokhtar. "Towards physical layer security in Internet of Things based on reconfigurable multiband diversification." In Information Technology, Electronics and Mobile Communication Conference (IEMCON), 2017 8th IEEE Annual, pp. 446–450. IEEE, 2017.

[25] Ghourab, Esraa M., Mohamed Azab, Mohamed F. Feteiha, and Hesham El-Sayed. "A novel approach to enhance the physical layer channel security of wireless cooperative vehicular communication using decode-and-forward best relaying selection." Wireless Communications and Mobile Computing 2018 (2018).

[26] Okimoto, Tenda, Naoto Ikegai, Katsumi Inoue, Hitoshi Okada, Tony Ribeiro, and Hiroshi Maruyama. "Cyber security problem based on multi-objective distributed constraint optimization technique." In Dependable Systems and

Networks Workshop (DSN-W), 2013 43rd Annual IEEE/IFIP Conference on, pp. 1–7. IEEE, 2013.

[27]   Jones, Stephen, Alexander Outkin, Jared Gearhart, *et al.* Evaluating moving target defense with PLADD. Sandia National Laboratories, 2015.

[28]   Crouse, Michael B., and Errin W. Fulp. "A moving target environment for computer configurations using genetic algorithms." In SafeConfig. 2011, October.

[29]   Falko Dressler "Self-organization in sensor and actor networks." John Wiley & Sons, Ltd, (2008). ISBN: 9780470028209, doi: 10.1002/9780470724460

[30]   Fister Jr, Iztok, Xin-She Yang, Iztok Fister, Janez Brest, and Dušan Fister. "A Brief Review of Nature-Inspired Algorithms for Optimization." arXiv preprint arXiv:1307.4186 (2013).

[31]   Zang, Hongnian, Shujun Zhang, and Kevin Hapeshi. "A review of nature-inspired algorithms." Journal of Bionic Engineering 7 (2010): S232–S237.

[32]   Yang, Xin-She. "Flower pollination algorithm for global optimization." In International Conference on Unconventional Computing and Natural Computation, pp. 240–249. Springer, Berlin, Heidelberg, 2012.

[33]   Zhang, Zhongshan, Keping Long, Jianping Wang, and Falko Dressler. "On swarm intelligence inspired self-organized networking: its bionic mechanisms, designing principles and optimization approaches." IEEE Communications Surveys & Tutorials 16, no. 1 (2014): 513–537.

[34]   Anuradha, V. P., and Sumathi, D. "A survey on resource allocation strategies in cloud computing." International Conference on Information Communication and Embedded Systems (ICICES2014), 2014. doi:10.1109/icices.2014.7033931

[35]   Dorigo, Marco, and Mauro Birattari. "Ant colony optimization." In Encyclopedia of machine learning, pp. 36–39. Springer, Boston, MA, 2011.

[36]   Roy, Bibhash, Suman Banik, Parthi Dey, Sugata Sanyal, and Nabendu Chaki. "Ant colony based routing for mobile ad-hoc networks towards improved quality of services." Journal of Emerging Trends in Computing and Information Sciences 3, no. 1 (2012): 10–14.

[37]   Leandro Nunes de Castro. "Fundamentals of natural computing basic concepts, algorithms, and applications." New York: Imprint Chapman and Hall/CRC, 2006. ISBN 9781420011449.

[38]   Binitha, S., and S. Siva Sathya. "A survey of bio inspired optimization algorithms." International Journal of Soft Computing and Engineering 2, no. 2 (2012): 137–151.

[39]   Sivanandam, S. N., and S. N. Deepa. "Genetic algorithm optimization problems." In Introduction to Genetic Algorithms, pp. 165–209. Springer, Berlin, Heidelberg, 2008.

[40]   Anderson-Cook, Christine M. Practical genetic algorithms. Journal of the American Statistical Association, 2005, pp. 1099–1099.

[41]   Fister, Iztok, Ponnuthurai Nagaratnam Suganthan, Salahuddin M. Kamal, Fahad M. Al-Marzouki, Matjaž Perc, and Damjan Strnad. "Artificial neural

network regression as a local search heuristic for ensemble strategies in differential evolution." Nonlinear Dynamics 84, no. 2 (2016): 895–914.

[42] Haykin, Simon. "A comprehensive foundation." Neural Networks 2, no. 2004 (2004): 41.

[43] Yang, Xin-She. "Firefly algorithms for multimodal optimization." In International symposium on stochastic algorithms, pp. 169–178. Springer, Berlin, Heidelberg, 2009.

[44] Camazine, Scott, Jean-Louis Deneubourg, Nigel R. Franks, James Sneyd, Eric Bonabeau, and Guy Theraula. Self-organization in biological systems. Vol. 7. Princeton University Press, 2003.

[45] Marichelvam, Mariappan Kadarkarainadar, Thirumoorthy Prabaharan, and Xin She Yang. "A discrete firefly algorithm for the multi-objective hybrid flow-shop scheduling problems." IEEE Transactions on Evolutionary Computation 18, no. 2 (2014): 301–305.

[46] Van Ryckeghem, Willy. "Domestic policy variables and foreign direct investment inflows in Latin America." In International Trade, Foreign Direct Investment and the Economic Environment, pp. 59–75. Palgrave Macmillan, London, 1998.

[47] Yang, Xin-She, and Xingshi He. "Bat algorithm: literature review and applications." International Journal of Bio-Inspired Computation 5, no. 3 (2013): 141–149.

[48] Yang, Xin-She. Nature-inspired optimization algorithms. Elsevier, 2014.

[49] Das, Sajal K., Nilanjan Banerjee, and Abhishek Roy. Solving optimization problems in wireless networks using genetic algorithms. Taylor & Francis Group, LLC, 2005, p. 219.

[50] Latah, Majd, and Levent Toker. "Application of artificial intelligence to software defined networking: a survey." Indian Journal of Science and Technology 9, no. 44 (2016).

[51] Sim, Kwang Mong, and Weng Hong Sun. "Ant colony optimization for routing and load-balancing: survey and new directions." IEEE Transactions on Systems, Man, and Cybernetics-Part A: Systems and Humans 33, no. 5 (2003): 560–572.

[52] Sim, Kwang Mong, and Weng Hong Sun. "Multiple ant-colony optimization for network routing." In Cyber Worlds, 2002. Proceedings. First International Symposium on, pp. 277–281. IEEE, 2002.

[53] Li, Kun, Gaochao Xu, Guangyu Zhao, Yushuang Dong, and Dan Wang. "Cloud task scheduling based on load balancing ant colony optimization." In Chinagrid Conference (ChinaGrid), 2011 Sixth Annual, pp. 3–9. IEEE, 2011.

[54] Mohan, B. Chandra, and Ramachandran Baskaran. "A survey: ant colony optimization based recent research and implementation on several engineering domain." Expert Systems with Applications 39, no. 4 (2012): 4618–4627.

[55] Mishra, Ratan, and Anant Jaiswal. "Ant colony optimization: a solution of load balancing in cloud." International Journal of Web & Semantic Technology 3, no. 2 (2012): 33.

[56]   Gao, Yongqiang, Haibing Guan, Zhengwei Qi, Yang Hou, and Liang Liu. "A multi-objective ant colony system algorithm for virtual machine placement in cloud computing." Journal of Computer and System Sciences 79, no. 8 (2013): 1230–1242.

[57]   Sathyanarayana, Sushma, and Melody Moh. "Joint route-server load balancing in software defined networks using ant colony optimization." In High Performance Computing & Simulation (HPCS), 2016 International Conference on, pp. 156–163. IEEE, 2016.

*Chapter 7*

# Towards nature-inspired machine-learning approach for cyber security

*Rafał Kozik[1] and Michał Choraś[1]*

This chapter provides an insight into bio-inspired techniques that applied the problems of machine learning and features extraction in the area of cyber security. We focus on the fundamental aspects of the intelligent systems, namely how relevant information can be extracted in order to build the knowledge and how then knowledge could be maintained and represented to solve various cyber security problems. Moreover, we give some practical examples of application and quantitative results to give the reader evidence of the usefulness of the presented algorithms.

## 7.1  Introduction

In many machine-learning cases, it turns out that the problems with the effectiveness of machine-learning algorithms often boil down to the feature extraction. Obviously, the extracted features have to be meaningful and correlated with the classification task. Recently, many techniques have been proposed for autonomous features extraction. As this task is crucial and highly relevant to the scope of this book, we give some practical examples how the nature-inspired techniques can be effectively used to extract meaningful information from the raw data. In particular, we show how evolutionary algorithms (EAs) can be used to learn the structure hidden in the data and how this could be successfully applied to protect web-based information system.

Another issue with the intelligent systems and the machine-learning algorithms applied in the area of cyber security is to mimic the human behaviour in the process of knowledge accumulation. Currently, one of the difficulties in machine learning is to build autonomous systems that are able to learn sequential tasks and to transfer the accumulated knowledge to solve new tasks more efficiently and effectively (e.g. shorter training time without deterioration of effectiveness). Such capability is termed as lifelong machine learning (LML) or as lifelong learning intelligent systems. This paradigm is intended to resemble the process of learning in the way the humans do. Human beings have the capability to use the knowledge from the past in order to

[1]Institute of Telecommunications and Computer Science, Department of Teleinformatics Systems, Poland

solve new and unknown tasks. This is in contradiction to the classic machine-learning algorithms, that in order to solve task A always starts the learning process from scratch. Obviously, the LML could be a good solution for detecting infected machines in the network. Such LML-enabled system can benefit from historical data obtained from various systems or attack scenarios without starting the training process from scratch. Naturally, there are various problems to address such as common language, knowledge representation, and scalability. Therefore, in this chapter, we give an insight into recently proposed lightweight and efficient lifelong learning framework.

## 7.2    Review of nature-inspired solutions for pattern extraction and machine learning

In the literature, we may find plenty of nature-inspired solutions proposed to solve problems in various fields of cyber security domain.

Obviously, one of the most intuitive solutions adapting the bio-inspired approaches is based on the mechanisms that follow the self-defence techniques of the living organisms in nature. The moving target strategy could be a good example here. This strategy ensures security by the diversity of the system. For example, one may develop a technique for continuous changes of system configuration. In that way, it would be way much difficult for the attacker to perform reconnaissance, find the target of attack, and execute an attack. Such technique has been adapted in [1] to protect cloud services from side-channels attacks (information leakage between virtual machines due to the sharing of physical resources). The technique is based on runtime live migration of the virtual machines between various physical hosts. On the other hand, in [2], authors have proposed to use an EA to avoid the problem of deterministic configuration. In the literature, there are also proposals following the moving target strategies that adapt dynamic IP addressing translation or techniques that intend to fool the network scanners [3].

Another bio-inspired strategy is to mimic behaviour of the immune system. In contrast to moving target strategy is fact that the nature-inspired algorithm is an element of a bigger architecture. An example of successfully used approach that adapts artificial immune system has been proposed in [4]. The authors used this technique to detect malwares. The key concept is based on information flows (generate by an application) to concurrently evolve the multiple detectors sets via negative selection.

In this work, we present our recent research that adapts nature-inspired approaches at two architectural levels, namely pattern extraction and knowledge management. Similar to analysed approaches, the pattern extraction adapts EA for optimisation. On the other hand, the nature-inspired knowledge management is essentially different. Is must be noted here that we will avoid introducing the recent advancements in deep learning, as it is out of the scope of this chapter. Instead we will focus on such aspects as multitask learning (MTL) and knowledge transfer. In our opinion, this topic of machine learning (in particular human-alike knowledge accumulation) in the area of cyber security has not been fully addressed yet.

## 7.3   From data to knowledge

### 7.3.1   Raw-requests and hidden structure

Probably, the most intuitive way to build the cyberattack detection algorithm for network-based systems is to intercept the communication channel and capture the raw data for the analysis. Despite the fact that such data are hard to get, due to the privacy implications, the data have also a variety of formats and encoding techniques. One of the most popular (and one of the most frequently used) protocols for data exchange is Hypertext Transfer Protocol (HTTP). As it is shown Figure 7.1, at a first glance, one may notice that the HTTP requests have rather form of byte sequences without formal structure. However, looking more carefully, one may also notice that the structure indeed exists, as specific characters (e.g. semicolon, plus sign, or colon) are used to separate various fields of various types. Unfortunately, inferring the structure form the raw data adds additional level of complication, that increases the computation time, requires additional computing resources, and imposes some challenges to scalability. Therefore, it is tempting to apply analysis to entire request and consider it as a monolithic sequence of bytes. However, we are going to show that this approach in not a good strategy.

### 7.3.2   Time-series of traffic statistics

It is common to use the NetFlows protocol to monitor the network behaviour. NetFlow should be understood as a standard format to describe the bidirectional communication. It contains the information such as IP source and destination address, destination

```
https://www.google.pl/webhp? sourceid=chrome-instant&ion=1&
espv=2&ie=UTF-8#q=serialization+ and+deserialization

https://www.google.pl/maps/place/ Stacja+PKP+Bydgoszcz+Fordon/
@53.1439362,18.16896,14z/data=
!4m2!3m1!1s0x4703166afe4d5843: 0x63ecc18530748e8f

http://chart.apis.google.com/ chart?cht=p&chs=500x250&chdl=
first+legend%7Csecond+legend% 7Cthird+legend&chl=first+label%
7Csecond+label%7Cthird+label&
chco=FF0000|00FFFF|00FF00,6699CC|
CC33FF|CCCC33&chp=0.436326388889&
chtt=My+Google+Chart&chts=000000, 24&chd=t:5,10,50|25,35,45
```

*Figure 7.1    Example of custom serialisation technique used in URL address. Some of the methods use classic 'key = value' separated by '&', while others use customised serialisation techniques, e.g. sequence of values separated by '—' or '+'*

*Table 7.1  NetFlow attributes*

| Attribute | Description |
|---|---|
| StartTime | Start time of the recorded NetFlow |
| Dur | Duration |
| Proto | IP protocol (e.g. UTP, TCP) |
| SrcAddr | Source address |
| Sport | Source port |
| Dir | Direction of the recorded communication |
| DstAddr | Destination address |
| Dport | Destination port |
| State | Protocol state |
| sTos | Source type of service |
| dTos | Destination type of service |
| TotPkts | Total number of packets that have been exchanged between source and destination |
| TotBytes | Total bytes exchanged |
| SrcBytes | Number of bytes sent by source |

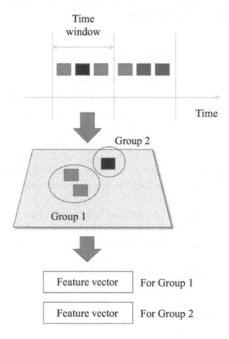

*Figure 7.2  General overview of the feature vectors extraction pipeline*

port, and the amount of the exchanged bytes. More detailed list of single NetFlow attributes is shown in Table 7.1.

The decision if the node is infected or not, or if requests are malicious or not, cannot be drawn on the basis of single NetFlow. What we need to perform is the

*Table 7.2   Time window-based statistic*

| Parameter | Description |
| --- | --- |
| $S_1$ | Number of flows |
| $S_2$ | Sum of transferred bytes |
| $S_3$ | Average sum of bytes per NetFlow |
| $S_4$ | Average communication time with each unique IP addresses |
| $S_5$ | Number of unique destination IP addresses |
| $S_6$ | Number of unique destination ports |
| $S_7$ | Most frequently used protocol (e.g. TCP, UDP) |

aggregation of the NetFlows in time-windows in order to extract more relevant data and record/detect malicious symptoms such as port scanning, packet flooding effects, etc. [5,6]. After the preprocessing and aggregation of NetFlows, the statistics can be calculated for each time window.

The general overview of the feature extraction pipeline has been presented in Figure 7.2. In general, the proposed feature extraction method aggregates the NetFlows within each time window. For each time window, we group the NetFlows by the IP source address. For each group (containing Netflows with the same time window and IP source address), we calculate feature vector $S = (S_1, \ldots, S_7)$. The feature vector holds the statistics described in Table 7.2.

## 7.4   Nature-inspired feature extraction algorithms

The general idea of structure extraction process is depicted in Figure 7.3. First, the sequence of request (byte sequences) is collected. Afterwards, the byte sequences are analysed in order to identify common parts (tokens). Next, the structure is encoded as graphs, so that each token is indicated as a vertex and each indicates the collection of bytes between tokens. The same tokens in the requests may appear in a different order. In result, the graph will have different paths (forks). To keep this example simple, let us assume that each edge in the graph maintains a histogram representing the bytes values distribution. The nature-inspired part is in the model, more precisely in the way the model is constructed with mutations and crossovers of the EA.

### 7.4.1   Using genetic algorithm to identify structure in HTTP requests

The application layer serves the user interfaces and other key purposes. It is the OSI model layer which is close to the user-end. Unfortunately, application layer provides the hacker with the broadest spectrum of attack opportunities. When exploited, user data can be stolen or in many cases, the entire application can be manipulated to serve malicious purposes. There were also successful attack on critical infrastructures that exploited application layer and, e.g., paralysed the energy grid in Ukraine.

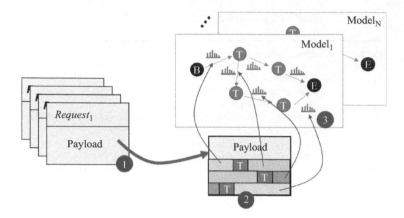

*Figure 7.3    The idea of extracting the structure model from a series of requests.
First, request are collected (1). Afterwards, common byte sequences
(indicated as T) are extracted (2). Finally, the model is constructed
using as a graph structure (3)*

Currently, various business services are now offered online in the form of variety of client–server applications. This is also the case of public administration and healthcare institutions. However, the threat of cyberattack on that bodies has become more and more serious over the last years. As it is reported in 2016 IBM X-Force Cyber Security Intelligence Index [7], healthcare domain is at the top of the list of the most threatened industries, even more, exposed on the data breaches than a financial, transportation, and governmental services. According to [8], three out of seven most serious data breaches in 2015 were related to the healthcare sector, and more than 100 million records from the healthcare databases were breached in 2016 [7].

HTTP is one of the most frequently used communication protocols in the application layer since it is a reliable mean enabling communication between computers in distributed networks and meets requirements of current web services. It is a request-response plain-text protocol. Basically, the request is a type of method that can be called (executed) on a resource uniquely identified by URL address. There are different types of methods that (among others) allow performing CRUD (Create, Read, Update, and Delete) operations. Other protocols using HTTP for transportation exhibit different structures of the payload. For example, the structure sent via plain HTML form will be different from JSON-RPC call.

In our approach, we define token as a sequence of bytes that appears in different requests. Clearly, requests sent by an application to a server will cluster together in groups, which will share common elements (e.g. parameters names, names of actions or name of resources that given action is executed). These common elements are of our interest as these will later help us to reconstruct the structure of the payload.

After generation of the tokens, we are able to apply genetic algorithm (GA) which aligns tokens for further processing and decision. In order to build the HTTP request model, we have to solve the challenge of selecting appropriate subset of tokens and their order. In our case, the single token represents the item. To each of the tokens, we assign the value and mass which represents the position of token in a sequence. It is worth to add that in the current implementation, we prefer longer tokens over the shorter ones. The limit is determined by the analysed sequences. More formally, the problem is challenged by the following problem:

$$\underset{x}{\text{maximise}} \quad C(x) = \sum_{i=0}^{n} v_i x_i$$

$$\text{subject to} \quad \sum_{i=0}^{n} w_i x_i \leq W, \ x_i \in \{0, 1\}. \tag{7.1}$$

To solve the above optimisation task, we propose to use the GA with the classical binary chromosome encoding schema and one point crossover. The chromosome in our algorithm represents the candidate solution. It is reflected by the string of bits (1 indicates that given token is chosen to build the structure of request, while 0 is used to reject a given token).

We use the GA as follows:

1. The population is initialised randomly. The chromosome length is determined by the number of tokens identified during the extraction procedure.
2. The fitness of each chromosome is measured. Individuals are ordered by fitness values.
3. Two chromosomes are selected randomly from the population.
4. Selected chromosomes are subjected to the crossover procedure.
5. The procedure is terminated (and individual with the best fitness is selected) if maximal number of iterations is exceeded; otherwise, it goes back to step 2.

The next step after the tokens are identified is the algorithm to describe the sequences between tokens using their statistical properties. Hereby we apply machine-learning algorithms to decide if the requests represented by tokens are anomalous or not. We have proposed to build histograms of characters.

## 7.4.2 Evolutionary approach for content validation

Usually, the EAs that mimic the biological evolution or social behaviour of the species from nature have been proposed to find near-optimum solutions to difficult optimisation challenges. Some of the widely known EAs in the literature are GAs, ant colonies, particle swarm, firefly algorithms, or shuffled frog leaping.

A practical implementation is proposed in [9], where authors implemented a GA to learn IF-THEN rules of the firewall from the historical data. Authors first extracted the relevant features describing Transmission Control Protocol/Internet Protocol (TCP/IP) connections using the Principal Component Analysis (PCA) technique, and then they encoded the rules as chromosomes within the typical GA framework. In [10], authors used the GA to increase the detection of insider threats on the basis of the fuzzy-classifier.

In one of our own previous works [11], we proposed the new anomaly detection method. It was designed to detect Structured Query Language (SQL) injection attack and worked on the basis of the GA for determining anomalous queries. Our proposed solution incorporated the GA implemented as a variant of social behaviour of species. The individuals in the population explored the lines in the log files that were generated by the SQL database. In our model, each individual delivers a generic rule (which was a regular expression) that describes the visited line of the log. The proposed algorithm is divided into the following steps:

- Initialisation. The line from the log file is assigned to each individual. Each newly selected individual is compared to the previously selected one in order to avoid duplicates.
- Adaptation phase. Each individual explores the fixed number of lines in the log file (the number is predefined and adjusted to obtain reasonable processing time of this phase).
- Fitness evaluation. The fitness of each individual is evaluated. The global population fitness as well as rule level of specificity is taken into consideration, because we want to obtain the set of rules that describe the lines in the log file.
- Crossover. Randomly selected two individuals are crossed over using algorithm for string alignment. If the newly created rule is too specific or too general, it is dropped in order to keep low false positives and false negatives.

Our method is based on the modified Needleman–Wunsch algorithm [12]. It was invented in order to find the best possible match between various DNA sequences. The idea is to find best match between two sequences by inserting gaps into the sequences. Such approach can be used not only for DNA but also, for example, for text strings and the logs, which are analysed by our system. The penalty is assigned for each gap (and for mismatch), while for correct matches, an award is given.

Therefore the task for the Needleman and Wunsch algorithm is to search for the best possible alignment between two sequences (it is the one with highest award). From anomaly detection point of view, the parts where gaps are inserted can in fact be the points of injections. We describe those with regular expressions using the following heuristics:

- The character sequences are encoded as [a-zA-Z]+ if they contain letters only.
- The character sequences are encoded as [0-9]+ if they contain numbers only.
- The sequences can also be encoded using both of the mentioned above sequences (e.g. [a-zA-Z0-9]+).
- Whenever encoded character sequences contain special characters (e.g. whitespace, brackets, etc.), those are included into the regular expression accordingly.

The fitness function used to evaluate each individual takes into account the effectiveness of the particular regular expression (number of times it fires), the level of specificity of such a rule, and the overall effectiveness of the whole population. The level of specificity indicates the balance between number of matches and number of gaps. This parameter enables the algorithm to penalise these individuals that try to find general rule for significantly different queries like SELECT and INSERT.

*Table 7.3    Effectiveness of different methods*

|  | True positives (%) | False positives (%) |
|---|---|---|
| $\chi^2$ (no structure extracted) | 33.2 | 0.1 |
| $\chi^2$ with our method | 91.1 | 0.7 |
| Our method with RF | 91.90 | 0.7 |

The fitness is computed using the following cost function:

$$E(i) = \alpha \sum_{j\in(I-i)} E_f(j) + \beta E_f(i) + \gamma E_s(i) \qquad (7.2)$$

In this formula, the $\alpha,\beta,\gamma$ are constants that normalise the overall score and balance the each coefficient importance. $E_f$ indicates of regular expression (number of times the rule fires) and $E_s$ indicates the level of specificity. The level of specificity indicates balance between number of matches and number of gaps.

### 7.4.3  Results

The proposed and described method based on the practical application of the GA achieves very good results. In fact, the reported results are better than state-of-the-art methods that also used the benchmark database called CSIC [13]. The results are provided in Table 7.3.

## 7.5  The concept of lifelong and nature-inspired machine learning

Originally, lifelong learning was stated as a sequence of learning tasks that need to be solved using the previous knowledge stored in previously learnt classifiers [14]. According to [15,16], theoretical considerations on lifelong learning are relatively widely described in the literature, in particular, in the light of growing popularity of machine-learning approaches and applications.

However, scientific communities usually put more attention to aspects of learning based on well-known knowledge domains and well-labelled training datasets, while approaches to lifelong learning (or "learning to learn") without observed data, e.g. to perform new, future tasks are not yet very popular. In [17], one of the first attempts to describe the model of lifelong learning can be found. The author introduced a formal model called inductive bias learning, that can be applied when the learner is able to learn novel tasks drawn from multiple, related tasks from the same environment. Those considerations focused only on the finite-dimensional output spaces, and mainly on linear machines rather than nonlinear ones, in contrary to [18] work, additionally extending earlier research with algorithmic stability aspects. In [19], there is proposed an approach to the problem of learning a number of different target functions over time, with assumptions that they are initially unknown for the learning system and that they share commonalities. Different approaches to solve this sequence of tasks include transfer learning [20], MTL, supervised, semi-supervised, reinforcement learning [21], and unsupervised techniques. There are also works defining strong theoretical foundations for LML concept. Particularly, in [16], authors worked on a Probably Approximately Correct (PAC)-Bayesian generalisation bound applied for lifelong learning allowing quantification of relation between expected losses in future-learning tasks and average losses in already observed (learned) tasks. Majority of the approaches so far assume that problem representation is not changing (i.e. feature space). However, recent works increasingly consider that also the underlying feature space can be shifting. To overcome different approaches, solutions such as changing kernels for feature extraction [22], changing latent topics [23], or the underlying manifold in manifold learning [24,25] are proposed. The hybrid intelligent systems paradigm addresses naturally all the challenges of LML such as learning new tasks while preserving knowledge of the previous ones. In fact, classifier ensemble management resembles some of the algorithms proposed for lifelong learning. For example, critical aspect of the lifelong learning systems is the ability to detect the task shift, which is quite similar to concept drift detection [26] and can be tackled by hyper-heuristics [27]. To deal with debatable cases in ensemble learning and to increase transparency in such debatable decisions, our hypothesis is that argumentation could be more effective than current resolution methods. Moreover, recent work on hybrid classifiers has demonstrated promising results of using an argumentation-based conflict resolution instead of voting-based methods for debatable cases in ensemble learning [28], showing that the hybridisation of ensemble learning and argumentation fits the decision patterns of human agents.

In the next section, we propose the practical application of lifelong learning framework to solve cyber security problems such as intrusion, anomalies, and cyberattacks detection.

## 7.5.1    The LML in cyber security

The concept of task, that appears in many formal definitions [15] of LML model, seems to be hard to match with many real life set-ups. For example, when considering telecommunication network monitoring for cyber security purposes, it is often difficult to distinguish when a particular task finishes and the subsequent one starts i.e. when a different family of attacks have started. Therefore, lifelong learning approach fits very well with the reality in cyber security domain.

In practice, while designing and developing intelligent systems for anomaly and cyber threats detection, one can draw following conclusions:

- When it comes to the cyber security and cyberattacks detection, there is no single classifier or IDS system that will allow recognising all kinds of attacks. Also the same system (even if learnt to detect the same type of attacks) have to be learnt again when changing the monitored network (topology, services, characteristics, etc.). In that regards, we will need transfer learning mechanism that will allow us to learn to detect attack B from knowledge learnt for attack A.

- There is an overlap of knowledge that intelligent and adaptive system will need to be aware of. One can leverage this both to facilitate learning of new tasks and improving the effectiveness, when executing the old ones. Using again the cyber security example, IDS learnt in one network will use already established knowledge to detect attacks in another new network in a more accurate way (than without lifelong learning approach).

## 7.5.2 Mathematical background behind LML

The ELLA framework [29] defines the lifelong learning problem as a series of supervised learning tasks, where each task $Z^{(t)} = (f^{(t)}, X^{(t)}, Y^{(t)})$ is defined by training data $X^{(t)}$, training labels $Y$, and prediction function (called in this paper also as a base learner) $f^{(t)} : X^{(t)} \rightarrow Y^{(t)}$.

The ELLA framework assumes that in each iteration, the training algorithm may receive a batch of labelled data for some task $t$ (a new one or previously trained). Moreover, it is assumed that number of task is large, and thus the ELLA algorithm must be scalable. As stated in [29], ELLA framework achieves equivalent accuracy to batch MTL [30], has faster learning times, and is able to train the model online.

ELLA framework uses parametric model to represent task-specific prediction function $f^{(t)}(x) = f(x, \theta^{(t)})$. The parameters $\theta$ are linear combination of a so-called shared basis $L$, in the way that $\theta^{(t)} = Ls^{(t)}$.

The optimisation goal of the ELLA framework is to minimise the predictive loss over all training tasks. Formally, the objective function is defined as

$$e(L) = \frac{1}{T} \sum_{t=1}^{T} \min_{s^{(t)}} \left\{ \frac{1}{n_t} \sum_{i=1}^{n_t} \mathcal{L} \left( f(x_i^{(t)}; Ls^{(t)}), y_i^{(t)} \right) + \mu \|s^{(t)}\|_1 \right\} + \lambda \|L\|_2^2 \quad (7.3)$$

However, to reduce the complexity related to the outer summation (over the number of training tasks $T$), the authors of the framework proposed to optimise $s^{(t)}$ only when training on task $t$. Moreover, the inner summation is approximated with the second order Taylor expansion around the optimal single task model. Therefore, the final objective function is defined as

$$g(L) = \frac{1}{T} \sum_{t=1}^{T} \min_{s^{(t)}} \left\{ \frac{1}{n_t} \|\theta^{(t)} - Ls^{(t)}\|_{D^{(t)}}^2 + \mu \|s^{(t)}\|_1 \right\} + \lambda \|L\|_2^2 \quad (7.4)$$

where $\theta^{(t)} = \min_{\theta} (1/n_t) \sum_i^{n_t} \mathcal{L} \left( f(x_i^{(t)}; \theta), y_i^{(t)} \right)$ is the optimal single task model and $D^{(t)}$ is the Hessian of the loss function evaluated at $\theta^{(t)}$. The optimisation process of the ELLA framework has following steps:

1. Using the base learner, optimal model parameters $\theta^{(t)}$ are calculated for a task $t$.
2. Using the current basis $L$, the model parameters vector $\theta^{(t)}$ is reconstructed in the way that $\theta^{(t)} = Ls^{(t)}$, where

$$s^{(t)} = \arg\min_{s^{(t)}} \left( \mu \|s^{(t)}\|_1 + \|\theta^{(t)} - Ls^{(t)}\|_{D^{(t)}}^2 \right) \quad (7.5)$$

3.  The updated matrix $L$ is calculated using the $s^{(t)}$ from a previous step, solving the convex optimisation problem:

$$L = \arg\min_{L} \left( \lambda \|L\|_2^2 + \frac{1}{T} \sum_{1}^{T} (\|\theta^{(t)} - Ls^{(t)}\|_{D^{(t)}}^2) \right) \tag{7.6}$$

From the optimisation point of view, formula (7.12) can be solved using LASSO (least absolute shrinkage and selection operator) regression method. On the other hand, to find the optimal $L$, one can first null the gradient and obtain the following formula:

$$\lambda L + \frac{1}{T} \sum_{1}^{T} D^{(t)} \left( \theta^{(t)} - Ls^{(t)} \right) s^{(t)^T} = 0 \tag{7.7}$$

It can be shown that this is a special case of linear matrix equation of form $AXB = C$,

$$B = \lambda I + \frac{1}{T} \sum_{1}^{T} D^{(t)} s^{(t)} s^{(t)^T} \tag{7.8}$$

and the constant $C$ is equal to

$$C = \frac{1}{T} \sum_{1}^{T} D^{(t)} \theta^{(t)} s^{(t)^T} \tag{7.9}$$

Thus, using the Kronecker product notation and the vectorisation operator, the equation can be rewritten as

$$(B^T \otimes A) vec(x) = vec(C) \tag{7.10}$$

which has closed-form solution in the form $H^{-1}b$, where

$$H = \lambda I + \frac{1}{T} \sum_{1}^{T} \left( s^{(t)} s^{(t)^T} \right) \otimes D^{(t)} \tag{7.11}$$

and

$$b = \frac{1}{T} \sum_{1}^{T} vec \left( s^{(t)^T} \otimes \left( \theta^{(t)} D^{(t)} \right) \right) \tag{7.12}$$

## 7.5.3  *Data imbalance*

The problem of data imbalance has recently been deeply studied [31,32] in the areas of machine learning and data mining. In many cases, this problem negatively impacts the machine-learning algorithms and deteriorates the effectiveness of the classifier. Typically, classifiers in such cases will achieve higher predictive accuracy for the majority class, but poorer predictive accuracy for the minority class.

This phenomenon is caused by the fact that the classifier will tend to bias towards the majority class. Therefore, the challenge here is to retain the classification effectiveness even if the proportion of class labels is not equal. The imbalance of labels in our case of cyber security is significant. We may expect that only a few machines in the network will be infected and produce malicious traffic, while the majority will behave normally. In other words, most data contains clean traffic, while only a few data samples indicate malware.

The solutions for solving such a problem can be categorised as data-related and algorithm-related. The methods belonging to the data-related category use data over-sampling and under-sampling techniques, while the algorithm-related ones introduce a modification to training procedures. This group can be further classified into categories using cost-sensitive classification (e.g. assigning a higher cost to majority class) or methods that use different performance metrics (e.g. Kappa metric).

Cost-sensitive learning is an effective solution for class imbalance in large-scale settings. The procedure can be expressed with the following optimisation formula:

$$\hat{\beta} = \min_{\beta} \left\{ \frac{1}{2} ||\beta||^2 + \frac{1}{2} \sum_{i=1}^{N} C_i ||e_i||^2 \right\} \tag{7.13}$$

where $\beta$ indicates classifier parameters, $e_i$ the error in classifier response for $i$th (out of $N$) data samples, and $C_i$ the importance of the $i$th data sample. In cost-sensitive learning, the idea is to give a higher importance to the minority class, so that the bias towards the majority class is reduced.

Similarly, the above optimisation can be expressed using a matrix notation, as it is shown below:

$$\hat{\beta} = \min_{\beta} \left\{ (Y - X\beta)^T C (Y - X\beta) + \lambda ||\beta||^2 \right\} \tag{7.14}$$

Setting the gradient to zero, it is easy to show that the closed form formula for finding the optimal $\beta$ is

$$\hat{\beta} = \left( \frac{I}{\lambda} + X^T C X \right)^{-1} X^T C Y \tag{7.15}$$

Therefore, the Hessian matrix for weighted linear classifier will also have closed-form solution $X^T C X$.

## 7.5.4   Practical application of LML concept

For the evaluation, we have used the CTU-13 dataset [5] and the same experimental setup as its authors (to be able to compare our results). This dataset includes different scenarios which represent various types of attacks including several types of botnets. Each of these scenarios contains collected traffic in the form of NetFlows. The data was collected to create a realistic test bed. Each of the scenarios has been recorded in a separate file as a NetFlow using CSV notation. Also each NetFlow in the data set is augmented with a label (Table 7.4).

Before using the ELLA framework to train the base classifiers, the raw NetFlows are processed in order to produce feature vectors. The procedure is detailed in the Section 7.3.2 (Table 7.5).

*Table 7.4    Effectiveness of compared methods*

| Compared methods | Detection ratio | False positive ratio | Accuracy |
|---|---|---|---|
| B-ELLA | $0.809 \pm 0.093$ | $0.017 \pm 0.002$ | $0.896 \pm 0.046$ |
| B-STL | $0.745 \pm 0.104$ | $0.034 \pm 0.001$ | $0.856 \pm 0.052$ |
| ELLA | $0.250 \pm 0.121$ | $0.000 \pm 0.000$ | $0.625 \pm 0.061$ |
| STL | $0.002 \pm 0.018$ | $0.000 \pm 0.0001$ | $0.501 \pm 0.009$ |

*Table 7.5    Balanced ELLA: per-task effectiveness*

| Task | Detection ratio | False positive ratio | Accuracy |
|---|---|---|---|
| 1 | $0.400 \pm 0.291$ | $0.025 \pm 0.003$ | $0.688 \pm 0.145$ |
| 2 | $0.300 \pm 0.085$ | $0.027 \pm 0.000$ | $0.636 \pm 0.042$ |
| 3 | $0.800 \pm 0.245$ | $0.040 \pm 0.002$ | $0.880 \pm 0.122$ |
| 4 | $0.944 \pm 0.045$ | $0.015 \pm 0.004$ | $0.964 \pm 0.022$ |
| 5 | $0.960 \pm 0.080$ | $0.003 \pm 0.002$ | $0.978 \pm 0.039$ |
| 6 | $0.839 \pm 0.072$ | $0.001 \pm 0.000$ | $0.919 \pm 0.036$ |
| 7 | $1.000 \pm 0.000$ | $0.010 \pm 0.001$ | $0.995 \pm 0.000$ |
| 8 | $0.988 \pm 0.025$ | $0.007 \pm 0.000$ | $0.990 \pm 0.013$ |
| 9 | $0.862 \pm 0.096$ | $0.037 \pm 0.001$ | $0.912 \pm 0.048$ |
| 10 | $1.000 \pm 0.000$ | $0.008 \pm 0.005$ | $0.996 \pm 0.003$ |
| | $0.809 \pm 0.093$ | $0.008 \pm 0.005$ | $0.996 \pm 0.003$ |

Each of the scenario in the CTU dataset is considered as a separate task. For the evaluation purposes, we have generated ten random splits of the dataset in order to produce training and the test datasets.

## 7.5.5    Remarks on effectiveness

The experimental results are presented in Tables 7.1 and 7.2. Table 7.1 contains the comparison of results obtained with the B-ELLA algorithm, balanced single task learner (STL) algorithm, the original ELLA algorithm, and imbalanced STL algorithm. The results shows that balancing the base classifier embedded within the ELLA frameworks yields great improvements over the other compared method.

In Table 7.2, we have presented the effectiveness of B-ELLA method at a single task level. The average detection ration is 80%, while the ratio of false positives (alarms) is less than 1%. As presented in Tables 7.1 and 7.2, the achieved results are very promising and motivate further work on both balanced lifelong learning systems (B-ELLA) and their application to cyber security.

## 7.6 Conclusions

The goal of this chapter was to provide the overview of the nature-inspired machine-learning solutions applied to solve cyber security problems. We presented our own nature-inspired methods and implementations, mainly dedicated to detect cyber-attacks in the application layer. Such attacks are very often obfuscated and the traditional means to protect IT systems and networks are not effective. Our goal was to demonstrate how nature inspired solutions might help in such situations and how they can be practically applied to counter emerging cyber threats. Most of our work, also presented here, is focused on anomaly detection which needs to be deployed besides traditional signature-based solutions. In this chapter, we have discussed and presented the practical solutions for the evolutionary-based optimisation techniques, collective intelligence, and techniques that mimic social behaviour of species. The proposed GAs improve detection of SQL injection attacks and anomalies within HTTP requests. We believe that the bio-inspired techniques will further find many applications in cyber security domain since, as proven, the readiness of such technology has increased and practical implementations give the promising results.

## References

[1]   Azab M, Eltoweissy M. MIGRATE: Towards a Lightweight Moving-Target Defense Against Cloud Side-Channels. In IEEE Security and Privacy Workshops (SPW), San Jose, CA. 2016;p. 96–103.

[2]   Lucas B, Fulp EW, John DJ, *et al.* An Initial Framework for Evolving Computer Configurations as a Moving Target Defense. In Proceedings of the 9th Annual Cyber and Information Security Research Conference (CISRC). 2014;p. 96–103.

[3]   Kewley D, Fink R, Lowry J, *et al.* Dynamic Approaches to Thwart Adversary Intelligence Gathering. In Proc of the DARPA Information Survivability Conference & Exposition II (DISCEX '01). 2001;p. 176–185.

[4]   Brown J, Anwar M, Dozier G. Detection of Mobile Malware: An Artificial Immunity Approach. In 2016 IEEE Security and Privacy Workshops (SPW), San Jose, CA. 2016;p. 74–80.

[5]   Garcia S, Grill M, Stiborek J, *et al.* An empirical comparison of botnet detection methods. Computers & Security. 2014;45:p. 100–123.

[6]   Garcia S. Identifying, Modeling and Detecting Botnet Behaviors in the Network. PhD Thesis. 2014.

[7]   IBM. 2017 IBM X-Force Threat Intelligence Index. IBM; 2017. Available from: https://www.ibm.com/security/data-breach/threat-intelligence-index.html.

[8]   Healthcare IT News. 7 Largest Data Breaches of 2015. Healthcare IT News; 2015. Available from: http://www.healthcareitnews.com/news/7-largest-data-breaches-2015.

[9]    Bankovic Z, Stepanovic D, Bojanic S, *et al.* Improving network security using genetic algorithm approach. Computers & Electrical Engineering. 2007;33:p. 438–451.

[10]   Bin Ahmad M, Akram A, Asif M, *et al.* Using genetic algorithm to minimize false alarms in insider threats detection of information misuse in windows environment. Mathematical Problems in Engineering. 2014;2014:p. 418–425.

[11]   Choraś M, Kozik R, Puchalski D, *et al.* Correlation Approach for SQL Injection Attacks Detection. Herrero Á, Snášel V, Abraham A, *et al.* (Eds.), Advances in Intelligent and Soft Computing. Springer, Berlin, Heidelberg. 2012;p. 177–186.

[12]   Needleman SB, Wunsch CD. A general method applicable to the search for similarities in the amino acid sequence of two proteins. Journal of Molecular Biology. 1970;48:p. 443–453.

[13]   Torrano-Giménez C, Prez-Villegas A, Alvarez G. The HTTP Dataset CSIC 2010; 2010. Available from: http://users.aber.ac.uk/pds7/csicdataset/csic2010http.html.

[14]   Chen Z, Bing L. Lifelong Machine Learning in the Big Data Era. In IJCAI 2015 tutorial. 2015.

[15]   Pentina A, Lampert CH. Lifelong Learning with Non-i.i.d. Tasks. In Advances in Neural Information Processing Systems. 2015.

[16]   Pentina A, Lampert CH. A PAC-Bayesian Bound for Lifelong Learning. In ICML. 2014.

[17]   Baxter J. A model of inductive bias learning. Journal of Artificial Intelligence Research (JAIR). 2000;12:p. 149–198.

[18]   Maurer A. A model of inductive bias learning. Algorithmic Stability and Meta-Learning. 2005;7:p. 967–994.

[19]   Balcan M, Blum A, Vempala S. Efficient Representations for Life-Long Learning and Autoencoding. In Workshop on Computational Learning Theory (COLT). 2015;p. 191–210.

[20]   Segev N. Learn on source, refine on target: a model transfer learning framework with random forests. IEEE Transactions on Pattern Analysis and Machine Intelligence. 2015;39:p. 1–10.

[21]   Ammar HB, Tutunov R, Eaton E. Safe policy search for lifelong reinforcement learning with sublinear regret. The Journal of Machine Learning Research (JMLR). 2015;37:2361–2369.

[22]   Qiu Q, Sapiro G. Learning transformations for clustering and classification. Journal of Machine Learning Research. 2015;16:p. 187–225.

[23]   Chen Z, Liu B. Topic Modeling using Topics from Many Domains, Lifelong Learning and Big Data. In Proceedings of the 31st International Conference on Machine Learning. 2014;32:p. 703–711.

[24]   Yang HL, Crawford MM. Domain adaptation with preservation of manifold geometry for hyperspectral image classification. IEEE Journal of Selected Topics in Applied Earth Observations and Remote Sensing. 2016;9:p. 703–711.

[25]   Yang HL, Crawford MM. Spectral and spatial proximity-based manifold alignment for multitemporal hyperspectral image classification. IEEE Transactions on Geoscience and Remote Sensing. 2016;54:p. 56–64.

[26]   Widmer G, Kubat M. Learning in the presence of concept drift and hidden contexts. Machine Learning. 1996;23:p. 69–101.

[27]   Sim K, Hart E, Paechter B. A lifelong learning hyper-heuristic method for bin packing. Evolutionary Computation. 2015;23:p. 37–67.

[28]   Contiu S, Groza A. Improving remote sensing crop classification by argumentation-based conflict resolution in ensemble learning. Expert Systems with Applications. 2016;64:p. 269–286.

[29]   Ruvolo P, Eaton E. An efficient lifelong learning algorithm. International Conference on Machine Learning, 2013.

[30]   Ruder S. An overview of multi-task learning in deep neural networks. CoRR – Computing Research Repository Journal. 2017. arXiv:1706.05098

[31]   Kozik R. Choraś M. Solution to Data Imbalance Problem in Application Layer Anomaly Detection Systems. Martinez-Alvarez F, Troncoso A, Quintian H, Corchado E (Eds.), Hybrid Artificial Intelligent Systems, HAIS 2016, LNAI. Springer, Cham. 2016;p. 441–450.

[32]   Woźniak M. Hybrid Classifiers: Methods of Data, Knowledge, and Classifiers Combination. Springer Series in Studies in Computational Intelligence. Springer, Berlin, Heidelberg. 2013.

## Chapter 8

# Artificial intelligence and data analytics for encrypted traffic classification on anonymity networks

*Khalid Shahbar[1] and Nur Zincir-Heywood[1]*

This chapter studies and analyzes multilayer-encryption anonymity networks. Multilayer-encryption anonymity networks aim to enable users to access the Internet without being tracked or traced. To achieve this, they use technologies to resist traffic analysis and network surveillance—or at least make it more difficult. However, for various reasons—from network operations to security—network packet and flow analysis have been employed to identify multilayer-encryption anonymity networks. In the following, we discuss the usage of traditional and nature-inspired artificial intelligence and data analytics techniques to classify encrypted anonymity network traffic.

## 8.1 Introduction

The main goal of anonymity networks is to provide a certain level of privacy to their users when they access different applications and services such as web browsing on the Internet. Anonymity networks employ a multilayer-encryption-based approach to achieve this goal. On multilayer-encryption anonymity networks, messages between sender and receiver pass through multiple stations (computers/nodes) with multiple layers of encryption. Each station only knows the information necessary for passing the message. In this way, they aim to avoid the destination station to link the message to the original sender. The onion router (Tor), JonDonym and I2P networks are some of the well-known examples of anonymity networks. The growth of the amount of information collected by services websites such as search engines, web servers or even Internet service providers for improving the services, data analysis, security enhancement, advertisement or other reasons increased the demand and growth of multilayer-encryption anonymity networks. Not only this, but these networks facilitated reporting any kind of illegal activities to the authorities without the fear of exposing the reporter's identity, provided space with freedom to express thoughts and ideas and ensured the person's (user's) privacy for the journalists' (or other) sources.

[1]Dalhousie University, Computer Science, Canada

On the other hand, the environment of multilayer-encryption anonymity networks offered the possibility of performing harmful activities with little or no probability of tracing back the source. For example, a botnet is one of the threats to Internet users which infect computers to gain control through the botmaster. One way of communication between the bot and the botmaster is to use a Command and Control (C&C) server where frequently the bots contact the C&C server to get instructions from the botmaster. By blocking the server, the bots could not communicate with the botmaster anymore. Therefore, botnet developers seek more complex methods to communicate without being detected such as using peer-to-peer (P2P) architectures, domain generation algorithms or IP flux. Moreover, one of the attempts to build undetectable communication on the botnet is by using multilayer-encryption anonymity networks [1,2]. One of the known examples of such cases is the 64-bit Zeus botnet that could use hidden services on the Tor network to communicate anonymously between the bots and the botmaster. The hidden services are one of Tor's services which allow anonymously hosting servers (such as a web server) on the Tor networks. The user accessing the server does not know the IP address of the server. Thus, the C&C server could be hosted anonymously on the Tor network. The Zeus botnet has not been the only attempt to implement an anonymous botnet over multilayer-encryption anonymity networks, there has been much research and multiple reports about using such an anonymous environment to hide botnet communications. Multilayer-encryption anonymity networks are blocked in some countries. Consequently, different obfuscation techniques are employed by some of these networks to bypass the censorship restrictions and enable access to the anonymity network by the users. In this book chapter, we aim to analyze and discuss multilayer-encryption anonymity networks using traditional as well as nature-inspired artificial intelligence techniques. The rest of the chapter is organized as the following: anonymity networks and the related works are discussed in Section 8.2. Traditional and nature-inspired artificial intelligence and data-analytics techniques as well as publicly available anonymity network datasets for encrypted traffic identification are introduced in Section 8.3. Evaluations using these techniques at the circuit, flow and packet level are presented in Section 8.4. Finally, conclusions are drawn and future works are discussed in Section 8.5.

## 8.2    Background

Studies of anonymity networks have dealt with multiple aspects. For example, part of these studies worked on the improvement and enhancement of the anonymity networks' performance. Others focused on analyzing vulnerabilities and performing attacks. The following subsections summarize the anonymity networks and the studies performed on them.

### 8.2.1    Anonymity networks

Multilayer-encryption anonymity networks relay users' traffic through multiple stations on the network on the way to their final destination. Furthermore, messages between sender and receiver pass through these stations with multiple layers of encryption. To the best of authors' knowledge, the most popular anonymity networks are I2P,[1] JonDonym[2] and Tor [3].

## 8.2.1.1   I2P

The I2P network is different from the other anonymity networks because it is designed as a private network. The users mainly communicate within the network. However, through outproxies, they can communicate with the services and users outside of the I2P network as well. I2P is decentralized and therefore has a distributed network database—netDb—using the Kademlia algorithm [4]. The information that users get from the netDb enables them to build tunnels. Each user builds two tunnels: inbound and outbound. The inbound tunnels are used to receive messages and the outbound tunnels are used to send messages on the P2P I2P network. The default configuration of the users' agents (clients) enables bandwidth participation, which means in addition to building his/her tunnels, the user can also participate in building other users' tunnels. The tunnels consist of two or more routers based on the client configuration and the tunnel type. Thus, when the user participates in building tunnels, his/her role could be the first or the last or one in the middle in forming the tunnel. This makes it harder to separate a specific user's tunnels from the other participating tunnels. I2P uses the concept of garlic routing,[3] where layered encryption is implemented in addition to binding multiple messages together. The messages within the I2P network are encrypted end-to-end as long as the end-systems are within the I2P network. However, when the user communicates with an end-system that is outside of the I2P network using an outproxy, then the encryption is not end-to-end. By default, the user within the network transfers their data and that of other users where the user's machine functions as a resource for the network. The users' contributions in passing the network data are restricted by passing the data only within the I2P network. A different configuration is required when a user wants to pass the I2P traffic to an end-system outside of the I2P network (outproxy). The number of outproxies in the I2P network is limited.

## 8.2.1.2   JonDonym

JonDonym, which is also known as AN.ON, is a network of mix cascades (paths) to provide anonymity to the users based on multilayer encryption.[4] The cascade consists of mix servers which could be paid or free. Currently, a user could choose from five free cascades and eleven paid cascades on the JonDonym network. Only one active connection to one cascade is possible during the user's connection to the JonDonym network. The path that the user's data takes is fixed based on the chosen cascade. To choose another path, the user has to start a new connection to the JonDonym. Multilayered encryption is used during the communication between the user and the last mix, which ensures that even the mixes cannot access the user's data. When the

[1] https://geti2p.net/en/faq#eepsite
[2] Jondonym InfoService. https://anonymous-proxy-servers.net/en/help/infoservice.html
[3] Garlic routing. https://geti2p.net/en/docs/how/garlic-routing
[4] Project: AN.ON anonymity. http://anon.inf.tu-dresden.de/index

connection is established, the IP address that is visible to the websites is the IP address of the last mix. JonDo is the client software that connects the user to the JonDonym network. Each Hypertext Transfer Protocol (HTTP) request will create a connection from the browser (JonDoFox) with the client software JonDo. The JonDoFox browser can generate multiple connections with the JonDo. All these connections are multiplexed into one connection to the first mix server, which receives connections from multiple users. All the users' connections are then multiplexed into one Transmission Control Protocol/Internet Protocol (TCP/IP) connection to the second mix and it continues using this approach till the last mix in the cascade. The user gets the information about the cascades from the InfoService, and the last mix sends the users' requests to cache proxies. Infoservice stores the information about the available cascades, the number of users and the mix status.[5]

### 8.2.1.3    The onion router

Tor project is a publicly available software that enables users to anonymize their identities while they use the Internet. The Tor network requires volunteers to run their machines as relay nodes to forward other users' traffic through Tor. Circuits and cells are the major components for Tor communication. The circuit is a virtual path from the user's machine to the last relay. The cell is the data block in Tor. The user's data is divided into small fixed size (512 bytes) Cells. There are two types of cells: control cells and relay cells. The control cells direct the relays what to do with the cell. The relay cells contain the user's data. On the Tor network, the user starts by establishing a virtual circuit. This circuit consists of three relays. A directory server is used to get the addresses of available relays (routers) and their keys to encrypt the data. User data is encrypted with three layers of encryption. First, the data is encrypted with the key of the last relay (exit router), then the middle relay and finally, by the first relay (entry router). This way, the entry router only knows the source of the data. The middle routers only know where to get the encrypted data and where to send them, but nothing about the source of the data or the destination. Finally, the exit router knows the destination of the data but knows nothing about the source. This ensures that the whole path is not known by any of the three nodes (routers) on the Tor network. After the circuit is established between the user and the exit relay, the user is ready to send the data into RELAY DATA cells. The circuit path changes each time the user makes a connection. The bandwidth of the relays and the policy of the exit relay play a key role in selecting the best circuit path. The user and the relay use encrypted Transport Layer Security (TLS) connections to communicate.

### 8.2.2    *Measuring anonymity*

Measuring the level of anonymity is a challenge for a number of reasons. One reason is the difference in the design and the goal of each anonymity network. In addition, the anonymity level is not directly quantifiable compared to other network traffic measurements as delay, bandwidth, volume, etc. Ries *et al.* [5] evaluated five

---

[5]Jondonym InfoService. https://anonymous-proxy-servers.net/en/help/infoservice.html

anonymization tools with regard to performance, usability, anonymity, network relia-bility and cost. The evaluated tools were Tor, I2P, JonDonym, Perfect Privacy and Free proxies. The performance factors used to evaluate and rank these tools were round trip time, inter-packet delay variation and throughput. Additionally, they used installation, configuration and verification of the anonymization connection as factors to define the usability of these tools. The anonymization of the tools was evaluated by using the rankings of the ability of an adversary to perform de-anonymization attacks against these tools. It should be noted here that these evaluations were limited to specific scenarios. Abou-Tair *et al.* [6] examined the usability of four anonymity tools (Tor, JonDo, I2P and Quicksilver) during the installation phase. They detailed the installa-tion process of these tools, applying four tasks to test the installation phase: success of installation, success of configuration, confirmation of anonymization and the ability to disable anonymization. To test the usability of these tools, the authors used eight guidelines taken from Clark [7], which focused on the user's ability to perform the four tasks mentioned above. Wendolsky *et al.* [8] compared Tor and JonDonym from the user's perspective, based on the performance and the number of users. Latency and bandwidth were used to measure the performance, and the results showed that Tor performs unpredictably based on the time of day. In contrast, JonDonym showed more consistent performance. The above studies focused mainly on evaluating anonymity services based on their performance or usability, where anonymity was not the focus of the evaluation. On the other hand, there are studies where measuring anonymity was the main goal. The idea of measuring anonymity is synchronized with the pro-posed ideas to develop anonymity by passing the message between the sender and the receiver through multiple stations until it reaches the final destination [9]. This aims to separate the ability of an attacker to link the sender and the receiver, even if they communicate over a channel observed by the attacker. To anonymize against such a threat model, Chaum [10] presented the concept of the anonymity set, in which the set is the total number of participants in the anonymity service which may include the sender. When the size of the set is increased, the anonymity level is con-sidered to increase as well. Consequently, if the size of the anonymity set is one, then there is no anonymity, and the attacker can identify the sender easily. Serjantov and Danezis [11] developed the concept of the anonymity set by using the information-theoretic metric based on anonymity probability distribution. Díaz *et al.* [12] also used an information-theoretic model to evaluate the anonymity level of a system under a particular attack scenario. The model aimed to evaluate the anonymity level of a sys-tem by finding the level of information the attacker can statistically gain to connect a user of the anonymity system to his messages. Shannon's definition of entropy is used to calculate this gain. Even though the above researches have studied measuring the anonymity levels, they all focused on the problem from the perspective of linking the message to the sender. However, there could be other factors that could be used in measure the anonymity as well. To this end, Shahbar *et al.* proposed five factors [13]. These include (i) the level of information available for the service provider, (ii) block-ing and obfuscation options, (iii) application and anonymity, (iv) authority and log files collected and (v) available threat models. They compared these factors with each other to rank their weights. They demonstrated that these weighted factors could be applied for measuring the anonymity level under different anonymity network use cases.

### 8.2.3    Identification of anonymity networks by infrastructure

Tor bridges[6] are special Tor nodes where their addresses are not announced publicly like the other nodes (relays). A Tor user can connect to the Tor network using Tor bridges in the cases where the IP addresses of normal nodes are blocked by censorship. The user can get up to three addresses of Tor bridges per day by sending an email or by accessing Tor bridges websites. Ling *et al.* [14] used two different methods to reveal the addresses of Tor bridges. The first method was using bulk email accounts to request many bridge IP addresses daily. The second method was to insert one router in the Tor network and let the directory server to choose it as a middle router. Then, they use this middle router to obtain the addresses of the other bridges. They discovered 2,365 bridges by using the email method and 2,369 bridges by using only one middle router for 14 days. Li *et al.* [15] classified Tor nodes depending on their uptime. Nodes which have a higher bandwidth and longer uptime considered as super nodes. Their hypothesis was that these super nodes could decrease the anonymity of the Tor network. They demonstrated the decrease in anonymity in a simulation using 3,000 nodes, Tor algorithms, a directory server and a path selection protocol. Results showed that when the super nodes were targeted with higher rates than the normal nodes, the failure on the network increased. Liu *et al.* [16] presented four methods to discover the I2P routers. They discovered about 95% of all the I2P routers in their 2-week experiment. On the other hand, Herrmann and Grothoff [17] presented an attack to determine the identity of the HTTP hosting router on the I2P network. They used a combination of three types of routers to identify the hosting router. Wilde [18] found out that censorship in China uses a scanner to discover where the bridge is. To do so, a connection from the user to the bridge must take place first. Should inspecting the packets show that that there is a connection using the Tor protocol, the scanner starts to search through random Chinese IP addresses. If a certain IP address seems to be a bridge, then it establishes a connection to this IP address. If the connection is a success, then this is a bridge IP and its ports are blocked. Tor connections could be recognized because Tor uses a special Tor TLS client hello message. The result of Wilde's work was used by Winter *et al.* [19] to get more details about how China blocks the Tor networks. They discovered that once the bridge IP address was discovered by the Chinese authorities, it was blocked within 15 min. In this case, the blocking was continuous as long as the scanners could connect to the bridge, otherwise the blocking was removed. They also found that only 1.6% of Tor relays could be reached from China. The packet inspection for Tor connections is applied only for the connection from China to the outside world. In summary, research on the identification of multilayer-encryption anonymity networks by discovering the network's infrastructure include (i) compromising parts

---

[6]Tor bridges. https://www.torproject.org/docs/bridges.html.en

of the anonymity network and/or (ii) employing resources outside of the anonymity network to track the anonymity network resources or users.

## 8.2.4   Identification of applications and services on the anonymity network

AlSabah *et al.* [20] used machine-learning algorithms to classify the application used by Tor's users. The applications are Browsing, Streaming and BitTorrent (BT). Given that Tor traffic is encrypted, they used the circuit level and the cell level information for the classification. The classification included online and off-line methods. The best result they achieved in the off-line classification was 91%, whereas the best results achieved in the online classification was 97.8%. It should be noted here that in order to employ this method, access to Tor nodes and code is necessary. Wagner *et al.* [21] proposed Torinj—a malware code that uses an image tag injection and a semi-supervised learning algorithm for identifying the number of users on Tor and their web-browsing activities. All HTTP sessions were collected for further analysis. To classify each user's session, a label propagation algorithm was used to relate a flow to a specific user. In this case, a compromised or controlled Tor exit node is necessary to collect the traffic flow between the users and the web servers. Moreover, for this attack to work, the user should not be able to detect/track the image tag. Panchenko *et al.* [22] used a support vector machine (SVM) classifier with the websites' fingerprints to show that Tor and JonDonym do not provide total anonymity. The volume, time and direction of the traffic were the features in SVM. They could reach up to 70%–80% accuracy to detect the websites. However, they require special features such as (i) the size of the packet that contains the acknowledgement control character (ACK) between the sender and the receiver; (ii) a special text label that shows the change in the direction of the packet and is used to sum up all packets in the same direction; (iii) an HTML marker for distinguishing between each HTML request and to check the size of the requested site; (iv) rounded transmitted bytes for the number of all transmitted packets in both directions (rounded in increments of 10,000); (v) the number of markers group the packet size for all the packets of a flow in one direction; (vi) the number of each site's packets in both directions; (vii) the percentage of incoming packets; and (viii) the number of packets. Barker *et al.* [23] used a simulated network to differentiate between encrypted traffic and Tor traffic. The simulated network contained three directory servers and fifteen relays. Different machine-learning algorithms (Random Forest, J4.8 and AdaBoost) were employed via WEKA. Their results showed that approximately 90% of the HTTP and HTTPS traffic on the Tor network could be detected with a false positive (FP) rate of 3.7%. Timpanaro *et al.* [24] proposed a monitoring architecture for the I2P network to describe how it is used. The applications that the monitoring architecture can identify were limited to web browsing and I2PSnark. On the other hand, Egger *et al.* [25] presented several attacks that could be implemented against the I2P network. They claimed that their attacks against the I2P network could reveal the services that the I2P user accesses, the time of access and the time spent using the service. Westermann and Kesdogan [26] presented two attacks against the DonDonym network: the redirection attack and the replay attack. The redirection attack aims to discover the websites which the user visited. The attacker controls a web server and tries to redirect the user to this controlled web server. The replay attack aims to correlate the user's HTTP request with a web server. The attacker monitors and records the user's communications with the first mix. Shahbar *et al.* analyzed the network flow behaviors using machine-learning algorithms to identify (i) the multilayer-encryption anonymity networks, (ii) the applications running on them [13,27] and (iii) the traffic generated by obfuscation tools which some of the multilayer-encryption anonymity networks have employed to avoid blockage or detection [28].

Furthermore, among the anonymity networks analyzed in this work, Tor is also used deploy hidden services. Ling *et al.* studied the Tor network to collect information on the hidden services [29]. In their work, several entry routers, a client, a rendezvous point and a central server were necessary to relate the hidden server with its Tor features. This requires the controlled client to connect to the hidden server while the entry routers are watching/tracking for different cell types that have special combinations. The important part for detecting the hidden server is to let it choose a specified entry router which depends on the number of entry routers and the bandwidth available. Biryukov *et al.* analyzed the security of hidden services by exploring the amount of information that could be obtained about hidden services on the Tor network [30]. The analysis included finding the popularity of any hidden service, denying access to the hidden service by impersonating the responsible hidden service directory and revealing the IP addresses of the hidden services. Two main techniques were used in this analysis. The first was inserting nodes with an incorrectly announced high bandwidth. The second technique used Sybil attacks to inject nodes to be selected as hidden service directories. In their analysis, they controlled the hidden service directory of the Silk Road hidden service and the DuckDuckgo hidden service. After controlling these directories for several days, they were able to get the number of requests for the hidden service descriptor. Elices *et al.* used a time fingerprint to mark a hidden server on the Tor network [31]. They estimated the time required for the HTTP request to get a response from a hidden web server on the Tor network by using the data field in the HTTP response message with statistical models.

## 8.3    Data analytics for encrypted network traffic

As discussed earlier, anonymity networks employ layers of encryption to provide the anonymity to users and hidden services. This makes any analysis of the traffic very challenging. As discussed above, most of the previous research requires the use of marking techniques for the users' traffic and/or compromising/operating resources within the anonymity network or resources at the final destination (such as web servers). This in return means that these approaches are limited to traffic passing through the compromised/operated resources. To overcome this challenge, more recently we have seen some research employing different artificial intelligence and data analytics techniques to analyze malicious (botnets, etc.) usage of anonymity networks. The following presents the datasets and algorithms employed in these studies.

## 8.3.1 Datasets

One of the difficulties that face researchers in the anonymity networks field is the lack of an anonymity dataset. In some of the anonymity research papers, the used data is collected in a simulated environment [23,32]. Others used data that were collected by the researchers themselves [16,20,26,33]. The most common issue that researchers face in the anonymity field is that these anonymity tools provide anonymity to the users; thus collecting the data and making it publicly available might affect the privacy of the users of the anonymity tools. Consequently, the research in this field ends up using data collected from a simulated environment or collected by the researchers themselves. The traffic on the anonymity networks relies on passing the users' data through multiple stations on the network (nodes, for example). These stations pass traffic for multiple users; collecting the data from these stations will include traffic for other users which means that usually the research needs to run a station (node) and modify the way they collect the data to include only their traffic. Anon17 [13] is a dataset for three anonymity tools: Tor, JonDonym and I2P. This data is prepared and made publicly available without affecting the privacy of the users. To this end, the IP addresses of the users have been removed. The payload information is used only for statistical measurement and then is removed. This is because Anon17 aims to provide a publicly available anonymity dataset which could be used to study the aforementioned anonymity tools. The dataset includes several applications used on these anonymity tools as well as several obfuscation techniques that are used on some of these tools. Consequently, the dataset could be used for multiple types of research. More detailed information regarding Anon17 could be found in [13].

## 8.3.2 Artificial intelligence and data analytics

In the following, we summarize the traditional and nature-inspired artificial intelligence techniques that are mostly used in the literature for encrypted traffic data analysis.

### 8.3.2.1 Decision tree—C4.5

C4.5 [34] decision tree is a well-known traditional artificial intelligence technique. The goal of C4.5 is to create a model that predicts the value of a target variable by learning simple decision rules inferred from the data features. It is supervised machine-learning algorithm where a tree is build. C4.5 decision tree defines a relation between the instances, attributes and classes on a training set of data. The trained tree can then be used to classify unseen instances based on the relationships built during the training phase. The tree divides the training set into subsets starting at a root node. The root node represents an attribute that split the training set best. The tree then split again on another decision node based on another attribute. The split decision is based on entropy and information gain. The entropy of a training data ($T$) with $c$ classes is calculated as shown in the following equation:

$$Entropy(T) = \sum p_i log_2 p_i \qquad (8.1)$$

The probability $p_i$ is calculated as the number of instances in class $i$ over the total number of instances, $c$. The information gain of an attribute $A$ on the training data $(T)$ is calculated as shown in (8.2) where $v$ represents the possible values of attribute $A$. $T_v$ is a subset of the training data $(T)$ that has the value $v$ of attribute $A$. More detailed information on C4.5 could be found in [34].

$$InformationGain(T, A) = Entropy(T) - \sum \frac{T_v}{T} Entropy(T_v) \qquad (8.2)$$

### 8.3.2.2    Random forests

Random forests [35] is an ensemble of trees working together as a supervised classifier to predict an outcome. Again, this algorithm can be categorized as a traditional artificial-intelligence technique. Random forests build multiple decision trees, then for a given input, a vote decides the classification results based on the majority of the results of the trees. A tree on the random forests ensemble is built by selecting a set of features randomly at each node and splitting on these features. The instances are selected randomly from the training set with replacement. The rest of the training set (out of bag) is used to calculate the error of the tree. One of the features that random forests offers is to avoid over-fitting. At the same time, random forests lacks the interpretability that C4.5 offers. More detailed information on random forests could be found in [35].

### 8.3.2.3    Naive Bayes

Naive Bayes [36] is a supervised classier known for its simplicity to build. It is a popular traditional artificial intelligence technique from the family of probabilistic classifiers. Naive Bayes is based on Bayes' theorem with an assumption of independence between features. The assumption that a feature $(x)$ on a class $(c)$ is independent from other features is called the class conditional independence. If the likelihood $P(x|c)$ is the probability of feature $x$ given class $c$, $P(c)$ is the prior probability of class $c$ and $P(x)$ is the prior probability of feature $x$. Then, the posterior probability of class $c$, given feature $x$, $P(c|x)$ is calculated as

$$P(c|x) = \frac{(P(x|c)P(c))}{P(x)} \qquad (8.3)$$

The likelihood function $P(x|c)$ is evaluated for the observed data $x$ (feature) and it is shown as a function of $c$ [37].

### 8.3.2.4    Bayesian network

Bayesian network (belief network) [38] is a probabilistic graphical model which uses a combination of graph theory and probability theory. The graph describes the relations among random variables shown as nodes on the graph. Links on the graph represent the relation (probabilistic dependencies) among the random variables. Bayesian uses a directed acyclic graph model where links are directed to show the causality among the random variables. Nodes on the graph are represented as well by conditional probability distribution which in a discrete model can be represented as a conditional probability table for quantifying the relations among the nodes. To demonstrate how the Bayesian Network represents a direct graph for a probability distribution [37], assume a joint distribution $p(a, b, c)$ for the variables $a$, $b$ and $c$. The joint distribution $p(a, b, c)$ can be rewritten using the following probability rule:

$$p(a, b, c) = p(c|a, b)p(b|a)p(a) \tag{8.4}$$

The above equation could be represented by a graph where the three random variables are represented by three nodes. The conditional probabilities are represented by links on the graph between the nodes. For example, the $p(c|a; b)$ could be presented by links from node $a$ and node $b$ to $c$. A link from node $a$ to node $b$ will present $p(b|a)$. The graph will not show any link for $p(a)$ because it has no conditional probability. Indeed, a graph could be drawn for more than three variables. Bayesian networks have become extremely popular in early 2000s as a traditional artificial intelligence technique. They are ideal for combining prior knowledge, which often comes in causal form, and observed data.

### 8.3.2.5 Self-organizing map

The self-organizing map (SOM) is an unsupervised learning algorithm based on artificial neural networks [39]. Therefore, it is a nature-inspired artificial intelligence technique that is inspired by the way biological nervous systems, such as the brain, process information. The key element of this paradigm is the novel structure of the information processing system. It is composed of a large number of highly interconnected processing elements (neurons) working in unison to solve specific problems. In the SOM framework, the topology of the resulting neurons resembles that of the original data given the interaction between the best matching unit (BMU), updating neighborhood and annealing schedule; albeit as projected into a typically 2D topology. In practice, the SOM training process usually consists of two phases: coarse training, during which the topographic order of the SOM is formed, and fine training, for obtaining a more accurate final state with the same total number of training steps as original training procedure. The trained SOM preserves the topological properties of the input space and therefore can be used as a data analytics tool to visualize and analyze the high-dimensional data. Moreover, SOM has the ability to generalize data from the training set. Characteristics of each new input can be derived by identifying its BMU and quantization error.

## 8.3.3 Flow exporters

A computer network traffic flow is a sequence of packets from a source computer to a destination. RFC 2722 defines traffic flow as "an artificial logical equivalent to a call or connection" [40]. Flow exporter tools use the following five tuples to aggregate network packets to define a traffic flow over a given duration of time. The five tuple information includes the source IP address, the destination IP address, the source port, the destination port and the protocol of a network packet. Flow analysis employs statistical information extracted from the packet headers of a flow.

There are many flow analysis tools [40] commercially available such as Cisco NetFlow,[7] Juniper J-Flow[8] and InMon sFlow[9] or open source ones such as Softflowd,[10] Argus[11] [40], YAF,[12] Maji,[13] Tcptrace[14] and Tranalyzer.[15] Most of these tools support extracting flows from captured network traffic logs (PCAP (packet capture), tcpdump, etc.) or directly from the network. Flow analysis first requires collecting (capturing) packets (data). Then, converting these packets into flows, and finally analyzing these flows. Some of the flow analysis tools contain the flow exporter only and require a collector, others have the collector and the exporter integrated into the tool itself [40].

Even though flow analysis tools use mostly the same five-tuple to extract flow information, they differ in multiple ways such as the number of generated features, the definition of flow timeout and the ability to configure this value, the number of generated flows, the supported form of captured traffic and so on. Few of the open-source flow analysis tools have been tested for the purpose of analyzing multilayer-encryption anonymity networks. As a results, Tranalyzer has been selected for use as the flow analysis tool in our research. Once the flows are exported using Tranalyzer, information such as the source IP address, the destination IP address, source and destination port numbers as well as flow start and end times are removed from the analysis to ensure that the classification process is not biased using this information. This is important since IP addresses could be spoofed and applications could use dynamic port numbers on today's Internet. Specifically, in most of the multilayer-encryption anonymity networks, the port number is configurable. For example, Pluggable transports can be configured even to use well-known ports such as port 80 or port 443.

## 8.4 Empirical evaluations

In this section, we present empirical evaluations performed on the publicly available ANON17 dataset using the traditional (conventional) and nature-inspired artificial intelligence and data-analytics-based approaches. In these evaluations, the following well-known performance metrics are used. The first metric Accuracy is defined as the summation of true positive (TP) and true negative (TN) values divided by the total number of instances (N), as shown in (8.5). For example, when measuring the accuracy of the classification for the browsing application, TP is the total number of instances classified correctly as browsing. TN is the total number of instances classified correctly as non-browsing. As shown in (8.6), precision is the ratio of TP

---

[7]Cisco Netow. http://www.cisco.com/c/en/us/products/ios-nx-os-software/ios-net

[8]Juniper J-Flow. https://www.juniper.net/documentation/enUS/junose10.3/information-products/topic-collections/swcong-ip-services/id-37225a.html

[9]InMon sFlow. http://www.inmon.com/technology/index.php

[10]Softowd. http://www.mindrot.org/projects/soft

[11]https://qosient.com/argus/

[12]http://tools.netsa.cert.org/yaf/index.html

[13]https://research.wand.net.nz/software/maji.php

[14]http://www.tcptrace.org/

[15]Tranalyzer2. http://tranalyzer.com/

divided by the summation of TP and FP. If the classifier classifies an instance as browsing and the right type is not browsing then this is considered as an FP measure. The opposite occurs when the classier classifies an instance to be non-browsing while it is a browsing instance, then this is a false negative (FN). Equation (8.7) defines the recall as the division of TP over the summation of TP and FN. The relation between the precision and recall is shown in (8.8).

$$Accuracy = \frac{TP + TN}{N} \tag{8.5}$$

$$Precision = \frac{TP}{TP + FP} \tag{8.6}$$

$$Recall = \frac{TP}{TP + FN} \tag{8.7}$$

$$F - Measure = \frac{2 \times Precision \times Recall}{Precision + Recall} \tag{8.8}$$

These evaluations employ flows, circuits and packets to understand and to model the encrypted traffic on the aforementioned anonymity networks. These evaluation aim to shed light into the amount of information that could be extracted from the encrypted traffic, and the possibility of identifying different behaviors of the applications (services) or hosts on the multilayer-encryption anonymity networks.

The circuit level and the flow level approaches both give a high level of classification accuracy. Even though the machine-learning algorithms used in this research are similar in both approaches, the same algorithm gives a different accuracy depending on the approach used. The details of these results are discussed in the following sections.

## 8.4.1   Using circuit level information

In this approach, the circuit level classification uses the attributes of the cell as described in [20,27]. The part of the ANON17 dataset used consists of 60% browsing, 20% streaming and 20% BT activities. Table 8.1 shows the results for the off-line circuit level classification. In this case, accuracy reached to 100% when using the C4.5 classier with 70% of the instances as the training set. When 10-fold cross-validation was used, the best accuracy was 94.9% using the random forest classier. In Table 8.1 (and thereafter), "split" refers to the results obtained on the test dataset (30% of the data) using the model generated from the training dataset (70% of the data). On the other hand, "CV" refers to the results obtained using the 10-fold cross-validation on the whole data.

## 8.4.2   Using flow level information

While the cell-based approach could only be used for the Tor anonymity network, flow-based approach could be used for all the aforementioned anonymity network.

*Table 8.1    Circuit level classification results using distribution of classes similar to [20] on Tor network*

| Classifier | Partition | Accuracy | F-measure | | |
|---|---|---|---|---|---|
| | | | Browsing | Streaming | BitTorrent |
| Bayesian networks | Split | 0.986 | 0.99 | 0.97 | 1 |
| | CV | 0.877 | 0.89 | 0.82 | 0.98 |
| Naive Bayes | Split | 0.986 | 0.99 | 0.97 | 1 |
| | CV | 0.945 | 0.95 | 0.88 | 1 |
| C4.5 | Split | 1 | 1 | 1 | 1 |
| | CV | 0.932 | 0.94 | 0.83 | 1 |
| Random forest | Split | 0.972 | 0.98 | 0.97 | 0.96 |
| | CV | 0.949 | 0.96 | 0.88 | 1 |

### 8.4.2.1    Experiments with I2P traffic

The I2P network uses separate tunnels for the outgoing and incoming traffic. The tunnels are used to send and receive messages, to communicate with the netDb and to manage the tunnels. Consequently, the messages which travel through the user's tunnels do not always represent only the messages traveling between the users. Given that the tunnels contain these control and user messages mixed together and the incoming/outgoing tunnels are separated, it becomes important to understand the effect of such a design in terms of anonymizing the traffic flow behaviors of a user's activities. In this section, we study (i) the ability to identify the type of application a user is using; (ii) the effect of bandwidth participation on the aforementioned ability; (iii) the effect of bandwidth participation on the ability to profile a user and (iv) regardless of the application used, the ability to profile the user and to distinguish between different users by observing the tunnels. To this end, we employ the part of the ANON17 dataset that includes the browsing, chat and file downloading applications running on the I2P network. The reason behind choosing these applications is that they are the most used ones on the I2P [41]. It should be noted here that before analyzing the traffic, all the IP addresses and payloads are removed. In addition, the encryption used on I2P anonymity network keeps the users' data private. The analysis of the collected data includes tunnel-based data analysis, applications and user-based data analysis and tunnel clustering as described below.

*Tunnel based data analysis*
Here, the focus is on differentiating application tunnels from exploratory and participating tunnels.[16] Exploratory tunnels are used for management (administration traffic of the I2P network) and also for testing purposes. The participating tunnels are used for relaying other users' traffic. Table 8.2 shows the results from the perspective

---

[16]I2P: Peer profiling and selection. https://geti2p.net/en/docs/how/peer-selection

*Table 8.2   Binary classier based on traffic flows on the I2P tunnels*

|  | TP-rate | FP-rate | TN-rate | FN-rate |
|---|---|---|---|---|
| Application tunnels | 0.875 | 0.288 | 0.712 | 0.125 |
| Others (exploratory and participating tunnels) | 0.712 | 0.125 | 0.875 | 0.288 |
| Accuracy | | 82.04% | | |

*Table 8.3   Tunnel based traffic flow analysis for different applications on the I2P*

|  | TP-rate | FP-rate | TN-rate | FN-rate |
|---|---|---|---|---|
| I2Psnark | 0.661 | 0.033 | 0.967 | 0.339 |
| jIRCii | 0.778 | 0.084 | 0.916 | 0.222 |
| Eepsites | 0.531 | 0.143 | 0.857 | 0.469 |
| Others (exploratory and participating tunnels) | 0.755 | 0.152 | 0.848 | 0.245 |
| Accuracy | | 70.3% | | |

of a binary classification problem in which one represents the "applications" and the other represents "other" shared traffic. In this case, the analysis shows that these two groups of traffic can be differentiated in I2P tunnels with up to 82% accuracy on the test data, which was unseen by the classier during the training phase.

The other goal is to analyze for what purpose a tunnel might be used. In this case, if an application is running, then the tunnels related to that application are extracted and labeled. In the experiments performed for this goal, the following three applications on the I2P network are employed: I2Psnark, jIRCii and Eepsites. The Eepsites tunnels, which are the client tunnels, might be used for another application on the I2P network. They also stay alive all the time that the user is online. On the other hand, the I2Psnark (jIRCii) tunnels stay alive as long as the user uses the application. The shared client tunnels could be used for I2Psnark (if the user changes the setting) but the default setting is for using the jIRCii tunnels. The exploratory and participating tunnels stay alive as they are. Aiming to shed light on the purpose for which a tunnel might be used is a very challenging problem. However, the results still achieved 70% accuracy (on the unseen test data) in predicting the potential purpose of a tunnel on the I2P network by just analyzing the traffic flow features, Table 8.3.

*Applications and user-based data analysis*
In this part of the analysis, the effect of bandwidth participation on the I2P network was examined using two scenarios: (i) traffic profiling and (ii) user profiling. In the traffic profiling scenario, we explore whether an attacker could identify the different applications running in encrypted I2P tunnels. Specifically, we want to understand the effect of the existence of exploratory and participant tunnels on the ability to identify application types. On the other hand, in the user profiling scenario, we explore whether an attacker could identify different users of the I2P tunnels based on

their behaviors. In this case, we want to understand the effects of shared bandwidth on this ability. What follows is a summary of the results of both scenarios in addition to the effect of the protocol separation – TCP vs UDP (Transmission Control Protocol vs User Datagram Protocol) on the test data. Table 8.4 shows the accuracy per application for the traffic and user profiling when the amount of shared bandwidth is 80%, which is the default case on the I2P network. The accuracy measures the percentage of correctly classified instances out of all instances. It should be noted here that even though both the IP addresses and the port numbers were not used in the analysis, the result could achieve 80%–86% accuracy for differentiating one user from another. However, it seems like differentiating traffic behavior in terms of protocols is much more challenging.

The configuration for the empirical evaluations presented in Table 8.3 was achieved under the default bandwidth configuration (300 kbps in, 60 kbps out) of an I2P client. Under this setting, the bandwidth participation is 80% which is equal to 48 kbps. Then, to observe and study the effect of the bandwidth participation on I2P anonymity, we changed this setting to 0%. In both cases, the floodfill was disabled. Table 8.5 presents the results of the analysis of the traffic and user profiling when the bandwidth participation was set to 0%. Effectively, this does not allow any bandwidth sharing. In this case, while the accuracy of user profiling decreases, the accuracy of traffic profiling increases. Intuitively, this was expected because with no traffic

*Table 8.4   Summary of application and user profiling on I2P*

| 80% Bandwidth participation | | |
| --- | --- | --- |
| | **Number of instances (flows)** | **Accuracy (%)** |
| Traffic profiling | 190,000 | 47.4 |
| Traffic profiling TCP only | 61,453 | 61.7 |
| Traffic profiling UDP only | 128,547 | 56.3 |
| User profiling | 189,906 | 81.8 |
| User profiling TCP only | 62,882 | 86.0 |
| User profiling UDP only | 127,024 | 79.8 |

*Table 8.5   Summary of application and user profiling on I2P without bandwidth sharing*

| 0% Bandwidth participation | | |
| --- | --- | --- |
| | **Number of instances (flows)** | **Accuracy (%)** |
| Traffic profiling | 195,081 | 73.7 |
| Traffic profiling TCP only | 40,075 | 65.6 |
| Traffic profiling UDP only | 155,006 | 75.7 |
| User profiling | 195,081 | 66.7 |
| User profiling TCP only | 40,075 | 81.7 |
| User profiling UDP only | 155,006 | 63.2 |

sharing, finding patterns in the tunnels is more likely to happen. However, under the same conditions, identifying users without using IP addresses and port numbers becomes more challenging.

### 8.4.2.2   Experiments with JonDonym traffic

JonDonym anonymity network has two forwarding options: TCP/IP forwarding and Skype forwarding. Moreover, the JonDo client software includes an option for the user to enable the obfuscation. This obfuscation on JonDonym counts on forwarding the connection to another JonDonym user, instead of connecting directly to the network to obfuscate the connection to the JonDonym network. This motivated us to study the traffic flow behavior of the forwarding techniques used on JonDonym. To this end, JonDonym traffic without any obfuscation will be studied first and then will be compared with the TCP/IP and Skype forwarders used on JonDonym.

The JonDonym data employed in this analysis is the JonDonym part of the Anon17 dataset. In addition, the LBNL/ICSI dataset [42] was employed as the background traffic. It contains network traces collected from more than 100 h of activities for several thousands of hosts. The data size is 11 GB. The data is publicly available in a PCAP form. The data is distributed over several small PCAP files. For this research, a total of 211,370 flows was extracted from approximately 1.5 GB of data. Table 8.6 shows that JonDonym traffic flows could be distinguished from the other background traffic with a high accuracy.

The background data contains a vast number of applications and protocols. Some of the applications or the protocols appear just a few times while others have a high number of appearances in the data. Thus, in the next part of the analysis, instead of having just one class (Background), the data is studied using 12 classes (HTTP, HTTPS, IMAPS, SNMP, NETBIOS-SSN, DNS, POP3, LPD, EPMAP, SMTP, SSH (Secure SHell) and Other). Table 8.7 shows the results of this analysis. In this case, the overall accuracy is decreased by 2% compared with the previous analysis.

Users on the JonDonym network also have the option of using the TCP/IP forwarding to connect to JonDonym through other users of the JonDonym network. To perform this, a user needs to solve a strong CAPTCHA (completely automated public turing test to tell computers and humans apart) before establishing the connection. The other option is to use the Skype forwarding option. In this case, a user needs to have a Skype account to log in. Then, the user selects Skype as the forwarding option. The JonDo client sends the connection to Skype to forward the connection to the JonDonym network. Table 8.8 shows the results on the analysis of JonDonym, Skype Forwarder, TCP/IP Forwarder and the background applications.

*Table 8.6   JonDonym flow analysis results*

|  | **TP-rate** | **FP-rate** | **Precision** | ***F*-measure** |
|---|---|---|---|---|
| JonDonym | 0.997 | 0 | 1 | 0.998 |
| Background (LBNL/ICSI) | 1 | 0.003 | 1 | 1 |
| Accuracy | | | 99.99% | |

*Table 8.7  Background applications and JonDonym flow analysis*

|  | TP-rate | FP-rate | Precision | *F*-measure |
|---|---|---|---|---|
| HTTP | 0.986 | 0.013 | 0.981 | 0.984 |
| HTTPS | 0.897 | 0.004 | 0.919 | 0.908 |
| IMAPS | 0.88 | 0.001 | 0.900 | 0.888 |
| SNMP | 0.998 | 0.000 | 0.996 | 0.997 |
| NETBIOS-SSN | 0.974 | 0.002 | 0.971 | 0.972 |
| DNS | 0.997 | 0.000 | 0.998 | 0.998 |
| POP3 | 0.982 | 0.000 | 0.969 | 0.975 |
| LPD | 0.998 | 0.000 | 0.998 | 0.998 |
| EPMAP | 0.993 | 0.000 | 0.988 | 0.990 |
| SMTP | 0.948 | 0.000 | 0.961 | 0.955 |
| SSH | 0.455 | 0.000 | 0.613 | 0.522 |
| OTHER | 0.973 | 0.006 | 0.976 | 0.974 |
| JonDonym | 0.999 | 0.000 | 1.000 | 1.000 |
| Accuracy | | 97.99% | | |

*Table 8.8  Background applications and obfuscated JonDonym flow analysis*

|  | TP-rate | FP-rate | Precision | *F*-measure |
|---|---|---|---|---|
| HTTP | 0.986 | 0.012 | 0.982 | 0.984 |
| HTTPS | 0.900 | 0.004 | 0.920 | 0.910 |
| IMAPS | 0.888 | 0.001 | 0.906 | 0.897 |
| SNMP | 0.997 | 0.000 | 0.997 | 0.997 |
| NETBIOS-SSN | 0.973 | 0.002 | 0.970 | 0.972 |
| DNS | 0.998 | 0.000 | 0.998 | 0.998 |
| POP3 | 0.979 | 0.000 | 0.977 | 0.978 |
| LPD | 0.998 | 0.000 | 0.998 | 0.998 |
| EPMAP | 0.992 | 0.000 | 0.991 | 0.992 |
| SMTP | 0.956 | 0.000 | 0.958 | 0.957 |
| SSH | 0.437 | 0.000 | 0.591 | 0.502 |
| OTHER | 0.974 | 0.006 | 0.977 | 0.975 |
| JonDonym | 0.999 | 0.000 | 1.000 | 1.000 |
| SKYPEFWD | 0.992 | 0.000 | 0.983 | 0.988 |
| TCPIPFWD | 0.988 | 0.000 | 0.996 | 0.992 |
| Accuracy | | 98.04% | | |

## 8.4.2.3  Experiments with Tor traffic

In this section, we explore the behavior of Tor network using flow analysis under two scenarios, specifically when Tor anonymity system is used without obfuscation and when it is used with obfuscation, i.e., Tor pluggable transports.

*Table 8.9    Flow level classification results using uniformly distributed classes of application on Tor network*

| Classifier | Partition | Accuracy | F-measure | | |
|---|---|---|---|---|---|
| | | | Browsing | Streaming | BitTorrent |
| Bayesian networks | Split | 1 | 1 | 1 | 1 |
| | CV | 0.992 | 0.99 | 0.99 | 1 |
| Naive Bayes | Split | 0.947 | 0.98 | 0.91 | 0.94 |
| | CV | 0.933 | 0.98 | 0.90 | 0.93 |
| C4.5 | Split | 0.987 | 0.98 | 0.98 | 1 |
| | CV | 0.972 | 0.96 | 0.98 | 0.98 |
| Random forest | Split | 0.987 | 0.98 | 0.98 | 1 |
| | CV | 0.988 | 0.99 | 0.98 | 0.99 |

*Table 8.10    Flow level classification results using distribution of classes similar to [20] on Tor network*

| Classifier | Partition | Accuracy | F-measure | | |
|---|---|---|---|---|---|
| | | | Browsing | Streaming | BitTorrent |
| Bayesian networks | Split | 1 | 1 | 1 | 1 |
| | CV | 1 | 1 | 1 | 1 |
| Naive Bayes | Split | 1 | 1 | 1 | 1 |
| | CV | 0.957 | 0.99 | 0.89 | 0.91 |
| C4.5 | Split | 0.976 | 0.98 | 1 | 0.93 |
| | CV | 0.993 | 0.99 | 1 | 0.98 |
| Random forest | Split | 1 | 1 | 1 | 1 |
| | CV | 0.986 | 1 | 0.96 | 0.96 |

*Tor without obfuscation*

In this scenario, the dataset consists of the uniform distribution of three classes: browsing, streaming and BT. The reason these three classes are chosen to be able to compare this analysis with the circuit-based analysis performed in section. Even though the amount of data transferred by the streaming and the BT circuits is larger than the browsing circuits, they are similar in terms of the number of flow instances. Thus, the number of flows is approximately the same for each class. Table 8.9 shows the results when using the uniform distribution of the three classes. The results are 88%–100% when using 70% of the instances as the training set. When using 10-fold cross-validation, results are 86%–99%. It should be noted here that the dataset employed in [20] consists of 60% browsing instances, 20% streaming instances and 20% BT instances. They generated such a dataset to mimic the traffic distributions of Tor users [20]. To make the results of this flow-level-based approach comparable to theirs, the data is down-sampled to the same percentages. In this case, Table 8.10, the results still show high accuracy in both the split and the cross-validation cases.

The circuit level classification requires access to the network connection traffic between the user's machine and the Tor relay. Moreover, in the circuit level classification, access to the relay itself is required. That means the circuit level classification has its limitations in terms of who can use it. On the other hand, the flow level classification can be performed on any captured data. From the availability perspective, flow level classification is easier to apply compared to the circuit level classification. The tools used in the flow level classification are available online. These tools include traffic capturing (such as Tcpdump) and flow exporters for generating the traffic flows (such as Tranalyzer). Capturing data in circuit level classification which is ready to be classified by the learning algorithms requires additional effort compared to the flow level classification data. Tor itself and Tor's tools can be used to provide such information about the usage of Tor's circuits and cells. However, both of these provide a limited amount of information. For instance, the cell statistics feature (CELL STAT) which was introduced in Tor version 0.2.5.2-alpha is only available when Tor is working in the test mode.[17] STEM[18] can provide the user with information about Tor as well. It provides a library for the user to communicate with Tor using the Tor control protocol. It can generate useful information about the circuit, bandwidth usage, etc. However, Tor, again, needs to be working in the test mode.

*Tor with obfuscation*

Tor pluggable transport systems[19] work to provide access to the Tor network in adversarial environments. They achieve this by focusing on obfuscating the traffic or hiding the content of the packets in a way that makes it hard for the adversaries when to detect the connection to the bridges or using deep packet inspection. In this study, the flow analysis technique is used to explore the resistance of Tor pluggable transports, i.e., Tor with obfuscation, against such adversaries.

Given that pluggable transports obfuscates (hides) the Tor traffic using different protocols, the part of the ANON17 data analyzed for this purpose include HTTP, HTTPS, SSH, BT and encrypted BT traffic as background traffic. Table 8.11 presents the number of flows for the background and the pluggable transports traffic for this analysis.

Again, we use Tranalyzer as the flow exporter and the C4.5 decision tree as the classifier. For this encrypted traffic analysis, we first explored whether obfuscated and encrypted Tor traffic could be differentiated from other encrypted or not encrypted network traffic. The results for this analysis is shown in Table 8.12.

Then, we explored whether different types of obfuscated and encrypted Tor traffic could be differentiated from other encrypted or not encrypted network traffic. The results for this multi-class traffic analysis is shown in Table 8.13. These results show that an adversary who has the means to perform flow analysis on Tor Traffic could achieve a high accuracy in detecting even the obfuscated Tor (pluggable transports) traffic. The pluggable transports are designed to hide or obfuscate the

---

[17] https://gitweb.torproject.org/torspec.git/tree/control-spec.txt
[18] https://stem.torproject.org/
[19] Tor pluggable transports. https://www.torproject.org/docs/pluggable-transports.html.en

*Table 8.11  Traffic employed for the analysis of Tor with obfuscation*

| Background traffic | | | | | |
|---|---|---|---|---|---|
| **Type** | **HTTP** | **HTTPS** | **SSH** | **BT** | **Encrypted BT** |
| Number of flows | 182,725 | 8,058 | 54,214 | 116,440 | 198,302 |
| Total | | | 559,739 | | |
| **Tor pluggable transports traffic** | | | | | |
| **Type** | **Obfs3** | **FTE** | **ScrambleSuit** | **Meek** | **Flashproxy** |
| Number of flows | 15,356 | 106,549 | 16,953 | 43,152 | 172,331 |
| Total | | | 354,341 | | |

*Table 8.12  Evaluation results for obfuscated Tor vs background traffic—binary classification*

| Traffic type | TP-rate | FP-rate | Precision | *F*-measure |
|---|---|---|---|---|
| Background (non-Tor) | 0.997 | 0.003 | 0.998 | 0.998 |
| Obfuscated Tor | 0.997 | 0.003 | 0.995 | 0.996 |
| Overall correctly classified instances | | 99.7% | | |

*Table 8.13  Evaluation results for obfuscated Tor vs background traffic—multi-class classification*

| | Traffic type | TP-rate | FP-rate | Precision | *F*-measure |
|---|---|---|---|---|---|
| Background (non-Tor) traffic | HTTP | 0.99 | 0.001 | 0.99 | 0.99 |
| | HTTPS | 0.94 | 0 | 0.95 | 0.95 |
| | SSH | 0.99 | 0 | 0.99 | 0.99 |
| | BT | 0.94 | 0.025 | 0.84 | 0.89 |
| | BT-Encrypted | 0.89 | 0.009 | 0.96 | 0.92 |
| Obfuscated Tor traffic | FTE | 0.99 | 0 | 0.99 | 0.99 |
| | ScrambleSuit | 0.98 | 0.001 | 0.92 | 0.95 |
| | Meek | 0.99 | 0 | 0.99 | 0.99 |
| | Flashproxy | 0.99 | 0.001 | 0.99 | 0.99 |
| | Obfs3 | 0.99 | 0 | 0.99 | 0.99 |
| Overall correctly classified instances | | | 97% | | |

content of the Tor connection, not the flow. Thus, the traffic flow analysis could identify Tor traffic even with the existence of such obfuscation techniques. For example, ScrambleSuit changes the distribution of the packet length and the inter-arrival time of the traffic, but the duration is still a factor in classifying this type of traffic. On the other hand, Obfs3 does neither change the distribution of the packet length nor the inter-arrival time. This makes the packet size an important feature that profiles the Obfs3 traffic. Moreover, Flashproxy changes the connection to the user based on the IP addresses of the Flashproxy-supported websites. Thus, in this case, the size gains more importance compared to the duration as well. These evaluations seem to indicate that pluggable transports, i.e., obfuscated Tor traffic, could be classified with a high (98%) accuracy. When the decision tree and information gain results are analyzed, the learned model shows that the most important features indicating the presence of these behaviors in the traffic are duration, number of bytes sent and maximum packet size. However, it should be noted here that the detection rate might change based on the background traffic characteristics. For example, FTE obfuscates by making the regex of the Tor encrypted traffic look like the regex of HTTPS traffic. This makes the inclusion of HTTPS traffic, in the training dataset, a very important factor for artificial intelligence/machine-learning-based classifiers.

In summary, flow analysis is used to identify both the obfuscated and the non-obfuscated traffic on the multi-layer-encryption anonymity networks, specifically I2P, JonDonym and Tor. On the I2P network, there are no obfuscation tools available yet. So our analysis of the encrypted traffic on I2P focused on the effects of tunneling and bandwidth sharing from the perspective of application and user classification. On the JonDonym network, there are two obfuscation tools, so we analyzed the encrypted traffic both with obfuscation (using each tool) and without obfuscation. In this case, we concentrated on application and as well as protocol classification. On the Tor network, there are many obfuscations tools available for users. Thus, we analyze the encrypted traffic created with each of these obfuscations tools on Tor as well as analyzing the encrypted traffic Tor generates without any obfuscation. Similar to JonDonym analysis, in this case we again focused on the application and protocol classification. In all cases, our results show that network metadata available in traffic flows do reveal enough information to classify applications and protocols with high accuracy. Similar trends and results are also obtained by Pescape *et al.* in [43].

### 8.4.3   Using packet level information

Flow-analysis-based encrypted traffic classification has satisfactory results in understanding anonymity networks even with the existence of the obfuscation techniques. However, flow analysis has its limitations as well. One of the obstacles in using flow analysis is the fact that the packets need to be aggregated to flows. Moreover, the higher the amount of data traffic and the number of features representing a flow, the higher the computational cost to export flows and extract features. In large scale networks, this may require high CPU resources and time. This was a big motivation for seeking the possibility of improving flow analysis to give better results in less time.

The anonymity networks have their way in dealing with traffic within the network. The unit that is used on the Tor network is the cell. The size of the cell is 512 bytes.

The Tor user (client) installed on the client's machine divides data sent by the client to the Tor network into fixed size cells. When these cells arrive at the transport layer and beyond, they are considered to be like any other normal traffic according to the protocol used. The cells will be packed inside packets and traverse like other packets on the network. There are research papers on studying the link between the packets and the cells. The point here is that the fixed size cells have some proportion to the number and the size of the packets. On the other hand, how applications or protocols work in general has a sort of repetition in the data flow. For example, accessing a web server starts by sending a request to the web server then waiting for the server to reply while data travels back and forth to the web server. Whenever another access to the web server is taking place, the process is repeated. This type of pattern exists to a certain level in many applications. On the anonymity network, the pattern is used as well but it is more complex. The obfuscation techniques aim to make identification of such patterns difficult. In addition, on all anonymity networks, the anonymity level is increased when there are more users. The reason behind this is the difficulty of finding patterns when the number of users is large. Also, on some of these anonymity networks, users relay data of other users in addition to their own data and messages related to managing the connection to the network.

On the anonymity networks, the users' data contains mostly overhead due to encryption operations and managing the connection to the network. This requires that the users maintain a connection to the network all the time. No matter what obfuscation technique is used to avoid inspecting packets, the aforementioned behavior cannot be hidden. ScrambleSuit aims to alter the this flow behavior between the user and the ScrambleSuit server. This produces a different pattern, but it is still identifiable. Another aspect of packets' behavior is the direction of dialog in the process of communication. For example, when watching a video stream, the direction of the data is mostly from the server to the user with little from the user to the server. The point here is that the application has its influence on the direction that the data will take back and forth.

Based on the above observations, Shahbar *et al.* proposed the following packet features to analyze the multi-layer encrypted anonymity networks traffic: maximum packet size, frequency of maximum packet size, second maximum packet size, frequency of the second maximum packet size, packet sequence and sequence speed. The authors proposed a new approach—called packet momentum—to integrate these packet features. Their results on ANON17 dataset show that the use of packet momentum to identify applications running on the anonymity networks and to identify obfuscated traffic used on anonymity networks is not only very successful (up to 98% accuracy) but also computationally very efficient. A more detailed discussion of their approach could be fund in [44].

## 8.4.4 *Nature-inspired learning for encrypted traffic analysis*

In all of the above evaluations, the results presented are obtained by well-known traditional artificial intelligence and learning techniques. These results show that these techniques tend to work well when labels, in other words, ground truth information is available for the training datasets used for this type of data analytics. However,

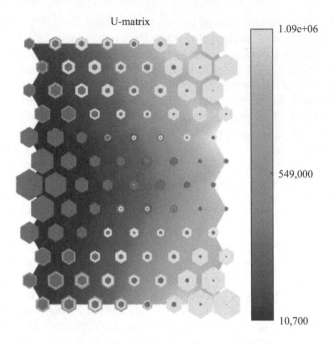

*Figure 8.1    Clustering of encrypted tunnels on the SOM*

in practice, even though network traffic data might be available to analyze, ground truth about such data may not be available, i.e., labels for network packets or network flows or circuits may not be known. In such cases, we found that nature-inspired unsupervised learning algorithms such as SOMs may be very effective to use for analyzing network traffic at all levels. Therefore, we employed SOMs to cluster and visualize the different patterns (if any), which may exist in the data of the tunnels captured in ANON17—I2P dataset. For this purpose, SOM toolbox [45] was used. Figure 8.1 presents the visualization of the data clusters on the SOM where the network traffic includes four tunnels, namely, (i) I2PSnark, (ii) jIRCii, (iii) Eepsites and (iv) exploratory and participating tunnels. In this figure, SOM is trained on unlabeled data and then to check the similarities that we know, we superimpose the four different colors to represent the four clusters after training the SOM map. In this case, the yellow hexagons represent the I2PSnark tunnels. The magenta hexagons represent the exploratory and participating tunnels. The red ones represent the jIRCii tunnels, whereas the green ones represent the Eepsite tunnels on the SOM. Based on how these clusters are distributed on the map, the Eepsite tunnels seem to overlap with the exploratory and participating tunnels, namely the magenta ones. Intuitively, this follows the process regarding how the I2P tunnels are used. The I2PSnark and the jIRCii both use separate tunnels. On the other hand, the client tunnels are the tunnels which are used for the Eepsites. Thus, if we merge the Eepsites tunnels with the

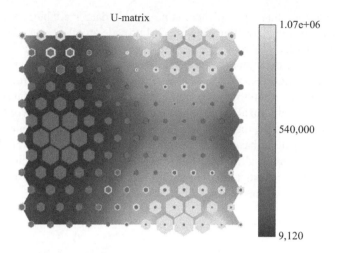

*Figure 8.2    Clustering of encrypted tunnels on the SOM after Eepsites tunnels are merged with the exploratory and participating tunnels*

exploratory and participating tunnels, the clustering of the behaviors would look like as shown in Figure 8.2. In summary, SOM results help us to understand the behavior of the tunnels in terms of which behaviors in the traffic are similar to which ones when running different applications. The evaluations show that the effect of bandwidth sharing on the anonymity level of the I2P network could be identified even if the ground truth about the data is not known as long as the similarities in the data could be identified.

## 8.5    Conclusions and future work

Multilayer-encryption anonymity networks provide privacy which has become a significant concern on today's Internet due to many attacks and privacy breaches. The anonymity and privacy these networks provide is a double-edged knife. Increasing attacks, threats and misuse of such valuable anonymity services trigger the need to identify such anonymity networks. Moreover, the implementation of the obfuscation techniques hardens the identification of such networks. Consequently, the artificial intelligence and data-analysis techniques used, the features and the data employed in the classification of encrypted traffic on such networks become very challenging. To this end, we have discussed ANON17 dataset, cell features, traffic flow features and packet features used as well as the traditional and nature-inspired artificial intelligence and data analysis techniques used in the literature. We studied the results in terms of traffic classification accuracy and efficiency. Our analysis and study indicate that traditional artificial intelligence techniques work accurately and efficiently when there is labeled data (ground truth) available to train the aforementioned techniques. On the other hand, if there is no labeled data available, nature-inspired unsupervised learning algorithm such as SOM provide an effective and clear way to analyze and visualize different behaviors in encrypted traffic flows. This in return provide an intuitive data analytics approach for network engineers and experts to understand the similarities in the data given the known behaviors in the traffic. Our research also indicates that there is more need for publicly available datasets such as Anon17. Including additional applications as they developed on anonymity networks would be a much needed research direction in the future. Furthermore, analyzing other anonymity systems based on the anonymity factors and evaluating them under adversarial conditions would increase the research community's knowledge in this area. Finally, further investigation into packet momentum type of approaches would be very necessary as our networks get faster and data gets bigger.

# References

[1]    Dennis Brown. Resilient botnet command and control with Tor. https:// www.defcon.org/images/defcon-18/dc-18-presentations/D.Brown/DEFCON-18-Brown-TorCnC.pdf, 2010.

[2]    Matteo Casenove and Armando Miraglia. Botnet over Tor: The illusion of hiding. In *International Conference on Cyber Conflict*, pages 273–282, 2014.

[3]    Roger Dingledine and Nick Mathewson. Tor path specification. https://gitweb.torproject.org/torspec.git/tree/path-spec.txt, 2016.

[4]    Petar Maymounkov and David Mazières. Kademlia: A peer-to-peer information system based on the XOR metric. In *International Workshop on Peer-to-Peer Systems*, volume 2429 of *Lecture Notes in Computer Science*, pages 53–65. Springer, 2002.

[5]    Thorsten Ries, Radu State, and Andriy Panchenko. Comparison of low-latency anonymous communication systems – Practical usage and performance. In *Australasian Information Security Conference*, pages 77–86, 2011.

[6]    Dhiah el Diehn Abou-Tair, Lexi Pimenidis, Jens Schomburg, and Benedikt Westermann. Usability inspection of anonymity networks. In *Privacy, Security, Trust and the Management of e-Business*, pages 100–109, 2009.

[7]    Jeremy Clark, Paul C. van Oorschot, and Carlisle Adams. Usability of anonymous web browsing: An examination of Tor interfaces and deployability. In *ACM Symposium on Usable Privacy and Security*, pages 41–51, 2007.

[8]    Rolf Wendolsky, Dominik Herrmann, and Hannes Federrath. Performance comparison of low-latency anonymisation services from a user perspective. In *International Symposium on Privacy Enhancing Technologies*, volume 4776 of *Lecture Notes in Computer Science*, pages 233–253. Springer, 2007.

[9]    David Chaum. Untraceable electronic mail, return addresses, and digital pseudonyms. *Communications of the ACM*, 24(2):84–88, 1981.

[10]    David Chaum. The dining cryptographers problem: Unconditional sender and recipient untraceability. *Journal of Cryptology*, 1(1):65–75, 1988.

[11] Andrei Serjantov and George Danezis. Towards an information theoretic metric for anonymity. In *International Workshop on Privacy Enhancing Technologies*, volume 2482 of *Lecture Notes in Computer Science*, pages 41–53. Springer, 2002.

[12] Claudia Díaz, Stefaan Seys, Joris Claessens, and Bart Preneel. Towards measuring anonymity. In *International Workshop on Privacy Enhancing Technologies*, volume 2482 of *Lecture Notes in Computer Science*, pages 54–68. Springer, 2002.

[13] Khalid Shahbar and A. Nur Zincir-Heywood. ANON17: Network traffic dataset of anonymity services. *Technical Report CS-2017-03*. Dalhousie University, 2017.

[14] Zhen Ling, Junzhou Luo, Wei Yu, Ming Yang, and Xinwen Fu. Extensive analysis and large-scale empirical evaluation of tor bridge discovery. In *Proceedings of the IEEE INFOCOM*, pages 2381–2389, 2012.

[15] Chenglong Li, Yibo Xue, Yingfei Dong, and Dongsheng Wang. "Super nodes" in Tor: Existence and security implication. In *ACM Annual Computer Security Applications Conference*, pages 217–226, 2011.

[16] Peipeng Liu, Lihong Wang, Qingfeng Tan, Quangang Li, Xuebin Wang, and Jinqiao Shi. Empirical measurement and analysis of I2P routers. *Journal of Networks*, 9(9):2269–2278, 2014.

[17] Michael Herrmann and Christian Grothoff. Privacy-implications of performance-based peer selection by onion-routers: A real-world case study using I2P. In *International Symposium on Privacy Enhancing Technologies*, volume 6794 of *Lecture Notes in Computer Science*, pages 155–174. Springer, 2011.

[18] Tim Wilde. Great firewall Tor probing. https://gist.github.com/twilde/da3c7a9af01d74cd7de7, January 2012.

[19] Philipp Winter and Stefan Lindskog. How the great firewall of china is blocking Tor. In *USENIX Workshop on Free and Open Communications on the Internet*, 2012.

[20] Mashael AlSabah, Kevin S. Bauer, and Ian Goldberg. Enhancing tor's performance using real-time traffic classification. In *ACM Conference on Computer and Communications Security*, pages 73–84, 2012.

[21] Cynthia Wagner, Gérard Wagener, Radu State, Alexandre Dulaunoy, and Thomas Engel. Breaking Tor anonymity with game theory and data mining. *Concurrency and Computation: Practice and Experience*, 24(10):1052–1065, 2012.

[22] Andriy Panchenko, Lukas Niessen, Andreas Zinnen, and Thomas Engel. Website fingerprinting in onion routing based anonymization networks. In *ACM Workshop on Privacy in the Electronic Society*, pages 103–114, 2011.

[23] John Barker, Peter Hannay, and Patryk Szewczyk. Using traffic analysis to identify the second generation onion router. In *IEEE/IFIP International Conference on Embedded and Ubiquitous Computing*, pages 72–78, 2011.

[24] Juan Pablo Timpanaro, Isabelle Chrisment, and Oliver Festor. Monitoring the I2P network. https://hal.archives-ouvertes.fr/hal-00653136/, December 2013.

[25] Christoph Egger, Johannes Schlumberger, Christopher Kruegel, and Giovanni Vigna. Practical attacks against the I2P network. In *International Symposium on Research in Attacks, Intrusions, and Defenses*, volume 8145 of *Lecture Notes in Computer Science*, pages 432–451. Springer, 2013.

[26] Benedikt Westermann and Dogan Kesdogan. Malice versus AN.ON: possible risks of missing replay and integrity protection. In *International Conference on Financial Cryptography and Data Security*, pages 62–76, 2011.

[27] Khalid Shahbar and A. Nur Zincir-Heywood. Benchmarking two techniques for Tor classification: Flow level and circuit level classification. In *IEEE Symposium on Computational Intelligence in Cyber Security*, pages 58–65, 2014.

[28] Khalid Shahbar and A. Nur Zincir-Heywood. Traffic flow analysis of Tor pluggable transports. In *IEEE International Conference on Network and Service Management*, pages 178–181, 2015.

[29] Zhen Ling, Junzhou Luo, Kui Wu, and Xinwen Fu. Protocol-level hidden server discovery. In *Proceedings of the IEEE INFOCOM*, pages 1043–1051, 2013.

[30] Alex Biryukov, Ivan Pustogarov, and Ralf-Philipp Weinmann. Trawling for Tor hidden services: Detection, measurement, deanonymization. In *IEEE Symposium on Security and Privacy*, pages 80–94, 2013.

[31] Juan A. Elices, Fernando Pérez-González, and Carmela Troncoso. Fingerprinting tor's hidden service log files using a timing channel. In *IEEE International Workshop on Information Forensics and Security*, pages 1–6, 2011.

[32] Kevin S. Bauer, Micah Sherr, and Dirk Grunwald. ExperimenTor: A testbed for safe and realistic Tor experimentation. In *USENIX Workshop on Cyber Security Experimentation and Test*, 2011.

[33] Chaabane Abdelberi, Pere Manils, and Mohamed Ali Kâafar. Digging into anonymous traffic: A deep analysis of the tor anonymizing network. In *IEEE International Conference on Network and System Security*, pages 167–174, 2010.

[34] J. Ross Quinlan. *C4.5: Programs for Machine Learning*. Morgan Kaufmann, San Francisco, CA, 1993.

[35] Leo Breiman. Random forests. *Machine Learning*, 45(1):5–32, 2001.

[36] Xindong Wu, Vipin Kumar, J. Ross Quinlan, *et al.* Top 10 algorithms in data mining. *Knowledge and Information Systems*, 14(1):1–37, 2008.

[37] Christopher M. Bishop. Pattern recognition and machine learning. *Information Science and Statistics*. Springer, 5th edition, Berlin, 2007.

[38] Nir Friedman, Dan Geiger, and Moisés Goldszmidt. Bayesian network classifiers. *Machine Learning*, 29(2–3):131–163, 1997.

[39] Teuvo Kohonen. *Self-Organizing Maps*. Springer, Berlin, 2001.

[40]  Fariba Haddadi and A. Nur Zincir-Heywood. Benchmarking the effect of flow exporters and protocol filters on botnet traffic classification. *IEEE Systems Journal*, 10(4):1390–1401, 2016.

[41]  Khalid Shahbar and A. Nur Zincir-Heywood. Effects of shared bandwidth on anonymity of the I2P network users. In *IEEE Symposium on Security and Privacy, International Workshop on Traffic Measurements for Cybersecurity*, pages 235–240, 2017.

[42]  Ruoming Pang, Mark Allman, Vern Paxson, and Jason Lee. The devil and packet trace anonymization. *Computer Communication Review*, 36(1):29–38, 2006.

[43]  Antonio Pescape, Antonio Montieri, Giuseppe Aceto, and Domenico Ciuonzo. Anonymity services Tor, I2P, JonDonym: Classifying in the dark (web). In *IEEE Transactions on Dependable and Secure Computing*, pp. 1–14, IEEE DL Early access, 2018.

[44]  Khalid Shahbar and A. Nur Zincir-Heywood. Packet momentum for identification of anonymity networks. *Journal of Cyber Security and Mobility*, pages 27–56, 2017.

[45]  SOM toolbox. http://www.cis.hut./somtoolbox/, January 2016.

*Chapter 9*

# Bio/nature-inspired algorithms in A.I. for malicious activity detection

*Andria Procopiou[1] and Nikos Komninos[1]*

## 9.1 Introduction

Malicious software [1] is one of the main threats to networks and its assets, as well as individual users. As we approach the Internet of Things (IoT) and cyber-physical systems era, network traffic becomes more complex and heterogeneous. In recent years, the number of devices connected to the Internet is increased exponentially as well as big data that is produced from them. Also, each device comes with its own protocols and standards. Furthermore, computing devices operate with different protocols and standards and effective traffic monitoring becomes harder. Hence, adversaries conduct more sophisticated attacks against networks, so the malicious behaviour can be more difficult to be detected. Simplistic and one-dimensional security countermeasures are likely to fail under such circumstances.

Artificial intelligence and particularly learning algorithms seems to be appropriate for detecting cyberattacks. Using machine learning, fast and accurate detection of malicious behaviour is more achievable than ever. A special branch of machine-learning algorithms includes nature and bio-inspired algorithms. Such algorithms followed models from nature, biology, social systems and life sciences. Some examples include genetic algorithms (GAs), swarm intelligence (SI), artificial immune systems (AISs), evolutionary algorithms (EAs), artificial neural networks (ANNs), fractal geometry, chaos theory and so on [2].

Nature/bio-inspired algorithms have an advantage against traditional machine-learning algorithms: they focus on optimisation. In detail, nature acts as a method of making something as perfect as possible or choosing the most fitted samples from a population. In practice, this family of algorithms applies these principles in the form of optimisation and finding the best solution to the problem assigned. In anomaly detection, the main objective is to identify the malicious behaviour, so these algorithms use their best fit mechanisms to detect malicious abnormalities. Another beneficial usage of nature/bio-inspired algorithms is to optimise the potential

[1]Centre for Software Reliability (CSR), Department of Computer Science, City, University of London, UK

features used in attack's detection. An optimal set of features is selected for efficient malware detection but also for reducing the complexity and computational burden. Additionally, nature/bio-inspired algorithms are highly flexible as they can accept a mixture of variables in terms of type and continuity. This gives us the opportunity to give a variety of different variable types which expand feature selection in such algorithms.

In this chapter, we will explore how nature/bio-inspired algorithms are applied in intrusion detection against different threats and attacks for various networks. The first section of this chapter gives an introduction and in-depth explanation of how the most popular nature/bio-inspired algorithms operate. Both the theoretical and practical concepts are explained and how these algorithms operate to detect malicious behaviour in the context of cyber security. The second section includes a selection of the most notable and complete studies of anomaly detection using nature/bio-inspired algorithms in networks and in low-resources systems such as cyber-physical systems and IoT. In the third section, the techniques used and the results produced are discussed. Finally, future direction on how nature-inspired algorithms could be applied in detecting anomalies in such systems is presented.

## 9.2   Towards technology through nature

It can safely be stated that nature is the most suitable entity of solving hard and complex problems. It is able to find the most suitable solution. It can also maintain the balance between various components. Hence, computer scientists have been inspired by it and created their own algorithms based on natural phenomena and procedures. Bio/Nature-inspired algorithms simulate the nature at solving optimisation problems. In the next section, we group and explain the most popular bio/nature-inspired algorithms as categorised in Figure 9.1.

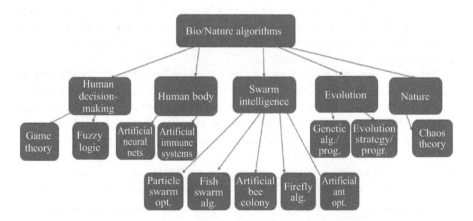

*Figure 9.1   Bio/Nature-inspired algorithms taxonomy*

## 9.2.1 Terminologies of bio/nature-inspired algorithms

### 9.2.1.1 Populations

The term population is an important and vital concept in the field of bio/nature-inspired algorithms. In biology and nature sciences, the term population defines a group of either animals or people that belong to a specific kind/type and live in a specific place [3]. In bio/nature-inspired algorithms, the term population refers to a set of possible solutions to a specific problem. In every bio/nature-inspired algorithm, the procedure starts with an initial population. An initial population is the first commencing set of solutions or candidates, before the algorithm starts functioning, with a specific size. Depending on the type of algorithm used, the population size can change.

The members of a population can be cooperative or competitive. In algorithms that consist of population members that are cooperative, no new members will be either added or deleted. On the other hand, in algorithms where the members of a population are competitive only the fittest members will be included. This process is iterative and on each iteration (called generation) the fitness of the current members is compared to the new members generated. The weakest already existing members are replaced with the strongest new members.

New members that can be potentially merged with the population must be evaluated through scoring. The score value is calculated based on the suitability of each member's solution [3].

### 9.2.1.2 Selection

The process of selection involves choosing one or more potential solutions to the problem from the population. Depending on the bio/nature-inspired algorithm chosen, a different selection procedure is adopted [3].

### 9.2.1.3 Crossover

In biology, crossover is the process in which a male and a female mate together to breed offspring. In bio/nature-inspired algorithms, crossover does not consider genders, any two candidates can mate to produce children. Crossover is mostly used in EAs [3].

### 9.2.1.4 Mutation

In biology, a mutation is a change in an organism's DNA sequence. This change can be either benign or malignant. In bio/nature-inspired algorithms "mutation" denotes the asexual reproduction, so a child could be created from a single parent. Mutation is mostly used in EAs. Through mutation, potential solutions can breed a child (new solution, that is potentially slightly better) in the next generation. If a solution has become optimal through mutation, it can become even more efficient [3].

## 9.2.2 Review of bio/nature-inspired algorithms

### 9.2.2.1 Artificial neural networks

ANNs have been inspired by the biological neural networks present in animal brains and was first introduced in 1943 by [4]. ANN models are inspired from biological neural networks that process an 'acceptable' information. Just as animal brains contain biological neurons, ANNs contain a set of interconnected nodes, called artificial neurons. Each connection between the different ANNs (analogous to synapses in animal brains) helps the model of interconnected neurons (nodes) that communicate with each other by exchanging information. The neurons are connected with a set of adaptive weights that are tuned by a learning algorithm that accepts a great set of inputs and decides how the weights between the nodes are going to be adapted.

ANNs are ideal for pattern recognition. In this simplest form, there are three types of layers in ANNs: the input layer that accepts the pattern data; the hidden layer that applies the algorithm for deciding what the result should be and the output layer that shows the result. Most of the models have at least an input and output layer. The input layer accepts the pattern and the output layer gives the output pattern. The hidden layer defines the interaction between the input and the output layers. A diagram of a typical ANN architecture is shown in Figure 9.2.

ANNs can be either supervised or unsupervised. Both of these processes are iterative. In supervised training, the similarity between the actual and the supposed output is calculated at each iteration. This is described in the form of a percentage error. The calculation of the error is called backpropagation. At each iteration the internal weights matrices are altered towards minimising this error at a low acceptable percentage.

In unsupervised training, calculating this error percentage is not straightforward due to the model not having an expected output. Hence, the model cannot estimate the current output is from the ideal output. Instead, the model is iterated for a fixed number of rounds.

There are different types of ANNs. All of them have common elements such as neurons, weights, activation functions and layers. However, each type fits for different tasks. Due to their versatile nature, not all of the types of ANNs can perform equally well in every problem. There are various problems ANNs in general can solve though, including clustering, regression, classification and prediction problems. In Table 9.1,

*Figure 9.2    Artificial neural network architecture*

*Table 9.1    ANN architectures*

| Clustering | Regression | Classification | Prediction |
|---|---|---|---|
| Self-org. map (1) | Feedforward (1) | Feedforward (1) | Recurrent (1) |
| – | Deep feedforward (1) | Deep belief network (1) | Deep feedforward (2) |
| – | Recurrent (2) | Deep feedforward (1) | Feedforward (2) |
| – | Convolutional (3) | Convolutional (1) | – |
| – | – | Recurrent (2) | – |
| – | – | – | – |

we present a table with the most popular ANN types and the problems they can solve best, inspired by [3]. The problem is at the top and in descending order the architecture that solves it best.

ANNs have been used extensively in intrusion and malware detection. The relevant features to differentiate between normal and malicious activity are extracted from the raw data collected and fed to the input neurons of the ANN architecture. The extracted data are processed in the hidden layers of neurons and the final result is output through the output neurons.

### 9.2.2.2 Evolutionary algorithms

EA is a branch of nature/bio-inspired algorithms in artificial intelligence that is very popular and considered classical from all the nature/bio-inspired techniques [5]. EAs comprise evolutionary techniques and mechanisms taken from the biological evolutions. Some examples include reproduction, mutation, selection and recombination. Since these biological models are considered nearly perfect when finding the most fitted individuals, their artificial equivalents are designed to find solutions to hard problems.

The procedure followed in different types of EAs is similar to the equivalent in nature. There is an initial population of random candidates in which natural selection occurs, otherwise called survival of the fittest. Each individual candidate is evaluated through a fitness/quality function. Then iteratively: the best candidates are chosen as parents to seed the next generation of candidates (reproduction). This is done by crossover and/or mutation applied to them. The generated candidates (offspring) are evaluated by the fitness/quality function and replace the least fitting candidates of the previous generation. This process can be iterative until a sufficient solution (set of candidates) is constructed or a computational limit is met.

During this process, the fitness of candidates in consecutive populations is improved, and the easiness of adaption to new environments is also improved. Below we briefly enlist and explain the most notable EAs and summarise the GA's flow in Figure 9.3.

*Genetic algorithm*
GA was first introduced by Holland in 1975 [6]. It is a very popular evolutionary-based algorithm especially for optimisation purposes. The algorithm functions as follows:

Step 1: It begins by initialising a population of solutions (chromosomes).
Step 2: Applying a fitness function, the current chromosomes are evaluated.
Step 3: The best chromosomes are selected to generate a new generation of chromosomes through crossover and mutation.
Step 4: The new chromosomes are evaluated and exchanged with the least fit of the previous generation of chromosomes.

In intrusion detection, certain procedures have to be made before the training. The different groups of data (two at least with normal and attack) represent the initial different groups of chromosomes. Then the training starts with the procedure

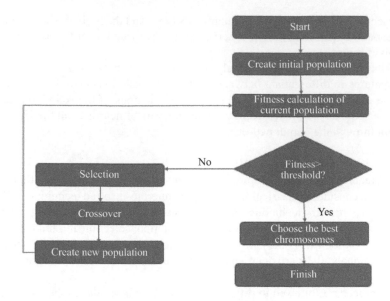

*Figure 9.3   GA algorithm*

described above. During the testing/detection part, the input data is taken and an initial population is created from it. The generated population is compared to the training population. The chromosomes that the new population's chromosomes are related, the closest are classified after them.

### Genetic programing

Genetic programing (GP) was first proposed by Koza in 1992 [7], and it is considered an extension of the GA. GP represents the solution in the form of a tree, and computer programs are generated (instead of chromosomes). GP functions as follows:

Step 1: An initial population of computer software programs is generated, which consists of functions and terminals.
Step 2: Each computer program solves a problem given and a fitness value is assigned based on its accuracy.
Step 3: Once again, the best programs are chosen to breed the next generation.
Step 4: Through mutation and crossover, new computer programs are created to form the next generation.
Step 5: Finally, the best programs of the new generation are exchanged with the worst ones of the previous generation.

### Evolutionary strategy

Evolutionary strategy (ES) methods were proposed by Bienert, Rechenberg and Schwefel in 1964 [8]. It is an optimisation algorithm which is based on the adaption of evolution theory. A special characteristic of the ES is that the mutation can be controlled depending on the type of the ES strategy chosen. Hence, both the search process and the solution are optimised, as well as the mutation parameters. Below, the most popular schemes are briefly explained [9].

*(1 + 1)-ES:* This is the scheme with the simplest selection mechanism. A real-valued vector of variables is created from the parent through mutation, by using standard deviation to each variable object. Then, newly constructed individual is evaluated and compared to its parent. The best of the two becomes the new parent for the next generation with the less fit being discarded.

*($\mu + \lambda$)-ES:* In this scheme, a $\mu$ number of parents is chosen from the current generation. These $\mu$ parents are responsible for creating the $\lambda$ offspring through mutation and crossover. Then the $\mu$ generation and $\lambda$ offspring are united into one group, with only the best $\mu$ remaining, and the rest being discarded.

*($\mu$, $\lambda$)-ES:* Once again, $\mu$ parents are chosen from the current generation to generate the $\lambda$ offspring (where $\lambda \geq \mu$). From the new generation, only the best $\mu$ offspring individuals survive, with the parents being discarded completely.

ESs are particularly effective against intrusion detection because they generate rules that can match the malicious traffic. To evaluate the population of suggested solutions, the dataset chosen is used to judge at which iteration the most optimal solution is obtained.

### Evolutionary programing

Evolutionary programing is again an extension of the ES methods, also using the theory of evolution [10]. It is very similar to the GP method as it encompasses of computer programs as well. Their major difference is that the structure of the program to be optimised is fixed.

### 9.2.2.3 Swarm intelligence algorithms

SI has been introduced by Beni and Wang in 1989 [11] for cellular robotic systems. The concept consists of collaborative functioning by a large number of small organisms such as bees, ants, birds and so on. Based on this concept, self-organising computer network systems can operate efficiently. Under this term, the most common technique used is the ant colony optimisation, which is based on the organisation of large ant colonies for food transporting reasons, artificial bee colonies, fish swarm algorithm (FSA), intelligent water drops algorithm, firefly algorithms (FAs) and so on. Below we briefly describe the common fundamental concepts all of the SI are based on. A summary of how SI algorithms operate is illustrated in Figure 9.4.

### Swarm intelligence fundamentals

*Proximity fundamental:* The population performs a series of time and space computation calculations to function properly.

*Quality fundamental:* In the presence of environment quality factors, the population shall be able to positively react.

*Diverse response methods:* In any procedures the population carries out, the means and ways shall not be limited and fixed.

*Stability fundamental:* The population shall be able to remain intact and fixed in its functioning, regardless of any changes in the environment.

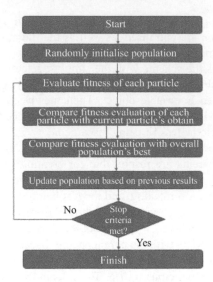

*Figure 9.4   SI algorithm*

*Adaptability fundamental:* The population must be 'intelligent' enough to realise that if the computational burden can be decreased, then it shall change its behaviour.

SI algorithms can be applied in intrusion detection by constructing a set of rules for effective classification. Each organism creates a set of rules that evaluates them with the training set it is provided with. With iterations, the rules are reconstructed and extended enough to have a high accuracy percentage.

### Particle swarm optimisation

Particle swarm optimisation (PSO) was first introduced by Kennedy and Eberhart in 1995 [12] and has been inspired by the food searching activity of birds. It is an optimisation type of algorithm and has been extensively used due to its simplicity, computational lightness and straightforward implementation. In detail, the 'particle' word of the name means the population members who are low in mass and volume can achieve a better behaviour. Every 'particle' in the population can be considered a solution. Each solution consists of four vectors in the high dimensional space: current position, best position discovered yet, best position discovered yet by neighbour and velocity. Each particle rearranges its position in the search space based on two factors, its best position and its neighbour's best position during the search process until a stopping criteria is met.

### Ant colony optimisation

Ant colony optimisation (ACO) was first introduced by Dorigo and Di Caro in 1999 [13]. It was inspired by the remarkable ability of ant species to collaboratively find the shortest path between their nest and the various food sources by making usage of pheromone trails. The more pheromone each path has, the stronger the probability is to follow it. This procedure is a type of reinforcement.

## Artificial bee colony algorithm

Artificial bee colony (ABC) algorithm was proposed by Karaboga in 2005 [14]. Inspired by the behaviour of bees, several SI algorithms have been proposed. Mainly, there are two types, foraging and mating. One of the most popular foraging algorithms is the ABC algorithm which simulates the behaviour of honeybees groups. This promotes intelligent and cooperative behaviour between bees with different roles. A bee can have one of the two following behaviours; the first is when a bee finds food, the other bees are led to the food source and the second is when bees leave food sources for others. The bee can have three roles in these scenarios, the employed bee, the onlooker bee and the scout bee. In the ABC algorithm, the place where the food is located can be a potential solution to the problem and the quality of the food maps to the fitness of the solution. The number of onlookers or employed bees corresponds to the number of the solutions to the problem. Concluding, there is only one employed bee for every food source.

## Fish swarm algorithm

The FSA is a relatively new population-based/swarm algorithm, proposed in 2002 by Li *et al.* [15]. The FSA was based on fish schooling behaviour to search for food. A fish in the FSA algorithm is represented by a D-dimensional position, and the fish food satisfaction is represented by a numerical metric. The relationship between the two fish is denoted by the Euclidean distance of the two. Three basic behaviours are consisted in this algorithm: 'searching for food', swarming against to a threat' and 'following towards a better result'. *Searching for food* means that the fish randomly search for food so they can minimise the food satisfaction. *Swarming* means that the objective is to keep the food levels of fish satisfactory, keep the existing fish happy and attract new fish. *Following* means that when a fish locates food, the others will follow.

## Firefly algorithm

The FA has first been introduced by Yang [16] in 2009 and has been inspired by the flashing behaviour of the fireflies. The algorithm consists of an iterative procedure with a population of agents (the fireflies) working together to solve an optimisation problem. The algorithm is based on the following concept of finding a solution: a better firefly glows more. Each firefly attracts other fireflies, regardless of their gender, so the searching for the optimal solution in the search space can be found more efficiently. The procedure is the following:

Step 1: All the fireflies will move towards the brightest one, regardless of their gender.
Step 2: The more a firefly glows, the more attractive it is towards the others. The brightness can be decreased though due to distance. If there is not a firefly that stands out in terms of brightness from the rest, then they will move randomly.
Step 3: The brightness of a firefly is based on the result of a calculation of the objective function for a given problem.

#### 9.2.2.4 Artificial immune systems

AISs algorithm has been first introduced in 1999 [17] by Dasgupta and was inspired by the human immune system. The human immune system is a true wonder, as it is highly evolving, works in a parallel and distributive way, it is robust and can be adapted easily to any environment. The human body generates various detector cells (antibodies) to guard against non-self cells (antigens/pathogens). Antibodies are distributed to the entire body, so there is no central coordinator. Each antigen is unique and independent in terms of detection. Hence, the set of body cells is mapped to the system/network/hosts to be protected, and the antibodies are the intrusion detection system (IDS) agents to detect the external entities (pathogens) (Figure 9.5).

There are various algorithms to create antibodies to protect cells from pathogens, such as the clonal selection algorithm (CSA) and the negative selection algorithm (NSA).

The CSA is based on the concept of acquired immunity where in a specific way B and T lymphocytes respond in a better way to antigens over time. The NSA is inspired by the biological concept of identifying and deleting self-reacting cells that attack self-tissues.

NSA operates as follows: normal data are defined as self-patterns. Then, a great number of random patterns is generated and compared to the self-patterns. If the new generated pattern matches one of the self-pattern, it becomes a detector otherwise it is discarded. Next in the monitoring state, if there is a match between a detector and an incoming traffic part, then an anomaly is present. NSS, on the other hand, operates in two stages. In the first stage, feature extraction takes place, and then these features are used to train the algorithm. The system extracts the duration/direction of the flow

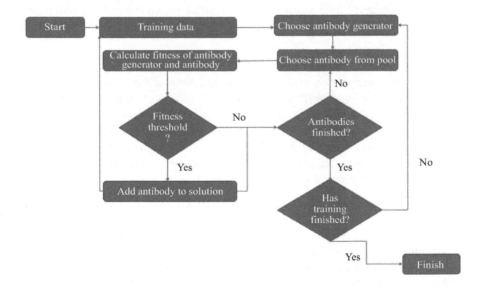

*Figure 9.5    AIS algorithm*

and the number of packets/bytes. In the second stage, the NSS algorithm is used for detection. A quantitative approach is adopted to detect instead of a single threshold. A less used algorithm of AIS is the dendritic cell algorithm (DCA). DCA is based on how dendritic cells operate in natural immune systems as activators.

AIS relies on mutation to make its decisions and operates in the following way:

Step 1: *Initialisation:* The potential solutions to the problem (antibodies) are initialised. Antigens mark the value of the objective function that must be optimised.

Step 2: *Cloning:* The antibodies are evaluated on how fit they are. The best antibodies are cloned proportionally, with the best being cloned the most.

Step 3: *Hypermutation:* In this stage, the best antibody's clones are mostly mutated, and the worst antibody's clones are lessly mutated. Next, the clones are evaluated with their original antibodies. The best antibodies are kept for the next generation, with the best being discarded, for the next generation. This mutation can be Gaussian, exponential or uniform.

In intrusion detection, AIS consists of three phases. First, the algorithm defines itself by learning the normal behaviour so that it can construct a baseline. Second, it generates detectors through the T-cells process. Third, the input data are compared to all the T-detectors. If there is a match, there is no intrusion.

## 9.2.2.5 Fuzzy logic

Fuzzy logic (FL) was proposed in 1965 [18] by Zadeh. FL concept mimics the human brain interpretation of uncertain information. Similar to the brain operation, FL replies to inputs with approximate (truthy/faulty) rather than distinct and exact reasoning. In reasoning, some questions have various answers, based on a set of knowledge and rules that form a specific solution to the problem. Likewise, each FL reply has a degree of truth, and in combination with probabilities they form a fuzzy set.

## 9.2.2.6 Chaos theory

Chaos is a sub-area of mathematics that was first formed by Lorenz in 1972 [19]. In contrast to most of the scientific models that are responsible for modelling predictive behaviour such as gravity, electricity, chemical reactions and so on, chaos theory can model non-linear behaviour that has no means of being predicted such as the weather, stock market and so on. Formally, in the context of complex systems, there are always subtle patterns, iterative feedbacks along with iteration itself, underlying similarities in behaviour and overall connections between the various states of a system. A very important aspect in chaos theory is that in a complex system, there is the so-called 'sensitive dependence on initial conditions', the 'butterfly effect'. In detail, this effect denotes that a small change in a single state of a complex deterministic non-linear system can cause major changes in a later state/outcome of it.

In the context of intrusion detection, the IDS system closely monitors the traffic and through calculations can understand at what extend it starts behaving chaotically. If there is an indication of chaos, then there is likely an intrusion.

### 9.2.2.7    Game theory

Game theory (GT) has been applied in many areas including mathematics, psychology, economics, computer science, political sciences and gambling. GT is inspired from mathematical modelling and decision-making. Although multiple and different approaches to GT have been proposed, it has been first introduced by Neumann in 1928 [20]. It studies cooperation and conflict between individuals who make decisions upon particular rule scenarios. The theory consists of games played between players where games can be cooperative or non-cooperative depending on the players' intentions. Games are also based on self-interest or common interest.

In the context of intrusion detection, a game is played between the IDS and the possible attacker. Based on the model constructed and the assumptions considered, a decision is made on whether there is an intrusion.

## 9.3    Cyberattacks and malware detection

In cyber space, there are numerous cyberattacks that can be conducted against networks and/or individual assets. These attacks can threaten one or more of the main cyber security principles: confidentiality, integrity and availability. Below we give a brief explanation of the most popular cyberattacks and malware and their impact on a network and/or asset, as well as which cyber security principle they mostly negatively affect.

### 9.3.1    Distributed/Denial of service attacks

A distributed/denial of service ((D)DoS) attack can be volumetric or vulnerability exploitation-based or reflection-based. A volumetric DoS attack consists of an attacker sending a massive volume of requests in an attempt to 'flood' the target machine and make it unable to accept legitimate requests from normal users [21]. In a vulnerability-exploitation (D)DoS attack, an attacker is taking advantage of a system or protocol or communication weakness to make the target machine unavailable to legitimate requests from normal users. In a reflection (D)DoS attack, the target is responding with the received challenge. A (D)DoS attack can also occur in any of the Transmission Control Protocol/Internet Protocol (TCP/IP) layers. (D)DoS attacks mainly threat the availability security principle.

(D)DoS attacks can occur in all the Open Systems Interconnection (OSI) layers. Below we briefly describe the most popular (D)DoS attacks across all layers.

**Physical layer:** In the physical layer, we have jamming attacks.

A *jamming* attack consists of an adversary flooding the physical medium with signals in order for legitimate packets not being able to be transmitted normally. A jamming attack has multiple forms. The most popular is the constant jamming (D)DoS attack where a burst amount of radio signals are constantly sent. The second type is the deceptive jamming (D)DoS which falsely sends radio signals in an attempt to make the target unavailable.

**Link (MAC) layer:** In the Media Access Control (MAC) layer, we have the Address Resolution Protocol (*ARP*) *poisoning* attack where the attacker performs MAC address spoofing so it can send ARP messages to a network. Hence, messages are redirected to him instead of the normal user. Therefore, the attacker can cause a (D)DoS attack by dropping the packets.

In wireless networks, a node that wants to connect to a wireless network, scans the environment to connect to an available network by sending probe requests. The access point responds back, providing information about the network. In a **probe request flooding** attack, the adversary sends a burst amount of probe requests to the access point to make it unavailable to legitimate requests.

Another popular attack in the MAC layer consists of the *authentication request flood*. The attacker has already performed a MAC spoofing attack to try and authenticate themselves to the access point by sending authentication requests. The attacker aims to flood the access point with authentication requests.

**Network/Transport layer:** In the network and transport layer, we have a variety of different types of (D)DoS attacks.

In a *SYN-Flood (TCP-Flood) (D)DoS*, the attacker sends a great number of SYN packets to the target until the target becomes unresponsive to legitimate requests. In a normal situation, a client initiates a TCP connection by sending a SYN message to the server. The server responds with a SYN-ACK to the client, the client responds back with an ACK message and the connection is established (three-way handshake).

In a User Datagram Protocol (*UDP*) *Flooding (D)DoS*, the attacker sends a large number of UDP packets to random ports of the target.

In a *Grey Hole (D)DoS*, the attacker selectively drops packets that are to reach a particular destination.

A *Black Hole (D)DoS* is similar to the grey-hole attack, but the attacker drops all packets passed by it.

An Internet Control Message Protocol (*ICMP*) *Flooding (D)DoS*, otherwise called ping flooding (D)DoS attack, sends a burst amount of ICMP echo request packets to the server.

In a *Low-Rate (D)DoS*, the attacker exploits TCP's retransmission timeout mechanism and sends low-rate traffic to the target so the connection can be kept alive. As time goes by, the attacker opens more and more connections and eventually makes the target unavailable to legitimate incoming connections.

In a *Ping of Death (D)DoS*, the attacker aims to make the target unavailable by sending either malformed or oversized packets using the ping command.

In a *Teardrop-DoS*, the attacker sends mingled IP fragments with either overlapping or over-sized payloads to the target server in an attempt to make it unavailable.

In a *Land-(D)DoS*, the attacker sends a TCP packet, which contains the targets IP Address as both the source and the destination. This causes the victim to send replies to itself over and over again, resulting into it becoming unavailable.

The *Fraggle (D)DoS* is similar to Smurf attack, but instead of ICMP echo packets, the attacker sends UDP echo packets to the target.

The *Smurf (D)DoS* attack can either be a simple or distributed DoS attack where the attacker(s) through IP Spoofing the victim's IP address sends a large number of ICMP echo requests to the IP broadcast address. As a result, the victim's computer is becoming extremely slow and eventually becoming unavailable. Finally, in the application layer, we have a fair number of different (D)DoS attacks.

The *Session Initiation Protocol (SIP) Flooding (D)DoS* attack is conducted in the SIP, which is an application layer protocol used in Internet telephony for both voice and video calls as well as instant messaging. The attack floods the target with either valid or invalid calls or messages.

In an HyperText Transfer Protocol (*HTTP*) *Flooding (D)DoS*, the attacker sends a burst amount of legitimate get or post request to the victim resulting into the target becoming unavailable to legitimate requests. Since the requests are perfectly legitimate, the server has no ways of rejecting them.

In a Domain Name System (*DNS*) *(D)DoS*, the attacker sends DNS queries that at first are small in size but then become large in size. The attacker redirects these messages to the victim's IP address resulting into a target's unavailable state.

In a *Slow Rate (Request and Post requests and Response) (D)DoS*, the attacker takes advantage of the server's waiting time for a get/post request to be completed (time-out time). The server is waiting for a specific amount of time for the client to send the request before closing the connection. The attacker instead sends a request very slowly, tricking the server into believing that simply the request is coming from a slow connection. In time, the attacker opens more and more connections to send requests that are never completed. As a result, the server becomes unavailable. In response attacks, the attacker reads the response sent to him very slowly by having a much smaller window-size than the server's send buffer size.

In Secure Socket Layer (*SSL*) *(D)DoS* attacks, the adversary exploits the SSL handshake authentication mechanism. In detail, the attacker sends bogus data to the target or exploits the functions to the SSL encryption key negotiation procedure.

## 9.3.2   Botnets

A botnet is a set of devices/machines that are connected to the Internet which, at some point, have been infected by a malware and are controlled by an adversary, the botmaster. A botnet can perform a (D)DoS attack, send spam mail or engage in click frauds [22]. This can result into the network/target not functioning fully thus, the availability principle is threatened.

## 9.3.3   Malware

Malware, an acronym for malicious software, is a general term encompassing any malicious or intrusive program. It can take the form of an executable code, script, active content and so on. A malware exploits any known or unknown vulnerabilities of a system, network, machine, protocol and so on so it can illegally execute malicious code to steal data, destroy assets or abuse services and/or functions [22]. The most popular types of malware are briefly explained below.

### 9.3.3.1   Viruses

A virus is a malicious software that once installed, through user interaction, starts making copies of itself and infects various types of files and/or programs. Through it, the confidentiality and integrity principles are affected [22].

### 9.3.3.2 (Remote access) Trojan horses

A Trojan horse is a type of malware that masquerades itself as a legitimate, useful program in order for the victim to be tricked and install it. It has taken its name from the Ancient Greek Trojan Horse used to stealthily invade the city of Troy. In contrast to viruses and worms, Trojans do not usually inject or propagate themselves in other files. A remote access Trojan is a special type of Trojan that gives to the adversary remote access to the victim's computer. Through it, the confidentiality and integrity principles are affected [22].

### 9.3.3.3 Rootkits

A rootkit is a special type of malware, its main strength being it remains undetected. To achieve that, it modifies the victim's operating system so that it remains hidden from the user. In detail, the rootkit is able to hide malicious processed from being visible in the list of active processes. It also eliminates any access to its files. Through it, the confidentiality and integrity principles are affected [22].

### 9.3.3.4 Backdoors

A backdoor gives the ability to the adversary to invisibly access and manipulate remotely a machine by bypassing any form of authentication. Through it, the confidentiality and integrity principles are affected [22].

### 9.3.3.5 Spyware

A spyware is a malicious software that once installed on a victim's computer, starts illegally gathering information about assets without the user's consent. Through it, the confidentiality and integrity principles are affected [22].

### 9.3.3.6 Worms

A worm is a type of malware that, unlike viruses, can replicate itself without any user interaction and spread to other computer when connected to a network. Through it, the confidentiality and integrity principles are affected [22].

### 9.3.3.7 Ransomware

A ransomware is a special type of malware that either aims to encrypt a victim's entire data and/or programs or block access to the entire machine. To reverse these malicious actions, a ransom must be paid to the adversary [22]. Through it, the confidentiality and integrity principles are affected as well as availability since the machine is unavailable to the user.

## 9.3.4 Probe attacks

Probe attacks are scanning procedures an attacker follows to collect useful about potential vulnerabilities a machine or an entire network has. Based on the gathered information, the attacker can attempt to exploit the victim at a later stage [22]. Through it, the confidentiality principle is affected.

## 9.3.5    Buffer overflow

Sometimes, due to poor programming code, applications and software have a serious vulnerability. While data is being written to the buffer during a process, the buffer's boundary is overrun and nearby memory locations are overwritten. An attacker can exploit this vulnerability through malformed inputs to gain unauthorised access. Through it, the confidentiality and integrity principles are affected [22].

## 9.3.6    Brute force attack

A brute force attack consists of an attacker attempting to break a password by trying a great amount of random combinations to get it right [54]. Here, the confidentiality principle is affected [22].

## 9.3.7    Masquerading attacks

In masquerading attacks, an adversary manages to steal the identity of a legitimate user and masquerades themselves as normal entities in an attempt to exploit a system or a network [22].

## 9.3.8    Datasets used in intrusion detection

### 9.3.8.1    DARPA dataset

The MIT Lincoln Laboratory along with the Defence Advanced Research Projects Agency (DARPA ITO) and Air Force Research Laboratory (AFRL/SNHS) have collaborated together to create an intrusion detection dataset from 1998 to 1999. The DARPA 1998 Dataset consists of seven weeks with normal and attack traffic. The dataset set consists of 2 weeks of attack-free traffic, with 1 week of new attacks along with the old ones from the DARPA 1998 Dataset [23].

### 9.3.8.2    KDD99 dataset

The KDD99 dataset became public in 1999 and has been one of the most popular IDS datasets used in literature. It has been based on the captured data of the DARPA 1998 Dataset. It contains 7 weeks of raw network traffic with an approximate total of 4,900,000 connections. A total of 41 features have been suggested and were used to differentiate between normal and malicious traffic. There are various types of cyberattacks present in the dataset. These attacks are categorised into four groups, DoS, user-to-root (U2R), remote-to-local (R2L) and probing attacks. DoS and probing attacks have already been explained above. U2R denotes a set of attacks in which the attacker manages to gain root access. R2L denotes a set of attacks in which the attacker exploits a certain vulnerability to gain access to a local machine in the network [24]. A newer version of the KDD99 dataset, the NSL-KDD dataset, attempts to improve the KDD99 dataset's issues highlighted in the literature studies [25].

### 9.3.8.3    ISCX IDS 2012 dataset

In the ISCX IDS 2012 dataset, various multi-stage attacks scenarios were conducted such as SSH Brute Force attacks, (D)DoS attacks and through IRC botnets and internal Infiltrating of the network [26].

#### 9.3.8.4 ISCX IDS 2017 dataset

In the ISCX IDS 2017 dataset, multi-stage attacks scenarios were conducted with more diversity. Some examples were various (D)DoS ADoS slowloris, DoS Slowhttptest, DoS Hulk, DoS LOIT and DoS GoldenEye as well as the botnet ARES. Brute Force attacks were also conducted such as SSH and Brute Force attacks. Also, web-based attacks were conducted such as web Brute Force, XSS and SQL Injection. Finally, port-scan malicious behaviour was simulated [27].

#### 9.3.8.5 Botnet dataset

In the botnet dataset, various botnets were used to attack the network such as Neris, Rbot, Virut, NSIS, IRCBot, Menti, Sogou, Zeus, Weasel, SmokeBot, Murlo [28].

#### 9.3.8.6 CIC DoS dataset

In the Canadian Institute for Cybersecurity (CIC) DoS dataset, the attack behaviour was focused on application layer (D)DoS attacks. The attacks conducted were of high-volume as well as low-volume. The high-volume attacks were HTTP GETs, DNS queries, SIP INVITEs. The Low-volume attacks were low-rate attacks, apache range header attack, slow-rate DoS Slowhttptest, DoS Hulk, DoS LOIT and DoS GoldenEye [29].

#### 9.3.8.7 The AWID dataset

The AWID dataset has been constructed in 2015 and consists of a dataset with normal and attack traffic targeting 802.11 networks [30].

#### 9.3.8.8 The UNSW-NB15 dataset

The UNSW-NB 15 dataset was constructed by the Cyber Range Lab of the Australian Centre for Cyber Security consisting both normal and attack data. This data set has nine types of attacks, namely Fuzzers, Analysis, Backdoors, DoS, Exploits, Generic, Reconnaissance, Shellcode and Worms [31].

## 9.4 Bio/Nature-inspired algorithm studies in intrusion detection

### 9.4.1 Game theoretic studies

The authors in [32] used GT with Nash equilibrium. They designed a cooperative IDS in an attempt to increase accuracy and to detect new threats. The authors proposed a trust management framework so that the IDSs could be connected in a trustful way, reduce the impact for compromised IDSs and reduce the false positive (FP) rates (FPRs) and be scalable. When an IDS evaluates traffic to detect potential DoS attacks but has limited knowledge, it seeks help from other IDS by sending requests to gain extra feedback from them. There is a central component that organises the communication between the different IDSs. The authors evaluated their solution against DoS attack, so when a malicious node is detected, it is removed from the network.

The authors in [33] also used GT to prevent and detect (D)DoS attack in ad hoc networks. The GT concept was applied as a form of multiplayer game in combination with cryptographic puzzles. In an ad-hoc network, when a node wishes to send a request, it needs to solve a puzzle first and then become a member in a group. The nodes belonging to each group play a multiplayer game that is divided into two-player sub-games. The winner of each group (highest score) is served by the requested node. The games are continued until all requests are served. In the end, there will be one player left at each group. In that case, that game is played between the last node and the node responsible for authorising the requests. By doing that the authors ensure that the bulk of the computation overhead is handled by the requesting node which checks the winning results. In case a malicious node is already present in the network, it will need to process a high computation puzzle. The authors found that the optimal number of players for each group would be between 2 and 20. The solution also is efficient for the ad hoc nodes of the network.

## 9.4.2    Evolution strategies studies

The authors in [34] have suggested an online intrusion detection framework able to detect SIP flooding attacks using various EAs, including evolving radial basis function, fuzzy AdaBoost, genetic classifier, extended classifier, supervised classifier and continuous ant miner classifier. Their framework consists of six components. The packet sniffer captures the SIP traffic and stores it in a buffer, which can hold up to 500 packets. As soon as this buffer is full, the feature extractor component begins analysing the packets and extracts values for a set of features selected. These features are invite, register, bye, ack, options, cancel, update, refer, subscribe, notify, message, info and prack requests. The values of the features are normalised according to the total number of SIP request messages. The features also include response messages, such as the number of success, redirection, client error, server error, global error that are normalised according to the total number of SIP messages. With the help of rules generated from the EAs, it is decided if there is an attack. Supervised classifier and extended classifier have been proved to be effective with 82.17% and 77.00% against chunk flood attacks and harmonic flood attacks.

The authors in [35] use ES to generate rules to match anomalous connections from the DARPA dataset, including DoS and (D)DoS attacks. As they have stated in their work, the majority of research is focused on GA approaches, so they are the first to use ES to generate rules for detecting anomalous connections. The attributes the authors have used for detecting anomalies are the source IP address, the destination IP address, the source port, the destination port, the duration of the connection, the state, the protocol, the number of bytes sent by the source and the number of bytes sent by the destination nodes. The range of values for each attribute have a predefined set of values and use ES to find the optimal range. The authors do not present experimental results, although their suggestion is important for research.

## 9.4.3    Genetic algorithms studies

There are numerous studies that make usage of GAs to detect various cyberattacks. GA is an excellent algorithm for optimising the features used in intrusion detection, managing to not only reduce the overall complexity of the system but also achieve a better detection rate (DR) against various cyberattacks.

The authors in [36] designed an IDS for MANETs using GA to detect black hole and dropping routing DoS attacks. They defined a set of characteristics for the GA algorithm to consider (whether connections was from/to similar port/host, number of wrong fragments within the connection, connection SYN errors, percentage of connections to similar/desimilar services and hosts and so on). Using a trained set, they constructed the population. Then, by introducing the test data to the GA and by performing analysis (selection, crossover, mutation), test data were categorised. The authors report a DR of 95%.

In [37], the authors have designed a multilayer approach IDS by using the GA. They followed a multilayer IDS to detect attacks from the KDD999 dataset. Each layer operates as a filter for each group of attacks (there were four layer, one for each group of attacks) and blocks any malicious activity so there is no need for further investigation. The authors report that as the number of rounds of the GA is increased, so does the accuracy of the results but the complexity as well. They report an overall of 90% of potential accuracy, but the time complexity is reported to be relatively high.

The authors in [38] have also made usage of GA to detect the same family of attacks from the KDD99 dataset in wireless networks. They have compared their results with other studies, which consist of studies using ANNs, and their solution is reported to have a DR 95.67% training accuracy and 97.57% testing accuracy. They have also made usage of only 16 features to achieve these results from a total of 41 features.

### 9.4.4 Fuzzy logic studies

In intrusion detection, FL is often used in combination with other bio-inspired algorithmic techniques such as GA. The authors in [39] combined GA with FL to detect KDD99 set of attacks, including DoS attacks. For the detection using the GA algorithm, they have used a set of characteristics; source IP address, destination IP address, connection duration, protocol type, source port, destination port, and destination host service. With FL specific rules, the DR is increased and the error rate (ER) is decreased when the input is ambiguous. The results indicate that solution being more accurate, faster and lighter in computational resources than GA and FL when used separately. Specifically, the DR is high (>95%), the execution time is 12,500 ms and the memory allocation in less than 25 MBs.

In [40], the authors have combined the GA along with FL to create the fuzzy GA (FGA) for their research. The algorithm was detecting all the attacks from the KDD99 dataset. The algorithm commences by randomly choosing rules and then using the EA to improve the rules during the training phase. Then, during the testing phase, the final rules are used for classification of the testing data. The new algorithm was trained with traffic collected by the researchers themselves and can also detect unknown attacks. Through a series of experiments, the FGA has DR percentage above 95% and FPR less than 1%.

GA was also used as a feature selection technique before proceeding to the detection part. In [41], the authors have used GA to choose the most relevant and accurate for detection features from the KDD99 dataset. In that way, the authors aimed to perform a faster, lighter and more accurate detection. For the detection part, an SVM-fuzzy-based algorithm was used for detection. Authors' report claims that their results are better when using their solution rather than Support Vector Machine (SVM) by itself or the SVM-fuzzy algorithm without the GA performing the feature selection. Specifically, for the detection of DoS attacks, the DR is reported to be 98.3% and the ER to be 2.7%.

The authors in [42] have used FL to detect (D)DoS jamming attacks at Physical and MAC layers in IEEE 802.15.4 low rate wireless personal area networks. They have taken into consideration bad packet and signal-to-noise ratios to detect such attacks. Bad packet ratio is measured at the receiver side and consists of the total number of bad packets received by a node, divided by the total number of all packets received by the node, over a specific amount of time. Signal-to-noise ratio consists of the ratio of the received signal power at a node to the received noise at the node. A collection of objects has a fuzzy set which maps each object of the collection to a membership value (by applying a membership function to it) from 0 to 1. In this case, two set of objects exist, one for the signal-to-noise ratio and one for bad packet ratio. Through fuzzification, each of the two values produced from the two metrics fall among low, medium and high. According to certain rules, one final result is produced that is defuzzied, and a final decision is made on whether there is jamming attack or not. Throughout simulating different types of jamming attacks, the DR has an average of 99.75% and an FPR of 0.01%.

## 9.4.5   Swarm intelligence studies

The authors in [43] used the ant-colony-optimisation (ACO) to detect UDP DoS attacks on port 7, specifically Fraggle and Teardrop attacks. The agents (ants) iteratively monitor the network activity flow. More specifically, each ant represents an IDS agent, which is responsible for monitoring the network activity. Each agent/ant moves from a state/step $a$ to a state/step $b$, where each state represents network pattern knowledge. On each state, depending on the incoming packets received, a set of feasible expansions to the ant colony is calculated and the agent moves to the highest probability expansion. The probability for each move is calculated based on step attractiveness and step trail. Trails values are automatically updated when all agents/ants complete their state transiting. An increase or decrease on trail levels indicates a good move/legitimate behaviour or a bad move/malicious behaviour. The results indicate that the DR is reaching 80%.

The authors in [44] used the ant-colony-optimisation algorithm and focused on detecting low-rate (D)DoS attacks. The system first collects information from incoming traffic such as traffic flow, packet arrival time, packet attack rate and arrival time interval by manual setting. Next, the multi-agents installed in the network are working cooperatively towards the detections of malicious activity and tracking down the IP addresses of the attackers in a cooperative way. To change state, the traffic flow and time density from router to router is calculated. The proposed technique can also be used to detect attacks in neighbouring paths. The average DR is 89%.

The authors in [45] designed an IDS to detect attacks of the KDD99 dataset, including various types of (D)DoS attacks using the ant colony optimisation algorithm.

To detect anomalies in the traffic, they used IP Protocol segments, the total length of each packet, the source port and destination port in the TCP and UDP. They report that their algorithm has a precision of 96.94%.

In [46], the authors have used the ABC algorithm to detect various MANET-specific attacks such as flooding attacks, blackhole attacks and wormhole attacks. The authors extend the ABC algorithm to dynamically update the generated profile as MANET networks are not static (due to the nodes mobility). Their system has three stages: training, detection and update states. Each of the nodes in the MANET create a set of spherical detectors. The ABC algorithm applies Monte Carlo estimation to prevent the overcreation of detectors and Gaussian local search to refine the detectors generated. The spherical detectors are responsible for differentiating malicious from normal behaviour. The spherical detectors at regular time intervals are partially updated. Monte Carlo estimates when the detectors shall be totally updated. In their results, they report a DR of 96.11% with FPR of 1.45%.

The authors in [47] combined PSO with fast learning networks (FLN) which is a specific type of ANN to detect malicious activity in the KDD99 dataset. FLN comes with the disadvantage of not consisting of optimal weights. Hence, its accuracy is decreased. For that reason, the authors use PSO to select optimal weights for the neurons. PSO creates particles, each of them representing one candidate solution for the weights of the FLN. The authors have compared their solution to other types of ANNs such as evolutionary learning models and showing that their solution has suppressed related solutions. Furthermore, they report the accuracy has increased for all models with increasing the number of hidden neurons. In detail, they report a true positive (TP) rate (TPR) for normal traffic of 99.7%, for (D)DoS attacks 98.11%, for U2R attacks 80.40%, for R2L attacks 54.55% and for probe attacks 80.01%.

## 9.4.6 Artificial neural network studies

In most of the bio/nature-inspired studies for intrusion detection, ANNs are used in combination with other bio/nature-inspired algorithms that their main objective is to optimise the features. Some notable studies are briefly described below.

The authors in [48] used a combination of SI and ANN to detect malicious activity in the KDD99 dataset. In detail, they have made usage of the ABC algorithm with a BP ANN in an attempt to construct an effective neural network architecture to avoid overfitting problems. The authors justify their choice through the following argument: the ABC algorithm's objective is to optimise the BP neural network's training process (construction of network weights and thresholds, initial training values) until it reaches an acceptable accuracy. For evaluating the model, they have used 10% of the KDD dataset. They report a squared error of approximately less than 0.25, while a traditional BP neural network is higher.

In [49], the authors have combined the GA along with ANN, attempting to increase the DR. The have used the Center for Applied Internet Data Analysis (CAIDA) dataset. The GA was used for feature selection to find the most important features from a total of 43 and exclude all the irrelevant or redundant ones. The ANN was used for detection by taking the most relevant features as inputs, using the Multi-Layer Perceptron (MLP) method for defining the architecture. The proposed solution had a DR of 99.997% and an FPR of 0.002%.

In [50], the authors designed a neural network IDS to detect DoS attacks with the KDD99 dataset. They used the LVQ algorithm to structure the architecture of the neural network. They conducted the experiment ten times using both BP and LVQ algorithms to compare results. The ANN using the LVQ algorithm achieved an average DR of 99.723% and a 0.277% FPR, while the BP-ANN achieved an average DR 89.9259% and a 0% FPR.

The authors in [51] have used ANNs and the MLP method to detect DoS attacks in the NSL-KDD dataset (11 in total). They have constructed 11 different MPL-Neural Networks, one responsible for detecting each attack. They have altered the features that are normally used to train the neural network differently. Specifically, they changed the "connection" feature. If the "connection" is legitimate the feature value is set to 0. If it is malicious it is set to 1–39, depending on the attack it corresponds to. For the flag feature instead of Boolean value they have defined 11 flags, each corresponding to a different state of the connection. In their results, they report an average DR of 96.6% and an FPR of 3.4%.

The authors in [52] have used MLP ANNs to detect (D)DoS attacks in the AMI of the smart grid. Their proposed method consists of three phases: the training, the feature extraction and traffic filtering phases. The features chosen are the packet headers, source and destination port, windows size and flags. The authors were particularly interested to evaluate their proposed method under the possibility of accepting impure traffic. Impure traffic consists of malicious traffic mixed with normal traffic. They have tested their technique under five impure datasets they have created. They report the best results to have a false acceptance rate of less than 8% and the false rejection rate to be less than 5%.

The authors in [53] have used ANNs to detect (D)DoS attacks in 802.16 (WiMax) networks, which is used in the smart grid. The proposed system consists of three stages: feature extraction, process of the features and features forward to the neural network for classification. The features extracted are the Hurst parameter incoming traffic, the average bit rate of received messages, the increment bit rate of the received message, the entropy and conditional entropy of received MAC address and the amount of mutual information that use entropy and conditional entropy of the received packet. For the maximum number of subseries size (=256), the maximum TPR is 85% and the minimum FPR is 15%.

## 9.4.7   Artificial immune systems studies

The authors in [54] used a variation of the NSA, the neighbourhood negative selection (NNS) algorithm to detect DoS flooding attacks focusing on the ICMP, TCP and UDP protocols, from the DARPA dataset. NSA operates as follows: normal data are defined as self-patterns. Then a great number of random patterns is generated and compared to the self-patterns. If the new generated pattern matches one of the self-pattern, it becomes a detector, otherwise it is discarded. Then, in the monitoring state, if there is a match between a detector and an incoming traffic part, then an anomaly is present. NSS has two stages. The system extracts from traffic protocol type, duration of the flow, number of packets/bytes from outside to inside and vice versa. In the first stage, feature extraction takes place and then the set is used to train the algorithm. In the second stage, the NSS algorithm is used for detection. Neighbourhoods represent data, so therefore no single threshold is used to detect anomalies but rather a quantitative approach is adopted. The results indicate that the proposed system can detect the attacks in an efficient way. In detail, the true negative rate (TNR) has not fallen below 8.5% and the maximum value for false negative (FN) rate (FNR) was no more than 15%.

The authors in [55] apply the CSA (AIS) algorithms. They proposed an IDS for the smart grid infrastructure. The attacks considered were from the KDD99 dataset and the DoS group of attacks were included. The FPR is only 0.7% while the FNR is 21.02% for the CSA and 1.3% and 26.32% for the AIS, respectively. Their high FNR value is because of the U2R attacks, so it is assumed that the proposed solution is effective against DoS attacks. U2R attack is when the attacker initiates the attack as a normal user and by exploiting the system's vulnerabilities attempts to gain root privileges.

The authors in [56] focused in detecting SYN-Flooding attacks using DCA. DCA correlates the different data-streams as signals and antigens. The signals represent the behaviour of the system while being categorised. The output signal value changes according to the input signals received. If that value changes in an abnormal way, it is removed from the population for analysis. Two series of experiments were conducted, one for selecting the best attributes to pass them to the algorithm and another for the actual detection. Through a series of experiments, the authors claim perfect DR and only 0.17 FPR.

The authors in [57] have used AIS generation algorithms in the NSL-KDD dataset. In particular, they have used NSA and the CSA with different set of features at each experiment. For the NSL-KDD dataset, the authors found the following thresholds showed the most promising results: 39 features used a threshold of 20, 22 features used a threshold of 9, and 13 features used a threshold of 6. For 39 features, the DR is 86.86, for 22 features, the DR is 77.23 and for 13, 21.56.

In [58], the authors have used AIS to design a distributed IDS to detect cyberattacks in the KDD99. Two types of antibodies are constructed (through positive and negative selection), one for malicious and one for normal traffic. In practice, antibodies are formed as hypersphere shapes with a specific centre and radius. The centre is denoted as a vector of the values for the features chosen. Hence, Euclidean distance is adopted for affinity measurement. Furthermore, the authors used PSO for updating the radiuses of the antigens. Through their simulation experiments, it is shown that the proposed algorithm achieved 99.1% TPR, while the FPR is 1.9%.

The authors in [59] have developed a multiple detector which consists of various types of AIS algorithms to detect attacks from the UNB ISCX intrusion detection evaluation dataset using various features such as connection duration, protocol type, service, flag type, source and destination ports and so on. Their results show the multiple-detector set AIS achieved a DR of 53.34% and an FPR of 0.20%.

The authors in [60] have used GA with one-point crossover instead of two to find an optimal set of features before using ML algorithms for detecting attacks from the NSL-KDD dataset. Multiple popular supervised classifiers were used on the dataset such as random forest (RF), decision trees (DTs), $K$-nearest neighbour ($K$-NN), Naive Bayes (NB) and Bayesian networks (BNs). The authors report RF as the algorithm producing the best results. The best ML algorithm was RF with 99.87% DR.

### 9.4.8   Chaos theory studies

Most of the studies making usage of chaos, also use ANNs for the effective malware and intrusions detections. Below, we briefly present some notable studies that combine chaos theory with ANNs.

In [61], the authors have created a (D)DoS detection system to detect (D)DoS attacks but also be robust against legitimate bursts of traffic. They aimed to discover patterns that can define how legitimate traffic behaves. Based on their observations, they developed a baseline to use it to train their neural network model to detect (D)DoS attacks.

Their system uses self-similarity theory to construct a self-similar neural network model to monitor the traffic and chaos theory's local Lyapunov exponents to distinguish between normal behaviour and (D)DoS attack. Normal and attack traffic are represented in a space graph. These points are the mappings of a non-linear function of the input variables, which includes sequences of normal, bursty normal and normal changed to attack traffic. It is assumed that legitimate traffic diminishes asymptotically with time. However, if traffic behaves chaotically as soon as new traffic enters the space, then it is likely there is a (D)DoS attack. They report a DR of 88%–94% with an FP of 0.45%–0.05%.

Based on the findings and the methods used in [61], the authors in [62] have followed a similar approach, managing to improve the DR. In detail, they have once again used chaos theory's Lyapunov exponents in a combination with neural networks to detect (D)DoS attacks. They report a 98.4% DR; however, they do not give any details regarding any FP or FNRs.

In [63], the authors again use the local Lyapunov exponent in combination with the ANNs to detect a (D)DoS attack from the DARPA dataset. They have used information regarding the packets flow to differentiate between (D)DoS traffic and normal burst traffic. With the results they gained they trained their neural network model to correctly detect (D)DoS attacks. The chaos theory model they used the AR time model to predict the network traffic and calculate the ER. They used DARPA dataset to evaluate their work and claimed 93.75% DR.

## 9.5   Case study: application layer (D)DoS detection

Smart homes consist of a great number of different devices, all deployed in a single network monitoring the environment, collecting and sharing important data and information with the owners and other smart IoT devices and external services through internal and external networks. The node responsible for this communication is the energy services interface (ESI). It acts as a bidirectional interface where information can be exchanged between the smart home and external domains. Furthermore, it protects internal energy resources from security failures and ensures secure internal communication between the devices deployed in the smart home. ESI's importance to the smart home and in the outside domains makes it an excellent target for cyberattacks.

(D)DoS attacks can be conducted across all the layers of the TCP/IP model. Application layer (D)DoS attacks are much more harder to be detected efficiently and accurately than their perspective ones in lower layers as they do not violate any protocol rules or make usage of malicious behaviour. The TCP connections are established successfully, and normal requests are sent to the target, in contrast to (D)DoS attacks in lower layer such as the TCP flooding which sends a burst amount of SYN packets without acknowledging the SYN, ACK packets sent from the server. The application layer flooding instead sends a burst amount of legitimate requests to the server, which the server cannot refuse but to reply. As a result, it becomes unresponsive due to great amount of incoming requests. On the contrary, slow-rate application layer (D)DoS attack exploits a server's ability to wait for a connection to be completed in a range of time, if the incoming connection is legitimately slow. As long as the client manages to send a subsequent packet in an attempt to complete the request the server is obliged to keep the connection open. Based on that, the slow-rate attack opens a great number of connections and initiates requests that never complete them. As time is passing by, more and more connections are open and that results in the target becoming once again unresponsive.

Based on these issues and concerns, it is important to develop effective security countermeasures to detect (D)DoS attacks in such critical systems. However, the majority of devices deployed in IoT networks are low in resources such as memory, processing power and power. Therefore, it is important for the detection algorithms to be as lightweight as possible. Since the most popular detection algorithms used belong to artificial intelligence and machine learning, it is even more important since they are particularly high in complexity and need a large dataset to be trained. One effective way to reduce an algorithm's complexity is to reduce the features. In that way, the algorithms are going to be trained faster, in less time and the model constructed is going to be less complex. Therefore, we have constructed a smart home IoT dataset which consists of both legitimate and application layer flooding and slow-rate (D)DoS attacks. The dataset consists of 197 attack instances and 257 normal instances.

## 9.5.1 Evaluation environment

### 9.5.1.1 Network simulator 3

For the simulation of the smart home network, network simulator 3 (NS-3) was used. NS-3 is an open-source discrete-event simulator developed in C++. A summary of the networks' parameters and protocols used is given in Table 9.2. Various IoT devices are deployed in the home area network that connect to the gateway, called ESI, to exchange data with the smart city infrastructures. For our IoT smart home network simulation, ten nodes were simulated. Nine of them represent IoT devices and smart appliances and the final node forms the ESI. All simulated nodes were static, with no mobility. In the physical layer, all the connections were wireless and the 802.11 protocol was used. The structure was set to ad hoc, using AODV routing protocol.

Table 9.2    Smart home protocols

| Layer | Protocol SH/SG-substations/SG-AMI |
|---|---|
| Physical | 802.11 |
| Data-link | SSID |
| Network | IPv4 |
| Transport | TCP |
| Application | HTTP, MQTT, CoAP, XMPP |

In the network layer, IPv4 was used and in the transport layer both UDP and TCP were used. In the application layer, a wide variety of application layer protocols were simulated including CoAP, MQTT, XMPP and AMQP and HTTP.

### 9.5.1.2    Simulation of (D)DoS attacks

Our proposed algorithm's accuracy is evaluated through experiments. Related (D)DoS detection studies make usage of popular datasets such as the KDD99, DARPA or NSL-KDD datasets. However, we cannot use these datasets as they do not have IoT traffic nor they contain application layer (D)DoS attacks. In IoT networks, the traffic is highly heterogeneous, therefore harder to detect any malicious behaviour. Hence, we had to create our own synthetic traffic using NS-3. A series of traffic containing normal and attack traffic files were generated. Both flooding and slow-rate attacks were simulated. In every scenario, seven nodes from the smart home were generating normal traffic, and the remaining two were generating malicious traffic.

In order for both normal and attack traffic to be simulated, degree of randomness was added in the network packet generation from the nodes. Randomness was introduced through Poisson distribution in the following metrics, at the time a packet was created and sent from the client to the server, at the size of the packet generated from both the client and the server and at the time the server needed to respond. Different speeds were also applied in IoT nodes to service application layer requests. Hence, we can simulate slow connections that are legitimate.

Most of the (D)DoS attacks, Flooding types in particular, can be classified as constant rate. In constant rate attacks, the attackers generate a high steady rate of traffic towards the target [5]. The impact of such an attack is fast, but it can easily be detected due to the its obvious intensity. Hence, attackers have moved towards more sophisticated ways of conducting (D)DoS attacks. One way to evade any security measures installed is to slowly but steadily flood the target in an increasing-rate attack, where the maximum impact of the attack is reached gradually over the attack period. To simulate increased-rate attacks in NS-3, we used open random connections after random time-intervals. To assess the results for chaos algorithm's effectiveness, we have calculated the most popular metrics used when assessing a detection algorithm's accuracy.

These are DR, ER, TPs, FPs, FNs and precision. In intrusion detection, positives instances are attacks and negative instances are normal. DR measures the algorithm's

*Table 9.3   List of features*

| Feature name | Description |
|---|---|
| Requests no | Total number of requests in a time-series interval |
| Packets no | Total number of packets in a time-series interval |
| Data rate | Average data rate in a time-series interval |
| Avg packet size | Average packet size in a time-series interval |
| Avg time betw requests | Average time between two requests in a time-series interval |
| Avg time betw response and request | Average time between the response and the first requests encountered in a time-series interval |
| Avg time betw responses | Average time between two responses in a time-series interval |
| Parallel requests | Total number of parallel requests in a time-series interval |

proportion in correctly classifying incoming instances and ER measures the algorithm's proportion errors incorrectly classifying incoming instances. The sum of DR and ER equals one. TP measures the proportion of positive instances that are correctly identified as such. FP measures the proportion of negative instances to have been misclassified as positive. FN measures the proportion of positive instances that have been misclassified as negative. Lastly, precision measures the proportion of relevant instances among the retrieved instances. Hence, precision measures the rate of TPs divided by all the positives, both correctly and incorrectly classified.

## 9.5.2   Feature selection

Most of the studies using forecasting techniques against (D)DoS attacks mentioned in the previous section usually make usage of a single feature for prediction and detect the possible deviations in the number of packets, the number of packets per IP, the packet flags and so on. However, these studies focus on detecting (D)DoS attacks on lower layers and not on the application layer. The adoption of one single feature on the application layer is likely not to produce satisfactory results since application (D)DoS attacks do not violate any protocol rules and do not produce malformed packets. Therefore we have designed a new set of features to detect application layer flooding and slow-rate (D)DoS attacks. All of the features are heavily dependent on time and form ideal features for forecasting-based algorithms and presented in Table 9.3.

### 9.5.2.1   Requests number

In a flooding scenario, the number of requests over a period of time will be much greater compared to normal traffic request rates. In a slow-rate attack, scenario, the number of requests over two consecutive periods of time will have large difference. Since slow-rate opens connections to send requests after an amount of minutes, there will be a pattern of low number of requests, then high number of requests, then low and so on.

### 9.5.2.2    Packets number

In a flooding attack, the number of packets on application layer is rapidly increased over a short period of time. In a slow-rate attack, the number of packets is lower due to the packets being sent slowly, just before a request can be rejected. Hence, the request stays alive but very few packets are sent.

### 9.5.2.3    Data rate

In a flooding attack, the data rate on application layer is rapidly increased over a short period of time. In a slow-rate attack, the data rate is lower due to the slow data rate of the malicious requests.

### 9.5.2.4    Average packet size

In a flooding attack, the average packet size is decreased due to the requests being simply a get request with no payload. In a slow-rate attack, the average size packet is decreased since a great series of connections send small incomplete packets over the attack period of time.

### 9.5.2.5    Average time between requests

In a flooding attack, the average time between each request is vastly decreased due to an outburst of requests being sent over a short period of time simultaneously. In a slow-rate attack, the average time between each request is decreased compared to the same value in a normal scenario. Instead, there are spikes of the number of requests being sent. When the attack is at the stage of opening new requests, their rate is increased. When the attack is at the stage of maintaining the connections open, normal subsequent packets are sent; therefore, the rate of the requests is less than the previous stage.

### 9.5.2.6    Average time between response and request

In a flooding attack, the average time between a response and the next request is vastly decreased. In a slow-rate attack the average time between a response and the next request the slow-rate attack causes malicious requests.

### 9.5.2.7    Average time between responses

In a flooding attack, the average time between two consecutive responses is vastly decreased since a burst of requests is being sent to the server; therefore, a great number of responses have to be generated. In a slow-rate attack, the same feature is increased since the slow-rate attack's requests are initiated but never completed.

### 9.5.2.8    Parallel requests

In a flooding attack, the average concurrent requests is decreased since the attackers send multiple requests that are very quickly finished. In a slow-rate attack, many requests are initiated and stay open over a period of time and the average number of parallel open requests is large.

## 9.5.3   *Intrusion detection evaluation metrics*

In the intrusion detection literature, studies use an extended series of evaluation metrics and statistical tests to assess their detection engines performance. Measuring the system's DR is not enough sometimes; therefore, to provide a more holistic evaluation, different metrics are adopted. In this section, we briefly describe the most popular evaluation metrics, the actual formulas and their application in intrusion detection. In intrusion detection research, the presence of a cyberattack is regarded as a positive instance and the absence of it as a negative instance.

### 9.5.3.1   True positive rate

TPR or otherwise called recall or sensitivity is when the detection algorithm is able to correctly identify an instance as an attack.

### 9.5.3.2   True negative rate

TNR or otherwise called specificity, is when the detection algorithm is able to correctly identify an instance as normal.

### 9.5.3.3   False positive rate

FPR, or otherwise called fall-out, is when the detection algorithm has incorrectly classified an instance as an attack, with it being normal.

### 9.5.3.4   False negative rate

FNR is when the detection algorithm has incorrectly classified an instance as normal, with it being an attack.

### 9.5.3.5   Precision

Precision, or otherwise called positive predictive value, denotes the rate at which the detection algorithm has correctly classified TP instances out of all the positive instances it has classified. In general, precision denotes the fraction of instances that are relevant from the total number of all retrieved instances.

## 9.5.4   *Experiments results analysis*

As it has been highlighted in [39–41,46,47,49,60], bio/nature-inspired algorithms have been used for feature reduction in an attempt to reduce the overall complexity of detection algorithms without affecting their accuracy. For finding an optimal set of features, we have used the available nature-inspired algorithms provided from Weka toolkit. Specifically, we used evolutionary search, ant and bee search, genetic search and PSO search algorithms. All algorithms have identified parallel requests, average data rate, average packet size and packet number as the necessary features. The machine-learning algorithms used were RFs, DTs, $K$-NN, SVM, BNs, Naive Bayesian, multilayer perceptron ANN, deep-MLP ANN. Two series of experiments have been conducted, one with all eight features and one with four features.

## 9.5.5   Results analysis and discussion

From our experiments, it was observed that the overall DR has been vastly decreased across all algorithms when the features were reduced. The specific rates are enlisted in Table 9.4 (with 8 features) and in Table 9.5 (with 4 features).

DR: MLP and $K$-NN have performed best with eight features, both with 98.69%, followed by RF with 96.74%, DT and Deep-MLP with 95.42%, and then BN with 91.50%, NB with 89.54% and SVM with 88.24%.

In the series of experiments using four features, $K$-NN has still been the most accurate in classifying unknown traffic but MLP's DR has been dropped. In detail, $K$-NN comes first in terms of DR, followed by SVM, MLP, BN, DT, RF, Deep-MLP and NB. Based on the results, we can observe that $K$-NN's distance metrics is accurate enough regardless of the features involved for effectively differentiating between normal and attack traffic.

The reduction of features clearly negatively affects MLP, Deep-MLP, RF and DT's accuracy. The feature reduction makes the ANNs models' characteristics such as the connections between the layers, weights and number of hidden layer in the deep-MLP less complex but also less accurate. The model generated is too simplistic to identify

*Table 9.4   Machine-learning algorithms results against application layer (D)DoS attacks smart home IoT dataset with eight features*

| Alg (dataset) | DR (%) | TP (%) | FP (%) | TN (%) | FN (%) | Prec (%) |
|---|---|---|---|---|---|---|
| NB(1) | 89.54 | 83.8 | 5.9 | 94.1 | 16.2 | 91.9 |
| BN(1) | 91.50 | 80.9 | 0 | 100 | 8.50 | 100 |
| SVM(1) | 88.24 | 73.5 | 0 | 100 | 26.5 | 100 |
| $K$-NN(1) | 98.69 | 97.1 | 0 | 100 | 1.31 | 100 |
| DT(1) | 95.42 | 97.1 | 5.9 | 94.1 | 2.9 | 93 |
| RF(1) | 96.73 | 97.1 | 3.5 | 96.5 | 2.9 | 95.7 |
| MLP(1) | 98.69 | 98.5 | 1.2 | 98.8 | 1.5 | 98.5 |
| DeepMLP(1) | 95.42 | 89.7 | 0 | 100 | 10.3 | 100 |

*Table 9.5   Machine learning algorithms results against application layer (D)DoS attacks smart home IoT dataset with four features*

| Alg (dataset) | DR (%) | TP (%) | FP (%) | TN (%) | FN (%) | Prec (%) |
|---|---|---|---|---|---|---|
| NB(1) | 86.61 | 82 | 7.8 | 92.2 | 18 | 92.6 |
| BN(1) | 89.29 | 85.2 | 5.9 | 94.1 | 14.8 | 94.5 |
| SVM(1) | 89.29 | 82 | 2 | 98 | 18 | 98 |
| $K$-NN(1) | 93.75 | 93.4 | 5.9 | 94.1 | 6.6 | 95 |
| DT(1) | 88.39 | 88.5 | 11.8 | 88.2 | 11.5 | 90 |
| RF(1) | 88.39 | 90.2 | 13.7 | 86.3 | 9.8 | 88.7 |
| MLP(1) | 89.29 | 86.9 | 7.8 | 92.2 | 13.1 | 93 |
| DeepMLP(1) | 87.5 | 83.6 | 7.8 | 92.2 | 16.4 | 92.7 |

the kind of incoming traffic. Also, the reduction of features makes DT and RF models to create less complex trees that have the same negative effect. On the other hand, the probabilistic models used, BN and NB, are not particularly negatively affected due to joint probabilities used. However, with the feature reduction, the SVM algorithm's DR is vastly increased. This could be because the hyperplane constructed with less features is actually more accurate than with eight features.

*TPR*: In the eight features series of experiments, MLP achieves the best TPR with 98.5%. $K$-NN, RF and DT have the highest TPRs, all with 97.1%. RF performed better than DT as expected due to RFs being an 'improved' DT version. The algorithms following are deep-MLP with 89.7%, NB 83.8%, BNs with 80.9% and SVM with 73.5%. The deep-MLP model although having a high TP, rate it can be highlighted that the construction of additional hidden layers does not necessarily mean they are going to be more accurate in detecting attacks so an MLP with a single hidden layer is a better solution. Also, it is indicated that probabilistic models and SVM have not been particularly effective in constructing models to detect the attacks accurately enough.

In the four features series of experiments, the TPR is generally decreased across all algorithms. Only $K$-NN and RF manage to get a TPR above 90 with 93.4% and 90.2%. Then DT follows with 88.5%, MLP with 86.9%, BN with 85.2%, deep-MLP with 83.6% and lastly NB and SVM with 82%.

It is worth highlighting that the feature reduction vastly decreases the algorithms' general accuracy and ability to detect the attacks. In sophisticated attacks such as the application layer *(D)DoS* attacks, features play an important role in the construction of the algorithmic models. Based on both of these series of experiments, it is evident that probabilistic approaches fail to identify the attack instances as BN and NB fail to get a TPR above at least 90%. This occurs because probabilistic models need a large dataset to construct accurate and robust probabilities. Furthermore due to the small dataset as well as the feature reduction, MLP and deep-MLP failed to create robust algorithmic models. On the other hand, $K$-NN proves to be robust in detecting unknown attacks along with RF and relatively DT.

*FPR*: In the series of eight features BN, SVM, deep-MLP and $K$-NN do not generate any FP instances. MLP generates a 1.2% FPR, RF generates a 3.5% FPR, and DT and NB generate 5.9% FPR. In the series of four features, SVM generates 2% FPR, BN and $K$-NN generate 5.9% FPR, MLP, deep-MLP and NB generate 7.8% FPR, DT generates 11.8% and RF 13.7% FPRs. In general, it is observed that with the reduction of features the FPR is increased. This indicates that the four features removed are quite important in understanding when normal behaviour can have anomalies but still be normal.

## 9.6 Discussion

Without a doubt, the work done in the field of intrusion detection using bio-inspired techniques is remarkable. There is a great diversity of different techniques used to both reduce the features and/or detect the various types of malicious behaviour. Bio/Nature-inspired algorithms have been proven particularly effective in finding an optimal set

*Table 9.6    Bio/Nature-inspired algorithms studies results*

| Algorithm/Reference | Attack | Result |
|---|---|---|
| GT [32] | (D)DoS attacks | Prevention |
| GT [33] | (D)DoS attacks | Prevention |
| EA [34] | SIP flooding attacks | 82.17% and 77.00% |
| ES [35] | DARPA (D)DoS attacks | No results |
| GA [36] | Blackhl. and Packt. Dr. | 95% |
| GA [37] | KDD99 attacks | 90% |
| GA [38] | KDD99 attacks | 97.57% |
| GA and FL [39] | KDD99 attacks | 95% |
| GA and FL [40] | KDD99 attacks | 95% and 1% FPR |
| GA and FL [41] | KDD99 attacks | 99.75% |
| FL [42] | Jamming DoS | 99.75% |
| ACO [43] | UDP DoS | 80% |
| ACO [44] | Low-rate DoS | 89% |
| ACO [45] | KDD99 Attacks | 96.94% |
| ABC and ANN [46] | KDD99 attacks | Less 0.025 squarer. |
| GA and ANN [49] | KDD99 attacks | 99.997% DR and 0.002% FPR |
| ANN [50] | KDD99 attacks | 99.723% DR and 0.277% FPR |
| ANN [51] | NSL-KDD attacks | 96.6% DR and 3.4% FPR |
| ANN [52] | KDD99 attacks | False accept. less 8% and false rej. less 5%. |
| ANN [53] | (D)DoS | 85% TPR |
| AIS [54] | DARPA (D)DoS | Max TN 8.5% and max FNR 15% |
| AIS [55] | KDD99 | FP 0.7% and FN 21.02% and 1.3% and 26.32% |
| AIS [56] | SYN attacks | 100% TPT and 0.17 FPR |
| CT [61] | (D)DoS attacks | 88%–94% and 0.45%–0.05% FPR |
| CT [62] | (D)DoS attacks | 98.4% |
| CT [63] | DARPA Attacks | 93.75% |
| PSO with FLN [47] | KDD99 | Norm. 99.7%, (D)DoS 98.11%, U2R 80.4%, R2L 54.55%, Probe 80.01% |
| AIS [57] | NSL-KDD | 86.8% |
| AIS [58] | KDD99 | TPR 99.1% and FPR 1.9% |
| AIS [59] | KDD99 | DR 53.34% and FPR 0.20% |
| GA with RF [60] | NSL-KDD | 99.87% DR |

of features that can achieve high rate of detection as well as a low rate of FPs. This is particularly beneficial as it reduces the algorithmic complexity of the detection model constructed as well as the time complexity. Furthermore, through the studies, it is highlighted that bio/nature-inspired algorithms are particularly effective in detecting different types of attacks that may or may not belong in the same attack family, such as the KDD99 dataset.

As discussed above, studies achieve results of DR above 77% and FPRs not below 2.7% as illustrated in Table 9.6.

ANNs are proved the most effective in terms of the detection technique, achieving the highest DR with 99.72%. This is reflected in the research literature as ANN is proved to be the most usable and popular bio-inspired algorithm in intrusion detection.

However, ANNs have an increased computational complexity [39]. To decrease and optimise the complexity threshold techniques, such as GAs and chaos theory, could be applied. Hence, ANN will need fewer resources.

GT is mainly used for preventing intrusions in systems. However, its ability to define how network nodes in the system should communicate makes it a suitable approach to detect malicious behaviour. For that reason, the authors in [14,15] have applied a combination of computational puzzle with GT to prevent an attack rather than just detecting it. GT can also be used for trust management between the nodes participating in detection of threats in the system.

GAs have a better DR as shown in [36–38] than evolution strategies [35] although both technologies follow a similar approach. GA algorithms are behaving effectively, from resources allocation and execution time [18], for feature reduction. In next generation, GA algorithms can be more effective as the dataset can be diverse and provide better detection with fewer errors. This is due to packet dropping, which is normal in communication networks, and it cannot be considered an attack unless it is examined more carefully. GA algorithms are behaving effectively for feature reduction before intrusion detection. Regarding detection, GA is able to achieve a DR between 90% and 97.57% for KDD99 attacks. This indicates that the evolutionary approach GA follows is effective against detecting different types of attacks as well as different variations of the same attack. Also, GA is able to detect other types of (D)DoS attacks such as grey-hole and packet dropping attacks as shown in [18] with a high DR (95%). GA can also be used in combination with other bio/nature-inspired algorithms such as [39–41,49]. In such case, GA is used for feature reduction in an attempt to reduce complexity of complex architectures (ANN and FL) without affecting the DR. This objective is achieved as the DR is between 95% and 99.997%.

AISs are particularly effective against intrusion detection in distributed systems since there is no need for central coordinator. In [54], authors detect (D)DoS attacks based on the AIS algorithm which is able to spread itself across the network for monitoring. Therefore, (D)DoS attacks are detected faster since the proposed NSS algorithm is able to mix antibodies and detect anomalies. In addition, from the studies of [54–56], it is shown that their proposals produce low FPRs since authors construct systems that can immediately detect abnormal instances. Hence, AIS algorithm is able to detect a wide range of (D)DoS attacks as well as other types of attacks, when KDD99 is used. However, AIS has a relatively high FNR, between 15% and 26.32%, whereas the FPR remains low, between 0.17% and 1.3%.

SI achieve a respectable DR against a range of cyberattacks as they take advantage of the algorithm's cooperative nature to detect various types of attacks that can be considered stealthy, such as low-rate (D)DoS attacks [44] and UDP DoS attacks [43], achieving a good DR of 89% and 80%, respectively. In the KDD99 attacks, SI algorithm is performing well while achieving a 96.94% DR.

FL also achieves high rates of detection as shown in [39–42]. FL is also effective in comparing classifications from many sources and deciding if an instance is either malicious or normal. FL promotes collaborative detection by effectively combining evidence from multiple IDS agents. Therefore, it is able to detect the multiple and different cyberattacks contained in the KDD99 dataset with a DR between 95% and 98.3%. FL in [54] has also been used against jamming DoS attacks with a very high DR of 99.75%.

Finally, chaos theory is proved to also be a promising approach in detecting abnormalities in real time traffic as shown in [61–63] when combined with ANNs achieving a DR between 88% and 98.4% against various (D)DoS attacks in different protocols.

Although the studies on bio-inspired techniques and their effective application in intrusion detection seem more than promising, they certainly have some limitations. Cyberattacks have become highly sophisticated and an attacker can stealthy bypass any security control.

It can be observed that current studies discuss how robust against cyberattacks and (D)DoS attacks in particular. However, there is no indication on how to detect compromised nodes/botnets acting maliciously. As a counter example, an attacker can constantly change IP addresses to bypass (D)DoS attack detection. In a similar example, botnets can flood the network and then 'sleep' for a while and 'wake' again to carry on so as to avoid detection. There are no studies that target such scenarios. This issue should have been at least considered since many (D)DoS attack scenarios are initiated from one machine being infected and gradually infecting the rest of the network so they can all become a part of a large botnet.

Furthermore, the U2R and R2L scenarios included in the KDD99 dataset have been used in multiple studies. Although these malicious types of behaviour are useful for detecting more complex cyberattacks scenarios, none of the related studies make usage of more complex cyberattack scenarios such as APTs. Hence, more sophisticated and recent datasets shall be used to evaluate bio-inspired algorithms.

Unfortunately, only a few studies exist that make usage of bio-inspired algorithms in the cyber-physical systems [42,51–53,55]. Other techniques could also be used to detect malicious behaviour in other cyber-physical systems such as the smart grid, IoT networks and the smart city. First, FL could be used and be particularly effective. As seen from the studies of [39–42], FL promotes collaboration, an essential concept for the detection of advanced persistent attacks in distributed systems such smart city networks.

Such systems are heterogeneous and complex, therefore, multiple information must be collected from different intrusion detection sensors to identify if there is malicious behaviour present. Another method that could be proved particularly effective for these infrastructures is the SI algorithm since it also promotes cooperation and it can be particularly effective against unknown attacks, or anomaly detection. A strong advantage of the chaos theory is that it can capture legitimate behaviour and define how much alteration can still be considered legitimate. Also, chaos theory could be used to detect other types of attacks that are relatively new, such as the application layer (D)DoS attacks. Lastly, GT would also be an effective solution for preventing (D)DoS attacks.

In smart city IoT networks and critical infrastructures, there is a vast amount of intelligent electronic devices interconnected together spread into large geographical distances. Due to their close mutual operation, they have higher possibilities of being compromised and participate in botnet attacks.

Another observed limitation is that researchers do not consider compromised IDS agents before actually launching the DoS or (D)DoS attacks. If one or more IDS agents are compromised, the attacker violates the 'trust' between the IDS agents. Hence, the compromised agent can 'fool' the network and act as legitimate. The only studies that address this issue are [32,33]. Such scenarios are critical to the system and can cause major consequences.

Additionally, bio-inspired techniques are proved to be particularly effective against (D)DoS attacks as it can be seen from the studies. We still believe they can be just as effective against other types of (D)DoS attacks, such as the slow-rate attack in the application layer [42]. Low-rate and slow-rate attacks follow similar approach but take place in different OSI Layer. Hence, detection can be efficiently achieved using bio-inspired techniques. Additional studies and extended experiments must be conducted for such an assumption to be validated. In addition, other (D)DoS attacks can be explored, such as the DNS amplification attack.

There have been studies to defend systems against application layer (D)DoS attacks but none of them have made usage of bio-inspired techniques or has examined how to defend against such attacks in the IoT networks and critical infrastructures [53–56]. However, since smart grid communicates on application level as well, such attacks are possible to be conducted on such environment. Bio-inspired techniques could be particularly effective in the smart grid due to its collaborative nature.

Another direction to consider effective detection of cyberattacks in the Smart Grid is the possibility of an attack being initiated from another infrastructure still targeting the smart grid. One example of such a circumstance is smart homes and the IoT. Smart homes are directly connected to the smart grid. It is much easier for an adversary to compromise a number of smart home devices and attack the smart grid than trying to harm the smart grid directly.

An important aspect to consider is that the majority of devices deployed in the smart grid are low in resources. On the other hand, most of the bio-inspired algorithms are resources demanding. Therefore, possible changes to the algorithms could be considered to make them lightweight and possibly adapt to such devices.

In the future, several bio-inspired techniques may combine with other machine-learning techniques, such as in [41] with SVM. Mitigating approaches rather than just detection be considered in the near future. Additionally, new solutions could expand to hybrid attacks and increase security confidence in networked systems.

Although the techniques used in intrusion detection are wide in range, there is still room for introducing new bio-inspired techniques as they could detect anomalies in a given set using nature-inspired models. An example is the self-healing technique used in the field of organic computing. In nature, self-healing is the automated process of recovery of a natural being. In research, most likely bioinformatics, the aim is to construct the self-X properties set depending on the goal. A self-detection approach could be designed as inspired by [37,38].

Another potential approach is the FA, inspired by the fireflies' behaviour. A firefly's main behaviour is flashing so that it can attract other fireflies. The concept is that the brighter the colour is, the greater the attractiveness is. Distance also plays a role as it increases brightness. FA could be potentially used for feature selection and reduction as well as used as an optimisation technique for ANN/SVM/FL techniques.

Besides detection, possible mitigation/prevention methods should be explored. A good example for this process is the cuckoo search optimisation technique as introduced in Section 2. It is motivated by the cuckoo species that let their eggs on hosts of other birds. If birds understand that their eggs are not their own, they throw them away or build a nest somewhere else. Eggs represent solutions and a cuckoo egg consists of a new solution that can potentially replace the old one. The algorithm can grow to a complex solution consisting a series of solutions. After detection, it can be used to find an optimised solution. Also, cuckoo technique could be used for feature reduction and possible weight training of ANNs.

## 9.7    Conclusion

As the technology rapidly progresses, it becomes a vital part of our lives with the smart city era approaching. Critical infrastructures and IoT networks become more complex in the smart city context but still need to be continuously available. Hence, the protection of critical infrastructures, such as the Smart Grid, against (D)DoS attacks is important. Since an attack can become highly sophisticated, the usage of natural systems to protect networks from intrusions could transform IDSs into fast, accurate and robust systems able to effectively detect plethora of (D)DoS attacks. Bio-inspired techniques are proved to be an efficient and practical solution to various attacks.

In this chapter, we discussed the importance of bio-inspired techniques in the field of intrusion detection. A brief explanation was given on the most popular cyber-attacks, as well as the most popular concepts of bio-inspired algorithm detection. Furthermore, the most recent and high-impact studies on this topic have been presented in a wide range of networks, and a detailed discussion was made regarding these studies. Concluding, future directions were highlighted for new research exploration in the bio-inspired era.

## References

[1]    C.C. Elisan, Malware, Rootkits & Botnets, McGraw-Hill, USA, 2013, pp. 9–82.
[2]    S. Olariu, A.Y. Zomaya, Handbook of Bioinspired Algorithms and Applications, Chapman and Hall/CRC, USA, 2005.
[3]    J. Heaton, Artificial Intelligence for Humans, Volume 2: Nature-Inspired Algorithms, CreateSpace Independent Publishing Platform, USA, 2014, pp. 1–38.
[4]    W. McCulloch, W. Pitts, 'A logical calculus of ideas immanent in nervous activity', Bulletin of Mathematical Biophysics, vol. 5, no. 4, pp. 115–133, 1943.

[5]   A.E. Eiben, J.E. Smith, Introduction to Evolutionary Computing, Springer, USA, 2003, pp. 25–48.

[6]   J.H. Holland, 'Genetic algorithms and the optimal allocation of trials', SIAM Journal on Computing, vol. 2, no. 2, pp. 88–105, 1973.

[7]   J.R. Koza, Genetic Programming: On the Programming of Computers by Means of Natural Selection, Cambridge, MA: The MIT Press, 1992.

[8]   H.G. Beyer, H.P. Schwefel, 'Evolution strategies', Natural Computing, vol. 1, pp. 3–52, 2002.

[9]   S. Binitha, S.S. Sathya, 'A survey of bio inspired optimization algorithms', International Journal of Soft Computing and Engineering (IJSCE), vol. 2, no. 2, 2012. ISSN: 2231-2307.

[10]  L.J. Fogel, A.J. Owens, M.J. Walsh, Artificial Intelligence through Simulated Evolution, John Wiley, USA, 1966.

[11]  G. Beni, J. 'Wang, Swarm Intelligence in Cellular Robotic Systems', in Proceedings of NATO Advanced Workshop on Robots and Biological Systems, Tuscany, Italy, June 26–30, 1989.

[12]  J. Kennedy, R. Eberhart, 'Particle Swarm Optimization', in Proceedings of IEEE International Conference on Neural Networks. IV, pp. 1942–1948, 1995.

[13]  M. Dorigo, V. Maniezzo, A. Colorni, 'Ant system: optimization by a colony of cooperating agents', IEEE Transactions on Systems, Man, and Cybernetics – Part B, vol. 26, pp. 29–41, 1995.

[14]  D. Karaboga, 'An idea based on honey bees warm for numerical optimization', Tech. Rep. TR06, Erciyes University, Engineering Faculty, Computer Engineering Department, USA, 2005.

[15]  X. Li, Z. Shao, J. Qian, 'An optimizing method base on autonomous animates: fish-swarm algorithm', Systems Engineering Theory and Practice, vol. 22, no. 2002, pp. 32–38, 1995.

[16]  X.S. Yang, 'Firefly algorithms for multimodal optimization', International symposium on stochastic algorithms. Springer, Berlin, Heidelberg, 2009.

[17]  H.G. Beyer, H.P. Schwefel, 'Evolution strategies', Natural Computing, vol. 1, pp. 3–52, 2002.

[18]  L.A. Zadeh, 'Fuzzy sets', Information and Control, vol. 8, no. 3, pp. 338–353, 1965.

[19]  E. Lorenz, 'Predictability: Does the flap of a butterfly's wings in Brazil set off a tornado in Texas', American Association for the Advancement of Science, Washington, DC, 1972.

[20]  J.V. Neumann, 'Zur Theorie der Gesellschaftsspiele', Mathematische Annalen, vol. 100, no. 1, pp. 295–320, doi:10.1007/BF01448847 English translation: Tucker, A. W.; Luce, R. D., eds. (1959), 'On the theory of games of strategy', Contributions to the Theory of Games, vol. 4, pp. 13–42, 1928.

[21]  M. McDowell, 'Understanding Denial-of-Service Attacks US-CERT', United States Computer Emergency Readiness Team, 2013.

[22]  C.C. Elisan, Malware, Rootkits & Botnets, McGraw-Hill, USA, 2013, pp. 9–82.

[23]  DARPA intrusion detection evaluation, 1998. Available on: http://www.ll.mit. edu/IST/ideval/data/data_index.html

[24]  KDD Cup, 1999. Available on: http://kdd.ics.uci.edu/databases/kddcup99/ kddcup99.html

[25]  NSL-KDD, 2009. Available on: http://www.unb.ca/cic/datasets/nsl.html

[26]  A. Shiravi, H. Shiravi, M. Tavallaee, A.A. Ghorbani, 'Toward developing a systematic approach to generate benchmark datasets for intrusion detection', Computers & Security, vol. 31, no. 3, pp. 357–374, 2012.

[27]  I. Sharafaldin, A.H. Lashkari, A.A. Ghorbani, 'Toward Generating a New Intrusion Detection Dataset and Intrusion Traffic Characterization', in Proceedings of the 4th International Conference on Information Systems Security and Privacy (ICISSP 2018), pp. 108–116, 2018.

[28]  E.B. Beigi, H.H. Jazi, N. Stakhanova, A.A. Ghorbani, 'Towards effective feature selection in machine learning-based botnet detection approaches', in Communications and Network Security (CNS), 2014 IEEE Conference on, pp. 247–255, 2014.

[29]  H.H. Jazi, H. Gonzalez, N. Stakhanova, A.A. Ghorbani, 'Detecting HTTP-based application layer DoS attacks on web servers in the presence of sampling', Computer Networks, vol. 121, pp. 25–36, 2017.

[30]  C. Kolias, G. Kambourakis, A. Stavrou, S. Gritzalis, 'Intrusion detection in 802.11 networks: empirical evaluation of threats and a public dataset', IEEE Communications Surveys & Tutorials, vol. 18, no. 1, pp. 184–208, 2018.

[31]  N. Moustafa, J. Slay, 'The evaluation of Network Anomaly Detection Systems: Statistical analysis of the UNSW-NB15 data set and the comparison with the KDD99 data set', Information Security Journal: A Global Perspective, vol. 25, no. 1–3, pp. 18–31, 2016.

[32]  Q. Zhu, C. Fung, R. Boutaba, T. Başar, 'Guidax: A game-theoretic incentive-based mechanism for intrusion detection networks', IEEE Journal on Selected Areas in Communications, Special Issue on Economics of Communication Networks & Systems (SI-NetEcon), pp. 2220–2230, 2012.

[33]  A. Michalas, N. Komninos, N.R. Prasad, 'Multiplayer Game for DDoS Attacks Resilience in Ad Hoc Networks', in 2nd International Wireless Communication, Vehicular Technology, Information Theory and Aerospace & Electronic Systems Technology, pp. 1–5, 2011.

[34]  M.A. Akbar, M. Farooq. 'Application of Evolutionary Algorithms in Detection of SIP Based Flooding Attacks', in Proc of the 11th Annual Conference on Genetic and Evolutionary Computation, GECCO'09, pp. 1419–1426, 2009.

[35]  H.K. Mbikayi, 'An evolution strategy approach toward rule-set generation for network intrusion detection systems (IDS)', International Journal of Soft Computing and Engineering (IJSCE), vol. 2, no. 5, pp. 201–205, 2012.

[36]  M. Lali, V. Palanisamy, 'Intrusion Detection for MANET to Detect Unknown Attacks Using Genetic Algorithm', in IEEE International Conference on Computational Intelligence and Computing Research, pp. 1–5, 2014.

[37]  M. Padmadas, N. Krishnan, J. Kanchana, M. Karthikeyan, 'Layered Approach for Intrusion Detection Systems based Genetic Algorithm', in International Conference on Computational Intelligence and Computing Research (ICCIC), pp. 1–4, 2013.

[38]  F.H. Khan, R. Shams, M. Aamir, M. Waseem, M. Memon, 'Intrusion detection in wireless networks using Genetic Algorithm', in Computing for Sustainable Global Development (INDIACom), 2015 2nd International Conference on, pp. 1830–1835, 2015.

[39]  Y. Danane, T. Parvat, 'Intrusion Detection System using Fuzzy Genetic Algorithm', in International Conference on Pervasive Computing, pp. 1–5, 2015.

[40]  P. Jongsuebsuk, N. Wattanapongsakorn, C. Charnsripinyo, 'Network Intrusion Detection with Fuzzy Genetic Algorithm for Unknown Attacks', in Information Networking (ICOIN), pp. 1–5, January 2013.

[41]  A. Kannan, G.Q. Maguire, 'Selection Algorithm for Effective Networks', in IEEE 12th International Workshops, pp. 416–423, 2012.

[42]  C. Balarengadurai, S. Saraswathi, 'A Fuzzy based Detection Technique for Jamming Attacks in IEEE 802.15.4 Low Rate Wireless Personal Area Network', in proceedings of Advances in Intelligent Systems and Computing-Springer Verlag-LNEE, pp. 422–433, 2012.

[43]  A. Gupta, O.J. Pandey, M. Shukla, A. Dadhich, A. Ingle, V. Ambhore, 'Intelligent Perpetual Echo Attack Detection on User Datagram Protocol Port 7 Using Ant Colony Optimization', in Electronic Systems, Signal Processing and Computing Technologies (ICESC), 2014 International Conference on, pp. 419–424, 2014.

[44]  H.H. Chen, S.K. Huang, 'L(D)DoS Attack Detection by Using Ant Colony Optimization Algorithms', Journal of Information Science and Engineering, vol. 32, no 4, PP. 995–1020, 2016.

[45]  C. Cai, L. Yuan, 'Intrusion detection system based on ant colony system', Journal of Networks, vol. 8, no. 4, p. 888, 2013.

[46]  F. Barani, A. Barani, 'Dynamic Intrusion Detection in AODV-based MANETs Using Memetic Artificial Bee Colony algorithm', in IEEE Conferences: 2014 22nd Iranian Conference on Electrical Engineering (ICEE), pp. 1040–1046, 2014.

[47]  M.H. Ali, B.A.D. Al Mohammed, A. Ismail, M.F. Zolkipli, 'A new intrusion detection system based on Fast Learning Network and Particle swarm optimization', IEEE Access, 6, pp. 20255–20261, 2018.

[48]  Q. Qian, J. Cai, R. Zhang, 'Intrusion Detection based on Neural Networks and Artificial Bee Colony', in IEEE/ACIS 13th International Conference on Computer and Information Science, pp. 257–262, 2014.

[49]  M. Barati, A. Abdullah, N.I. Udzir, R. Mahmod, N. Mustapha, 'Distributed Denial of Service Detection using hybrid machine learning techniques', International Symposium on Biometrics and Security Technologies, IEEE, pp. 268–273, 2014.

[50]   L. Jin, Y. Liu, L. Gu, 'DDoS Attack Detection Based on Neural Network', in International Symposium on Aware Computing, pp. 196–199, 2014.

[51]   M.M. Javidi, M.H. Nattaj, 'A new and quick method to detect DoS attacks by Neural Networks', Journal of Mathematics and Computer Science, vol. 6, pp. 85–96, 2013.

[52]   H. Atashazar, H. Modaghegh, 'Hybrid packet filtering for overcoming DDoS attacks against AMI components', Smart Grid Electrical Grids Technology, pp. 1–5, 2013.

[53]   M. Shojaei, N. Movahhedinia, B.T. Ladani, 'DDoS attack detection in IEEE 802.16 based networks', Wireless Networks, vol. 20, no. 8, pp. 2543–2559, 2014.

[54]   D. Wang, L. He, Y. Xue, Y. Dong, 'Exploiting Artificial Immune systems to detect unknown DoS attacks in real-time', in Cloud Computing and Intelligent Systems (CCIS), 2012 IEEE 2nd International Conference on, vol. 2, pp. 646–650, 2012.

[55]   Y. Zhang, L. Wang, W. Sun, R.C. Green, M. Alam, 'Distributed intrusion detection system in a multi-layer network architecture of smart grids', IEEE Transactions on Smart Grid, vol. 2, no. 99, pp. 796–808, 2011.

[56]   N.B.I. Al-Dabagh, I.A. Ali, 'Design and Implementation of Artificial Immune System for Detecting Flooding Attacks', in High Performance Computing and Simulation (HPCS), 2011 International Conference on, pp. 381,390, 4–8 July 2011.

[57]   D. Hooks, X. Yuan, K. Roy, A. Esterline, J. Hernandez, 'Applying Artificial Immune System for Intrusion Detection', in 2018 IEEE Fourth International Conference on Big Data Computing Service and Applications (BigDataService), pp. 287–292, 2018.

[58]   M. Tabatabaefar, M. Miriestahbanati, J.C. Grégoire, 'Network intrusion detection through artificial immune system', in Systems Conference (SysCon), 2017 Annual IEEE International, IEEE, pp. 1–6, 2017.

[59]   J. Brown, M. Anwar, G. Dozier, 'Intrusion Detection Using a Multiple-Detector Set Artificial Immune System', in 2016 IEEE 17th International Conference on Information Reuse and Integration, pp. 283–286, 2016.

[60]   A. Ferriyan, A.H. Thamrin, K. Takeda, J. Murai, 'Feature selection using genetic algorithm to improve classification in network intrusion detection system', in Knowledge Creation and Intelligent Computing (IES-KCIC), 2017 International Electronics Symposium on, pp. 46–49, 2017.

[61]   A. Chonka, J. Singh, W. Zhou, 'Chaos theory based detection against network mimicking DDoS attacks', IEEE Communications Letters, vol. 13, no. 9, pp. 717–719, 2009.

[62]   X. Wu, Y. Chen, 'Validation of chaos hypothesis in NADA and improved DDoS detection algorithm', IEEE Communications Letters, vol. 17, no. 12, pp. 2396–2399, 2013.

[63]   Y. Chen, X. Ma, X. Wu, 'DDoS detection algorithm based on pre-processing network traffic predicted method and Chaos theory', IEEE Communications Letters, vol. 17, no. 5, pp. 1052–1054, 2013.

*Chapter 10*
# DNA-inspired characterization and detection of novel social Twitter spambots

*Stefano Cresci[1], Roberto Di Pietro[2], Marinella Petrocchi[1], Angelo Spognardi[3], and Maurizio Tesconi[1]*

Spambot detection is a must for the protection of cyberspace, in terms of both threats to sensitive information of users and trolls that may want to cheat and influence the public opinion. Unfortunately, new waves of malicious accounts are characterized by advanced features, making their detection extremely challenging. In contrast with the supervised spambot detectors largely used in recent years and inspired by biological DNA, we propose an alternative, unsupervised detection approach. Its novelty is based on the idea of modeling online user behaviors with strings of characters representing the sequence of the user's online actions. Exploiting this nature-inspired behavioral model, the proposed technique lets groups of spambots emerge from the crowd, by comparing the accounts' behaviors. Results show that the proposal outperforms the best-of-breed algorithms commonly employed for spambot detection.

## 10.1 Introduction

Ranging over a time period spanning the last 10 years, the academic literature has seen the flowering of scientific approaches to model and analyze deceptive accounts in online social networks (OSNs). Deception in OSNs can take many different forms, each one having its own characteristics and being associated to a specific kind of anomalous accounts. In particular, OSNs currently feature the following different kinds of anomalous subscribers: *spammers*, *bots*, *cyborgs*, *compromised accounts*, *sybils*, and *fake followers* [1].

In a nutshell, spammers are those accounts that advertise unsolicited and often harmful content—e.g., messages that contain links to malicious pages [2]. Bots are computer programs that control social accounts, as stealthy as to mimic real

[1]Institute of Informatics and Telematics, National Research Council (IIT-CNR), Italy
[2]College of Science and Engineering, Hamad Bin Khalifa University (HBKU), Qatar
[3]Department of Computer Science, "La Sapienza" University of Rome, Italy

users [3]. Instead, cyborgs interweave characteristics of both manual and automated behavior [4]. Despite the heterogeneous behavior, these accounts are typically controlled by their rightful owners, by means of both manual and programmatic (i.e., via web APIs) interaction. Compromised accounts are similar to cyborgs, in that they alternate legitimate and automated behavior. However, compromised accounts are accounts that have been taken over my malicious users and are no longer under the control of their rightful owners [5]. Sybils are instead multiple fake identities, created by a malicious user in order to unfairly increase their power and influence within a target community [6]. Finally, there are fake followers, massively created accounts that can be bought from online markets to follow a target account and apparently inflate its popularity [7,8]. Each of these categories has been the matter of several investigations, all sharing the ultimate goal of developing techniques for automatically detecting (and consequently removing) the different kinds of deceptive accounts.

The vast majority of such detection techniques make large use of machine learning, in order to infer the nature (whether legitimate or malicious/deceptive) of the social media accounts under investigation. They have been proved to represent consolidated mechanisms for detecting spammers and bots, henceforth *spambots*. However, one of the most fascinating peculiarities of spambots is that they "evolve" over time, adopting sophisticated techniques to evade early established detection approaches. As evolving spambots became clever in escaping detection, for instance by changing discussion topics and posting activities, Academia and OSN administrators tried to keep pace and proposed more complex detection models. Investigations went beyond mere textual analyses on the content of shared messages [9] and considered also social relationships and/or interaction graphs of the accounts under investigation [10–12]. Most noticeably, spambots evolution still goes on. Indeed, recent investigations anecdotally highlight that new waves of *social spambots* are rising [13,14].

## 10.1.1 Contributions

This chapter targets these new waves, by

1.  benchmarking a number of recently proposed spambots detection applications and scientific techniques. Results presented in Section 10.4 demonstrate that social spambots feature evolved and sophisticated characteristics and that they cannot be assimilated to previous waves of malicious accounts. As such, they deserve dedicated detection mechanisms.
2.  describing a novel, biologically inspired, behavioral modeling technique. Such technique, presented in Section 10.5, exploits historic behavioral data of an account, in order to produce a compact and efficient behavioral representation. The behavioral representation of an account is particularly suitable to be compared with others, thus supporting efficient group analyses.
3.  presenting an unsupervised detection technique, together with its thorough evaluation, also comparing it with the state-of-the-art tools and algorithms surveyed in Section 10.4. Results in Section 10.6 show the effectiveness of the proposed social spambots detection technique.

## 10.2 Datasets

In this section, we present the datasets that we exploited for studying the new waves of deceptive accounts. Such datasets have been collected with the underlying idea to compare the characteristics of novel deceptive accounts with those of legitimate, human-operated accounts. The differences uncovered by this comparison can then be leveraged to design novel detection techniques for automatically identifying deceptive accounts. Detailed statistics about all the datasets are also reported in Table 10.1.

### 10.2.1 Social spambots

In general, spambots are automated accounts (i.e., accounts driven by a bot) that repeatedly advertise unsolicited and often harmful content (e.g., malware, URLs to phishing websites, fake news, etc.). Recent studies in social media spam and automation provide anecdotal argumentation of the rise of a new generation of spambots, so-called social spambots [13]. In [15], we extensively studied this novel phenomenon on Twitter and we provided quantitative evidence that a paradigm-shift exists in spambot design.

In [8], we had the chance to benchmark the efficiency of a novel classifier to detect the so-called fake followers, created to inflate the number of followers of a specific Twitter account (such as a celebrity, a politician, a popular brand, etc.). For that study, we relied on a ground truth of fake followers publicly available on online markets. Contrary to that first investigation, in [15], we considered social spambots directly found in the Twitter ecosystem.

A first dataset of social spambots (henceforth SPAM-POL) was created after observing the activities of a suspicious group of accounts that we discovered on Twitter during the Mayoral election in Rome, in 2014. One of the runners-up employed a social media marketing firm for his electoral campaign that made use of almost 1,000 automated accounts to publicize his policies. Surprisingly, we found such automated accounts to be similar to genuine ones in every way. Every profile was accurately filled with detailed—yet fake—personal information such as a stolen photo, short-bio, location, etc. Those accounts also represented credible sources of information

*Table 10.1 Statistics about the datasets of Twitter accounts used in the remainder of this chapter*

| Dataset | Description | Accounts | Tweets | Year |
|---|---|---|---|---|
| HUM-HYB | Random accounts that answered questions | 3,474 | 8,377,522 | 2011 |
| SPAM-POL | Retweeters of an Italian political candidate | 991 | 1,610,176 | 2012 |
| SPAM-AMZ | Spammers of products on sale at *Amazon.com* | 464 | 1,418,626 | 2011 |

The **year** column reports the average creation year of the accounts belonging to the different groups.

since they all had thousands of followers and friends, the majority of which were genuine users. Furthermore, the accounts showed a tweeting behavior which was apparently similar to those of genuine accounts, with a few tweets posted every day, mainly quotes from popular people. However, every time the political candidate posted a new tweet from his official account, all the automated accounts retweeted it in a time span of just a few minutes. By resorting to this farm of bot accounts, the political candidate was able to reach many more genuine accounts in addition to his direct followers and managed to alter Twitter engagement metrics during the electoral campaign. Amazingly, we also witnessed tens of human accounts who tried to engage in conversation with some of the spambots. The most common form of such human-to-spambot interaction was represented by a human reply to one of the spambot tweets quotes. Quite obviously, no human account who tried interacting with the spambots ever received a meaningful reply from them.

Furthermore, we uncovered a second group of social bots, labeled SPAM-AMZ, which advertise products on sale on *Amazon.com*. The deceitful activity was carried out by spamming URLs pointing to the advertised products. Similar to the retweeters of the Italian political candidate, also this family of spambots interleaved spam tweets with harmless and genuine ones.

## 10.2.2   Legitimate accounts

The HUM-HYB dataset is a random sample of genuine (human-operated) accounts. Following a hybrid crowdsensing approach [16], we randomly contacted Twitter users by asking them a simple question in natural language. All the replies to our questions were manually verified, and all the 3,474 accounts that answered were certified as legitimate. The accounts that did not answer to our questions were discarded and are not used in this study. In addition to the abovementioned accounts, we also randomly contacted Twitter users to build a genuine set. We mentioned such users in tweets about our research, and we further asked them simple questions in natural language. Possible answers to our questions were given by contacted users in the form of replies to our tweets. Such answers were then manually verified, and all the 3,474 accounts that answered were certified as legitimate, becoming our HUM-HYB dataset.

In Sections 10.4 and 10.6, we leverage two test sets in order to benchmark and compare a number of spambot detection techniques and applications. Specifically, the first of such test datasets, labeled SPAM-TEST1, is a balanced combination of social spambots from the SPAM-POL dataset and legitimate accounts from HUM-HYB. Similarly, SPAM-TEST2 is a balanced combination of social spambots from the SPAM-AMZ dataset and legitimate accounts from HUM-HYB.

## 10.2.3   Reproducibility

For the sake of reproducibility, the datasets have been made publicly available for scientific purposes. In particular, they are included within the data catalogue of the

SoBigData European research infrastructure.[1] Moreover, they are hosted within the Bot Repository website,[2] maintained by the Indiana University, and within the My Information Bubble project website,[3] hosted by IIT-CNR in Italy.

## 10.3 Classification task and classification metrics

In the next sections, we will evaluate state-of-the-art detection mechanisms, in order to assess their effectiveness in detecting the new waves of social spambots introduced in Section 10.2. Here, we briefly recall the standard classification metrics we employed to carry out the evaluation.

A classification task, in its simplest form (i.e., binary classification), involves the development of a statistical model (called *classifier*) capable of automatically distinguishing between data instances of a *positive* class and those of a *negative* class. For example, one could cast the fake detection problem as a binary classification task, where the positive class is associated to fake accounts, and the negative class to genuine, human-operated accounts. A classification task can be extended beyond its binary form by considering any finite number of classes. Classification results—either binary or multiclass—are evaluated with metrics that are based on the following four standard indicators:

- *True positives (TP)*: The absolute number of positive data samples correctly recognized as such by the classifier.
- *True negatives (TN)*: The absolute number of negative data samples correctly recognized as such by the classifier.
- *False positives (FP)*: The absolute number of negative data samples wrongly recognized as positive ones by the classifier.
- *False negatives (FN)*: The absolute number of positive data samples wrongly recognized as negative ones by the classifier.

The meaning of each indicator is graphically highlighted by the so-called *confusion matrix* of Table 10.2, where each column represents the instances in the predicted class, while each row represents the instances in the actual class [17].

In order to provide thorough classification results, we consider the following standard evaluation metrics, based on the four indicators defined above:

- *Accuracy*: The proportion of predicted true results (both TP and TN) in the population,

$$Accuracy = \frac{TP + TN}{TP + TN + FP + FN}$$

[1] https://sobigdata.d4science.org/explore
[2] https://botometer.iuni.iu.edu/bot-repository/
[3] http://mib.projects.iit.cnr.it/dataset.html

*Table 10.2    Confusion matrix*

| | Predicted class | |
| Actual class | Negative | Positive |
| --- | --- | --- |
| *Negative* | TN | FP |
| *Positive* | FN | TP |

The grey shade highlights the 4 values of
the confusion matrix.

- *Precision*: The proportion of predicted positive cases that are indeed real positive,

$$Precision = \frac{TP}{TP + FP}$$

- *Recall* (also known as *sensitivity*): The proportion of real positive cases that are indeed predicted positive,

$$Recall = \frac{TP}{TP + FN}$$

- *Specificity*: The proportion of real negative cases that are indeed predicted negatives,

$$Specificity = \frac{TN}{TN + FP}$$

- *F-measure* (also known as *F1-score*): The harmonic mean of precision and recall,

$$F\text{-}measure = 2 \cdot \frac{Precision \cdot Recall}{Precision + Recall}$$

- *Matthews correlation coefficient* (*MCC*): The estimator of the correlation between the predicted class and the real class of the samples [18],

$$MCC = \frac{TP \cdot TN - FP \cdot FN}{\sqrt{(TP+FN) \cdot (TP+FP) \cdot (TN+FP) \cdot (TN+FN)}}$$

Each of the above metrics captures a different aspect of the classification performance. In detail, *accuracy* measures how many samples are correctly identified in both of the classes, but it does not express if the positive class is better recognized than the negative one. Moreover, there are situations where some predictive models perform better than others, even having a lower *Accuracy* [19]. A high *Precision* indicates that many of the samples identified as positive are indeed correctly classified, but it does not give any information about the positive samples that have not been identified. This information is instead provided by the *Recall* metric, that expresses how many positive samples have been correctly classified as such. A low recall means that many positive samples are left unidentified. The *F-measure* and *MCC* try to convey in one single value the overall quality of a prediction, combining all the other metrics. Furthermore, *MCC* is considered the unbiased version of the *F-measure*, since it uses all the four elements of the confusion matrix [19]. An *MCC* value close to 1 means that the prediction is really accurate; a value close to 0 means that the prediction is no better than random guess, and a value close to $-1$ means that the prediction is heavily in disagreement with the real class (namely, the classifier almost always places a sample in the wrong class).

## 10.4 Benchmarking current spambot detection techniques

Here, we investigate whether established tools and techniques are able of identifying the novel social spambots introduced in Section 10.2.

### 10.4.1 The BotOrNot? service

BotOrNot? (recently renamed Botometer) is a publicly available service to evaluate the similarity of a Twitter account with the known characteristics of social spambots [20]. Similarly to most already established techniques, BotOrNot? performs its analyses on an account-by-account basis. Despite being specifically designed for the detection of social spambots, authors state that the detection performances of BotOrNot? against evolved spambots might be worse than those reported in [20]. Here, we aim at evaluating this point by querying the service with a set of legitimate and social spambot accounts. As shown in Table 10.3, BotOrNot? achieves rather unsatisfactory results for the accounts of both SPAM-TEST1 and SPAM-TEST2. Its detection performances are particularly bad for the accounts of SPAM-TEST1 – where the spambots are retweeters of a political candidate from the SPAM-POL dataset. The low values of *F-measure* and *MCC*, respectively, 0.288 and 0.174, are mainly due to the low *Recall*. In turn, this represents a tendency of wrongly labeling SPAM-POL spambots as legitimate accounts.

### 10.4.2 Supervised spambot classification

Among the many supervised classification approaches to spambot detection proposed in recent years by Academia, we included in our analysis the one presented by Yang *et al.* in [11], since it focuses on the detection of *evolving* Twitter spambots. Thus, it is interesting to evaluate if the system recently presented in [11] is actually able to detect the sophisticated social spambots. This supervised system provides a machine-learning classifier that infers whether a Twitter account is genuine or spambot by relying on account's relationships, tweeting timing, and level of automation. We have reproduced such a classifier by implementing and computing all the features proposed in [11], and by training the classifier with its original dataset. Results in Table 10.3 show that the system fails to correctly classify the novel social spambots. Similar to the results of the BotOrNot? service, the worst results of this system in both SPAM-TEST1 and SPAM-TEST2 are related to the *Recall* metric. This means that also this classifier labeled social spambots as genuine accounts.

Table 10.3    Comparison among the spambot detection techniques, tools, and
algorithms surveyed in this section

| Technique | Type | Detection results | | | | | |
|---|---|---|---|---|---|---|---|
| | | *Precision* | *Recall* | *Specificity* | *Accuracy* | *F-measure* | *MCC* |
| Test set: `SPAM-TEST1` | | | | | | | |
| BotOrNot? [20] | Supervised | 0.471 | 0.208 | 0.918 | 0.734 | 0.288 | 0.174 |
| Yang *et al.* [11] | Supervised | 0.563 | 0.170 | 0.860 | 0.506 | 0.261 | 0.043 |
| Miller *et al.* [21] | Unsupervised | 0.555 | 0.358 | 0.698 | 0.526 | 0.435 | 0.059 |
| Ahmed *et al.* [22]* | Unsupervised | 0.945 | **0.944** | 0.945 | **0.943** | **0.944** | **0.886** |
| Test set: `SPAM-TEST2` | | | | | | | |
| BotOrNot? [20] | Supervised | 0.635 | **0.950** | 0.981 | 0.922 | 0.761 | 0.738 |
| Yang *et al.* [11] | Supervised | 0.727 | 0.409 | 0.848 | 0.629 | 0.524 | 0.287 |
| Miller *et al.* [21] | Unsupervised | 0.467 | 0.306 | 0.654 | 0.481 | 0.370 | −0.043 |
| Ahmed *et al.* [22]* | Unsupervised | 0.913 | 0.935 | 0.912 | **0.923** | **0.923** | **0.847** |

For each test set, the highest values in each evaluation metric are shown in **bold**.
*Modified by employing *fastgreedy* instead of *MCL* for the graph clustering step.

## 10.4.3    *Unsupervised spambot detection via Twitter stream clustering*

Observing the results of traditional spambot classifiers, we can claim that social
spambots might be so sophisticatedly designed to make it very difficult to distinguish
them from genuine accounts, *if observed one by one*, as also supported by preliminary
work [13,14]. If demonstrated, this claim would imply that traditional supervised
classification approaches—where the evaluation of a set of features of the single
account is considered to assign to that account the genuine/spambot label—do not
represent the best methodology for the detection of social spambots. Supervised
classifiers, in facts, need to observe and learn the statistical characteristics of datasets
made of labeled samples in order to give a label to a new, probably unseen, sample.
Unsupervised classifiers, instead, do not need to know *in advance* the type of label
to assign, but can cluster together samples that share common characteristics, being
unaware if any label even exists. For this reason, we have also experimented with
unsupervised approaches for spambot detection.

The approach in [21] considers vectors made of 126 features extracted from
both accounts and tweets as input of modified versions of the DenStream [23] and
StreamKM++ [24] clustering algorithms, to cluster feature vectors of a set of unlabeled accounts. We have implemented the system proposed in [21] to cluster the
accounts of the two test sets. As shown in Table 10.3, this achieved the worst performances among all those that we have benchmarked in this study. Low values of both
*Precision* and *Recall* mean incomplete and unreliable spambot detection. Among the
126 features, 95 are based on the textual content of tweets. However, novel social
spambots use texts with contents similar to that of genuine accounts (e.g., retweets of

genuine tweets and famous quotes). For this reason, an approach almost solely based on tweet content will not be able to achieve satisfactory results.

### 10.4.4 Unsupervised spambot detection via graph clustering

The approach in [22] exploits statistical features related to URLs, hashtags, mentions, and retweets. Feature vectors generated in this way are then compared with one another via an Euclidean distance measure. Distances between accounts are organized in an adjacency matrix, which is later used to construct an undirected weighted graph of the accounts. Then, graph clustering and community detection algorithms are applied in order to identify groups of similar accounts. Graph clustering is done by employing the *Markov cluster algorithm* (*MCL*) [25]. We fully implemented this solution and experimented with the proposed datasets. However, the approach failed to identify two distinct clusters, since accounts of both the SPAM-TEST1 and SPAM-TEST2 test sets were assigned to a single cluster. We also performed a grid search simulation in order to test the best parameter configuration for *MCL*,[4] but to no avail. To achieve effective detection results, instead of the *MCL*, we adopted the *fastgreedy* community-detection algorithm [26]. As reported in Table 10.3, this modified implementation proved effective in detecting social spambots, with an $MCC = 0.886$ for SPAM-TEST1 and $MCC = 0.847$ for SPAM-TEST2.

## 10.5 Toward an accurate detection of social spambots

As shown in Table 10.3, the techniques and the established scientific works benchmarked in Section 10.4 largely failed to detect the new wave of social spambots, one notable exception being the (modified) unsupervised approach proposed by Ahmed *et al.* in [22]. On the one hand, these unsatisfactory results call for novel analytic tools able to keep pace with the latest evolutionary step of spambots. On the other hand, the comforting results, achieved by the unsupervised system of Ahmed *et al.*, seem to support the intuition that the novel social spambots can hardly be detected by carrying out analyses on an "account-by-account" basis. Instead, one promising research direction for the detection of the much sophisticated social spambots might stem from the analysis of *collective behaviors*. Studying the behavior of *groups* of accounts as a whole, rather than focusing on a single account at a time, opens up the possibility to exploit much more data for the analysis. In turn, this approach might hopefully allow to amplify those weak signals left behind by the sophisticated social spambots, ultimately leading to their detection.

Thus, in this section, we focus on providing a novel and effective way of modeling online collective behaviors [27]. The behavioral modeling technique proposed in this section is subsequently exploited in Section 10.6 to design and implement an accurate social spambot detection system.

---

[4]*MCL* admits two fundamental parameters: *inflation* and *expansion*.

## 10.5.1   The digital DNA behavioral modeling technique

Building on the considerations emerged in the previous section, here we provide a novel online behavioral modeling technique that is particularly suitable to be applied for social spambot detection, by focusing the analysis on large groups of users.

### 10.5.1.1   Digital DNA sequences

The human genome is the complete set of human genetic information encoded as nucleic-acid sequences. DNA sequences are successions of characters (strings) indicating the order of nucleotides within DNA molecules. The possible characters are A, C, G, and T, representing the four nucleotide bases of a DNA strand: adenine, cytosine, guanine, and thymine. Biological DNA stores the information that directs a living organism's functions and characteristics. DNA sequences are analyzed via bioinformatics techniques, which feature a rich set of different algorithms for arranging the sequences to identify regions of similarity. By analyzing common sequence patterns, it is possible to predict an individual's specific characteristics and uncover relationships among different families of individuals.

Inspired by biological DNA, we propose modeling online user behaviors with strings of characters representing the sequence of a user's online actions. Each action type (such as posting new content, or following, or replying to a user) can be encoded with a different character, just as in DNA sequences, where characters encode nucleotide bases. According to this paradigm, online user actions would represent the bases of their *digital DNA*. Different kinds of user behavior can be observed on the Internet [12], and digital DNA is a flexible and compact way of modeling such behaviors [28]. The flexibility lies in the possibility of choosing which actions form the sequence. For example, digital DNA sequences on Facebook could include a different base for each user-to-user interaction type: comments (C), likes (L), shares (S), and mentions (M). Then, interactions can be encoded as strings formed by such characters according to the sequence of user-performed actions. Similarly, user-to-item interactions on an e-commerce platform could be modeled by using a base for every product category. User purchasing behaviors could be encoded as a sequence of characters according to the category of products they buy. In this regard, digital DNA shows a major difference from biological DNA, where the four nucleotide bases are fixed. In digital DNA, both the number and the meaning of the bases can change according to the behavior or interaction to be modeled. Just like its biological predecessor, digital DNA is a compact representation of information—for example, a Twitter user's timeline could be encoded as a single string of 3,200 characters (one character per tweet).

### 10.5.1.2   Definition of digital DNA

A digital DNA sequence can be defined as a row-vector of characters (i.e., a string),

$$\mathbf{s} = (b_1, b_2, \ldots, b_n) \quad b_i \in \mathbb{B} \ \forall \ i = 1, \ldots, n$$

Characters $b_i$ in **s** are drawn from a finite set, called *alphabet*,

$$\mathbb{B} = \{B_1, B_2, \ldots, B_N\} \quad B_i \neq B_j \ \forall \ i, j = 1, \ldots, N \quad i \neq j$$

The $B_i$ characters are also called the (DNA) *bases* of the alphabet $\mathbb{B}$. A user's behavior can be represented with a digital DNA sequence by encoding each action of the user with an alphabet base. Then, by scanning the user's actions in chronological order and by assigning the appropriate base to each action, one can obtain the sequence of characters that make up the digital DNA sequence of the user. For example, Figure 10.1 shows the process of extracting the digital DNA sequence of a Twitter user, by scanning its timeline according to the alphabet $\mathbb{B}^3_{type}$ defined in Table 10.4.

Table 10.4 contains the definitions of some of the possible alphabets we can rely on for modeling users' behaviors. Each alphabet's name is characterized by a subscript (e.g., *type*), which identifies the kind of information captured by the bases; and by a superscript (e.g., 3), which denotes the number $N$ of bases in the alphabet. These two indices are typically enough to univocally identify an alphabet. As demonstrated by the examples proposed in Table 10.4, the superscript is useful to distinguish alphabets modeling the same facet with a different number of bases. These alphabets represent different possible encodings for OSNs actions. In detail, the $\mathbb{B}^3_{type}$ alphabet encodes

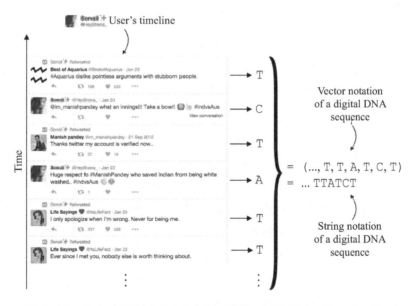

*Figure 10.1*  *The digital DNA behavioral modeling technique. Excerpt of a digital DNA extraction process for a Twitter user with the $\mathbb{B}^3_{type}$ alphabet. By scanning the user's actions in chronological order and by assigning the appropriate base to each action, one can obtain the sequence of characters that makes up the digital DNA sequence of the user*

*Table 10.4    Naming and definition of some digital DNA alphabets*

| Label | Definition |
|---|---|
| $\mathbb{B}^3_{type}$ | $= \begin{cases} \text{A} \Leftarrow \text{tweet,} \\ \text{C} \Leftarrow \text{reply,} \\ \text{T} \Leftarrow \text{retweet} \end{cases}$ |
| $\mathbb{B}^3_{content}$ | $= \begin{cases} \text{N} \Leftarrow \text{tweet contains no entities (plain text),} \\ \text{E} \Leftarrow \text{tweet contains one or more entities of one type,} \\ \text{X} \Leftarrow \text{tweet contains entities of mixed types} \end{cases}$ |
| $\mathbb{B}^6_{content}$ | $= \begin{cases} \text{N} \Leftarrow \text{tweet contains no entities (plain text),} \\ \text{U} \Leftarrow \text{tweet contains one or more URLs,} \\ \text{H} \Leftarrow \text{tweet contains one or more hashtags,} \\ \text{M} \Leftarrow \text{tweet contains one or more mentions,} \\ \text{D} \Leftarrow \text{tweet contains one or more media,} \\ \text{X} \Leftarrow \text{tweet contains entities of mixed types} \end{cases}$ |
| $\mathbb{B}^3_{interaction}$ | $= \begin{cases} \text{W} \Leftarrow \text{tweet without interaction,} \\ \text{O} \Leftarrow \text{interaction with ordinary user,} \\ \text{C} \Leftarrow \text{interaction with celebrity user} \end{cases}$ |
| $\mathbb{B}^6_{interaction}$ | $= \begin{cases} \text{W} \Leftarrow \text{tweet without interaction,} \\ \text{L} \Leftarrow \text{interaction with low popularity user,} \\ \text{D} \Leftarrow \text{interaction with middle-low popularity user,} \\ \text{M} \Leftarrow \text{interaction with middle popularity user,} \\ \text{H} \Leftarrow \text{interaction with middle-high popularity user,} \\ \text{C} \Leftarrow \text{interaction with celebrity user} \end{cases}$ |
| $\mathbb{B}^3_{account\text{-}age}$ | $= \begin{cases} \text{N} \Leftarrow \text{interaction with new user,} \\ \text{M} \Leftarrow \text{interaction with middle-aged user,} \\ \text{L} \Leftarrow \text{interaction with longtime user} \end{cases}$ |

user behaviors according to their type of tweets produced, either *tweets*, *retweets*, or *replies*. Alphabets $\mathbb{B}^3_{content}$ and $\mathbb{B}^6_{content}$ provide a way to model Twitter actions, with different granularities, by looking at the content of tweets rather than the type. In order to easily classify a tweet based on its content, we exploited Twitter's notion of entities.[5] The idea underlying the alphabets $\mathbb{B}^3_{interaction}$ and $\mathbb{B}^6_{interaction}$ is to employ different bases with respect to the popularity level of the peers with whom a given user interacts. Specifically, we exploited retweets and replies between users as a form of interaction and an account's followers count as a measure of popularity for that account. For this purpose, we computed the distribution of followers counts among a random sample of 400,000 Twitter users: such distribution is skewed towards low followers count values for ordinary users, since only few outliers count up to millions of followers, representing the Twitter celebrities. Then, in the definition of the alphabets, we represent interactions with celebrity users, ordinary users, and tweets that are not interactions. These types of alphabets could be adopted to understand whether users with a given level of popularity in a social network typically interact with other users on the same level, thus following an assortativity law [29,30]. $\mathbb{B}^3_{account\text{-}age}$ shows another possible way of modeling user interactions. In contrast with the two $\mathbb{B}_{interaction}$ alphabets, here the different bases represent the age of the accounts (i.e., time since the account's creation) with whom users interact, rather than their popularity. We used fixed thresholds to classify accounts as being new users in the Twitter platform (account age < 6 months), middle-aged users (6 months $\leq$ account age < 3 years), or longtime users (accounts age $\geq$ 3 years). We defined the alphabet as having one base for each of these three classes of accounts. Notably, to mark a difference with $\mathbb{B}_{interaction}$ alphabets, in $\mathbb{B}^3_{account\text{-}age}$ we did not include a base for tweets that do not represent interactions. As a consequence, such tweets are not represented in digital DNA sequences obtained with $\mathbb{B}^3_{account\text{-}age}$.

Although we show here only the six alphabets defined in Table 10.4, the proposed modeling technique is suitable to encode a broad range of different behaviors and interactions, thus representing a flexible framework for online behavioral analyses. For instance, it would have been possible to easily model via digital DNA sequences both the web-based online behavioral features recently studied in [31–33] and the behavioral features studied in [34] that are derived from the fields of market analysis and social-security analysis.

### 10.5.1.3 Similarity between digital DNA sequences

In order to analyze groups of users rather than single users, we need to study multiple digital DNA sequences as a whole. A group $\mathbf{A}$ of $M = |\mathbf{A}|$ users can be described by the digital DNA sequences of the $M$ users, where all the sequences are formed according to the same alphabet,

$$
\mathbf{A} = \begin{pmatrix} \mathbf{s}_1 \\ \mathbf{s}_2 \\ \vdots \\ \mathbf{s}_M \end{pmatrix} = \begin{pmatrix} (b_{1,1}, b_{1,2}, \ldots, b_{1,n}) \\ (b_{2,1}, b_{2,2}, \ldots, b_{2,m}) \\ \vdots \\ (b_{M,1}, b_{M,2}, \ldots, b_{M,p}) \end{pmatrix}
$$

---

[5]Twitter defines the following types of entities: URLs, #hashtags, @mentions, and media (images, videos). For a complete reference of Twitter entities, see *https://dev.twitter.com/overview/api/entities*

The group **A** is defined as a column-vector of $M$ digital DNA sequences of variable length, one sequence for each user of the group.

To perform analyses on groups of digital DNA sequences, we can rely on recent advances in the fields of bioinformatics and string mining. In fact, many efficient algorithms and techniques for the analysis of biological strings have been continually proposed in such fields [35]. One of the possible means to quantify similarities between sequential data representations, such as the digital DNA sequences, is the *longest common substring (LCS)* [36]. Intuitively, users that share long behavioral patterns are much more likely to be similar than those that share short behavioral patterns. Given two strings, $s_i$ of length $n$ and $s_j$ of length $m$, their LCS is the longest string that is a substring of both $s_i$ and $s_j$. For example, given $s_i$ = MASSACHUSETTS and $s_j$ = PARACHUTE, their LCS is the string ACHU and the LCS length is 4. The extended version of this problem that considers an arbitrary finite number of strings, is called the *k-common substring* problem [37]. In this case, given a vector $\mathbf{A} = (s_1, \dots, s_M)$ of $M$ strings, the problem is that of finding the LCS that is common to at least $k$ of these strings, for each $2 \leq k \leq M$. Notably, both the *LCS* and the *k-common substring* problems can be solved in linear time and space, by resorting to the generalized suffix tree and by implementing state-of-the-art algorithms, such as those proposed in [36]. Given that, in the *k-common substring* problem, the LCS is computed for each $2 \leq k \leq M$, it is possible to plot an *LCS curve*, showing the relationship between the length of the LCS and the number $k$ of strings.

For example, Figure 10.2(a) and (b) depicts the LCS curves computed for the Twitter accounts of the HUM-HYB dataset, via the $\mathbb{B}^3_{type}$ and $\mathbb{B}^3_{content}$ alphabets. On the $x$ axis is reported the number $k$ of accounts (corresponding to the $k$ strings, or digital

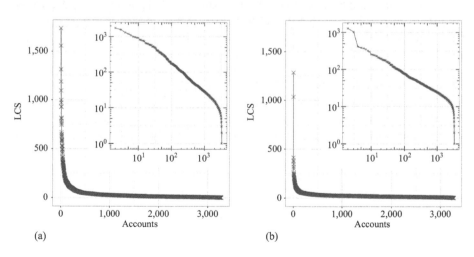

*Figure 10.2    Measuring behavioral similarity of a group of legitimate accounts*
*(HUM-HYB). Examples of the LCS curves obtained with the*
*application of different alphabets. (a) $\mathbb{B}^3_{type}$ alphabet and (b) $\mathbb{B}^3_{content}$*
*alphabet*

DNA sequences, used to compute LCS values) and on the $y$ axis the length of the LCS common to at least $k$ accounts. Therefore, each point in an LCS curve corresponds to a subset of $k$ accounts that share the longest substring (of length $y$) among all those shared between all the other possible subsets of $k$ accounts.

As a direct consequence of the definition of LCS, as the number $k$ of accounts grows, the length of the LCS common to all of them shortens. In other words, LCS curves are *monotonic nonincreasing* functions, such that,

$$\text{LCS}[k-1] \geq \text{LCS}[k] \quad \forall \; 3 \leq k \leq M$$

Thus, it is more likely to find a long LCS among a few accounts rather than among large groups.

In our scenario, an LCS curve is a *representation* of the behavioral similarities among a group of users, since it is an ordered sequence of substring lengths, namely users' actions. To obtain a single value that acts as a *measure* of similarity for the whole group, it is possible to compute the area under the LCS curve (AUC) [38,39]. Since LCS curves are discrete functions defined over the $[2, M]$ range, their AUC can be computed straightaway, without approximations, with the following trapezoid rule,

$$\text{AUC} = \sum_{k=3}^{M} \frac{(\text{LCS}[k-1] + \text{LCS}[k])\Delta_k}{2}$$

$$= \frac{1}{2} \sum_{k=3}^{M} \text{LCS}[k-1] + \text{LCS}[k] \tag{10.1}$$

Compared to LCS, the definition of AUC given in (10.1) allows to directly and quantitatively compare the overall similarity among different groups.

## 10.6 DNA-inspired detection of social spambots

In this section, we leverage the online behavioral modeling technique presented in the previous Section 10.5 to design an efficient social spambot detection system. In order to evaluate the proposed system, we leverage the SPAM-TEST1 and the SPAM-TEST2 test sets already used in the previous sections.

### 10.6.1 LCS curves of legitimate and malicious accounts

To exploit at its best the potential of digital DNA, we need a deeper understanding of the elements that mark the distinction between legitimate accounts and social spambots. Hence, building on the definitions of digital DNA and LCS curves given in Section 10.5.1, in this section, we show how it is possible to capture the characteristics of the LCS curves of different groups of accounts. In particular, we are interested in evaluating the differences and similarities among those groups of accounts, as seen through the lenses of digital DNA sequences.

### 10.6.1.1   LCS curves of a group of homogeneous accounts

Figure 10.3 shows a comparison between the LCS curves of legitimate accounts and social spambots of the SPAM-POL (Figure 10.3(a)) and SPAM-AMZ (Figure 10.3(b)) groups. As shown, the LCSs of both groups of spambots are rather long even when the number of accounts grows. This is strikingly evident in Figure 10.3(b) (SPAM-AMZ – spammers of *Amazon.com* products). For both the spambot groups, we observe a sudden drop in LCS length when the number of accounts gets close to the group size, namely, at the end of the $x$ axis. In contrast to the remarkably high LCS curves of spambots, genuine accounts show little to no similarity—as represented by LCS curves that exponentially decay, rapidly reaching the smallest values of LCS length.

This preliminary yet considerable differences between the LCS curves of legitimate accounts and spambots suggest that, despite the advanced characteristics of these novel spambots, the $\mathbb{B}^3_{type}$ digital DNA is able to uncover traces of their automated and synchronized activity. In turn, the automated behaviors of a large group of accounts results in exceptionally high LCS curves for such accounts. Indeed, we consider high behavioral similarity as a proxy for automation and, thus, an exceptionally high level of similarity among a large group of accounts might serve as a red flag for anomalous behaviors. In the following, we preliminarily compare groups of heterogeneous users, looking for features that could be used to design a detection mechanism, while in Section 10.6.2, we detail how to leverage such elements for an effective detection mechanism.

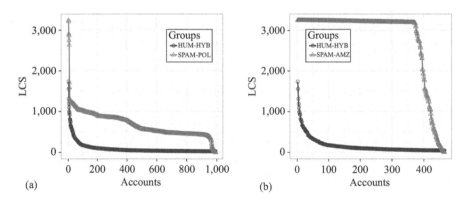

*Figure 10.3    Measuring behavioral similarity for different groups of accounts. Comparison between LCS curves of social spambots and legitimate accounts, obtained with the $\mathbb{B}^3_{type}$ alphabet. Social spambots feature much greater behavioral similarities than legitimate accounts. (a) Social spambots (SPAM-POL) versus legitimate accounts (HUM-HYB) and (b) social spambots (SPAM-AMZ) versus legitimate accounts (HUM-HYB)*

## 10.6.1.2 LCS curves of a group of heterogeneous accounts

In the previous section, we analyzed LCS curves derived from digital DNA sequences of users with similar characteristics, such as legitimate Twitter accounts and spambots of a given family. We demonstrated that groups with different characteristics lead to qualitatively different LCS curves. However, we have not yet considered LCS curves that are obtained from sequences of an unknown, heterogeneous group of users. Thus, we leveraged the SPAM-TEST1 and SPAM-TEST2 mixed groups of legitimate accounts and spambots, and we repeated the analysis with LCS curves. In detail, Figure 10.4 shows the LCS curves obtained via the $\mathbb{B}^3_{type}$ alphabet.

In the left hand plot of Figure 10.4, we observe a continuous decrease in the LCS length as the number of considered accounts grows. Such slow decrease is sometimes interleaved by steeper drops, such as those occurring in the region of 500 and 1,000 accounts. Another—and even more evident—steep drop is shown in the right hand plot of Figure 10.4, in the region of 400 accounts. LCS curves in both plots asymptotically reach their minimum value as the number of accounts grows. Overall, such LCS curves show a different behavior than those related to a single group of similar accounts, such as the ones shown in Figure 10.3(a) and (b). Indeed, the plots of Figure 10.4 lack a single trend that spans for the whole domain of the LCS curves. Instead, they depict a situation where a trend seems to be dominant only until reaching a certain threshold. Then, a steep fall occurs and another trend—possibly different—kicks in. Notably, such portions of the LCS curves separated by the steep drops resemble LCS curves of the single groups of similar accounts (i.e., SPAM-POL, SPAM-AMZ,

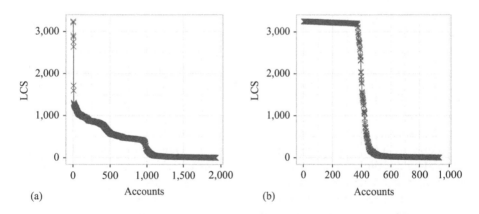

*Figure 10.4    Measuring behavioral similarity for an heterogeneous group composed of legitimate accounts and social spambots. LCS curves obtained via the $\mathbb{B}^3_{type}$ alphabet. These LCS curves lack a single trend that spans for the whole domain. Instead, they depict a situation where a trend seems to be dominant only until reaching a certain threshold. Then, a steep fall occurs and another trend kicks in. (a) Dataset: SPAM-TEST1 and (b) dataset: SPAM-TEST2*

HUM-HYB) used to obtain the sets of heterogeneous accounts (i.e., SPAM-TEST1, SPAM-TEST2). The steep drops of LCS curves separate areas where the length of the LCS remains practically unchanged, even for significantly different numbers of considered accounts. In the left hand plot of Figure 10.4, for instance, the LCS remains almost unchanged when considering a number of accounts between 500 and 1,000. The same also applies to the right-hand plot of Figure 10.4, for a number of accounts lower than 400. Such *plateaux* in LCS curves are strictly related to homogeneous groups of highly similar accounts. Note that it is possible to observe multiple plateaux in a single LCS curve, as in the case of Figure 10.4(a). This represents a situation where multiple (sub)groups exist among the whole set of considered accounts. Furthermore, the steeper and the more pronounced is a drop in an LCS curve, the more different are the two subgroups of accounts split by that drop.

To summarize, LCS curves of an unknown and heterogeneous group of accounts can present one or more *plateaux*, which are related to subgroups of homogeneous (i.e., with highly similar behaviors) users. Conversely, *steep drops* represent points marking big differences between distinct subgroups. Finally, *slow and gradual decreases* in LCS curves represent areas of uncertainty, where it might be difficult to make strong hypotheses about the characteristics of the underlying accounts. In conclusion, we argue that LCS curves of an unknown and heterogeneous group of users are capable of conveying information about relevant and homogeneous subgroups of highly similar users.

### 10.6.2    An unsupervised detection technique

Here, we discuss an unsupervised methodology that leverages previous findings and exploits the shape of LCS curves of heterogeneous accounts in order to find subgroups of accounts with similar behaviors [40]. Specifically, we propose to exploit the discrete derivative of an LCS curve to recognize the points corresponding to the steep drops. This approach is applicable to a broad range of situations, since it requires no information other than the LCS curve of the heterogeneous group of accounts.

The steep drops of LCS curves appear as sharp peaks in the derivative plot and represent suitable splitting points to isolate different subgroups among the whole set of accounts. All the suitable splitting points might be ranked according to their corresponding derivative value (i.e., how steep is the corresponding drop) and then, a hierarchical top-down (i.e., divisive) approach may be applied, by repeatedly dividing the whole set of accounts based on the ranked points, leading to a dendrogram structure. For instance, this approach can be exploited in situations where the LCS curve exhibits multiple plateaux and steep drops, in order to find the best possible clusters that can be used to divide the original set of heterogeneous accounts.

The discrete derivative of the LCS curve of a set of $M$ accounts can be easily computed as

$$\text{LCS}'[k] = \frac{\Delta_k \text{ LCS}}{\Delta_k \text{ accounts}} = \text{LCS}[k] - \text{LCS}[k-1]$$

for $k = 3, \ldots, M$. Given that LCS curves are monotonic nonincreasing functions defined over the $[2, M]$ range, their derivatives LCS′ will assume only zero or negative values, with steep drops in the LCS corresponding to sharp negative peaks in LCS′. Simple peak-detection algorithms can be employed in order to automatically detect the relevant peaks in LCS′ [41]. Notably, this approach does not require a training phase and can be employed pretty much like a clustering algorithm, in an unsupervised fashion. We can notice that finding the splitting points is very efficient. In facts, evaluating the derivative peaks has a cost (in number of operations) that is linear with respect to the size of the dataset, while comparing and choosing the different split candidates is a customizable step that can be as easy as choosing the one corresponding to the highest (absolute) peak. Building the dendrogram and comparing the different split is an additional and optional step that can help representing the possible splits, if one needs to carefully explore the possible groups of accounts.

To prove the effectiveness of this unsupervised approach, we applied it to the LCS obtained from the unlabeled SPAM-TEST1 and SPAM-TEST2 test sets, with the goal of separating social spambots from legitimate accounts. Figure 10.5(a) and (b) shows stacked plots of the LCS of the SPAM-TEST1 and SPAM-TEST2 groups, respectively, together with their discrete derivative LCS′, both in linear and logarithmic scale. The logarithmic scale plots of the derivatives have been computed as $\log_{10} |\text{LCS}′|$, and they have been added for the sake of clarity, since they highlight the less visible peaks of the linear scale plots. In order to facilitate the detection of peaks in LCS′, we

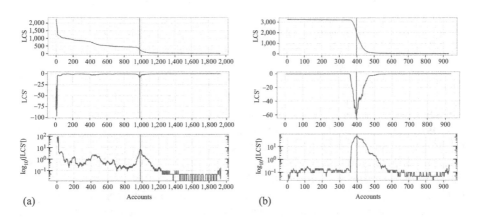

*Figure 10.5*   *Application of the unsupervised approach for discriminating between spambots and legitimate users among an unknown set of accounts. The peaks in the LCS derivatives that represent the best candidate points for the split are marked in all graphs with a vertical solid line. Accounts to the left of the splitting points are identified as spambots, while those to the right are identified as legitimate users. (a) Dataset: SPAM-TEST1 and (b) dataset: SPAM-TEST2*

smoothed the original LCS curves before computing their derivatives [42]. This pre-processing step acts pretty much like a low-pass filter, allowing to flatten the majority of noisy fluctuations.

In Figure 10.5, the solid vertical lines correspond to the most pronounced peaks in the LCS′ of SPAM-TEST1 and SPAM-TEST2. As shown, the proposed methodology accurately identified reasonable splitting points in order to find two clusters among the whole sets of unlabeled accounts. In detail, those accounts laying on the left of the vertical splitting line—that is, accounts sharing long behavioral patterns (i.e., long LCS)—are labeled as spambots. Conversely, the accounts to the right of the vertical splitting line—i.e., accounts sharing little similarities—are labeled as legitimate ones. Together with this qualitative assessment, in Section 10.6.3, we also perform a thorough quantitative evaluation of our spambots detection techniques, by means of well-known performance metrics of the machine-learning algorithms.

We remark that, although the SPAM-TEST1 and SPAM-TEST2 datasets feature an equal number of genuine and spambot accounts, the ratio between the two types of accounts is generally different when considering the whole Twittersphere [43]. The balance in SPAM-TEST1 and SPAM-TEST2 is because we mostly envision the application of this digital DNA technique to spot anomalous groups within devoted events/campaigns—e.g., those accounts retweeting a specific hashtag, or participating in an electoral campaign, or which are followers of a certain account. Whereas the analysis is concentrated on a subset of accounts acting around a particular event, the ratio between legitimate and spambot accounts can drastically vary, even leading to a balance in the cardinality of the two groups. For the sake of completeness, we carried out a series of further experiments with the aim of investigating the applicability of this technique to the whole Twittersphere, in order to gain insights into its effectiveness when the ratio between spambot accounts and legitimate ones is likely different than the one in the SPAM-TEST1 and SPAM-TEST2 test sets. Results of this experiment are presented in the next section (Tables 10.5 and 10.6).

We evaluate the performances of the unsupervised approach with a dataset that reflects a real word scenario, where the number of spambots is supposed to be much smaller than the number of human-operated accounts. In particular, Figure 10.6 reports the *MCC* resulted from the experiments obtained considering the ratio between the number of spambots and legitimate accounts spanning from 0.01 to 0.10, within a dataset of 5,000 total accounts. For each experiment, we firstly set the spambots ratio. Then, we randomly picked the DNA sequences of the two original test sets (SPAM-TEST1 and SPAM-TEST2) so as to build mixed datasets with the correct numbers of spambots and legitimate accounts. Finally, we executed the unsupervised detection approach on such datasets and evaluated the detection performance, averaging the results over 20 executions. From the plot in Figure 10.6, it is noticeable that the performance improves as the number of spambots in the dataset increases. Considering that the number of spambot accounts in this experiment is extremely low (the smallest one is only of 50 spambots), the reliability of the unsupervised approach is still noticeable.

*Table 10.5   Social spambots detection results*

| | | Detection results | | | |
|---|---|---|---|---|---|
| Technique | Type | TP | TN | FP | FN |
| Test set: SPAM-TEST1 | | | | | |
| Social Fingerprinting | Unsupervised | 963 | 924 | 18 | 28 |
| Yang *et al.* [11] | Supervised | 169 | 811 | 131 | 822 |
| Miller *et al.* [21] | Unsupervised | 355 | 657 | 285 | 636 |
| Ahmed *et al.* [22]* | Unsupervised | 935 | 888 | 54 | 56 |
| Test set: SPAM-TEST2 | | | | | |
| Social Fingerprinting | Unsupervised | 398 | 468 | 0 | 66 |
| Yang *et al.* [11] | Supervised | 190 | 397 | 71 | 274 |
| Miller *et al.* [21] | Unsupervised | 142 | 306 | 162 | 322 |
| Ahmed *et al.* [22]*,† | Unsupervised | 428 | 427 | 41 | 30 |

Comparison between the Social Fingerprinting splitting technique and other state-of-the-art algorithms toward the detection of social spambots among the accounts of the SPAM-TEST1 and SPAM-TEST2 test sets. Original contributions, represented by the proposed Social Fingerprinting technique, are highlighted
*Modified by employing *fastgreedy* instead of *MCL* for the graph clustering step.
†With regard to the feature set of [22], a few accounts had null values for all the features thus resulting in the impossibility to apply the clustering algorithm to such accounts.

*Table 10.6   Evaluation metrics for social spambots detection*

| | | Evaluation metrics | | | | | |
|---|---|---|---|---|---|---|---|
| Technique | Type | Precision | Recall | Specificity | Accuracy | F-measure | MCC |
| Test set: SPAM-TEST1 | | | | | | | |
| Social Fingerprinting | Unsupervised | **0.982** | 0.972 | **0.981** | 0.976 | **0.977** | 0.952 |
| Yang *et al.* [11] | Supervised | 0.563 | 0.170 | 0.860 | 0.506 | 0.261 | 0.043 |
| Miller *et al.* [21] | Unsupervised | 0.555 | 0.358 | 0.698 | 0.526 | 0.435 | 0.059 |
| Ahmed *et al.* [22]* | Unsupervised | 0.945 | 0.944 | 0.945 | 0.943 | 0.944 | 0.886 |
| Test set: SPAM-TEST2 | | | | | | | |
| Social Fingerprinting | Unsupervised | **1.000** | 0.858 | **1.000** | 0.929 | 0.923 | 0.867 |
| Yang *et al.* [11] | Supervised | 0.727 | 0.409 | 0.848 | 0.629 | 0.524 | 0.287 |
| Miller *et al.* [21] | Unsupervised | 0.467 | 0.306 | 0.654 | 0.481 | 0.370 | −0.043 |
| Ahmed *et al.* [22]* | Unsupervised | 0.913 | 0.935 | 0.912 | 0.923 | 0.923 | 0.847 |

Comparison between the Social Fingerprinting splitting technique and other state-of-the-art algorithms toward the detection of social spambots among the accounts of the SPAM-TEST1 and SPAM-TEST2 test sets. For each test set, the highest values in each evaluation metric are shown in **bold**. Original contributions, represented by the proposed Social Fingerprinting technique, are highlighted.
*Modified by employing *fastgreedy* instead of *MCL* for the graph clustering step.

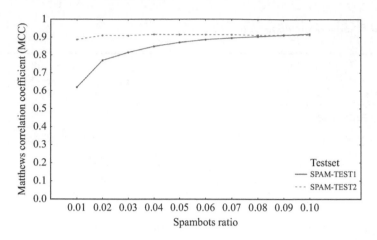

*Figure 10.6    Detection performances, in terms of MCC, of the Social
Fingerprinting unsupervised approach with heavily imbalanced data.
The SPAM-TEST1 and SPAM-TEST2 datasets have been resampled
for this experiment so as to obtain a spambots-to-legitimate-accounts
ratio = 0.01/0.1*

## 10.6.3    Comparison with state-of-the-art detection techniques

To thoroughly evaluate the Social Fingerprinting technique, we compared its detection
results with those obtained by different state-of-the-art spambot detection techniques,
namely, the supervised one by Yang *et al.* [11], and the unsupervised approaches by
Miller *et al.* [21] and by Ahmed *et al.* [22].

Notably, the Social Fingerprinting detection technique outperforms the other
approaches for all the considered metrics, achieving $MCC = 0.952$ and 0.955 for
SPAM-TEST1, and $MCC = 0.867$ and 0.940 for SPAM-TEST2. Specifically, there
is a clear performance gap between the approaches of [11] and [21] with respect to the
*Social Fingerprinting* approaches and that of [22]. The supervised approach by Yang
*et al.* [11] proved unable to accurately distinguish spambots from legitimate accounts,
as demonstrated by the considerable number of *FN* and the resulting very low *Recall*.
This result supports the initial claim that this new wave of bots is surprisingly similar
to legitimate accounts: they are exceptionally hard to detect if considered one by one.
Moreover, also the unsupervised approach in [21] provided unsatisfactory results.
Instead, the approach in [22] proved effective in detecting our considered spambots,
showing an $MCC = 0.886$ for SPAM-TEST1 and $MCC = 0.847$ for SPAM-TEST2.
With only seven features, the modified version of [22] focuses on retweets, hashtags,
mentions, and URLs, thus analyzing the accounts along the dimensions exploited
by these spammers. However, although achieving an overall good performance for
the considered spambots, the approach in [22] might lack reusability across other
groups of spambots with different behaviors, such as those perpetrating a follower

fraud [8,44]. *Social Fingerprinting*, instead, is flexible enough to highlight suspicious similarities among groups of accounts without focusing on specific characteristics.

## 10.7   Conclusions and future directions

In this chapter, we highlighted that recent waves of spambots have been thoroughly engineered so as to mimic the human behavior of OSNs genuine users. We showed that these novel species of spambots escape state-of-the-art algorithms specifically designed to detect them. Later, we described the digital DNA behavioral modeling technique. Leveraging this methodology, we have been able to find that there are still low intensity signals that make humans different from bots, when considering users not on an account-by-account basis, but rather on collective behaviors. Our Social Fingerprinting detection approach and coupled algorithmic toolbox—drawn from the bioinformatics and string mining domains—have shown excellent detection capabilities for all of the most relevant detection metrics, outperforming state-of-the-art solutions.

   As future research, we aim at exploiting the combined application of the digital DNA behavioral modeling technique and the effective heuristics represented by genetic algorithms. Since decades, the latter have been successfully used to solve optimization problems. However, in order to be applied, genetic algorithms require a string-based genetic encoding of information, which severely limited their applicability when dealing with online accounts. The combination of (i) digital DNA modeling—and, hence, the possibility to even create synthetic digital DNA sequences—and (ii) the evolutionary simulations allowed by genetic algorithms, open up the unprecedented opportunity to study the evolutionary patterns of modern social spambots.

## References

[1]   Liu H, Han J, Motoda H. Uncovering deception in social media. Social Network Analysis and Mining. 2014;4(1):1–2.

[2]   Stringhini G, Kruegel C, Vigna G. Detecting spammers on social networks. In: Proceedings of the 26th Annual Computer Security Applications Conference (ACSAC'10). ACM; 2010. p. 1–9.

[3]   Boshmaf Y, Muslukhov I, Beznosov K, *et al.* The socialbot network: When bots socialize for fame and money. In: Proceedings of the 27th Annual Computer Security Applications Conference (ACSAC'11). ACM; 2011. p. 93–102.

[4]   Chu Z, Gianvecchio S, Wang H, *et al.* Detecting automation of Twitter accounts: Are you a human, bot, or cyborg? IEEE Transactions on Dependable and Secure Computing. 2012;9(6):811–824.

[5]   Zangerle E, Specht G. Sorry, I was hacked: A classification of compromised Twitter accounts. In: Proceedings of the 29th Symposium on Applied Computing (SAC'14). ACM; 2014. p. 587–593.

[6]    Yang Z, Wilson C, Wang X, *et al.* Uncovering social network sybils in the wild. ACM Transactions on Knowledge Discovery from Data (TKDD). 2014;8(1):2:1–2:29.

[7]    Stringhini G, Wang G, Egele M, *et al.* Follow the green: Growth and dynamics in Twitter follower markets. In: Proceedings of the 13th Internet Measurement Conference (IMC'13). ACM; 2013. p. 163–176.

[8]    Cresci S, Di Pietro R, Petrocchi M, *et al.* Fame for sale: Efficient detection of fake Twitter followers. Decision Support Systems. 2015;80:56–71.

[9]    Lee K, Caverlee J, Webb S. Uncovering social spammers: Social honeypots + machine learning. In: Proceedings of the 33rd International Conference on Research and Development in Information Retrieval (SIGIR'10). ACM; 2010. p. 435–442.

[10]   Ghosh S, Viswanath B, Kooti F, *et al.* Understanding and combating link farming in the Twitter social network. In: Proceedings of the 21st International Conference on World Wide Web (WWW'12). ACM; 2012. p. 61–70.

[11]   Yang C, Harkreader R, Gu G. Empirical evaluation and new design for fighting evolving Twitter spammers. IEEE Transactions on Information Forensics and Security. 2013;8(8):1280–1293.

[12]   Hu X, Tang J, Liu H. Online social spammer detection. In: 28th International Conference on Artificial Intelligence (AAAI). AAAI; 2014. p. 59–65.

[13]   Ferrara E, Varol O, Davis C, *et al.* The rise of social bots. Communications of the ACM. 2016;59(7):96–104.

[14]   Zhang J, Zhang R, Zhang Y, *et al.* The rise of social botnets: Attacks and countermeasures. IEEE Transactions on Dependable and Secure Computing. 2016;15(6):1068–1082.

[15]   Cresci S, Di Pietro R, Petrocchi M, *et al.* The paradigm-shift of social spambots: Evidence, theories, and tools for the arms race. In: Proceedings of the 26th International Conference on World Wide Web (WWW'17 Companion). ACM; 2017. p. 963–972.

[16]   Avvenuti M, Bellomo S, Cresci S, *et al.* Hybrid crowdsensing: A novel paradigm to combine the strengths of opportunistic and participatory crowdsensing. In: Proceedings of the 26th International Conference on World Wide Web (WWW'17 Companion). ACM; 2017. p. 1413–1421.

[17]   Kohavi R, Provost F. Glossary of terms. Machine Learning. 1998;30(2-3): 271–274.

[18]   Baldi P, Brunak S, Chauvin Y, *et al.* Assessing the accuracy of prediction algorithms for classification: An overview. Bioinformatics. 2000;16(5): 412–424.

[19]   Powers DM. Evaluation: from precision, recall and F-measure to ROC, informedness, markedness and correlation. International Journal of Machine Learning Technologies. 2011;2(1):37–63.

[20]   Davis CA, Varol O, Ferrara E, *et al.* BotOrNot: A system to evaluate social bots. In: Proceedings of the 25th International Conference on World Wide Web (WWW'16 Companion). ACM; 2016. p. 273–274.

[21] Miller Z, Dickinson B, Deitrick W, *et al.* Twitter spammer detection using data stream clustering. Information Sciences. 2014;260:64–73.

[22] Ahmed F, Abulaish M. A generic statistical approach for spam detection in online social networks. Computer Communications. 2013;36(10): 1120–1129.

[23] Cao F, Estert M, Qian W, *et al.* Density-based clustering over an evolving data stream with noise. In: Proceedings of the SIAM International Conference on Data Mining (SDM'06). SIAM; 2006. p. 328–339.

[24] Ackermann MR, Märtens M, Raupach C, *et al.* StreamKM++: A clustering algorithm for data streams. Experimental Algorithmics. 2012;17:2–4.

[25] Van Dongen SM. Graph clustering via a discrete uncoupling process. SIAM Journal on Matrix Analysis and Applications. 2008;30(1):121–141.

[26] Clauset A, Newman ME, Moore C. Finding community structure in very large networks. Physical Review E. 2004;70(6):066111.

[27] Cresci S, Di Pietro R, Petrocchi M, *et al.* DNA-inspired online behavioral modeling and its application to spambot detection. IEEE Intelligent Systems. 2016;5(31):58–64.

[28] Cresci S, Di Pietro R, Petrocchi M, *et al.* Exploiting digital DNA for the analysis of similarities in Twitter behaviours. In: Proceedings of the 4th International Conference on Data Science and Advanced Analytics (DSAA'17). IEEE; 2017. p. 686–695.

[29] Benevenuto F, Rodrigues T, Almeida V, *et al.* Detecting spammers and content promoters in online video social networks. In: Proceedings of the 32nd International Conference on Research and Development in Information Retrieval (SIGIR'09). ACM; 2009. p. 620–627.

[30] Wilson C, Sala A, Puttaswamy KP, *et al.* Beyond social graphs: User interactions in online social networks and their implications. ACM Transactions on the Web. 2012;6(4):17.

[31] Benevenuto F, Rodrigues T, Cha M, *et al.* Characterizing user navigation and interactions in online social networks. Information Sciences. 2012;195:1–24.

[32] Viswanath B, Bashir MA, Crovella M, *et al.* Towards detecting anomalous user behavior in online social networks. In: Proceedings of the 23rd USENIX Security Symposium (SEC'14). USENIX; 2014. p. 223–238.

[33] Ruan X, Wu Z, Wang H, *et al.* Profiling online social behaviors for compromised account detection. IEEE Transactions on Information Forensics and Security. 2016;11(1):176–187.

[34] Cao L. In-depth behavior understanding and use: The behavior informatics approach. Information Sciences. 2010;180(17):3067–3085.

[35] Gusfield D. Algorithms on strings, trees and sequences: Computer science and computational biology. Cambridge: Cambridge University Press; 1997.

[36] Arnold M, Ohlebusch E. Linear time algorithms for generalizations of the longest common substring problem. Algorithmica. 2011;60(4):806–818.

[37] Chi L, Hui K. Color set size problem with applications to string matching. In: Combinatorial Pattern Matching. Berlin, Heidelberg: Springer; 1992. p. 230–243.

[38]   Friedman J, Hastie T, Tibshirani R. The elements of statistical learning. vol. 1. New York: Springer Series in Statistics; 2001.
[39]   Fawcett T. An introduction to ROC analysis. Pattern Recognition Letters. 2006;27(8):861–874.
[40]   Cresci S, Di Pietro R, Petrocchi M, *et al.* Social fingerprinting: Detection of spambot groups through DNA-inspired behavioral modeling. IEEE Transactions on Dependable and Secure Computing; 2017;15(4):561–576.
[41]   Palshikar G. Simple algorithms for peak detection in time-series. In: Proceedings of the 1st International Conference on Advanced Data Analysis, Business Analytics and Intelligence. IIMA; 2009.
[42]   Lampos V, Cristianini N. Nowcasting events from the social web with statistical learning. ACM Transactions on Intelligent Systems and Technology (TIST). 2012;3(4):72.
[43]   Twitter Inc. Twitter's IPO filing; 2013. https://goo.gl/pbXxHh (Last checked 31/10/17).
[44]   Jiang M, Cui P, Beutel A, *et al.* Catching synchronized behaviors in large networks: A graph mining approach. ACM Transactions on Knowledge Discovery from Data (TKDD). 2016;10(4):35:1–35:27.

*Chapter 11*

# Nature-inspired approaches for social network security

*Indu Valsaladevi[1,2] and Sabu M. Thampi[2]*

---

*Study Nature, Love Nature, Stay Close to Nature. It will never fail you.*

Frank Lloyd Wright

## 11.1 Introduction

Nature is one of the best teachers in the whole Universe. It constantly experiences the transitions happening in the environment and adapts itself to the changes and has its own inherent capability to evolve according to the changing environment. It has powerful features of self-learning, self-optimisation, self-processing and self-healing, and it has been a rich source of inspiration for philosophers and researchers from ancient times. Nature has the ability to solve extremely complicated problems in its own unique way, and humans are always allured by the mesmerising ways by which it tackles different circumstances [1]. Scientists and philosophers have always been observing the amazing phenomena happening in the nature, and they have been trying to analyse and replicate them as algorithms in novel problem-solving techniques [2]. Here comes the relevance of nature-inspired algorithms since they emerge from the fact that they imitate the best characteristics in the nature. The area of nature-inspired algorithms in social network security is a highly unexplored area, and this chapter is an attempt to throw lights into the amazing world of nature-inspired techniques that find application in the social network arena. This chapter sketches various bio-inspired algorithms that can be applied for social network analysis (SNA) problems and also summarises the state-of-the-art nature-inspired techniques prevailing in social network security, their open challenges and future research directions in this area.

### 11.1.1 An overview of nature-inspired algorithms

Humans are greatly inspired by the nature and they try to mimic many techniques through which it solves different problems and adapts itself to the dynamic

[1]Faculty of Engineering (Department of Computer Science and Engineering), University of Kerala, India
[2]Center for Research and Innovation in Cyber Threat Resilience (CRICTR), Indian Institute of Information Technology and Management – Kerala (IIITM-K), India

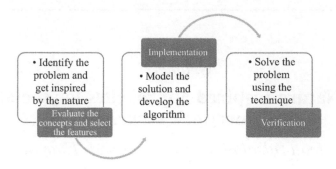

*Figure 11.1    Workflow of nature-inspired algorithms*

environment. Drawing inspiration from the real-world events, researchers have been trying to develop more logical and effective ways of problem-solving in the form of algorithms for cracking many real-world optimisation problems. The collective and emerging behaviour of individuals, self-organisation, the division of labour, food searching habits, communication and interaction among animals, birds, fishes and even insects like ants, bees, fireflies, termites, wasps, etc. have drawn the attention of researchers and numerous optimisation algorithms have been developed based on their behaviour analysis [3,4]. The algorithms which are developed taking inspiration from nature are called *nature-inspired algorithms* or *bio-inspired algorithms*. The beauty of the nature-inspired algorithms lies in the fact that they draw their sole inspiration from the nature and its efficiency and success depend on the selection of the fittest features of biological systems that have evolved through natural selection over millions of years [5]. Figure 11.1 shows the general workflow of nature-inspired algorithms.

Nature-inspired algorithms can be broadly classified into *evolutionary algorithms (EAs)* and *swarm intelligence algorithms*. There are also several other nature-inspired approaches which involve the combination of evolutionary and swarm intelligence approaches, techniques which take inspiration from different biological structures found in the nature and their organisational principles, occurrences of natural hazards, the spread of epidemics, human behaviour, stimulus action of organisms, bacterial diffusion and so on which may be categorised under *miscellaneous approaches* [6]. Classification of nature-inspired algorithms is depicted in Figure 11.2.

## 11.1.1.1    Evolutionary algorithms

EAs utilise the concepts of natural evolution. These algorithms get their inspiration from the famous Theory of Natural Selection proposed by Charles Darwin. The basic concept behind natural selection is the *survival of the fittest* which means individuals which are well suited to the environment survive, reproduce and pass their genetic traits to their offspring [1], i.e. a major population adapts itself to the changing environment and the variations in individuals accumulate over time and generate a new species. The underlying concept in all EAs is that if there is a given population

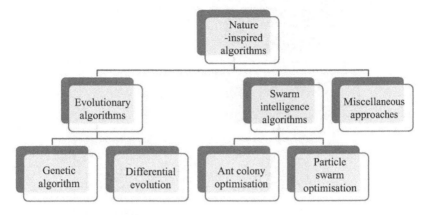

*Figure 11.2 Classification of nature-inspired algorithms*

of individuals, the environmental pressure causes natural selection and this causes a rise in the fitness of the population. The major components of an EA are as follows:

- **Representation**: The first step is to set up a link between the original problem context and the problem-solving space where the evolution takes place. Objects forming a possible solution with the original problem context are referred to as phenotypes and their encoding is referred to as genotypes and the mapping of phenotypes on to a set of genotypes is called representation.
- **Evaluation (fitness function)**: Evaluation function or fitness function represents the requirements to adapt to. It forms the basis for selection and facilitates for improvements.
- **Population**: Population represents the set of possible solutions. It is a multiset of genotypes and forms the basic unit of evolution.
- **Parent selection mechanism**: Parent selection or mating selection process is to determine the individuals based on their quality so that better quality individuals get a higher chance to become parents of the next generation than lower quality individuals.
- **Variation operators, recombination and mutation**: Variation operators create new individuals from the old ones. Mutation is a unary variation operator which when applied to one genotype delivers a slightly modified mutant called the child or offspring of it. Recombination or crossover is a binary variation operator which combines information from two-parent genotypes into one or two offspring genotypes.
- **Survivor selection mechanism (replacement)**: The main purpose of the survivor selection or environmental selection is to distinguish among individuals based on their quality in order to create offsprings from the selected parents so as to retain the best and discard the worst. It is also called replacement or replacement strategy. It is similar to parent selection but is used in a different stage of the evolutionary cycle.

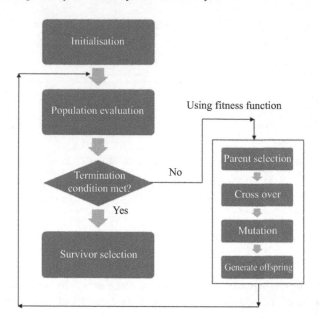

*Figure 11.3    Workflow of evolutionary algorithms*

Each of these components must be specified in order to define a particular EA. Moreover, to obtain a running algorithm, an initialisation procedure and a termination condition must also be defined [7]. The general workflow of EAs is illustrated in Figure 11.3.

EAs can be subdivided as *genetic algorithm (GA)* and *differential evolution (DE)*.

**GA**: It is a class of EA for solving constrained and unconstrained optimisation problems based on natural selection to select an optimised solution from a set of candidate solutions. To evolve good solutions and to perform the natural selection, there should be a measure for distinguishing good solutions from bad solutions. The measure could be an objective function or a computer simulation or a subjective function where humans choose better solutions from a set of available solutions. GA finds the optimal solution by maximising or minimising the fitness function where the fitness measure determines the candidate solution's relative fitness [8].

**DE**: It is a method that optimises a problem by repeatedly trying to improve a candidate solution with respect to a given measure of quality. DE creates new parameter vectors by adding the weighted difference vector between two population members to a third member. If the resulting vector yields a lower objective function value than a predetermined population member, then the newly generated vector substitutes the vector with which it was compared. In addition, the best parameter vector is evaluated for every generation in order to keep track of the progress that is made during the optimisation process. It is a population-based approach for minimising functions where a maximising function is converted to a minimising function [9].

### 11.1.1.2 Swarm intelligence algorithms

The second category of nature-inspired algorithms is called swarm intelligence algorithms where the algorithms work on the principle of the collective behaviour of decentralised, self-organising systems including both natural and artificial. The concept of swarm intelligence was introduced by Gerardo Beni and Jing Wang in 1989, in the context of cellular robotic systems. These algorithms are developed based on how the individuals in a population interact with each other and with their environment. Algorithms based on ant colonies, bird flocking, animal herding, bacterial growth, fish schooling and microbial intelligence can be categorised under swarm intelligence. In nature, such systems are commonly used to unfold problems such as effective foraging for food, prey evading or colony relocation. The information is typically stored around the participating homogeneous agents or is stored or communicated in the environment itself such as through the use of pheromones in ants, dancing in bees and proximity in fishes and birds. This area can be broadly classified into two subareas as *ant colony optimisation (ACO)* and *particle swarm optimisation (PSO)* [10].

**ACO**: The ACO algorithm is inspired by the foraging behaviour of ants; specifically, all the ants use pheromone as a chemical messenger for finding a good path between the colony and a food source in an environment. This mechanism is called *stigmergy* [10]. This idea was initially proposed by Marco Dorigo in 1992 in his PhD thesis, and the first algorithm was developed to find out an optimal path in a graph, based on the behaviour of ants seeking a path between their colony and a source of food. Solutions are related to the pheromone concentration and if the pheromone concentration is higher, more ants gather and more pheromone is left by then, showing a positive feedback mechanism of information. The higher concentration of pheromone path indicates the shortest path, so the path attracts more ants and finally, all the ants would choose this path. Normally, the ant colony algorithm works without any prior knowledge, it initially selects a random search path, with an understanding of the solution space and gradually the search becomes regular until the approximate global optimal solution is found [11].

**PSO**: PSO draws inspiration from the social foraging behaviour of some animals such as flocking behaviour of birds and the schooling behaviour of fishes. A flock of birds and shoal of fishes moving together follow certain patterns and they constantly update their position and direction of motion. Based on their overall information and by adjusting their speed and position, they achieve the best position of the individual through continuous iteration and ensure that all the team members maintain the optimum state [12]. In PSO, an individual in the swarm, called a particle, represents a potential solution. Each particle has a fitness value and a velocity, and it learns the experiences of the swarm to search for the global optima. Particles move around the search space being influenced by their own best past location and the best past location of the whole swarm or a close neighbour [10]. Traditional PSO includes the

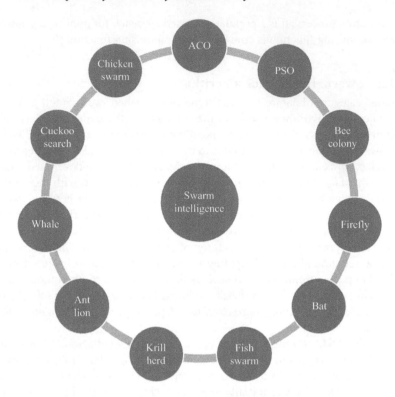

*Figure 11.4    Various swarm intelligence algorithms*

following steps as (1) particle initialisation, (2) velocity update, (3) particle position update, (4) memory update and (5) termination checking [13].

Apart from these two major classifications, a variety of algorithms inspired from the collective behaviour of various organisms, their food searching habits, self-protection mechanisms from predators and colony relocation have been put forward by many researchers which could be categorised under swarm intelligence algorithms. Algorithms like artificial bee colony (ABC), firefly algorithm (FA), bat algorithm, artificial fish swarm optimisation, krill herd swarm optimisation, ant lion optimisation, whale optimisation algorithm (WOA), etc. are some of them. All these algorithms are variants of the above-mentioned two main categories and utilise the principles of swarm behaviour of organisms. Figure 11.4 illustrates some of the various swarm intelligence algorithms.

## 11.2   Social network: terms and terminologies

The social behaviour of individuals, their communication skills and eagerness for information sharing have paved way for the emergence and popularity of social networks. Social networks provide an efficient way of connecting people around the globe through a common platform. These networks bring people closer to each other where people can share their thoughts, opinions, images, videos and even day-to-day events with family, friends, relatives, colleagues and among a wide community of people. Generally, a social network can be equated to a graph, $G = (V, E)$ where $V$ represents the set of individuals or nodes and $E$ represents the connections or inter-actions between them. Thus, a social network is a graph of individuals connected by different types of interactions such as friendship, acquaintanceship, co-authorship, etc. *SNA* is the method of investigating network structures with the help of graph theory and network-based techniques to retrieve meaningful knowledge from the net-works formed by various actors [14]. Some of the common terminologies associated with social networks are discussed below:

- **Node degree**: The degree of a node in a network is the number of connections it has to other nodes.
- **Modularity**: It is the measure of the structure of networks or graphs and it measures the strength of the division of a network into communities.
- **Centrality**: Centrality conveys the importance or prominence of a vertex and helps to identify the most important vertices in a graph.
  - *Closeness centrality*: In connected graphs, there is a natural distance measure between all pairs of nodes, which tells how close a node is to all the other nodes in a network. Closeness centrality of a node is defined as the inverse of the sum of the distances between a node to all other nodes in the network.
  - *Betweenness centrality*: It refers to the number of times a node acts as a bridge along the shortest path between two other nodes.
  - *Eigenvector centrality*: It is a measure of the number of other prominent nodes that are connected to a particular node.
- **Average path length**: It is defined as the average number of steps along the shortest paths for all possible pairs of network nodes [15].

## 11.2.1  The relevance of social network security and privacy

Social networks offer people a good medium for fun and recreation, and it also helps people in staying connected and act as a crucial element in the faster dissemination of information. Apart from the benefits showered to its users, social networks also have a darker side of hidden dangers and numerous pitfalls.

Most of the social network users publish a large amount of their private informa-tion including demographic information, contact details, images and videos in their social network space without any caution and thus social networks have become a huge trove of sensitive data. Due to the increasing popularity and ease of accessibil-ity, social networking websites have become new targets that attract cybercriminals. Security attacks are a very common issue in social networks which include various forms of attacks including privacy breaches, information leakage, phishing, spam-ming, hacking and malware which pose a severe threat to the online users. Another serious menace faced by social network users is the spread of misinformation or rumours through social networks which exploits users trust in an application and it also destroys the credibility of the target source. The increasing popularity, ease of access, lack of proper filtering mechanisms and the immense trust users place in these networks open door for several security breaches and online deceptions via social networks [16]. Researchers have been thriving to solve these problems and many have come up with effective solutions to provide better protection and enhance the security of social network users.

Online social networks (OSNs) have become an integral part of our day-to-day life, and online users are spending a majority of their time browsing these networks. Every day, more and more people are attracted towards the magnificent world of social networks and thereby a large number of people are unknowingly exposed to many of these security breaches. So, it is relevant to enhance the current safety and security measures in social networks in order to provide better security and privacy to social network users for savouring its benefits to the fullest.

## 11.3 The significance of nature-inspired approaches in social network security

Social network security has a greater significance in today's world since the number of security breaches and privacy violations are increasing day-by-day. Researchers have come up with effective remedies for deciphering the different security issues prevailing in social networks, and they have developed many techniques and algorithms involving machine learning, natural language processing, information retrieval and graph theory to enhance the security and privacy in OSNs. The performances of these existing techniques are not much promising. Security researchers are continually thriving to provide better solutions to online threats, and they are trying to improve the present solutions to provide better and more accurate protection against social network threats. The major research gaps identified in this domain are as follows:

- Most of the methods employed for threat detection and for enhancing social network security follow a supervised approach. To deal with problems involving a massive amount of diverse data as in the case of social networks, it is very difficult to train machines with a large set of labelled training data.
- There is a lack of self-learning and adaptive approaches in this area. It is advisable to use self-learning approaches for handling problems with no specific solutions like fake news detection and spam identification in social networks since it is hard to select relevant features for training a particular machine-learning model.

Taking this into consideration, novel and transformative methods can be utilised in the social network area to better safeguard social network users. Deviating from the contemporary methods and techniques, researches started looking into natural systems for inspiration and methods for solving problems in the human-created artificial environments.

Nature always tries to survive by creating a successful generation of descendants who can defend themselves against the predators and the negative conditions and adapt themselves to the rapid changes in the environment. Similarly, social networks and other communication systems rely on cyber security to safeguard their assets from cybercriminals, hackers, hostile organisations and even abrupt changes in the network environment. Many of the defence mechanisms used by natural organisms such as immune systems, predator detection, camouflage and mimicry may be mapped to the social network space to implement effective cyber security. Some of the social network security methods and algorithms developed for intrusion detection, malware attack, rumour detection have their roots in nature-inspired techniques, and they are found to perform well than the current security mechanisms. As the security attacks and threats are evading the state-of-the-art techniques, there is an immense need for developing novel bio-inspired security and defence mechanisms to counter these threats [17]. This has resulted in the development of bio-inspired algorithms involving evolutionary and swarm intelligence approaches for addressing the social network security problems.

## 11.4 Nature-inspired techniques in social network paradigm

Nature-inspired algorithms with novel concepts and efficient techniques can be used to handle challenging problems faced by social network users that are not resolved by the state-of-the-art techniques. Apart from existing methods and algorithms, nature-inspired approaches offer a diverse range of efficient, intelligent, self-adaptive and self-learning algorithms to address social network problems of crucial importance [18]. This section outlines some of the nature-inspired approaches that find application in SNA and security. It gives an overview of the different categories of bio-inspired algorithms that can be applied for SNA such as influence maximisation (IM), community detection (CD), link prediction (LP), and rumour detection. Nature-inspired techniques for trust management and for addressing various other security issues in the social network arena are also being discussed in this section.

### 11.4.1 Nature-inspired algorithms for influence maximisation in social networks

Influence Maximisation is the problem of finding a small subset of nodes (termed as seed nodes or key influentials) in a social network that could maximise the spread of influence. Due to the massive number of online users and strong person-to-person interaction, social networks have emerged as an important platform in the quick spread of news, rumours and opinions and a piece of information may go viral within seconds. Events, issues, interests, etc. happen and evolve very quickly in social networks and their capture, understanding, visualisation and prediction are becoming critical expectations for both the end-users and researchers [19].

Since social networks have now become a strong medium for information dissemination, influence maximisation problem helps to identify the most influential individuals in a network who can play the key roles in the information spread. It has a wide variety of applications such as how to spread ideas or information to a large community of people within a short span of time, identify the influential spreaders who are involved in the spread of rumours or false information through social media and how to market products, services, and promote innovative ideas to a wide circle of people by identifying the key initial users who could influence a huge number of people in the network within a minimum period of time [20].

### 11.4.1.1    Evolutionary algorithms for influence maximisation

In 2017, Doina Bucur *et al.* proposed a novel multi-objective EA (MOEA) to address the influence maximisation problem in social networks. MOEAs are a natural flavour of EAs specially designed for minimising the number of seed nodes in an influence campaign so as to identify the best set of seed nodes that spread the influence to the maximum. The proposed mechanism is then tested on two real-world case studies: the ego-Facebook network, which describes social circles from Facebook, and ca-GrQc, which covers the scientific collaborations between the authors using two different influence propagation models. This method was an attempt to maximise the influence campaign utilising a minimum number of seed nodes, thereby limiting the budget and it was said to outperform the state-of-the-art techniques. But, this approach solely depends on the size of the seed nodes, so the incorporation of other features into this method and its experimentation in a wide range of social networks is necessary to assess the effective potential of the proposed approach [21].

*Genetic algorithms for influence maximisation*
The concept of GAs was also utilised by the researchers to solve the influence maximisation problem in social networks. In 2016, Doina Bucur and Giovanni Iacca addressed the influence maximisation problem by means of a GA which uses simple genetic operators typically used in discrete optimisation. The candidate solution generated by the GA is encoded as a fixed size sequence of a seed node and the fitness value is evaluated by using a Cascade algorithm and after several iterations of the algorithm, the average value is assigned to each candidate solution as its fitness [22]. Another method based on GA which generates multiple seed nodes is presented in [23] where a clone operation is set in GA with which the range in local search can be expanded, thereby offering a diverse range of solutions for a fixed choice of thresholds. One of the main limitations of this approach is that GA gets affected by the network parameters and the process of optimisation becomes more complex when compared with the other methods.

Another technique for leveraging the capabilities of GA and greedy algorithm is discussed in [24] where the greedy algorithm keeps on adding a new node to the seed set on each iteration, so that the influence of the seed set will be increased until the size of the seed set has reached a predefined limit. Mayank Lahiri and Manuel Cebrian proposed a GA diffusion model to model the information flow in social networks. A canonical GA (one with binary string chromosomes and one-point crossover) with a spatially distributed population combined with specific forms of Holland's synthetic hyperplane-defined objective functions is used to simulate a large class of diffusion models for social networks [25].

GAs are a feasible solution for the influence maximisation problem when there is no prior knowledge about the network topology and the characteristics of the underlying social network graph. Even though some methods get affected by certain network parameters, GAs can be effectively paired with graph-based heuristics, in order to create domain-specific memetic algorithms.

### 11.4.1.2 Swarm intelligence algorithms for influence maximisation

Various swarm intelligence approaches have also been put forward by the researchers besides evolutionary approaches to address the influence maximisation problem and some are discussed below:

**ACO**: Wan-Shiou Yang and Shi-Xin Weng exploited the search capacity of the ACO algorithm for unfolding the influence maximisation problem in social networks, and their approach uses three metrics: degree centrality, distance centrality and simulated influence methods for determining the heuristic values of nodes and was evaluated in a competitive and non-competitive environment on a real-world co-authorship dataset [26].

**PSO**: In 2016, Maoguo Gong *et al.* addressed the problem of influence maximisation using discrete PSO (DPSO) algorithm where the influence maximisation is converted into an optimisation problem by developing a function named local influence evaluation. Proposed DPSO redefines the representations and update rules for velocity and position to solve the influence maximisation problem with lower time consumption [27]. An improved PSO algorithm is presented in [28] for finding the microblog users with maximum influence on the popular Chinese microblogging platform Sina Weibo. The influences of microblog users are determined by the various user behaviours, which are mapped with the five fundamental principles of swarm intelligence as proximity principle, quality principle, diverse response principle, stability principle, and adaptability principle, and in addition, the retweeting behaviour of users is also taken into consideration which is described as a variable of the user influence space.

A Hajibagheri *et al.* proposed a PSO diffusion model that utilises a stochastic method to model the information flow in a network by creating particle swarms for local network neighbourhoods that optimise a continuous version of Holland's hyperplane-defined objective functions. In this method, each node of the graph is considered as a selfish agent which locally optimises a utility function to increase its information share. The proposed method can be also used for identifying the community structure of the underlying network [29].

**ABC**: ABC is another swarm intelligence concept which was used for modelling information diffusion in social networks. ABC algorithm introduced by Karaboga *et al.* in 2005 is a meta-heuristic approach inspired by the natural foraging behaviour of a honey bee to find the optimal food resources through a *waggle dance*. A colony of honey bees called employer bees constantly search the environment for new flower patches and the bees (onlooker bees) which find a highly profitable food source would perform a waggle dance in an area in the hive called the dance floor. With the waggle dance, a scout bee communicates the location it has discovered to other bees, which may join in the exploration of the flower patch. Since the length of the dance is proportional to the scouts' rating of the food source, more bees get recruited to harvest the best rated flower patches [30].

G Sperlì *et al.* explored the efficiency of ABC algorithm and they utilised the same to inspect the social network and discover the key influential vertices through the process of the waggle dance. Each node in the network will be marked as a food source, and the employer bees locate the key influential opinion leaders in the propagation process, scout bees analyse the nearest neighbours of the employer bees for better solutions and the onlooker bees represent the followers of the opinion leaders and proposed approach was a good trigger for future researches in this area [18]. C P Sankar *et al.* also studied the communication process of the honey bees through the waggle dance and they used the global-local search capacity of the ABC algorithm for solving the influence maximisation problem. They introduced a node ranking procedure which combines user profile features and message activities for selecting a set of key influential nodes who are involved in the maximum influence diffusion during viral campaigns through online micro-blogging platforms [30].

**PhysarumSpreader**: An algorithm called PhysarumSpreader inspired from an amoeboid organism called Physarum polycephalum is introduced in [31] for identifying the influential spreaders in complex networks. Physarum polycephalum is a single-celled amoeboid organism that can form a dynamic tubular network within the discovered food sources. During the process of food search, Physarum will cut off those non-competing long tubes and reinforce shorter tubes depending on the flux and conductivity through the tubes. Here, the idea of PhysarumSpreader is used in combination with the well-known graph structure analysis technique called K-shell index to identify the influential nodes in weighted networks. A positive feedback mechanism is employed to accelerate the convergence of the algorithm and by taking the edge weights into consideration; the algorithm is used for identifying the spreading capability of nodes in a network. One of the advantages of using Physarum is that it can adapt itself to the dynamics of the network and take only less computational time.

**FA**: Another swarm intelligence based approach using FA was presented by Hema Banati and Monika Bajaj for promoting the online products. FA takes inspiration from the biochemical and social aspects of fireflies where fireflies emit cold light due to a chemical reaction called *bioluminescence* that helps them in attracting their mating partners and also serves as a protective warning mechanism. Attractiveness is proportional to their brightness and the less brighter fly will move towards the brighter one. This algorithm identifies the users who have a high potential of influencing the maximum number of other web users over a selected segment. The selection of the most potential segment and the number of segments to be considered for product promotion depend upon the type of the product to be promoted as well as the marketing budget. The social connectivity and influencing capabilities of the users are also considered to identify the most influential users called seeds who can maximise the product awareness through social networks [32].

### 11.4.1.3 Other nature-inspired approaches for influence maximisation

**Using GA, DE and PSO**: An algorithm combining the features of GA, DE and PSO is presented in [33] to address the problem of viral marketing via OSNs. The selection of initial seed users to maximise the profit is a challenging task due to the large scale of the network. By employing these methods, the authors were able to reduce the scalability of the network, and results indicate that these nature-inspired techniques outperformed the conventional methods in addressing the viral marketing problem.

**Using stimulus amplification**: Inspired by the nonlinear amplification of stimuli, S Pei *et al.* proposed a method to construct excitable sensor networks for analysing the influence of spreading in social networks. Here, the stimuli can be regarded as infections, and the response of the excited system can be considered as the detected influence. The amplifying effect of excitable sensors to external stimuli is utilised in this method, and the spreading of different topics in the Twitter platform is tracked and the excitable sensor networks are more likely to detect the spreading instances from high-degree and well-connected sources. The dynamics of excitable sensor networks are highly related to the network topology and the coupling strength which may affect the performance to some extent [34].

**Yeast cell cycle**: David L. Gibbs and Ilya Shmulevich conducted studies in the regulatory organisation of the yeast cell cycle, and the same concept was used for solving the influence maximisation problem. More than 26,000 regulatory edges from YeastMine were utilised and the gene expression dynamics were encoded as edge weights using time-lagged transfer entropy to analyse the diffusion process over a network [35].

**Memetic algorithm**: Another approach for addressing the community-based influence maximisation problem in social networks was introduced by M Gong *et al.* by using a memetic algorithm. Memetic algorithms are a division of evolutionary computing utilising both local and global search procedures for solving complex optimisation problems in social networks. Proposed method optimise the two-hop influence spread which can determine the influence spread of a node-set, and the community property has also been incorporated to reduce the search space of seed nodes effectively [36].

Due to the increasing popularity of social networks, the problem of influence maximisation is gaining more and more importance. Most of the traditional solutions concentrate on traversing each and every node in the network which is time-consuming and ineffective. Addressing this problem using nature-inspired approaches is a good starting point for the new researches and developments in this area.

## 11.4.2 *Nature-inspired algorithms for community detection in social networks*

A community is defined as a group of individuals who are strongly connected to each other than to other individuals who are outside the group, and the members of the community share some features in common [37]. The tendency of people with similar choices, opinions, and interests to get connected in a social network leads to the formation of virtual clusters or communities. CD is a hot topic for the researchers in network security since many illegal groups and communities prevailing in social networks are involved in antisocial activities, terrorism, criminal activities, information campaigns, cyberattacks and social media propaganda. These communities are involved in the strong manipulation of the public mind, and the social networking space has recently emerged as a new battlefield for political conflicts. Propaganda through social media let out by the different communities of people has emerged into a methodological process capable of influencing the whole nations in a short span of time, and it has recently become a powerful tool in the cyber warfare.

CD is also useful for various other applications such as finding a common research area in collaboration networks, finding a set of likeminded users for marketing and recommendations, locating people who are professionally connected, searching for collaborations among movie actors and finding protein interaction networks in biological networks [38].

### 11.4.2.1    Evolutionary algorithms for community detection

With the growing complexity of social networks, the EA gains considerable attention due to its high efficiency in solving several problems which the traditional approaches are hard to deal with. Various evolutionary approaches have been proposed by the researchers for dynamic CD, link clustering and for identifying overlapping communities in social networks in the past few years and some of them are summarised below:

*Differential evolution algorithms for community detection*

An algorithm named *DESSO/CD (DE using social spider optimisation (SSO) for CD)* is discussed in [39] by simulating the spider cooperative operators, marriage and operator selection. Here, a random cloud crossover model strategy is used to maintain the population diversity and the mating radius of the SSO algorithm is automatically adjusted according to the fitness value in the dominant individuals. This method has less dependence on parameters, shows better adaptability, higher efficiency and has greater accuracy. Another method called *DECD* is presented in [40] where an improved version of the standard binomial crossover in DE is used to extract some important information regarding the community structure. The method uses different objective functions such as conductance, normalised cut and average degree for calculating the fitness function, and it does not require any prior knowledge about the community structure.

Table 11.1 lists of some of the major GAs that have been developed for addressing CD in social networks. Analysis of the methods in the aforementioned table indicates that most of the GAs for CD suffer from slow convergence and low precision due to the presence of commonly used crossover operators that are not fit for CD. By suitably modifying the mutation and crossover operators or by successfully generating an initial population, many other efficient algorithms using evolutionary approaches have been proposed by the researchers for handling the CD problem in social networks and a few are discussed in Table 11.2.

A number of evolutionary approaches have been proposed so far to detect community structures in complex networks, but most of the existing EAs require a prior knowledge of the community structure and perform poorly in large complex networks because of their time complexity.

*Table 11.1    Genetic algorithms for community detection*

| Method | Inferences |
| --- | --- |
| Community detection based on Genetic Algorithm (2006) [41] | Detects the best community structure by maximising the network modularity which is used as the fitness value |
| GA-Net for Community Detection (2008) [42] | Uses a fitness function to identify the groups of nodes in the network having dense intra-connections, and sparse inter-connections |
| Genetic Algorithm with Ensemble Learning (GAEL) (2009) [43] | Traditional crossover operator of GA is replaced with a multi-individual crossover operator based on ensemble learning which improves the global search ability of GAEL |
| Genetic Algorithm for Community Detection (GACD) (2010) [44] | Locus-based adjacency encoding schema is applied to represent the community partition. |
| DYNamic Multi-Objective Genetic Algorithms (DYN-MOGA) (2010) [45] | The concept of community score is utilised to detect communities with better quality |
| Genetic algorithm for overlapping Community Detection (GaoCD) (2011) [46] | Detects the overlapping communities utilising link (edge) clustering |
| Overlap-Detection Genetic Algorithm (OGA) (2013) [47] | An edge-based representation for clustering is used to detect the overlapping communities of nodes by maximising an overlapping modularity function |
| Modularity and an Improved Genetic Algorithm (MIGA) (2013) [48] | Uses modularity as the objective function and exploits prior information regarding the community structures to improve the stability and accuracy of the CD |
| Matrix Encoding and Nodes Similarity Genetic Algorithm (MENSGA) (2013) [49] | Here, network modularity function is set as the target and fitness function, adopts matrix encoding and uses nodes' similarity to initialise the population |
| Genetic Algorithm for Fuzzy Community Detection (GAFCD) (2014) [50] | Uses two main operations: crossover and mutation. Crossover helps to converge quickly to the best solution and mutation aims to find the best partition |
| Overlapping community detection algorithm based on Genetic Algorithm (OGA) (2014) [51] | Matrix-based encoding is adopted to improve the efficiency of the crossover and decoding operations |
| Generational Genetic Algorithm (GGA+) (2017) [52] | Concentrates on the efficient initialisation methods and search operators giving importance to modularity |

*Table 11.2    Other evolutionary approaches for community detection*

| Method | Inferences |
| --- | --- |
| Non-dominated neighbour Immune Algorithm (NNIA) (2012) [53] | Uses non-dominated neighbour-based selection technique, an immune-inspired operator, two heuristic search operators and elitism |
| Dynamic Networks Community Detection-Multi-Objective Evolutionary Algorithm (DNCD-MOEA) (2013) [54] | Modularity density and normalised mutual information (NMI) are employed to measure the snapshot cost and temporal cost, and a local search operator is designed to improve the efficiency |
| Evolutionary Community Detection Algorithm (ECDA) (2014) [55] | Uses a fitness function to find the connections within and between the communities, novel cross over operator and a special mutation operator called self-evolution (SE) to speed up the evolutionary process |
| Multi-Objective Evolutionary Algorithm based on Decomposition and Membrane Structure (MOEA/DM) (2016) [56] | Role of membranes in the functioning of living cells is utilised and EA is applied to the membrane structure where a population is divided into different membrane structures |

### 11.4.2.2    Swarm intelligence algorithms for community detection

A wide variety of algorithms from swarm intelligence have been recommended for solving the CD problem utilising the social behaviour and group activities of different organisms. Table 11.3 presents some of the major swarm intelligence algorithms using divergent approaches for uncovering the underlying community structure and determining the number of different communities in various complex networks.

Apart from the traditional methods for CD which rely on graph partitioning, spectral or hierarchical clustering, swarm intelligence algorithms provide a rich variety of methods which can be effectively utilised for CD. From Table 11.3, it can be inferred that one of the important problems faced by PSO is the lack of diversity and different solutions are proposed for it; whereas other swarm intelligence methods could automatically identify the number of communities and easily find the global optimal solution to overcome the shortcomings of traditional algorithms.

## 11.4.3    Nature-inspired algorithms for link prediction in social networks

The relationships among people unfold with time; new connections may appear and sometimes old ones may fade away, and hence the edges in a social network keep on changing with time. For these reasons, social networks are highly dynamic in nature and they evolve very fast which makes it a challenging task to analyse and predict their future behaviour. Link prediction problem helps us identify the possibility

Table 11.3  Swarm intelligence approaches for community detection

| Approach | Basic methodology | Major works |
|---|---|---|
| Artificial bee colony (ABC) | Inspired by the food searching behaviour of the bee swarm | Heuristic artificial bee colony (HABC) algorithm [57] |
| Ant colony optimisation (ACO) | Each ant detects its community with the aid of pheromones. Detect community structures in networks using ACO by maximising the modularity measure | Ant colony optimisation (ACO) (2010) [58]<br>Multi-layer ant colony optimisation (MACO) (2011) [59]<br>ACO for detecting community structures (2012) [60]<br>Max–min ant system (MMAS) algorithm (2013) [61]<br>Divisive algorithm based on ACO (2014) [62]<br>Clustering using ACO and ant cemetery (2016) [63] |
| Particle swarm optimisation (PSO) | Based on the particle positions and velocity update rules. Also utilises the global search capability of PSO | PSO based community detection (2009) [64]<br>PSO with external optimisation (EO) (2013) [65]<br>Multi objective discrete PSO (MODPSO) (2014) [66]<br>Memetic particle swarm optimisation algorithm (MPSOA) (2016) [67]<br>Multi-objective particle swarm optimisation called CNLPSO-DE (2017) [68] |
| Bat algorithm (BA) | Depends on the echolocation behaviour of bats. Frequency and loudness of the emitted pulse is used to sense the obstacles   – | Bat Algorithm for Overlapping Community Detection (2015) [69]<br>Discrete Bat Algorithm (D-BA) for CD (2015) [70]<br>Metaheuristic approach by modifying Bat algorithm (2016) [71]<br>Hybrid Bat Algorithm with Tabu search (2016) [72] |

(Continued)

*Table 11.3* *(Continued)*

| Approach | Basic methodology | Major works |
|---|---|---|
| FireFly algorithm (FFA) | Inspired by the bioluminescence property and the social aspects of fireflies | Multi-objective optimisation problem (MOP) + enhanced firefly algorithm (EFA) (2013) [73]<br><br>Surprise maximisation based on firefly algorithm (2016) [74] |
| Artificial fish swarm optimisation | Exploiting the behaviour of fish swarm | Artificial fish swarm optimisation (AFSO) (2015) [75] |
| Krill Herd algorithm | Based on the behaviour of the individual krills in a herd while searching for food | Discrete Krill Herd swarm optimisation algorithm for community detection (AKSHO) (2015) [76] |
| Lion optimisation algorithm | Based on the hunting mechanism of ant lion | Ant lion optimisation (ALO) (2015) [37] |
| Cuckoo search algorithm | Inspired by the obligate brood parasitism of some cuckoo species by laying their eggs in the nests of other host birds | Metaheuristic cuckoo search optimisation algorithm with Levy flight for community detection (2017) [77] |
| Chicken swarm optimisation algorithm | Imitating the hierarchal order in the chicken swarm and the behaviours of the chicken swarm | Adaptive approach based on chicken swarm optimisation algorithm for community detection (ACSO) (2016) [78] |
| Elephant swarm optimisation | Based on the group behaviour of elephants and their leadership qualities | Efficient elephant swarm optimisation algorithm for community detection (EESO) (2017) [79] |
| Other approaches | Inspired by the human parliamentary system, where the members are elected and grouped into different clusters | Parliamentary optimisation algorithm (POA) (2015) [80] |

of the connections that are likely to occur and disappear in near future in a network. It also helps us identify the strength of connectivity between the nodes by analysing the proximity of nodes within a network and also identifies the missing links in a network structure [81]. Link prediction can be applied in a variety of networks for predicting the outbreak of an epidemic disease, identifying traffic congestion in particular areas and providing alternate paths for possible navigation, detecting spam emails, finding new friends in social networks, recommending interesting products, and items in online shopping based on their purchase history, locating potential collaborators or experts working in similar research domains, predicting cell phone contacts in large communication networks and so on [82]. It has wide applications in public security such as to predict the possibility of crimes to be committed in near future and the people who are supposed to be involved in it by closely analysing the links in terrorist and criminal networks.

### 11.4.3.1 Evolutionary algorithm for link prediction

An evolutionary approach for predicting the future links in dynamic social networks is mentioned in [83] by applying the covariance matrix adaptation evolution strategy which is used for optimising the weights of predicted links. The method highlights that the combination of topological similarity indices and node-specific similarity indices could yield better results for link prediction. Proposed method neither requires any parametric thresholds nor undersampling which reduces the computational complexity and is also network independent which makes it different from the conventional approaches.

### 11.4.3.2 Swarm intelligence algorithms for link prediction

Several algorithms based on swarm intelligence principles are successfully employed for link prediction in social networks and a few of them are listed below:

**ACO**: A modified version of the classical ACO is presented in [84] called SoS–ACO (sense of smell–ant colony optimisation) to search the path between the nodes in a network. Two novel concepts, *food* and *food odour*, are incorporated into the nodes having high centrality which help to find the shortest paths between the source node and the destination node since they use these food nodes as the meeting points of ants. Since the diffusion of the odour reduces the time to reach the food source, the same concept will reduce the time complexity in the path search to a considerable level. Another method called ACO-LP is proposed in [85] for link prediction using ACO where each ant chooses the path based on the pheromone and heuristic information in the links and the pheromone information is updated based on the quality of the path selected. Node and structural attributes are also considered which improve the performance of the algorithm.

**PSO**: A framework combining the features of matrix factorisation and hybrid PSO termed as *itelliPrediction* is presented in [86] for online user relation prediction. Utilising the best characteristics of both PSO and factorisation, the population is initialised, the fitness value is calculated and the particle position is updated using the *itelliPrediction* framework. This method is domain independent and shows high accuracy in user relationship prediction.

**WOA**: Link prediction based on the whale optimisation algorithm (WOA) discussed in [87] mimic the social activities and hunting approach of the humpback whales. Here the network is divided into a number of communities where the individuals are represented as adjacency matrices and each individual is evaluated to find the best solution in terms of a cost function and the proposed method yields better results.

**Bacterial diffusion**: A multistrain bacterial model is presented in [88] to predict the existence of links between nodes drawing inspiration from the natural process of bacterial growth and its spread through social contact. Information spread between the nodes in a network is similar to the bacterial diffusion among individuals in a community and the likelihood of developing a link between two nodes is proportional to their mutual infection level. This concept has been experimented in Facebook friendship graph, retweet graph of Twitter and many other similar datasets and the results generated are satisfactory.

There are different approaches for addressing the link prediction in social networks, but most of them are based on the proximity and similarity indices and in the case of supervised approaches, there exist a lot of limitations including the selection of feature sets, little information about the evolutionary processes of the networks and the computational complexity while handling large networks. Nature-inspired approaches help to surmount these challenges to a great extent and these methods provide more transparency and aid in the detection of indices which can serve as good predictors of future links in social networks.

## 11.4.4    Nature-inspired algorithms for rumour detection in social networks

Rumour or misinformation propagation is another serious menace faced by the OSN users. Everyday a massive amount of unverified information travel through these networks including false information which can mislead a large population. During emergency situations, natural disasters and other hazardous events, people widely use social networks to disseminate, search and curate event-related information. Along with this, a great amount of misinformation also spreads in social networks which may create panic and public provocation [89]. Modelling rumour diffusion helps us analyse the propagation pattern of rumours or misinformation in social networks. It helps us identify which pieces of information or topics are popular and diffuse the most, how, why and through which paths information is diffusing and will be diffused in the future, and which members of the network play the key roles in the spreading process [19]. Traditional machine-learning methods find it challenging to detect rumours in huge volumes of data; hence, some of the nature-inspired methods for confronting this problem are discussed below:

**Epidemic model**: This model maps the rumour spreading in a social network to the spread of epidemics from one individual to another in a community. The epidemic model discussed in [90] categorises users into three classes as spreaders, ignorants and stiflers and based on the chance of being infected, an infectious probability is defined which is a function based on the strength of ties. This work indicates that the strength of ties has a great significance in the rumour spreading process and the maximum number of spreaders depends on the immune and decay probability. Another model named *SEIZ* was proposed in [91] based on the concept of the epidemic model for modelling the spread of news events and rumours in the Twitter platform. Modifying the traditional SIR model which categorises users as suspected (S), infected (I) and recovered (R), here the social network users are categorised into four classes as suspected (S), exposed (E), infected (I) and sceptical (Z). Epidemic models suggest a new bio-inspired attempt for modelling rumours and information diffusion in social networks and the results are quite promising.

**Artificial immune system**: Drawing inspiration from two main areas: the spread of communicable diseases in the human population and how the human body builds immunity against diseases, an artificial immune system is developed in [92] for developing immunity in social networks. Based on the concept that a highly connected infected node can spread the infection faster to its neighbouring nodes, the proposed method identifies such nodes and introduces a weighing factor to the message passing through these nodes, and it can be effectively used for countering the spread of malicious information through social networks.

**Energy model**: Another important nature-inspired model for addressing the rumour propagation is presented in [93] which utilises the concept of heat-energy relationship. Substances absorb or release energy when the temperature of the surroundings changes; likewise the probability of rumour sharing is affected by the characteristics of the individuals who are involved in rumour sharing, and the attraction of rumours towards individuals is high at the initial time and gradually degrades with time. The energy model uses the heat energy equation to calculate the relationship between the rumour's attraction, the infected individual's authority and the infected individual's discriminability of the rumour, and it also utilises the concept of simulated annealing and metropolis rule to determine the characteristics of rumour and its propagation.

**Physarum mathematical model**: Inspired by the foraging behaviour of physarum, a new mathematical model is used in [94] to model the diffusion of information or epidemics in a network. Food and nutrient transportation in physarum is used to model the information diffusion, and the method can also locate the diffusion source which is independent of the propagation delays. This method gives better accuracy and needs only a limited amount of initial information.

Detection of rumours or misinformation in huge volumes of data traveling through social networks is a very challenging task, and several methods inspired by the nature, mentioned above, can be effectively used for modelling and countering the rumour propagation which performs well compared to the state-of-the-art techniques.

## 11.4.5 Nature-inspired algorithms for trust management in social networks

Most of the social network users publish their information unconsciously, and thus social networks have become a huge trove of sensitive data. One of the basic reasons for the vast sharing of private data is the immense trust users place in these networks and network relationships. Attackers exploit users' trust in these social-networking applications which open the door for several security breaches and online deceptions in social networks. Hence, trust management is an important domain in social networks where active research is happening nowadays. A few bio-inspired approaches applied for efficient trust management in social networks are described below:

**PSO**: A method using modified PSO is used in [95] for deploying a personalised evaluation system to manage the resources judiciously in a personalised manner. Here the resources are users and the modified version of PSO, by slightly changing the motion rules tend to find the clusters of people in online media who exhibit homogeneous characteristics. This method focuses on identifying the clusters of good users who can improve the trust and reputation of the system.

**ACO**: A novel algorithm called trust-ACO for calculating the trust path between different nodes is proposed in [96] using ACO. It combines the structural and behavioural properties of the users and the data shared among the users is calculated by assigning a weight to it. Data sharing between users is equated to the pheromone communication between the ants, and the more data sharing between the users indicate more trust among them, and this theory is projected for evaluating a trust cycle within the members of OSNs.

Deviating from the conventional approaches which depend on the structural properties of a network for evaluating the trust, nature-inspired approaches come up with new attempts combining topological features and users' behavioural patterns to establish trust-management systems.

### 11.4.6   Nature-inspired algorithms for addressing other social network issues

Table 11.4 lists some of the bio-inspired approaches for tackling different issues faced by OSN users. Analysis of the table indicates that a variety of problems in the social network paradigm can be effectively addressed by different bio-inspired approaches which exhibit improved performance and less complexity compared to other approaches.

## 11.5   Security in emerging areas

### 11.5.1   Decentralised social networks

Decentralised social networks (DSNs) is a budding area in the social network arena where the OSN is built on the top of a distributed information management platform, such as a network of trusted servers or peer-to-peer systems. Increasing cost incurred on the maintenance of infrastructures, performance scalability issues in the centralised social networking services, lack of privacy preservation schemes, and rupture of trust in social network users have created a demand for the decentralisation of the backend infrastructure. The basic idea behind a DSN is to provide the social network functionalities without the need of a central trusted entity. In contrast to the centralised OSNs, DSNs offer users a cost-effective platform, better service and improved user privacy since there is no single provider but a set of peers which take on a share of the tasks

Table 11.4 Nature-inspired algorithms for addressing various social network issues

| Approach | Problem addressed | Method and inferences |
| --- | --- | --- |
| Bacterial colony persistence [97] | To control viral spreading in social networks | Bacteria in the colony hibernate or switch to dormant states so as to reduce their exposure to antibiotics and to help the colony withstand the effects of the antibiotic attack |
| | | Determine the optimal conditions for a node to be in the sleep state so as to reduce the spread of infection |
| Combination of ACO and PSO [98] | To find the maximum clique in social networks | Some ants are placed initially on the graph and they follow paths to find the maximal clique and after the evaporation of the existing pheromones, proper path is updated by its amount on the edges using PSO |
| | | Advantage: Shows less complexity compared to other methods |
| Bio-inspired packet dropping [99] | To avoid packet dropping in intermediate nodes in a network | Adopts the immune system (IS) detection policy to detect the packet congestion in the intermediate nodes and IS selection policy to determine the availability of prioritised packets |
| | | Advantage: Provides maximum throughput, shows less delay, and performs better, compared to existing techniques |
| Particle swarm optimisation (PSO) [100] | To maintain the structural balance in social networks | Network structural balance is established by minimising an energy function based on discrete PSO |
| | | Topological features are integrated and particle properties are redefined to achieve a balanced structure and it also reveals the hidden community structure |
| Hybrid approach using ABC and k-nearest neighbour [101] | To identify buzz in social media | Proposed hybrid algorithm along with a set of 11 attributes comprising of created discussions, increase in authors, attention level, burstiness level, contribution sparseness, author interaction, author count and average length of discussions are used to segregate buzz discussions from the remaining topic discussions |
| | | Advantage: performs better in terms of accuracy and computational speed |
| Artificial bee colony (ABC) [102] | To optimise network attacks | Applies a destructive-constructive neighbourhood operator for generating new candidate solutions when bees explore the vicinity of food sources. Here, the selection of nodes is removed to minimise the maximum betweenness centrality value of the graph |
| Integration of k-means and Levy flight firefly algorithm [103] | To detect spammers in social network | Proposed approach tunes absorption and attractiveness coefficient of traditional firefly algorithm to speed up the detection and improves the accuracy |
| | | Limitation: Performance may be affected by the use of satire and use of non-English vocabulary |

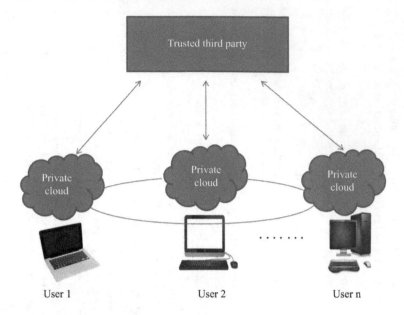

*Figure 11.5   Decentralised social networks*

needed to run the system. Migration from a centralised to a decentralised platform also makes different operations possible like using one's own storage or cloud storage, delay-tolerant social networks and local treatment of the local content [104]. The DSN is in the very early stage of its development, and certain companies like DECENT, DATT, AKASHA, Diaspora, Synereo, etc. are working on its development. DECENT is an open-source decentralised content distribution platform that uses the blockchain technology to ensure the privacy and security. The general architecture of a DSN is illustrated in Figure 11.5.

## 11.5.2   Mobile social networks

Mobile social networks (MSNs) is an integration of mobile computing and social computing where people with similar interests and opinions connect together and communicate with each other via mobile phones or tablets. MSNs can be represented as in Figure 11.6. MSNs leverage the capabilities of both mobile communication networks and social networks and offer a virtual environment where mobile applications utilise the services and collaborations of social networks and social networks take advantage of the mobile features and its ubiquitous accessibility. Unlike existing social networks which are built around individuals, MSNs exploit the additional features of smartphones such as location-related services, novel visualisation mechanisms and

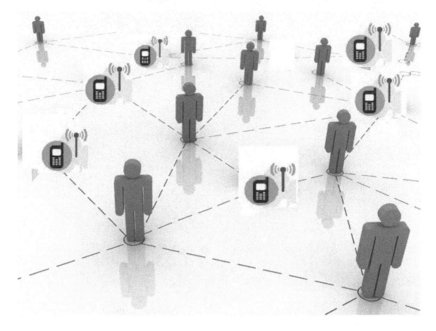

*Figure 11.6    Mobile social networks*

the ability to interact asynchronously. Besides popular commercial MSN platforms like Facebook, Twitter, Instagram, Foursquare and Strava; there are many more frameworks such as MobiSN, RoadSPeak, AmbientTalk, MobiSoC, MobiClique, Haggle, etc. which support MSNs [105].

## 11.5.3    Social Internet of Things

Social Internet of Things (SIoT) offers a platform where worldwide interconnected things could establish social relationships by sacrificing their individuality to the common interest and provide better service to the users. This relationship among the objects can be of co-location, co-work, parental, social or co-ownership. It enables the autonomous interaction between the social networks and the Internet of Things. Integration of social network principles with IoT can have several benefits like improved network navigability and scalability, increased level of trustworthiness and a more flexible approach to address the IoT-related issues. Through the SIoT paradigm, the ability of humans and devices to discover, select and use objects with their services in the IoT is elevated [106]. The communication among the different entities including people and objects using social networks in SIoT is shown in Figure 11.7.

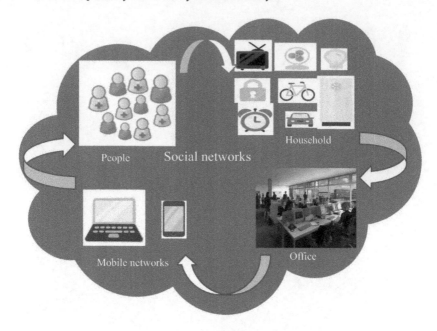

*Figure 11.7   Social Internet of Things*

## 11.6   Security challenges and future research directions

### 11.6.1   Research challenges in social networks

Nature offers a diverse range of solutions for handling problems and providing better security for social network users but even these techniques are not free from challenges. Some of the open challenges faced by the researchers in the social network paradigm are the following:

*Dynamic nature of social networks*: The number of people joining and becoming active in the social network world is increasing day-by-day and some people may leave the network over time. So social networks are highly dynamic in nature, and this unstable network topology creates a challenging environment for bio-inspired algorithms to work with, as most of the bio-inspired algorithms require prior knowledge about the network structure.

*Huge volume of unstructured data*: Daily a huge volume of unverified information including text, images, videos, hyperlinks or meta-data travel through social networks, and the amount of information in the social networking space is increasing at a fast pace. Detection of security breaches in social networks using bio-inspired approaches is quite challenging due to a large amount of heterogeneous content and complexity of unstructured data which makes information extraction and classification a very tedious task.

*Low quality and noisy data*: A social network page contains too much of data such as OSN content, navigation links, advertisements, copyright notices, privacy policies, hyperlinks, images, location, etc. which even include false information that can mislead a large population. Lack of proper filtering mechanisms for the contents posted in the web pages results in low quality, irrelevant and sometimes erroneous data. For a particular application, only a part of this information is required, and the rest should be filtered out as noise which poses a serious research challenge.

*Data representation*: Another serious challenge faced by the researchers in SNA is finding and representing the network data and patterns from the data source. This challenge is faced due to the presence of multiple aliases for the same user, ambiguity while using mixed languages, incompatibility in representing the information and ambiguity of relationships between individuals, different authorship styles, usage of the different set of words like abbreviations, data types and other personal styles.

*Non-availability of dynamic data*: Collection of live data from social networking sites is a serious problem faced by the researchers. Most of the researchers working in this area have shared their datasets which are static in nature and are suitable for specific research problems. Popular social networking sites impose a lot of restrictions in streaming their live data and there are certain limitations for the amount of data to be downloaded.

## 11.6.2    Future research directions

The rapid growth in the popularity of social networks has made it an active area of research, and a large number of people are attracted towards this research arena. The following section outlines some of the future research directions in this area which can be addressed using nature-inspired approaches:

*Spam behaviour analysis*: Explosive increase in the number of users has resulted in the sudden increase of spam content over social networks. Most of the spam blogs are copied from recent web content or web sources with specific keywords to remain undetected and promote spam links. Researchers struggle to use the links structure of the web and rely on traditional algorithms for detecting online spammers through real-time data and feature collection. Novel nature-inspired algorithms with lower training time and higher accuracy are required to facilitate detection of online spammers in real-time.

*User behaviour analysis*: Diverse range of users are members of the social network community and the frequency of online activity depends on their nature or behaviour which could range from updating statuses, uploading photos or videos on a daily basis to users who act like free-riders to just enjoy the public content. Gathering and analysis of user attributes details regarding social interactions and attributes pertaining to online activity help in identifying dominant users' behaviours which can be explored using bio-inspired algorithms.

*Security in DSNs*: With the advent of decentralised and distributed networks, architecture and network topology of the current social networks may drift from centralised to the decentralised one. Storage and communication become more distributed, shared and dynamic which creates new challenges in the security aspects and trust management of the participating peers. Nature-inspired approaches find wide applicability in this area where security could be enhanced by developing suitable approaches.

***Security in emerging areas***: As social networks are becoming more and more popular, vulnerabilities within the network are also increasing at an alarming rate. Emerging areas like location-based social networks, SIoT, MSNs, trust networks, social networks for business intelligence, networks for social gaming, trend analysis, opinion mining in social networks, etc. are coming with a lot of research challenges which can be addressed using nature-inspired techniques.

***Fog and social networks***: The level of trust within the OSN users can be enhanced by creating trust relationships among the users and providing more sustainable resource sharing mechanisms. Fog physically and functionally bridges the capabilities offered in the cloud, and those on the edge of networks and cloud capabilities can be leveraged and applied to social networks to create a dynamic cloud infrastructure within social network environment which opens up new research directions in this field.

## 11.7   Conclusion

Nature-inspired algorithms are becoming powerful and are gaining more popularity since real-world problems are becoming increasingly large, complex and dynamic. This chapter attempts to unfold some of the nature-inspired approaches that find application in social network security. It gives an overview of the various categories of bio-inspired algorithms that can be used for SNA such as information diffusion, CD, link prediction, influence maximisation, rumour detection and for trust management. This chapter outlines the state-of-the-art nature-inspired techniques for addressing the different security issues prevailing in social networks, their open challenges and future research directions in this area. It also aims to explore the scope of novel bio-inspired algorithms for deciphering issues concerned with social network security that are not addressed by the existing techniques. Since cyberattacks and cyber terrorism are increasing at an alarming rate, the need for developing algorithms that enhance the secure use of these networks is of great significance.

## Acknowledgement

This research was supported by the fellowship released by the Kerala State Council for Science, Technology and Environment [No.001/FSHP-MAIN/2014/KSCSTE].

## References

[1]    Dixit M, Upadhyay N, Silakari S. An exhaustive survey on nature inspired optimization algorithms. International Journal of Software Engineering and Its Applications. 2015;9(4):91–104.

[2]    Siddique N, Adeli H. Nature inspired computing: An overview and some future directions. Cognitive Computation. 2015;7(6):706–714.

[3]    Yang XS. Nature-inspired optimization algorithms. Elsevier. ISBN:978-0-12-416743-8; 2014, Feb 17.

[4]    Yang XS. Nature-inspired metaheuristic algorithms: Second Edition. Luniver Press. ISBN:10:1-905986-28-9; 2010.

[5]    Binitha S, Sathya SS. A survey of bio inspired optimization algorithms. International Journal of Soft Computing and Engineering. 2012;2(2): 137–151.

[6]    Zang H, Zhang S, Hapeshi K. A review of nature-inspired algorithms. Journal of Bionic Engineering. 2010;7:S232–S237.

[7]    Eiben AE, Smith JE. What is an evolutionary algorithm? In: Introduction to Evolutionary Computing. Springer, Berlin, Heidelberg; 2015. p. 25–48.

[8]    Sastry K, Goldberg DE, Kendall G. Genetic algorithms. In: Search methodologies. Springer, Boston, MA; 2014. p. 93–117.

[9]    Vasan A, Raju KS. Application of differential evolution for irrigation planning: An Indian case study. Water Resources Management. 2007;21(8): 1393.

[10]   Brownlee J. Clever algorithms: Nature-inspired programming recipes. Lulu (2011), pages: 436. ISBN 978-1-4467-8506-5; 2011.

[11]   Yang XS. Swarm intelligence based algorithms: A critical analysis. Evolutionary Intelligence. 2014;7(1):17–28.

[12]   Yu T, Wang L, Han X, *et al.* Swarm intelligence optimization algorithms and their application. In: WHICEB 2015 Proceedings; 2015. http://aiselaisnetorg/whiceb2015/3.

[13]   Chu SC, Huang HC, Roddick JF, *et al.* Overview of algorithms for swarm intelligence. In: International Conference on Computational Collective Intelligence. Springer; 2011. p. 28–41.

[14]   Mincer M, Niewiadomska-Szynkiewicz E. Application of social network analysis to the investigation of interpersonal connections. Journal of Telecommunications and Information Technology. 2012;2:83–91.

[15]   Terminology – Social Network Analysis. Available from: https://sites. google.com/a/umn.edu/social-network-analysis/terminology.

[16]   Kumar KK, Geethakumari G. Detecting misinformation in online social networks using cognitive psychology. Human-Centric Computing and Information Sciences. 2014;4(1):14.

[17]   Mazurczyk W, Moore S, Fulp EW, *et al.* Bio-inspired cyber security for communications and networking. IEEE Communications Magazine. 2016;54(6):58–59.

[18]   Sperlì G, del Puente G. Online Social Networks Influence Maximization, Bio-Inspired Approaches. 2016/2017. https://www.overleaf.com/articles/ online-social-networks-influence-maximizationbioinspiredapproaches/ qfpmqqrfbtdz/viewer.pdf.

[19]   Guille A, Hacid H, Favre C, *et al.* Information diffusion in online social networks: A survey. ACM Sigmod Record. 2013;42(2):17–28.

[20]    Chen W, Wang Y, Yang S. Efficient influence maximization in social networks. In: Proceedings of the 15th ACM SIGKDD International Conference on Knowledge Discovery and Data Mining. ACM; 2009. p. 199–208.

[21]    Bucur D, Iacca G, Marcelli A, *et al.* Multi-objective evolutionary algorithms for influence maximization in social networks. In: European Conference on the Applications of Evolutionary Computation. Springer; 2017. p. 221–233.

[22]    Bucur D, Iacca G. Influence maximization in social networks with genetic algorithms. In: European Conference on the Applications of Evolutionary Computation. Springer; 2016. p. 379–392.

[23]    Zhang K, Du H, Feldman MW. Maximizing influence in a social network: Improved results using a genetic algorithm. Physica A: Statistical Mechanics and its Applications. 2017;478:20–30.

[24]    Tsai CW, Yang YC, Chiang MC. A genetic NewGreedy algorithm for influence maximization in social network. In: IEEE International Conference on Systems, Man, and Cybernetics (SMC). IEEE; 2015. p. 2549–2554.

[25]    Lahiri M, Cebrian M. The genetic algorithm as a general diffusion model for social networks. In: Proceedings of the Twenty-Fourth AAAI Conference on Artificial Intelligence (AAAI'10). AAAI Press; 2010. p. 494–499.

[26]    Yang WS, Weng SX, Guestrin C, *et al.* Application of the ant colony optimization algorithm to the influence-maximization problem. International Journal of Swarm Intelligence and Evolutionary Computation. 2012;1(1)1–8.

[27]    Gong M, Yan J, Shen B, *et al.* Influence maximization in social networks based on discrete particle swarm optimization. Information Sciences. 2016;367:600–614.

[28]    Zhang B, Zhong S, Wen K, *et al.* Finding high-influence microblog users with an improved PSO algorithm. International Journal of Modelling, Identification and Control. 2013;18(4):349–356.

[29]    Hajibagheri A, Hamzeh A, Sukthankar G. Modeling information diffusion and community membership using stochastic optimization. In: IEEE/ACM International Conference on Advances in Social Networks Analysis and Mining (ASONAM). IEEE; 2013. p. 175–182.

[30]    Sankar CP, Asharaf S, Kumar KS. Learning from bees: An approach for influence maximization on viral campaigns. PLoS One. 2016;11(12):e0168125.

[31]    Wang H, Zhang Y, Zhang Z, *et al.* PhysarumSpreader: A new bio-inspired methodology for identifying influential spreaders in complex networks. PLoS One. 2015;10(12):e0145028.

[32]    Banati H, Bajaj M. Promoting products online using firefly algorithm. In: 12th International Conference on Intelligent Systems Design and Applications (ISDA). IEEE; 2012. p. 580–585.

[33]    Gao C, Lan X, Zhang X, *et al.* A bio-inspired methodology of identifying influential nodes in complex networks. PLoS One. 2013;8(6):e66732.

[34]    Pei S, Tang S, Zheng Z. Detecting the influence of spreading in social networks with excitable sensor networks. PLoS One. 2015;10(5):e0124848.

[35]    Gibbs DL, Shmulevich I. Solving the influence maximization problem reveals regulatory organization of the yeast cell cycle. PLoS Computational Biology. 2017;13(6):e1005591.

[36] Gong M, Song C, Duan C, *et al.* An efficient memetic algorithm for influence maximization in social networks. IEEE Computational Intelligence Magazine. 2016;11(3):22–33.

[37] Babers R, Hassanien AE, Ghali NI. A nature-inspired metaheuristic lion optimization algorithm for community detection. In: 11th International Computer Engineering Conference (ICENCO). IEEE; 2015. p. 217–222.

[38] Bedi P, Sharma C. Community detection in social networks. Wiley Interdisciplinary Reviews: Data Mining and Knowledge Discovery. 2016;6(3): 115–135.

[39] Li YH, Wang JQ, Wang XJ, *et al.* Community detection based on differential evolution using social spider optimization. Symmetry. 2017;9(9):183.

[40] Shakya HK, Singh K, Biswas B. Community detection using differential evolution algorithm with multiple objective function. International Journal of Urban Design for Ubiquitous Computing. 2014;2(1):7–14. Available from: doi:10.21742/ijuduc.2014.2.1.02.

[41] Tasgin M, Herdagdelen A, Bingol H. Community detection in complex networks using genetic algorithms. arXiv preprint arXiv:0711.0491 v1 [physics.soc-ph]. 4 Nov 2007.

[42] Pizzuti C. GA-net: A genetic algorithm for community detection in social networks. In: PPSN. Springer; 2008. p. 1081–1090.

[43] He D, Wang Z, Yang B, *et al.* Genetic algorithm with ensemble learning for detecting community structure in complex networks. In: Fourth International Conference on Computer Sciences and Convergence Information Technology, 2009. ICCIT'09. IEEE; 2009. p. 702–707.

[44] Shi C, Yan Z, Wang Y, *et al.* A genetic algorithm for detecting communities in large-scale complex networks. Advances in Complex Systems. 2010;13(01):3–17.

[45] Folino F, Pizzuti C. Multiobjective evolutionary community detection for dynamic networks. In: Proceedings of the 12th annual conference on Genetic and Evolutionary Computation. ACM; 2010. p. 535–536.

[46] Cai Y, Shi C, Dong Y, *et al.* A novel genetic algorithm for overlapping community detection. Advanced Data Mining and Applications. 2011;LNCS 7120: 97–108.

[47] Dickinson B, Valyou B, Hu W. A genetic algorithm for identifying overlapping communities in social networks using an optimized search space. Social Networking. 2013;2(04):193.

[48] Shang R, Bai J, Jiao L, *et al.* Community detection based on modularity and an improved genetic algorithm. Physica A: Statistical Mechanics and Its Applications. 2013;392(5):1215–1231.

[49] Li Y, Liu G, Lao Sy. A genetic algorithm for community detection in complex networks. Journal of Central South University. 2013;20(5):1269–1276.

[50] Su J, Havens TC. Fuzzy community detection in social networks using a genetic algorithm. In: IEEE International Conference on Fuzzy Systems (FUZZ-IEEE). IEEE; 2014. p. 2039–2046.

[51] Shen B, Wang N, Qiu H. A new genetic algorithm for overlapping community detection. In: Tenth International Conference on Intelligent

Information Hiding and Multimedia Signal Processing (IIH-MSP). IEEE; 2014. p. 766–769.

[52]    Guerrero M, Montoya FG, Baños R, *et al.* Adaptive community detection in complex networks using genetic algorithms. Neurocomputing. 2017;266:101–113. Available from: doi:10.1016/j.neucom.2017.05.029.

[53]    Gong MG, Zhang LJ, Ma JJ, *et al.* Community detection in dynamic social networks based on multiobjective immune algorithm. Journal of Computer Science and Technology. 2012;27(3):455–467.

[54]    Chen G, Wang Y, Wei J. A new multiobjective evolutionary algorithm for community detection in dynamic complex networks. Mathematical Problems in Engineering. 2013;2013:1–7. Available from: doi:10.1155/2013/161670.

[55]    He T, Chan KC. Evolutionary graph clustering for protein complex identification. IEEE/ACM Transactions on Computational Biology and Bioinformatics. 2016:1–1. Available from: doi:10.1109/tcbb.2016.2642107.

[56]    Ju Y, Zhang S, Ding N, *et al.* Complex network clustering by a multi-objective evolutionary algorithm based on decomposition and membrane structure. Scientific Reports. 2016;6(1). Available from: doi:10.1038/srep33870.

[57]    Guo Y, Li X, Tang Y, *et al.* Heuristic artificial bee colony algorithm for uncovering community in complex networks. Mathematical Problems in Engineering. 2017:1–12. Available from: doi:10.1155/2017/4143638.

[58]    Mandala SR, Kumara SR, Rao CR, *et al.* Clustering social networks using ant colony optimization. Operational Research. 2013;13(1):47–65.

[59]    He D, Liu J, Liu D, *et al.* Ant colony optimization for community detection in large-scale complex networks. In: Seventh International Conference on Natural Computation (ICNC). vol. 2. IEEE; 2011. p. 1151–1155.

[60]    Chen B, Chen L, Chen Y. Detecting community structure in networks based on ant colony optimization. In: Proceedings of the International Conference on Information and Knowledge Engineering (IKE). The Steering Committee of The World Congress in Computer Science, Computer Engineering and Applied Computing (WorldComp); 2012. p. 1.

[61]    Honghao C, Zuren F, Zhigang R. Community detection using ant colony optimization. In: IEEE Congress on Evolutionary Computation (CEC). IEEE; 2013. p. 3072–3078.

[62]    Javadi SH, Khadivi S, Shiri ME, *et al.* An ant colony optimization method to detect communities in social networks. In: IEEE/ACM International Conference on Advances in Social Networks Analysis and Mining (ASONAM). IEEE; 2014. p. 200–203.

[63]    Shahzad W, Qamber S. Finding user groups in social networks using ant cemetery. Procedia Computer Science. 2016;98:548–553.

[64]    Shi Z, Liu Y, Liang J. PSO-based community detection in complex networks. In: Second International Symposium on Knowledge Acquisition and Modeling, 2009. KAM'09. vol. 3. IEEE; 2009. p. 114–119.

[65]    Qu J. A hybrid algorithm for community detection using PSO and EO. Advances in Information Sciences and Service Sciences. 2013;5(7):187.

[66]  Gong M, Cai Q, Chen X, *et al.* Complex network clustering by multiobjective discrete particle swarm optimization based on decomposition. IEEE Transactions on Evolutionary Computation. 2014;18(1):82–97.

[67]  Zhang C, Hei X, Yang D, *et al.* A memetic particle swarm optimization algorithm for community detection in complex networks. International Journal of Pattern Recognition and Artificial Intelligence. 2016;30(02):1659003.

[68]  Pourkazemi M, Keyvanpour MR. Community detection in social network by using a multi-objective evolutionary algorithm. Intelligent Data Analysis. 2017;21(2):385–409.

[69]  Imane M, Nadjet K. Bat algorithm for overlapping community detection. In: SAI Intelligent Systems Conference (IntelliSys). IEEE; 2015. p. 664–667.

[70]  Chunyu W, Yun P. Discrete bat algorithm and application in community detection. Open Cybernetics & Systemics Journal. 2015;9:967–972.

[71]  Sharma J, Annappa B. Community detection using meta-heuristic approach: Bat algorithm variants. In: Ninth International Conference on Contemporary Computing (IC3). IEEE; 2016. p. 1–7.

[72]  Imane M, Nadjet K. Hybrid Bat algorithm for overlapping community detection. IFAC-PapersOnLine. 2016;49(12):1454–1459.

[73]  Babak A, Liaquat H, John C, *et al.* Multiobjective enhanced firefly algorithm for community detection in complex networks. Knowledge-Based Systems. 2013;46:1–11.

[74]  Del Ser J, Lobo JL, Villar-Rodriguez E, *et al.* Community detection in graphs based on surprise maximization using firefly heuristics. In: IEEE Congress on Evolutionary Computation (CEC). IEEE; 2016. p. 2233–2239.

[75]  Hassan EA, Hafez AI, Hassanien AE, *et al.* Community detection algorithm based on artificial fish swarm optimization. In: Intelligent Systems' 2014. Springer; 2015. p. 509–521.

[76]  Ahmed K, Hafez AI, Hassanien AE. A discrete krill herd optimization algorithm for community detection. In: 11th International Computer Engineering Conference (ICENCO). IEEE; 2015. p. 297–302.

[77]  Babers R, Hassanien AE. A nature-inspired metaheuristic cuckoo search algorithm for community detection in social networks. International Journal of Service Science, Management, Engineering, and Technology (IJSSMET). 2017;8(1):50–62.

[78]  Ahmed K, Hassanien AE, Ezzat E, *et al.* An adaptive approach for community detection based on chicken swarm optimization algorithm. In: International Conference on Genetic and Evolutionary Computing. Springer; 2016. p. 281–288.

[79]  Ahmed K, Hassanien AE, Ezzat E. An efficient approach for community detection in complex social networks based on elephant swarm optimization algorithm. In: Handbook of Research on Machine Learning Innovations and Trends. IGI Global; 2017. p. 1062–1075.

[80]  Altunbey F, Alatas B. Overlapping community detection in social networks using parliamentary optimization algorithm. International Journal of Computer Networks and Applications. 2015;2(1):12–19.

[81]    Liben-Nowell D, Kleinberg J. The link-prediction problem for social networks. Journal of the Association for Information Science and Technology. 2007;58(7):1019–1031.

[82]    Srinivas V, Mitra P. Link prediction in social networks: Role of power law distribution. SpringerBriefs in Computer Science. Springer, Cham. ISBN: 978-3-319-28922-9; 2016.

[83]    Bliss CA, Frank MR, Danforth CM, *et al.* An evolutionary algorithm approach to link prediction in dynamic social networks. Journal of Computational Science. 2014;5(5):750–764.

[84]    Rivero J, Cuadra D, Calle FJ, *et al.* A bio-inspired algorithm for searching relationships in social networks. IEEE; 2011. p. 60–65.

[85]    Chen B, Chen L. A link prediction algorithm based on ant colony optimization. Applied Intelligence. 2014;41(3):694–708.

[86]    Shi Z, Zuo W, Chen W, *et al.* User relation prediction based on matrix factorization and hybrid particle swarm optimization. In: Proceedings of the 26th International Conference on World Wide Web Companion. International World Wide Web Conferences Steering Committee; 2017. p. 1335–1341.

[87]    Barham R, Aljarah I. Link prediction based on whale optimization algorithm. In: Proc International Conference on New Trends in Computing Sciences; 2017. p. 55–60. Available from: DOI: http://10.1109/ICTCS.2017.41.

[88]    Chiancone A, Milani A, Poggioni V, *et al.* A multistrain bacterial model for link prediction andrea chiancone. In: 11th International Conference on Natural Computation (ICNC). IEEE; 2015. p. 1075–1079.

[89]    Shariff SM, Zhang X. A survey on deceptions in online social networks. In: International Conference on Computer and Information Sciences (ICCOINS). IEEE; 2014. p. 1–6.

[90]    Cheng JJ, Liu Y, Shen B, *et al.* An epidemic model of rumor diffusion in online social networks. The European Physical Journal B. 2013;86(1):1–7.

[91]    Jin F, Dougherty E, Saraf P, *et al.* Epidemiological modeling of news and rumors on twitter. In: Proceedings of the 7th Workshop on Social Network Mining and Analysis. ACM; 2013. p. 8.

[92]    Rathore H, Samant A. A system for building immunity in social networks. In: Fourth World Congress on Nature and Biologically Inspired Computing (NaBIC). IEEE; 2012. p. 20–24.

[93]    Han S, Zhuang F, He Q, *et al.* Energy model for rumor propagation on social networks. Physica A: Statistical Mechanics and Its Applications. 2014;394:99–109.

[94]    Liu Y, Gao C, She X, *et al.* A bio-inspired method for locating the diffusion source with limited observers. In: IEEE Congress on Evolutionary Computation (CEC). IEEE; 2016. p. 508–514.

[95]    Alboaie L, Vaida MF. Trust and reputation model for various online communities. Studies in Informatics and Control. 2011;20(2):143–156.

[96]    Sanadhya S, Singh S. Trust calculation with ant colony optimization in online social networks. Procedia Computer Science. 2015;54:186–195.

[97]    Enyioha C, Preciado V, Pappas G. Bio-inspired strategy for control of viral spreading in networks. In: Proceedings of the 2nd ACM International Conference on High Confidence Networked Systems. ACM; 2013. p. 33–40.

[98]    Soleimani-Pouri M, Rezvanian A, Meybodi MR. Finding a maximum clique using ant colony optimization and particle swarm optimization in social networks. In: Proceedings of the 2012 International Conference on Advances in Social Networks Analysis and Mining (ASONAM 2012). IEEE Computer Society; 2012. p. 58–61.

[99]    Liaqat HB, Xia F, Yang Q, *et al.* Bio-inspired packet dropping for ad-hoc social networks. International Journal of Communication Systems. 2017;30(1):e2857.

[100]   Xing LZ, Le HL, Hui Z. A novel social network structural balance based on the particle swarm optimization algorithm. Cybernetics and Information Technologies. 2015;15(2):23–35.

[101]   Aswani R, Ghrera S, Kar AK, *et al.* Identifying buzz in social media: A hybrid approach using artificial bee colony and $k$-nearest neighbors for outlier detection. Social Network Analysis and Mining. 2017;7(1):38.

[102]   Lozano M, García-Martínez C, Rodríguez FJ, *et al.* Optimizing network attacks by artificial bee colony. Information Sciences. 2017;377:30–50.

[103]   Aswani R, Kar AK, Ilavarasan PV. Detection of spammers in twitter marketing: A hybrid approach using social media analytics and bio inspired computing. Information Systems Frontiers. 2017;20(3):1–16.

[104]   Datta A, Buchegger S, Vu LH, *et al.* Decentralized online social networks. In: Handbook of Social Network Technologies and Applications. Springer; 2010. p. 349–378.

[105]   Hu X, Chu TH, Leung VC, *et al.* A survey on mobile social networks: Applications, platforms, system architectures, and future research directions. IEEE Communications Surveys & Tutorials. 2015;17(3):1557–1581.

[106]   Atzori L, Iera A, Morabito G, *et al.* The social internet of things (SIoT)– when social networks meet the internet of things: Concept, architecture and network characterization. Computer Networks. 2012;56(16):3594–3608.

*Chapter 12*

# Software diversity for cyber resilience: percolation theoretic approach

*Jin-Hee Cho[1] and Terrence J. Moore[2]*

## 12.1 Introduction

### 12.1.1 Motivation

In ecology, it has been well known that more species are closely related to higher resilience [1]. Inspired by this close relationship between diversity of species and resilience of ecosystems, information and software assurance research has evolved by introducing the concept of *software diversity* for enhanced security [2–6]. Due to the dominant trend of monoculture software deployment, attackers have had significant advantages in acquiring the intelligence needed so that a single attack can more efficiently compromise other homogeneous system components, such as operating systems, software packages, and/or hardware packages [7]. In the network science domain, some well-elaborated network models have shown that software diversity is closely related to enhancing the immunization of a computer system that halts multiple outbreaks of malware infections simultaneously occurring with heterogeneous and sparse spreading patterns [8]. Hence, the rationale that software diversity reduces malware spreading is quite well known and has been validated for its effectiveness to some extent [3,4]. Simply, this underlying philosophy leads a simple principle: *software polyculture* enhances security [3]. Thanks to the Internet, which allows distributing individualized software and cloud computing with the computational power to perform diversification, massive-scale software diversity has become realistic for the practical use of software diversity to enhance security [5]. Although the benefit of software diversity seems obvious, secure and transparent implementation of automatic software diversity is highly challenging [6].

Percolation theory has been substantially used to investigate network resilience (or robustness) in the network science domain. In percolation theory, the concepts of *site percolation* and *bond percolation* are used to select a node or an edge to remove, add, or choose to immunize in the context of epidemic networks, such as in disease transmission, computer malware spreading, or behavior propagation (e.g., product

[1]Department of Computer Science, Virginia Tech, Falls Church, USA
[2]US Army Research Laboratory, Adelphi, USA

adoption behavior) [8,9]. Recently, percolation theory was leveraged to develop software diversity techniques particularly to solve a software assignment problem [7,10]. Which nodes to be connected matters in the propagation of malware infection while choosing nodes or edges to connect or disconnect exactly follows the concept of site or bond percolation in percolation theory [8]. The software assignment problem addressed in [7,10] is another way to achieve network diversity by having each node not be adjacent to same software versions. However, this approach is different from our proposed approach in which it does not change a network topology (i.e., no adjustment of edges between nodes) but provides an algorithm on how to assign a different software version to each node in a given network.

Software diversity is one of the well-known moving target defense (MTD) techniques [11]. The goal of MTD techniques is to increase confusion and/or uncertainty for attackers to perform their attacks by changing attack surfaces. The underlying concept of the MTD techniques is to mislead attackers to waste their resources (e.g., time and/or effort) or lose their attack directions as system or network configurations dynamically change by the MTD launched by defenders. In a line of MTD strategies, this work is interested in addressing a software-assignment problem by proposing percolation-based network adaptability strategies based on the concept of bond percolation (i.e., removing or adding edges). To be specific, our main concern to a given software-assignment problem is how to choose nodes to be connected or disconnected in order to maximize software diversity while maximizing the size of the giant component (i.e., a largest cluster in a network) and minimizing adaptation cost based on the rationale that software diversity enhances system security. In order to measure a node's software diversity, this work proposed a software diversity metric based on the concept of the eigenvector centrality metric such that an individual node's software diversity metric is estimated based on the software diversity of the node's neighbors.

## 12.1.2   Research goal

In this work, we solve a software-assignment problem in a network in order to achieve the following goals: (1) maximizing the software diversity of a given network based on the developed software diversity metric; (2) maximizing the size of the giant component, which has been used as a metric to represent the degree of network resilience (i.e., higher connectivity with more nodes leads to attaining better resource/service availability); and (3) minimizing adaptation cost caused by removing or adding edges from an original network to the network that has adapted by the proposed adaptation strategies (i.e., removing or adding edges) and an intrusion detection mechanism (i.e., removing all edges of a detected attacker).

We leverage the notion of *percolation theory* (which is used to describe the process/paths for some liquid to pass through some material) in order to model and analyze attack processes as well as defense/recovery processes based on the concepts of site and bond percolation. When an attacker compromises a node, it means the node is percolated (i.e., infected). At the same time, depending on the percolation states of nodes in the network, network topology can be adjusted by adding or cutting an edge (i.e., bond percolation) for enhancing resilience, so that the infection does not spread further to homogeneous nodes installed with same software/hardware.

Although many centrality metrics have been used for a node to be connected or disconnected, few algorithms have been proposed by considering the nature of the distributed selection process based on each node's local view. In this work, we propose a software diversity metric based on the concept of the eigenvector centrality metric [12]. A node's eigenvector centrality is estimated based on the centrality of the node's neighbors [12]. Similarly, we devised the software diversity metric based on the dissimilarity between a node and its neighbors in terms of their software versions installed. We set the maximum number of hops to determine the range of a node's neighbors and use a decay factor in terms of the physical distance (i.e., a number of hops the node is distant from its neighbor). Note that the proposed software-diversity-based network adaptation strategies can be applied for the type of overlay networks where the connections between nodes can be considered as local connections and may be adjusted as necessary. As an example to adjust edges in a given network, a software-defined networking (SDN) technology allows each node's edge to be adjusted by a centralized SDN controller [13]. Also, another example is that in a fully distributed network such as a mobile ad hoc network, when a node wants to communicate with other nodes which are ensured for secure communications, it can establish a secure channel only with its neighbors in its ego network [14].

## 12.1.3 Key contributions

This work has the following **key contributions**:

1. We proposed a node's software diversity metric based on the concept of eigen-vector centrality metric in which a node's software diversity is derived from the software diversity of its neighbors. This represents that an entity's influence is derived from not only its own influence but also its friends' influence recursively. Taking a similar strategy, the dissimilarity of software installed in a node with its neighbor is also captured based on that of the software installed in the node's neighbors with their neighbors.
2. Percolation-based adaptability strategies are considered to maximize the degree of software diversity based on the rationale that polyculture software enhances security. We used the concept of bond percolation by removing or adding edges to maximize software diversity while maximizing the size of the giant component (representing network resilience) and minimizing adaptation cost.
3. Through the extensive simulation study, we demonstrate the effect of key design parameters, including network density, attack density, and the number of software versions available, on the three metrics measuring software diversity, the size of the giant component, and adaptation cost. From the simulation experiments, we investigate the relationships between the degree of software diversity and the degree of enhanced network resilience or adaptation cost under various environmental settings.

## 12.1.4   Structure of this chapter

The rest of this chapter is organized by the following sections:

- Section 12.2 discusses the related work including existing approaches using software diversity, graph coloring, epidemic models, percolation theory, and eigenvector centrality.
- Section 12.3 provides the system model characterizing a network, a node, an attack, and a defense.
- Section 12.4 describes the software diversity metric and the proposed software-diversity-based adaptation (SDA) strategy.
- Section 12.5 discusses the experimental setup, metrics, the counterpart schemes compared against the proposed SDA scheme, and the overall trends of the demonstrated simulation results.
- Section 12.6 concludes the chapter and suggests future work directions.


## 12.2   Background and related work

This section first provides the literature review to provide background knowledge for readers to easily understand the proposed work. For the background knowledge, we provide a brief overview of graph coloring algorithms, epidemic models, and percolation theory. As the related work to our work, we also discuss the state-of-the-art approaches to address enhanced security based on the concept of software diversity.

### 12.2.1   Graph coloring

Graph coloring traces its origins to the map-coloring problem, which can be translated to a graph coloring problem on planar graphs. The problem entails coloring territories on a map so that no two adjacent territories (having a measurable border) share the same color. The map-coloring problem is associated with Francis Guthrie's famous four-color conjecture (i.e., maps require no more than four colors), which was proven with the aid of a computer after more than a century by Kenneth Appel and Wolfgang Hake in 1976. For maps, the territories can be represented as vertices with edges between them if they have a measurable border, then the equivalent planar graph coloring problem entails labeling vertices with colors such that adjacent vertices have different colors. This notion can easily be generalized beyond planar graphs. If the graph can be colored in such a fashion with $k$ colors, it is said to be $k$-colorable and the color sets form $k$ independent sets of a $k$-partite graph. Tasks within this problem include determining if the graph is $k$-colorable for a given $k$, determining the chromatic number $\chi(G)$ or optimal (minimal) number of colors needed for the coloring and developing algorithms for solving the problem (either exactly or approximately) and their time-complexity.

Graph coloring has applications in scheduling, radio frequency and optical wavelength assignment, and pattern matching. More recently it was used as a strategy to enhance network resilience, which is also used as a counterpart to be compared against our proposed network-adaptation scheme. Colors in these cases represent labels that correspond to assignments in the particular application, and edges in the graph represent assignment conflicts. As such, significant interest in algorithms have been explored to tackle various scenarios or aspects of the graph coloring problem. For example, as used in this work, when creating a network with high software diversity, each color represents a software version where the different colors refer to distinct software versions. To enhance network resilience, a different software should be used between two connected nodes in a network. In general, an exact algorithm for finding a coloring will be exponential with respect to the size of the graph unless the graph has a particularly advantageous structure. Various strategies also exist for suboptimal greedy algorithms that assign colors given an ordering of the vertices.

There have been many nature-inspired approaches that have been adopted to solve the graph coloring problem. A sampling of these includes the behavior of ants in searching for food [15–17], bees reproductive [18] and food-search processes [19], bird-flocking-inspired particle swarm optimization [20,21], firefly synchronization [22], and cuckoo egg-laying behavior [23,24]. Several evolutionary-inspired approaches for solving the graph coloring problem include the use of genetic algorithms [25–27] and culturally inspired memetic algorithms [28].

O'Donnell and Sethu [2] used a graph coloring algorithm to develop software assignment strategies with the goal of maximizing attack tolerance. The authors used a real network topology based on email traffic logs between users in their institution and showed the outperformance of the proposed hybrid approach compared to the state-of-the-art counterparts. Yang *et al.* [10] mapped sensors in a network to geographic locations, which correspond to territories in the map-coloring problem, and used a backtracking color assignment to assign software to sensors by location. This enables the use of fewer colors since the coloring problem is effectively solved on the corresponding planar graph where the vertices are the geographic locations. Sensor neighbors that reside in the same geographic location are labeled with the same color but will have different colors with neighbors that are mapped to different adjacent geographic locations. Liu *et al.* [29] first categorized nodes according to their roles or local topological properties in order to determine software version assignment priority. The nodes in the highest priority class, termed ambassadors, are colored first or given the first choice of software versions before the nodes in the next two classes, bridges and loners, are assigned software.

## 12.2.2  Epidemic models

Simple epidemic models characterize the effect of disease transmission on a population. The population is separated into compartments, statuses, or states that describe condition of the total number or fraction of the population. The most common states describing the number of the population having a certain condition with respect to the disease are susceptible ($S$), infected ($I$), and recovered ($R$), although many other states exist, e.g., passive immunity ($M$), exposed ($E$). Traditional epidemiological models characterize the transitions from one state to another, typically under a homogeneous interaction or mixing bowl assumption, and usually described by a collection of ordinary differential equations. Popularly common models are the SIR model and the SIS model.

The SIR model only uses three statuses, where $(S, I, R)$ denotes the number of people in each status. Transitions are only possible from the susceptible status to the infected status and from the infected status to the recovered status. Since the interactions are treated as random and one-on-one, a susceptible individual has a probability $I/N$ of interacting with an infected individual, where $I$ refers to the number of infected nodes and $N$ is the total number of nodes in a network. Hence, given an infection rate $\beta$ and recovery rate $\gamma$, the dynamics of each condition's population can be described by ordinary differential equations, e.g.,

$$\frac{dS(t)}{dt} = -\beta S(t)I(t)/N, \quad \frac{dI(t)}{dt} = \beta S(t)I(t)/N - \gamma I(t), \quad \frac{dR(t)}{dt} = \gamma I(t),$$

$$(12.1)$$

where $S(t)$ is the number of susceptible nodes at time $t$, $I(t)$ is the number of infected nodes at time $t$, and $R(t)$ is the number of recovered nodes at time $t$. The SIS model only uses the susceptible $(S)$ and infectious $(I)$ statuses. Here, instead of a potential transition from infected status to recovered status, infected individuals can return to a susceptible status. This changes the equations describing the dynamics, e.g.,

$$\frac{dS(t)}{dt} = -\beta S(t)I(t)/N + \gamma I(t), \quad \frac{dI(t)}{dt} = \beta S(t)I(t)/N - \gamma I(t). \quad (12.2)$$

Given the recognition that individuals do not interact randomly but within a network of contacts, the extension of these ideas to networks has received considerable attention [30]. In particular, considering the relevance to computer security, the notion of modeling of harmful computer processes, such as computer viruses or email worms, using epidemic models was first suggested in the late 1980s [31,32]. Kephart and White [33] applied the SIS model on several network models including directed random graphs, hierarchical models, and spatial models (lattices). They found theoretical epidemic thresholds similar to that in classical homogeneous interactions and that match simulation results when the connectivity is high (but not when it is low).

However, a common feature of many real networks is the characteristic of being scale-free or having a degree distribution that follows a power law. Pastor-Satorras and Vespignani [34] adapted the SIS model to scale-free networks to study the spreading of computer viruses on the Internet. They arrived at the surprising discovery that there is no threshold for epidemic spreading of viruses over such a network, i.e., the virus will survive regardless of the infection rate although its probability of infecting a large portion of the network typically remains small. In studying finite-size effects, they also discovered a threshold determined by the ratio $\gamma/\beta$ [35]. When this exceeds the ratio of the mean connectivity or degree to its second moment, i.e., $\gamma/\beta > \langle d \rangle / \langle d^2 \rangle$ where $\langle d \rangle$ is a mean degree and $\langle d^2 \rangle$ is a mean second degree, then the infection spreads and becomes endemic, otherwise it dies out exponentially fast.

Wang *et al.* [36] discovered that for arbitrary graphs (i.e., not necessarily random or scale-free), the spectral radius $\rho(\mathbf{A})$ or largest eigenvalue of the adjacency matrix $\mathbf{A}$ determines if the epidemic dies out and if the number of infections decays exponentially fast. They showed that this occurs when the ratio $\gamma/\beta$ is less than $\rho(\mathbf{A})$. Ganesh *et al.* [37] also used the ratio $\gamma/\beta$ to determine the lifetime of an epidemic following the SIS model over a general network. If this ratio exceeds the spectral radius $\rho(\mathbf{A})$

of the adjacency matrix, then the lifetime is on the order of $\log n$. On the other hand, if the generalized isoperimetric constant $\eta(G, m) = \inf_{S \subset V, |S| \le m} E(S, \bar{S})/|S|$ (where $E(S, \bar{S})$ is the min cut of $S$ and its complement) exceeds the ratio, then the lifetime is exponential on the order of $e^{n^\alpha}$ for some constant $\alpha$.

Zou *et al.* [38] introduced an email worm model that accounts for user behavior, e.g., the time delay in checking email and the probability of opening up an infected email. This approach demonstrates that prior topological epidemic models tend to overestimate the spreading speed of the infection. Temporal aspects have more often been considered by introducing dynamics on the network structure with an epidemic model. Gross *et al.* [39] examined the SIS model on networks where susceptible nodes are able to rewire with constant probability their links with infected neighbors to avoid infection, thereby increasing the epidemic threshold. Volz and Meyers [40] studied the SIR model on simple dynamic random networks with random edge rewiring, demonstrating that the rate of rewiring and the heterogeneity of the node degrees also affect the likelihood of an epidemic. Prakash *et al.* [41] studied the SIS model over a periodic sequence of networks. Sanatkar *et al.* [42] investigated the model over a random sequence of a finite set of networks. Both approaches [41,42] determine an epidemic threshold dependent on versions of a joint spectral radius on the set of adjacency matrices of the networks.

## 12.2.3 Percolation theory

The origin of percolation theory comes from the mathematical formalization of statistical physics research on the flow of liquid through a medium [43]. Originally while it was studied on lattice structures, percolation theory has been applied to networks to study connectivity, robustness [8,44], and epidemics [45,46]. The percolation process was studied in the computer sciences under the notion of "network resilience" [47,48], independent of its development in the statistical physics literature. More recent developments in the physic literature have profoundly influenced studies in the computer sciences. These contributions have incorporated the recognition that networks are not derived from a random structure, and failures of nodes, whether from attacks or due to dependent correlations, are not uniformly random [49]. Hence, significant interest has developed in removal processes that model targeted attacks on the network, e.g., removal of nodes based on centrality measures such as degree or betweenness.

The ability of a liquid to pass through a medium is classically modeled using percolation over an infinite square lattice. Passage or flow is allowed through the edge (or intersection or vertex) with a given occupation probability $\phi$ that is a priori chosen before the flow and uniform for each edge (or vertex). This process is called *bond (or site) percolation* [50]. For low $\phi$, it is difficult for the liquid to flow as most edges are closed. As $\phi$ increases, more edges are open and the liquid has greater potential to flow. The natural question that arises is as follows: *At what $\phi$ will the liquid be able to pass through the lattice?* Because of the nature of the question, there exists a critical value $\phi_c$, called the percolation threshold, such that the liquid can find a passage through the lattice almost surely if $\phi > \phi_c$ and cannot find a passage almost surely if $\phi < \phi_c$. Effectively, $\phi_c$ determines the phase transition where many isolated subcomponents of open edges (or vertices) are connected into a unique infinite cluster.

In many structures, this percolation threshold is known, either theoretically or approximately, via extensive simulation. For example, in the two-dimensional infinite lattice, the bond percolation threshold is theoretically known to be $\phi_c = .5$ and the site percolation threshold is approximated to be near $\phi_c \approx .59$ [51]. Finding this threshold for a particular structure (e.g., higher dimensional lattices, particular network models) is a primary area of study in percolation theory in networks. Other key interests include, for a given $\phi$, the distribution of the sizes of the finite clusters, the correlation length (or the average path length of two vertices in the same cluster), the order parameter (or the probability of an edge or vertex residing in the infinite cluster), and the scale of the infinite cluster (or the fraction of nodes in it).

For network robustness, we are interested in the complementary occupation probability, i.e., the probability that the node or edge is removed from the existing network. Instead of being interested in structural changes when vertices (sites) or edges (bonds) are added to the network, the network scientist is interested in determining the topological changes that occur as vertices or edges are removed from an existing network structure. One problem with theoretical percolation results in this context is that many results apply to infinite networks, whereas real networks are finite. This introduces finite-size effects, or a smoothing of phase transitions, when percolation is studied via simulation experiments on real networks. Another problem is the definition of network failure. In a real network, this occurs well before the complete dissolution of the giant component or cluster, motivating the relevance of the size of the giant component as a fraction of the original network in simulated experiments on networks.

Percolation theory has been used to model various processes on networks in the context of network failures and attacks, e.g., connectivity, routing, and epidemic spreading. In the prior section, we discussed how epidemic spreading can be used to model the infection of a computer network by a computer virus or botnet. In fact, a particularly famous result in percolation theory on scale-free networks, the Molloy–Reed criterion [52], i.e., $\langle d^2 \rangle / \langle d \rangle = 2$, also relies on (the inverse of) the ratio of the mean connectivity or degree to its second moment, as mentioned in the last section. The second moment is also a factor in determining if an epidemic becomes an endemic for the SIS model on finite-size networks [35]. This percolation threshold is given by

$$\phi_c = \frac{1}{\langle d^2 \rangle / \langle d \rangle - 1}, \tag{12.3}$$

meaning that the expected fraction of nodes removed at random needs to be $f_c = 1 - \phi_c = 1 - 1/(\langle d^2 \rangle / \langle d \rangle - 1)$ to destroy the giant component. For random networks, this can occur with a relatively small fraction of node removals, e.g., $f_c = 1 - 1/\langle d \rangle$. But for scale-free networks, if the power law exponent is small enough, then the second moment becomes unbounded and $f_c = 1$, implying scale-free networks are robust to random failures. When a network is targeted for attacks, there may be a strategy taking advantage of the topological structure of the network. The simplest example is targeting nodes with high degree centrality [49,52]. In this scenario, random networks are robust while scale-free networks are found to be fragile. We can clearly observe the fragility of scale-free networks under epidemic attacks in our experiments as well (see Section 12.5).

## 12.2.4 Software diversity

The concept of the philosophy of "survivability through heterogeneity" derived in ecology has been also applied to enhance security through software or network diversity in the security domain. Many approaches have been explored to validate the usefulness of the software or network diversity for system security. Chen and May [53] investigated the new argumentation in principle to prove the usefulness of software diversity on the enhanced safety. This work used fault injection methods to analyze the effect of failure distributions on software diversity. Huang *et al.* [54,55] solved a software-assignment problem by isolating nodes with a same software in order to minimize the epidemic worm attacks. This work considered not only the constraints of host functionality and software availability but also the degree and effect of vulnerability to maximize system security based on the balance between these two key factors. Franz [56] proposed an approach to introduce compiler-generated software diversity for a large-scale network in order to make it harder for attackers to take advantage of vulnerabilities of a single software. An "App Store" with a diversification engine automatically generates a different version of every program, which is functionally identical whenever a download is requested.

Hole [3,4] investigated the benefit of software diversity in order to stop infectious malware spreading and discussed how software diversity can increase the time required for attackers to infect enterprise systems and the likelihood of detecting and mitigating the outbreaks of malware infection in the early stage. In these works [3,4], the underlying idea of the proposed *malware halting technique* is to immunize hubs in order to mitigate the number of infected nodes by injecting and/or increasing software diversity. This idea has been proposed by Dezsö and Barabási [9] and studied in scale-free networks considering general epidemic models, which treat viruses in either disease transmission or computer virus. Their finding shows that a biased policy to immune hubs can significantly reduce cost to eradicate or limit the fraction of infected entities.

Homescu *et al.* [57] presented a large-scale automated software diversification to mitigate the vulnerabilities exposed by software monoculture. This work gives the description of the implementation of the developed automated software diversity tool and proposed a generic method to measure the effectiveness of software diversity as a potential cure to remove code-reuse attacks. Yang *et al.* [10] proposed a software diversity technique to combat sensor worms by solving a software assignment problem, given a limited number of software versions available. Taking the key philosophy of software diversity to prolong system survivability, this work uses percolation theory to model the design features of software diversity to defend against sensor worms. The authors also extended this work to investigate the effect of sensors with multiple software versions, rather than a single version in terms of network robustness under sensor worm attacks [7]. Salako and Strigini [58] questioned the assumption of complete independence of different software versions, which does not reflect reality in practice. This work extended probability models to consider the commonalities in developing multiple versions of software and proposed alternative ways to consider software diversity in the presence of dependencies between the different versions of software.

Zhang *et al.* [59] proposed a method to enhance network resilience by building a heterogeneous networking-based system based on the rationale of the "survivability through heterogeneity philosophy" where a single solution was common to increase interoperability. Recently, *network diversity* is proposed as a security metric to measure network resilience against zero-day attacks [60]. This work designed and evaluated a suite of network-diversity metrics such as a biodiversity-inspired metric based on the number of different resources, which has positively impacted in enhancing security.

Unlike the above works discussed [3,4,7,9,10,53–57,59,60], our work proposes a node's software diversity metric that is obtained from the software diversity of the node's neighbors. This idea is borrowed from the concept of eigenvector centrality metric [12], which measures a node's influence based on the influence of its neighbors. Based on the devised software diversity metric, we proposed percolation-based adaptation strategies, which determine an edge to remove or add to make a network more resilient.

## 12.3    System model

This section describes the design models of key components in terms of network model, node model, attack model, and defense model.

### 12.3.1    Network model

A temporal network, denoted by $\mathbf{G}(t)$, is given as an undirected network and evolves dynamically over time $t$. The topology evolution (or change) of the network occurs due to node failures or nodes being compromised by attackers. In addition, the network may change its topology when some types of adaptability strategies are performed by connecting between two nodes or disconnecting all the edges associated with compromised nodes to mitigate the spread of infecting other nodes in the network. The set of nodes in the network is denoted by $\mathbf{V}(t)$ where node $v_i$ is characterized by its attributes, which is described in Section 12.3.2. The set of edges between nodes with respect to time $t$ is represented by $\mathbf{E}(t)$ where an edge between nodes, $e_{ij}$, can be on and off depending on the dynamics caused by node failures, node recovery, and/or edge adaptations (i.e., an edge can be added or removed). We maintain an adjacency matrix $\mathbf{A}(t)$ with respect to time $t$ in order to keep track of direct or indirect connectivities between nodes in the network where $a_{ij} = 1$ indicates there exists an edge between $v_i$ and $v_j$, while no edges exist with $a_{ij} = 0$ otherwise.

### 12.3.2    Node model

Nodes in set $V(t)$ are characterized by their attributes as follows:

- A node's status on whether it is active or not, denoted by $na_i$, indicating whether it is alive ($= 1$) or failed ($= 0$), respectively.

- A node's status on whether the node is compromised ($= 1$) or non-compromised ($= 0$), denoted by $nc_i$.
- A node's software version, denoted by $sv_i$, that refers to which software version is installed in node $i$, given a limited number of software versions available, $N_{sv}$, where $sv_i$ refers to an integer, ranged in $[1, N_{sv}]$.
- A node's degree of software diversity, $sd_i$, whose physical meaning is how different node $i$'s software version is from its neighbors'. We use the concept of an eigenvector centrality in order to compute the dissimilarity of $i$'s software version from its neighbors' software versions in a network. The details on the computation of $i$'s software diversity are elaborated in (12.6) of Section 12.4.1.

Based on the above four attributes of a node, each node is characterized by

$$\mathbf{node}(v_i) = [na_i, nc_i, sv_i, sd_i] \tag{12.4}$$

If attacker $j$ targets susceptible node $i$, which is one of its direct neighbors, the probability that $j$ infects $i$, denoted by $\beta_{ji}$, is estimated based on the probability that $j$ can exploit $sv_i$. We call this probability $i$'s exploitability by $j$, which is simply estimated by [3]

$$\beta_{ji} = \begin{cases} 1 & \text{if } \sigma_j(i) > 0; \\ \frac{1}{N_{sv} - |\sigma_j| + 1} & \text{otherwise.} \end{cases} \tag{12.5}$$

where $\sigma_j$ is a vector of software versions $j$ knows about their security vulnerabilities. The cardinality of $\sigma_j$, denoted by $|\sigma_j|$, refers to the number of software versions $j$ can exploit, which is a dynamic value learned after $j$ compromises $i$ via reconnaissance even if $sv_i \neq sv_j$. Algorithm 1 describes the epidemic process of attackers compromising susceptible nodes.

## 12.3.3 Attack model

In this work, we model an attacker's infection behavior based on an epidemic model, called the SIR model [8]. The attacker $j$ can infect its direct neighbor node $i$ when the following two conditions are met:

- Node $i$ has not been compromised by other attackers (i.e., $nc_i = 0$).
- Node $i$ uses a software version that attacker $j$ can exploit because the attacker knows the vulnerability of the software version. This case happens when $sv_i$ is the same as $sv_j$ or attacker $j$ learned $sv_i$'s vulnerability in the past (i.e., $\sigma_j(i) > 0$). When node $j$ is installed with a particular software version, $sv_j$, and selected as a seeding attacker, we assume that $j$ knows the vulnerability of its own software version, $sv_j$. Hence, attacker $j$ can learn the vulnerabilities of other software versions although it needs to commit more time and use its resource to obtain the information of their security vulnerabilities. Node $i$'s exploitability by attacker $j$ based on these two cases is reflected in (12.5).

---

**Algorithm 1:** Epidemic attacks

---

1: **Input:**
2:   **A** ← an adjacency matrix
3:   $\sigma_i$ ← attacker $i$'s vector of exploitable software versions
4:   $N_{sv}$ ← a number of software versions available
5:   $\gamma$ ← an intrusion detection probability
6: **node** ← nodes' attributes, defined in (12.4)
7: **procedure** PERFORMEPIDEMICATTACKS(**A**, **node** $\sigma_j$, $N_{sv}$, $\gamma$)
8:     $spreadDone \leftarrow 0$
9:     **spread**: a list with length $N$    ▷ To check if node $i$ attempted to compromise its direct neighbors
10:     **while** $spreadDone == 0$ **do**
11:         **for** $i := 1$ to $N$ **do**                      ▷ check if $i$ is an attacker
12:             **if** $nc_i > 0 \land na_i > 0$ **then**        ▷ If $i$ is an active attacker
13:                 $r \leftarrow$ a random real number in $[0, 1]$ based on uniform distribution
14:                 **if** $r < \gamma$ **then**
15:                     $\text{spread}(i) = 1$
16:                     **for** $j := 1$ to $N$ **do**
17:                         **if** $a_{ij} > 0 \land na_i > 0 \land nc_i > 0$ **then**       ▷ if $j$ is susceptible
18:                             **if** $\sigma_i$ includes $sv_j$ **then**    ▷ $i$ knows $sv_j$'s vulnerability
19:                                 $nc_j = 1$                    ▷ $j$ is compromised by $i$
20:                             **else**
21:                                 $r \leftarrow$ a random real number in $[0, 1]$
22:                                 $d \leftarrow \frac{1}{N_{sv}-|\sigma_i|+1}$   ▷ $|\sigma_i|$ is # of software versions $i$ knows
23:                                 **if** $r < d$ **then**
24:                                     $nc_j = 1$                    ▷ $j$ is compromised by $i$
25:                                     $\sigma_i(j) = 1$           ▷ $i$ learned $sv_j$'s vulnerability
26:                                 **end if**
27:                             **end if**
28:                         **end if**
29:                     **end for**
30:                 **else**
31:                     $na_i = 0$       ▷ $i$ is detected and deactivated for infecting behavior
32:                     $a_{ij} = 0, a_{ji} = 0$             ▷ disconnecting all edges connected to $i$
33:                 **end if**
34:             **end if**
35:         **end for**
36:         **for** $k := 1$ to $N$ **do**
37:             **if** $na_i > 0 \land nc_i > 0 \land \text{spread}(k) < 2$ **then**   ▷ each node has two chances to compromise each of its direct neighbors
38:                 $spreadDone = 0$
39:                 $break$
40:             **else**
41:                 $spreadDone = 1$
42:             **end if**
43:         **end for**
44:     **end while**
45: **end procedure**

---

When node $i$ meets the above two conditions, $i$'s status is changed from "susceptible" to "infected" indicating that $i$ is now an attacker. Then, $i$ can infect other nodes and learn their software vulnerabilities, which are unknown to it. The details of the attack procedures are described in Algorithm 1.

### 12.3.4   Defense model

In this work, we assume that a system is equipped with an intrusion detection system (IDS), which detects infected (i.e., compromised) nodes. When infected node $i$ is detected by the IDS, we model the detection rate with $\gamma$ representing the removal rate in the SIR model. We interpret $1/\gamma$ as the delay incurred to detect an infected node and take a response action to isolate the infected node. The response to the detected node will be performed by disconnecting all the edges connected to the detected attacker, which corresponds to removing the node from the system based on the concept of *site percolation*.

## 12.4   Software-diversity-based adaptation strategies

In this section, the proposed adaptation strategy is discussed where software diversity is used as a key determinant to select an edge to percolate (i.e., add or remove) in order to mitigate the spreading of compromised nodes by attackers.

### 12.4.1   Software diversity metric

A node's vulnerability is commonly computed based on its software version installed [3,4]. However, if the node is connected with many other nodes that are directly or indirectly connected, its potential vulnerability is not simply restricted by the vulnerability of its own software version. We use the broad concept of the node's vulnerability to attacks based on network structure the node is associated with. Based on this concept of the node's vulnerability, node $i$'s software diversity via $k$ iterations is measured by

$$sd_i^k = \sum_{j \in \mathbf{A}_i} \frac{sd_j^{k-1}/k}{|\mathbf{A}_i|} \qquad (12.6)$$

where $k$ ($> 1$) refers to a particular round of iterations to calculate a node's software diversity based on the software diversity of its direct neighbors. $\mathbf{A}_i$ is a set of $i$'s direct neighboring nodes $j$'s and $|\mathbf{A}_i|$ refers to the cardinality of the set $\mathbf{A}_i$. The influence of the software diversity of neighbors decays inversely proportional as $k$ increases. This implies that using higher $k$ allows us to consider the software diversity of other nodes on the paths to reach $i$. In the first round with $k = 1$, node $i$'s software diversity with respect to $j$, denoted by $sd_j^0$, is initialized by

$$sd_j^0 = \frac{\sum_{u \in \mathbf{A}_j} sd_{ju}}{|\mathbf{A}_j|} \qquad (12.7)$$

where $sd_{ju}$ is obtained by

$$sd_{ju} = \begin{cases} 1 & \text{if } sv_j \neq sv_u; \\ 0 & \text{otherwise.} \end{cases} \tag{12.8}$$

---

**Algorithm 2:** Software diversity based adaptation (SDA)

---

1: **DN** ← a vector with the length $N$ indicating whether a node's edges are disconnected, 1 for disconnected; 0 otherwise.
2: **A** ← an adjacency matrix for a given network
3:
4: **Step 1:** Remove edges between two connected nodes when they use a same software version
5: **for** $i := 1$ to $N$ **do**
6:     **for** $j := 1$ to $N$ **do**
7:         **if** $(a_{ij} > 0) \wedge sv_i == sv_j$ **then**
8:             $a_{ij} = 0; a_{ji} = 0$
9:             **DN**$(i) = $ **DN**$(i) + 1$                  ▷ counting # of disconnected nodes per $i$
10:         **end if**
11:     **end for**
12: **end for**
13:
14: **Step 2:** Add edges between two disconnected nodes when they don't use a same software version
15: $\rho$ ← a threshold of software diversity
16: **for** $i := 1$ to $N$ **do**
17:     **candidate** ← a vector of nodes that can be connected with node $i$ where $sd_i \leq \rho \wedge a(i,j) == 0 \wedge (na_i \cdot na_j > 0)$ for node $j$ in a given network **G**
18:     **visited** ← a vector with $length$(**candidate**)
19:     **for** $j := 1$ to **DN**$(i)$ **do**              ▷ **DN**$(i)$ is # of edges that node $i$ lost in Step 1
20:         $r$ ← a random integer in $[0, length($**candidate**$)]$ based on uniform distribution
21:         **if** visited$(r) == 0$ **then**
22:             $k \leftarrow$ **candidate**$(r), a_{ik} = 1; a_{ki} = 1$
23:             visited$(r) = 1$
24:         **else**
25:             $j = j - 1$
26:         **end if**
27:         **if** $sum($**visited**$) == length($**visited**$)$ **then**      ▷ all candidate nodes are selected
28:             *break*
29:         **end if**
30:     **end for**
31: **end for**

---

## 12.4.2   *Adaptations based on software diversity*

In this work, our research problem is to answer which edge to connect or disconnect in order to maximize the size of the giant component (i.e., the largest network cluster in a network) with minimum cost estimated based on the network topology changes from the original network to the adapted network (see the adaptation cost metric in Section 12.5.1). Bond percolation for a non-compromised, active node $i$ to remove or add an edge with other nodes can be performed to meet this goal as follows:

1.  When $(sv_i == sv_j)$ for $a_{ij} > 0 \land i \neq j$, meaning that when two connected nodes use a same software version, then remove an edge between $i$ and $j$, $e(i,j) = 0$.
2.  When $(sv_i \neq sv_j) \land (sd_j \geq \rho)$ for $a_{ij} == 0$, meaning that when two disconnected nodes do not have a same software version *and* $j$'s software diversity is no less than the threshold $\rho$, then add an edge between $i$ and $j$.

---

**Algorithm 3:** Graph-coloring based adaptation (Graph-C)

---

1: **DN** ← a vector with the length $N$ indicating whether a node's edges are disconnected, 1 for disconnected; 0 otherwise.
2: **A** ← an adjacency matrix for a given network
3:
4: **Step 1:** Remove edges between two connected nodes when they use a same software version
5: **for** $i := 1$ to $N$ **do**
6:     **for** $j := 1$ to $N$ **do**
7:         **if** $(a_{ij} > 0) \land (sv_i == sv_j)$ **then**
8:             $a_{ij} = 0; a_{ji} = 0$     ▷ disconnect edges if $i$ and $j$ have a same software version
9:             **DN**$(i) =$ **DN**$(i) + 1$     ▷ counting # of disconnected nodes per $i$
10:         **end if**
11:     **end for**
12: **end for**
13:
14: **Step 2:** Add edges between two disconnected nodes when they don't use a same software version
15: **for** $i := 1$ to $N$ **do**
16:     **candidate** ← a vector of nodes that can be connected with node $i$ where $a(i,j) == 0 \land (na_i \cdot na_j > 0)$ for node $j$ in a given network **G**
17:     **visited** ← a vector with *length*(**candidate**)
18:     **for** $j := 1$ to **DN**$(i)$ **do**     ▷ **DN**$(i)$ is # of edges that node $i$ lost in Step 1
19:         $r$ ← a random integer in $[0, length(\textbf{candidate})]$ based on uniform distribution
20:         **if** **visited**$(r) == 0$ **then**
21:             $k$ ← **candidate**$(r), a_{ik} = 1; a_{ki} = 1$
22:             **visited**$(r) = 1$
23:         **else**
24:             $j = j - 1$
25:         **end if**
26:         **if** $sum(\textbf{visited}) == length(\textbf{visited})$ **then**     ▷ all candidate nodes are selected
27:             *break*
28:         **end if**
29:     **end for**
30: **end for**

---

Here $a_{ij}$ is an entry of an adjacency matrix **A** for vertices $i$ and $j$ for a given undirected network $G$ in which $a_{ij} = 1$ means there is an edge between $i$ and $j$; no edge otherwise. The first condition is equally applied as in the Graph-C scheme described in Algorithm 3. For the second condition, the number of edges disconnected from the first removal process will be restored by adding new edges with the same number of edges lost in the removing bond-percolation process.

## 12.5    Numerical results and analysis

In this section, we describe the experimental setup used for our simulation study, metrics, and schemes that are compared against the proposed network adaptation strategies. Finally, we demonstrate the simulation results and discuss the overall trends observed from the results.

### 12.5.1    Metrics

In this work, the following metrics are used to evaluate the performance of the proposed schemes and other counterparts:

- **Software diversity ($D_s$):** This metric measures the degree of software diversity in an ego network with which a node is associated within $k_{max}$ hops from the node. This metric implies that a node's software diversity is measured based on the software diversity of its neighbors within $k_{max}$ hops from itself. This metric is computed based on (12.6) and the average software diversity of nodes in the network is simply obtained by

$$D_s = \frac{\sum_{i=1}^{N} sd_i}{N} \qquad (12.9)$$

  In this metric, higher is more desirable implying that a system with more software diversity is less likely to be compromised by attackers than the system with less software diversity.
- **Size of the giant component ($S_g$):** This metric captures the degree of network connectivity composed of non-compromised (uninfected), active nodes in a network. $S_g$ is computed by

$$S_g = \frac{N_g}{N} \qquad (12.10)$$

  where $N$ is the total number of nodes in the network and $N_g$ is the number of nodes in the giant component. Higher is more desirable in this metric.
- **Adaptability cost ($A_c$):** This metric measures the cost associated with any edge adaptations (i.e., adjustments by adding or removing edges) to isolate detected attackers by the IDS (i.e., removing all edges connected to the detected attackers) and to maximize software diversity of nodes in a network, which can more likely

lead to a larger size of the giant component than counterparts that do not consider software diversity. This metric is obtained by

$$A_c = \frac{sum(|A - B|)}{sum(A + B)} \qquad (12.11)$$

where the numerator refers to the differences of edges between the adjacency matrix of an original network and that of an adjusted network after edges adaptations are made. The denominator is the sum of the additive two matrices. Lower is more desirable in this metric.

## 12.5.2 Comparing schemes

For the experimentation, we compare the performance of the following schemes in terms of the metrics explained in Section 12.5.1:

- **Non-adaptation (NA)**: This represents the case when no adaptation strategy is applied, showing the pure effect of attacks on the performance metrics in an original network topology. However, we allow an IDS to detect attackers after a set of seeding attackers is spread out to compromise other nodes that are directly connected to them in the network. When the IDS detects compromised nodes with the probability $\gamma$, all edges connected to the detected attacker will be disconnected in order to isolate the attackers, ultimately resulting in mitigating the spread of compromised nodes in the network. Therefore, even if NA is used, adaptation cost can be high because the number of edges to be disconnected is affected by the network topology, which is one of the key factors impacting the degree of network vulnerability.
- **Graph-C**: This scheme uses a graph coloring technique by simply removing an edge between two nodes with a same software version or adding an edge between two nodes with a different software version. To do this, we first disconnect all the edges between two directly connected nodes that have the same software version. And then add the number of edges between two randomly selected, disconnected nodes with different software versions. To be fair, the number of nodes removed will be added by connecting two nodes that have two different software versions.
- **SDA**: This scheme uses the software diversity-based metric in (12.6) in selecting an edge to remove or add based on the concept of bond percolation, which is discussed in Section 12.4.2. To be specific, first all edges between two connected nodes with the same software versions are removed. And then to determine which edges to add are determined based on Algorithm 2 where different threshold values of software diversity, $\rho$, are used to investigate its impact on the metrics described in Section 12.5.1.

We provide the details of *SDA* and *Graph-C*, in Algorithms 2 and 3, respectively. In our experiments, we will compare NA, Graph-C, and three variants of SDA with three different thresholds, $\rho$ (i.e., $= 0.2, 0.5, 0.7$). Basically Graph-C and the SDA schemes belong to adaptation schemes, while NA indicates no adaptation.

## 12.5.3   Experimental setup

The scenario considered in this work is that an original network is generated under a given network condition. On top of the original network, we apply five different schemes: (1) NA; (2) Graph-C; (3) SDA with $\rho = 0.1$; (4) SDA with $\rho = 0.2$; and (5) SDA with $\rho = 0.3$. After then, given a certain % of seeding attackers that are selected uniformly at random, each seeding attacker's epidemic attacks are performed based on Algorithm 1. Based on the three metrics described in Section 12.5.1, we show the effect of varying key design parameter values.

To be specific, we aim to investigate the effect of the key design parameters as follows:

- *Effect of network density*: Network density affects the number of edges each node has. For the Erdös–Rényi (ER) network (i.e., a random network), the density is the connection probability between two nodes, $p$, which we vary from 0.005 to 0.025 with the increment of 0.005. For the Barabási–Albert (BA) network (i.e., a scale-free network), the density is approximately $mN/2$, where $m$ is the connection rate as nodes are added to the network, which we vary from 3 to 13 to have a comparable density with the ER network.
- *Effect of attack density*: Attack density refers to the percentage of initial seeding attackers over the total number of nodes in a network, with respect 0.01, 0.05, 0.1, 0.2, and 0.3 (i.e., 1%–30%). Each attacker will perform epidemic attacks based on Algorithm 1.
- *Effect of the number of software versions*: The number of software versions available, $N_{sv}$, is varied with respect to $2, 3, 5, 7$, and $9$.

Two types of network topologies are used as synthetic network datasets: ER random network and BA scale-free network [8]. The ER network is commonly represented by $G(N, p)$ where $N$ is the total number of nodes and $p$ is the connection probability of two randomly chosen nodes. The BA network is represented, in this case, as $BA(N, m)$, where each node is introduced to a small initial connected network (in this case, a chain of length $m$) attaching $m$ links with preferential attachment based on the existing node degrees.

All other key design parameters, their meaning, and their default values are summarized in Table 12.1. Each data point is collected based on the average of 100 simulation runs.

## 12.5.4   Simulation results under a random network

**Effect of network density under a random network:** Figure 12.1 shows how network density (i.e., degree of node connectedness in terms of the number of edges each node has) impacts the three metrics in Section 12.5.1. To see this effect, we varied the connection probability $p$ between two nodes in a given random network from 0.005 to 0.025 with 0.005 increment. In Figure 12.1(a), the overall trend observed from all schemes is the decreasing software diversity as $p$ increases. Since being more connected can be easily leveraged by epidemic attackers to infect more of their neighbors, after the network with or without adaptations is attacked, the network with

*Table 12.1   Key design parameters, their meanings, and their default values*

| Param. | Meaning | Value |
|---|---|---|
| $N$ | Total number of nodes in a network | 1,000 |
| $\gamma$ | Intrusion detection probability | 0.9 |
| $k_{max}$ | The upper bound of hops considered in calculating the degree of software diversity, $n_i^{sd}$ | 3 |
| $n_r$ | Number of simulation runs | 100 |
| $N_{sv}$ | Number of software versions available | 3 |
| $p$ | Connection probability between pairs of nodes in an ER network | 0.02 |
| $m$ | Connection rate/initial network size in an BA network | 10 |
| $P_a$ | Percentage of seeding attackers in a network | 10% |
| $\rho$ | Threshold of software diversity in SDA | $0.2, 0.5, 0.7$ |

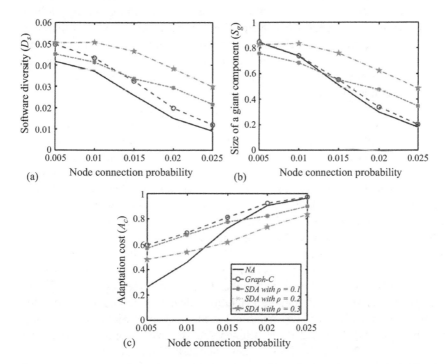

*Figure 12.1   (a) Effect of network density on the software diversity ($D_s$), (b) the size of the giant component ($S_g$), and (c) adaptation cost ($A_c$) under a random network*

higher connectedness (i.e., higher $p$) is more adversely impacted than one with lower connectedness. However, we can clearly observe the outperformance of adapted networks by adaptation strategies, including both Graph-C and SDA. To be specific, the overall performance order in software diversity (where higher is better in this metric) is as follows: "SDA schemes with $\rho = 0.2$ and $\rho = 0.3$" $\geq$ "SDA with $\rho = 0.1$" $\geq$ "Graph-C" $\geq$ "NA." For SDA, we observe the same performance for $\rho = 0.2$ and $\rho = 0.3$. From this observation, we infer that approximately $\rho = 0.2$ seems an upper bound that can maximally improve the software diversity in this random network environment. In particular, as the network is more vulnerable with higher $p$, SDA's performance with all thresholds, $\rho$'s, in the software diversity metric is more resilient against the higher network vulnerability, showing significant outperformance over Graph-C and NA. In Figure 12.1(b), we investigated how varying $p$ affects the size of the giant component ($S_g$). Similar to Figure 12.1(a), better connectivity in the original network reveals high vulnerability, which is proven that the size of the giant component decreases as $p$ increases in all schemes. Also we can clearly observe that the adaptation schemes, including both Graph-C and SDA, outperforms the NA scheme particularly when $p$ is sufficiently high (i.e., $p > 0.01$). In particular, SDA schemes with $\rho \geq 0.2$ show significant resilience as even $p$ becomes higher, which means higher resilience under more vulnerable network conditions. Lastly, in Figure 12.1(c), as intuitively understood, adaptation schemes incur more cost than NA scheme because the adaptation schemes incur additional cost to make percolation-based adaptations. However, as $p$ becomes higher, SDA schemes (with all thresholds) give even high efficiency by saving adaptation cost. We can infer the cause with two aspects: (1) after removing the vulnerable edges between two nodes with a same software version, a fewer number of edges are qualified to meet the threshold (to be added), which leads to less adaptation cost incurred and (2) due to better adjustments of edges in the adaptation stage, not many edges are removed from the network by the IDS's site percolation process (i.e., cutting all edges of a detected attacker). Due to the second reason, in this cost metric, SDA schemes even outperform NA which does not perform any adaptations. In Figure 12.1, we can clearly observe that higher software diversity can be more aligned with a larger size of the giant component particularly under more vulnerable network conditions with higher network density.

**Effect of attack density under a random network:** Figure 12.2 shows how attack density (i.e., % of seeding attackers, $P_a$) affects the three metrics under a random network. Figure 12.2(a) shows how the attack density impacts the degree of software diversity. Overall, as expected, higher $P_a$ decreases the degree of software diversity in all schemes. In addition, the adaptation schemes, both Graph-C and SDA, clearly outperform the NA scheme. In particular, SDA schemes with $\rho \geq 0.2$ clearly outperform among all. This is also well aligned with the size of the giant component as shown in Figure 12.2(b). This implies that a network with high software diversity also provides high network resilience in terms of the size of the giant component. Lastly, Figure 12.2(c) shows how the degree of attack density changes adaptation cost. Where lower cost is more desirable, in Figure 12.2(c), the performance order is as follows: "SDA schemes with $\rho \geq 0.2$" > "SDA with $\rho = 0.1$" > "NA" > "Graph-C," particularly when $P_a > 0.01$. The less cost incurred in SDA schemes are also because of the similar reasons described in Figure 12.1 with the two reasons.

**Effect of software versions available under a random network:** Figure 12.3 shows how the number of available software versions affects the performance in the three metrics. Figure 12.3(a) shows how the number of software versions available

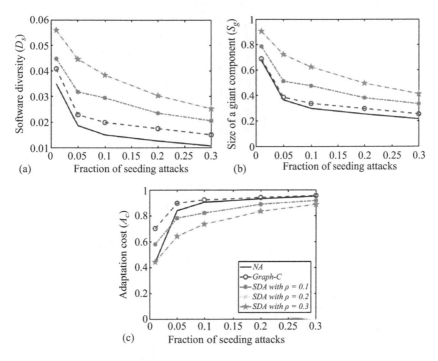

*Figure 12.2*   *(a) Effect of attack density on the software diversity $(D_s)$, (b) the size of the giant component $(S_g)$, and (c) adaptation cost $(A_c)$ under a random network*

$(N_{sv})$ affects the performance in the software diversity metric. It is evident that adaptation schemes (i.e., Graph-C and SDA schemes) perform better than their NA counterpart. Similar to what we observed from Figures 12.1 and 12.2, SDA schemes with $\rho \geq 0.2$ outperform among all, showing the highest software diversity and the size of the giant component while incurring the least cost compared to other schemes. In addition, more interestingly under $N_{sv} = 2$, SDA's performance is even better than under $N_{sv} = 3$, which naturally shows the significant outperformance over NA and Graph-C in $D_s$ and $S_g$. The reason can be inferred in two-fold: (1) for SDA schemes under $N_{sv} = 2$, an individual node's many neighbors are cut but all the edges that are cut are not necessarily restored by being connected with other nodes because of the lack of eligible nodes that can meet its software diversity higher than the given threshold $\rho$. This condition makes the software diversity fairly high because the sum of software versions of a node's neighbors do not have to be divided by a greater number of neighbors. In addition, this allows the network to maintain lower connectivity but still be sufficiently connected to form a larger giant component and (2) the choice of nodes in SDA schemes focuses more on better connected indirectly while Graph-C makes an near-sight decision to maximize the immediate payoff which allows a simple choice of a node to connect only based on the different version of a node's software

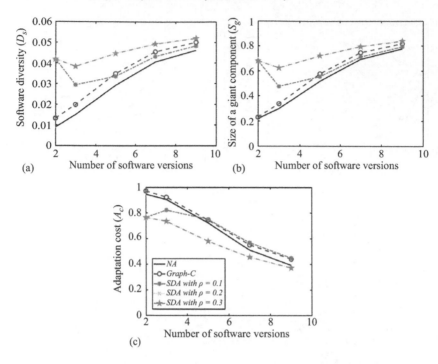

*Figure 12.3   (a) Effect of the number of software versions available on the software diversity ($D_s$), (b) the size of the giant component ($S_g$), and (c) adaptation cost ($A_c$) under a random network*

version. These two reasons can make the software diversity high enough while also making the network better connected under $N_{sv} = 2$ than under $N_{sv} = 3$. However, as $N_{sv}$ significantly increases, the benefit of using more software versions exceeds the trade-off condition observed under $N_{sv} = 2$. From the results observed in Figure 12.3, we can draw the conclusion that SDA with a fine-tuned software diversity threshold (i.e., $\rho = 0.2$ or 0.3) outperforms among all schemes with respect to all three metrics. This means that software-diversity-based bond percolation with a fine-tuned threshold can make a network more resilient against epidemic attacks with minimum cost based on the comparative performance analysis conducted in this study.

## 12.5.5   Simulation results under a scale-free network

In this section, we investigate how the nature of a scale-free network can impact the trends of varying key design parameters on the three metrics. Recall that the scale-free network is highly vulnerable to targeted attacks [8]. Although attackers are randomly selected in this work, they perform epidemic attacks, which are significantly affected by the network topology. Hence, in general, the scale-free network is much more vulnerable to epidemic attacks compared to the random network.

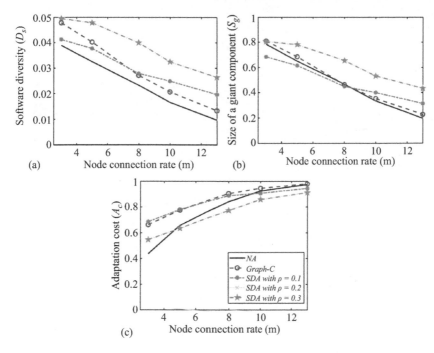

*Figure 12.4 (a) Effect of network density on the software diversity ($D_s$), (b) the size of the giant component ($S_g$), and (c) adaptation cost ($A_c$) under a scale-free network*

**Effect of network density under a scale-free network:** Figure 12.4 shows the effect of network density on the three metrics under a scale-free network. Recall that the scale-free network has the property of preferential attachment, which creates a set of nodes with high degree because each node is more likely to be connected with nodes with high influence (i.e., high degree). When we compare the results of Figure 12.1 with those of Figure 12.4, the overall performance under a scale-free network is similar to the performance under a random network over a similar range of network density. Recall that the number of edges for the ER network is approximately $p\binom{N}{2}$ and for the BA network is approximately $mN$, so the number of edges in the ranges in Figures 12.1 and 12.4 are similar. The performance trends observed in Figure 12.4 are very similar to the trends in Figure 12.1 by showing the following performance order: "SDA schemes with $\rho = 0.2$ and $\rho = 0.3$" ≥ "SDA with $\rho = 0.1$" ≥ "Graph-C" ≥ "NA." We also observe the same behavior wherein one scheme performs poorer than another scheme in a less dense network but better in a more dense network, e.g., SDA with $\rho = 0.1$ compared with Graph-C in the software diversity and the giant component size metrics.

**Effect of attack density under a scale-free network:** Figure 12.5 shows the effect of attack density ($P_a$) under a scale-free network. The overall trends are very

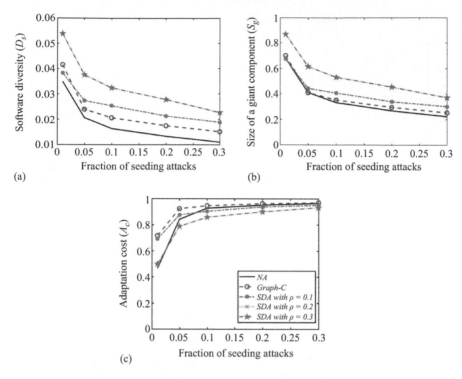

*Figure 12.5*   *(a) Effect of attack density on the software diversity ($D_s$), (b) the size of the giant component ($S_g$), and (c) adaptation cost ($A_c$) under a scale-free network*

similar to what we observed from Figure 12.2 in the ER network when the degree of attack density is varied. Figure 12.5(a) shows the impact of varying attack density on the software diversity. Overall, the software diversity has an initial significant decrease as more attackers are added to the network and, afterwards, becomes less sensitive to the increasing attack density, $P_a$, as shown in Figure 12.5(a). This trend is also similarly observed in Figure 12.5(b). But in Figure 12.5(a) and (b), all three SDA schemes outperform NA/Graph-C although we observe each absolute performance much lower than the performance under the random network in Figure 12.5. The trends here are similar to the case of the random network with two very subtle differences. First, the performance differences between the several schemes are more compressed for the BA networks than for the ER networks. Second, the initial effect of increasing attackers (from 1% to 5%) has a slightly initial impact in the BA network than the ER network before becoming more gradual. This is most clear in adaptation cost, where in Figure 12.5(c) the range of $A_c$ is less than 0.2 at a 5% attack density, whereas in Figure 12.2(c), this does not occur until the attack density is at least 20%.

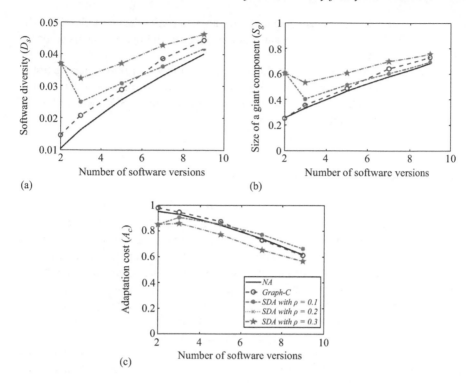

Figure 12.6   (a) Effect of the number of software versions available on the software
diversity (D_s), (b) the size of the giant component (S_g), and
(c) adaptation cost (A_c) under a scale-free network

**Effect of software versions available under a scale-free network:** Lastly, we
discuss how the number of software versions available ($N_{sv}$) impacts the performance
in the three metrics under a scale-free network, as shown in Figure 12.6. Overall,
as more $N_{sv}$ is considered, a higher software diversity and size of the giant component is observed while lower adaptation cost incurs. As in the previous results, the
performance order is similar. However, we can notice the significant increase of performance by Graph-C as more $N_{sv}$ are available in the system although SDA with
$\rho \geq 0.2$ still performs the best. In comparison with the random network, the relative
performances observed in all schemes are similar. One difference is that the BA network results are more compressed in the range of values of adaptation cost $A_c$, while
giant component size $S_g$ is narrower in Figure 12.6 than in Figure 12.3 over the range
of the number of software versions. However, the opposite is true with respect to the
software diversity $D_s$. There is also generally a greater adaptation cost for the BA
network in Figure 12.6(c) compared with the ER network in Figure 12.3(c), perhaps
due to the network topology with highly heterogeneous nodes in their degrees. If a
hub node in the BA network gets infected, significantly more edges will be cut by the

IDS or adaptation schemes as compared with an arbitrarily chosen node in the ER network. This also leads to smaller giant component sizes in Figure 12.6(b) compared with Figure 12.3(b).

Although we considered a fairly large network with $N = 1,000$, when we tested with a smaller network such as $N = 100$, the overall trends are still observed in a same way. Based on this finding, we can say that the proposed SDA scheme can be applicable in a wide range of network size.

## 12.6 Conclusions and future work

We investigated how software diversity is related to network resilience measured by the size of the giant component (i.e., the largest cluster in the network), which often represents connectivity-based network resilience implying high network availability. We proposed a software diversity metric based on the concept of the eigenvector centrality metric, which measures a node's software diversity based on its neighbor's software diversity. In order to examine the relationship between software diversity and the network resilience through the extensive simulation experiments, we conducted comprehensive performance analysis by comparing our proposed software diversity adaptation schemes with two existing counterparts, including graph coloring and no adaptation baseline model, under two different network models, ER random network and BA scale-free network. From our simulation experiments, the following **new findings** are observed:

- The degree of software diversity is well aligned with the size of the giant component. In addition, SDA strategies, particularly with an optimal threshold, outperform the NA scheme and the existing counterpart (i.e., Graph-C) with respect to the high software diversity, the larger size of the giant component, and the lower adaptation cost.
- When a network is more connected, this implies higher vulnerability, resulting in the higher adverse impact of epidemic attacks. In this sense, the overall performance trend is that a scale-free network gives slightly reduced software diversity, slightly smaller size of the giant component, and higher adaptation cost than a random network.
- To achieve both high network availability (i.e., having a large size of the giant component) and low network vulnerability (i.e., not easily adversely impacted by attacks), a node needs to make a good balance between the following two strategies: sufficiently being connected with nodes with a different software version or high software diversity while being less connected with nodes with a same software version or low software diversity.

We plan to have the following **future research directions**:

- We will study performance on other network models, e.g., the Watts–Strogatz small world model [8] is specifically relevant to determine the effect of a clustered density in the metrics, and alternative scale-free models can elucidate the effect of the exponent in the power law degree distribution.

- We will revisit our software diversity metric that can even be well aligned with other performance and security metrics (e.g., mean time to security failure as a security metric or service availability metric as a performance metric) under less vulnerable, less hostile environments.
- We will develop a closed-form mathematical model to predict the size of the giant component by deriving the infection rate $\beta$ to describe the average system behavior.
- We will revisit the design of the dissimilarity computation between two nodes in terms of each node's configuration vector, instead of only considering a single software functionality as considered in this work.
- We will consider a *shuffling* technique, as an MTD technique, by shuffling a node's software version where multiple versions are available to provide a same service. The decision for shuffling can be modeled based on a game theoretic approach in order to meet multiple system objectives.
- We will investigate the interdependencies between software versions in terms of their vulnerabilities and evaluate their impact on the performance metrics based on the comparative performance analysis of the schemes compared in this work.

# References

[1] Walker B, Kinzig A, Langridge J. Original articles: Plant attribute diversity, resilience, and ecosystem function: The nature and significance of dominant and minor species. Ecosystems. 1999;2(2):95–113.

[2] O'Donnell AJ, Sethu H. On achieving software diversity for improved network security using distributed coloring algorithms. In: Proceedings of the 11th ACM Conference on Computer and Communications Security. CCS'04; 2004. p. 121–131.

[3] Hole KJ. Diversity reduces the impact of malware. IEEE Security Privacy. 2015;13(3):48–54.

[4] Hole KJ. Toward anti-fragility: A malware-halting technique. IEEE Security Privacy. 2015;13(4):40–46.

[5] Larsen P, Brunthaler S, Franz M. Security through diversity: Are we there yet?. IEEE Security & Privacy. 2014;12(2):28–35.

[6] Larsen P, Brunthaler S, Franz M. Automatic software diversity. IEEE Security & Privacy. 2015;13(2):30–37.

[7] Yang Y, Zhu S, Cao G. Improving sensor network immunity under worm attacks: A software diversity approach. Ad Hoc Networks. 2016;47(Supplement C): 26–40.

[8] Newman MEJ. Networks: An Introduction. 1st ed. New York: Oxford University Press; 2010.

[9] Dezsö Z, Barabási AL. Halting viruses in scale-free networks. Physical Review E. 2002;65:055103.

[10]    Yang Y, Zhu S, Cao G. Improving sensor network immunity under worm attacks: A software diversity approach. In: Proceedings of the 9th ACM International Symposium on Mobile Ad Hoc Networking and Computing. MobiHoc'08; 2008. p. 149–158.

[11]    Hong JB, Kim DS. Assessing the effectiveness of moving target defenses using security models. IEEE Transactions on Dependable and Secure Computing. 2016;13(2):163–177.

[12]    Bonacich P. Power and centrality: A family of measures. American Journal of Sociology. 1987;92(5):1170–1182.

[13]    Kreutz D, Ramos FMV, Verissimo PE, *et al.* Software-defined networking: A comprehensive survey. Proceedings of the IEEE. 2015;103(1):14–76.

[14]    Cho JH, Chen IR, Eltoweissy M. On optimal batch rekeying for secure group communications in wireless networks. Wireless Networks. 2008;14(6): 915–927.

[15]    Costa D, Hertz A. Ants can colour graphs. Journal of the Operational Research Society. 1997;48(3):295–305.

[16]    Hertz A, Zufferey N. A new ant algorithm for graph coloring. In: Workshop on Nature Inspired Cooperative Strategies for Optimization NICSO; 2006. p. 51–60.

[17]    Plumettaz M, Schindl D, Zufferey N. Ant local search and its efficient adaptation to graph colouring. Journal of the Operational Research Society. 2010;61(5):819–826.

[18]    Bessedik M, Toufik B, Drias H. How can bees colour graphs. International Journal of Bio-Inspired Computation. 2011;3(1):67–76.

[19]    Dorrigiv M, Markib HY. Algorithms for the graph coloring problem based on swarm intelligence. In: Artificial Intelligence and Signal Processing (AISP), 2012 16th CSI International Symposium on. IEEE; 2012. p. 473–478.

[20]    Cui G, Qin L, Liu S, *et al.* Modified PSO algorithm for solving planar graph coloring problem. Progress in Natural Science. 2008;18(3):353–357.

[21]    Hsu LY, Horng SJ, Fan P, *et al.* MTPSO algorithm for solving planar graph coloring problem. Expert Systems with Applications. 2011;38(5):5525–5531.

[22]    Fister Jr I, Yang XS, Fister I, *et al.* Memetic firefly algorithm for combinatorial optimization. In: Bioinspired Optimization Methods and their Applications (BIOMA 2012), B. Filipic, J. Silc (Eds.). Jozef Stefan Institute, Ljubljana, Slovenia, 2012.

[23]    Mahmoudi S, Lotfi S. Modified cuckoo optimization algorithm (MCOA) to solve graph coloring problem. Applied Soft Computing. 2015;33:48–64.

[24]    Zhou Y, Zheng H, Luo Q, *et al.* An improved cuckoo search algorithm for solving planar graph coloring problem. Applied Mathematics & Information Sciences. 2013;7(2):785.

[25]    Costa D, Hertz A, Dubuis C. Embedding a sequential procedure within an evolutionary algorithm for coloring problems in graphs. Journal of Heuristics. 1995;1(1):105–128.

[26]    Galinier P, Hao JK. Hybrid evolutionary algorithms for graph coloring. Journal of Combinatorial Optimization. 1999;3(4):379–397.

[27]  Dorne R, Hao JK. A new genetic local search algorithm for graph coloring. In: International Conference on Parallel Problem Solving from Nature. Springer; 1998. p. 745–754.

[28]  Lü Z, Hao JK. A memetic algorithm for graph coloring. European Journal of Operational Research. 2010;203(1):241–250.

[29]  Liu Y, Zhang W, Bai S, *et al.* Defending sensor worm attack using software diversity approach. In: Communications (ICC), 2011 IEEE International Conference on. IEEE; 2011. p. 1–5.

[30]  Keeling MJ, Eames KT. Networks and epidemic models. Journal of the Royal Society Interface. 2005;2(4):295–307.

[31]  Cohen F. Computer viruses: Theory and experiments. Computers & Security. 1987;6(1):22–35.

[32]  Murray WH. The application of epidemiology to computer viruses. Computers & Security. 1988;7(2):139–145.

[33]  Kephart JO, White SR. Directed-graph epidemiological models of computer viruses. In: Proceedings of IEEE Computer Society Symposium on Research in Security and Privacy; 1991. p. 343–359.

[34]  Pastor-Satorras R, Vespignani A. Epidemic spreading in scale-free networks. Physical Review Letters. 2001;86(14):3200.

[35]  Pastor-Satorras R, Vespignani A. Epidemic dynamics in finite size scale-free networks. Physical Review E. 2002;65(3):035108.

[36]  Wang Y, Chakrabarti D, Wang C, *et al.* Epidemic spreading in real networks: An eigenvalue viewpoint. In: Proceedings of IEEE 22nd International Symposium on Reliable Distributed Systems; 2003, p. 25–34.

[37]  Ganesh A, Massoulié L, Towsley D. The effect of network topology on the spread of epidemics. In: INFOCOM 2005. 24th Annual Joint Conference of the IEEE Computer and Communications Societies. Proceedings IEEE. vol. 2. IEEE; 2005. p. 1455–1466.

[38]  Zou CC, Towsley D, Gong W. Modeling and simulation study of the propagation and defense of internet e-mail worms. IEEE Transactions on Dependable and Secure Computing. 2007;4(2):104–118.

[39]  Gross T, D'Lima CJD, Blasius B. Epidemic dynamics on an adaptive network. Physical Review Letters. 2006;96(20):208701.

[40]  Volz E, Meyers LA. Epidemic thresholds in dynamic contact networks. Journal of the Royal Society Interface. 2009;6(32):233–241.

[41]  Prakash BA, Tong H, Valler N, *et al.* Virus propagation on time-varying networks: Theory and immunization algorithms. In: Joint European Conference on Machine Learning and Knowledge Discovery in Databases. Springer; 2010. p. 99–114.

[42]  Sanatkar MR, White WN, Natarajan B, *et al.* Epidemic threshold of an SIS model in dynamic switching networks. IEEE Transactions on Systems, Man, and Cybernetics: Systems. 2016;46(3):345–355.

[43]  Grimmett G. Percolation and disordered systems. In: Lectures on Probability and Statistics. Springer, Berlin Heidelberg; 1997. p. 153–300.

[44]  Barabási AL. Network Science. 1st ed. Cambridge: Cambridge University Press; 2016.

[45]  Cardy JL, Grassberger P. Epidemic models and percolation. Journal of Physics A: Mathematical and General. 1985;18(6):L267.

[46]  Moore C, Newman ME. Epidemics and percolation in small-world networks. Physical Review E. 2000;61(5):5678.

[47]  Colbourn C. Network resilience. SIAM Journal on Algebraic Discrete Methods. 1987;8(3):404–409.

[48]  Najjar W, Gaudiot JL. Network resilience: A measure of network fault tolerance. IEEE Transactions on Computers. 1990;39(2):174–181.

[49]  Albert R, Jeong H, Barabási AL. Error and attack tolerance of complex networks. Nature. 2000;406(6794):378–382.

[50]  Broadbent SR, Hammersley JM. Percolation processes: I. Crystals and mazes. In: Mathematical Proceedings of the Cambridge Philosophical Society. vol. 53. Cambridge University Press; 1957. p. 629–641.

[51]  Newman ME, Ziff RM. Fast Monte Carlo algorithm for site or bond percolation. Physical Review E. 2001;64(1):016706.

[52]  Cohen R, Erez K, Ben-Avraham D, *et al.* Resilience of the internet to random breakdowns. Physical Review Letters. 2000;85(21):4626.

[53]  Chen L, May JHR. A diversity model based on failure distribution and its application in safety cases. IEEE Transactions on Reliability. 2016;65(3): 1149–1162.

[54]  Huang C, Zhu S, Erbacher R. Toward Software Diversity in Heterogeneous Networked Systems. In: Data and Applications Security and Privacy XXVIII, V. Atluri, G. Pernul (Eds.). Springer, Berlin, Heidelberg; 2014. p. 114–129.

[55]  Huang C, Zhu S, Guan Q, *et al.* A software assignment algorithm for minimizing worm damage in networked systems. Journal of Information Security and Applications. 2017;35(Supplement C):55–67.

[56]  Franz M. E unibus pluram: Massive-scale software diversity as a defense mechanism. In: Proceedings of the 2010 New Security Paradigms Workshop. NSPW'10. New York, NY, USA: ACM; 2010. p. 7–16.

[57]  Homescu A, Jackson T, Crane S, *et al.* Large-scale automated software diversity–program evolution redux. IEEE Transactions on Dependable and Secure Computing. 2017;14(2):158–171.

[58]  Salako K, Strigini L. When does "diversity" in development reduce common failures? Insights from probabilistic modeling. IEEE Transactions on Dependable and Secure Computing. 2014;11(2):193–206.

[59]  Zhang Y, Vin H, Alvisi L, *et al.* Heterogeneous networking: A new survivability paradigm. In: Proceedings of Network Security Paradigms Workshop (NSPW'01). Cloudcroft, New Mexico, USA: ACM; 2001.

[60]  Zhang M, Wang L, Jajodia S, *et al.* Network diversity: A security metric for evaluating the resilience of networks against zero-day attacks. IEEE Transactions on Information Forensics and Security. 2016;11(5):1071–1086.

## Chapter 13
# Hunting bugs with nature-inspired fuzzing
### *Konstantin Böttinger[1]*

Motivated by the urgent need for secure software, we construct new testing methods inspired by biology to improve current development life cycles. We connect probability theory with current testing technologies by formulating feedback-driven fuzzing in the language of stochastic processes. This mathematical model allows us to translate deep results from probability theory into algorithms for software testing. Exploring the full capabilities of our model leads us to the application of reinforcement learning methods, which turns out to be a fruitful new direction in software testing.

## 13.1 Research challenge

The ever increasing complexity of software systems in the core infrastructures of society demands advanced methods for testing their robustness. In recent years, we observe an increasing proliferation of serious software vulnerabilities in the technologies that surround us. The perfectly secure piece of software is far out of reach, and the common practice in hardening software often boils down to finding vulnerabilities before the adversary does. Undisclosed security-critical bugs known as *zero-days* will continue to emerge on the surface of black markets to attract players of a variety of backgrounds. A common strategy to decrease the risk of being successfully attacked is to increase the effort it takes to compromise our assets. From the perspective of practical risk assessment, this chapter presents advanced methods to lower this probability in efficient ways. Efforts in reducing the attack surface and increasing attack efforts directly point us to research secure software development life cycles.

Besides secure design and implementation, state-of-the-art in secure software engineering always includes several verification steps prior to release. In practice, there is always a certain mismatch between functionality intended by the architect and actually provided by the implementation at hand. This mismatch gives rise to unintended and unexpected behavior in terms of security critical vulnerabilities. To discover such flaws, a magnitude of different verification methods has emerged over time. From a practical point of view, we especially need automated methods that allow

[1] Fraunhofer Institute for Applied and Integrated Security (AISEC), Germany

344 Nature-inspired cyber security and resiliency

us to systematically perform vulnerability analysis of software. The modern world of software engineering strongly requires fully automated testing tools that scale to the ever growing application landscape.

Nowadays, the most effective way to proceed in this direction is random testing of software, also called fuzzing. There exists a substantial diversity of test case generation strategies for random testing of software. All these approaches have in common to a greater or lesser extent the random generation of test cases with the aim of driving the targeted program to an unexpected and possibly exploitable state. The prime advantage of fuzzing is its relative ease of use. Most software that processes any input data is a suitable target for random test generation, and simple fuzzers are implemented in a short time. This ease of use comes with a lack of completeness: Fuzzing does not guarantee the absence of vulnerabilities but only reduces the probability of their existence. However, from point of view of practical risk assessment, decreasing the number of security critical vulnerabilities exactly corresponds to the required risk reduction.

Looking at state-of-the art in *random* testing, we see the discipline of randomness very much underrepresented. Rooted in ancient times, the theory of probability gained momentum in the correspondence of Gerolamo Cardano, Pierre de Fermat, and Blaise Pascal beginning in 1654 [1]. From Christiaan Huygens' 1657 discourse *De ratiociniis in ludo aleae* ("On Reasoning in Games of Chance") over Andrey Kolmogorov's foundations of the field in 1933 [2] up to the powerful methods of modern stochastics [3], the theory of randomness has developed into an influential and rich mathematical discipline. When comparing the deep results of this theory to simple random bit flips in state-of-the-art random testing, three major research questions arise:

- How can we connect probability theory to state-of-the-art software testing?
- How can we transfer the deep results from probability theory into the world of software testing in order to discover new algorithms?
- How can biology help us to find inspiration in answering these questions?

To answer the first question, we construct a mathematical model of fuzzing. This provides a common language that functions as gateway between both fields of research. To answer the second question, we identify stochastic structures and processes underlying this model and translate their essence into algorithms for software testing. All presented methods are strongly inspired by biological processes, and at the end of this chapter, the reader will clearly see the answer to the third question.

In the first section of this chapter, we connect fuzzing with the field of stochastic processes. On the one hand, fuzzing in its essence deals with controlling a feedback loop in the sense of classic cybernetics [4]: The fuzzer generates an input, injects it to the program under test, observes what the program does, and adapts its behavior for generating the next input accordingly. On the other hand, the rich field of probability theory offers deep results for feedback-driven stochastic processes. Formulating fuzzing in the language of mathematics enables us to directly transfer results from probability theory to fuzzing. Well-established methods and search strategies proven to be stable and effective suddenly give rise to novel fuzzing algorithms. This way, we open the door to a variety of new perspectives on software testing.

To guide our choice of perspectives, we find inspiration in the field of biology. In Section 13.3 of this chapter, we investigate fuzzing strategies inspired by animal foraging and swarm theory. We construct self-adaptive feedback loops for fuzzing and evaluate their efficiency on realistic targets. Further, we enhance the random nature of input generation with deterministic and precise methods: The combination of fuzzing with symbolic reasoning turns out to be effective in reaching deep layers of the program under test. Next, we introduce a novel method for distributed large-scale fuzzing in computer clusters based on the biological concept of chemotaxis in order to maximize coverage of execution paths in the target under test. This approach is inspired by colonies with dedicated explorers and the concept of chemotaxis. Section 13.3 deals with predefined behavior in the sense that input mutation and synchronization follow a fixed sequence of actions.

We research fuzzers with learning behavior in Section 13.4. At a certain level of abstraction controlling, the fuzzing loop can be interpreted as a game against the program. Motivated by the success in Backgammon [5,6], Atari games [7], and the game of Go [8], we apply machine learning to fuzzing. Again, our mathematical model provides a direct interface to reinforcement learning, which has its historical roots in the psychology of animal learning [9]. And in fact, the deep $Q$ learning algorithm that achieved super-human behavior in [7,8] turns out to be an exciting new direction in software testing.

This chapter summarizes ideas from papers presented at the IEEE Symposium on Security and Privacy [10–12] and in two journal papers [13,14].

## 13.2 The stochastic process of fuzzing

In this section, we connect fuzzing with stochastics. We formulate fuzzing in terms of stochastic processes, which allows us to construct a mathematical model of generic fuzzing architectures. The essence of this section is captured in Figure 13.1: the mutator (M), input (I), and program (P), which are concepts of fuzzing, are connected via rewards, states, and actions, which in turn are concepts of certain stochastic processes. The mutator (M) generates an input (I) that is injected into the program under test (P). This input generation is interpreted as an action that causes a state transition and a reward. At the end of this section, the reader will understand each aspect of this view.

First, we present the essential background necessary to understand state-of-the-art fuzzing in Section 13.2.1. This includes historical notes, an introduction of common terminology, and a short note on testing taxonomies as well as an abstraction of a generic architecture.

Second, we introduce the language required for mathematically modeling fuzzing in Section 13.2.2. We keep the discussion of Markov decision processes at an assessable level to keep the overall presentation as clear as possible.

Third, in Section 13.2.3, we capture the generic architecture abstracted in Section 13.2.1 in the language introduced in Section 13.2.2. This mathematical model of fuzzing provides the basis for Sections 13.3 and 13.4 of this chapter.

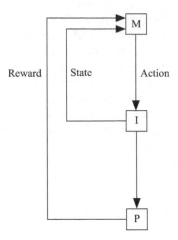

*Figure 13.1    The stochastic process of fuzzing*

## 13.2.1    Fuzzing essentials

In this section, we introduce everything necessary to understand state-of-the-art fuzzing. We trace the development of random test generation beginning at its origins in the 1950s to the advanced feedback-driven frameworks for modern software testing. This leads us to characteristic properties of modern fuzzers, based on which we construct a generic architecture to obtain an abstract view on the fuzzing process. Extracting the essentials of fuzzing this way will prepare us for the challenges of a formal analysis that lie ahead.

### 13.2.1.1    Fuzzing origins

Reasoning about the correctness of the computer is as old as computing itself. Even if we go back to the stepped reckoner, a digital mechanical calculator invented by Gottfried Wilhelm Leibniz [15], we find the abyss that ever since opened up between intent and reality of computation: Beyond calculation errors in the precision gearwork that drove fine mechanics technology in those days over its limits, a design error in the carrying mechanism was detected in 1893—199 years after construction of the machine. The first attempt to systematically reason about the correctness of a program can be dated back to 1949 when Turing indicated a general proof method for program correctness on three foolscap pages of text [16,17]. Research of the following decades established the field of program verification [18–20], which aims for proving correctness of a program with respect to formal specifications and properties. However, proving correct system behavior for large programs suffers from explosion of possible states inherent in complex software. Further, verification techniques require a system model to prove properties of the program. Constructing such models counters the aim of fully automated testing and may even miss system properties [21].

Parallel to the discipline of formal verification, another kind of software testing was established. As Weinberg [22] recalls, *We didn't call it fuzzing back in the 1950s, but it was our standard practice to test programs by inputting decks of punch cards taken from the trash. We also used decks of random number punch cards. We weren't networked in those days, so we weren't much worried about security, but our random trash decks often turned up undesirable behavior.* Networking evolved and the rise of the internet exacerbated the situation of complex systems facing a lack of scalable testing methods. Software ever increased in size and complexity—so did the proliferation of software bugs—and finding flaws in systems becomes even harder when they are distributed. A computer connected to the ARPANET [23,24] was much more likely to process data from untrusted sources. From security perspective, a system without air-gap means an increased attack surface, which was famously demonstrated by the Morris worm in 1988 [25]. Although testing with random program inputs was considered far inferior compared to the theory of formal verification (and sometimes even viewed as the *worst case of program testing* [26]), it was applied as a cost-effective alternative in practical software engineering. Duran and Ntafos [26,27] justified the use of random testing in the early 1980s by evaluating its effectiveness in relation to more formal methods. Random testing, meanwhile referred to as *monkey testing* due to the eponymous tool *The Monkey* that released 1983 by Steve Capps to test user interfaces for the Macintosh, was established among the programming practitioners of the late 1980s. But it was lacking the theoretical background needed to increase trust in this method. Just in the same fall of the year 1988 when the Morris worm spread, the perils of interconnected systems themselves gave rise to a systematic approach in the spirit of the 1950s random decks: when Barton Miller remotely connected to his Unix system during a fall thunderstorm, the rain caused noise on the line and thereby in the commands he entered to the shell leading programs to crash [28]. This motivated him to systematically execute programs with random and unstructured input data, which he referred to as *fuzzing* [29]. Since then the fuzzing discipline has evolved to an active area of research providing a rich diversity of fuzzing tools available, each focusing on specialized approaches. Fuzzing is nowadays the prevalent method used for detecting vulnerabilities in binaries. In a nutshell, inputs are randomly generated and injected into the target program with the aim to drive the program to an unexpected and exploitable state.

### 13.2.1.2 Modern fuzzing

The overall goal of fuzzing a target executable is to drive it to an unexpected and unintended state. Informally, we want to cause error signals, program crashes, and timeouts and refer to such program behavior as a bug. In this section, we first show how to actually sense bugs in a program during testing and discuss aspects of bug classification and criticality. Subsequently, we motivate currently applied search strategies that aim for maximization of code coverage. Such coverage information can be interpreted as a feedback mechanism that gives rise to feedback-driven fuzzing.

*Bug observation and identification*
Finding bugs in the program under test requires a mechanism to sense them. Current state-of-the-art fuzzers detect bugs that cause the target to timeout or crash.

*Timeouts* The former refers to delay or complete absence of an expected program response. In most situations such timeouts simply require a specified amount of time the fuzzer waits for a responds. Therefore, sensing timeouts is straight forward in most cases and current state-of-the-art fuzzers come with default time values around 1 s. Only very rare settings require more caution: The Windows Operating systems (from Windows Vista upwards), for example, come with the *Timeout Detection and Recovery* functionality, which detects problems in the response from graphic cards and upon detection of a frozen GPU resets the relevant drivers. In such cases, where timeouts of subsystems of the fuzzing target are handled by the target itself or its execution environment, timeout handling of the target must be disabled or more advanced sensing mechanisms are required.

*Crashes* A program crash refers to termination of the program due to a failure condition. Such conditions can happen inside the processor or in processor-external hardware modules. The latter indicate failure conditions by sending an interrupt to the processor. Since such external interrupt signals are usually asynchronous to the processor clock, they are referred to as *asynchronous events*. Processor-internal failure conditions in turn are generated synchronous to the processor clock and we refer to them as *exception events*.

Our definition of interrupts and exceptions is compliant with standard texts on processor design [30] and the Intel ×86 and ×86-64 software developer manuals [31]. However, this distinction is not always consistently followed in the literature and even standard references on the Linux kernel [32] occasionally refer to interrupts as both, synchronous and asynchronous, events. Considering the broad spectrum of different processor architectures, such vagueness of notation in the related literature seems natural: the ARM processor manuals, for example, include software interrupts (not to be confused with the hardware interrupts in our definition) as exceptions. Further, it depends on the processor architecture if the failure condition is labeled an interrupt or an exception. For example, a processor-external memory management unit detecting an unauthorized memory access indicates an interrupt, whereas a memory-management unit integrated in the processor (as implemented most often in modern CPU designs) per our definition rises an exception. In any case, our definition of crashes is sufficient for the presentation of this thesis as it covers both, synchronously and asynchronously, generated events: we are interested in software bugs and mainly abstract away the specific processor architecture.

The causes of crashes are manifold and typically fall into one of the following classes: division error, invalid opcode, overflow, page fault, unauthorized memory access, and unauthorized call of a routine with higher privileges. The exact types of failure conditions depend on the specific processor. For example, the Intel ×86 and ×86-64 architecture defines exceptions and interrupts related to coprocessor segment overrun, floating-point errors, virtualization exceptions and many more (see [31] Chapter 6). Each time a crash occurs, the operating system takes care of its handling. For example, the Linux routine for processors implementing the ×86 and ×86-64 instruction set architecture proceeds as follows. Upon receiving such interrupt or exception, the processor stops execution of the current process, saves all process registers, and switches to the operating system event handler indicated by the interrupt descriptor table. The operating system handler in turn sends a signal to the target process that evoked the interrupt. To eventually sense the crash at software side, we catch the signals that are sent from the operating system to the target process and filter the fatal ones.

Each operating system comes with its own types of signals. For Unix-like operating systems, famous fatal signals include SIGABRT (abnormal termination signal), SIGSEGV (invalid memory access signal), SIGSYS (bad argument to system call), SIGFPE (erroneous arithmetic operation), and SIGILL (illegal instruction). We refer to the POSIX programmers guide [33] for a complete list of fatal signals in the UNIX environment.

Software vulnerabilities come in a large spectrum of different characteristics, which motivated a diversity of research efforts to categorize them. For example, we could just take the criticality of bugs depending on their effect on the defined assets into account. If the asset to safeguard is availability of a server, a bug $B_1$ that crashes the server should be considered critical. If a second bug $B_2$ only crashes a server submodule that gets restarted automatically, it does not affect the overall stability of the program and is less critical with regard to server availability. In contrast, if the asset is data confidentiality and $B_2$ allows an attacker to read out confidential data, it should be considered critical. The famous *Heartbleed* bug from 2014 that allowed remote read of protected memory in estimated up to 55% of popular HTTPS internet sites [34] belongs to the latter kind. Besides criticality, there is a magnitude of other characteristics that give rise to a variety of different vulnerability taxonomies. However, discussing this active area of research is out of scope of this chapter and we refer to [35–38] for a first overview. Practically, the *Common Vulnerabilities and Exposures* data provides a standardized corpus of specific software bugs that facilitates identification and communication of concrete vulnerabilities. Similarly, the *Common Weakness Enumeration* provides a more general accumulation of common software vulnerabilities separate from specific products.

Intuitively, the likelihood of finding a bug rises with the percentage of code that we execute. In fact, the idea that code coverage leads to bug coverage was proven fruitful in the early days of fuzzing [39]. As a natural evolution, coverage levels were not only reported as minimal adequacy criteria in development life cycles but also used as reward feedback during the actual fuzzing process to generate inputs that potentially explore new code regions. We systematically define such rewards in Section 13.2.3.3.

## Fuzzer taxonomy

In this section, we briefly discuss a common basic taxonomy to classify modern fuzzing frameworks. First, we distinct fuzzers depending on the level of target information they have access to: while white-box fuzzers [40] have full sight on the target source code and therefore can theoretically gain detailed information about the program, black-box fuzzers [28,41] are basically blind in the sense that they only sense program crashes or timeouts during testing. Grey-box methods are settled in between and often make use of instrumentation frameworks (such as Pin [42], Valgrind [43], DynamoRIO [44], Dyninst [45], DTrace [46], and QEMU [47]) to gain detailed information regarding program execution. Evolutionary and white-box fuzzers such as AFL, Driller (enhancing AFL with symbolic execution), EFS, Sage,

Choronzon, Honggfuzz, libFuzzer, Kasan, Kcov, and BFF belong to this category. While binary instrumentation provides advanced test case generation based on run-time feedback, it comes with relatively high overhead (see [42] for a benchmark) and resulting moderate test case throughput. In contrast, black-box fuzzers (such as zzuf, Peach, and Radamsa) pitch test cases into the targeted binary without gathering feedback from dynamic instrumentation, which makes them significantly faster compared to feedback-driven fuzzers.

Second, we can distinct fuzzers with respect to the information they have regarding the input format. Generation fuzzers create and mutate inputs with respect to such input structure information, which may come as a predefined or dynamically learned grammar but also a less formal format specification. In contrast, mutation fuzzers are unaware of the input format. Both classes have advanced representatives within modern state-of-the art fuzzers: Peach and SPIKE, for example, are generation fuzzers that deploy a grammar, while AFL, zzuf, VUzzer [48], and Radamsa are powerful examples of mutation fuzzers.

Third, we distinct fuzzers between host and network-based fuzzers. In contrast to host-based fuzzers, network frameworks have to keep a state machine to handle communication sequences over time.

It is easy to extend this basic taxonomy to much more distinction features, as discussed in [28] and [41]. However, even the three presented basic differentiators sometimes fail: in Section 13.4 of this chapter, we present a fuzzer that learns a generalized grammar for input formats and therefore evolves from a pure mutation fuzzer towards a generation fuzzer over time.

### 13.2.1.3    Generic architecture and processes

Now we are ready to abstract a generic architecture common for modern fuzzing frameworks and identify basic processes within the components. This abstract view will allow us model fuzzing in the language of mathematics and therefore acts as a bridge between stochastic analysis and software testing.

In principle, a fuzzer generates an input using a set of predefined actions for bit string manipulation and generation. It injects this input into the target under test and observes the result. While black-box fuzzers are limited to sensing crashes and timeouts, feedback-driven frameworks gather detailed runtime information of the program executing the generated input, as discussed in Section 13.2.1.2. Subsequently, the fuzzer evaluates the extracted information from target execution and generates a new input based on this evaluation. This abstract loop is depicted in Figure 13.2.

## 13.2.2    Markov decision processes

In this section, we introduce the formal background that gives us the expressiveness to formulate fuzzing in a mathematically rigorous shape. We abstract the concepts as introduced in Section 13.2.1 to obtain a generic model of fuzzing. This model directly connects fuzzing with the rich and deep theory of stochastic processes and allows us to infer fuzzing strategies based on mathematical reasoning. At the end of

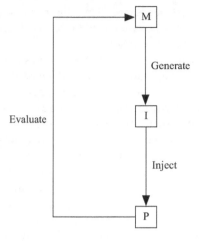

*Figure 13.2   Generic architecture for feedback-driven fuzzing*

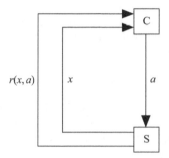

*Figure 13.3   Markov decision process*

this chapter, the reader will fully understand the mathematical background of Markov decision processes as depicted in Figure 13.3.

### 13.2.2.1   Policies and behavior

We begin the construction of our mathematical model of fuzzing with only two entities, namely, a controller and a system. As depicted in Figure 13.3, we assume the controller $C$ to interact with the system $S$ via state observations $x$, actions $a$, and rewards $r(x, a)$. In this generic model, the controller observes a state of the system and decides to take a corresponding action, which in turn results in a state transition of the system and an associated reward. Repeating this sequence gives rise to a feedback loop in which the controller aggregates rewards over time. The overall goal for the controller is to maximize the total reward. This scenario is commonly referred to as the reinforcement learning problem. Reinforcement learning as a subfield of machine learning is an active area of research and is best captured in the framework of Markov decision processes. The following introduction follows the notation of Szepesvári [49]. As usual in the probability theory literature, capital letters indicate stochastic variables while lower cases denote their realizations.

Let $\mathscr{X}$ and $\mathscr{A}$ denote the set of all possible system states and controller actions, respectively. Let us first get an intuitive picture of a *probability kernel* $\mathscr{P}_0$. Assume the system to be in state $x \in \mathscr{X}$. Upon observing $x$, the controller takes action $a \in \mathscr{A}$, which causes the system to perform a state transition associated with a corresponding reward to the controller. We assume the system to behave stochastically so that there is uncertainty regarding the new state $y \in \mathscr{X}$ of the system as well as the associated reward $\rho \in \mathbb{R}$. We can only provide the probability $\mathscr{P}_0(y, \rho|x, a)$ that the system transits from $x$ to $y$ with reward $r$ upon action $a$. Formally, for each state $x \in \mathscr{X}$ and action $a \in \mathscr{A}$ let $\mathscr{P}_0( \cdot \ |x, a)$ denote a probability measure on the measurable space $(\mathscr{X} \times \mathbb{R}, \sigma(\mathscr{X} \times \mathbb{R}))$, where $\sigma(\mathscr{X} \times \mathbb{R})$ is the $\sigma$-algebra generated by $\mathscr{X} \times \mathbb{R}$. In other words, for each $(x, a) \in \mathscr{X} \times \mathscr{A}$, the probability kernel $\mathscr{P}_0$ gives rise to the probability space $(\mathscr{X} \times \mathbb{R}, \sigma(\mathscr{X} \times \mathbb{R}), \mathscr{P}_0( \cdot \ |x, a))$. Then we define a *Markov decision process*

$$\mathscr{M} := (\mathscr{X}, \mathscr{A}, \mathscr{P}_0) \tag{13.1}$$

to be a set of states, actions, and an assigned probability kernel. As we will shortly see, $\mathscr{M}$ directly induces a stochastic process, which gives $\mathscr{M}$ its name. $\mathscr{P}_0$ directly determines the *state transition probability*

$$P(x, a, y) := \mathscr{P}_0(\{y\} \times \mathbb{R} \mid x, a) \tag{13.2}$$

for $(x, a, y) \in \mathscr{X} \times \mathscr{A} \times \mathscr{X}$, which denotes the probability that the system transits from state $x$ to state $y$ upon action $a$ associated with any reward as indicated by the argument $\{y\} \times \mathbb{R}$. Further, $\mathscr{P}_0$ determines the expected reward upon action $a$ and thus the *immediate reward function*

$$r : \mathscr{A} \rightarrow \mathbb{R} \tag{13.3}$$

$$r(x, a) := \mathbb{E}\left[R_{(x,a)}\right] \tag{13.4}$$

where the random variables $Y_{(x,a)}$ and $R_{(x,a)}$ are distributed according to

$$\left(Y_{(x,a)}, R_{(x,a)}\right) \sim \mathscr{P}_0( \cdot \ |x, a). \tag{13.5}$$

We assume all rewards to be bound such that

$$\exists \hat{R} > 0 \ \forall (x, a) \in \mathscr{X} \times \mathscr{A} : |R_{(x,a)} \leq \hat{R}| \tag{13.6}$$

almost surely. This also bounds the expected reward

$$\|r\|_\infty = \sup_{(x,a) \in \mathscr{X} \times \mathscr{A}} |r(x, a)| \leq \hat{R}. \tag{13.7}$$

The repeated loop of state observation and action by the controller, state transition by the system, and resulting reward generation gives rise to the discrete time stochastic process $(X_t, A_t, R_{t+1})_{t \in \mathbb{N}}$, where transition states and associated rewards are distributed according to the probability kernel $(X_{t+1}, R_{t+1}) \sim \mathscr{P}_0( \cdot \ |X_t, A_t)$. The probability that the system transits from state $x \in \mathcal{X}$ to state $\in \mathcal{X}$ upon controller action $a \in \mathcal{A}$ is then given by the state transition probability

$$p(X_{t+1} = y | X_t = x, A_t = a) = P(x, a, y). \tag{13.8}$$

The reward of this transition is expected to be

$$\mathbb{E}[R_{t+1} | X_t, A_t] = r(X_t, A_t). \tag{13.9}$$

Next we formalize the process of action selection by the controller in more detail. We assume the controller makes decisions based on the whole history of actions, state transitions, and associated rewards. Formally, this is captured by an infinite sequence of probability kernels $(\pi_t)_{t \in \mathbb{N}}$, each mapping the process history to probability distributions over $\mathcal{A}$. The decision making by the controller is then determined by the current system state and experience of the past:

$$\forall a \in \mathcal{A} : \pi_t(a) = \pi_t(a | x_0, a_0, r_0, \ldots, x_{t-1}, a_{t-1}, r_{t-1}, x_t). \tag{13.10}$$

We refer to the sequence $(\pi_t)_{t \in \mathbb{N}}$ as a **behavior** and denote the set of all possible behaviors as $\Pi$. An initial system sate $X_0 \in \mathcal{X}$ and a behavior fully govern the process $(X_t, \Lambda_t, R_{t+1})_{t \in \mathbb{N}}$. A controller that behaves according to $(\pi_t)_{t \in \mathbb{N}}$ accumulates the *total discounted sum of rewards*, also called *return*,

$$\mathcal{R} = \sum_{t=0}^{\infty} \gamma^t R_{t+1}, \tag{13.11}$$

where $\gamma \in [0, 1]$ is a discount factor. A lower value of $\gamma$ prioritizes rewards in the near future while discounting rewards in the far future and vice versa. We already stated that the overall goal of the controller is to maximize its expected return. Such maximization requires the controller to behave optimally.

We can identify two special classes of behavior, namely, *stochastic stationary policies* and *deterministic stationary policies*. Stochastic stationary policies

$$\pi : \mathcal{X} \to D(\mathcal{A}, \sigma(\mathcal{A})), \tag{13.12}$$

map system states to probability distributions (indicated by $D$) over the action space. For $\pi(X) = \pi' \in D(\mathcal{A}, \sigma(\mathcal{A}))$ we directly write

$$A_t \sim \pi( \cdot | X_t) \tag{13.13}$$

instead of $A_t \sim \pi'( \cdot | X_t)$ in the following. For our purposes, this short notation does not introduce ambiguity. Deterministic stationary policies

$$\pi : \mathcal{X} \to \mathcal{A}, \ A_t = \pi(X_t) \tag{13.14}$$

assign a fixed predefined action $A_t$ to each observed state $X_t$. Such deterministic policies are special cases of stochastic stationary policies: Determinism corresponds to distributions with $\pi(A_t | X_t) = 1$ such that the probability mass of $\pi$ for other actions than $A_t$ is distributed only on a null set in $\mathcal{A} \setminus \{A_t\}$.

### 13.2.2.2   Value functions

We define the *value function* for states $x \in \mathcal{X}$ to be the expected total reward

$$V^{\pi}(x) := \mathbb{E}\left[\sum_{t=0}^{\infty} \gamma^t R_{t+1} | X_0 = x\right] \tag{13.15}$$

the controller accumulates when behaving according to $\pi \in \Pi$. This gives rise to the *optimal value function* $V^* : \mathcal{X} \to \mathbb{R}$ which indicates the highest possible return for the controller interacting with a system starting in state $x$. With this in mind, we define the *optimal behavior* to achieve optimal return values for all initial states $x \in \mathcal{X}$. In other words, an optimal behavior yields the optimal return value

$$V^*(x) = \sup_{\pi \in \Pi} V^{\pi}(x). \tag{13.16}$$

Similarly, we define the *action-value function*

$$Q^{\pi} : \mathcal{X} \times \mathcal{A} \to \mathbb{R}, \ Q^{\pi}(x,a) := \mathbb{E}\left[\sum_{t=0}^{\infty} \gamma^t R_{t+1} | X_0 = x, A_0 = a\right] \tag{13.17}$$

to be the expected return when initially reacting with action $a \in \mathcal{A}$ to system state $x \in \mathcal{X}$ and then following behavior $\pi \in \Pi$. Analog to the above, let $Q^*(x, a) : \mathcal{X} \times \mathcal{A} \to \mathbb{R}$ denote the *optimal action-value function*. We refer to an action that maximizes $Q(x, \cdot)$ as a *greedy action* and to a policy that always prioritizes greedy actions as a *greedy policy*. With this notation in mind, we can already state the Bellman equation

$$V^{\pi}(x) = r(x, \pi(x)) + \gamma \sum_{y \in \mathcal{X}} P(x, \pi(x), y) V^{\pi}(y). \tag{13.18}$$

The Bellman equation shall for now close our presentation of Markov decision processes and we refer to Szepesvári [49] for a more comprehensive introduction to this theory. The Bellman equations will guide us in constructing reward maximization strategies in later sections. In essence, they allow us to break down our overall goal of maximizing code coverage during fuzzing into smaller and local subproblems. This motivates the algorithms of Part 13.3, where we predefine policies that lead to determined fuzzing behavior. Further, the Bellman equations give rise to the algorithms for reinforcement learning fuzzers as discussed in Part 13.4. Such algorithms mimic learning behavior and self-adapt their policies as given in (13.10).

### 13.2.3   Fuzzing as a Markov decision process

Now that we know the nature of fuzzing and the language of decision processes as formulated in Section 13.2.2, we enter the final phase of constructing our mathematical model. In the following we formulate each part of the generic architecture for feedback fuzzers (as presented in Section 13.2.1.3 and depicted in Figure 13.2) in the language of probability theory. This reformulation directly connects fuzzing with the theory of stochastic processes. Translating all essential aspects of fuzzing into abstract system states, controller actions, and process rewards opens the door for applying powerful methods from the field of search optimization and reinforcement

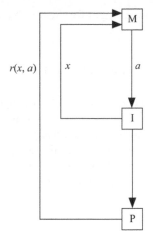

*Figure 13.4   Modeling fuzzing as a Markov decision process*

learning. In the following sections, we map the states $x$, actions $a$, and rewards $r(x, a)$ of a Markov decision process $\mathcal{M}$ (see (13.1)) to their fuzzing counterparts as depicted in Figure 13.4.

### 13.2.3.1   States

In this section, we introduce the states of feedback-driven fuzzing as input strings of symbols. The input $x \in \Sigma^*$ as a string of symbols within an alphabet $\Sigma$ further gives rise to a multitude of string features we could take into account for adapting the policy. The spectrum reaches from processed characteristics such as entropy of fractions of the input to augmented input fractions obtained from dynamic taint analysis. While we operate on the bit level in Sections 13.3 and 13.4 of this chapter, we do not limit our approach to this choice and formulate our model to be compatible with generic alphabets $\Sigma$.

We can consider the system that the reinforcement learning agent learns to interact with to be a raw input string of alphabet symbols $\Sigma$. To realize this, we define the states that the agent observes to be substrings of consecutive symbols within such an input. Formally, let $\Sigma$ denote a finite set of symbols. The set of possible target program inputs $\mathcal{I}$ written in this alphabet is then defined by the Kleene closure $\mathcal{I} := \Sigma^*$. For an input string $x = (x_1, \ldots, x_n) \in \mathcal{I}$ let

$$S(x) := \{(x_{1+i}, \ldots, x_{m+i}) \mid i \geq 0, \ m + i \leq n)\} \tag{13.19}$$

denote the set of all substrings of $x$. Clearly, $\cup_{x \in \mathcal{I}} S(x) = \mathcal{I}$ holds. We define the states of our Markov decision process to be

$$\mathcal{X} := \mathcal{I} = \Sigma^*. \tag{13.20}$$

In the following, $x \in \mathscr{I}$ denotes an input for the target program and $x' \in S(x) \subset \mathscr{I}$ a substring of this input.

*State features*

Based on the raw input strings, we can extract further refined state features as indicated in the following examples.

*Offset and Width* Again, let $\mathscr{I} = \Sigma^*$ denote the input space. For the given seed $x \in \mathscr{I}$ we can extract a strict substring $x' \in S(x)$ at offset $o \in \{0, \ldots, |x| - |x'|\}$ of width $|x'|$ as state features. In words, the reinforcement agent observes a fragment of the whole system via the substring $x'$. In this setting, we can specifically define actions to move the offset and vary the width of the observed substring.

*String Entropy* Let $|x'| = n$ denote the length of a string $x' = (x'_1, \ldots, x'_n) \in \mathscr{I}$. The entropy of $x'$ is then defined as

$$H(x') = \sum_{s \in \sigma(x')} p_s \log(p_s^{-1}), \tag{13.21}$$

where $\sigma(x')$ denotes the set of symbols represented in $x'$ and $p_s$ the probability of appearance of symbol $s$ in string $x'$. As possible state we could take this entropy of substrings of an input $x$ into account. The fuzzer then observes the changes in entropy during the fuzzing process.

*Tainted bytes* We can further augment the input with taint information extracted from target program execution. Here, each symbol in $x'$ is tracked with regard to subroutines that access it during execution. Symbols that are processed by the same subroutines are then grouped together and assigned with a label. These labels can then be taken into account as features for reinforcement learning. For example, Cui *et al.* [50] can automatically detect record sequences and types in the input by identification of chunks based on taint tracking input data in respective subroutine calls. Similarly, the authors of [51] apply dynamic tainting to identify failure-relevant inputs. Another recent approach was proposed by Höschele *et al.* [52], who mine input grammars from valid inputs based on feedback from dynamic instrumentation of the target by tracking input characters.

Since state-of-the-art taint tracking is computationally too expensive, we leave this set of features for future work.

### 13.2.3.2 Actions

In this section, we introduce reinforcement fuzzing actions as rewriting rules for symbols in $x$.

Similar to the one-step rewriting relations in a semi-Thue system, we define the set of possible actions $\mathscr{A}$ of our Markov decision process to be random variables mapping substrings of an input to probabilistic rewriting rules

$$\mathscr{A} := \{a : \mathscr{I} \rightarrow (\mathscr{I} \times \mathscr{I}, \mathscr{F}, P) \mid a \sim \pi(x)\}, \tag{13.22}$$

where $\mathscr{F} = \sigma(\mathscr{I} \times \mathscr{I})$ denotes the $\sigma$-algebra of the sample space $(\mathscr{I} \times \mathscr{I})$ and $P$ gives the probability for a given rewrite rule.

In the upcoming sections of this chapter, we define both probabilistic and deterministic actions. This is still in line with our definition in (13.22), where deterministic actions $a(x) = (x, x')$ correspond to $P((x, x')) = 1$ almost surely. Examples for probabilistic actions are random bit flips and shuffling bytes and sequences of bytes within $x$, while deterministic actions include string manipulation based on symbolic execution (as presented in [53]) and insertion of dictionary tokens.

The choice of actions is a crucial design decision for feedback-driven fuzzing. We experiment with a whole set of different actions in the following presentation and describe them in further detail in the corresponding sections. In fact, one major difference between Parts 13.3 and 13.4 is how the fuzzer chooses between a set of given actions: While Part 13.3 discusses predefined behavior, where actions are given by a deterministic policy $a = \pi(x)$, Part 13.4 deals with actions $a \sim \pi(x)$ distributed according to a stochastic policy. In the latter case, we will show that reinforcement fuzzing is able to learn a high rewarding policy, i.e., picking high rewarding actions given observed states $x$.

### 13.2.3.3 Rewards

We define rewards for both characteristics of the performed action and program execution of the generated input independently, i.e.,

$$R(x, a) = E(x) + G(a). \tag{13.23}$$

As described in Section 13.2.2, the stochastic variables $(y(x, a), R(x, a))$ are distributed according to $P_0(\cdot | x, a)$. $G$ is provided by performing action $a$ on $x$ to generate a new mutation and $E$ measured during execution of the target program with input $x$.

We experiment with $E$ providing number of newly discovered basic blocks, execution path length, and the execution time of the target that processes the input $x$. Formally, let $c_x$ denote the execution path the target program takes when processing input $x$ and $B(c_x)$ the set of unique basic blocks of this path. Here, we define a basic block to be a sequence of instructions without branch instructions between block entry and exit. Given a history of previously processed inputs $I' \subset I$, we can write the number of newly discovered blocks as

$$E_1(x, I') := \left| B(c_x) \setminus \left( \bigcup_{\chi \in I'} B(c_\chi) \right) \right|. \tag{13.24}$$

Another choice of $E$ is taking the execution time $E_2 = T(x)$ of the target into account. Similarly, we could define $G$ to be the time it takes to generate a mutation based on the seed $x$. This would reinforce the fuzzer to find a balance between coverage advancements and action-processing costs.

The idea to generate program inputs that maximize execution path coverage in order to trigger vulnerabilities has been discussed in the field of test case prioritization some time ago, see, e.g., [54,55] for a comparison of coverage-based techniques. Rebert *et al.* [56] discuss and compare methods to gain optimal seed selection with respect to fuzzing, and their findings support our decision to select code coverage for evaluating the quality of test cases.

We could further introduce rewards based on the execution graph. For example, it is conceivable to distribute negative rewards for execution paths that correspond to error handling code or in turn reward paths that enter a desired code area. We leave such types of reward for future work and concentrate on coverage and time in the following.

## 13.3 Fuzzing with predefined behavior

In this section, we discuss fuzzing with predefined behavior. Now that we have a mathematical model for fuzzing, we can identify stochastic structures and processes underlying this model. The language of Markov decision processes allows us to directly translate the nature stochastic processes with well-known behavior into effective algorithms for software testing.

As introduced in (13.10), we refer to the sequence $(\pi_t)_{t\in\mathbb{N}}$ as a *behavior* and denote the set of all possible behaviors as $\Pi$. We can generally distinct the behaviors in two classes: policies based on stochastic processes whose behavior is well researched and policies based on learning processes whose behavior depends on the applied machine-learning methods. In this second part, we focus on the former class.

In Section 13.3.1, we investigate certain processes called Lévy flights that provably minimize search time in specific situations that suffice our conditions. The application of Lévy flights yields self-adaptive fuzzing behavior by adjusting the process parameters according to the feedback reward.

While the approach of Section 13.3.1 yields generally good results, it is purely stochastic in nature. However, reaching deep layers of a targeted program sometimes requires exact calculations, e.g., of checksums within the input. To pass the first parsing layers of the program, we enhance our mathematical model based on stochastics with powerful formal methods based on symbolic execution. This upgrade provides the best characteristics of both worlds: the properties of search optimization from stochastic processes and partial input correctness required for deep fuzzing. We discuss this approach in detail in [53].

Upgrading purely stochastic fuzzing with symbolic execution comes with a high price. Such formal methods are computationally expensive and slow our algorithms down. Therefore, instead of packing our efficient stochastic fuzzers with formal sandbags, in Section 13.3.2, we give them hints and guide them toward high rewarding input regions. This introduces an elegant way to combine stochastic with formal methods while keeping the overall fuzzing process efficient.

### 13.3.1 Hunting bugs with Lévy flight foraging

In this section, we describe a method for random testing of binary executables inspired by biology. We refer to [10,13] for a more detailed presentation of our ideas. In our approach, we introduce the first fuzzer based on a mathematical model for optimal foraging. To minimize search time for possible vulnerabilities, we generate test cases with Lévy flights in the input space. In order to dynamically adapt test generation behavior to actual path exploration performance, we define a suitable measure for quality evaluation of test cases. This measure takes into account previously discovered code

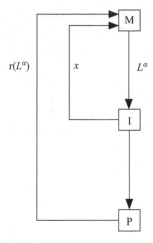

*Figure 13.5    Fuzzing with Lévy flights*

regions and allows us to construct a feedback mechanism. By controlling diffusivity of the test-case generating Lévy processes with evaluation feedback from dynamic instrumentation, we are able to define a fully self-adaptive fuzzing algorithm.

The overall approach of this section is depicted in Figure 13.5. The mutator engine (M), input (I), and target program (P) are connected via rewards, states, and actions as introduced in Section 13.2.3 of this chapter. Within the space of actions $\mathscr{A}$ as defined in (13.22), we focus on a special subset $\mathscr{L}^\alpha \subset \mathscr{A}$ based on Lévy flights. While the global behavior is determined by Lévy flights, the actual shapes of the flights are automatically adapted via parameters $\alpha$, which in turn are adjusted according to the reward $r(\mathscr{L}^\alpha)$. Here, the reward $R(x, a)$ as introduced in (13.23) is inferred from effects of Lévy flight actions denoted by $r(\mathscr{L}^\alpha)$.

In the course of researching new effective search strategies, we find similar problems in biology, particularly in the field of optimal foraging. A variety of biological systems let us observe optimal strategies for finding energy sources by simultaneously avoiding predators. When we identify sources of food with possible vulnerabilities in binary executables and predators with the overhead of execution runtime, we are inspired to adapt mathematical models of optimal foraging to test case generation. This approach enables us to take stochastic models of optimal foraging as a basis for input mutation. In particular, we rely on Lévy flights to search for bug triggering test cases in input space.

Before summarizing our contributions, we first give some short background on optimal foraging and the Lévy flight hypothesis.

### 13.3.1.1    Optimal foraging

Observing biological systems has led to speculation that there might be simple laws of motion for animals searching for sources of energy in the face of predators. Regardless of whether we look at bumblebees[57], fish and hunting marine predators in the sea

[58,59], grey seals [60], spider monkeys [61], the flight search patterns of albatrosses [62], the wandering of reindeer [63], the reaction pathways of DNA-binding proteins [64], or the neutralization of pathogens by white blood cells [65], we can discover emerging movement patterns all those examples have in common. Mathematical modeling of such common patterns is an active field of research in biology and is more generally referred to as *movement ecology*. While the physics of foraging [66] provides us several possible models our choice is not guided by accuracy with respect to the biological process but by minimization of software bug search time. This leads us to the special class of stochastic processes called *Lévy flights*.

### 13.3.1.2    Lévy flight hypothesis

Within the variety of models for optimal foraging Lévy flights have several characteristic properties that show promise for software testing. In particular, the Lévy flight hypothesis accentuates the most significant property of these kinds of stochastic processes for our purposes. It states that Lévy flights minimize search time when foraging sources of food that are sparsely and randomly distributed, resting, and refillable. These assumptions match to the properties of bugs in software (with the interpretation that *refillable* translates to the fact that software bugs stay until fix). In addition to the mathematical Lévy flight hypothesis, the Lévy flight *foraging* hypothesis in theoretical biology states that these processes actually model real foraging behavior in certain biological systems due to natural selection. The Lévy flight hypothesis constitutes the major connection link between optimal foraging theory and random software testing.

### 13.3.1.3    Swarm behavior

While moving patterns of foraging animals inspire us to define the behavior of a single fuzzer, we are further guided by biology when accumulating multiple fuzzer instances to a parallelized testing framework. Again we take a look at nature to discover a whole branch of science that researches swarm behavior [67]. For example, the ants of a colony collectively find the shortest path to a food source. Based on simple rules for modeling natural swarm behavior, we construct a *fuzzing swarm* that mimics colony clustering observed in biology. Our algorithm navigates the fuzzing swarm without a central control and provides self-organization of the fuzzers as they flexibly adapt to the binary structure under test.

In [10,13], we propose a novel method for random software testing based on the theory of optimal foraging. In summary, we make the following contributions:

- We introduce a novel fuzzing method based on Lévy flights in the input space in order to maximize coverage of execution paths.
- We define a suitable measure for quality evaluation of test cases in input space with respect to previously explored code regions.
- In order to control diffusivity of the test generation processes, we define a feedback mechanism connecting current path exploration performance to the test generation module.
- We enable self-adaptive fuzzing behavior by adjusting the Lévy flight parameters according to feedback from dynamic instrumentation of the target executable.

- We aggregate multiple instances of such Lévy flights to fuzzing swarms which reveal flexible, robust, decentralized, and self-organized behavior.
- We implement the presented algorithm to show the feasibility of our approach.

Inspired by moving patterns of foraging animals we introduce the first self-adaptive fuzzer based on Lévy flights. Just like search patterns in biology have evolved to optimal foraging strategies due to natural selection, so have evolved mathematical models to describe those patterns. Lévy flights are emerging as successful models for describing optimal search behavior, which leads us to their application of hunting bugs in binary executables. By defining corresponding stochastic processes within the input space of the program under test, we achieve an effective new method for test case generation. Further, we define an algorithm that dynamically controls diffusivity of the defined Lévy flights depending on actual quality of generated test cases. To achieve this, we construct a measure of quality for new test cases that takes already explored execution paths into account. During fuzzing, the quality of actually generated test cases is constantly forwarded to the test case generating Lévy flights. High-quality test case generation with respect to path coverage causes the Lévy flight to enter sub-diffusion and focus its search on nearby inputs, whereas a low-quality rating results in super-diffusion and expanding search behavior. This feedback loop yields a fully self-adaptive fuzzer. Inspired by the collective behavior of certain animal colonies, we aggregate multiple individual fuzzers to a fuzzing swarm which is guided by simple rules to reveal flexible, robust, decentralized, and self-organized behavior. Our proposed algorithm is modular in the sense that it allows integration of other fuzzing goals beyond code coverage, which is subject to future work.

## 13.3.2 Guiding a colony of Fuzzers with chemotaxis

In this section, we introduce an elegant way to combine stochastic with formal methods while keeping the overall fuzzing process efficient. We refer to [11,14] for a more detailed presentation of our ideas. Blending stochastic fuzzing with, e.g., symbolic methods [53] for fuzzing combines the best of both worlds but also comes with a high price: formal methods are computationally expensive and slow our algorithms down. Larger fuzzing campaigns would therefore greatly benefit, if fast and efficient *worker* fuzzers could run isolated from symbolic execution while being guided by explorers. How can we create an information channel between isolated fuzzing instances in order to allow such strategies? We approach this question via a state synchronization mechanism.

In [11,14], we present a biology-inspired method for large-scale fuzzing to detect vulnerabilities in binary executables. In our approach, we deploy small groups of feedback-driven explorers that guide colonies of high throughput fuzzers to promising regions in input space. We achieve this by applying the biological concept of chemotaxis: the explorer fuzzers mark test case regions that drive the target binary to previously undiscovered execution paths with an attractant. This allows us to construct a force of attraction that draws the trailing fuzzers to high-quality test cases. By introducing hierarchies of explorers, we construct a colony of fuzzers that is divided into multiple subgroups. Each subgroup is guiding a trailing group and simultaneously drawn itself by the traces of their respective explorers. We implement a prototype and evaluate our presented algorithm to show the feasibility of our approach.

As introduced in Section 13.2.1 of this chapter, state-of-the-art fuzzing frameworks all share one overall goal: generating and pitching suitable program inputs into the target in order to eventually trigger an exploitable bug. For suchlike bug hunting there is a straight forward track: The more input we generate to test a binary target the more code coverage we achieve during program execution and the more likely we will find what we are looking for. This results in parallel large-scale testing by running distributed fuzzer instances on a computer cluster. However, state-of-the-art in distributed large-scale fuzzing basically reduces to pure parallelization. Recent research focuses on advancing single fuzzers and optimal scheduling of fuzzers, test case corpora, and targets during fuzzing campaigns [68]. But how can we optimize the interaction between fuzzers? How can we transform a cluster of isolated fuzzers into a colony that works together and collectively adapts to the binary under test?

Inspired by biology, two observations in particular guide our research: colonies with dedicated explorers and the concept of chemotaxis.

### 13.3.2.1 Colonies with explorers

Several species such as honeybees, ants, rats, and bats reveal dedicated exploring behavior of colony individuals that primarily function as scouts. Investigation of the environment by just a small fraction of explorers seems to be an efficient way for some colonies to gain information regarding the surrounding territory. In case the explorer found an interesting spot (for example a source of food during foraging), it reports its findings back to the colony. The famous dance of the honeybees [69] is just one example for this behavior. Hence, we define dedicated subgroups of explorer fuzzers that guide higher throughput worker fuzzers. In fact, we can divide modern fuzzing frameworks into two categories, namely, (1) feedback fuzzers that instrument their targets in order to gain runtime information during program execution and (2) black-box fuzzers that are blind to what happens during execution and only see program crashes in the case of a triggered bug. While fuzzers of the first category (including white-box and evolutionary fuzzers) are relatively slow, they nowadays achieve similar levels of code coverage compared to traditional fast executing black-box fuzzers. Both categories, the relatively slow feedback driven explorers as well as the fast and efficient black-box worker fuzzers have their right to exist in modern fuzzing campaigns and both provide comparable results. Inspired by colony behavior in biology, is there a way to combine the explorer sight into runtime (gained by dynamic instrumentation) with the speed of black-box worker fuzzers? How can we achieve guidance by the explorers and transfer information to the blind black-box fuzzers? This brings us to the second observation found in biology.

### 13.3.2.2 Chemotaxis

Regardless, if we look at bacteria, mold fungus, termites, ciliates, or algae, all those species have one thing in common: they make use of chemical substances to transmit information between individuals of the colony in order to trigger collective behavior. The movement of organisms responding to chemical stimuli is called *chemotaxis*.

Positive chemotaxis causes the individuals to move towards regions of higher concentration of an attractant. Ant colonies [70] coordinating their foraging behavior using attracting trail pheromones impressively illustrate the power of chemotaxis. Can we mimic social behavior of biological colonies using the concept of chemotaxis?

In this section, we construct an algorithm for distributed large-scale fuzzing that equips feedback-driven explorer fuzzers with the ability to attract high throughput fuzzers by marking regions in the input space with an attractant. First, we develop the main idea on a single subgroup of explorers guiding a single subgroup of workers: by controlling the attractant concentration among promising test case regions, the *seeing* feedback-driven explorers guide the colony of *blind* (but fast) black-box fuzzers in order to maximize code coverage. Second, we generalize this approach to multiple hierarchies of fuzzers: we introduce multiple hierarchies of explorers by further subdividing our scouts according to their overall test case throughput.

In [11,14], we make the following contributions:

- We introduce a novel method for distributed large-scale fuzzing in computer clusters based on the biological concept of chemotaxis in order to maximize coverage of execution paths in the target under test.
- We construct a mechanism for distributing attractants in input space and define the resulting force field of attraction exerted on high throughput fuzzers.
- We implement and evaluate our presented algorithm to show the feasibility of our approach.

Inspired by insect and animal colonies that reveal a rich diversity of scouts and explorers, we introduce the first framework for large-scale random testing of binary executables based on the concept of chemotaxis. In order to maximize coverage of execution paths in the target under test, we draw fast and efficient (but blind regarding runtime information) black-box workers to regions in input space discovered by feedback-driven explorers. We realize this by constructing a mechanism for distributing attractants in input space and defining the resulting force field of attraction exerted on black-box fuzzers. This approach combines the best of both worlds: the sight into runtime information from dynamic instrumentation by the explorers and the speed of black-box worker fuzzers. Next, we generalize this approach to multiple hierarchies of fuzzers to capture their attraction network in a graph. Such a graph definition is especially useful when distributing fuzzing instances on actual computing clusters, as we can adjust the graph of attraction to the hardware infrastructure. We show the feasibility of our approach by evaluating it on a real-world target with different parameter settings. Further, we discuss modifications and expansions of our algorithm. Especially customized testing frameworks would allow us to distribute attractant concentration significantly more fine-grained, which probably results in faster code coverage and is subject to future work.

## 13.4   Fuzzing with learning behavior

We finally enter the third and last phase of our journey. Let us take the bird's eye view first. Our mathematical model of Section 13.2 enabled us to translate specific stochastic processes into algorithms for software testing in Section 13.3. The model spans a rich world that invites for exploration with different techniques and search strategies. Up to now, we only explored a small part of this world as we did not take multiple action classes or actual state structures into account. If we do so, we need to enhance our equipment and means of transportation. How can we explore the full range of our model? In this section, we approach this question with some help from the field of machine learning.

Considering the full capabilities of our model, we soon realize the complexity we have to deal with. In the reduced setting of similar actions and rewards independent of states, we were able to find adequate fuzzing strategies: we got inspired by biology in choosing processes with suitable characteristics which directly determine fuzzing behavior (as formalized in (13.10)). For example, while the algorithm introduced in Section 13.3.1 self-adapts its diffusivity and corresponding actions according to the received reward, it always performs a Lévy flight in nature. From the bird's eye view, we constructed a subset of actions with known similar characteristics within $\mathscr{A}$ (as defined in (13.22)) based on stochastic processes and defined a reward-based decision mechanism for the actions to take (in terms of (13.23)).

Let us enlarge our problem space by (1) offering the system multiple different classes of actions and (2) taking the system state into account. In this setting, two questions arise:

- Do optimal behaviors $(\pi_t)_{t\in\mathbb{N}} \in \Pi$ exist?
- Is the definition of such a behavior accessible for a human?

For discrete and finite state and action spaces, Watkins [71] theoretically provides a positive answer to the first question. However, our state space (as defined in (13.20)) is huge, and our action-value function $Q(x, a)$ cannot be represented in a look-up table. Therefore, we are in a similar situation as in chess or the game of Go: while an optimal strategy might exist, we are currently bound to playing the game in the search for it. In the same spirit, while we currently cannot give a satisfactory answer to the first question, we can play the game against the program. In fact, we can apply the same techniques that achieved super-human behavior in Backgammon [5,6], Atari games [7], and the game of Go [8]. We can do so because the mathematical model of Section 13.2 provides a direct interface to reinforcement learning. And similar to gaming, we expect that the definition of winning behaviors for fuzzing are not accessible for the human, especially if we take into account states from binary input. In the following, we will see that deep $Q$ learning turns out to be a fruitful new direction in software testing.

In [12], we formulate random test generation for fuzzing as a reinforcement learning problem (as depicted in Figure 13.6). Modeling basic characteristics of random test generation as a Markov decision process as described in detail in Section 13.2 enables us to apply state-of-the-art deep $Q$-learning algorithms that optimize predefined rewards measured during runtime of the program under test. By observing the reward effects caused by mutating with a set of actions performed on the seed file, the fuzzing agent learns a policy that converges to the optimal behavior within the defined setting. To indicate the feasibility of our approach, we implement and

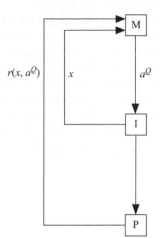

*Figure 13.6    Reinforcement fuzzing*

evaluate a prototype of such a reinforcement learning agent. We experiment with two different types of rewards to show that our fuzzing algorithm learns to select highly rewarded string mutation actions better than a baseline of purely random strategies.

Our mathematical model presented in Section 13.2 theoretically captures rewards that directly take the system state as defined in (13.23) into account. Further, instead of a single class of similar actions, our model permits a generic actions space $\mathscr{A}$ (as defined in (13.22)) that covers all possible string mutations. As discussed at the beginning of this part, in the following we will explore the full range of our model: We enlarge our problem space by offering the system multiple different classes of actions and taking the system state into account.

We propose an effective fuzzing method within the given problem space by formulating random test generation for fuzzing as a reinforcement learning problem. The reinforcement learning setting defines an agent that interacts with a system. Each performed action causes a state transition of the system. Upon each performed action, the agent observes the next state and receives a reward. The goal of the agent is to maximize the total reward over time. We introduced this setting in Section 13.2 of this chapter. In particular, we experiment with $Q$-learning, that just recently has successfully applied similarly complex scenarios [5–8].

In [12], we make the following contributions:

- We formulate fuzzing as a reinforcement learning problem.
- We introduce a fuzzing algorithm based on deep $Q$-learning that learns to choose highly rewarded actions given an observed input string.
- We implement and evaluate a prototype of our defined approach.

Inspired by the similar nature of feedback-driven random testing and reinforcement learning, we introduce the first fuzzer that learns to perform highly rewarded mutations with respect to a predefined search heuristics. By automatically rewarding runtime characteristics of the target program, we obtain inputs that likely drive program execution toward a predefined goal, e.g., maximization of code coverage or processing time. To achieve this, we formulate fuzzing as a reinforcement learning problem based on the language of Markov decision processes as introduced in Section 13.2 of this chapter. This allows us to construct an algorithm based on deep $Q$-learning that learns to choose highly rewarded actions given an input seed. Adapting the $Q$ function iteratively yields a policy that encodes the behavior of the Markov decision process. We indicate the feasibility of our approach by implementing a prototype targeted against PDF parsers.

## 13.5    Outlook

We embed our thoughts into a broader view on the subject and open the gates to two general directions for future research.

### 13.5.1    Hierarchies of learning agents

Let us place two illustrative examples first. In order to drive our fuzzers toward a predefined goal, we gave them rewards as discussed in Section 13.2.3.3 to award good mutation actions and sanction ineffective ones. With the help of machine-learning techniques, we were able to take performed actions as well as raw system states into account for learning rewarding policies and therefore establishing effective behavior. We applied deep neural networks to be able to deal with the complex state structures. However, the measurements for the concrete values were quite simple. We measured coverage of code, execution time, or the time it takes to perform the mutation. We did this because these values are correlated with finding bugs fast (as discussed in detail in Section 13.2). How can we bridge those indirect measures and reward the presence or neighborhood of bugs directly? If we could find a way to detect characteristic conditions of certain bug classes during program execution, we could feedback this information as a reward. If we could further find some kind of similarity measure, we could define a distance to such bug conditions and directly reward the fuzzer to generate inputs that drive the program towards the bug. Machine-learning techniques helped us to deal with complex actions and system states in Section 13.4. Intuitively, machine learning might also help us in detecting complex bug characteristics in the program flow.

Further, we could proceed to research the interaction between multiple fuzzers. In Section 13.3.2, we discussed an approach to organize large-scale fuzzing in computer clusters. In the spirit of Section 13.4, we could introduce learning techniques to this interaction. A swarm of fuzzers that is controlled by an overall learning agent might reveal efficient strategies for larger fuzzing campaigns.

Both examples, the sensing mechanism for characteristic bug classes and the controlling agent for a swarm of fuzzers, have one thing in common: they introduce machine learning into the overall testing process, the former via subagents within the feedback-loop, the latter via super-agents above multiple fuzzing instances. Considering such hierarchies of learning agents might be a fruitful new direction in software testing.

### 13.5.2 Alternative models

The work at hand was motivated by two research challenges, namely, to connect probability theory to software testing and to translate stochastic processes into fuzzing algorithms. We approached this adventure with constructing a mathematical model for fuzzing. All results of the work at hand are findings from explorations within this model. It is important to realize that this model is just one possibility within a manifold of alternatives. Other models will most likely reveal very different techniques. To illustrate this thought very impressively, let us have a look at the way we defined actions. In Section 13.2.3.2, we modeled actions as random variables mapping substrings of an input to probabilistic rewriting rules. Let us consider the following variant: what if actions could not only transform the input of the program under test but also the program itself? Imagine an action that transforms a program into representations that are more accessible to fuzzing. As an example, such an action could replace compare instructions with large operands by multiple comparisons with small operands, increasing the probability to pass them during input generation. Such actions that translate the target into equivalent representations open the door to completely undiscovered fields of research. Similarly, alternative mathematical models will reveal interesting new characteristics and novel approaches for testing.

## 13.6 Conclusion

This conclusion ends our journey through the world of nature-inspired fuzzing. Motivated by the urgent need for automated software testing and the lack of probability theory in state-of-the-art random testing tools, we set the target to connect the deep knowledge of stochastic processes with software testing. We achieved this by modeling feedback-driven fuzzing in the language of Markov decision processes in Section 13.2. This formulation allowed us to translate processes with suitable characteristics into concrete fuzzing algorithms in Section 13.3. In order to explore the full capabilities of our mathematical model, we made use of very recent results from the field of reinforcement learning. Similar to chess and the game of Go, we conjecture that machine-learning techniques will continue to surpass purely human fuzzing strategies in the future.

All presented ideas are closely related to processes in nature. We were inspired by animal foraging, swarm theory, the concept of chemotaxis, colonies with dedicated explorers, and the psychology of animal learning. We strongly believe that future nature-inspired approaches will reveal exciting discoveries in vulnerability research.

# References

[1]    Hacking I. The emergence of probability: A philosophical study of early ideas about probability, induction and statistical inference. Cambridge University Press, Cambridge; 2006.

[2]    Kolmogoroff A. Grundbegriffe der Wahrscheinlichkeitsrechnung. Springer, Springer-Verlag, Berlin, Heidelberg; 1933.

[3]    Jacod J, Protter P. Probability essentials. Springer Science & Business Media, Springer-Verlag, Berlin, Heidelberg; 2004.

[4]    Wiener N. Cybernetics: Or control and communication in the animal and the machine. vol. 25. MIT Press, Cambridge, MA; 1961.

[5]    Tesauro G. Practical Issues in Temporal Difference Learning. In: Advances in Neural Information Processing Systems; 1992. p. 259–266.

[6]    Tesauro G. TD-Gammon: A self-teaching backgammon program. In: Applications of Neural Networks. Springer, Springer-Verlag, Berlin, Heidelberg; 1995. p. 267–285.

[7]    Mnih V, Kavukcuoglu K, Silver D, *et al.* Human-level control through deep reinforcement learning. Nature. 2015;518(7540):529–533.

[8]    Silver D, Huang A, Maddison CJ, *et al.* Mastering the game of Go with deep neural networks and tree search. Nature. 2016;529(7587):484–489.

[9]    Sutton RS, Barto AG. Reinforcement learning: An introduction. MIT Press, Cambridge; 1998.

[10]   Böttinger K. Hunting Bugs with Lévy Flight Foraging. In: IEEE Symposium on Security and Privacy Workshops 2016; 2016. p. 111–117.

[11]   Böttinger K. Guiding a Colony of Black-box Fuzzers with Chemotaxis. In: IEEE Symposium on Security and Privacy Workshops 2017; 2017. p. 11–16.

[12]   Böttinger K, Singh R, Godefroid P. Deep Reinforcement Fuzzing. In: IEEE Symposium on Security and Privacy Workshops; 2018.

[13]   Böttinger K. Fuzzing binaries with Lévy flight swarms. EURASIP Journal on Information Security. 2016;28:1–10.

[14]   Böttinger K. Chemotactic test case recombination for large-scale fuzzing. Journal of Cyber Security and Mobility. 2017;5(4):269–286.

[15]   Kidwell PA, Williams MR. The calculating machines: Their history and development. MIT Press, Cambridge, MA; 1992.

[16]   Turing A. Checking a large routine. In: Report of a Conference on High Speed Automatic Calculating Machines. University Mathematical Laboratory, Cambridge, England; 1949. p. 67–69.

[17]   Morris FL, Jones CB. An early program proof by Alan Turing. IEEE Annals of the History of Computing. 1984;6(2):139–143.

[18]   Naur P. Proof of algorithms by general snapshots. BIT Numerical Mathematics. 1966;6(4):310–316.

[19]   Floyd RW. Assigning meanings to programs. Mathematical Aspects of Computer Science. 1967;19(19–32):1.

[20]   Hoare CAR. An axiomatic basis for computer programming. Communications of the ACM. 1969;12(10):576–580.

[21] Ruthruff J, Armstrong RC, Davis BG, *et al.* Leveraging formal methods and fuzzing to verify security and reliability properties of large-scale high-consequence systems. Sandia National Laboratories (SNL-CA), Livermore, CA, United States; 2012.

[22] Weinberg GM. Perfect software: And other Illusions about testing. Dorset House Publishing Co., New York; 2008.

[23] Salus PH, Vinton G. Casting the net: From ARPANET to Internet and beyond. Addison-Wesley Longman Publishing Co., Reading, MA; 1995.

[24] Hafner K, Lyon M. Where wizards stay up late: The origins of the Internet. Simon and Schuster, New York; 1998.

[25] Orman H. The Morris worm: A fifteen-year perspective. IEEE Security & Privacy. 2003;99(5):35–43.

[26] Duran JW, Ntafos SC. An evaluation of random testing. IEEE Transactions on Software Engineering. 1984;10(4):438–444. Available from: http://dx.doi.org/10.1109/TSE.1984.5010257.

[27] Duran JW, Ntafos S. A Report on Random Testing. In: Proceedings of the 5th International Conference on Software Engineering. IEEE Press; 1981. p. 179–183.

[28] Takanen A, DeMott J, Miller C. Fuzzing for software security testing and quality assurance. 1st ed. Artech House, Inc., Norwood, MA, USA; 2008.

[29] Miller BP, Fredriksen L, So B. An empirical study of the reliability of UNIX utilities. Communications of the ACM. 1990;33(12):32–44.

[30] Wüst K. Mikroprozessortechnik: Grundlagen, Architekturen, Schaltungstechnik und Betrieb von Mikroprozessoren und Mikrocontrollern. Springer-Verlag, Berlin, Heidelberg; 2010.

[31] Corporation I. Intel 64 and IA-32 architectures software developer manuals. Intel Corporation, Santa Clara, CA; 2016.

[32] Daniel P, Marco C. Understanding the Linux kernel. O'Reilly, Sebastopol, CA; 2007.

[33] Lewine D. POSIX programmers guide. O'Reilly, Sebastopol, CA; 1991.

[34] Durumeric Z, Kasten J, Adrian D, *et al.* The Matter of Heartbleed. In: Proceedings of the 2014 Conference on Internet Measurement Conference. ACM; 2014. p. 475–488.

[35] Van der Veen V, Dutt-Sharma N, Cavallaro L, *et al.* Memory Errors: The Past, the Present, and the Future. In: Research in Attacks, Intrusions, and Defenses; 2012. p. 86–106.

[36] Berghe CV, Riordan J, Piessens F, *et al.* A Vulnerability Taxonomy Methodology Applied to Web Services. In: Proceedings of the 10th Nordic Workshop on Secure IT Systems (NordSec 2005); 2005. p. 49–62.

[37] Mell P, Scarfone K, Romanosky S. Common vulnerability scoring system. IEEE Security & Privacy. 2006;4(6):1–23.

[38] Szekeres L, Payer M, Wei T, *et al.* Sok: Eternal War in Memory. In: Security and Privacy (SP), 2013 IEEE Symposium on. IEEE; 2013. p. 48–62. Available from: http://ieeexplore.ieee.org/xpls/abs_all.jsp?arnumber=6547101.

[39]    Hutchins M, Foster H, Goradia T, *et al.* Experiments of the Effectiveness of Dataflow- and Controlflow-based Test Adequacy Criteria. In: Proceedings of the 16th International Conference on Software Engineering. ICSE'94. Los Alamitos, CA, USA: IEEE Computer Society Press; 1994. p. 191–200. Available from: http://dl.acm.org/citation.cfm?id=257734.257766.

[40]    Cadar C, Ganesh V, Pawlowski PM, *et al.* EXE: automatically generating inputs of death. ACM Transactions on Information and System Security (TISSEC). 2008;12(2):10.

[41]    Sutton M, Greene A, Amini P. Fuzzing: Brute force vulnerability discovery. 1st ed. Addison-Wesley Professional, Boston, MA, USA; 2007.

[42]    Luk CK, Cohn R, Muth R, *et al.* Pin: Building Customized Program Analysis Tools with Dynamic Instrumentation. In: Proceedings of the 2005 ACM SIG-PLAN Conference on Programming Language Design and Implementation. PLDI'05. New York, NY, USA: ACM; 2005. p. 190–200.

[43]    Nethercote N, Seward J. Valgrind: A Framework for Heavyweight Dynamic Binary Instrumentation. In: Proceedings of the 28th ACM SIGPLAN Conference on Programming Language Design and Implementation. PLDI'07. New York, NY, USA: ACM; 2007. p. 89–100. Available from: http://doi.acm.org/10.1145/1250734.1250746.

[44]    Bruening D, Zhao Q, Amarasinghe S. Transparent Dynamic Instrumentation. In: Proceedings of the 8th ACM SIGPLAN/SIGOPS Conference on Virtual Execution Environments. VEE'12. New York, NY, USA: ACM; 2012. p. 133–144. Available from: http://doi.acm.org/10.1145/2151024.2151043.

[45]    Buck B, Hollingsworth JK. An API for runtime code patching. International Journal of High Performance Computing Applications. 2000;14(4):317–329. Available from: http://dx.doi.org/10.1177/109434200001400404.

[46]    Cantrill BM, Shapiro MW, Leventhal AH. Dynamic Instrumentation of Production Systems. In: Proceedings of the Annual Conference on USENIX Annual Technical Conference. ATEC'04. Berkeley, CA, USA: USENIX Association; 2004. Available from: http://dl.acm.org/citation. cfm?id=1247415.1247417.

[47]    Bellard F. QEMU, a Fast and Portable Dynamic Translator. In: USENIX Annual Technical Conference, FREENIX Track; 2005. p. 41–46.

[48]    Rawat S, Jain V, Kumar A, *et al.* VUzzer: Application-aware Evolutionary Fuzzing. In: Symposium on Network and Distributed System Security (NDSS); 2017.

[49]    Szepesvári C. Algorithms for reinforcement learning. Synthesis Lectures on Artificial Intelligence and Machine Learning. 2010;4(1):1–103.

[50]    Cui W, Peinado M, Chen K, *et al.* Tupni: Automatic Reverse Engineering of Input Formats. In: Proceedings of the 15th ACM Conference on Computer and Communications Security. CCS'08. New York, NY, USA: ACM; 2008. p. 391–402. Available from: http://doi.acm.org/10.1145/1455770.1455820.

[51]    Clause J, Orso A. Penumbra: Automatically Identifying Failure-relevant Inputs Using Dynamic Tainting. In: Proceedings of the Eighteenth International Symposium on Software Testing and Analysis. ISSTA'09. New York, NY,

USA: ACM; 2009. p. 249–260. Available from: http://doi.acm.org/10.1145/1572272.1572301.

[52] Höschele M, Zeller A. Mining Input Grammars with AUTOGRAM. In: Proceedings of the 39th International Conference on Software Engineering Companion. ICSE-C'17. Piscataway, NJ, USA: IEEE Press; 2017. p. 31–34. Available from: https://doi.org/10.1109/ICSE-C.2017.14.

[53] Böttinger K, Eckert C. DeepFuzz: Triggering Vulnerabilities Deeply Hidden in Binaries. In: Conference on Detection of Intrusions and Malware, and Vulnerability Assessment. Springer; 2016. p. 25–34.

[54] Leon D, Podgurski A. A Comparison of Coverage-Based and Distribution-Based Techniques for Filtering and Prioritizing Test Cases. In: Proceedings of the 14th International Symposium on Software Reliability Engineering. ISSRE'03. Washington, DC, USA: IEEE Computer Society; 2003. p. 442–456.

[55] Rothermel G, Untch RH, Chu C, *et al.* Test Case Prioritization: An Empirical Study. In: Proceedings of the IEEE International Conference on Software Maintenance. ICSM'99. Washington, DC, USA: IEEE Computer Society; 1999. p. 179–188.

[56] Rebert A, Cha SK, Avgerinos T, *et al.* Optimizing Seed Selection for Fuzzing. In: Proceedings of the 23rd USENIX Conference on Security Symposium. SEC'14. Berkeley, CA, USA: USENIX Association; 2014. p. 861–875.

[57] Lenz F, Ings TC, Chittka L, *et al.* Spatiotemporal dynamics of bumblebees foraging under predation risk. Physical Review Letters. 2012;108(9):098103.

[58] Viswanathan GM. Ecology: Fish in Lévy-flight foraging. Nature. 2010;465(7301):1018–1019.

[59] Humphries NE, Queiroz N, Dyer JR, *et al.* Environmental context explains Lévy and Brownian movement patterns of marine predators. Nature. 2010;465(7301):1066–1069.

[60] Austin D, Bowen WD, McMillan JI. Intraspecific variation in movement patterns: modeling individual behaviour in a large marine predator. Oikos. 2004;105:15–30.

[61] Ramos-Fernández G, Mateos JL, Miramontes O, *et al.* Lévy walk patterns in the foraging movements of spider monkeys (*Ateles geoffroyi*). Behavioral Ecology and Sociobiology. 2004;55(3):223–230.

[62] Viswanathan GM, Afanasyev V, Buldyrev S, *et al.* Lévy flight search patterns of wandering albatrosses. Nature. 1996;381(6581):413–415.

[63] Mårell A, Ball JP, Hofgaard A. Foraging and movement paths of female reindeer: Insights from fractal analysis, correlated random walks, and Lévy flights. Canadian Journal of Zoology-revue Canadienne De Zoologie. 2002;80:854–865.

[64] Bénichou O, Loverdo C, Moreau M, *et al.* Intermittent search strategies. Reviews of Modern Physics. 2011;83(1):81.

[65] Harris TH, Banigan EJ, Christian DA, *et al.* Generalized Lévy walks and the role of chemokines in migration of effector CD8+ T cells. Nature. 2012;486(7404):545–548.

[66]  Viswanathan GM, Da Luz MG, Raposo EP, *et al.* The physics of foraging: an introduction to random searches and biological encounters. Cambridge University Press, Cambridge, England; 2011.
[67]  Bonabeau E, Dorigo M, Theraulaz G. Swarm intelligence: From natural to artificial systems. Oxford University Press, Inc., New York, NY, USA; 1999.
[68]  Woo M, Cha SK, Gottlieb S, *et al.* Scheduling Black-box Mutational Fuzzing. In: Proceedings of the 2013 ACM SIGSAC Conference on Computer & Communications Security (CCS). New York, NY, USA: ACM; 2013. p. 511–522.
[69]  Riley JR, Greggers U, Smith AD, *et al.* The flight paths of honeybees recruited by the waggle dance. Nature. 2005;435(7039):205–207.
[70]  Sumpter DJ, Beekman M. From nonlinearity to optimality: Pheromone trail foraging by ants. Animal Behaviour. 2003;66(2):273–280.
[71]  Watkins CJ, Dayan P. Q-learning. Machine Learning. 1992;8(3–4):279–292.

*Chapter 14*

# Bio-inspired cyber-security for the smart grid

*Naeem Firdous Syed[1], Ahmed Ibrahim[1], Zubair Baig[2], and Craig Valli[1]*

Critical infrastructures (CIs) are vital to a nation's economy, security and public safety of nations. Any threats to these infrastructures can result in cascading consequences ranging from severe financial loss to loss of human lives. The electric power industry is going through major transformations in order to become more energy efficient, environment friendly and sustainable. The modernised and transformed electricity grid is known as the 'smart grid (SG)' [1]. The United States Department of Homeland Security considers the energy sector as one among 16 CIs [2].

SGs are changing the way traditional power grids operate from being islands of automation to interconnected systems with a two-way flow of energy and information. They are designed to enhance the efficiency and reliability of power grids using a large number of interconnected electronic devices. Even though the SG has many advantages over the traditional power grid, heterogeneity of devices and standards introduces cyber security issues in the SG which can have adverse impact on grid operations [3].

Successful cyberattacks against industrial control systems include Slammer worm [4], which attacked the critical monitoring systems of the nuclear power plant in USA, and Stuxnet [5], which caused the failure of centrifuges of a nuclear plant in Iran [6]. In addition, the attack on Ukraine power grid in December 2015 resulted in a major power disruption affecting 225,000 customers across several Ukrainian cities [7]. Such attacks show the adverse impact of cyberattacks on power grids.

As more and more complex cyberattacks that target the power grids are discovered, the need to build secure SGs becomes critical. The challenges faced in securing SGs are similar to the challenges faced in traditional information and communication technology (ICT) systems. However, the cyber-physical nature of SGs and complex architecture makes traditional security measures ineffective [8]. Conventional cyber defence systems typically follow a centralised approach, putting the central nodes under heavy loads, which can cause certain attacks to remain undetected [9]. In addition, conventional security systems do not scale well in a complex environment with millions of devices generating a large amount of data [9].

[1]School of Science, Security Research Institute, Edith Cowan University, Australia
[2]School of Information Technology, Deakin University & CSIRO, Data61, Australia

The answer to the problems faced by conventional security systems lie in natural phenomenon. With over a billion years of survival, biological systems have developed mechanisms that allow them to protect and defend themselves from threats in a constantly changing environment. Biological factors have been influencing cyber security since the term 'computer virus' was first coined to describe malicious software [10]. Cyber security concepts such as artificial immune system (AIS) inspired from biological immune system (BIS), fault-tolerant systems inspired from animal diversity and autonomic computing inspired from homeostasis are classic examples of bio-inspired techniques for computing systems [10]. As the biological processes become comprehensible with the advancement of scientific research, it is inevitable that biological inspirations will play a critical role in computer security in the future. Efforts have been made to develop novel bio-inspired cyber defence techniques suitable for large and complex environments such as SGs [8,11–13]. In this chapter, the security issues in the SG are elaborated, and the various nature inspired defence techniques applied for cyber security of the SG are discussed.

## 14.1 Smart grid security

SGs bear enormous benefits for both electricity providers and consumers alike, as they reduce the energy demands, global warming and consequently utility costs. However, several security and privacy issues arise with this new way of interaction between consumers and power grid [3]. A brief description of a typical SG communication network is presented in this section to better structure the discussion on the cyber security issues faced.

### 14.1.1 Smart grid architecture

Based on the National Institute of Standards and Technology (NIST) conceptual model [14], the SG can be divided into seven domains: bulk generation, transmission, distribution, customers, markets, service providers and operations. Figure 14.1 illustrates the NIST SG conceptual framework. Electricity flow occurs from bulk generation to customers, and information flow occurs between all domain pairs. Each of these seven domains comprises actors and applications which represent the devices, systems or programs and their corresponding tasks. In this SG framework, communication and data management play a pivotal role, which introduce a layer of intelligence over the current and future SG infrastructures [1].

A distributed and hierarchical communication network is mandatory for connecting the various domains of an SG [15]. Various devices and applications such as smart meters, thermostats, phasor measurement units, substation controllers, supervisory control and data acquisition (SCADA) form the network endpoints within the SG communication network. Inter-domain and intra-domain data communication will be essential to provide end-to-end services to various endpoints [14]. The SG network consists of a backbone network supporting the inter-domain communications

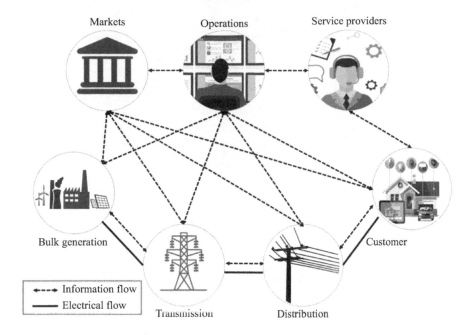

*Figure 14.1    NIST conceptual smart grid framework. © 2018. Based on, with permission, from Reference [14]*

and several subnetworks or local area networks to support intra-domain communications [15]. The subnetworks can consist of various types such as home area networks (HANs), personal area network, wireless access network, local area networks and wide area networks (WANs).

SG is a large network of many subnetworks with information and control data flowing between various networks and stakeholders. Hence, it is critical to secure the communication between various endpoints for its reliable and smooth operations. In such large interconnected systems, it is essential that compromise in network or domain does not compromise the security in other networks. Hence, the security measures should simultaneously prevent intrusions as well as allow access to information for relevant stakeholders [14].

## 14.1.2   Smart grid cyber security requirements

The SG communication network plays a pivotal role in the successful transformation of traditional power grids from one-way electricity flow to two-way information and electricity flow. The SG communication network ensures secure and reliable exchange of information between its various critical components. The main challenge for cyber security here is to maintain reliability and resilience of the infrastructure even under a cyberattack [16]. Unlike traditional information and technology (IT) systems, the control systems of an SG cannot be disconnected easily during a cyberattack as this

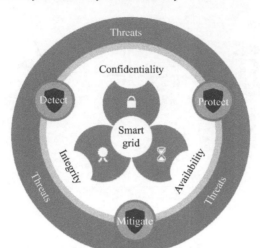

*Figure 14.2   Smart grid security objectives and defence measures*

could adversely impact the safety and stability of the system and lead to blackouts [16]. The primary goal of cyber security in traditional IT systems is to protect the confidentiality, integrity and availability of the system. However, in an SG, availability has the highest priority as many critical services depend on it [17]. In addition, various domains have different security objectives. For example, data integrity and timely delivery of data are critical in power generation and transmission as altered or delayed data could impact the reliability of the system. In the customer domain, confidentiality of customer data is deemed most important [16]. Figure 14.2 shows the three security objectives of SG and the necessary defence techniques against threats. The main cyber security objectives of SG are

- Availability: SG should be tolerant to faults and cyberattacks in order to continue its operations without disruptions. This requires attack detection and resilient operations by means of constant monitoring and evaluation of Cyber-Physical System (CPS) to detect and prevent security breaches. The SG should also be capable of self-healing in the event of attacks and continue operations to prevent blackouts [15].
- Integrity: Relates to preventing messages from being modified and ensuring its timely delivery. Measures such as access control, secure as well as timely delivery of messages and authenticating command sources [18] can be applied to preserve the integrity of SG. Message modification can result in incorrect decisions and can have cascading impact on power management [15].
- Confidentiality: Includes measures that restrict access to and disclosure of information in SG. Sensitive information such as personal details of customers, energy usage data and proprietary grid information are to be protected from unauthorised access and disclosure in public domains [15].

## 14.1.3   Smart grid cyber security threats

The introduction of ICT into traditional electricity grid attracts adversaries to target critical operations in order to cause damage and disruption. Cyber security threats from adversaries can come from various devices, applications and networks of the SG [17]. Several security and privacy issues arise in a complex SG system [3]. McDaniel and McLaughlin [3] envisioned the SG's cyber security future to comprise smart meter bots, i.e. distributed denial of service (DoS) attack facilitators, usage loggers, meter rootkits, viruses, and malware. McDaniel and McLaughlin also predicted that utility companies will exploit the energy use information stored in smart meters to mine behavioural data which will affect consumer privacy.

Some of the security issues arise through the introduction of two-way information and energy flow. In the communications model, consumers are required to share information about their energy consumption with their utility providers, over a communication channel. The interconnection of multiple smart meters and computerised infrastructure of the grid makes them vulnerable to several network-based attacks [3]. In addition, the introduction of smart meters attracts cybercriminals and other malicious users to alter the smart meters and to attack the core ICT infrastructure.

With a complex architecture, the cyber security issues pertaining to SGs are also numerous. On a high level, the various security threats to SG can be categorised based on the security objectives of the SG which are stated as follows [15]:

- Availability attacks: These attacks target the availability of SGs by causing DoS to legitimate services and its users. These attacks can either cause message delay or block messages from being delivered to end services or users. In time-sensitive SG applications, message delay can have adverse impact on operations.
- Integrity attacks: Attacks targeting the integrity of messages try to alter the messages or corrupt the message parameters to cause misconfiguration or undesirable effects in the SG operations.
- Confidentiality attacks: These attacks attempt to gain unauthorised access to the data stored in the SG. Such attacks lead to data leakage or breach of customer privacy.

Additionally, the security issues in SG can be classified based on the various ICT components and functions as summarised by Liu *et al.* [17]:

- Device issues: Security issues related to smart meters, customer appliances, electric vehicles, and sensors.
- Network issues: Security issues related to the Internet, wireless network, sensor networks, and wired network.
- Dispatching and management: Security issues related to SCADA, energy management systems, distribution management system, asset management, cipher key management and real time operations.
- Anomaly detection: Security issues with temporal information and data and services.
- Others: Issues with demand and response system, protocols and standards.

The perpetrators first need to exploit the entry points to launch attacks. The common entry points include smart meters, infected USB media, network-based intrusion (like vulnerabilities in ICT infrastructure or dialup access to remote terminal units) compromised supply chain and malicious insiders [19]. Once the intruder enters the network, he/she can launch attacks through spreading malware. These attackers may be capable of accessing databases, eavesdropping, compromising communication equipment and fabricating meter data.

In order to protect the SG from threats mentioned above, robust and effective solutions must be in place. These solutions must be scalable and be resilient to cyberattacks. In order to identify the measures required to protect SGs from cyberattacks, the various cyber defence techniques used in ICT systems are reviewed in the following section.

## 14.2    Defence techniques

Vulnerabilities in computing systems are a plenty, owing to system or programming errors [20]. A large number of cyber security professionals and researchers are involved in developing a variety of cyber defence techniques. The main aim of these cyber defence techniques is to protect a system from attacks against the three pillars of cyber security, namely confidentiality, integrity and availability. Based on these objectives, multiple control mechanisms can be implemented to protect computing systems from cyberattacks. The cyber defence techniques used for SG security need to be both scalable and resilient. The measures against attacks can be summarised into three main categories as follows [21]:

1. **Detect**: Detect on-going attacks or attacks that already took place so that appropriate actions can be taken,
2. **Prevent**: Prevent and deter attacks from reaching and harming the targets by hardening the system. Attacks can also be deflected by using decoy systems or making other targets attractive [21].
3. **Mitigate**: Mitigate or recover from the side effects of attacks and enable routine operations.

These measures are explained in detail in the following sections.

### 14.2.1    Attack detection

Detecting attacks and analysing their impact on computing systems is an important phase for all cyber defence techniques. In SG systems, attack detection techniques are designed and deployed to prevent and to detect cyberattacks against CIs. Various detection techniques exist. One of the most important classes of cyber defence tools is intrusion prevention system (IPS) and intrusion detection system (IDS). IPS uses attack-detection techniques to proactively defend against attacks and take rapid preventive actions to thwart intrusion attempts. On the other hand an IDS uses detection techniques to detect and report any intrusions that have already occurred, which can help assess the damage, track the intruders and prevent future attacks [20].

Traditional detection techniques are either signature or anomaly based. Signature-based detection techniques use known attack patterns discovered from prior attacks to predict or detect future attacks. Signature-based detection methods are effective in detecting known attacks; however, these methods fail to detect new or unknown attacks. They also require a constant effort to update the existing signature databases to effectively detect attacks. In contrast, anomaly-based detection techniques use statistical tools to differentiate between normal and abnormal patterns. Even though anomaly-based detection techniques do not require prior knowledge of cyberattacks to detect them, they suffer from high false positives causing operational difficulties. In addition, a complex, distributed and massive system like an SG with multiple components can cause centralised IPS and IDS systems to suffer from high false positives [22]. Hence, a more distributed and scalable IDS or IPS techniques suitable to CPS systems need to be applied in protecting an SG.

## 14.2.2 Attack prevention

Cyberattack prevention is an important defence technique that prevents attacks from compromising the target system by actively defending. Attack prevention measures use various techniques to prevent the attacks from reaching and harming the target system. Most measures employed are preventive in nature, as they are intended to prevent unauthorised access and control of target-computing resources. Notable attack prevention methods used in cyber infrastructures are access control and IPSs [23]. Access control is a cyber security measure used to regulate who or what can view or modify a resource in a cyber infrastructure. Access control measures first need to identify who or what is requesting the access and then verify their permissions to access the resource. It plays a crucial role in SGs as they apply to a large number of devices (both conventional ICT devices and cyber-physical devices) (CPS) spread across various subnetworks and stakeholders. Strict access control rules must be in place to prevent access to critical systems with in the SG. Some of the attack prevention measures useful for an SG are listed in Table 14.1.

## 14.2.3 Attack mitigation

Mitigating the adverse effects of cyberattacks is critical for effective reinstating of affected computing systems. Vulnerabilities in cyber security tools and techniques is inevitable due to design flaws, programming errors or implementation errors [20]. Hence, it is important to have cyberattack mitigation measures in place to prevent the adverse effects of successful attacks. Especially in an SG with time critical CPS systems, mitigation measures must ensure grid stability during cyberattacks. Mitigation measures must use tools that detect attacks (such as IDS systems) and monitor grid operations (such as measuring the voltage, temperature, power, frequency, phase, etc.) to automatically launch countermeasures in optimal way to stabilise the grid [24]. The priority of any mitigation measure must be to act rapidly before the adverse effect of the attack causes failure of the system [18]. In other words, the detection and

*Table 14.1   Attack prevention methods applicable for smart grids*

| Prevention measure | Description |
| --- | --- |
| Access control list | Used to authenticate and authorise users or devices to access a certain resource in the smart grid. Unauthorised users are prevented from accessing the resources |
| Firewall | Prevents and controls internal users from accessing untrusted outside network. It also prevents unauthorised connection attempts to the internal network |
| Encryption | Prevents adversaries from intercepting or modifying the contents of the messages passed between endpoints in the smart grid |
| Command source authentication [18] | Prevents endpoints in cyber-physical systems to accept commands from unauthorised users |
| Intrusion prevention system (IPS) | Detects and stops attacks targeting smart grid resources |

response to an attack must happen before the time to criticality is reached to ensure safe operations [18].

The cyber security challenges faced by SGs will be similar to the challenges in conventional IT systems; however, there will be many differences due to the cyber-physical nature of SGs and complex interconnections of various subnetworks. Systems depending on central nodes for detecting and identifying threats will face challenges in processing large volumes of data produced by the system. Scalability is another factor that will impair the conventional systems in effective cyberattack detection [9]. Furthermore, according to Symantec corporation, only 45% of malware infections are detected by antivirus software due to the complex and evolving cyberattacks [25].

So the question arises: where to take inspirations from to enhance security solutions? Nature holds the key to this problem faced by cyber security professionals. Living systems have developed unique ways to protect and defend themselves from predators and natural phenomena. Many examples of intelligent and autonomous techniques employed by living organisms to protect themselves is proving to be a great source of inspiration to build solutions in a constantly changing cyber security landscape. The following sections explain in detail the role of bio-inspired cyber security solutions when applied to SG security.

## 14.3   Bio-inspired cyber security architectures

Over many millions of years, living systems have been coping with the ever changing surroundings in a constant struggle to survive and reproduce. Nature has inspired researchers and engineers from various fields in developing novel solutions. Some of the well-known examples of bio-inspired solutions include Velcro, a fabric hook inspired from burdock plant burrs, retro-reflective road markings inspired from a cat's eye reflections in dark when light falls on them, fast swim suit design inspired from sharks, energy-efficient buildings inspired from termite mounds, etc. Even computing systems have adopted many of the bio-inspired techniques to build intelligent solutions. Genetic algorithms (GAs) [26], neural networks [27], ant algorithms (algorithms inspired by foraging behavior of ants) [28], swarm intelligence [28] and AIS [29] are few examples of bio-inspired solutions in computing systems [30].

### 14.3.1 Mapping between biological systems and cyber security systems

Before explaining the bio-inspired methods for cyber security, there is a need to understand how biology maps to the cyber security world. These mappings will help in evaluating the various biological concepts applied to cyber security. Ecology is the study of interactions among the various actors (organisms) and their environments. It also relates to the functioning and structure of community of living and nonliving components comprising an ecosystem. The main driving force within an ecosystem is the flow of energy from plants (producers) to higher order living things (predators) in the food chain. Similarly a cyber ecosystem can be viewed as a community of various applications, programs and processes, which are either offensive or defensive, and their interactions [31].

Similar to energy flow in biological ecosystems, various information types is the key driving force in cyber ecosystem, and it can be transformed, stored or circulated to higher order consumers including attackers [31]. The mappings between biological and the cyber world start with observations of organisms and their behaviour in a natural setting. These observations help in defining various phenomena, which can be mapped to a computing system to mimic nature. The mapping of ecological theories to the cyber world forms the basis of cyber ecology (CE) [31].

CE can thus be defined as the set of interactions between the cyber components and their environment subtypes [31]. Figure 14.3 shows the various subtypes of CE.

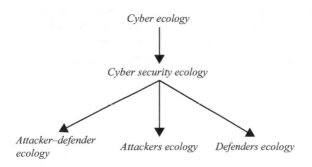

*Figure 14.3   Cyber ecology and its subtypes. © 2018. Based on, with permission, from Reference [31]*

The cyber security ecology looks into the interactions between various cyber components and the impact of its environment on security. This is a subtype of CE. The attacker–defender ecology describes the interactions between cyber components that take roles of attacker and defenders (e.g. biological behaviours such as predation or parasitism which aim to obtain resources from other organism). Attacker ecology is the study of interactions among the various adversaries that attack other cyber components (e.g. symbiotic relationship among predators and parasites in targeting other organisms). Defender ecology studies the interactions between the various cyber components that defend and protect other cyber components (e.g. BIS which defends the animals from diseases).

Living systems use both offensive and defensive techniques to protect themselves from adversaries. Offensive techniques are similar to attacks launched by cybercriminals. Some of the examples of such behaviour in the animal world are [30]

- Angler fish using its fleshy growth protruding from its head as bait to attract victims. This is similar to phishing websites or emails of a cyberattack.
- *Ophiocordyceps unilateralis* fungus infects a species of ants and alters the ants behavioural patterns to help the fungus growth. This is similar to botnet operations, where victim hosts are exploited for various malicious operations.
- Kudzu group of plants grow over trees and shrubs and can eventually kill them by preventing sunlight. This is analogous to a DoS attack which prevents legitimate users from accessing services.

In contrast, defensive techniques try to protect the living system from attackers. Some of the examples of defensive behaviour in the animal world are as follows [30]:

- Hedgehog's spines and turtle shells or plants with thorns to prevent external threats. This is similar to firewalls or access control measures deployed in the cyber world.
- The ability of living systems to differentiate between self and non-self cells by immune systems, thereby protecting from diseases. This is similar to IPSs which can detect anomalies and prevent cyberattacks.

The mappings between the biological and the cyber world helps identify and implement some of the important features exhibited by nature. One of the key features of living organisms in a constantly changing environment is adaptability, which has helped living systems to survive and reproduce [32]. The five factors key to adaptability [32,33] are decentralisation, redundancy, cooperation, responsiveness and heterogeneity. These adaptability factors found in nature are applied in cyber security solutions to make them robust and effective. A comparison of the applications of these factors [33] in nature and their respective mapping to cyber security are described in Table 14.2.

## 14.3.2 *Bio-inspired solutions for smart grid security*

In a large and complex system such as the SG, a robust, scalable and effective cyber security solution is required to protect from adversarial threats. Bio-inspired

*Table 14.2    Mapping of adaptability factors with cyber security. © 2018. Based on, with permission, from Reference [33]*

| Feature | Application in nature | Application in cyber security |
|---|---|---|
| Responsiveness | An instantaneous, accurate and reactive behaviour of body sensors when provoked | IPS systems have a reactive behaviour to prevent intrusions |
| Heterogeneity | Genetic diversity in same species allows cumulative chance of survival when faced by challenges | Using multiple combinations of security measures to protect from intrusions |
| Decentralisation | Social animals (e.g. ants or bees) using complex communication methods to protect the group when intruders attack | The use of probes or multiple IDS/IPS sensors to better detect threats |
| Redundancy | Community animals duplicating roles to increase the chance of success | Using redundant computing systems to increase the resilience of the system and prevent single point of failure |
| Cooperation | Symbiotic relationships in animals to counter common threats | Sharing threat information between multiple security solutions to protect a common threat |

techniques are effectively applied in developing SG security solutions. Bio-inspired solutions that have been proposed for SG cyber security are based on digital ants framework (DAF) [8], multi-flock technique [13] and immune system [11,12,34]. Here, these solutions are described. Some of the solutions mentioned in this section are directly applicable to SGs security. In addition, CPS-based security solutions that are also applicable in SGs have been included.

### 14.3.2.1    Digital ants framework

As the name suggests, this framework is inspired from the foraging behaviour seen in ant colonies. Ant colonies that span a few million ants have to handle a variety of tasks and risks. The assignment of tasks to individual ants is through coordination rather than central planning. Older ants forage to find food. Ant species use chemical marking (known as pheromone) to create foraging trails to help other ants find food through a shortest route to the nest. Other ants are also attracted by the left behind pheromone to follow the trail. This makes it easy for ants to quickly gather around food or in case of a threat. The foraging and communication behaviour of ants inspired McKinnon *et al.* [8] to propose a DAF to protect SGs from cyber threats.

The DAF uses a hierarchical structure with mobile sensors in the bottom layer and human supervisors in the top layer. The middle layers consist of sentinel and sergeants [8]. Figure 14.4 shows the DAF hierarchy. The mobile sensors move from device to device looking for anomalies in the device. Based on the measurements

*Figure 14.4    Digital ants framework hierarchy. © 2018. Based on, with permission, from Reference [8]*

from neighbouring devices, the sentinels decide if the findings of sensors are normal or anomalous. The sentinel then rewards the sensors following which, these sensors move to other devices by leaving behind messages that act as pheromones. This attracts other sensors to move towards the device to find other anomalies. The sergeants take responsibility of larger networks of devices, and the sentinels report their findings to a single sergeant. Sergeants can correlate the events at different locations to detect a distributed threat that spans multiple sentinel areas [8]. The sergeants report their findings to human supervisors who manage bigger enclaves consisting of many sergeants. Most of the problems are resolved by the lower levels, and human supervisors are only involved when certain problems require their involvement. The decentralised and scalable DAF framework makes it suitable for securing the complex SG.

### 14.3.2.2    Multi-flock technique

A measurement based multi-flock approach was proposed by Wei *et al.*[13] to identify real-time generator coherency in the presence of faults or cyberattacks. Inter-area oscillations occur between generators that form coherent groups and are detrimental to the power grid's stability. Especially, in a complex and large scale SG where in these devices will operate under increased pressure and are more susceptible to these oscillations. The inter-area oscillations adversely impact the power systems and affect their achieving of maximum power transfer and optimal power flow. Generators naturally form clusters, and any disturbance causes generator angles within the same cluster to oscillate faster than the generators in distinct groups. Wide-area monitoring, protection and control systems are designed to detect and mitigate the issues of inter-area oscillations. In order to maintain stability of the power grids, these monitoring and control systems need to operate even in the presence of noise or cyber threats. The proposed bio-inspired solution [13] is designed to rapidly detect the inter-area oscillations even in the presence of noise or cyberattacks.

The operations that prevent this phenomenon require groups of coherent generators to be identified first. In this work [13], the flocking feature of birds is used to detect coherent generator clustering. In flocking behaviour exhibited by certain groups of birds, the birds cooperate to achieve a collective goal of reaching a particular destination. A single flock of birds might have cooperation rules such as flock centring, velocity matching, collision avoidance and obstacle avoidance [13]. In addition, the birds also try to remain close to the flock that belongs to the same species. This bio-inspired algorithm is robust to measurement errors or data corruption and reduces the requirement of advanced computation with reduced observation window, when compared to other techniques. The robustness and low computation requirements of the multi-flock approach are suitable in rapidly detecting anomalous behaviour in SG systems.

### 14.3.2.3 Multi-agent immunologically inspired model

Immunity inspired SG protection (IISGP) model provides an end-to-end protection model for a complex SG system [12]. The SG system can be viewed as a complex adaptive system (CAS) which needs to adapt to changes in its own environment or changes occurring in other interconnected systems. The analogy between a CAS for SG and an immune system can be made based on latter's complex system, adaptive environment, resilient and robust operations in the presence of external agents. The IISGP model uses the decentralised and self-protective properties of BIS by including techniques such as [12]

- Immune network theory: The entire power grid is considered as a human body protected by an immune system. Network nodes act as tissues and nodes are connected to nearby nodes to form an immune network.
- Danger theory: Monitors the immune network for any anomalies and deals with the threat in a decentralised manner.
- Negative selection theory: Explains the method used in discriminating between self and non-self cells.
- Clonal selection theory: Explains the functioning of lymphocytes in response to the invading antigens.

Based on IISGP, each node will have an immune-inspired algorithm running to detect and prevent malicious attacks. Specifically, the clonal selection and negative selection algorithms will identify and respond to local attacks. Once a malicious event occurs, multiple elements get involved to analyse the attack and handle it at the node level. Occurrence of the event and its response is then propagated throughout the network to deal with similar attacks in other locations of the SG. IISGP is a high-level model which needs to be further tested in order to assess the effectiveness and robustness of the solution. However, the adaptive and decentralised approach in IISGP is suitable for large and complex SG.

### 14.3.2.4 Smart grid immune system

SG immune system (SGIS) is a bio-inspired solution for SG and is based on the human immune system [11]. SGIS builds an immune wall around the SG architecture to enhance the security of the grid. Two levels of immune walls are proposed: network-based immune wall (NIW) and host-based immune wall (HIW). The immune walls take inspiration from the adaptive immune system and has the following functionality built into it:

- Packet filtering,
- Classification,
- Anomaly detection,
- Synchronised intrusion and malware database cloning and
- Self-healing and incident response.

The SGIS operates by filtering traffic flowing in and out of the endpoints and uses IPS or IDS to classify intrusions. Memory is used to store information on attacks and normal data to classify future connections. All incoming connections go through the NIW which applies packet filtering in the first stage. Filtered connections are classified into normal or anomalous by random forest classifier built into NIW. Anomalous connections are blocked and normal connections are reclassified by a $K$-nearest neighbour classifier to block any anomalous connections undetected in previous phase. The HIW functions similarly to NIW but at host level and includes a MAC filtering system and antivirus engine to detect local attacks. This two-layered security approach is beneficial to vulnerable endpoints in the SG.

### 14.3.3    Future bio-inspired solutions for smart grid

Other bio-inspired measures applied to computing systems security can also prove to be useful in protecting SGs from cyberattacks. Especially the security solutions which are applicable for distributed environments can be used in the SGs. Methods such as GA, AIS, etc. have been used in developing novel cyber defence systems for CPS systems. Some of the most useful techniques that are applicable to an SG are described below.

#### 14.3.3.1    Genetic algorithm

GAs represent a class of bio-inspired evolutionary algorithms which help in generating the best in class solutions through gene operations such as mutation, crossover and selection. It was used by Fulp *et al.* [35] to propose a resilient cyber defence strategy. Figure 14.5 shows the steps involved in a generic GA algorithm. Based on GA, a moving target is created by constantly evolving computer configurations which will be diverse and secure. In this study, configurations are considered as chromosomes and the associated security as the fitness. The chromosomes (here configurations) go through a series of mutation, crossover and selection processes to find the most secure configuration. The fitness of the configurations also decays with the length of time which allows newer configurations to replace older insecure configurations. The adaptable and evolving nature of GA are suitable to secure the various endpoints of the SG system. In addition, this method can be applied to detection and prevention systems of SGs to constantly update their security configurations. However its application in CPS systems and the scalability in a complex and large SG system is a topic of further research.

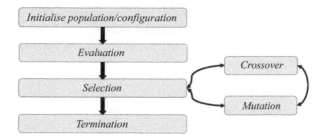

*Figure 14.5   Genetic algorithm flow chart*

### 14.3.3.2   Artificial immune system

The BIS is an autonomous system performing many operations without the central systems intervention. BIS also uses multiple agents to recognise external pathogens and learns the response produced by the immune system to protect from future infections. This model was applied to enhance the security of distributed systems such as grid computing [36]. The model is inspired by the BIS and uses four groups of autonomous agents that can learn and interact with other agents. These agents were presenter, helper, memory and killer agents. The presenter agents move between various nodes to detect faults or failures through cyberattacks. When an anomaly is detected, the presenter agents instruct the helper agents to find a specific killer agent to eliminate the anomaly and its effects. The memory agents learn and instruct killer agents. The killer agents migrate to the nodes where presenter agents discover anomaly. In addition, these agents take information from other killer agents about unsuccessful ways to eliminate the anomaly. Once it identifies a method to eliminate, it acts upon the anomaly by taking actions such as killing a process, disabling intruder access, etc. The memory agents are similar to the lymphocytes (a type of white blood cells) that are known as killer cells. As SGs have a distributed architecture similar to grid computing this security technique can be extended to protect SGs from cyberattacks.

In an AIS-inspired technique [34], Zhang *et al.* used a distributed IDS system, which incorporates analysing modules (AM) in multiple layers of an SG. The AM uses AIS algorithms to classify attacks and is deployed in HAN, neighbour area network and WAN zones. AM uses training datasets relevant to each zone in order to detect attacks pertaining to it. This distributed model of IDS for SG enhances the detection rate [34].

### 14.3.3.3   Hive oversight for network intrusion early warning

Another interesting bio-inspired work that can be used in SG security is the Hive oversight for network intrusion early warning, through distributed intrusion/anomaly monitoring for nonparametric detection (DIAMoND) [37]. This is a fully distributed cyber defence technique inspired from bees. Honey bees live in colonies and have complex communications systems to share information on flowering plants and their locations. In order to survive in a competitive environment of other bees and insects, the bees need to efficiently search for locations rich in resources and communicate this location to other members of the colony and exploit the resources quickly. Honey bees do not set the search target locations before foraging, instead they encounter these locations during their foraging. The bees then communicate it back to other members along with the level of excitement that the bee has regarding the location. Other bees decide to either go to that location or search for new location based on the excitement level exhibited by the bee. A similar approach is applied in cyber defence using sensors searching for anomalies.

A DIAMoND framework is used to build an overlay network on top of the physical network. DIAMoND separates the network intrusion detection function from network wide coordination [37]. The framework combines the direct observations by local IDS devices with the observations of neighbouring devices to detect anomalies in the underlying system. The coordinating nodes in DIAMoND act as honey bees to exchange a nonparametric level of concern similar to the excitement levels shown by bees. This information reflects the observed probability of malicious attacks. In a large and complex SG with multiple networks and millions of endpoints, a distributed framework such as DIAMoND will play a crucial role in securing the system.

#### 14.3.3.4  Digital epidemics: transmissive attacks

A useful work that discusses the relations between transmissive attacks and spread of epidemics in real life was done by Chen *et al.* [38]. Transmissive attacks are cyberattacks that spread via various communication paths and adversaries to reach the target via multiple intermediate hosts. This study is particularly useful for SG security, as it is composed of multiple subnetworks and stakeholders, which could attract transmissive attacks to target SG operations. With the proliferation of IoT, such attacks could be a digital epidemic [38]. Chen *et al.* evaluated the effectiveness of transmissive attacks using epidemic models. This study can be used to evaluate features of transmissive attacks in the context of biological epidemics. In addition, bio-inspired control measures can be developed to prevent the spread of such attacks. With millions of connected devices in the SG, rapid detection of transmissive attacks will prevent malwares and other malicious attacks from spreading and disrupting its operations.

### 14.3.4  Taxonomy

The bio-inspired techniques that are suitable for SG security can be categorised based on the biological factors that are behind the system or organisms behaviour. The various biological factors used in developing the cyber security solutions and the corresponding security measures are presented in Figure 14.6. The main biological factors that were applied in various solutions are

- evolution,
- ethology (study of animal behaviour),
- immunology and
- epidemics.

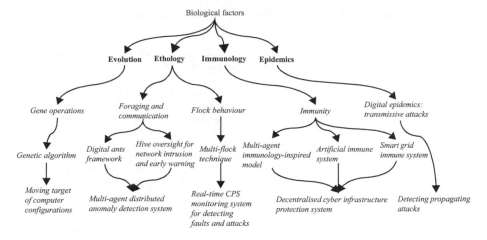

*Figure 14.6   Taxonomy of bio-inspired techniques for smart grids*

Evolution deals with the changes that occur in natural system over a period of time. It is usually triggered by environmental changes or by introduction of new challenges to the biological systems. One of the important evolutionary processes is the changes in genes. GAs are inspired by these gene changes which help in selecting the best characteristics for new environments. Ethology deals with the study of animal behaviour in natural surroundings. Many important inspirational factors emerge from the behavioural study of animals. Especially, decentralised and complex communication systems developed by many organisms are important factors in developing SG cyber defence techniques based on them. Immunology and epidemics primarily deal with the study of spread of diseases and the response to foreign antibodies by the biological systems. This can be replicated in SG cyber defence systems to protect from threats. An SG security defence system that can be developed using the various bio-inspired techniques are highlighted in Table 14.3.

## 14.4   Summary

In this chapter, the challenges in SG security and appertaining bio-inspired cyber security solutions to tackle those challenges were presented. At first, the SG architecture was presented and then the cyber security requirements of the SG were introduced. Among the three security objectives, availability was considered the most important in SGs. The various cyber security threats to SG cyber infrastructures were elaborated. These threats to SGs might be similar to the threats faced by traditional IT systems, but there are many differences due to the dynamics in the cyber-physical nature of the grid. Many bio-inspired security measures have been proposed in the literature.

*Table 14.3   Mapping bio-inspired cyber security measures with smart grid cyber defence*

| Security feature | Application in smart grid |
| --- | --- |
| Moving target of computer configuration | Useful in attack prevention techniques in smart grid environment. Generating best configuration parameters from time to time can prevent unauthorised access to critical systems |
| Multi agent, distributed anomaly detection system | Critical for IPS and IDS systems used with in smart grids for attack prevention and detection. Improves the detection of anomalies by using multi agent system which uses a distributed architecture suitable for large and complex smart grid cyber infrastructure |
| Real time CPS monitoring system for detecting faults and attacks | Useful for attack detection and mitigation as it monitors the physical devices for faults and potential cyberattack effect |
| Decentralised cyber infrastructure protection system | A comprehensive system to detect and mitigate attacks by rapidly responding to on-going attacks similar to immune system. Also builds immunity to future attacks |
| Detecting propagating attacks | Useful in detecting attacks that propagate multiple networks to target the main smart grid operations |

The various bio-inspired cyber security techniques suitable for SG systems and the taxonomy of biological factors that inspired these methods were presented.

# References

[1]   Farhangi H. The path of the smart grid. IEEE Power and Energy Magazine. 2010;8(1):18–28.
[2]   Critical Infrastructure Sectors. Department of Homeland Security; [updated 2018 Nov 21; cited 2013 Mar 5]. Available from: https://www.dhs.gov/critical-infrastructure-sectors.
[3]   McDaniel P, McLaughlin S. Security and privacy challenges in the smart grid. IEEE Security and Privacy. 2009;7(3):75–77.
[4]   Poulsen K. Slammer worm crashed Ohio nuke plant network. SecurityFocus. 2003;19.
[5]   Langner R. Stuxnet: Dissecting a cyberwarfare weapon. IEEE Security & Privacy. 2011;9(3):49–51.
[6]   Sadeghi AR, Wachsmann C, Waidner M. Security and privacy challenges in industrial internet of things. In: Design Automation Conference (DAC), 2015 52nd ACM/EDAC/IEEE. IEEE; 2015. p. 1–6.

[7] Lee TRM, Assante MJ, Conway T. Analysis of the cyber attack on the Ukranian power grid. Defense use case. SANS ICS; Mar 2016.

[8] McKinnon AD, Thompson SR, Doroshchuk RA, *et al.* Bio-inspired cyber security for smart grid deployments. In: Innovative Smart Grid Technologies (ISGT), 2013 IEEE PES. IEEE; 2013. p. 1–6.

[9] Bitam S, Zeadally S, Mellouk A. Bio-inspired cybersecurity for wireless sensor networks. IEEE Communications Magazine. 2016;54(6):68–74.

[10] Somayaji A. Immunology, diversity, and homeostasis: The past and future of biologically inspired computer defenses. Information Security Technical Report. 2007;12(4):228–234.

[11] Faisal MMA, Chowdhury MAI. Bio inspired cyber security architecture for smart grid. In: 2016 International Conference on Innovations in Science, Engineering and Technology (ICISET); 2016. p. 1–5.

[12] Mavee SMA, Ehlers EM. A multi-agent immunologically-inspired model for critical information infrastructure protection – An immunologically-inspired conceptual model for security on the power grid. In: 2012 IEEE 11th International Conference on Trust, Security and Privacy in Computing and Communications; 2012. p. 1089–1096.

[13] Wei J, Kundur D, Butler-Purry KL. A novel bio-inspired technique for rapid real-time generator coherency identification. IEEE Transactions on Smart Grid. 2015;6(1):178–188.

[14] NIST Framework and Roadmap for Smart Grid Interoperability Standards, Release 1.0. NIST Special Publication. 2010. Available from: https://www.nist.gov/sites/default/files/documents/public_affairs/releases/smartgrid_interoperability_final.pdf.

[15] Wang W, Lu Z. Cyber security in the smart grid: Survey and challenges. Computer Networks. 2013;57(5):1344–1371.

[16] Cyber Security in Energy Sector. 2017. Available from: https://ec.europa.eu/energy/sites/ener/files/documents/eecsp_report_final.pdf.

[17] Liu J, Xiao Y, Li S, *et al.* Cyber security and privacy issues in smart grids. IEEE Communications Surveys & Tutorials. 2012;14(4):981–997.

[18] Rice EB, AlMajali A. Mitigating the risk of cyber attack on smart grid systems. Procedia Computer Science. 2014;28:575–582. 2014 Conference on Systems Engineering Research. Available from: http://www.sciencedirect.com/science/article/pii/S1877050914001331.

[19] Mo Y, Kim THJ, Brancik K, *et al.* Cyber–physical security of a smart grid infrastructure. Proceedings of the IEEE. 2012;100(1):195–209.

[20] Dua S, Du X. Data mining and machine learning in cybersecurity. Boca Raton, FL: Auerbach Publications, Taylor & Francis Group; 2016.

[21] Pfleeger CP, Pfleeger SL. Security in computing, 4th Edition. Upper Saddle River, NJ: Prentice Hall PTR; 2006.

[22] MacDermott Á, Shi Q, Merabti M, *et al.* Intrusion detection for critical infrastructure protection. In: 13th Annual Postgraduate Symposium on Convergence of Telecommunications, Networking and Broadcasting (PGNet 2012); 2012.

[23]    Kruegel C, Valeur F, Vigna G. Intrusion detection and correlation: Challenges and solutions. vol. 14. Boston, MA: Springer Science & Business Media; 2004.

[24]    Friedberg I, McLaughlin K, Smith P. Towards a cyber-physical resilience framework for smart grids. In: IFIP International Conference on Autonomous Infrastructure, Management and Security. Springer; 2015. p. 140–144.

[25]    Gibbs S. Antivirus software is dead, says security expert at Symantec. The Guardian; 2014 May 6. Available from: https://www.theguardian.com/technology/2014/may/06/antivirus-software-fails-catch-attacks-security-expert-symantec.

[26]    Owais S, Snasel V, Kromer P, *et al.* Survey: Using genetic algorithm approach in intrusion detection systems techniques. In: 2008 7th Computer Information Systems and Industrial Management Applications; 2008. p. 300–307.

[27]    Buczak AL, Guven E. A survey of data mining and machine learning methods for cyber security intrusion detection. IEEE Communications Surveys & Tutorials. 2016;18(2):1153–1176.

[28]    Zelinka I. A survey on evolutionary algorithms dynamics and its complexity–Mutual relations, past, present and future. Swarm and Evolutionary Computation. 2015;25:2–14.

[29]    Dasgupta D. Advances in artificial immune systems. IEEE Computational Intelligence Magazine. 2006;1(4):40–49.

[30]    Mazurczyk W, Rzeszutko E. Security – A perpetual war: Lessons from nature. IT Professional. 2015;17(1):16–22.

[31]    Mazurczyk W, Drobniak S, Moore S. Towards a systematic view on cybersecurity ecology. In: Combatting Cybercrime and Cyberterrorism. Springer; 2016. p. 17–37.

[32]    Sagarin R. Bio-hacking: Tapping life's code to deal with unpredictable risk. IEEE Security Privacy. 2013;11(4):93–95.

[33]    Rzeszutko E, Mazurczyk W. Insights from nature for cybersecurity. Health Security. 2015;13(2):82–87.

[34]    Zhang Y, Wang L, Sun W, *et al.* Artificial immune system based intrusion detection in a distributed hierarchical network architecture of smart grid. In: 2011 IEEE Power and Energy Society General Meeting; 2011. p. 1–8.

[35]    Fulp EW, Gage HD, John DJ, *et al.* An evolutionary strategy for resilient cyber defense. In: Global Communications Conference (GLOBECOM), 2015 IEEE. IEEE; 2015. p. 1–6.

[36]    Noeparast EB, Banirostam T. A cognitive model of immune system for increasing security in distributed systems. In: 2012 UKSim 14th International Conference on Computer Modelling and Simulation; 2012. p. 181–186.

[37]    Korczynski M, Hamieh A, Huh JH, *et al.* Hive oversight for network intrusion early warning using DIAMoND: A bee-inspired method for fully distributed cyber defense. IEEE Communications Magazine. 2016;54(6):60–67.

[38]    Chen PY, Lin CC, Cheng SM, *et al.* Decapitation via digital epidemics: A bio-inspired transmissive attack. IEEE Communications Magazine. 2016; 54(6):75–81.

*Chapter 15*

# Nature-inspired cryptography and cryptanalysis

*Jörg Keller\* and Gabriele Spenger\**

## 15.1 Introduction

Cryptography, i.e., the study of keeping information confidential and authentic, and cryptanalysis, i.e., the practice and study of analyzing cryptographic techniques,[1] have developed over the centuries in an arms race. Advantages on one side always have led to advantages on the other side. Thus, lots of talented scientists have invested their energy in improving either cryptographic algorithms, protocols, implementations and the like, or their analysis. In this strive, a broad spectrum of methods and approaches is used, ranging from pure mathematics to quantum physics. It is not surprising that also nature has been used as a guide, ranging from genetic algorithms (GAs) to design new cryptographic primitives to ant-colony algorithms to pursue most promising paths first in cryptanalysis. Consequently, a number of nature-inspired approaches have found their way into *cryptology*, comprising both cryptography itself and cryptanalysis.

This chapter is structured into four parts. After the brief introduction into the importance of nature-inspired cryptology given above, some background and preliminary information will be presented. The central parts will cover general ideas (including classical approaches) and recent developments in nature-inspired cryptography and cryptanalysis, respectively.

## 15.2 Background and basics

### 15.2.1 Cryptography and cryptanalysis

According to [1], *cryptography* "is the study of mathematical techniques related to aspects of information security such as confidentiality, data integrity, entity authentication, and data origin authentication. Cryptography is not the only means of providing information security, but rather one set of techniques." Generally spoken,

---

\*Faculty of Mathematics and Computer Science, FernUniversität in Hagen, Germany
[1]Such techniques include decrypting messages without possession of the key, or forging signatures by exploiting weakness of cryptographic hash functions.

*Table 15.1    Security objectives [1]*

| Privacy or confidentiality | Keeping information secret from all but those who are authorized to see it |
| --- | --- |
| Data integrity | Ensuring information has not been altered by unauthorized or unknown means |
| Entity authentication or identification | Corroboration of the identity of an entity (e.g., a person, a computer terminal, a credit card, etc.) |
| Message authentication | Corroborating the source of information; also known as data origin authentication |
| Signature | A means to bind information to an entity |
| Authorization | Conveyance, to another entity, of official sanction to do or be something |
| Validation | A means to provide timeliness of authorization to use or manipulate information or resources |
| Access control | Restricting access to resources to privileged entities |
| Certification | Endorsement of information by a trusted entity |
| Time stamping | Recording the time of creation or existence of information |
| Witnessing | Verifying the creation or existence of information by an entity other than the creator |
| Receipt | Acknowledgment that information has been received |
| Confirmation | Acknowledgment that services have been provided |
| Ownership | A means to provide an entity with the legal right to use or transfer a resource to others |
| Anonymity | Concealing the identity of an entity involved in some process |
| Non-repudiation | Preventing the denial of previous commitments or actions |
| Revocation | Retraction of certification or authorization |

cryptography is the modern answer to the question how to achieve the security objectives as listed in Table 15.1. *Cryptanalysis* comprises techniques to validate, and possibly break, crypto algorithms. We will view cryptology in a wide sense and include also information hiding, i.e., techniques to hide the very existence of information transfer, under this umbrella term.

Cryptography rests on a number of cryptographic primitives. A prominent one is *encryption*. Given a set $S$ of symbols (such as 128-bit words), and a set $K$ of keys, an encryption algorithm is a function $enc : S \times K \rightarrow S$, that transforms a plain-text symbol $m$ under a key $k$ into a cipher-text symbol $c$, i.e., $enc(k, m) = c$. Given a fixed key $k$, $enc(k, \dots)$ is injective, to allow decryption of the ciphertext. Thus, there exists a *decryption* algorithm $dec : S \times K \rightarrow S$ such that for every encryption key $k$, there is a corresponding decryption key $k^*$ so that $dec(k^*, c) = m$. An encryption realizes the goal of confidentiality if the chance of an attacker to get the plain-text $m$ from the cipher-text $c$ without knowing the key is not better than guessing. This means that the cipher-text should look like a random string and not reveal any structure or content of the underlying plain-text. If a cryptanalysis reveals that an attacker needs to try out notably fewer than $|K|$ keys to derive the plain-text from a cipher-text, then the encryption algorithm is considered insecure. Encryption algorithms have to fulfill some more objectives besides the above, e.g., they should be quick to compute. Thus, developing a crypto-algorithm is a form of (multi-criteria) optimization. There are more cryptographic primitives like cryptographic hash functions and digital signatures, and for each primitive there have been hundreds of concrete proposals over the decades. A good overview about the subject, e.g., can be found in [1].

## 15.2.2 Nature-inspired algorithms

In the past decades, the interest in nature-inspired algorithms has increased significantly, and a large amount of research effort has been put into finding applications for these algorithms. Nature is a great source of inspiration for problem solving, providing diverse, dynamic and robust solutions using inspiring and creative approaches. Binitha states in [2] that "[Nature] always finds the optimal solution to solve its problem maintaining perfect balance among its components. This is the thrust behind Bio-inspired computing." He defines nature-inspired algorithms to be meta-heuristics that mimic nature for solving optimization problems, opening a new era in computation. While optimization algorithms are not the only inspirations by nature in the context of cryptography, they are the major subject for research publications in this area.

Nature-inspired optimization algorithms can be divided into three different categories, as shown in Figure 15.1.

**Evolutionary computation** [3] orients on collective phenomena in adaptive populations of problem solvers. It makes progress iteratively by implementing aspects that can be observed in populations like growth, development, reproduction, selection and survival. These aspects are the foundation of the existence of living beings and the basis for their interaction with each other. Research on evolutionary algorithms (EAs) has already started in the 1950s, and EAs are probably the most well-known and classical approach in nature-inspired algorithms. EAs are nondeterministic algorithms or cost based optimization algorithms. As an example, Figure 15.2 depicts the cycle of a GA, where a number of promising (partial) solutions to a problem form a population, from which the best are selected, combined (by mating) and some new (mutated, i.e., randomly modified) solutions added to form a new population. The cycle continues

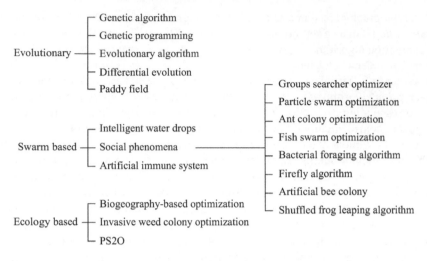

*Figure 15.1    Taxonomy of various bio-inspired optimization algorithms [2]*

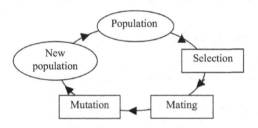

*Figure 15.2    A basic cycle of GA [5]*

until a certain number of generations whereby the surviving individuals represent a solution to the problem [4].

According to [5], GA mimics the evolutionary principles rooted in biological evolution inspired by neo-Darwinian theory and has been successfully applied to numerous applications in the field of search and optimization. It was developed by Prof. J. Holland *et al.* at the University of Michigan in 1965 [6].

A related approach is **DNA-based computing**,[2] where large numbers of molecules are used to solve an optimization problem.

A new and rapidly growing field of computer science is the **artificial immune system** (AIS). According to [5], it adopted three immunological principles:

1.    Negative selection: The main role of the immune system is to provide defense mechanisms against foreign cells and to remove the malfunctioning cells. In order to defend against foreign and malfunctioning cells, the immune system needs to

---

[2] DNA is an acronym for desoxyribonucleid acid, which carries the genetic information used in development, functioning and reproduction of living organisms.

distinguish between good cells (known as self) and the bad ones (non-self). The self-elements that recognize any element of the self are eliminated. This process creates self elements that react only to non-self elements.

2.  Clonal selection: In contrast to the process toward negative selection, according to this theory, the immune system does not eliminate cells but instead replicates cells whose receptors can recognize and bind with an antigen. The replication is proportional to the degree of recognition and is accompanied by a mutation, leading to individual cells that will be more adapted to the antigen recognition.

3.  Immune network theory: According to this theory which was proposed by Jerne in 1974, immune cells and molecules are capable of recognizing each other in addition to recognizing invading antigens [7,8]. Cells that recognize an antigen are stimulated, resulting in an increased life span, cell activation and antibody secretion. Cells that are recognized by other immune cells are suppressed on the other hand [8].

One further approach that might be considered as a form of evolutionary computation but has become a large research domain of its own is **artificial neural networks** (ANNs). Those networks of connected "neurons," each of them a basic computational unit, are first trained by examples, like networks of synapses in the brain, and are subsequently used, e.g., to classify unknown inputs into the categories learned with the examples. ANNs are also used in many other fields, including approximation, prediction, control, pattern recognition, estimation and optimization. A good overview about ANNs is presented in [9].

Each neuron can receive input, change its internal state and produce output depending on the input and its internal state. The network created by the connected neurons forms a directed, weighted graph. The modification of the weights as well as of the function that calculates the modification of the internal state is inspired by the learning process of the human brain.

ANNs can be classified according to their topology. Common topologies include feed-forward ANNs, recurrent ANNs, Hopfield ANNs, Elman and Jordan ANNs, long short-term memory, bidirectional ANNs, self-organizing maps, stochastic ANNs and physical ANNs.

The selection of a topology that describes the problem as good as possible is the key to a solution that employs simple principles to model a complex behavior. Similar to the human brain, ANNs can be trained using real world data and will come up with a generalized solution. Another similarity to the human brain is the potential to make use of parallel processing, which can decrease the time for computations significantly on hardware that is specifically designed for ANNs or modern CPU and GPU architectures.

Reference [9] describes the different generations of ANNs as they have developed in the past decades. Figure 15.3 shows the first generation, which is based on digital in- and outputs. Each neuron consists of a sum and a threshold section. Neurons of first generation ANNs are also known as perceptrons.

The second generation of ANNs extended the concept by allowing for any real-valued numbers as input and calculating a transfer function, resulting in a real-valued output.

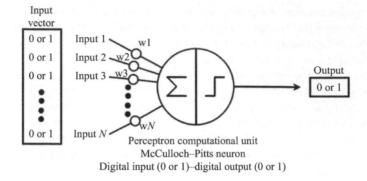

*Figure 15.3    The first generation of artificial neural networks [9]*

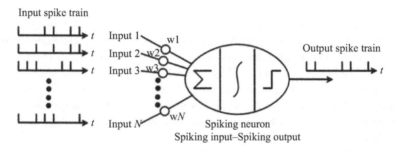

*Figure 15.4    The third generation of artificial neural networks [9]*

The third generation of ANNs added the concept of time to the model by using timed impulses (so-called spikes) as input. This models the neurons of the human brain even closer, as the signals transmitted by real neurons exhibit a similar behavior (Figure 15.4).

**Swarm intelligence (SI)** [10] is a newer approach to nature-inspired algorithms. Contrary to EA, it focuses on the collective social behavior of groups of individuals, typically called agents in this context. Inspirations for these kind of algorithms involve, e.g., flocks of birds maneuvering in the air, swarms of fish or swarms of insects. Typical for these flocks or swarms is the irregular movement of the agents in the problem space. The respective trajectories exhibit decentralized and self-organized patterns, leading to an intelligent global behavior, although the single agents have no knowledge of this behavior. For example, an ant marks its trail by some pheromone. A trail to some food source is marked by several ants, so that other ants tend to follow that trail more often than going at random.

According to [2], SI can be described by considering five fundamental principles:

1.  Proximity principle: The population should be able to carry out simple space and time computations.

2.  Quality principle: The population should be able to respond to quality factors in the environment.
3.  Diverse response principle: The population should not commit its activity along excessively narrow channels.
4.  Stability principle: The population should not change its mode of behavior every time the environment changes.
5.  Adaptability principle: The population should be able to change its behavior mode when it is worth the computational price.

A related approach is **cellular automata** (CA). The basic element of CA is a biological cell which has a fixed set of states and a fixed position within the nodes of a spatial grid. It uses a simple mathematical abstraction of the principles of interaction between biological cells. Toffoli and Margolus showed that CA leads to the definition of a computing medium whose computational power is equivalent to the Turing machine [11]. CAs model and try to explain real-world problems, e.g., about growth and decline of animal or human population in a certain environment. The CA represents the idea that like in SI, complex behavior can result from simple rules.

**Ecology** is inspired by the widest view on nature among the three categories of nature-inspired algorithms. The view comprises the living organisms together with their interaction with an abiotic environment, e.g., air, soil, water, etc. The kind of interactions among species in an ecosystem can be complex, roughly dividable into cooperative (e.g., division of labor) and competitive interactions. An example for such an interaction is the interaction with invasive species. The abiotic environment is taken into account, e.g., in biogeography by analyzing the distribution of species over a given time and space. Cheng described an ecology-inspired approach to a Denial of Service (DoS) attack in cognitive radio networks [12]. He interpreted such networks as ecosystems with inhabitants following the survival of the fittest phenomenon. He showed that inserting a "new species" with a different aim into this ecosystem, members of this species can motivate the other members of the ecosystem to misbehave, thereby causing a collapse of the network.

## 15.3   Application in cryptology

Many tasks in cryptology are a form of optimization, which becomes most obvious when a solution is sought among a multitude of candidates which—other properties achieved—either in cryptography best withstands some form of attack or in cryptanalysis most efficiently can achieve some attack. Hence, nature-inspired methods have been used again and again in cryptology for this and other purposes. In particular, GA, ANN, DNA, CA and ant colony have been exploited in cryptology. For example, Binitha [2] lists a number of nature-inspired approaches that have been used for different purposes in cryptology, see Table 15.2. Over the years, a number of works have tried to provide an overview over parts of the field [2,9,13–15] but do either not consider latest results, or focus on a particular branch within cryptology or

*Table 15.2   Use of nature-inspired approaches in cryptology [2]*

| Biological approach | Cryptology sub-field | Research details | |
| --- | --- | --- | --- |
| GA | Cryptanalysis | Classical cipher | Simple substitution, transposition, polyalphabetic, rotor machine, Knapsack |
| | | Modern cipher | TEA, RSA |
| | Cryptographic primitive | Boolean function and S-Box | |
| | Cryptographic protocols | Protocol design | |
| NN | Cryptanalysis | Unix crypt | |
| | Cryptographic protocols | Key exchange | |
| DNA | Cryptographic algorithm | Encryption | |
| CA | Cryptographic algorithm | Encryption for stream and block cipher | |
| Ant colony | Cryptanalysis | Encryption for block cipher | |

among nature-inspired approaches, or consider cryptology only within a wider focus, or have not been primarily been designed as a survey but as a thesis.

## 15.3.1   Genetic cryptology

Several research papers have applied GA on cryptanalysis or on the design of cryptographic algorithms. Clark provides a good summary of many of the most relevant results in his PhD work [14], including the application of GA on substitution ciphers, transposition ciphers and polyalphabetic ciphers.

Further work is referred to by Bagnall in [16]. In the following, some of the more relevant research papers are listed as examples.

Spillman *et al.* employed GA on the cryptanalysis of simple substitution ciphers in [17] successfully. He derived a cost function from the fact that a well-known cryptographic attack on such ciphers exists, which exploits a weakness against the frequency distribution of characters in the clear text. Spillman could show that a GA algorithm could be used to discover the key for a simple substitution cipher. He recommended to research the use of trigram frequency distribution on crossover and mutation procedures. Spillman did further investigations on the use of GA on the cryptanalysis of Knapsack ciphers, which are based on the NP-complete, i.e., hard Knapsack problem.

Matthews [14,18] applied GA on transposition ciphers. He based the cost function on the message length, the frequency distribution of bigrams and trigrams (sequences of two resp. three characters) and the probability of the occurrence in successfully deciphered messages.

Clark and Dawson proposed new attacks on classical ciphers, making use of simulated annealing and tabu search [4]. They showed the tabu search to be superior to other techniques when used in the cryptanalysis of such ciphers. They furthermore applied a parallel GA to attack a polyalphabetic substitution cipher, effectively solving each of the key positions simultaneously [19]. This was proven to be a highly efficient method to in solve polyalphabetic ciphers even with large periods.

Bagnall did not only provide a good summary of existing research on the field of GA in cryptography but also did a cryptanalysis of the rotor machine [16]. He based the cost function on the phi-test for nonrandomness of text and was able to break a three-rotor machine with only 4,000 letters of ciphertext.

There are more notable works employing GA on cryptanalysis of classic ciphers, including [20–24]. At the same time, work is ramping up on GA for modern ciphers, e.g., on the Tiny Encryption Algorithm (TEA) [25] as well as on RSA [26] (named after the initials of the inventors Rivest, Shamir and Adleman). In addition, GA was applied successfully to the design of S-boxes (a substitution table used as primitive in ciphers) and Boolean functions (that describe the linear combinations of columns of S-boxes, thereby adding nonlinearity). Usually, Boolean functions are created either randomly (with accordingly random properties), or constructed directly according to given design criteria (typically only fulfilling exactly those, but no others). In [27], Millan combined GA with a two-step hill climbing algorithm for the generation of Boolean functions, improving the performance of the GA significantly. In [28], Dimovski did a direct comparison of the result of random and GA methods, showing that GA was more efficient. Last but not least, it is mentionable that Clark could extend the design using GA toward the development of security protocols, being able to prove the correctness of the evolved protocols [29].

## 15.3.2 *Neural cryptology*

The two main application areas of ANNs in cryptology are cryptanalysis and key exchange [5]. Ramzan performed a cryptanalysis on the Unix crypt cryptosystems in 1998, proving that the ANN could predict many of the plain text bits with a high confidence, although the used transfer function of the ANN was simple [30].

The work on neural key exchange is a comparably new research area [31–33]. The purpose of key exchange protocols is to exchange cryptographic keys for a subsequent encryption over public channels in a secure way. Classic key exchange protocols are based on mathematical trapdoor functions that are easy to calculate but very hard to revert. A typical example of such a function is the discrete logarithm that is the basis for the Diffie–Hellman protocol. Neural key exchange protocols are not based on number theory, but instead on the synchronization of neural networks by mutual learning [31]. Kanter showed that two perceptrons (classifiers consisting of a simplified form of an artificial network) being trained on their mutual outputs develop an antiparallel state of their synaptic weights (see Figure 15.5).

The synchronized weights can be used to construct a key exchange protocol that is supposedly hard to break, because the tracking of the weights is a hard problem compared to the synchronization of the networks. Klimov *et al.* were able to

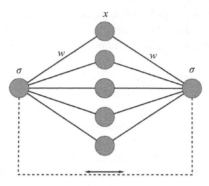

*Figure 15.5    Two perceptrons receive an identical input x and learn their mutual output bits σ [32]*

demonstrate that there are at least three different approaches to break the protocol shortly after though [33]. Kinzel extended the research work to multilayer networks [32]. Mislovaty combined this approach with the synchronization of chaotic systems, resulting in a higher security of the resulting key-exchange protocols. Ruttor combined neural cryptography with a feedback mechanism, which also results in increased security [34].

Another example for the use of ANN is [35], where continuous authentication is achieved not by reentering a password (which annoys users) but by repeatedly checking keystroke dynamics by a neural network, to reliably distinguish the logged in user from other users.

### 15.3.3    Artificial immune systems in cryptology

Ibrahim compares in [5] AIS with GA and ANN, coming to the conclusion that they share certain properties that might make AIS usable for cryptographic applications. He mentions the ability to solve hard problems [36], as well as the similarity between the clonal selection and GA [8,37]. He refers to de Castro, who stated that the clonal selection can be interpreted as Charles Darwin's law of evolution, with the three major principles of repertoire: diversity, genetic variation and natural selection [37]. These similarities lead him to the conclusion that AIS algorithms may be applied in the same cryptology subfield where GA is applied successfully. Furthermore, he lists successful applications of immune network models to improve ANN models [7,38]. In addition, Tarakanov showed the general possibility of using formal immune network for encryption in [39]. While none of these research works employed AIS successfully directly in cryptographic applications, the existing investigations indicate that further research is worth conducting.

### 15.3.4    Other biological approaches in cryptology

In addition to the nature-inspired approaches to cryptology mentioned above, different other methods can be found in literature. CA have been used by Wolfram already in

1985 [40]. Nandi used them for hardware implementations of block and stream ciphers [41]. DNA has been used successfully to create one-time-pads, taking advantage of its ultrascale computation and compact storage [42]. Also, ant colony algorithms have been applied in the context of cryptography, e.g., by Bafghi to perform a differential cryptanalysis on the Serpent algorithm [43].

## 15.4 Recent developments

In this section, several research publications from the recent years are described, which either deepen the approaches from the previous sections or incorporate new methods. Two areas with significant research activity in the context of cryptography seem to be evolutionary computation and artificial neural networks which gain a lot of attention in all applications recently. Furthermore, a completely different approach is secure data exchange inspired by nature is presented as an example for out-of-the-box thinking.

### *15.4.1 Evolutionary approaches*

Several recent publications focus on EAs. A good general overview of the potential of these algorithms is given in [15], with the goal to show that evolutionary computation can (and should) be considered as a viable choice when addressing certain difficult problems in cryptology.

Picek claims in this publication that GAs are "not only genetic, but also generic." His work is based on a framework, called GET, that is used to conduct experiments regarding the evolution of Boolean functions and S-boxes. Picek evaluates (among others) the effectiveness of different methods, including genetic programing, Cartesian genetic programming, GAs and evolution strategy when applying them on cryptographic Boolean functions. He shows that for this particular problem, the two variations of genetic programming are much more effective in finding a solution than the other approaches.

Picek's conclusion is that although the application of EC in the cryptology area is not a large research domain, it is a rewarding area that has still a lot to offer in respect of research. He urges the crypto community to work together with the evolutionary computation community and to combine their strengths, as he sees this as an area where the complementary work of both communities has larger impact than the sum of those two communities.

Two recent publications have taken on the challenge, although due to their publication date not necessarily motivated by Picek's work. In [44], Polak applies GAs in order to break line feedback shift registers as depicted in Figure 15.6, which are commonly used to create pseudorandom numbers, e.g., formerly used in cryptographic protocols. She successfully determines the state and parameters of the Linear Feedback Shift Register (LFSR), allowing her to calculate any further pseudo random numbers generated by the algorithm and therefore break any encryption that is based on such an LFSR. This practical experiment shows how powerful GAs can be,

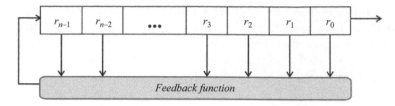

*Figure 15.6    Feedback shift register [44]*

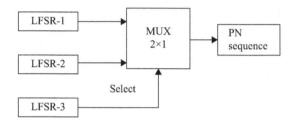

*Figure 15.7    Geffe generator [45]*

although LFSRs are comparably easy to break using other methods. This is particularly interesting, because GAs due to their heuristic nature usually give only approximate solutions.

In [45], Din successfully determines the states of a Geffe generator as shown in Figure 15.7, a nonlinear binary key sequence generator based on several LFSRs. A GA-based search approach and a divide-and-conquer attack are employed, with simulation results showing that the proposed scheme obtains the initial states correctly in optimal time. The author suggests that the proposed scheme can be applied to solve other nonlinear random binary key sequence generators, too.

### 15.4.2    Artificial neural networks

An area of nature-inspired approaches toward cryptography and cryptanalysis that recently seems to get increased attention is the application of ANNs. In [9], ANNs and GAs are suggested to be used to extract certain information about ciphers. Proposals are made how to identify properties like the language of the plain text, or the cipher type for classical ciphers from the cipher text only. As future research, the authors target to not only identify the general type of encryption algorithms (e.g., classical cipher, block cipher and public-key cipher) but extend the method to identify the exact algorithm (e.g., Data Encryption Standard (DES), Advanced Encryption Standard (AES) and Twofish).

### 15.4.3    Out-of-the-box thinking

Nature continues to inspire researchers to new creative solutions. These inspirations are not only limited to algorithmic optimizations but foster an out-of-the-box thinking

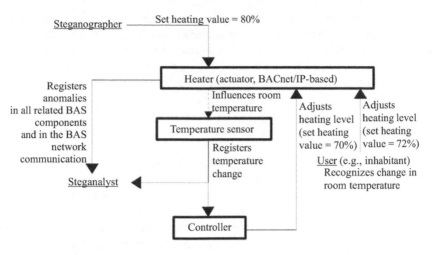

*Figure 15.8   Hiding information in actuator values [46]*

and a look onto a problem from fresh viewing angles. A good example for this is [46], where scatter hoarding (the distribution of food over many widely spaced caches with only few items in each, done by animals) was inspiring a method for covert information exchange using cyber physical systems like actuators used in smart buildings. The method makes either use of unused registers of devices or modifies actuator states in a way that it does not draw attention to it (cf. Figure 15.8). This allows steganographers (people who are exchanging information in an inconspicuous rather than encrypted way) to use public facilities like airports or train stations for their means. This method typically only allows a small amount of data to be exchanged, because the availability of unused registers and of possible modifications of used registers that lead to a negligible impact on the behavior of the smart building is limited. On the upside, this is a new method for which currently no counter-measures seem to exist, which makes cyber physical systems well suited, secure steganographic storage objects.

## 15.4.4   Conclusion and outlook

The examples shown in this chapter demonstrate that nature-inspired algorithms and methods have been applied very successfully to cryptographic problems. With the ongoing development toward faster hardware and the ubiquitousness of highly parallel processing power, e.g., by recent GPUs, the application areas of existing optimization algorithms will become larger and larger. The problems that can be solved will become more and more complex and the arms race between cryptanalysts and cryptographers will continue.

Several of the cited research works came to the conclusion that the combination of different algorithms, e.g., of ANN, AIS and GA can lead to better results. Therefore, it can be expected that this area will be a focus of future research work. Furthermore, some of the classes of nature-inspired algorithms are very wide, e.g., SI and ecology. For these classes, probably only the surface of possibilities has been scratched, and there is still a lot of room left to extend research. At the same time, researchers will continue to draw inspiration from nature, leaving the classical paths of solutions and coming up with unexpected ideas that approach problems in a new way.

# References

[1]    Menezes AJ, van Oorschot PC, Vanstone SA. Handbook of Applied Cryptography. Boca Raton, FL: CRC Press; 1996.
[2]    Binitha S and Sathya SS. A Survey of Bio Inspired Optimization Algorithms. International Journal of Soft Computing and Engineering. 2012;2(2):137–151.
[3]    Back T. Evolutionary Algorithms in Theory and Practice: Evolution Strategies, Evolutionary Programming, Genetic Algorithms. Oxford, UK: Oxford University Press; 1996.
[4]    Clark A, Dawson E. Optimisation Heuristics for the Automated Cryptanalysis of Classical Ciphers. Journal of Combinatorial Mathematics and Combinatorial Computing. 1998;28:63–86.
[5]    Ibrahim S, Maarof MA. A Review on Biological Inspired Computation in Cryptology. Jurnal Teknologi Maklumat. 2005;17(1):90–98.
[6]    Deb K. Genetic Algorithm in Search and Optimization: The Technique and Applications. In: Proceedings of International Workshop on Soft Computing and Intelligent Systems; 1998. p. 58–87.
[7]    De Castro LN, Timmis JI. Artificial Immune Systems as a Novel Soft Computing Paradigm. Soft Computing. 2003;7(8):526–544.
[8]    De Castro LN. Immune, Swarm, and Evolutionary Algorithms. Part I: Basic Models. In: Neural Information Processing, 2002. ICONIP'02. Proceedings of the 9th International Conference on. vol. 3. IEEE; 2002. p. 1464–1468.
[9]    Al-Janabi S, Al-Khateeb B, Abd A. Intelligent Techniques in Cryptanalysis: Review and Future Directions. UHD Journal of Science and Technology. 2017;1(1):1–10.
[10]   Kennedy J, Eberhart R. Particle Swarm Optimization. In: Proceedings of IEEE International Conference on Neural Networks. IEEE; 1995. p. 1942–1948.
[11]   Tarakanov AO, Skormin VA, Sokolova SP. Immunocomputing: Principles and Applications. Luxembourg: Springer Science & Business Media; 2013.
[12]   Cheng SM, Chen PY. Ecology-Based DoS Attack in Cognitive Radio Networks. In: IEEE Security and Privacy Workshops (SPW); 2016. p. 104–110.
[13]   Bergmann KP. Cryptanalysis Using Nature-Inspired Optimization Algorithms [Master thesis]. University of Calgary; 2007.
[14]   Clark JA. Nature-Inspired Cryptography: Past, Present and Future. In: The 2003 Congress on Evolutionary Computation (CEC '03). vol. 3; 2003. p. 1647–1654.
[15]   Picek S. Applications of Evolutionary Computation to Cryptology [Thesis]. Radboud University Nijmegen and University of Zagreb; 2015.

[16] Bagnall AJ. The Applications of Genetic Algorithms in Cryptanalysis. School of Information Systems, University of East Anglia; 1996.

[17] Spillman R, Janssen M, Nelson B, *et al.* Use of a Genetic Algorithm in the Cryptanalysis of Simple Substitution Ciphers. Cryptologia. 1993;17(1): 31–44.

[18] Matthews RA. The Use of Genetic Algorithms in Cryptanalysis. Cryptologia. 1993;17(2):187–201.

[19] Clark A, Dawson E. A Parallel Genetic Algorithm for Cryptanalysis of the Polyalphabetic Substitution Cipher. Cryptologia. 1997;21(2):129–138.

[20] Dimovski A, Gligoroski D. Attack on the Polyalphabetic Substitution Cipher using a Parallel Genetic Algorithm. Swiss-Macedonian Scientific Cooperation through SCOPES Project; 2003.

[21] Dimovski A, Gligoroski D. Attacks on the Transposition Ciphers Using Optimization Heuristics. In: Proceedings of ICEST; 2003. p. 1–4.

[22] Morelli R, Walde R. A Word-Based Genetic Algorithm for Cryptanalysis of Short Cryptograms. In: FLAIRS Conference; 2003. p. 229–233.

[23] Morelli R, Walde R, Servos W. A Study of Heuristic Approaches for Breaking Short Cryptograms. International Journal on Artificial Intelligence Tools. 2004;13(01):45–64.

[24] Servos W. Using a Genetic Algorithm to Break Alberti Cipher. Journal of Computing Sciences in Colleges. 2004;19(5):294–295.

[25] Hernández JC, Sierra JM, Isasi P, *et al.* Genetic Cryptoanalysis of Two Rounds TEA. In: International Conference on Computational Science. Springer; 2002. p. 1024–1031.

[26] Ali H, Al-Salami M. Timing Attack Prospect for RSA Cryptanalysis Using Genetic Algorithm Technique. The International Arab Journal of Information Technology. 2004;1(1):80–85.

[27] Millan W, Clark A, Dawson E. Heuristic Design of Cryptographically Strong Balanced Boolean Functions. In: Advances in Cryptology—EUROCRYPT'98; 1998. p. 489–499.

[28] Dimovski A, Gligoroski D. Generating Highly Nonlinear Boolean Functions Using a Genetic Algorithm. In: Telecommunications in Modern Satellite, Cable and Broadcasting Service, 2003. TELSIKS 2003. 6th International Conference on. vol. 2. IEEE; 2003. p. 604–607.

[29] Clark JA. Metaheuristic Search as a Cryptological Tool [PhD]. University of York; 2002.

[30] Ramzan Z. On Using Neural Networks to Break Cryptosystems. Cambridge, MA: MIT Press; 1998.

[31] Kanter I, Kinzel W, Kanter E. Secure Exchange of Information by Synchronization of Neural Networks. EPL (Europhysics Letters). 2002;57(1):141.

[32] Kinzel W, Kanter I. Interacting Neural Networks and Cryptography. In: Advances in Solid State Physics. Berlin: Springer; 2002. p. 383–391.

[33] Klimov A, Mityagin A, Shamir A. Analysis of Neural Cryptography. In: International Conference on the Theory and Application of Cryptology and Information Security. Springer; 2002. p. 288–298.

[34]    Ruttor A, Kinzel W, Shacham L, *et al.* Neural Cryptography with Feedback. Physical Review E. 2004;69(4):046110.

[35]    Acar A, Aksu H, Uluagac AS, *et al.* WACA: Wearable-Assisted Continuous Authentication. In: Proc. 3rd Workshop on Bio-inspired Security, Trust, Assurance and Resilience (BioSTAR 2018); 2018.

[36]    Tomassini M. Evolutionary Algorithms. In: Towards Evolvable Hardware. Berlin: Springer Verlag; 1996. p. 19–47.

[37]    De Castro LN, Von Zuben FJ. Learning and Optimization Using the Clonal Selection Principle. IEEE Transactions on Evolutionary Computation. 2002;6(3):239–251.

[38]    De Castro LN, Von Zuben FJ. An Immunological Approach to Initialize Feedforward Neural Network Weights. In: Artificial Neural Nets and Genetic Algorithms. Berlin: Springer; 2001. p. 126–129.

[39]    Tarakanov AO. Information Security with Formal Immune Networks. In: International Workshop on Mathematical Methods, Models, and Architectures for Network Security. Berlin: Springer; 2001. p. 115–126.

[40]    Wolfram S. Cryptography with Cellular Automata. In: Conference on the Theory and Application of Cryptographic Techniques. Springer; 1985. p. 429–432.

[41]    Nandi S, Kar BK, Chaudhuri PP. Theory and Applications of Cellular Automata in Cryptography. IEEE Transactions on computers. 1994;43(12):1346–1357.

[42]    Gehani A, LaBean T, Reif J. DNA-Based Cryptography. Lecture Notes in Computer Science. 2003;2950:167–188.

[43]    Bafghi AG, Sadeghiyan B. Differential Model of Block Ciphers with Ant Colony Technique. In: Proceedings of the Second International Symposium on Telecommunications, Iran; 2003. p. 556–560.

[44]    Polak I, Boryczka M. Breaking LFSR Using Genetic Algorithm. In: International Conference on Computational Collective Intelligence. Springer; 2013. p. 731–738.

[45]    Din M, Bhateja AK, Ratan R. Cryptanalysis of Geffe Generator Using Genetic Algorithm. In: Proceedings of the Third International Conference on Soft Computing for Problem Solving. Springer; 2014. p. 509–515.

[46]    Wendzel S, Mazurczyk W, Haas G. Don't You Touch My Nuts: Information Hiding in Cyber Physical Systems. In: IEEE Security and Privacy Workshops (SPW). River Publishers; 2017. p. 29–34.

*Chapter 16*

# Generation of access-control schemes in computer networks based on genetic algorithms

*Igor Kotenko[1] and Igor Saenko[1]*

The nature-inspired approaches and methods are widely used now for the solution of problems in cases when classical mathematical ones fail. Fully it concerns also the problems solved in the field of computer security. One of such types of problems is the optimization of access-control schemes in computer networks. A common example of such problem is the formation of access-control schemes in databases, which use a role-based access-control (RBAC) model. This problem was singled out in a separate direction in data mining and received the name "role mining problem" (RMP). Another example is to generate a scheme of the virtual local computer network (VLAN) where network hosts must be distributed among the minimum quantity of virtual subnets. Both problems are NP-complete. A set of different approaches was offered to solve these problems. However, none of them can be considered as universal one. At the same time, genetic algorithms, which are one of the most characteristic representatives of nature-inspired approaches and methods, can be considered as a basis for such universal solutions. The chapter outlines the mathematical foundations for generation of access-control schemes in computer networks, and examples of generating the RBAC and VLAN schemes are considered. The chapter demonstrates that these optimization problems belong to the class of Boolean matrix factorization (BMF) problems. Besides, it shows how to use genetic algorithms for their solving. Some enhancements in these algorithms which allow increasing the speed of their operation and accuracy of decisions are considered.

## 16.1 State of the art

Access control is one of the most important sides of information and computer security in modern computer networks. Access-control mechanisms consist in establishment for each user of a computer network a set of allowed permissions, or the rights for making any actions over the resources that are available in the network and also

[1]St. Petersburg Institute for Informatics and Automation of Russian Academy of Sciences (SPIIRAS), Laboratory of Computer Security Problems, Russia

in provision of compliance with these permissions. A set of rules regulating the accessibility or deviation of these permissions is an *access-control policy*. If the rules have a simple form and can be presented in the form of assignments connecting users to allowed permissions, then in this case instead of an access-control policy it is possible to speak about a *configuration*, or an *access-control scheme* (similar to a database scheme when considering the database structure).

The type of the access-control scheme depends on the access-control model which is used in the computer network. One of the first such models was the discretionary access-control (DAC) model, or Harrison, Ruzzo, Ullman model [1]. Using the DAC model, the access-control scheme may be presented in the form of a matrix, which columns correspond to users; rows—to network resources; and allowed user's permissions are written in its cells. Other representation form for the DAC scheme is access-control lists (ACL) which are created for each user. Each ACL element contains a set of user's permissions concerning the resources of the computer network.

Access-control schemes for the DAC model are evident and simple to implement. However, they have the following essential shortcoming. In the case of substantial increase of the number of users or resources of the computer network, these schemes become very large, superfluous, and very difficult to be controlled. This shortcoming becomes especially noticeable when it is possible to select user groups among the users of the computer network, where all users in the user group have the same set of permissions to a limited set of resources. In this case, the access matrix will contain very large number of empty (and for this reason superfluous) cells, and the ACL will be duplicated.

For overcoming this shortcoming, Sandhu offered an access-control model in which besides a set of users and a set of permissions, the third set of elements called *roles* is selected [2]. In this model, the user has the right to implement the required permissions if the user belongs to a role, and this role has these permissions. This access-control model received the name of the RBAC model. Now the RBAC model is used everywhere in many areas of computer networks, for example, for access to database records, to accounts of operating systems, and others. Besides, the RBAC model is standardized [3,4].

The RBAC scheme, unlike the DAC scheme, can be represented not by one but two Boolean matrixes: the matrix "users–roles" and the matrix "roles–permissions." The matrix "users–permissions" which shall conform to the requirements determined by an access-control policy is the result of the multiplication of these matrixes.

Determination of a set of roles and a type of the related matrixes "users–roles" and "roles–permissions" separated in computer science into an individual scientific direction called *role engineering* [5]. At the same time, two approaches are selected here. The first approach is *top-down* one in which the set of roles is searched out by analyzing the tasks fulfilled by users. Some works, the most interesting of which are [6–10], are devoted to this approach. However, in this approach, as a rule, there are no complex optimization problems and, therefore, there is no need in genetic algorithms.

The second approach is *bottom-up* one. In it, a set of roles and matrixes related with them is found by analyzing the required matrix "users–permissions." However, it is necessary to note that if some conditions (criteria) are not superimposed on the resultant set of roles, then there will be rather large number of possible RBAC schemes which differ in the quantity of roles and the type of matrixes "users–roles" and "roles–permissions." Therefore, the RBAC schemes satisfying some criteria are searched out. This approach, due to its complexity, is named *role mining*. *RMP* is considered as one of the problems related to data mining [11].

Several variants of the problem statement for RMP, which differ in the used criteria to search for access-control schemes, are offered [12]. For example, the variant in which it is required to provide the minimum quantity of roles in the case of complete coincidence of the given and resultant matrixes "users–permissions" is named *Basic RMP*. The variant in which it is required to provide the minimum quantity of assignments (i.e., nonzero elements in matrixes "users–roles" and "roles–permissions") is named *Edge RMP*. These and other possible RMP variants belong to problems of nonlinear integer programing with different types of objective functions and restrictions. More precisely, different RMP variants belong to the problems of *BMF*, and the BMF problem is NP-complete [13]. At the same time, a dimensionality of this problem is rather large. For solving such problems, traditional methods of mathematical programing (methods of "branches and boundaries" and "directional descent" and others) are not effective as they cannot be used in real or in close to real timescale.

Different approaches were offered for solving different RMP variants. For instance, a cluster approach was offered by Kuhlmann *et al.* [14]. However, it requires to account the additional parameters characterizing business processes and users. Vaidya *et al.* [15] and Blundo *et al.* [16] suggested simple heuristic techniques for solving the basic RMP variant. These solutions are based on combinatorial algorithms. For lowering their complexity, Colantonio *et al.* [17] and Frank *et al.* [18] developed probability models. However, the accuracy of solving the problem using this approach is not guaranteed. An approach based on a clustering model of Boolean data was offered in [19], where it is shown that this model is applicable for solving particular variants of RMP. A cost-driven approach was proposed in [20] where the criterion on administration expenses is used. This criterion will be used by us further for solving the problem of reconfiguring access-control schemes.

Despite existence of a variety of different algorithms for solving RMP, there is no universal, suitable one for all of RMP variants. Genetic algorithms were proposed and investigated by authors for solving different variants of RMP in [21–23]. The results of this research were generalized and used for another type of the access-control scheme implemented in VLAN.

It is known that implementation of VLAN technology in local computer networks means that a set of logical fragments known as *virtual subnets* is created in the network. Each node of the local area network (LAN) can belong to one or several virtual subnets. Creation of VLAN can be carried out by different methods— port-based, MAC-based, protocol-based, and authentication-based ones [24]. These methods guarantee that if two hosts do not belong to the same virtual subnet, then data exchange does not happen between them. Using the VLAN technology to protect information flows in the computer network is very convenient for security administrators as all actions necessary for this purpose can be localized in one place, for example, in the switch or the router. The alternative protection method based on using the ACL in operating systems is also possible, but it is not same flexible. To reconfigure the organization scheme of information flows, this approach requires that the security administrator should visit remote workstations, but that is not always possible.

The problem of creating an additional level of computer protection against the insider attacks on the basis of virtual subnets is insufficiently considered in scientific literature. As a rule, creation of virtual subnets based on the VLAN technology happens on the basis of other factors which are not related with solving this problem. Now, creation of virtual networks in computer networks is fulfilled mainly by functional features. According to this approach, as a rule, the virtual area networks are created around separate servers, forbidding access of computers from other groups. Thus, the legitimate information exchange between workstations can be forbidden.

More effective is an approach when for a given matrix of logical computer connectivity (i.e., a Boolean matrix "computers–computers"), there is a Boolean matrix "computers–subnets" such that the matrix "computers–computers" is a result of the multiplication of the matrix "computers–subnets" on the matrix "subnets–computers," where the last matrix is the transposed resultant matrix "computers–subnets." If we do not superimpose any conditions on quantity of subnets, then this problem will have many solutions. If we require that the quantity of the virtual subnets must be minimum, then the problem becomes a kind of the data mining problems, and it can be named *VLAN mining problem (VMP)*. It will be, as well as RMP, a kind of the BMF problem. Besides, it will be NP-complete for this reason and will require effective methods to solve it.

The works, devoted to solving VMP, are not enough. For example, Tai *et al.* [25] suggested to apply cluster analysis for solving this problem. However, this approach is oriented generally on mobile ad hoc networks. We showed in [26] that VMP can be reduced to the problem of *Boolean matrix self-factorization (BMSF)*. We did not find the works containing algorithms for solving it. There are some papers considering the algorithms to solve the BMF problem [13,27]. However, they have restrictions on scalability. Snasel *et al.* [28] offered the genetic algorithm for the BMF problem. However, it cannot be applied for solving the BMSF problem and, therefore, cannot be applied for VMP. Using the genetic algorithm for optimization of the VLAN structure was proposed in [29]. However, the BMSF problem was not considered in this work, and it is possible to claim that the development of effective algorithms is still required to solve the VMP.

The given above statements of problems for generation of the RBAC and VLAN access-control schemes reflect the *static case* of access control, when the access-control policy was not changed during a long time. In *dynamic case*, this policy can be changed rather often due to changing the structure of a set of users and a set of the permissions allowed them. Now this direction is researched actively within a kind of RBAC models named *temporal RBAC (TBAC)* [30,31]. However, TBAC did not gain yet the same wide propagation as RBAC and is not supported broadly by developers of access-control software. Therefore, together with the static case which we will name as the problems of *initial design of RBAC and VLAN schemes*, we will consider the problems of *reconfiguring these schemes*. In these problems, it is required to transform the previous access-control scheme to new one taking into account the happened changes in the access-control policy. A search criterion for the new access-control scheme will be the minimum of actions needed to be executed for implementation of such transformation. In other words, the criterion of such problem will be the minimum of administration costs. Accounting such criterion is quite reasonable as it allows to transfer to new access-control schemes for the minimal time.

The problem of reconfiguring the access-control schemes is considered in literature rather seldom. A risk-based approach is offered for solving this problem in [32]. However, the criterion of risk minimization used at this approach does not guarantee the complete satisfaction of new requirements of an access-control policy. Besides, it does not consider time required for reconfiguring. In our approach, which is considered in [33,34], the reconfiguring time is minimal. At the same time, the complete satisfaction of new requirements of an access-control policy is provided.

Among a large number of works about genetic algorithms, we are interested in the works applying these algorithms for the purposes of access control and computer security. One of the first such examples is provided in [35]. However, in this work, the genetic algorithms are used not for a generation of RBAC schemes. Classification of genetic algorithms and propositions on their application for wireless networks design are given in [36]. Multi-objective optimization problem to search for the medium access-control protocol parameters in network architecture is considered in [37]. In this paper, the genetic algorithm showed high performance to search for Pareto optimal solutions. However, the variables of this problem had scalar values. Therefore, this problem is less difficult than RMP. Genetic algorithms were proposed for access control of web services in [38] and for intrusion detection in [39]. However, problems solved in these works also are less difficult than RMP. The genetic algorithms used for solving these problems had a standard form. Each individual in these algorithms had one chromosome, and genes of chromosomes were binary elements.

Thus, the analysis of relevant works allows to draw the following conclusions. First, the known works on generation of the required access-control schemes on the example of RBAC and VLAN are not integrated by a uniform approach. Second, the known works on the design of RBAC and VLAN schemes do not investigate the issues of their reconfiguring though this problem is no less important than the design one. At last, the known works on applying genetic algorithms for computer security do not consider RMP and VPN. The solutions, which are considered in the chapter, are directed on elimination of all these shortcomings.

## 16.2 Mathematical foundations

In this section, we will discuss three problem statements: first, for the RBAC scheme design; second, for the VLAN scheme design, and, finally, for reconfiguring the RBAC and VLAN access-control schemes.

## 16.2.1    RBAC scheme design

Let us suppose that the RBAC model defines conditions of an access of $m$ users to $n$ permissions by $k$ roles. Let us introduce the following necessary formal designations (these designations are taken from [11,12,17]):

- $U = \{u_i\},$  $i = 1, \ldots, m,$  $m = |U|$ —set of users;
- $PRMS = \{p_j\},$  $j = 1, \ldots, n,$  $n = |PRMS|$ —set of permissions;
- $ROLES = \{r_l\},$  $l = 1, \ldots, k,$  $k = |ROLES|$ —set of roles;
- $UA \subseteq U \times ROLES$—a many-to-many mapping of user-to-role assignments;
- $PA \subseteq PRMS \times ROLES$—a many-to-many mapping of role-to-permission assignments;
- $UPA \subseteq U \times PRMS$—a many-to-many mapping of user-to-permission assignments.

A tuple <$U$, *PRMS*, *ROLES*, *UA*, *PA*> is usually called *RBAC configuration* or *RBAC scheme*. We will adhere further to the second definition.

Traditional RMP, or RBAC scheme design problem, claims that for the given $U$, *PRMS*, *ROLES,* and *UPA* it is required to search for *UA* and *PA*, which would meet some criterion. The type of this criterion defines different variants of RMP. The most popular RMP variants are as follows:

- Basic RMP, if the quantity of roles $k$ must be minimum.
- Edge RMP, if the total number of assignments in *UA* and *PA* mappings must be minimum.
- Minimal Noise RMP, if under the given $k$ the discrepancy between the given *UPA* mapping and the mapping of user-to-permission assignments which turns out by means of the *UA* and *PA* mappings is minimum.
- $\delta$-*Approx*. RMP, if the discrepancy between a given *UPA* mapping and the mapping of user-to-permission assignments which turns out by means of the *UA* and *PA* mappings does not exceed the preset value $\delta$, and the value $k$ is minimum.

The example of graphical representation of the RBAC scheme is given in Figure 16.1. This example is borrowed from [12].

Figure 16.1(a) shows the mapping between $U$ and *PRMS* which is required to be received by means of the RBAC scheme. Figure 16.1(b) shows how the mapping between $U$ and *PRMS* is formed, if consistently to connect two mappings *UA* and *PA*. The mapping turning out as a result of consecutive connection of *UA* and *PA* mappings is called *direct UPA*, or *DUPA*. The *UA* and *PA* mappings need to be found. The *UPA* mapping is given.

It is easy to find out that the example given in Figure 16.1 corresponds to the basic RMP and edge RMP variants. The *DUPA* mapping, which turns out at the consecutive connection of *UA* and *PA* mappings, completely coincides with the required *UPA* mapping. At the same time, the value $k$ accepts the minimal value equaled to three, and the total number of assignments in the *UA* and *PA* mappings is equal to 13.

*UPA, DUPA, UA,* and *PA* mappings are represented using Boolean matrices. We assume that the *UPA* mapping corresponds to an $m \times n$ Boolean matrix $\mathbf{A} = M(UPA)$,

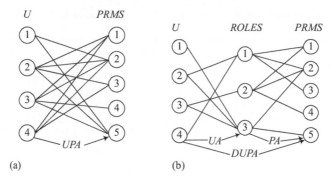

*Figure 16.1   Example of mappings between sets of users, permissions, and roles: (a) UPA mapping and (b) UA and PA mappings*

where 1 in cell $\{ij\}$ indicates the assignment of permission $j$ to user $i$. Similarly, we define the matrixes $\mathbf{DA} = M(DUPA)$, $\mathbf{X} = M(UA)$, and $\mathbf{Y} = M(PA)$.

It is not hard to see that the matrixes $\mathbf{DA}$, $\mathbf{X}$, and $\mathbf{Y}$ are related to each other by the following expression:

$$\mathbf{DA} = \mathbf{X} \otimes \mathbf{Y}, \tag{16.1}$$

where the symbol $\otimes$ denotes Boolean matrix multiplication, which is a form of matrix multiplication, based on the rules of Boolean algebra. Boolean matrix multiplication allows to obtain the elements of matrix $\mathbf{DA}$ according to the following expression: $da_{il} = \bigvee_{j=1}^{n} (x_{ij} \wedge y_{jl})$, where $x_{ij}$ is the element of matrix $\mathbf{X}$ in the cell $\{i, j\}$, $y_{jl}$ is the element of matrix $\mathbf{Y}$ in the cell $\{j, l\}$.

Using expression (16.1), the example given in Figure 16.1 can be written by the following expression:

$$\begin{pmatrix} 0 & 1 & 0 & 0 & 1 \\ 1 & 1 & 1 & 0 & 1 \\ 1 & 1 & 0 & 1 & 1 \\ 1 & 1 & 1 & 0 & 0 \end{pmatrix} = \begin{pmatrix} 0 & 0 & 1 \\ 1 & 0 & 1 \\ 0 & 1 & 1 \\ 1 & 0 & 0 \end{pmatrix} \otimes \begin{pmatrix} 1 & 1 & 1 & 0 & 0 \\ 1 & 1 & 0 & 1 & 0 \\ 0 & 1 & 0 & 0 & 1 \end{pmatrix}.$$

In order to define the distance between Boolean matrixes, the concept of $L_1$-*norm* is used [12]. For two matrixes $\mathbf{A}$ and $\mathbf{B}$ of identical dimensionalities, this metrics is calculated as follows:

$$\|\mathbf{A} - \mathbf{B}\|_1 = \sum_{i=1}^{m} \sum_{j=1}^{n} |a_{ij} - b_{ij}|. \tag{16.2}$$

Using (16.2), the criteria of the generation of RBAC schemes for different variants of RMP can be presented in the form shown in Table 16.1.

Thus, for basic variant of the criterion is as follows: if the *UPA* and *DUPA* are identical, it is necessary to obtain the minimal number of roles $k = |ROLES|$. For the variant edge, we require the complete coincidence of *UPA* and *DUPA* and the

*Table 16.1   Criteria for the problems of RBAC scheme design*

| No. | Variants | Criteria | |
|-----|----------|----------|---|
| 1 | Basic RMP | $\|UPA - DUPA\|_1 = 0$, | $\|ROLES\| \Rightarrow$ min |
| 2 | Edge RMP | $\|UPA - DUPA\|_1 = 0$, | $\|UA\| + \|PA\| \Rightarrow$ min |
| 3 | Minimal noise RMP | $\|UPA - DUPA\|_1 \Rightarrow$ min, | $\|ROLES\| =$ const |
| 4 | $\delta-$ Approx. RMP | $\|UPA - DUPA\|_1 \leq \delta$, | $\|ROLES\| =$ min |

minimum of the sum $|UA| + |PA|$. For the variant minimal noise, it is necessary for the fixed number of roles $k = |ROLES|$ to obtain the minimal difference between *UPA* and *DUPA*. For the variant $\delta$-Approx., we should get the minimal number of roles $k = |ROLES|$ if the difference between *UPA* and *DUPA* does not exceed the specified value $\delta$.

Using (16.1), the problem statement for the variant basic is as follows. For given $U$, *PRMS*, and $\mathbf{A} = M(UPA)$, we should find *ROLES*, $\mathbf{X} = M(UA)$, and $\mathbf{Y} = M(PA)$, so that $|ROLES| \rightarrow$ min and the following expression is true:

$$\mathbf{A} = \mathbf{X} \otimes \mathbf{Y}. \tag{16.3}$$

The expression (16.3) is an expression of the problem of BMF. The essence of this problem is to decompose the Boolean matrix $\mathbf{A}$ into two matrixes $\mathbf{X}$ and $\mathbf{Y}$, the Boolean matrix multiplication of which gives $\mathbf{A}$ as a result. This decomposition has many solutions, but we want to find such one in which the maximal value of the total index of these matrices will be minimal.

The problem statement for the edge variant differs from the basic variant that instead of criteria $|ROLES| \rightarrow$ min the criterion $|UA| + |PA| \rightarrow$ min is used.

In the minimal noise variant, the criterion would be $\|\mathbf{X} \otimes \mathbf{Y} - \mathbf{A}\|_1 \rightarrow$ min, and the value $|ROLES|$ is given and is included in the initial data.

In the $\delta$-Approx. variant, the first criterion has the same form as in the basic variant, and the second criterion is the condition $\|\mathbf{X} \otimes \mathbf{Y} - \mathbf{A}\|_1 \leq \delta$.

It is shown in [12] that all variants of RMP are NP-complete problems.

## 16.2.2   VLAN scheme design

The access-control scheme on the basis of the VLAN technology is formed by creation of a set of virtual subnets in LAN. Exchange between hosts in VLAN is regulated by the following conditions:

- Both hosts between which exchange is allowed must belong to the same virtual subnet.
- The same host can be in different subnets at the same time.
- The number of the virtual subnets is not restricted.

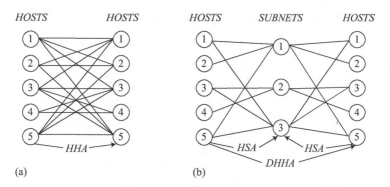

*Figure 16.2   Example of mappings between sets of hosts and virtual subnets:*
*(a) HHA mapping and (b) HSA and DHHA mappings*

Let us introduce necessary formal designations for a formal problem statement:

- $HOSTS = \{h_i\}$,    $i = 1, \ldots, n$,   $n = |HOSTS|$—set of hosts in LAN;
- $SUBNETS = \{s_j\}$,    $j = 1, \ldots, k$,   $k = |SUBNETS|$—set of virtual subnets formed in LAN;
- $HHA \subseteq HOSTS \times HOSTS$—a many-to-many mapping of host-to-host assignments; and
- $HSA \subseteq HOSTS \times SUBNETS$—a many-to-many mapping of host-to-subnet assignments.

A tuple *<HOSTS, SUBNETS, HSA>* will be called *VLAN scheme. HHA* mapping is not included into this scheme. This mapping defines the required logical connectivity of hosts and is a part of initial data of the problem. In other words, *HHA* is a required mapping.

By analogy with RBAC, let us designate a direct mapping of host-to-host assignments, which turns out due to using the virtual subnets as *DHHA*.

Figure 16.2 shows an example of all mappings between the set of hosts and the set of virtual subnets, introduced into consideration in the VLAN scheme. It is visible from this figure that the subnet $s_1$ consists of hosts $h_1$, $h_2$, and $h_5$, the subnet $s_2$—of hosts $h_3$ and $h_4$, and the subnet $s_3$—of hosts $h_1$, $h_3$, and $h_5$.

Let us suppose that *HHA* mapping corresponds to the Boolean matrix $\mathbf{A} = M(HHA)$, *DHHA* mapping—to the Boolean matrix $\mathbf{DA} = M(DHHA)$, and *HSA* mapping—to the Boolean matrix $\mathbf{X} = M(HSA)$.

Then the relation between matrixes $\mathbf{DA}$ and $\mathbf{X}$ is determined by the following theorem.

**Theorem 1.** *Theorem (on relation between the matrixes DA and X in the VLAN):* *If in the VLAN scheme the matrix* $\mathbf{DA}$ *is related to a direct mapping of host-to-host assignments and the matrix* $\mathbf{X}$ *is related to a mapping of host-to-subnet assignments, then the matrix* $\mathbf{DA}$ *equals to the Boolean matrix multiplication of the matrix* $\mathbf{X}$ *and its transposed matrix.*

This theorem can be written formally as follows:

$$\mathbf{DA} = \mathbf{X} \otimes \mathbf{X}^{\mathrm{T}}, \tag{16.4}$$

where $\mathbf{X}^{\mathrm{T}}$ is the transposed matrix $\mathbf{X}$.

Boolean matrix multiplication allows to get elements of the matrix $\mathbf{DA}$ in (16.4) according to the following expression: $da_{ij} = \vee_{j=1}^{n} (x_{ij} \wedge x_{ji})$.

Let us prove this theorem. Let us designate the set *HOSTS* as $\mathbf{C}$ and the set *SUBNETS* as $\mathbf{V}$. Then there is a mapping $\mathbf{X} : \mathbf{C} \rightarrow \mathbf{V}$ between a set of hosts and the set of subnets, and there is a mapping $\mathbf{X}^{\mathrm{T}} : \mathbf{V} \rightarrow \mathbf{C}$ between the set of subnets and the set of hosts. It is easy to see in Figure 16.2 that $\mathbf{DA}$ mapping from the set $\mathbf{C}$ in the set $\mathbf{C}$ will be defined in this case by multiplication $\mathbf{X}$ and $\mathbf{X}^{\mathrm{T}}$ mappings. It proves the expression (16.4) and the formulated theorem.

From the example given in Figure 16.2, it is visible that the following expressions between the matrixes $\mathbf{DA}$, $\mathbf{X}$, and $\mathbf{X}^{\mathrm{T}}$ are true:

$$\mathbf{X} = \begin{pmatrix} 1 & 0 & 1 \\ 1 & 1 & 0 \\ 0 & 1 & 0 \\ 1 & 0 & 1 \\ 0 & 1 & 1 \end{pmatrix}, \mathbf{X}^{\mathrm{T}} = \begin{pmatrix} 1 & 1 & 0 & 1 & 0 \\ 0 & 1 & 1 & 0 & 1 \\ 1 & 0 & 0 & 1 & 1 \end{pmatrix}$$

$$\mathbf{DA} = \begin{pmatrix} 1 & 0 & 1 \\ 1 & 1 & 0 \\ 0 & 1 & 0 \\ 1 & 0 & 1 \\ 0 & 1 & 1 \end{pmatrix} \otimes \begin{pmatrix} 1 & 1 & 0 & 1 & 0 \\ 0 & 1 & 1 & 0 & 1 \\ 1 & 0 & 0 & 1 & 1 \end{pmatrix} = \begin{pmatrix} 1 & 1 & 0 & 1 & 1 \\ 1 & 1 & 1 & 1 & 1 \\ 0 & 1 & 1 & 0 & 1 \\ 1 & 1 & 0 & 1 & 1 \\ 1 & 1 & 1 & 1 & 1 \end{pmatrix}$$

It is easy to notice that the matrix $\mathbf{DA}$ is always symmetric.

Now we will show that the problem consisting in searching for $\mathbf{X}$ from Expression (16.4) is a variety of the BMF problem. As it is well-known [13,28], the BMF problem comes down to searching for the Boolean matrixes $\mathbf{W}$ and $\mathbf{H}$ related to the given Boolean matrix $\mathbf{DA}$ by the following equation:

$$\mathbf{DA} = \mathbf{W} \otimes \mathbf{H}, \tag{16.5}$$

where $\mathbf{DA} = \mathbf{DA}\ [n, m]$, $\mathbf{W} = \mathbf{W}\ [n, k]$, and $\mathbf{H} = \mathbf{H}\ [k, m]$. Comparing (16.4) and (16.5), it is possible to note that the problem (16.4) is a special case of (16.5) in the case of execution of two conditions. The first condition is the equality $m = n$. The second condition has the following appearance:

$$w_{ij} = h_{ji} \text{ for any } i = 1, \ldots, n \text{ and } j = 1, \ldots, k. \tag{16.6}$$

From the fact that the considered problem is a variety of the BMF problem, it is followed that this problem is NP-complete. At the same time, we consider that the problem (16.4) is more difficult, than the BMF problem as in (16.4) both matrixes, on which the matrix $\mathbf{DA}$ is decomposed, are related, and in the BMF problem they are not related. For this reason, we propose to call the problem (16.4) as the problem of BMSF.

Because of (16.6), direct application of the methods for solving the problem (16.5) to the problem (16.4) is difficult. This reason describes our proposition to solve this problem by heuristic methods namely by genetic algorithms. However, for this purpose, it is necessary to introduce a criterion of optimization. In order to make it, let us pay attention to the fact that in the problem (16.4), the value $k$ can be arbitrary. Let us show how it is possible to restrict it on top. For this purpose, we will create the partition of the network on subnets so that only two computers $i$ and $j$ entered in each subnet if $a_{ij} = 1$. In this case, for the example given in Figure 16.2, the matrix $X$ will have the next five rows and eight columns:

$$X_{tr} = \begin{pmatrix} 1 & 1 & 1 & 0 & 0 & 0 & 0 & 0 \\ 1 & 0 & 0 & 1 & 1 & 1 & 0 & 0 \\ 0 & 0 & 0 & 1 & 0 & 0 & 1 & 0 \\ 0 & 1 & 0 & 0 & 1 & 0 & 0 & 1 \\ 0 & 0 & 1 & 0 & 0 & 1 & 1 & 1 \end{pmatrix}.$$

Matrix $X_{tr}^T$, respectively, will have eight rows and five columns. However, their Boolean multiplication anyway gives as a result the matrix $A$ that it is not difficult to check. At the same time, the sequence of columns can be arbitrary.

We will call the matrix $X_{tr}$ as *a trivial solution*. The trivial solution has the following properties. First, the number of columns in the matrix $X_{tr}$ is equal to the number of "1"-values in the matrix $DA$ located above the main diagonal. We denote this value as $M$. Then $k = M = 8$. Second, in each column of the matrix $X$, there is just two "1"-values. Finally, the number of trivial solutions is equal to the number $P$ of permutations of columns in the matrix $X$. It is obvious that $P = 2^M$. For this reason, the trivial solutions cannot be considered as good. At the same time, we see that for the example shown in Figure 16.2, there is a good solution, in which $k = 3$. Therefore, we can assume that the optimization criterion of the VLAN scheme-generation problem is the minimum of value $k$ under full coincidence of matrixes $A$ and $DA$.

Formally, this criterion is written as follows:

$$\|A - X \otimes X^T\|_1 = 0, \quad |SUBNETS| \to \min \tag{16.7}$$

By analogy with RMP, we will call the problem (16.7) as *VMP*.

## 16.2.3 Reconfiguring the access-control schemes

The essence of the problem of reconfiguring the access-control schemes consists in the following. The security administrator, as a rule, designs the access-control scheme once in the computer network—at the beginning of its operation. Then, during operation of the computer network, the security policy can be changed. This is expressed either in appearance, or in deletion, or in changing users and/or permissions. Thus, it is needed to realize *reconfiguring* the access-control scheme.

If for reconfiguring the access-control scheme to design it repeatedly, the new access scheme can strongly differ from the previous scheme. Such solution of the problem cannot be always good because it can involve large administration costs. Therefore, it is better to search for such access scheme which, on the one hand, would meet requirements of the changed access-control policy, and, on another hand, would have the minimal differences from the previous scheme. Thereby, this solution would involve the minimum of administration costs.

Thus, unlike the design problem, in the problem of reconfiguring the access scheme, it is necessary to consider the current access-control scheme as initial data and use the criteria that minimize administrative costs. In other words, the difference of the problem of reconfiguring the access-control scheme from the problem of its design consists in the following:

1.   The current access-control scheme is introduced into initial data.
2.   The main criterion is the minimum of administration costs.

Let us consider the formal problem statement for reconfiguring the access-control schemes for cases of RBAC and VLAN.

### 16.2.3.1   Reconfiguring the RBAC scheme

Let us suppose there is initially the RBAC scheme, presented by a tuple $<U$, *PRMS*, $ROLES_0$, $UA_0$, $PA_0>$, which reflects the existing access-control policy expressed by the $UPA_0$ mapping. This scheme was formed as a result of solving the basic variant for the problem of designing the RBAC scheme shown in Figure 16.1.

Let us assume next that during the operation of the computer network, the need arose to change the access-control policy in the following way. It is necessary to remove in $UPA_0$ the connection between the user $u_1$ and the permission $p_5$. Thus, the transition from $UPA_0$ to $UPA_1 = UPA_0 \backslash (u_1, p_5)$ is done. It is necessary to find appropriate changes in the $UA_0$ and $PA_0$ mappings, and possibly in the set *ROLES*, to minimize the administration costs during the transition to the new RBAC scheme.

If we evaluate the administration costs using the sum of changes made in the $UA_0$ and $PA_0$ mappings, the result will be the solution for the problem of reconfiguration of the RBAC scheme presented In Figure 16.3 by the scheme $<U, PRMS, ROLES_1,$ $UA_1, PA_1>$. It is easy to notice that in this scheme, a new role $r_4$ is added and three links in the $UA_0$ and $PA_0$ mappings are changed (one link is removed and two links are inserted).

If we solve this problem as the problem of designing the RBAC scheme, for example, in the basic or edge variants, assuming that the required access-control policy is the mapping of user-to-permission assignments $UPA_1$, then we get the RBAC scheme presented in Figure 16.4. When solving this problem in the basic variant to get the resultant scheme (Figure 16.4(a)), there is a need to make six changes in links (three links are removed and three links are inserted). When solving this problem in the edge variant to get the resultant scheme (Figure 16.4(b)), it is necessary to make 11 changes in the links (five links are removed and six links are inserted).

Therefore, the solution for the problem of reconfiguring the RBAC scheme that is based on the problem of the RBAC scheme design cannot be considered as the best by the criterion of minimal administration cost.

Initial data of this problem are

- a set of users $U$ and a set of permissions *PRMS*;
- $UPA_0 \subseteq U \times PRMS$ —an initial mapping of user-to-permission assignments;

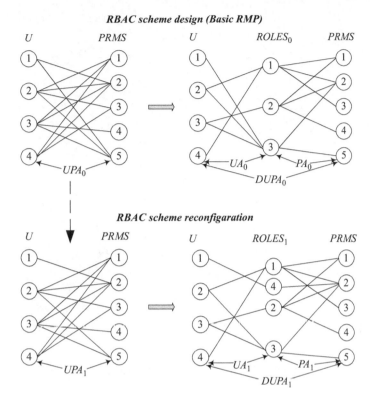

**RBAC scheme design (Basic RMP)**

**RBAC scheme reconfiguration**

*Figure 16.3   Example of reconfiguring the RBAC schemes*

- $ROLES_0 = \{r_l\}$,     $l = 1, \ldots, k$,    $k = |ROLES_0|$—an initial set of roles;
- $UA_0 \subseteq U \times ROLES_0$—an initial mapping of user-to-role assignments;
- $PA_0 \subseteq PRMS \times ROLES_0$—an initial mapping of role-to-permission assignments;
- $UPA_1 \subseteq U \times PRMS$—new mapping of user-to-permission assignments, to which it is necessary to pass.

It is required to find

- $ROLES_1 = \{r_l\}$,     $l = 1, \ldots, k_1$,    $k_1 = |ROLES_1|$ —a new set of roles;
- $UA_1 \subseteq U \times ROLES_1$—new mapping of user-to-role assignments;
- $PA_1 \subseteq PRMS \times ROLES_1$—new mapping of role-to-permission assignments.

Let is move to the matrix representation: $\mathbf{A}_0 = M(UPA_0)$, $\mathbf{X}_0 = M(UA_0)$, $\mathbf{Y}_0 = M(PA_0)$, $\mathbf{A}_1 = M(UPA_1)$, $\mathbf{X}_1 = M(UA_1)$, and $\mathbf{Y}_1 = M(PA_1)$. We introduce as variables of the problem two matrices: $\Delta \mathbf{X}$ and $\Delta \mathbf{Y}$. The matrix $\Delta \mathbf{X}$ is defined as $\Delta \mathbf{X} = \mathbf{X}_0 \oplus \mathbf{X}_1$, and the matrix $\Delta \mathbf{Y}$—as $\Delta \mathbf{Y} = \mathbf{Y}_0 \oplus \mathbf{Y}_1$, where the symbol "$\oplus$" means "exclusive OR." Then criteria for reconfiguring the RBAC scheme are as follows:

$$(\mathbf{X}_0 \oplus \Delta \mathbf{X}) \otimes (\mathbf{Y}_0 \oplus \Delta \mathbf{Y}) = \mathbf{A}_1, \|\Delta \mathbf{X}\|_1 + \|\Delta \mathbf{Y}\|_1 \rightarrow \min. \tag{16.8}$$

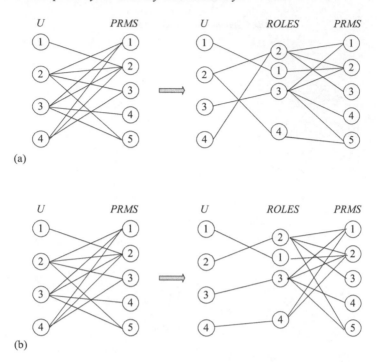

*Figure 16.4   Reconfiguring the RBAC scheme using (a) basic and (b) edge variants*

First expression in (16.8) defines the condition that the new mapping of user-to-permission assignments, which is formed by using the new $UA_1$ and $PA_1$ mappings, fully coincides with the new desired $UPA_1$ mapping. Second expression in (16.8) defines the requirement to minimize the number of changes in the $UA_0$ and $PA_0$ mappings. In other words, this expression is the criterion of minimizing the administration costs under reconfiguring the RBAC scheme.

As well as the RMP variants considered above, the problem of reconfiguring the RBAC scheme stated by (16.8) is one of the varieties of BMF problems. Therefore, it is the NP-complete optimization problem.

### 16.2.3.2   Reconfiguring the VLAN scheme

Let there is an access-control scheme $\mathbf{X}_0$, which satisfies to a connectivity matrix $\mathbf{A}_0$. Let us suppose that due to change of an access-control policy, there is a need to change the matrix $\mathbf{A}_0$ to the value $\Delta\mathbf{A}$; thus a new connectivity matrix $\mathbf{A}_1 = \mathbf{A}_0 \oplus \Delta\mathbf{A}$ can be defined. Therefore, it is necessary to create a new access-control scheme $\mathbf{X}_1$. It is possible to determine $\mathbf{X}_1$, solving the design problem. However, as a result we can get the matrix, which is different from the initial matrix $\mathbf{X}_0$. This decision can demand from the administrator to perform a large number of actions to change the access-control scheme. Therefore as a criterion of the solution search, we choose the minimum of actions spent by the administrator on reconfiguration.

Thus, the initial data in the problem of reconfiguring the VLAN scheme are

- An initial matrix $A_0[n, n]$ defining the current mapping of host-to-host assignments;
- A new matrix $A_1[n, n]$ defining the new mapping of host-to-host assignments; and
- An initial matrix $X_0[n, k]$ defining the current mapping of host-to-subnet assignments.

Let us suppose that $X_1 = X_0 \oplus \Delta X$, where $\Delta X[n, k]$ is a matrix showed what elements of the matrixes $X_1$ and $X_0$ have no coincidences. Then criteria of reconfiguring the VLAN scheme can be written as follows:

$$(X_0 \oplus \Delta X) \otimes (X_0 \oplus \Delta X)^T = A_1, \|\Delta X\|_1 \to \min. \tag{16.9}$$

Comparing (16.9) and (16.8), it is visible that the problem of reconfiguration, as well as the problem of design, is a BMSF problem. Comparing (16.9) and (16.7), it is visible that in the problem of reconfiguring the VLAN scheme, unlike VMP, the minimization of the number of virtual subnets is not required. It means that if to solve the problem of reconfiguring the VLAN scheme as VMP, the solution not meeting the criterion (16.9) can be generated. We will show it on an example.

Let in the network presented in Figure 16.2 it is necessary to pass to a new logical connectivity matrix:

$$A_1 = \begin{pmatrix} 1 & 1 & 0 & 1 & 1 \\ 1 & 1 & 1 & 0 & 1 \\ 0 & 1 & 1 & 0 & 0 \\ 1 & 0 & 0 & 1 & 1 \\ 1 & 1 & 0 & 1 & 1 \end{pmatrix}.$$

If to solve this problem in the form (16.7), we get the solution $X_2$ with the number of subnets $k = 3$. In the first subnet there are hosts $h_1$, $h_4$, and $h_5$, in the second—$h_1$ and $h_2$, and in the third—$h_2$, $h_4$, and $h_5$. In this case, the measure of administration costs $\|\Delta X\|_1$ is equal seven that is confirmed as follows:

$$\Delta X = X_2 + X_0 = \begin{pmatrix} 1 & 1 & 0 \\ 0 & 1 & 1 \\ 0 & 0 & 1 \\ 1 & 0 & 0 \\ 1 & 0 & 1 \end{pmatrix} + \begin{pmatrix} 1 & 0 & 1 \\ 1 & 0 & 0 \\ 0 & 1 & 1 \\ 0 & 1 & 0 \\ 1 & 0 & 1 \end{pmatrix} = \begin{pmatrix} 0 & 1 & 1 \\ 0 & 1 & 1 \\ 0 & 0 & 1 \\ 1 & 0 & 1 \\ 0 & 0 & 0 \end{pmatrix}.$$

When solving the problem (16.9), one of the possible decisions is the matrix $X_1$, corresponding to a quantity of subnets plus 1, i.e., $k = 4$. In the first subnet, there are hosts $h_1$, $h_2$, and $h_5$; in the second—$h_4$ и $h_5$; in the third—$h_1$, $h_2$ and $h_5$; and in the fourth—$h_2$ и $h_3$. In this case, the matrix $\Delta \mathbf{X}$ is as follows:

$$\Delta \mathbf{X} = \mathbf{X}_1 + \mathbf{X}_0 = \begin{pmatrix} 1 & 0 & 1 & 0 \\ 1 & 0 & 1 & 1 \\ 0 & 0 & 0 & 1 \\ 0 & 1 & 0 & 0 \\ 1 & 1 & 1 & 0 \end{pmatrix} + \begin{pmatrix} 1 & 0 & 1 & 0 \\ 1 & 0 & 0 & 0 \\ 0 & 1 & 1 & 0 \\ 0 & 1 & 0 & 0 \\ 1 & 0 & 1 & 0 \end{pmatrix} = \begin{pmatrix} 0 & 0 & 0 & 0 \\ 0 & 0 & 1 & 1 \\ 0 & 1 & 1 & 1 \\ 0 & 0 & 0 & 0 \\ 0 & 1 & 0 & 0 \end{pmatrix}.$$

In this case, the measure $\|\Delta \mathbf{X}\|_1$ is less, than in the previous case, and is equal to six. Therefore, the solution $\mathbf{X}_1$, in spite of the fact that there are more subnets than in previous case, is considered as better than $\mathbf{X}_2$ from the point of view of administration costs.

## 16.3    Genetic algorithm development

### 16.3.1    General provisions

Nowadays, genetic algorithms [40] are sufficiently well known and efficient methods to solve optimization problems in cases when the problem is NP-complete and has large dimension. In general case, the idea, put into a genetic algorithm, is as following. All potential solutions of the problem (individuals) are coded as symbol strings (chromosomes). To each individual, the value of the fitness function is put into correspondence. In this case, it is assumed, for certainty, that individuals with lower fitness function value correspond to better solutions of the problem. Before the start of the algorithm, some initial set of individuals (initial population) is formed randomly. Then the algorithm starts to execute a sequence of iterations. At every iteration, the population is improved by application of three basic operations: crossover, mutation, and selection. Crossover selects from the population randomly a pair of individuals (parents) and forms new individuals (descendants) by means of exchange of parts of the parental chromosomes. Mutation randomly selects individuals from population and changes codes in their chromosomes. Selection deletes from population individuals with the worst (i.e., maximal) values of the fitness function. Key aspects that should be developed when implementing a genetic algorithm to generate the access-control schemes are as follows: generation of chromosomes, generation of initial population, definition of the fitness function, and development of crossover and mutation operators.

### 16.3.2    Generation of chromosomes

As a rule, chromosomes are formed from variables of the optimization problem. In the case of the problem of the RBAC scheme design, the variables are Boolean matrixes $\mathbf{X} = M(UA)$ and $\mathbf{Y} = M(PA)$. For the problem of the VLAN scheme design, the variable is a Boolean matrix $\mathbf{X} = M(HSA)$.

For the problem of reconfiguring the RBAC scheme, the variables are the matrices $\Delta \mathbf{X}$ and $\Delta \mathbf{Y}$. They can be found using the following expressions: $\Delta \mathbf{X} = \mathbf{X}_0 \oplus \mathbf{X}_1$,

$\Delta Y = Y_0 \oplus Y_1$, where $X_0$ and $Y_0$ are known matrices. Therefore, the matrixes $X_1$ and $Y_1$ can be considered as alternative variables for this problem. Similarly, for the problem of reconfiguring the VLAN scheme, the basic variable is the matrix $\Delta X$ and the alternative variable is the matrix $X_1 = X_0 \oplus \Delta X$.

All matrices considered above are not symmetric. Usually in that case, the chromosome is created in the form of the string made from rows of these matrixes. However, such representation of the chromosome has essential shortcomings. It is obvious that it is most easy to realize crossing the parent individuals if their chromosomes are divided in one point. But in this case for the problem of the RBAC scheme design, for example, descendants will inherit unchanged code of either $X$ or $Y$. It significantly reduces the operation speed of the algorithm. For eliminating this shortcoming, it is necessary to divide the parent chromosomes into two and more points. However, it considerably complicates the algorithm implementation. Besides, in this case, it is possible to get invalid descendants under crossing parent individuals. It also significantly reduces an operation speed of the algorithm. For elimination of these shortcomings, we offer the following enhancements of genetic algorithms:

- Multi-chromosomal coding of the problem solutions if in the problem two variable matrixes are applied, for example, in the case of the RBAC scheme design. One chromosome encodes the matrix $X$, and the second—the matrix $Y$.
- As separate genes of chromosomes not elements of matrixes, but their columns are used. In the problem of the RBAC scheme design, they correspond to roles. Then lengths of these chromosomes will be restricted by the greatest possible number of roles in the RBAC scheme which is defined as $K = \min \{m, n\}$.

As in columns of the matrixes $X$ and $Y$, there are Boolean values, then for convenience of processing chromosomes we will encode further their genes in the form of integral decimal numbers. These numbers correspond to binary numbers which are formed from elements of the appropriate columns. For example, the first gene of the chromosome $X$ for the RBAC scheme in Figure 16.1 can be represented as $(0101)^T$, second—$(0010)^T$, and third—$(1101)^T$. In the form of a decimal number, their representation will be as follows: (5), (4), and (15), respectively.

### 16.3.3 Generation of initial population

Both for the problems of designing and reconfiguring the RBAC and VLAN schemes, the initial population of individuals shall be restricted. Otherwise, it is impossible to execute selection of individuals. The number of individuals in the population is the algorithm parameter $N_{pop}$ which does not change during algorithm operation.

Initial population for generation of the RBAC and VLAN schemes is created randomly. It occurs in two stages. In the beginning, the number of roles (the virtual subnets) is defined randomly. Then the *UA* and *PA* mappings, forming a basis of creation of chromosomes $X$ and $Y$ (in the case of the RBAC scheme), or the *HSA* mapping, which is the basis of the chromosomes $X$ (in the case of the VLAN scheme), are created randomly. Further the structure of the population changes on each iteration of the algorithm in the case of execution of the crossover operation (adding new individuals), the mutation (changing separate individuals), and the selection (deleting worst individuals). However, before entering new individuals in the population, we offer one more enhancement of the algorithm: to check new individuals on uniqueness within the current population.

This procedure, in our opinion, is necessary for preventing the avalanche rise of identical individuals in the population. Thereby, it gives an opportunity to move from area of a local minimum with continuation of searching for the global minimum.

## 16.3.4   Fitness functions

The fitness function provides a measure to choose the best of two individuals. We assume that the smaller the value of fitness function, the better the individual. The kind of the fitness function depends upon the search criteria used in the problem.

For all the above-mentioned variants of the problem of RBAC scheme generation, we offer a unified approach to create the fitness function. All criteria considered above for different variants of designing the RMP (Table 16.1) and VMP (16.7) schemes and for reconfiguring the RBAC (16.8) and VLAN (16.9) schemes consist of two parts. The first part represents some function, which needs to be minimized. The second part represents some equality or some inequality.

We offer a unified form for the fitness function as follows:

$$F = w_1 F_1 + w_2 F_2, \tag{16.10}$$

where $w_1$ and $w_2$ are weights; $F_1$ is a function that should be minimized; and $F_2$ is a function that reflects equality or inequality. Between weights, the ratio of $w_1 \ll w_2$ is set. This ratio ensures that during operation of the genetic algorithm, the search for solutions that have $F_2 = 0$ happens first, and then the search for solutions with smaller values of $F_1$ is fulfilled. As a result in the case of each next iteration, the population will be replenished by individuals for whom the given equality or given inequality is satisfied in the beginning. When all or the majority of individuals in the population reach this criterion, on the following iterations among such individuals, the individuals with minimal value of function $F_1$ will be found.

Using this approach, we get expressions for $F_1$ and $F_2$ to create the fitness functions in different variants of the problem statements given in Table 16.2.

*Variant 1* corresponds to the *basic RMP*. The function $F_1$ specifies the number of roles $k$ in the scheme. This value is determined algorithmically by determining the number of nonzero columns in the matrix **X**. The function $F_2$ displays the measure of discrepancy between the *UPA* and *DUPA* mappings. This discrepancy should be zero.

*Variant 2* corresponds to the *edge RMP*. The function $F_1$ determines the total number of links in the RBAC scheme. It should be minimal. The function $F_2$, as in the variant 1, displays the measure of discrepancy between the *UPA* and *DUPA* mappings. This discrepancy should be zero.

*Variant 3* corresponds to the *minimal noise RMP*. The function $F_1$ determines the measure of discrepancy between the *UPA* and *DUPA* mappings. This discrepancy should be minimal. Function $F_2$ shows measure of dissimilarity between the value $k$ and the prespecified constant $C$. This difference should be zero. In this case, the

*Table 16.2 Expressions to form fitness functions*

| No. | Problem variants | Functions $F_1$ and $F_2$ |
|-----|------------------|---------------------------|
| 1 | Basic RMP | $F_1 = k$ <br> $F_2 = \sum_{i=1}^{n} \sum_{j=1}^{m} \left| a_{ij} - \sum_{l=1}^{K} x_{il} y_{lj} \right|$ |
| 2 | Edge RMP | $F_1 = \sum_{i=1}^{n} \sum_{j=1}^{m} \left| x_{ij} \right| + \left| y_{ji} \right|$ <br> $F_2 = \sum_{i=1}^{n} \sum_{j=1}^{m} \left| a_{ij} - \sum_{l=1}^{K} x_{il} y_{lj} \right|$ |
| 3 | Minimal noise RMP | $F_1 = \sum_{i=1}^{n} \sum_{j=1}^{m} \left| a_{ij} - \sum_{l=1}^{K} x_{il} y_{lj} \right|$ <br> $F_2 = k - C$ |
| 4 | $\delta-$ Approx. RMP | $F_1 = \text{sign} \left( \left[ \sum_{i=1}^{n} \sum_{j=1}^{m} \left| a_{ij} - \sum_{l=1}^{K} x_{il} y_{lj} \right| \right] - \delta \right)$ <br> $F_2 = k - C$ |
| 5 | VMP | $F_1 = k$ <br> $F_2 = \sum_{i=1}^{n} \sum_{j=1}^{m} \left| a_{ij} - \sum_{l=1}^{K} x_{il} x_{lj} \right|$ |
| 6 | RBAC reconfiguration | $F_1 = \sum_{i=1}^{m} \sum_{l=1}^{K} \left| x0_{il} \oplus x1_{il} \right| + \sum_{j=1}^{n} \sum_{l=1}^{K} \left| y0_{jl} \oplus y1_{jl} \right|$ <br> $F_2 = \sum_{i=1}^{n} \sum_{j=1}^{m} \left| a1_{ij} - \sum_{l=1}^{K} x1_{il} y1_{lj} \right|$ |
| 7 | VLAN reconfiguration | $F_1 = \sum_{i=1}^{m} \sum_{l=1}^{K} \left| x0_{il} \oplus x1_{il} \right|$ <br> $F_2 = \sum_{i=1}^{n} \sum_{j=1}^{m} \left| a1_{ij} - \sum_{l=1}^{K} x1_{il} x1_{lj} \right|$ |

condition will be satisfied that the number of roles in the RBAC scheme must be equal to the specified number.

*Variant 4* corresponds to $\Delta$-*Approx. RMP*. The function $F_1$ uses the function sign $(u)$, which is equal to 1, if $u \geq 0$, and to 0, if $u < 0$. Thus, if a condition $\|UPA - DUPA\|_1 \leq \delta$ is met, then $F_1 = 0$, and the individual is considered to be good. However, at first this individual must have the number of roles $k$, which is equal to the constant C.

*Variant 5* corresponds to *VMP*. The function $F_1$ specifies the number of virtual subnets $k$ in the scheme. This value corresponds to the number of nonzero columns in the matrix **X**. The function $F_2$ displays the measure of discrepancy between the current and requested matrixes of host logical connectivity. This discrepancy should be zero.

*Variant 6* corresponds to the problem of *reconfiguring the RBAC scheme*. In the expressions for $F_1$ and $F_2$, the following designations are used: $\{x0_{il}\}$—elements of the matrix $\mathbf{X}_0$, $\{x1_{il}\}$—elements of the matrix $\mathbf{X}_1 = \mathbf{X}_0 \oplus \Delta\mathbf{X}$, $\{y0_{jl}\}$—elements of the matrix $\mathbf{Y}_0$, $\{y1_{jl}\}$—elements of the matrix $\mathbf{Y}_1 = \mathbf{Y}_0 \oplus \Delta\mathbf{Y}$, $\{a1_{ij}\}$—elements of the matrix $\mathbf{A}_1$. Function $F_1$ shows the number of links that need to be changed in the RBAC scheme, and the function $F_2$ shows the difference between $UPA_1$ and $DUPA_1$. This discrepancy should be zero.

*Variant 7* corresponds to the problem of *reconfiguring the VLAN scheme*. The function $F_1$ specifies the number of links that need to be changed in the VLAN

*Table 16.3    Representation of chromosomes in the case of crossover execution*

| Parent X-chromosomes | Parent Y-chromosomes | Descendant X-chromosomes | Descendant Y-chromosomes | $F_2$ |
|---|---|---|---|---|
| **X1** = (5 \| 8; 6) | **Y1** = (28 \| 18; 5) | **X3** = (5 \| 4; 14) | **Y3** = (28 \| 30; 9) | 0 |
| | | **X4** = (5 \| 4; 14) | **Y4** = (20 \| 18; 5) | 7 |
| **X2** = (9 \| 4; 14) | **Y2** = (20 \| 30; 9) | **X5** = (9 \| 8; 6) | **Y5** = (28 \| 30; 9) | 7 |
| | | **X6** = (9 \| 8; 6) | **Y6** = (20 \| 18; 5) | 10 |

scheme, and the function $F_2$ shows the difference between current and requested matrixes of host logical connectivity. This discrepancy should be zero.

## 16.3.5    Crossover

The crossover operation starts with the selection of pairs of individuals, which will be the parents for individuals' descendants. The selection is performed randomly in accordance with the probability $W_{cross}$, which is a parameter of the genetic algorithm.

Crossover execution in case when each individual has one chromosome (VLAN schemes) has no essential peculiarities. Chromosomes of parent individuals are divided in the same crossover point. Therefore, we will consider further a case of RBAC schemes when each individual has two chromosomes. Then each of chromosomes of parent descendants may have different crossover points. In this case, the parent individuals will have two channels of exchange. On the first channel, the exchange of parts of the first chromosome will take place, and on the second channel—that of the second chromosome. In this case, in the result of crossover execution there will be formed $2^2 = 4$ different descendants. All of them are included into the population. This will allow to significantly increase the operational speed of the algorithm.

Due to possible appearance of different numbers of roles in the intermediate problem solutions, it should be necessary to ensure individuals' crossover, thus reflecting solutions with different number of roles. For this purpose, it is proposed before and after the crossover to carry out additional processing of chromosomes. Before crossover, this processing involves sorting of genes, when genes with zero columns are moved to the end of the chromosome. After crossover, if in one of the two chromosomes a zero column appears, it is necessary to nullify the column with the same number from the other chromosome. This ensures consistency of both chromosomes. They will display the same number of roles in the mappings *UA* and *PA*.

The offered method of implementation of the crossover for basic RMP is displayed in Table 16.3 and illustrated in Figure 16.5.

**Parent 1** has chromosomes **X1** and **Y1**, **Parent 2** has chromosomes **X2** and **Y2**. For simplicity of consideration, the crossover point in chromosomes is between first and second roles. In the table, it is designated by the character "|". **Descendants 3** and **4** have chromosomes **X3** and **X4** formed from the left part of the chromosome

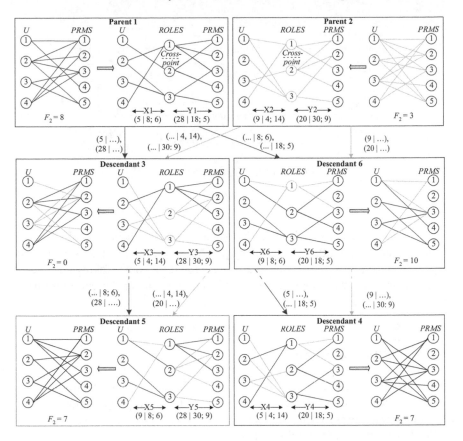

*Figure 16.5   The crossover in the genetic algorithm for basic RMP*

**X1** and the right part of the chromosome **X2**, and **Descendants 5** and **6**—otherwise. For **Y**-chromosome other situation is fair. **Descendants 3** and **5** have chromosomes **Y3** and **Y5** formed of the left part of the chromosome **Y1** and the right part of the chromosome **Y2**, and **Descendants 4** and **6**—otherwise.

The *DUPA*-mapping formed from the matrixes **X** and **Y** according to (16.1) corresponds to each parent and descendant individuals. For each individual, the value $F_2$ is calculated according to Table 16.2, No. 2. Let us get required *UPA*-mapping from [12]. It corresponds to the *DUPA*-mapping for **Descendant 3** in Figure 16.5. Let us calculate the value $F_2$ for all individuals participating in a crossover. For **Descendant 3** it is true $F_2 = 0$. Remaining values of $F_2$ are shown in Table 16.3 and Figure 16.5.

## 16.3.6   Mutation

The mutation begins with the selection of an individual from the population in order to change genes in their chromosomes. The selection is performed randomly in accordance with the probability $W_{\text{mut0}}$, which is a parameter of the genetic algorithm.

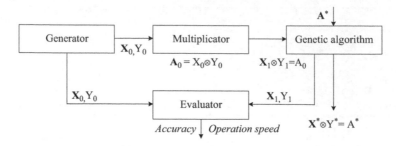

*Figure 16.6    Test bed structure*

The mutation operator is affected by two additional probabilities which will be parameters of the algorithm: $W_{\text{mut1}}$ is the probability of selection of a column and $W_{\text{mut2}}$ is the probability of selection of an element in the column. Taking into account these probabilities, the values of elements in the columns of the chromosome are changed to its opposite value randomly.

## 16.4    Evaluation test bed

For the purpose of estimation of accuracy and efficiency for the developed genetic algorithms, the test bed was created. Test bed is written in the programming language C#, and its structure is shown in Figure 16.6.

Test bed consists of the following modules:

- **Generator**, which randomly generates matrixes $X_0$ and $Y_0$, that determine the control variant of the scheme;
- **Multiplicator**, calculating the control matrix $A_0$ by performing the Boolean matrix multiplication of $X_0$ and $Y_0$;
- **Genetic algorithm**, which searches for the matrixes $X_1$ and $Y_1$ on the base of the matrix $A_0$;
- **Evaluator**, which fulfills the comparative estimation of the control matrixes $X_0$ and $Y_0$ and the resultant matrixes $X_1$ and $Y_1$ and makes conclusions about the accuracy and operation speed of the genetic algorithm.

Besides, test bed allows to search for the matrixes $X^*$ and $Y^*$ for the arbitrary external matrix $A^*$, which can be loaded to the module **genetic algorithm** directly from an external system.

The operating procedure of modules given above corresponds to the RBAC scheme design. In the case of reconfiguring the RBAC scheme, in the module **generator** the matrix $\Delta X$ is formed, in the module **multiplicator** the previous matrix $A_0$ is preserved and the new matrix $A_1$ is calculated, and in the module **genetic algorithm** the matrixes $X_1$ and $Y_1$ are generated according to the criteria shown in Table 16.2,

No. 6. For the case of the VLAN scheme design or reconfiguration, the test bed works similarly, using instead of the matrices $\mathbf{X}_0$ and $\mathbf{Y}_0$ only the matrix $\mathbf{X}_0$.

For assessment of the *algorithm accuracy*, the metric $\delta = \Delta/\|\mathbf{A}_0\|_1 \times 100\%$ is used, where $\Delta$ is the number of coincidences between the control matrixes $\mathbf{X}_0$ and $\mathbf{Y}_0$ and resulting the matrixes $\mathbf{X}_1$ and $\mathbf{Y}_1$. For assessment of the *algorithm, speed* the number of iterations $T$ spent for searching for $\mathbf{X}_1$ and $\mathbf{Y}_1$ is used.

## 16.5 Experiments

We will consider details of experiments with the developed genetic algorithms in two directions: (1) evaluation of accuracy and speed and (2) generation of access-control schemes for different real-world case studies.

### 16.5.1 Evaluation of accuracy and speed

Experiments were made for different categories of dimensionalities of the problem. For RBAC-scheme, the following couples of values $(m, n)$ are considered: (9, 30), (21, 100), and (36, 500). For the VLAN scheme, the next network sizes were considered: $n = 10$; 25; 50. The number of assignments in the generated scheme was estimated as $L_0 = \|\mathbf{A}_0\|_1$. Besides, for reconfiguration problem, the coefficient $\gamma = \|\Delta\mathbf{A}\|_1 / \|\mathbf{A}_0\|_1$ named *reconfiguration power* was considered. The coefficient $\gamma$ had the values 0.1, 0.25, and 0.5. Experiments were made ten times for each combination of the problem parameters. Then the mean value of the metrics was considered as the final assessment results. Parameters of the genetic algorithms had the following values: $N_{\text{pop}} = 200$; $P_{\text{mut}} = 0.1$; $P_{\text{cros}} = 0.01$.

To define the kind of work of the genetic algorithm at searching the optimal solution, the dependence of the fitness function from the number of the iterations made was probed. Results of this research for the case of the RBAC design and the dimensionality (9, 30) are provided in Figure 16.7.

In Figure 16.7(a), it is shown how values of the components $F_1$ and $F_2$ in the case of increasing the number of iterations are changed. By means of these components, the fitness function $F$ according to (16.10) is calculated. The dependence of a value of the fitness function $F$ from the number of iterations is shown in Figure 16.7(b). At the same time, the following values of the weight factors which are contained in the expression (16.10) were selected: $w_1 = 1$, $w_2 = 10$.

Apparently from Figure 16.7, at the beginning of the genetic algorithm functioning, i.e., after generating the initial population, the optimum individual had rather big discrepancy ($F_2 = 45$) between the *UPA* and *DUPA* mappings. The number of roles $F_1$ was equal to 7. Then in the case of increasing the number of iterations, the discrepancy between the *UPA* and *DUPA* mappings began to decrease sharply. On the iteration 350, the discrepancy became equal to zero and remained such until the end of the algorithm functioning. From this iteration, the value $F_1$ began to decrease too. At the end of the algorithm functioning, the number of roles was reached to 4.

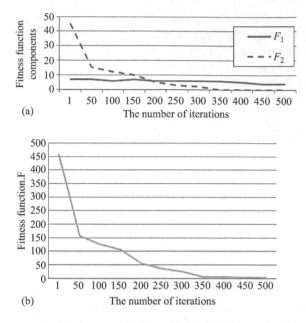

*Figure 16.7    Dependences of the fitness function and its components from the*
*number of the iterations: (a) components and (b) the fitness function*

Results of the experimental assessment of accuracy and speed of the genetic algorithms for design and reconfiguration of the RBAC and VLAN schemes are provided in Figure 16.8.

Analyzing the results of the algorithm speed, it is possible to draw the following conclusions. With increase in dimensionality of the problem, the number of the required iterations of the algorithms has dependence closing to the linear. This result should be considered as acceptable for solving the NP-complete problem. Therefore, it is possible to draw a conclusion that the offered genetic algorithms are applicable to the problems of generation of RBAC and VLAN schemes and have rather high performance.

In the case of small dimensionality of the problem and different values of $\gamma$, the values of $T$ are approximately equal. It means that the results of solving the problem of reconfiguring the access-control schemes in traditional way (through their design) and by means of the genetic algorithms proposed for reconfiguration are practically the same. In the case of middle or large dimensionalities, the results of solving the reconfiguration problems by the suggested reconfiguration approach have essential advantage in comparison with the results of their solving by the traditional manner. This effect becomes more significant, when the dimensionality of the problem rises.

Analyzing the results of the accuracy assessment, it is possible to draw the following conclusions. In the case of small dimensionality of the problem for the RBAC scheme design, the accuracy is about 100%. Lowering of the accuracy at increasing

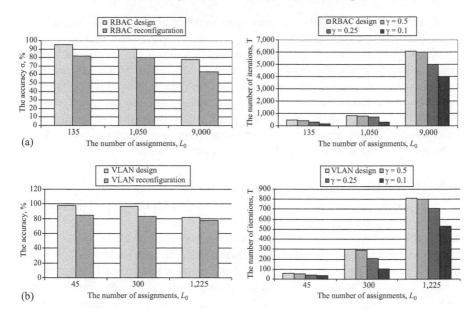

*Figure 16.8   Results of the experimental assessment of accuracy (δ) and speed (T): (a) RBAC design and reconfiguration (γ is reconfiguration power) and (b) VLAN design and reconfiguration*

in dimensionality has an explanation that the test bed for the allowed time could find only alternative solutions which can be considered as satisfactory (good). Smaller accuracy of the solutions of the problem of reconfiguring the access-control schemes in comparison with the problem of designing them is also explained by finding of satisfactory alternative solutions. In general, the results of assessment of the developed genetic algorithms show their rather high performance both in the case of small and in the case of big dimensionalities, considering that the problems of the generation of access-control schemes are NP-complete.

## 16.5.2   Real-world case studies

### 16.5.2.1   Generation of RBAC schemes

To assess the genetic algorithm efficiency for generation of RBAC schemes in real-world case studies, the enterprise resource planning (ERP) system "1C: Enterprise 7.7," installed at the manufacturing enterprise, was used. In ERP system about 200 users worked. Metadata of the system contained 65 document types, 185 types of reference manuals, and 255 report types. The main permissions, which were considered when forming roles, were "read" and "read and write."

Originally, the RBAC scheme had six roles: "administrator," "director," "marketing," "finance," "enterprise," and "warehouse." Within 10 years after exploitation of the ERP system, the number of roles grew to 35. New roles were created by the administrator "manually."

After application of the developed genetic algorithms for optimization of the access-control schemes, the number of roles was reduced to 19, i.e., almost twice. Searching of this solution demanded to execute 15 thousand iterations. Further reconfiguration of the RBAC scheme, when the permissions of one user were changed, required 12 thousand iterations. Thus, the given case study demonstrated that (1) the developed genetic algorithms can be successfully applied in real-world RBAC systems and (2) the algorithms have rather high performance.

### 16.5.2.2 VLAN design and reconfiguration

Efficiency of the genetic algorithms for solving the VLAN design problem was estimated on the example of a computer network that was physically deployed on three floors of a building. The network used Cisco Catalyst 5000 Series switches. The dynamic VLAN technology was implemented based on MAC addresses. For each host, the access lists to the neighboring hosts both at the level of one floor and between floors was made by the system administrator. Access lists have served as the basis to generate the initial matrix **A**. The total number of hosts specified by the matrix **A** is equal to 100. The larger number of hosts was considered inappropriate because of difficulties in forming the matrix **A**. The VLAN scheme was optimized by the genetic algorithm proposed. There were formed about 50 of large and small virtual subnets in the network. At the same time, users have not identified the decrease of the network performance. However, the users were protected from making unauthorized access to neighboring computers.

Efficiency of the genetic algorithm for solving the VLAN reconfiguration problem was carried out for a case study that imitates the Internet of Things network for "the smart house." The network includes four servers (supervisor, application server, database server, and web-server), from four to ten workstations, and from four to thirty-six user's devises ("things"). For imitation of "things," the Arduino Yún set was used. The network node consists of the ATmega 32u4 microcontroller and the Atheros AR9331 processor working under control of OS Linux. In general, the dimension of the network was changed from 10 to 50 elements. Experiments confirmed data on the satisfactory operation speed of the genetic algorithms.

## 16.6 Conclusions

The chapter proposed a new approach to solve the problems of access-control scheme generation in computer networks and evaluated this approach for RBAC and VLAN schemes. The approach is based on using genetic algorithms to search for solutions of optimization problems. The chapter discussed the state of the art in this domain, outlined the mathematical foundations, and features of the genetic algorithm development, evaluation, and implementation in real word. It considered some enhancements for genetic algorithms concerned: multi-chromosomal coding of solutions, usage of columns of matrixes as genes of chromosomes, and checking new individuals in population on uniqueness.

Experimental assessment of the proposed genetic algorithms on the specially designed test bed showed satisfactory efficiency. The operation speed of the algorithms grew by linear law at growing of the problem's dimension. Taking into consideration that the problems being solved are NP-complete, the result obtained may be considered sufficiently good.

Further research directions may be associated with several areas. First, the proposed genetic algorithms may be transferred to new domains of access control, e.g., firewalls. Second, the usage of other varieties of nature-inspired algorithms for solving various problems of access-control scheme generation is of interest. The following domains are considered: varieties of RBAC, for example, TBAC; other access-control models, for example, attribute-based access control. As other nature-inspired algorithms, it is possible to use differential evolution, swarm of particles, ant colony, bee colony, etc.

## Acknowledgment

This research is being partially supported by the grants of the RFBR (16-29-09482, 18-07-01369, 18-07-01488) and the budgetary subject AAAA-A16-116033 110102-5.

## References

[1] Harrison M.A., Ruzzo W.L., Ullman J.D. "Protection in operating systems". *Commun. ACM.* 1976, vol. 19(8), pp. 461–71.

[2] Sandhu R.S., Coyne E.J., Feinstein H.L., Youman Ch.E. "Role-based access control models". *Computer.* 1996, vol. 29(2), pp. 38–47.

[3] Sandhu R., Ferraiolo D., Kuhn R. "The NIST model for role-based access control: towards a unified standard". *Proceedings of the Fifth ACM Workshop on Role-Based Access Control*; Berlin, Germany, Jul 2000. New York: ACM Press, 2000. pp. 47–63.

[4] Ferraiolo D.F., Sandhu R., Gavrila S., Kuhn D.R., Chandramouli R. "Proposed NIST standard for role-based access control". *ACM Trans. Inf. Syst. Secur.* 2001, vol. 4(3), pp. 224–74.

[5] Coyne E.J., Weil T.R., Kuhn D.R. "Role engineering: methods and standards". *IT Prof.* 2011, vol. 13(6), pp. 54–7.

[6] Epstein P., Sandhu R. "Towards a UML based approach to role engineering". *Proceedings of the Fourth ACM Workshop on Role-Based Access Control*; Fairfax, Virginia, USA, Oct 1999. New York: ACM Press, 1999. pp. 135–43.

[7] Fernandez E.B., Hawkins J.C. "Determining role rights from use cases". *Proceedings of the Second ACM Workshop on Role-Based Access Control*; Fairfax, Virginia, USA, Nov 1997. New York: ACM Press, 1997. pp. 121–5.

[8]   Roeckle H., Schimpf G., Weidinger R. "Process-oriented approach for role-finding to implement role-based security administration in a large industrial organization". *Proceedings of the Fifth ACM Workshop on Role-Based Access Control*; Berlin, Germany, Jul 2000. New York: ACM Press, 2000. pp. 103–10.

[9]   Neumann G., Strembeck M. "A scenario-driven role engineering process for functional RBAC roles". *Proceedings of the Seventh ACM Symposium on Access Control Models and Technologies*; Monterey, CA, USA, Jun 2002. New York: ACM Press, 2002. pp. 33–42.

[10]  Narouei M., Takabi H. "Towards an automatic top-down role engineering approach using natural language processing techniques". *Proceedings of the 20th ACM Symposium on Access Control Models and Technologies*; Vienna, Austria, Jun 2015. New York: ACM Press, 2015. pp. 157–60.

[11]  Frank M., Buhmann J.M., Basin D. "On the definition of role mining". *Proceedings of the 15th ACM Symposium on Access Control Models and Technologies*; Pittsburgh, PA, USA, Jun 2010. New York: ACM Press, 2010. pp. 35–44.

[12]  Vaidya J., Atluri V., Guo Q. "The role mining problem: finding a minimal descriptive set of roles". *Proceedings of the 12th ACM Symposium on Access Control Models and Technologies*; Sophia Antipolis, France, Jun 2007. New York: ACM Press, 2007. pp. 175–84.

[13]  Miettinen P., Vreeken J. "Model order selection for Boolean matrix factorization". *Proceedings of the 17th ACM SIGKDD Conference on Knowledge Discovery and Data Mining*; San Diego, CA, USA, Aug 2011. New York: ACM Press, 2011. pp. 51–9.

[14]  Kuhlmann M., Shohat D., Schimpf G. "Role mining – revealing business roles for security administration using data mining technology". *Proceedings of the Eighth ACM Symposium on Access Control Models and Technologies*; Como, Italy, Jun 2003. New York: ACM Press, 2003. pp. 179–86.

[15]  Vaidya J., Atluri V., Warner J. "RoleMiner: mining roles using subset enumeration". *Proceedings of the 13th ACM Conference on Computer and Communications Security*; Alexandria, VA, USA, Oct 2006. New York: ACM Press, 2006. pp. 144–53.

[16]  Blundo C., Cimato S. "A simple role mining algorithm". *Proceedings of the 2010 ACM Symposium on Applied Computing*; Sierre, Switzerland, Mar 2010. New York: ACM Press, 2010. pp. 1958–62.

[17]  Colantonio A., Pietro R.D., Ocello A., Verde N.V. "A probabilistic bound on the basic role mining problem and its applications". *Proceedings of the 24th IFIP TC 11 International Information Security Conference*; Pafos, Cyprus, May 2009. Berlin: Springer-Verlag, 2009. pp. 376–86.

[18]  Frank M., Buhmann J.M., Basin D. "Role mining with probabilistic models". *ACM Trans. Inform. Syst. Secur.*, 2013, vol. 15(4), pp. 15:1–15:28.

[19]  Frank M., Streich A.P., Basin D., Buhmann J.M. "Multi-assignment clustering for Boolean data". *J. Mach. Learn. Res.*, 2012, vol. 13(1), pp. 459–89.

[20]  Colantonio A., Pietro R.D., Ocello A. "A cost-driven approach to role engineering". *Proceedings of the 2008 ACM Symposium on Applied Computing*; Fortaleza, Ceara, Brazil, Mar 2008. New York: ACM Press, 2008. pp. 2129–36.

[21] Saenko I., Kotenko I. "Genetic algorithms for role mining problem". *Proceedings of the 19th International Euromicro Conference on Parallel, Distributed and Network-Based Processing*; Ayia Napa, Cyprus, Feb 2011. Washington: IEEE Computer Society, 2011. pp. 646–50.

[22] Saenko I., Kotenko I. "Design and performance evaluation of improved genetic algorithm for role mining problem". *Proceedings of the 20th International Euromicro Conference on Parallel, Distributed and Network-based Processing*; Garching, Germany, Feb 2012. Washington: IEEE Computer Society, 2012. pp. 269–74.

[23] Saenko I., Kotenko I. "Using genetic algorithms for design and reconfiguration of RBAC schemes". *Proceedings of the 1st International Workshop on AI for Privacy and Security*; The Hague, Netherlands, Aug 2016. New York: ACM Press, 2016. Article 4.

[24] Teare D., Vachon B., Graziani R., Froom R., Frahim E., Ranjbar A. *CCNP Routing and Switching Foundation Learning Guide Library: ROUTE 300-101, SWITCH 300-115, TSHOOT 300-135*. Indianapolis: Cisco Press; 2015. p. 2700.

[25] Tai Ch.-F., Chiang Tz.-Ch., Hou T.-W. "A virtual subnet scheme on clustering algorithms for mobile ad hoc networks". *Expert Syst. Appl.*, 2011, vol. 38(3), pp. 2099–109.

[26] Saenko I., Kotenko I. "A genetic approach for virtual computer network design". *Proceedings of the 8th International Symposium on Intelligent Distributed Computing*; Madrid, Spain, Sep 2015. Berlin: Springer-Verlag, 2015. pp. 95–105.

[27] Cergani E., Miettinen P. "Discovering relations using matrix factorization methods". *Proceedings of the 22nd ACM International Conference on Information & Knowledge Management*; San Francisco, CA, USA, Oct 2013. New York: ACM Press, 2013. pp. 1549–52.

[28] Snasel V., Platos J., Kromer P. "On genetic algorithms for Boolean matrix factorization". *Proceedings of the Eighth International Conference on Intelligent Systems Design and Applications*; Kaohsiung, Taiwan, Nov 2008. Vol. 2. New York: IEEE Press, 2008. pp. 170–5.

[29] Saenko I., Kotenko I. "Genetic optimization of access control schemes in virtual local area networks". *Proceedings of the 5th International Conference on Mathematical Methods, Models and Architectures for Computer Network Security*; St. Petersburg, Russia, Sep 2010. Berlin: Springer-Verlag, 2010. pp. 209–16.

[30] Joshi J.B.D., Bertino E., Latif U., Ghafoor A. "A generalized temporal role-based access control model". *IEEE Trans. Knowl. Data Eng.* 2005, vol. 17(1), pp. 4–23.

[31] Thi K.T.L., Dang T.Kh., Kuonen P., Drissi H.Ch. "STRoBAC: spatial temporal role based access control". *Proceedings of the 4th International Conference on Computational Collective Intelligence: Technologies and Applications – Volume Part II*; Ho Chi Minh city, Vietnam, Nov 2012. Berlin: Springer-Verlag, 2012. pp. 201–11.

[32]   Aziz B., Foley S.N., Herbert J., Swart G. "Reconfiguring role based access control policies using risk semantics". *J. High Speed Netw.* 2006, vol. 15(3), pp. 261–73.

[33]   Saenko I., Kotenko I. "Reconfiguration of access schemes in virtual networks of the internet of things by genetic algorithms". *Proceedings of the 9th International Symposium on Intelligent Distributed Computing*; Guimarães, Portugal, Oct 2015. New York: Springer International Publishing, 2016. pp. 155–65.

[34]   Saenko I., Kotenko I. "Reconfiguration of RBAC schemes by genetic algorithms". *Proceedings of the 10th International Symposium on Intelligent Distributed Computing*; Paris, France, Oct 2016. New York: Springer International Publishing, 2017. pp. 89–98.

[35]   Hu N., Bradford Ph.G., Liu J. "Applying role based access control and genetic algorithms to insider threat detection". *Proceedings of the 44th ACM Annual Southeast Regional Conference*; Melbourne, FL, Mar 2006. pp. 790–1.

[36]   Yang H.-S., Maier M., Reisslein M., Carlyle W.M. "A genetic algorithm based methodology for optimizing multi-service convergence". *Metro WDM Network. J. Lightwave Technol.* 2003, vol. 21(5), pp. 1114–46.

[37]   Semmanche N., Selka S. "Access control of web services using genetic algorithms". *Proceedings of the 2008 High Performance Computing & Simulation Conference*; Nicosia, Cyprus, 2008. pp. 249–54.

[38]   Mehboob U., Qadir J., Ali S., Vasilakos A. *Genetic Algorithms in Wireless Networking: Techniques, Applications, and Issues* [online]. 2014. Available from https://arxiv.org/pdf/1411.5323.pdf [Accessed 30 Jan 2018].

[39]   Rai N., Rai Kh. "Genetic algorithm based intrusion detection system". *Int. J. Comput. Sci. Inf. Technol.* 2014, vol. 5(4), pp. 4952–7.

[40]   Goldberg D.E. *Genetic Algorithms in Search, Optimization and Machine Learning*. Boston; Addison-Wesley, 1989. p. 432.

# Index